OLYMPIC CITIES

City Agendas, Planning and the
World's Games, 1896–2032

Fourth Edition

edited by

John R. Gold

and

Margaret M. Gold

Routledge
Taylor & Francis Group

LONDON AND NEW YORK

First published 2024
by Routledge
4 Park Square, Milton Park, Abingdon, Oxfordshire OX14 4RN

and by Routledge
605 Third Avenue, New York, NY 10158

Routledge is an imprint of the Taylor & Francis Group, an informa business

British Library Cataloguing in Publication Data
A catalogue record of this book is available from the British Library

Library of Congress Cataloging in Publication Data
Names: Gold, John R., 1949– editor. | Gold, Margaret M., editor.
Title: Olympic cities : city agendas, planning and the world's games, 1896-2032 /
edited by John R. Gold and Margaret M. Gold.
Description: Fourth edition. | London ; New York : Routledge, 2024. |
Series: Planning, history and environment series | Includes bibliographical references and index. |
Identifiers: LCCN 2023052456 (print) | LCCN 2023052457 (ebook) | ISBN 9781032287119
(hardback) | ISBN 9781032287096 (paperback) | ISBN 9781003298175 (ebook)
Subjects: LCSH: City planning—History. | Municipal government—History. | Municipal services—
History. | Olympics—History. | Olympics—Planning. | Olympics—Management—History.
Classification: LCC HT166 .O4 2024 (print) | LCC HT166 (ebook) | DDC 307.1/216—dc23/
eng/20231120
LC record available at https://lccn.loc.gov/2023052456
LC ebook record available at https://lccn.loc.gov/2023052457

ISBN: 978–1–032–28711–9 (hbk)
ISBN: 978–1–032–28709–6 (pbk)
ISBN: 978–1–003–29817–5 (ebk)

DOI: 10.4324/9781003298175

Typeset in Aktiv Grotesk and ITC Galliard Pro by PNR Design, Didcot

IN MEMORIAM

David Pepper

(1940–2021)

Contents

PART III : CITY PORTRAITS

Preface

Much has occurred since the first edition of this book appeared in 2007. Summer and Winter Games have come and gone, with the relentless onward movement of the clock meaning that there are now further Olympics and Paralympics that need attention. Games that had not yet been allocated to the roster of host cities when the previous editions went to press are now part of the extensive roll call of Olympic Cities, with Sochi 2014, Rio de Janeiro 2016, Pyeongchang 2018, Tokyo 2020, Beijing 2022, Paris 2024, Milan 2026, Los Angeles 2028 and Brisbane 2032 joining the list since the first edition appeared. Beijing, at the point of running test events for the following year's Summer Games in 2007, has already reused some of the same facilities for the 2022 Winter Olympics and Paralympics. London 2012 – still a distant prospect in 2007 – has become a magnet for those interested in tracking the course of long-term post-Games legacy.

Understandably, every successive Games brings fresh developments. Beyond their implications for the sports and cultural communities, each succeeding event brings challenges and necessary innovations regarding funding, stakeholder partnerships, architecture and planning, construction, spectacle, ticketing, volunteering, and legacy. As a result, new knowledge is generated that needs to be chronicled, analysed, categorised and, hopefully, made available to successors through processes of knowledge transfer. In addition, the Olympics have shown a remarkable tendency to become the focal point of controversies, crystallising debate over such matters as funding priorities, corruption scandals, public accountability, environmental sustainability, security, legacy and, most recently, epidemiology.

The need to take stock of these developments and account for change has prompted the staging of innumerable specialist seminars and conferences. Often involving a mixture of academics and practitioners and sponsored by publishers or funding agencies, these events have stimulated new waves of publications about emerging problems and shared challenges that, at their best, have helped to move scholarship decisively forward. Understandably, therefore, an essential part of the purpose of this edition has been to take stock of the new literature and give adequate recognition to its findings. This amounts to rather more than might have been expected from the mere extension of the concluding date in the book's subtitle from 2012, as in the first edition, to 2032 as in this one.

Yet having emphasized the need for change, we also stress that this book's core aim remains precisely the same as its predecessors. In broad outline, it seeks to draw on the expertise of an international group of authors to examine the comparative experience of cities that have hosted the Olympics in the years from the creation of the modern Games in 1896 through to the present day and then beyond to 2032. As such, it remains a book framed around historical analysis, seeking not just to account for past Games but also to study recent and future Olympics in light of established and emerging narratives. For a festival as deeply immersed in precedent and invented tradition as the Olympics, we believe that this comprises an eminently appropriate approach to set alongside much of the instant punditry about the subject that is now on offer in conventional and social media.

Further similarities concern structure. We have retained the same multi-layered approach to our subject matter as in the previous editions, with an introduction followed by twenty chapters that are arranged into three main parts. The book opens with chronologically arranged surveys of the component festivals; followed by chapters that scrutinize significant planning and managerial themes arising from cities acting as hosts; and then by a representative selection of portraits of cities staging the Summer Games. The third section understandably concentrates on the twenty-first century but also includes a chapter on Rome 1960 – an event that heralded the period in which host cities became increasingly interested in using the Olympics as an economic stimulus and a catalyst for urban renewal. The continuity of structure also allows us to bring in new chapters that reflect recent developments and debates, but to do so within the original terms of reference. As a result, previous editions can be seen as resources in their own right. Rather than being superseded and redundant, each edition testifies to ideas and debate current at the time of writing. Moreover, the various editions essentially supply a series of snapshots of the *progress* on the Games of the twenty-first century, plotting sequentially the various positions that cities such as Beijing. London, Rio de Janeiro, and Tokyo had reached in the decade or more between thinking about bidding for the Olympics to the works necessary for post-event site conversion and potential legacy.

Adopting a tripartite structure that seeks both thematic insight and chronological coverage inevitably means revisiting the same festivals at several points in the text from different angles and perspectives. In addition, the correct balance between allowing authors scope for initial context and removing unnecessary repetition by employing cross-references is difficult to achieve, but we hope that the results are acceptable. Certainly, we have not regarded it as part of our task to remove differences of interpretation or even fundamental disagreements that may emerge from the ensuing chapters of this book. As befits a subject as complex and as controversial as the modern Olympics and Paralympics, there is no party line to which authors have had to adhere.

Certain elements of standardization and conventions deserve some clarification. Statements of expenditure frequently occur in local currencies and exchange rates at points in the past are not always easy to obtain, especially when sources are unclear about precise dates. Although Euros and various local currencies are occasionally used, wherever possible we have attempted to use the pound Sterling or US dollar equivalents. All sums where dollars are shown without qualification relate to the US currency. In addition, anyone familiar with using Olympic documentation, especially Official Reports, will realize that there are normally different language versions available. We have retained the linguistic version used by our contributors in cited references, even though this means that different language versions of the same publication might be listed separately in the consolidated bibliography. Finally, Olympic sport is a realm in which institutional acronyms abound. Our policy is to present acronyms in their most common form regardless of the language from which they are derived. Thus, for example, the abbreviation COJO (standing for Comité d'Organisation des Jeux Olympiques) is used in relation to Games held in Francophone nations, whereas elsewhere the equivalent Anglophone body is usually referred to as an OCOG (Organizing Committee for the Olympic Games). To avoid confusion, a full listing of all such acronyms occurs at the start of this text, with our practice being to provide names of bodies in full wherever they first occur in a chapter.

As ever, we have incurred a variety of debts in the lengthy process of preparing this book. First and foremost, we would like to express our sincere gratitude to our contributors for their patience with the editorial process and for their willingness to redraft material to benefit the book as a whole. Dennis Hardy and Ann Rudkin hatched the original idea and Graeme Evans provided valuable contacts when initiating the first edition. The International Planning History Society's Barcelona conference in 2004 supplied an invaluable opportunity to gather an initial group of contributors together. We would particularly like to acknowledge the assistance of the British Olympic Association for allowing us access to source materials and Martin McElhatton, Chief Executive of Wheel Power, for sparing generous amounts of time to show us round the Stoke Mandeville Stadium. A considerable debt of gratitude goes to the archivists and librarians of the Olympic Studies Centre in Lausanne. As any visiting scholar knows, its superb resources are enhanced by the knowledge and enthusiasm of its staff.

Next, our insights into the staging of the games and the problems faced by Olympic cities have been helped immeasurably by invitations that have allowed us to see the development of three recent Summer Games at first hand. Tony Sainsbury and James Bulley gave large amounts of their time while working at LOCOG to assist with an oral historical study of London 2012. Professor Yasushi Aoyama arranged a visiting professorial position at Meiji University, which allowed us to witness the progress of Tokyo 2020 from 2014 onwards. Louise Wagner generously supplied us with photographs that spoke elegantly of people as well as place. We very much share the sense of disappointment felt by our Japanese friends and colleagues at the way in which the pandemic destroyed the atmosphere of much of what, we are certain, would have been a great Olympic festival. Finally, we are grateful to Daphne Bolz, Marie Delaplace, Cécile Doustaly, Sylvain Feroz, Charly Machemehl, Luc Robène and Pierre-Olaf Schut, all of whom have created opportunities for us to watch the progress of Paris 2024 and to understand the tasks and challenges involved.

Moving on, it is a pleasure to record our thanks to Michael Barke, Brian Chalkley, Ruth Craggs, Jiska de Groot, Jo Foord, Vassil Girginov, Simon Gunasekara, Willy Guneriussen, Elsa-Minni Heimgard, Paul Kitchin, Lorraine Johnson, Eva Kassens-Noor, James Kennell, Peter Larkham, Daniel Latouche, Chuck Little, Sarah Loy, Kat Martindale, Martha McIntosh, Monika Meyer, Javier Monclús, Martin Müller, Jill Pearlman, Verity Postlethwaite, George Revill, Matthew Taylor, and Steve Ward for various contributions and sundry kindnesses. Oxford Brookes University and London Metropolitan University provided finance and other assistance to facilitate our work, with the Bartlett School of Architecture at University College London supplying a marvellously welcoming base from which to write. Iain, Josie, Thomas, Jenny, David, and Mathilda tolerated the things that did not happen in order to allow us time and space to complete this text and its predecessors. Finally, we respectfully dedicate this book to the memory of David Pepper, a giant of environmentalism but also a man for whom sport occupied its proper place in life.

West Ealing
October 2023

Acknowledgements

We are grateful to the following for permission to reproduce the illustrations as recorded below:

Yasushi Aoyama: Figures 18.4, 18.5 and 18.6

Christopher Balch: Figure 3.5

Brisbane City Council: Figure 21.7

Bruno Bartholini/CDURP: Figure 17.5

CanonStarGal: Figure 20.3

Chabe01: Figure 9.3

Ian Cook: Figure 15.1

Auguste Couttet: Figure 3.2

Aysin Dedekorkut-Howes: Figure 21.1

Cécile Doustaly: Figures 19.1, 19.2, 19.4 and 19.5

Stephen Essex: Figures 3.3, 3.4 and 3.8

Graeme Evans: Figures 16.3, 16.4 and 16.5

Lucas Faulhaber: Figure 17.8

Beatriz García: Figures 4.3 and 4.4

Greater London Authority: Figure 16.1

Gzzz: Figure 7.1

International Olympic Committee: Figures 3.1, 3.6, 3.7, 4.2, 4.5, 4.6, 4.7, 6.5, 6.6, 16.2, 18.3, 18.11 and 20.1

John and Margaret Gold: Figures 2.2, 2.11, 2.12, 2.13, 2.14, 2.15, 5.1, 5.2, 5.3, 5.4, 14.1, 14.2 and 14.3

Major Events Gold Coast: Figure 21.8

Tiia Monto: Figure 2.10

Norbert Müller: Figure 4.1

Hetarllen Mumriken: Figure 5.5

N509FZ: Part 3 Title Page and Figure 15.2

Nelma Gusmão de Oliveira: Figure 17.7

Mike O'Dwyer/Lendlease: Figure 8.6

The Contributors

Yasushi Aoyama is a Professor Emeritus at the Graduate School of Governance Studies at Meiji University in Tokyo and was also a Lecturer on the Faculty of Engineering at Tokyo University. His courses focus on international policy, crisis management, and policy development at the local government level. He was a Vice Governor and Chairman of the Personnel Commission of Tokyo Metropolitan Government, the body that held the 2020 Summer Olympic and Paralympic Games.

Giorgos Chatzinakos is an urban and cultural geographer from Thessaloniki in Greece. He received his PhD at Manchester Metropolitan University for his research on the everyday and cultural life of the suburbs. His research interests are focused on critical event studies, cultural consumption, neighbourhood-building, and the commons. He is a visiting Research Fellow at the Policy Evaluation and Research Unit at Manchester Metropolitan University.

Jon Coaffee is Professor in Urban Geography in the Department of Politics and International Studies at the University of Warwick. He is an international researcher of counterterrorism, security, and urban resilience. He is the author/coauthor of *The Everyday Resilience of the City* (2008), *Terrorism, Risk and the Global City* (2009), *Sustaining and Securing the Olympic City* (2011) and *The War on Terror and The Normalisation of Urban Security* (2021).

Ian G. Cook is Professor Emeritus of Human Geography at Liverpool John Moores University and formerly Head of the Centre for Pacific Rim Studies and Head of Geography. He is widely published in journals and book chapters and is the joint editor or author of ten books including *Aging in Asia* (2009), *Aging in Comparative Perspective: Processes and Policies* (2012) and *Sociability, Social Capital and Community Development: A Public Health Perspective* (2015).

Aysin Dedekorkut-Howes is Senior Lecturer in Urban and Environmental Planning at Griffith University and a member of the Cities Research Institute. Before moving to Australia, she taught and conducted research at the Florida State University, USA and İzmir Institute of Technology, Turkey. Her research interests include climate change adaptation and disaster resilience, water-resource management, and urbanization in subtropical areas and coastal cities. She also conducts historical research on the development of the Gold Coast and Southeast Queensland as well as on current issues and problems that the region is facing. She is the co-editor of *Off the Plan: The Urbanisation of the Gold Coast* (2016).

Cécile Doustaly is Reader (Habilitation Thesis) at the research centre Héritages at CY Cergy Paris Université (Greater Paris) and Fellow at the Centre for Cultural and Media Policy Studies-SCAPVC, University of Warwick (in 2012 for the London Olympic Games, and since 2020). Her interdisciplinary research draws on comparative cultural policy to analyse cultural glocalization and new cultural quarters (notably in London and Paris) and the role of the IOC, UNESCO, EU in framing cultural mega urban events and projects (Olympic Games, World Heritage Sites, Cities of Culture): policy and management models, creation and heritagization; cultural rights, public space and participation; tourism and sustainable development.

Özlem Edizel-Tasci is a Senior Associate and Proposal Writer at the Institute for Engagement & Negotiation at the University of Virginia, USA. Her recent work includes projects on environmental justice, community engagement and climate change policies. Her PhD thesis focused on London 2012: Sustainable Games.

Stephen Essex is Associate Professor (Reader) in Human Geography at the School of Geography, Earth and Environmental Science, University of Plymouth. His teaching and research focus on urban and rural planning, especially the infrastructural implications of the Olympic Games and post-war reconstruction planning. He has co-authored journal articles and book chapters on the urban impacts and planning of both the Summer and Winter Olympic Games with Professor Brian Chalkley (also at the University of Plymouth).

Graeme Evans is Professor Emeritus at University of the Arts London. He convened the Regional Studies Association international research network on mega-events and edited the recent book on *Mega Events and Place-Making* (2020). He is currently working on an AHRC-funded research project into UK Cities of Culture and led the research programme for Maastricht's Euregional European Capital of Culture bid at Maastricht University.

Robert Freestone is Professor of Planning in the School of Built Environment at UNSW Sydney, Australia. His research interests are in urban planning history, metropolitan change, heritage conservation, and planning education. He is Chair of the Editorial Board of *Planning Perspectives* and a former President of the International Planning History Society. His recent books include *Campus: Building Modern Australian Universities* (2022), *Iconic Planned Communities and the Challenge of Change* (2019), *Designing Global Sydney* (2019), and *Planning Metropolitan Australia* (2018).

Peter Fussey is a Professor of Sociology at the University of Essex. His main research interests concern the uses and wider human rights implications of digital security practices. He has authored books on urban security and mega events and human trafficking. He has also worked with national governments and supra-national organizations including UN agencies and the EU Fundamental Rights Agency on the human rights implications of biometric surveillance. He recently led the independent review of the Metropolitan Police's trials of facial recognition technology, and he leads the human rights and ethics strand of the national Biometrics and Surveillance Camera Commissioner's strategy.

Beatriz García is Senior Research Fellow in International Cultural Policy and Mega Events at the University of Liverpool and Associate Director at the Centre for Cultural Value. She is a member of the Culture and Olympic Heritage Commission and the European Capital of Culture Selection Panel. She has been at the forefront of research on the rhetoric, impact, and long-term legacy of culture-led regeneration interventions since 1999, conducting fieldwork on the cultural dimension of every edition of the Olympic Games since Sydney 2000. She has pioneered longitudinal methods to capture cultural value and has led UK-wide and international exercises to set up common evaluation principles for culture and major event interventions. She is the author of *The Olympics. The Basics* and *The Olympic Games and Cultural Policy* (both 2012).

John R. Gold is Honorary Senior Research Fellow at the Bartlett School of Architecture at University College London and Professor Emeritus at Oxford Brookes University. From 2014–2021, he was Special Appointed Professor in the Graduate School of Governance Studies at Meiji University (Tokyo, Japan). He is joint editor of the journal *Planning Perspectives* and the author or editor of twenty-three books on urban and cultural subjects. He is currently working on the third of his trilogy on architectural modernism in Great Britain, entitled *The Legacy of Modernism: Modern architects, the city and the collapse of orthodoxy, 1973–1990* and, with Margaret Gold, on a prequel to their book *Festival Cities* (2020) entitled *The Necessary Huddle: Festivals in the European urban experience.*

Margaret Gold is Senior Lecturer in Creative Industries at London Metropolitan University. With John Gold, she is joint editor of the journal *Planning Perspectives,* and shares authorship of *Imagining Scotland* (1995), *Cities of Culture* (2005) and *Festival Cities: Culture, Planning and Urban*

Life since 1945 (2020). She is also joint editor of *The Making of Olympic Cities* (2012). She is currently working with John Gold on *The Necessary Huddle: Festivals in the European urban experience*, a prequel to their book *Festival Cities*.

Steven Miles is Professor at Manchester Metropolitan University and author of a number of books including *The Experience Society* (2021), *Retail and the Artifice of Social Change* (2015) and *Consumerism as a Way of Life* (1998). He is Principal Investigator on the Leverhulme Unit for the Design of Cities of the Future (LUDeC) – a doctoral scholarship programme which is concerned with moving beyond a market-driven orthodoxy of the urban space, to promote a more playful, experimental, and change-oriented approach to the socially-just city. He is Editor-in-Chief of the *Journal of Consumer Culture*.

Erick Omena is Lecturer at the Institute of Research on Urban and Regional Planning, Federal University of Rio de Janeiro (IPPUR-UFRJ) and member of the Observatório das Metrópoles research network. His research interests include the interface of social theory, urban planning, and political economy, with a focus on city transformation related to major development projects and mega-events.

Holger Preuss is Professor of Sport Economics and Sport Sociology at the Johannes Gutenberg University in Mainz, Germany, Adjunct Professor at the University of Ottawa, Canada and International Scholar at the State University of New York (SUNY, Cortland). His field of research is directed at the economic and socio-economic aspects of sport, in particular looking at the socio-economic impact analysis of mega-sport events such as Olympic Games (since 1972) and the FIFA Football World Cup (since 2006). He is currently working with the Federal Ministry of the Interior regarding the development of a national strategy for mega sports events. He is President of the Evaluation Commission for the Paris 2024 Olympic Games and is working with the EU Bureau of Sports (Brussels) on a project designed to help NOCs in Europe to apply strategic management. He is also a member of the IOC's commission on Legacy and Sustainability.

Cerianne Robertson is a PhD candidate in Communication at the University of Southern California. Her research and journalistic work have examined urban development, gentrification, sports mega-events, media narratives, and social movements from Rio de Janeiro to Los Angeles. Cerianne previously worked as the Editor and Media Monitoring Coordinator for RioOnWatch. org, a Rio de Janeiro-based media platform that emerged to amplify favela resident perspectives and monitor urban transformations in the build-up to the 2016 Olympics.

Tony Sainsbury was LOCOG's Head of Villages for the 2012 London Summer Olympic and Paralympic Games for ten years. His previous professional career was initially as a PE teacher and then local government sport and leisure services director, which concluded as Director of Sport at the University of Manchester. He has been extensively involved in the planning, delivery, and management of Olympic and other multi-sport Villages for more than thirty years. His previous twenty-year voluntary role as Paralympics GB Chef de Mission and Paralympic Refugee Chef de Mission Rio 2016 has made an invaluable contribution to the legacy outcomes for those residential projects. He was awarded the OBE for his contribution to Paralympic sport in 1995.

Gabriel Silvestre is Senior Lecturer in Urban Planning in the School of Architecture, Planning and Landscape at Newcastle University. He is the author of several articles published in English, Portuguese, and Spanish examining the planning and delivery of the 2016 Olympic Games in Rio de Janeiro. His research interests include the areas of urban governance and policy analysis with a focus on circulating knowledge and policy mobilities. His most recent Olympic-related work compares the planning experience of BRICS countries in hosting mega-events.

Andrew Smith is Professor of Urban Experiences in the School of Architecture and Cities at the University of Westminster. He leads the university's multi-disciplinary research community dedicated to Sustainable Cities and the Urban Environment. His research focuses on the relationships between events and host cities, and he has written several books on this theme, including *Events and Urban Regeneration: The Strategic Use of Events to Revitalise Cities* (2012) and *Events in the City: Using Public Spaces as Event Venues* (2016). He has also published numerous journal papers on mega-events, including several on the London 2012 Olympic Games.

Giuseppe Telesca is Research Fellow at the Robert Schuman Centre for Advanced Studies, European University Institute (Florence), where he works on the European Research Council funded project: 'The Memory of Financial Crises: Financial Actors and Global Risk'. His work focuses on the economic and urban impact of big sport events on host cities/countries, with particular reference to Rome 1960, on the use of the memory of financial crises and on British and Italian economic and financial history.

Mike Weed is Professor of Applied Policy Sciences, Strategic Director of the Centre for Sport, Physical Education and Activity Research (SPEAR), and Senior Pro Vice-Chancellor for Research, Enterprise and Business Development at Canterbury Christ Church University. Drawing on a wide range of social science disciplines, his work has focused on informing, improving, and interrogating policy in the applied domains of public health, physical activity, physical education, sport, tourism, transport, urban development, and major events. He is editor-in-chief of the *Journal of Sport & Tourism*, editor of the *SAGE Library of Sport and Leisure Management*, and co-editor of the *Routledge Handbook of Physical Activity Policy and Practice*.

Sven Daniel Wolfe is Swiss National Science Foundation Ambizione Fellow at the ETH Zurich. An urban and political geographer, he works on the socio-spatial impacts of mega-events, urban sustainable development, and geopolitics. He has authored and co-authored a variety of articles about the impacts of mega-events worldwide, and has focused on case studies primarily in Russia, France, and the United States. He is the author of *More Than Sport: Soft Power and Potemkinism in the 2018 Men's Football World Cup in Russia* (2021).

List of Acronyms

The list below contains an alphabetical listing of acronyms used substantively in the text rather than simply for bibliographic purposes:

ACOG	Atlanta Committee for the Olympic Games
AOBC	Athens 2004 Olympic Bid Committee
AOC	Australian Olympic Committee
ATHOC	Athens Organizing Committee for the Olympic Games
BBC	British Broadcasting Corporation
COJO	Comité d'Organisation des Jeux Olympiques
COJOP	Comité d'Organisation des Jeux Olympiques et Paralympiques
COMSEQ	Council of Mayors South East Queensland
CONI	Comitato Olimpico Nazionale Italiano
COOB	Barcelona Olympic Organizing Committee
COVID-19	Coronavirus Disease, identified in 2019
CNOSF	Comité National Olympique et Sportif Français
DCMS	Department of Culture, Media and Sport (UK)
DIJOP	Délégué Interministériel aux Jeux Olympiques et Paralympiques
DSDILGP	Department of State Development, Infrastructure, Local Government and Planning (Queensland)
FDI	Foreign Direct Investment
FIFA	Fédération Internationale de Football Association
IBC	International Broadcast Centre
ICC	International Coordinating Committee of the World Sports Organisations
IFs	International Sports Federations
IOC	International Olympic Committee
IPC	International Paralympic Committee
ISMGF	International Stoke Mandeville Games Foundation
LAOOC	Los Angeles Olympic Organizing Committee
LDA	London Development Agency
LLDC	London Legacy Development Corporation
LOCOG	London Organizing Committee for the Olympic Games
NOC	National Organizing Committee
OCOG	Organizing Committee for the Olympic Games

ODA	Olympic Delivery Authority
OGI	Olympic Games Impact Study
PDA	Priority Development Area
SARS	Severe Acute Respiratory Syndrome
SEQ	South East Queensland
SOCOG	Sydney Organizing Committee for the Olympic Games
SOLIDEO	Société de Livraison des Ouvrages Olympiques
TOP	The Olympic Partner programme
TOROC	Organizing Committee of the XX Turin 2006 Olympic Winter Games
WWF	World Wildlife Fund

Chapter 1

Introduction

John R. Gold and *Margaret M. Gold*

The Olympic movement is wedded to chronology. Olympiads last four years and are numbered. Each year that ends in an even number sees the staging of a major Games, either Summer or Winter. Until recently, host cities were routinely given seven years to prepare for Games of fixed duration, with precise dates for their Opening and Closing Ceremonies agreed long in advance. Over the course of a long history and with very few exceptions, all have gone ahead according to plan, even if Organizing Committees (OCOGs) and their host cities have occasionally resorted to extreme measures to ensure that the venues and associated infrastructures were ready when required.

Normal circumstances, however, did not apply in the case of the Games of the XXXII Olympiad, due to be held in Tokyo from 22 July to 9 August 2020. Towards the end of December 2019, reports started to circulate about a new severe acute respiratory syndrome (SARS) coronavirus that was first identified in Wuhan (China). Officially named SARS-CoV-2 or 'COVID-19' after the year in which it was first identified, its highly contagious properties and marked propensity to mutate allowed it to spread rapidly and cause spiralling death tolls. By 30 January 2020, the World Health Organization declared it to be a Public Health Emergency of International Concern. On 11 March COVID-19 was reclassified as a global pandemic, just three months after it had first been isolated (Rothan and Byrareddy, 2020). Faced with the virus's continuing spread and the absence of any effective treatments or preventative vaccines, governments worldwide adopted the strategy of legally enforced restrictions on social interaction, colloquially known as 'lockdown'. Cancellation of public gatherings occurred almost immediately.

The Tokyo Olympics were then just four months away. All the venues had been completed, with only minor works remaining on tasks such as provision of overlay (temporary infrastructure) and furnishings. Test events had been completed. The Japanese were also uncomfortably aware that a previous Tokyo Summer Games, scheduled for 1940, had been cancelled for political reasons: a precedent they did not want to see repeated. They had also long cherished the idea that these would be the 'Recovery Games', indicating the nation's progress after the 2011 Tōhoku earthquake, which had brought the devastation of tsunami and nuclear meltdown (Boykoff and Gaffney, 2020). Hence there was great reluctance to countenance the idea of postponing or cancelling the Games despite the increasing clamour for one or other of those courses of action.

Initially, therefore, the International Olympic Committee (IOC) and the Japanese government stridently asserted that the event would proceed as planned. Staging the festival, they suggested, might be 'the balm the world needed to show victory over the coronavirus pandemic' (Rich *et al.*, 2020). On 12 March 2020, a day when the worldwide total of COVID-19 cases first exceeded 130,000, the Olympic flame lighting ceremony took place as scheduled in Greece. After a meeting with the international sports federations on 17 March, the IOC optimistically declared that measures against the virus were delivering results and that the Games could proceed with suitable precautions (Kihara, 2020). The next day, Chief Cabinet Secretary Yoshihide Suga told the Japanese parliament that: 'We're not making any adjustments to postpone the Games' (*ibid.*). On 20 March, a plane decked out in Tokyo 2020 livery transported the Olympic flame to Japan.

Nevertheless, their determination to stick to business as usual soon foundered. A mounting groundswell of resistance from the international media and from National Olympic Committees quickly took shape. On 22 March, the Canadian Olympic Committee was the first to warn that it would not send its athletes to the Tokyo Olympics unless the Games were postponed for a year. Their sentiments were quickly echoed by their Australian counterparts, with murmurs from other nations. Finally accepting the inevitable, the Japanese Government – the guarantors of the Tokyo Games – decided to act. As the host city contract specifies that the IOC alone has the right to cancel or postpone an Olympics, Prime Minister Shinzō Abe contacted the IOC on 24 March to seek a postponement.[1] This request came with two provisos: first, that the delayed event would be held no later than the Summer of 2021; and secondly, that the Games would still be known as Tokyo 2020. The IOC's President Thomas Bach accepted these points and agreed to the postponement but warned that finalizing the details of a new schedule and negotiating adjustments in the global sports calendar would take time (Rich *et al.*, 2020).

This was uncharted territory. Games had been cancelled in the past – as was the case during the two World Wars – and Denver had withdrawn from being host city for the 1976 Winter Games, but postponement was new. Commentators quickly recognized that this would create an unprecedented set of problems, which included:

How to renegotiate corporate sponsorships for another year? What to do with the Athletes' Village condominiums, which have already been sold to new tenants expecting to move in by Fall 2020? How to maintain the 110,000 Olympic volunteers?

With millions of moving parts involved, the most unpredictable aspect is the virus itself. Will Tokyo 2020 outrun COVID-19? (Holthus *et al.*, 2020, p. xvii)

For the host city, decisions had to be made, *inter alia*, about, whether to keep overlay in place, rescheduling the transport and mobility arrangements, compensating ticketholders, and resolving the specific problems connected with the legacy use of the Athletes' Village. There were questions of upkeep and maintenance of the stadia and of renegotiating contracts for the temporary use of buildings. For example, the conference and exhibition hall complex known as Tokyo Big Sight, intended to house the International Broadcasting and Main Press Centres, needed to be rebooked for 2021. In the process, another year's bookings would have to be set aside, if indeed the situation had improved sufficiently for those bookings to be fulfilled. Beyond these material considerations lay the realms of conjecture as to what state the pandemic might have reached twelve months hence and whatever further preventative measures might then be needed.

The necessary responses to these myriad complexities would come at considerable cost, later estimated at $2.8 billion; expense that needed to be set against an uncertain future income stream. For example, measures designed to tackle contagion rates had dramatically curtailed movement, with foreign tourism to Japan virtually ceasing. Would normality have returned sufficiently by July 2021 to allow the lifting of travel restrictions? Would spectators then be able to attend the rescheduled Games? Would international tourists be filling the city's hotels and hospitality outlets? Would the related packages of conferences, academic symposia and commercial fairs take place?

The doubts raised by these considerations were largely justified. The Games, which opened after a year's delay in July 2021, were a media event staged in venues occupied primarily by those within the Olympic 'bubble' (predominantly comprising other athletes and officials). The main stadia were fenced off from the public (figure 1.1). The fan zones and the specially created gathering places were empty (figure 1.2). Few conferences were held if these involved sizeable numbers of foreign participants. The forecasts made by economic think tanks about the economic impact and legacy of staging the Games took a battering. Most had subscribed to the view that the 2020 Olympics would sharply bolster not only the country's tourism industry but also the construction sector, while generally encouraging consumer spending. The estimates rose extravagantly in the years leading up to 2020. As reported by Shibata and Ito (2021):

Mitsubishi Research Institute Inc. in 2014 forecast 11 trillion yen in economic effects from the Games. The estimate of Mizuho Financial Group Inc. in 2017 reached 30 trillion yen. The Tokyo metropolitan government in 2017 went even higher, predicting 32 trillion yen in economic benefits from the sporting event... They also said a trickle-down effect would occur, helping smaller contractors in the construction industry, such as cement producers. Tokyo officials emphasized that the long-term economic 'legacy effects' from the Olympics would total 27.1 trillion yen. About 20 trillion yen of legacy effects would come from the post-Olympic use of the Athletes' Village and construction of an international business base.

Yet when reviewing the gross inaccuracy of these figures, it is important to recognize two points. First, there has always been a temptation to stress the unalloyed economic benefits of the Games as a strategy designed to head off criticism, especially given that staging them sees revenue only accruing after a long period of sustained expenditure. While protest was not necessarily as pronounced as in the USA and elsewhere (e.g. see Boykoff, 2020; Reef, 2021), there had been opposition at various stages to the Olympics in Japan (Richter *et al.*, 2020), with thoughts of civic pride, spectacle, and long-term cultural kudos frequently seeming secondary to considerations of price and value-for-money. Even Shinzō Abe had admitted in 2015 that there had been 'criticisms from the public which made me believe that we will not

Figure 1.1. Passers-by pose for selfies with the Japan National Stadium, Tokyo in the background on 24 July 2021, the first day of the Summer Olympic Games. Designed to prevent public access to the stadium, the fence symbolizes the difficult decisions necessary to stage the Games. (*Source*: Photo © Louise Claire Wagner)

Figure 1.2. Deserted entrance to Fan Park, Tokyo 2020 Summer Olympic Games. Photo taken in July 2021. (*Source*: Photo © Louise Claire Wagner)

be able to host a Games that everyone in this country would celebrate' (Wingfield-Hayes, 2015). Given the volatility of public opinion, therefore, these apparently authoritative and inherently positive econometric forecasts were used to address residual concerns about hosting the Games and to counter concerns about soaring costs as the planning and implementation phases proceeded (Shibata and Ito, 2021).

Secondly, and while not downplaying the unique features of the delivery of Tokyo 2020, other features of the project's development to date have mirrored rather than contrasted with those of its predecessors as Olympic cities. The same may well apply as its legacy phase unfolds. These parallels reinforce a central idea, namely that a proper appreciation of the staging of the modern Olympics rests on understanding the relationship between the IOC and its host cities (Gold and Gold, 2012). This complex and richly textured relationship, which shapes every Games, has emerged over the course of a long history, but is far from static. Indeed, its flexibility and capacity to absorb change has been a vital factor in ensuring the extraordinary longevity of the Olympics despite the trials and tribulations presented by changing times.

The IOC-Host City Relationship

The IOC's decision in the 1890s to re-establish the modern Games as an ambulatory event that moved to a new destination every four years immediately placed the relationship between the IOC and its host cities at the centre of the Olympic project. Like any contract entered into by two parties with different starting positions, it was always likely to be a fluid and occasionally uneasy partnership. This was particularly so because that partnership often rested on changing and sometimes conflicting views, first, about the ways in which the increasing size of the Games should be accommodated and, secondly, about the extent to which the hosts could or should use the Games as vehicles for achieving positive outcomes for their cities as opposed to the Olympic movement.

To elaborate, in the early days the Olympic movement sought to use the Games' ambulatory path to encourage longer-term sporting outcomes in host nations around the globe. Members of the IOC tended to nominate cities in their own countries as potential hosts, believing that the value of the event came from the prestige that accrued to centres that held the Games. Naturally, the organizers of earlier Olympiads were aware of the economic potential that the Games might have, especially with regard to tourism but, given the attachment to amateurism and antipathy to profit on the part of the IOC, it was considered inappropriate to glory in what the Games would do for the city rather than for sport and the pleasure of its citizens (McIntosh, 2003, pp. 450, 452).

This arrangement was perfectly feasible when the financial burden for the host city was small, with the local organizers staging the early Games in adapted stadia or temporary arenas. However, the rapid growth in the scale and complexity of the Olympics quickly created new challenges, with host cities increasingly expected to act as risk-takers. Special venues were needed, with London's White City Stadium, purpose-built for the 1908 Olympics, setting the trend. Five years later, the Swedish organizers of the 1912 Games wistfully concluded that: 'to carry out the Olympic Games of the present day … required not only personal effort on the part of the organizers, but also the most ample financial resources' (SOC, 1913, p. 51).

In the fullness of time, the Games' organizers saw that much more could be achieved as by-products of being nominated to stage the Olympics. Los Angeles' bid for the 1932 Games, for example, was crafted by aggressive local entrepreneurs and political leaders who wished to boost the city's credentials on the national and international stage. The organizers of Berlin 1936 saw the Summer Games used as a medium for the Third Reich's spectacular representations of the New Germany, albeit with a surprisingly small impact on the host city apart from the completion of an enormous sports complex on the city's outskirts. Rome 1960, the first Games held after the end of the Austerity that followed the Second World War, set the precedent for thoroughgoing attempts by a host city to attach general exercises in urban development to the festival. Over time, a tacit bargain effectively developed between the IOC and the host city, particularly as mediated by the OCOG.

In broad terms, this allowed the Games to be used to address the needs of the home city in return for the extraordinary investment of time, effort and resources needed to stage the event. By the time of Barcelona 1992, the balance had altered so dramatically that only 17 per cent of total expenditure actually went on the sports element of the Games compared with 83 per cent on urban improvement.

In the 1990s, the issue of sustainability entered the frame. In 1994, the IOC adopted the principle that the candidate cities for the Summer and Winter Games should also be evaluated on the environmental consequences of their plans (Gold and Gold, 2013). This was matched by the decision to construe 'environment' as a 'third pillar' of the Olympic movement's core philosophy of Olympism, alongside 'sport' and 'culture'. In 1996, the Olympic Charter was itself amended to assert that one of the IOC's roles is 'to encourage and support a responsible concern for environmental issues, to promote sustainable development in sport and require that the Olympic Games are held accordingly' (quoted in Pitts and Liao, 2009, p. 67). In October 1999, the Olympic Movement published its own Agenda 21 document as a response to the recommendations of the 1992 Rio Earth Summit to serve as a 'useful reference tool for the sports community at all levels in the protection of the environment and enhancement of sustainable development' (IOC, 2006, p. 10).

To a large extent, the idealistic tenor of environmentalism conveyed by these measures struck a resonant note with the Olympic Movement – itself not adverse to idealism. Yet it may also be argued that the sustainability agenda gave the IOC the chance to respond to accusations of 'gigantism', whereby host cities were seemingly required to spend ever larger amounts to stage one-off events that have steadily grown in size and complexity over the years (Geeraert and Gauthier, 2018, p. 19; also Preuss, 2004). Direct advocacy of environmental responsibility helped to show that the movement was addressing these issues by seeking to reduce the impact of the Games and to ensure that the future generations of the city's residents gained lasting benefits from the expenditure.

If sustainability led the way in renegotiating the core relationship between host cities and the IOC, it was quickly joined by a new and explicit concern for 'legacy' – a notion that now exerts a powerful sway over the way in which the outcomes of the Games are imagined, conceptualized, negotiated, and realized (Gold and Gold, 2014, 2017*b*). Historically, the word 'legacy' had had sporadic and non-specific usage in Olympic parlance, but largely lacked the conceptual impedimenta now attached to it. The first significant mention of the word *per se* appeared in the city of Melbourne's bid document for the 1956 Games (McIntosh, 2003, p. 450), but that was an isolated occurrence – particularly as there was no further use of the term in the Official Reports either prepared for the Melbourne Games or its successors for several decades thereafter. This did not mean, of course, that organizers were indifferent to achieving beneficial outcomes for their host cities. At Melbourne, for example, the OCOG's Official Report talked of putting resources to good use and creating 'a continuing asset' (Organizing Committee, 1958). For Rome 1960, the Official Report comments on 'meeting ever-increasing needs' (CONI, 1963) and the Montreal Summer Games in 1976 were intended to leave an 'inheritance of benefit' (Organizing Committee, 1976).

Legacy, in the contemporary sense, started to be used in a concerted manner in the Official Reports for Los Angeles with eleven mentions (LAOOC, 1985) and the Winter Games in Calgary 1988 with forty-two mentions (COWGOC, 1988). As measured by the Official Reports, the notion of legacy became increasingly entrenched in thinking over the last three decades, with Atlanta 1996 recording seventy-one mentions, forty-three for Sydney 2000, fifty-five for Salt Lake City 2002, and twenty-three for Athens 2004 (see respectively ACOG, 1990; SOCOG, 2000; SLOC, 2002; and ATHOC, 2005). The informal and *ad hoc* usages of the term, however, were in many ways racing ahead of substantive definition. It could clearly consist of a mélange of sporting, urban regenerative, social, and environmental elements. Equally, the term could encompass a disparate range of intangible ingredients that include skills, sports and cultural participation, volunteering, national pride, and city status.

In attempting to come to terms with the growing diversity, therefore, a symposium met under IOC auspices in 2002 to consider the relevant theory and practice. After extensive deliberations, it concluded (IOC, 2003*a*, p. 2) that:

> The effects of the legacy have many aspects and dimensions, ranging from the more commonly recognised aspects – architecture, urban planning, city marketing, sports infrastructures, economic and tourist development – to others ... that are less well recognised ... the so called intangible legacies, such as production of ideas and cultural values, intercultural and non-exclusionary experiences (based on gender, ethnicity or physical abilities), popular memory, education, archives, collective effort and voluntarism, new sport practitioners, notoriety on a global scale, experience and know-how...

This all-encompassing definition delimited a broad category within which further differentiation has been made by establishing dichotomies. The one recognized by the symposium was tangible (measurable) versus intangible legacy (non-measurable), but other dichotomies, often sharing common ground, have subsequently been added. They include direct (arising from investment in the Olympics) versus indirect (associated) legacy; short-term versus long-term; and hard (physical structures and infrastructure) versus soft (other tangible and intangible outcomes). In addition, other terms like 'pregacy' have become a jocular way of identifying impacts occurring before the event. The term pre-legacy was employed more formally by the Rio de Janeiro Organizing Committee for infrastructure completed before the Games; a phase considered to have begun when Olympic venues were opened to underprivileged communities (Anon, 2015).

The Ascendance of Legacy

Considerations of the hydra-headed beast known as legacy now comprises a shared frame within which policymakers and scholars alike have started to think about the trajectory of the development of the Olympic project over time in the host city.[2] Viewed analytically, the workings of legacy in each instance rest on a 'narrative', understood here as a structured account of a sequence of events that connect actions (actual or putative) with specific outcomes. The nature of that narrative, however, has changed over time and varies with the values of the observer. For most policymakers, the underlying narrative is one that links positive outcomes back to decisive actions. By contrast, for Olympic critics the corresponding narrative might well portray connections that lead from ideologically motivated actions to outcomes that are variously conceived as being unintended, dysfunctional, or even undemocratic (Gold and Gold, 2011).

With these thoughts in mind, it is worth making five points that help to contextualize the discussions of legacy that arise at many points in this text. The first is that the concept remains in its infancy in terms of its practical application. Despite now ostensibly being central to the *raison d'être* of the Games, no city to date has yet undergone a full and rigorous longitudinal evaluation of the legacy from an Olympic Games: a process that might easily take several decades to run its course. In attempting to gain better data, for example, the IOC established the Olympic Games Global Impact project in 2003, retitled the Olympic Games Impact Study (OGI) in 2006 (Dubi and Felli, 2006). Under OGI arrangements, candidate and then host cities are committed to look at the economic, environmental and social impact of the Games over a period of eleven years, namely when the city applies (baseline report); in the preparation phase; a report on staging the Games completed a year after the Games have ended; and a closing report supplied three years after the end. Although Athens 2004, Turin 2006 and Beijing 2008 cooperated in limited ways with this project, Vancouver 2010 and London 2012 were the first hosts to go through the full cycle. Nevertheless, what has emerged from the reports to date has been meagre and often more concerned with the problems of methodology than with supplying concrete evidence about legacy. The first of London 2012's OGI reports, for example, had reported:

No negative impacts were found as a result of preparing for the 2012 Games, some positive impacts were found but many indicators were inconclusive. Such inconclusiveness is not a criticism; it may stem from data issues, but also from the diverse policy landscape of the UK, London and East London. (UEL/TGIS, 2010, p. 125)

The next report – published in December 2015 – concluded by repeating the above finding (UEL, 2015, p. 183), before understandably underlining the complexity of the task and justifying the broad absence of more substantive findings by adding:

As with any long term project that is intended to be a catalyst for long term change and transformation, the analysis of three years into legacy that this report presents is only the beginning. The urban transformation of the Olympic Park is not expected to be complete before 2030. As we have noted, cultural changes towards, say, more healthy and active lifestyles can take a long time, may even be generational. That London 2012 has been a catalyst for positive change is not in doubt, but when and where the process ends and what will be the full magnitude of the effect is not yet known. The story of London 2012 will continue to unfold for a long time to come.

That point remains valid, even more than a decade after the process of legacy formally began (see Bernstock *et al.*, 2022).

The second contextual point about legacy concerns the role of values. Although many researchers would choose to see the term 'legacy' as representing a balance of negative as well as positive elements, IOC practice has accented the latter. Tomlinson (2014, p. 152), for example, noted that a bibliography from the IOC's Library and Study Centre contrasted 'legacy' with 'impact'. 'Legacy' was used in 'presenting positive effects … also … in association with those effects that are of longer duration', whereas 'impacts' was regarded 'as implying an adverse effect or a damaging or destructive result' (IOC, 2013*a*, p. 3; quoted in Tomlinson, 2014, p. 152). Games organizers and local growth coalitions[3] have adopted similar policies. Elsewhere (Gold and Gold, 2011, 2016), we have written about the prevalence of the Whig interpretations of history (Butterfield, 1931) that have long dominated writings about the Olympics: an interpretative approach that stands for historical narratives that selectively view the past in terms of the march towards ever greater achievement and enlightenment. Equally many academic observers have tended towards suspicion or hostility towards the assumptions linked to Olympic legacy, especially in light of instances of inadequate or overambitious planning, poor stadia design, financial corruption, heavy cost overruns, environmental damage, and lack of accountability (e.g. see Cohen, 2013; Raco, 2014; Pavoni, 2015).[4]

It is neither part of the function of this book to lionize or debunk the Games nor to argue that their impact on host cities is positive or adverse on *a priori* grounds. Nevertheless, what is apparent from the standpoint of Olympic cities is that staging the Games is now divorced from the economic rationale that surrounds almost all other festivals. The Olympics are commonly recognized as being mega-events[5] – cultural and sporting festivals that achieve sufficient size and scope to affect whole economies and to command sustained global media attention (Gold and Gold, 2005, p. 4; see also Roche, 2000; Preuss, 2015; Gruneau and Horne, 2016; Müller, 2017; Lauermann, 2019). Through their size and prestige, such events are held to bring a highly desirable package of benefits to the host city. *Inter alia*, these include boosting a city's economy, improving its international standing, repositioning it in the global tourist market, promoting urban regeneration, revamping transport and service infrastructures, creating vibrant cultural quarters, establishing a network of high-grade facilities that could serve as the basis for future bids, and gaining a competitive advantage over rivals. Some of these benefits are visible and readily measurable; others are confidently proclaimed but intangible; yet others are a mixture of the two. Shortfalls in one area might be offset by reference to another, with disagreements largely unresolvable due to incompatibilities in the evidence cited and the conflicting values of the parties to the argument.

Moreover, the Olympic festivals are also prime candidates for classification as 'megaprojects'. Defined as prestige schemes involving large-scale and high-risk investment over a lengthy period, megaprojects notoriously suffer heavy cost overruns, often failing to deliver the supposed benefits and regularly provoking financial crises (Flyvbjerg *et al.*, 2003; Flyvbjerg and Stewart, 2012; see also Hall, 1980; Söderlund *et al.*, 2017). Indeed, as Flyvbjerg and Stewart (2012, p. 3) have noted from their analyses of the costs and cost overruns for the Olympic Games from 1960 to 2012:

> We discovered that the Games stand out in two distinct ways compared to other megaprojects: (1) The Games overrun with 100 per cent consistency. No other type of megaproject is this consistent regarding cost overrun. Other project types are typically on budget from time to time, but not the Olympics. (2) With an average cost overrun in real terms of 179 per cent – and 324 per cent in nominal terms – overruns in the Games have historically been significantly larger than for other types of megaprojects, including infrastructure, construction, ICT, and dams.

The Olympics may suffer more in this respect than other megaprojects by virtue of having an immutable deadline for completion. Compromises that run counter to the goal of keeping public spending within bounds are inevitable. The swift cooperation of the private sector is required but often at the cost of providing incentives for investment in the form of grants of land, loans on favourable terms, and adjustments to building regulations.[6] The eventual appearance of gentrification in the housing market by private developers eager to generate income on their investment is a seemingly inevitable concomitant of such policies. In addition, works running behind timetable can add further cost pressures by forcing organizers to instigate high-cost emergency building programmes, with round-the-clock working and additional sub-contractors, in order to get laggard projects back on schedule.

Acknowledgment of these unwelcome characteristics and the degree of risk attached is rarely countenanced before winning the bid and almost never voluntarily voiced once the Games have been awarded. The right to host the Olympics represents the ultimate accolade that a city can earn on the world stage. Expenditures might be disputed and lower priority events, such as the Cultural Olympiad or associated youth programmes, might have their budgets slashed, but the prestige element of the marquee events generally means that expenditure will go ahead regardless. Ways will be found to finance the Games notwithstanding the apparently compelling logic of the balance sheet. If necessary, the nation as a whole rather than the Olympic city will pick up the bulk of the bill. Without cost as an effective constraint, therefore, debate inevitably centres on the seductive promise of legacy to sustain popular enthusiasm and drive the project forward.

The third contextual point that needs recognition at the outset concerns the balance of sports to non-sports legacy. It goes without saying that sports-related elements are a key element in the equation, particularly for the IOC which is not altogether happy about the over-identification of notions of legacy with the housing and infrastructural interests of the host city and the approach that this appears to embody. Certainly, bid documents by candidate cities pay close attention to sports legacy, which routinely incorporates four interrelated and overlapping themes. The first is sports *infrastructure*. With the Summer Games requiring new, renovated or temporary facilities for an ever-increasing number of sports, there is always likely to be a stock of new facilities available for local use or, if dismantled, for use elsewhere. The second, sports *development*, comprises encouraging sports participation for its own sake or for instrumental reasons (for example, promotion of public health or for tackling unequal access to sports opportunities). The third, sports *performance*, relates to raising standards and promoting excellence. The final element, sports *tourism*, involves travel to participate in or watch sporting events. Taken collectively, though, these various aspects of sports legacy are often easier to propose conceptually than to achieve, especially in terms of sports participation and inculcation of public health.

The fourth contextual point involves inclusion and exclusion. Anything that involves major long-term investment for an Olympic Games immediately evokes questions of equity. Although detailed discussion of these matters lies beyond the scope of this chapter,[7] it is possible to recognize, in outline, at least five dimensions of equity connected with Olympic legacy.[8] These are: *intergenerational* equity or the passing of resources from one generation to the next; *social* equity, whereby people within society have equal rights and opportunities with respect to the gains to be realized from legacy, regardless of their class or status; *economic* equity, in which wealth created as part of the legacy of the Games is distributed fairly throughout the community; *environmental* equity, which offers a safe, healthy, productive, and sustainable environment for all; and *spatial* equity or fairness of distribution of legacy outcomes regardless of location. These five loosely defined dimensions, of course, represent ideal states that are difficult to implement and pursuit of one may create tensions with others. Nevertheless, there is little doubt that these problems of definition and tensions need to be resolved if host cities are to make full sense of the still indeterminate notion of legacy.

Finally, thinking about legacy must now be seen within the context of the IOC's Agenda 2020 strategic initiative and its succeeding revisions. As originally initiated by IOC President Thomas Bach in December 2013 and approved by the IOC in December 2014, Agenda 2020 consisted of a set of forty detailed recommendations designed to clarify where the Olympic movement was headed and how it could 'protect the uniqueness of the Games and strengthen Olympic values in society' (IOC, 2014*b*, p. 1). Although the point had much wider considerations than purely a matter concerning legacy, it recognized legacy as a persuasive notion for gaining public support for and demonstrating public benefit from staging the Games. It also paved the way for explicitly tailoring the Olympic project to the needs and characteristics of aspirant host cities. Under Agenda 2020, legacy is now to be embedded more emphatically from the outset: '[it] should be at the heart of informing the decision whether or not to bid for the Games' before the city has even entered the bidding procedure formally (IOC, 2015*b*, p. 167). Moreover, it is a key element of the evaluation of the candidature as cities proceed through the bidding process (see also IOC, 2014*b*).

In 2017, the IOC published a strategic review of the role of legacy, clarifying its thinking and proffering a new approach for moving forwards (IOC, 2017*b*). A key aspect of this review was to provide a new definition, which is described as 'a tool for alignment within the Olympic Movement, rather than a theoretical endeavour' (*ibid.*, p. 13). Briefer and more focused than the version originally offered by the 2002 symposium (see above), it asserted that:

> Olympic legacy is the result of a vision. It encompasses all the tangible and intangible long-term benefits initiated or accelerated by the hosting of the Olympic Games/sport events for people, cities/territories and the Olympic Movement. (IOC, 2017*b*)

After then reiterating the point about vision for the purpose of emphasis, the report's authors (*ibid.*) argued:

> Olympic legacy comes from the implementation of a vision which originates from the

alignment of the Olympic Movement core vision of 'building a better world through sport' with the vision of a city (or a territory) of what a 'better world through sport' looks like in a specific place and time. (*Ibid.*)

For many years, legacy had essentially been the province of the host city; part of the *quid pro quo* for organizing the Games. Efforts were now being made to recentre matters so that legacy should be a joint project in which:

the alignment of the city/territory vision with the vision of building a better world through sport leads to the development of a joint vision, which in turn sets the scene for the development of the Olympic Games concept. (*Ibid.*, p. 14)

Examined in the context of the shifting pendulum of influence between the Olympic movement and the host city, it is hard to avoid the conclusion that the sense of even-handed partnership imparted by this statement also masks an underlying ideological steer.

Aims

The unfolding dialogue instigated by Agenda 2020 and subsequent initiatives (e.g. IOC, 2021*a*) forms a backdrop to discussions found in many points in this book. Selection by the IOC as an 'Olympic city' invites the host to contribute to a process that is now more than a century old but continues to evolve. The Olympic city gains the right to stage a festival carefully wrapped in the trappings of historical precedent, but which also possesses a remarkable malleability that has allowed the event to survive repeated crises and emerge, by the start of the twenty-first century, as unquestionably the 'World's Games'.[9] Olympic cities are risk-taking partners in the staging of the Olympics rather than nominees that run a festival crafted by its sponsoring body. The IOC guards the continuing traditions of its festival aided by fierce insistence on legal protection for its brand and intellectual property (Grady, 2020), but each recipient city shapes the Games to greater or lesser extent and contributes to the body of customs and practices associated with the Olympics. Constantly in a process of adaptation and change, the Olympics and host cities enjoy a flexible and symbiotic relationship.

This book explores that relationship, examining the experience of Olympic cities and the balance sheet of success and failure from the revival of the Games in Athens in 1896 to the plans for the Summer Games in Paris 2024, Los Angeles 2028, and Brisbane 2032.[10] As such, it has three main aims. First, it examines the city's role in *staging* the modern Games, a word that covers the full spectrum of activity from selection of sites to final modification of these sites to their post-festival condition. Secondly, it explores the underlying *agendas* that host cities have brought to bear on hosting the Games, recognizing the different blends of social, political, cultural, and economic aspirations that have emerged over time. Finally, it recognizes that, despite being an exceptional event in the life of a specific city, the business of staging the Games is now commonly related to the wider *planning* process. In this respect, we focus particularly on issues concerned with legacy, including infrastructural development and urban regeneration projects, which are now regarded as central to the process of planning for the Olympics.

Against that background, two points are important in understanding the scope of this book. First, while rightly giving prominence to the Summer Games as by far the largest, most prestigious and visible of the Olympic events, we seek a more comprehensive approach. The Olympics are not a single event. The advent of the Winter Olympics in 1924 and the gradual convergence of the Paralympics with both the Summer and Winter Games have added further strands to the Olympic sporting competitions. In addition, the revival of the modern Games predicated a cultural festival, now usually formulated as a four-year Cultural Olympiad, to exist alongside the sports events. Each of these strands merits coverage as intrinsic parts of the experience of being an Olympic city.[11]

Secondly, the prevailing focus is historical. This does not mean that we have confined the scope of this book to dealing purely with the past since later chapters deal with Olympics that, at the time of writing, are yet-to-come. What this volume does stress, however, is the value of seeing even these forthcoming Games as the product of a chain of events that reaches back into the late nineteenth century and has been steadily developing since that time. The staging of the Olympics assuredly invites historical analysis. Continuity between Games arises from each new Organizing Committee scrutinizing the experience of previous OCOGs, with transfer of knowledge from one to another facilitated both by the IOC's own procedures and a small army of freelance consultants and specialists who offer their services to Games organizers. In addition, each new host city prepares its Olympic festivals in the sure and certain knowledge that its efforts will be assessed against those of predecessors and will, in turn, provide a new point of comparison for successors.

Structure

As befits the multi-stranded nature of the narratives that surround the Games, the ensuing chapters divide into three main sections, each of which offers different perspectives on the Olympics. Part 1 contains four parallel but complementary essays that look chronologically at the progress of the individual Olympic festivals from inception to the early twenty-first century. Chapter 2 provides an overview of the relationship between the Summer Olympics and their host cities, acting as a general framework for the case studies of selected cities found in Part 3 as well as adding coverage of Summer Games, particularly from the early years, which are not tackled there. After examining the circumstances behind the revival of the Olympics, it traces eight phases in the history of staging the festival from the opening Games in Athens 1896 to their most recent manifestation in Tokyo 2020.

In a similar vein, chapter 3 provides a historic overview that identifies a five-phase framework for analysing the role of the Winter Olympics in changing and modernizing the built environment of its host cities. In looking to the future, it touches briefly on potential developments given the thinking that emerged from deliberations over the IOC's Agenda 2020. Chapter 4 examines the cultural dimension of the Games and its attachment to both the Summer and Winter Games. It provides an overview of the programme's evolution, from initial art competitions through to more recent four-year Olympiads, examining the problems and challenges encountered. After emphasizing how recent developments have seen the cultural festivals growing in scale, particularly in response to the economic interests of host cities, it also notes the relationship between the Cultural Olympiad and the evolving Agenda 2020 frameworks. Chapter 5 examines the Paralympic Games. It charts their development from small beginnings as a competition for disabled ex-servicemen and women in England in the late 1940s to the present day ambulatory international festivals for athletes with disabilities, which now take place in the Olympic city shortly after both the Summer and Winter Games.

Part 2 provides surveys of six key aspects of activity involved in planning and managing the Olympics. Chapter 6 examines the finance of the Olympics. It provides an economic overview of the development of the Games and identifies the broad group of stakeholders who benefit from staging them; a group that goes well beyond the main shareholders (the Olympic family). Chapter 7 deals with the emergence of sustainability as a key feature in the thought and practice of staging the Olympic Games. It looks at the ways in which the Olympic Movement has responded to growing concerns about the environmental impact of the Games historically and the agenda of environmentalism in the context of sustainability and in the face of global warming. It explores the evolution of IOC thinking as it has sought to carve out a role in shaping the relationship between sport and the environment in the Games themselves but also in the wider Olympic Movement. In doing this it also shows how sustainability and legacy have become part of a single discourse of positive impact for the Olympics. Chapter 8 draws on the experience of a practitioner with thirty years' experience to consider the provision and role of Olympic and Paralympic Villages. It reflects on the historical development of Villages as an integral part of staging the Games, identifying six strands that materially influenced the approach that was manifested at London 2012.

Turning to issues involving event spaces, their surrounding areas and subsequent use, chapter 9 switches attention to the question of security, which has rapidly become one of the key parameters for site organization. It discusses the gradual but inexorable increase in the securitization of Olympic sites, offering perspectives that include London 2012's response to international terrorism and Rio de Janeiro 2016's problems relating to tensions arising from the pacification of the city's *favelas* and drug-related violence. Chapter 10 reviews how and why the Olympic Games is used as a vehicle for regeneration, and how conclusions drawn from the Olympics are also applied to regeneration processes in general. Critical comment is directed against commonly expressed rhetoric, such as the notion that staging the Olympic Games provides 'flagship' urban projects and 'catalysts' for regeneration. The discussion of specific Games then focuses particularly on those Games which were staged on brownfield sites. Chapter 11 addresses Olympic tourism. It outlines a range of Olympic tourism products, before outlining how the Summer and Winter Games can be leveraged to generate tourism. The two substantive parts of this chapter then examine how cities staging the Winter Games can act as tourism gateways to their wider regions and how Summer Games can contribute to the development of their host cities' tourism product and image.

Part 3 offers ten portraits of Olympic Cities, arranged in chronological order. Its prime focus is staging the nine Olympic and Paralympic Games held or scheduled to be held in the twenty-first century, but it is also instructive to consider the experience of Rome 1960 – a watershed in the use of the Games to address the urban agenda. Chapter 12 places these Games in the contexts of Italian history, before pointing to their key importance in the evolution of the Summer Games as a vehicle for achieving urban development and legacy. It then offers reflections on the role that the 1960 Olympics played in heralding new opportunities for cities willing to bid for hosting the summer Games, indicating how the city itself would on numerous occasions seek in vain to repeat the exercise.

Chapter 13 focuses attention on Sydney 2000, examining in particular the physical planning and transformation of the main site at Homebush Bay. The author considers the process of development through the lens of legacy, briefly considering the nature of that concept before identifying a chronology of thinking that frames the narrative. The Sydney experience is characterized as comprising four main stages before reflecting on the broader implications of this episode in both Olympic and planning history. Next, chapter 14 analyses the Games' return to Athens in 2004. It discusses the serious delays incurred by belatedly switching from a nucleated to a dispersed locational policy for Olympic facilities. It also highlights the lip-service paid to the much-heralded goal of environmental sustainability before the event and the continuing desolation of the Olympic sites in their transfer to post-Games usage. Nevertheless, recent progress at several of the Olympic sites do offer a more positive view of the long-awaited legacy process.

Chapter 15 examines the astonishing expenditure and associated spectacle that was part and parcel of Beijing 2008. In doing so, it recognizes not only the urban dimension of these Games but their significance within wider processes of development taking place within the city of Beijing, in its region, and in the People's Republic of China as a whole. If place promotion took centre stage at Beijing, its successor at London 2012 saw the prospect for regeneration of a deprived and environmentally blighted area of East London as much a part of the bidding process as the image of an inclusive and spectacular Olympic festival. Chapter 16 takes stock of the event process, its legacy and the future planning of the Olympic Park and its environs. From their critical review of the emerging legacy experience, the authors argue for the importance of continuing longitudinal analysis of the Olympic project.

Chapter 17 charts the history of the Games in Rio de Janeiro, the first city in South America to host the Games, looking particularly at the urban changes associated with preparing the venues and the course of subsequent legacy. It examines the different Olympic bids the city had prepared in the last two decades and the course of the 2016 project – which was realized in a very different economic environment than applied at the time when the bid was formulated. It analyses the spatial planning of the Games and the course of the ambitious legacy programmes with which it was associated. It ends by attempting to answer social, political and environment challenges still associated with the event and questions that remain unanswered, even after the passage of more than seven years.

Drawing on the insights available from an academic observer and former politician who was part of the bid team, chapter 18 surveys Tokyo's history as an Olympic city. It notes the importance of the 1964 Games in the city's development, especially in acting as a catalyst for the reshaping of transport networks. With that event as a role model, the planners of the 2020 games sought to create an event that might also bring about social and economic benefit, only to be thrown off course by having to stage the event a year late and to spectatorless stadia due to the COVID-19 pandemic. After outlining the plans and the unique set of challenges that occurred in their implementation, it takes stock of the larger purposes of Olympic-inspired improvements, what visions they are serving, and how the continuing legacy of Tokyo 2020 might act in transforming Tokyo and Japanese society as a whole.

The three remaining chapters look ahead to Games that are yet to be held; festivals that by definition are at hugely different stages of preparation. Despite what was thought to be known about the bidding process from Agenda 2020 discussions, surprises were in store when the IOC session in

Lima in 2017 simultaneously selected Paris for 2024 and Los Angeles for 2028. Chapter 19 considers Paris 2024 which, at the time of writing in 2023, had entered full operational mode ready for test events. It is noted, however, that a variety of challenges remained, particularly around security, transport, funding, and sustainability. After considering the presentation of the bid for 2024, its context and governance, the discussion focuses on the urban dimension of the event, its sustainable dimensions and consideration of its urban legacy.

Looking forward into the longer-term future, chapter 20 turns attention to Los Angeles 2028. Gaining the nomination consolidated the city's claims to be *the* American Olympic city, given that this was to be the third staging of the Games. The chapter opens with an overview of the two previous Olympics staged in the city (1932 and 1984), along with the innovations that they introduced and the controversies that they engendered. This supplies context for considering the awarding of the 2028 Games, themselves seen against the background of changing Olympic strategies on hosting. Finally, the authors detail the preparations for 2028 and unpack three emblematic sites of contestation tied to the Games linked respectively to: transit systems; decorations and festivities; governance and budget.

Chapter 21 turns the spotlight on to Brisbane 2032, still more than nine years away at the time of writing. Identified as the IOC's approved candidate in February 2021 and confirmed as host city for 2032 at the IOC's meeting in the following July, the selection of Brisbane reflected bidding procedures first introduced in 2019 – themselves very different from those proposed in the original Agenda 2020 documents in 2014. This chapter reflects on that bidding process before analysing the master plan for venues and the Olympic Village and how these will fit into planning for Brisbane and the Southeast Queensland region. Consideration is then given to the Games' legacy in terms of their economic, social and environmental sustainability.

Notes

1. Seeking postponement rather than cancellation avoided a course of action that if taken would have caused the largest insurance claims in history (Zimbalist, 2021).

2. For a selection of a diverse and rapidly growing literature, see Thornley (2012); Graham *et al.* (2013); Thompson *et al.* (2013); Davis (2014); Gold and Gold (2015); Nichols and Ralston (2015); Girginov (2018); and Byun and Leopkey (2022).

3. For more on the nature of growth coalitions and their influence, see Andranovich *et al.* (2001); Kearins and Pavlovich (2002); Zhang and Wu (2008); and Boykoff (2014).

4. Compare, for example, the very different positions taken by Bernstock *et al.* (2022) and Owens and Ward (2022).

5. The term 'mega-event' was first used in 1987 at the 37th Congress of the Association Internationale d'Experts Scientifiques du Tourisme in Calgary in 1987 (Müller, 2015b, p. 2).

6. Practices clearly identified at many points in this book: *inter alia,* see chapters 6, 10, 16 and 17.

7. For further information and contrasting perspectives, see Chalip and Leyns (2002); Swart and Bob (2004); Vigor *et al.* (2004); Shipway (2007); Short (2008; 2018); O'Bonsawin (2010); Minnaert (2012); Noland and Stahler (2015); Kennelly (2016); Tjønndal (2019); and Wolfe (2023).

8. Originally based on http://gladstone.uoregon.edu/~caer/ej_definitions.html, accessed 25 March 2010.

9. It is important to distinguish this commonly applied aphorism for the Olympics from the 'World Games', a multi-sport event staged at four-yearly intervals since 1981 by the International World Games Association and covering sports not represented in the Olympics, such as billiards, netball, and bodybuilding. These aspire, as yet unconvincingly, to equal or even exceed the importance of the world championships that are organized individually by each individual participant federation.

10. Source papers relating to the contents of this book can be found in the four-volume set: *The Making of Olympic Cities* (Gold and Gold, 2012).

11. While recognizing the recent creation of youth editions of both the Summer and Winter Games – the former in 2010 (Singapore); the latter in 2012 (Innsbruck) – these much smaller events are not yet considered within the scope of this book. For more information, see Judge *et al.* (2009); Parry (2012); and Parent *et al.* (2015).

PART 1

THE OLYMPIC FESTIVALS

Chapter 2

THE SUMMER OLYMPICS 1896–2020

John R. Gold and *Margaret M. Gold*

Yet let us all together to our troops,
And give them leave to fly that will not stay;
And call them pillars that will stand to us;
And, if we thrive, promise them such rewards
As victors wear at the Olympian games

William Shakespeare[1]

The significance of ancient Greek thought and practices for the formation of modern Western culture effectively ensured that memories of the classical world never faded from European consciousness. Whatever vicissitudes had subsequently befallen the Greek state, notions of democracy and the pursuit of knowledge, scientific achievement and artistic excellence had reverberated down the years. Shakespeare's matter-of-fact reference to the Olympics in *Henry VI, Part 3*, for instance, 'was a shared, not isolated reference' in the arts throughout Western Europe (Segrave, 2005, p. 22). Indeed, although the Roman Emperor Theodosius I had prohibited the Games in 393 AD, the Olympics were 'probably the one' among the 'incalculable influences of the Greeks in the modern world … of which the general public [were] the most aware' (Littlewood, 2000, p. 1179).

Much the same sense of cultural resonance extended to Olympia, the place with which the Games were associated. As the English theologian Richard Chandler (1766, p. 308) remarked, its name would 'ever be respected as venerable for its precious era by the chronologer and historian', for whom:

[it] had been rendered excessively illustrious by the power and reputation of its ancient princes, among whom were Œnomaus and Pelops; by the Oracle and temple of the Olympian Jupiter; by the celebrity of the grand *Panegyris* or general assembly held at

it; and by the renown of the *Agon* or Games, in which to be victorious was deemed the very summit of human felicity. (*Ibid.*, p. 303)

Yet despite its lasting reputation, no one was sure about Olympia's exact whereabouts. Despite being indicated on maps since 1516, when the Venetian cartographer Battista Palnese referred to it as 'Andilalo',[2] the passage of time meant that 'Olympia has since been forgotten in its vicinity'. (*Ibid.*, p. 308).

Matters changed in the 1770s when travellers ventured to the Peloponnesus on the west coast of Greece, then an obscure corner of the Ottoman Empire. Towards the end of a trip in 1776 sponsored by the Society of Dilettanti, Richard Chandler and his companions Nicholas Revett (an architect) and William Pars (an artist) took local advice as to where Olympia might have been. They were directed to a spot situated at the confluence of the rivers Cladeos and Alpheios. It was a place that had already been examined in 1723 by the French archaeologist Bernard de Montfaucon, who neither realized its significance nor found much of interest (Mapanti, 1999, p. 27). This was understandable because the evidence had been concealed, first, by sixth century earthquakes that had levelled what was left of the buildings (Fellmann, 1973, p. 109) and, secondly, by river floods which had coated the remains with an alluvial layer several metres thick.

Yet despite the site appearing 'almost naked', closer inspection revealed some wall footings and a massive capital from a Doric column that had recently emerged from the river mud. The latter, Chandler correctly inferred, was a fragment of the Temple of Jupiter (Zeus). He also deduced that 'a deep hollow, with stagnant water and brickwork' was the site of the stadium (Chandler, 1766, p. 308). From these fragments, Chandler supplied a mind's eye account of classical Olympia, drawing on ancient descriptions to outline the grandeur of buildings, temples and stadium that had made this 'no inconsiderable place'.

Chandler simply made passing reference to these observations in his travelogue, but the site's rediscovery brought new waves of visitors. Surveys carried out for Lord Spencer Stanhope in 1807 mapped the ground plan of an imposing complex replete with temples, gymnasia, stadium, hippodrome, and accommodation. Noticeably, Stanhope's account extended to the ruined city of Elis, the prime settlement of the *polis* in which the festival site was located, thereby recognizing the links between the two (Stanhope, 1824, p. 1). Adopting a similar approach, William Leake (1830, I, pp. 23–44) described Elis as the 'place of ordination and preparation for the *athletæ* of the Olympic Games' (*ibid.*, II, p. 220) and the point from which participants set out in procession to traverse the 36 kilometres to Olympia. The journey, complete with ceremonies of ritual purification *en route*, took place before the start of each Games (see also S.G. Miller, 2003, p. 9). The complex of permanent structures at Olympia also contained administrative buildings belonging to the Elis-based civil government that had neither religious nor sports functions (Crowther, 2003; see also Drees, 1968). These were early and intriguing indications of the close relationship between host city and the Games, not least because Elis's claims to authority over the site were disputed by Pisa, situated 2.1 kilometres (1.3 miles) east of Olympia, and also occasionally contested by Sparta and Arcadia (Scott, 2010, p. 31).

Understandably, discovery of the ruins excited archaeologists, especially because it permitted free rein for the imagination. As Leake (1830, I, p. 44) observed, 'there is every reason to believe that the most interesting discoveries in illustration of the arts, language, customs and history of Greece, may yet be made by excavations at Olympia'. Digs first by English and then French archaeologists in the early nineteenth century proved short and inconclusive, particularly because they quickly awakened Greek sensitivities about removal of artefacts. Admittedly, at times the transfer of materials was undertaken with Greek governmental approval in order to protect antiquities from treasure hunting. The French expedition led by Albert Blouet in 1828–1829, for example, had excavated parts of the Temple of Zeus and transferred fragments of the Heracles metopes to the Louvre (Fischer-Lichte, 2005, p. 69). More often, however, looters and antiquity smugglers showed little respect for the sites, leading to prohibition of further expeditions. Systematic excavations would only recommence once agreement was reached to ensure that uncovered artefacts did not leave the country. Notably, negotiations between the Greek and German governments enabled teams from the Imperial German Archaeological Institute led by Ernst Curtius to carry out excavations between 1875 and 1881. These methodically analysed Olympia's core sites (Kyrieleis, 2003; Bohotis, 2017), creating a plan of the 192-metre running track (as shown in the middle-right of figure 2.1) and the associated complexes of religious and secular buildings (Perrottet, 2004; Barringer, 2021).

The annual reports of the German team's excavations aroused widespread interest, simultaneously exposing the material culture of ancient Olympia and supplying fuel for speculation for those eager to reflect on the place of sport in classical Greek society (Fischer-Lichte, 2005, p. 69). Their interest was not simply antiquarian. During the nineteenth century, many classicists embraced a 'vision of a "pure" and "original" Greece … [that] was driven by romantic and racist notions of European and Christian (especially Protestant) superiority' (Harloe and Momigliano, 2018, p. 2; see also Bernal, 1987). Thus appropriated, scholars also saw the achievements of the Olympian past as offering parallels for the modern age. For example, in a public lecture Sidney Colvin, the Director of Cambridge University's Fitzwilliam Museum, enthused over the new archaeological findings, but wistfully remarked that:

Figure 2.1. An imaginative graphic representation of Olympia in ancient Greece. (*Source*: Pierers Universal-Lexikon, 1891)

> It has been said that Englishmen and ancient Greeks are much like one another in two respects. One is their ignorance of all languages except their own, and the other is their love of physical sports. We have our Epsom and our Grand National, our games of cricket and football, our rowing and our running matches, and we despise Frenchmen and foreigners, generally, with the most impartial disdain; but somehow we don't make of our athletic sports so much as these ancient Greeks did. (Colvin, 1878, p. 7)

Colvin primarily had the link between sport and art in mind, seeing the Games as bridging the sacred and secular and creating a vital exemplar for contemporary cultural life that might be revived. Although the close connection between athletic contest and war in classical Greece was freely recognized (Reid, 2017), Colvin and his contemporaries preferred to envisage the Olympics as a peaceful yet competitive sporting festival that brought nations together notwithstanding the pressures of a turbulent world. It was a model that would prove pervasive when the moment arrived in the 1890s for the modern revival of the Games.

This chapter reviews the principal phases in the development of what are now known as the Summer Olympic Games from their reintroduction in Athens 1896 through to Tokyo 2020 (see table 2.1). In doing so, we focus on three phases. The first, lasting from 1896 to 1906, was characterized by revival and initial innovation. The second (1908–1956) was marked by steady evolution and consolidation of the Games, with local Organizing Committees (OCOGs) devoting increasing resources to preparing stadia and associated facilities. The third phase (1960–present) has seen the relationship between the Summer Olympics and their host cities actively and continually reinvented.

Table 2.1. Cities bidding for the Summer Olympic Games, 1896–2020. (*Source*: Partly based on Buchanan and Mallon, 2001)

Games	Year awarded	Host City	Other Candidates
1896	1894	Athens	London
1900	1894	Paris	
1904	1901	St Louis*	Chicago
1908	1904	London**	Berlin, Milan, Rome
1912	1909	Stockholm	
1916	1912		Berlin, Alexandria (Egypt), Budapest, Cleveland, Brussels
1920	1914	Antwerp	Amsterdam, Atlanta, Brussels, Budapest, Cleveland, Lyon, Havana, Philadelphia
1924	1921	Paris	Los Angeles, Atlantic City, Chicago, Pasadena, Rome, Barcelona, Amsterdam, Lyon, Paris
1928	1921	Amsterdam	Los Angeles
1932	1923	Los Angeles	
1936	1931	Berlin	Barcelona, Buenos Aires, Rome
1940	1936		Tokyo, Helsinki. Rome
1944	1939		London, Athens, Budapest, Lausanne, Helsinki, Rome, Detroit
1948	1946	London	Baltimore, Lausanne, Los Angeles, Minneapolis, Philadelphia
1952	1947	Helsinki	Amsterdam, Chicago, Detroit, Los Angeles, Minneapolis, Philadelphia
1956	1949	Melbourne	Buenos Aires, Chicago, Detroit, Los Angeles, Mexico City, Minneapolis, Montreal, Philadelphia
1960	1955	Rome	Budapest, Brussels, Detroit, Lausanne, Mexico City, Tokyo
1964	1959	Tokyo	Brussels, Detroit, Vienna
1968	1963	Mexico City	Buenos Aires, Lyon, Detroit
1972	1966	Munich	Detroit, Madrid, Montreal
1976	1970	Montreal	Los Angeles, Moscow
1980	1974	Moscow	Los Angeles
1984	1978	Los Angeles	Teheran
1988	1981	Seoul	Nagoya (Japan)
1992	1986	Barcelona	Amsterdam, Belgrade, Birmingham, Brisbane, Paris
1996	1990	Atlanta	Athens, Belgrade, Manchester, Melbourne, Toronto
2000	1993	Sydney	Beijing, Berlin, Brasilia, Istanbul, Manchester, Milan, Tashkent
2004	1997	Athens	Buenos Aires, Cape Town, Istanbul, Lille, Rio de Janeiro, Rome, San Juan, St. Petersburg, Seville, Stockholm
2008	2001	Beijing	Bangkok, Cairo, Havana, Istanbul[SL], Kuala Lumpur, Osaka[SL], Paris[SL], Seville, Toronto[SL]
2012	2005	London	Istanbul, Havana, Leipzig, Paris[SL], Madrid[SL], Moscow[SL], New York[SL], Rio de Janeiro
2016	2009	Rio de Janeiro	Baku, Chicago[SL], Doha, Madrid[SL], Prague, Tokyo[SL]
2020	2013	Tokyo	Baku, Doha, Istanbul[SL], Madrid

* The nomination was originally to Chicago.
** The nomination was originally to Rome.
[SL] Short Listed.

Revival

Groundwork

The modern Olympics may be considered part of a 'clustering' of 'invented traditions'[3] that emerged in Western nations in the period between 1870 and 1914 (Hobsbawm, 1983, p. 303), but the idea of appropriating the title 'Olympic' had appealed to organizers of sporting events for much longer (Redmond, 1988; Buchanan and Mallon, 2001). Robert Dover, described as an 'English captain and attorney' (Anon, 1910, p. 453), established a 'Cotswold Games' on his estate in 1604, largely as a protest against Puritan proscriptions of sporting pastimes and other apparent frivolities (Mandell, 1976, p. 29). The festival that contemporary writers described as 'Mr Robert Dover's Olimpick Games upon the Cotswold Hills' included 'cudgel-playing, wrestling, running at the quintain, casting the ball and hammer, hand-ball, gymnastics, rural dances and games, and horse-racing, the winners in which received valuable prizes' (Anon, 1910, p. 453). The Cotswold Games lasted until 1644, although were briefly revived during the reign of Charles II, with a separate 'Olympics', largely devoted to dog racing, occurring at Hampton Court Palace in 1679.[4] By the late Georgian and early Victorian periods the words 'Olympian' and 'Olympic Games' were routinely appropriated by English promoters to lend an aura of status to commercial entertainments and to exhibitions of sporting prowess (Polley, 2011, p. 19).

During the first half of the nineteenth century, a series of separate initiatives consciously sought to use Olympic sport to cement nationalist or pan-national aspirations. The Scandinavian Olympic Games of 1834 and 1836, founded at Ramlösa (Sweden) by the sports educator Gustav Johan Schartau, were designed as national festivals for the 'strong sons of Scandinavia' (Øresundstid, 2003). The Anglophone community in Montreal staged an Olympics in 1844 to assert their identity against the Francophone majority. The influential Much Wenlock Games, founded by Dr William Penny Brookes, grew from an initially limited affair to subsequent grander aims. Founded in October 1850 and still held annually, they aimed 'to promote the moral, physical and intellectual improvement of the inhabitants of the Town and neighbourhood of Wenlock' (WOS, 2006). Gradually, Brookes's vision expanded, most notably assisting the establishment of a National Olympian Association (NOA) in the 1860s. This eventually foundered, particularly due to opposition from the Amateur Athletic Club – an aristocratic and elitist group founded in 1866 to counter the NOA. Nevertheless, during its brief lifespan the NOA stimulated a brief flowering of athletics events in British cities, including the London Olympics – which attracted 10,000 spectators to Crystal Palace between 31 July and 2 August 1866 (Jefferys, 2014).

Understandably, there was considerable interest in reviving the Olympics in Greece. Having achieved political independence in 1830, groups within the country campaigned to restore the Games as a symbol of their re-emerging nationhood (see chapter 14). In 1859, an Olympic sports festival took place in Athens, assisted by sponsorship from Evangelis Zappas, a wealthy expatriate Greek landowner living in Romania (figure 2.2). The so-called 'Zappas Games', held again in 1870 and 1875, constituted a different scale of competition and spectacle than other events previously styled as 'Olympian'. The 1870 meeting, for example, attracted 30,000 spectators to watch Greek athletes compete in the partially restored Panathenian stadium. Significantly too, in the light of future developments, the festival opened with athletes swearing an oath to abide by the rules of fair play and it also included an arts competition alongside the sporting events (Margaritis *et al.*, 2017).

Historians, however, show considerable selectivity when dealing with these events. Official renditions of Olympic history typically styled them as 'pseudo-Olympics' (Redmond, 1988); interesting enough as expressions of

Figure 2.2. Statue of Evangelis Zappas, situated outside the Zappeion, the building named in his honour and used for the fencing competitions at the Athens 1896 games. (*Source*: Photograph, John and Margaret Gold)

the desire to create prestige sporting competitions, but not representing true progenitors of the revived Games as developed by the International Olympic Committee (IOC) under Baron Pierre de Coubertin's leadership.[5] This selectivity had ideological roots since, by emphasizing the originality of Coubertin's vision and downplaying the contribution of others, it privileged the IOC's claims for ownership of the Games – something that would now be regarded as equivalent to intellectual property.

The traditional treatment of the personal relationship between Pierre de Coubertin and William Penny Brookes is a case in point.[6] Historical accounts recognize that the two men actively corresponded. Brookes had also staged a special Autumn version of the Wenlock Games in Coubertin's honour when he visited England in October 1890; an event which featured award ceremonies and pageantry that greatly impressed Coubertin (Young, 1996, p. 78). By contrast, official Olympic histories routinely ignore both the 1866 London Olympics and the speeches in which Brookes proposed establishing the Games on an international basis with a permanent home in Athens (Young, 1998, p. 31; Toohey and Veal, 2000, p. 29). The English contribution was thereby downplayed, notably with Brookes portrayed as the organizer of a small rural sporting festival rather than one of the lynchpins of the Games' revival.

The ideological dimension was even stronger in the disparagement of Greece's attempts to reinstate the Games. Playing down the significance of the Zappas Games denied approval to any proprietorial claims by Greece to the revived Olympics, even though they were clearly based on a classical festival held on Greek soil for almost 1,200 years. In one sense, this ran counter to the mood of the times which favoured folk revival and saw collectors scouring the margins of Western nations in a nationalistic search for the 'authentic' roots of folk culture (Gold and Revill, 2006). Instead, the founders of the modern Olympics perceived their task as resuscitating an event that represented the quintessence of ancient cultural achievement to which Western civilization in general, rather than the late nineteenth-century Greek state, was heir (Christensen and Kyle, 2014). That outlook, in turn, imbued the modern Olympics with an internationalist stance, able continually to move to new host cities without loss of meaning, rather than needing to return permanently to Greece as a geographic hearth that would give the revived Games authenticity. Ceding control to the Greeks would have interfered with the freedom of action to pursue that policy.

Yet recognition of alternative antecedents scarcely detracts from the importance of Coubertin's role in campaigning for the reinstatement of the Olympics and subsequently for his influence on the Games' early development. Commentators (e.g. Mandell, 1976; MacAloon, 1981) rightly identify Coubertin's contribution as a reformer who gradually moved beyond specific concern with promoting sports education within France as a medium for fostering national regeneration to addressing the 'democratic and international' dimension of sport. On 25 November 1892, his speech at the Sorbonne in Paris urged a somewhat sceptical audience to aid 'this grandiose and salutary task, the restoration of the Olympic Games' (quoted in Müller, 2000, p. 297).[7] Coubertin repeated his exhortation, with greater success, at an international Sports Congress that he organized in 1894, which supported the re-establishment of the Games and laid down key principles for organizing them.

To summarize its recommendations, the revived Olympics would reprise the ancient Games' four-yearly cycle, but the Games would be ambulatory rather than based at a permanent site. They would be open to amateur sportsmen and should comprise modern rather than classical sports, although there was no definitive list of which sports to include or exclude. The Games would also have a cultural dimension that was intended to be co-equal with sport. For Coubertin in particular, the revived Games would seek to mirror the spirit of their classical counterparts by serving as a *panegyris* – a festive assembly in which the entire people came together to participate in religious rites, sporting competitions and artistic performance. To recreate this distinguishing characteristic in a modern idiom represented a considerable challenge, especially because 'ancient olympism was a constitutive part and element of religion… People went to Olympia in order to sacrifice and play sports – in this precise order and not the other way round' (Fischer-Lichte, 2005, p. 69).

Nevertheless, Coubertin felt that much could be done, first, by adding ceremonies to dignify the Games, secondly, by creating festivities to accompany the Games and, thirdly, by introducing artistic competitions as part of the Olympic programme. To help codify these ideas, the Congress initiated the process of constructing a Charter of 'fundamental principles, rules and by-laws' to run the Games, henceforth normally known as the Olympic Charter. Central to its outlook was 'Olympism', a humanistic philosophy that mediated the cultural construction of the revived Games and guided the development of the supporting ceremonial content (see chapter 4). Finally, it founded the IOC as the institution that would control the movement and select the host cities, although local Organizing Committees would still plan the Olympics to be held in their domains.[8]

Surviving the Fairground (1896–1906)

The first two Games were pragmatically scheduled for Athens in 1896 and Paris in 1900 (Young, 1987, p. 271). In spite of wanting to resist Greek claims to ownership of the Games and having given serious consideration to London in view of the advantages that it offered regarding access and venues, the Congress accepted the inevitable and recognized the symbolic associations that made Athens the only city that could effectively launch the modern Olympics. Dimitrios Vikelis, the delegate representing the Panhellenic Gymnastic Society at the Sorbonne Congress, was invited to be the IOC's first President.

Athens 1896 proceeded against an uncertain political and economic background that made preparations difficult and saw the first airing of a perennial question: should money be spent on the Olympics given their opportunity cost in relation to competing needs? In this instance, one side, led by Prime Minister Charilaos Tricoupis, argued against the Games for economic reasons; the other, led by opposition leader Theodorus Delyannis and supported by the monarchy, sympathized with the Games as a prestigious project that might well burnish the image of Greece and proclaim Greek identity (MacAloon, 1981, p. 182). The latter camp won the day, with the necessary finance raised through a mixture of public funds, appeals for subscriptions, private sponsors, and the first special issue of commemorative Olympic postage stamps (*ibid.*, p. 196).

The organizers established an early, low-expenditure model. The existing Zappeion Building and the restored Panathenian stadium were pressed into service, with new construction confined to the velodrome at Neo Faliro (funded by the Athens-Piraeus Railway Company), the rifle range at Kallithea, and seating for the swimming events (Davenport, 1996, pp. 4–5; Gordon, 1983). This parsimonious policy posed problems. The Panathenian stadium, for instance, successfully held crowds of more than 50,000 and accommodated a modern running surface, but its traditional elongated horseshoe shape with accentuated curves at each end, hindered athletic performance (figure 2.3). Nevertheless, the revived festival worked

Figure 2.3. The Panathenian stadium, Athens during the 1896 Olympic Games. (*Source*: Historic postcard)

well. The Games, symbolically opening on Greek Independence Day (6 April), attracted 245 athletes from fourteen countries to compete in forty-five events. The Opening Ceremony filled the stadium, with the spectators occupying the surrounding hillsides and streets swelling the audience to an estimated 80,000–120,000.

The city beyond the stadium readily embraced the Games. The Athenian authorities decorated the streets, illuminated the Acropolis and arranged an entertainments programme that included torchlight processions, parades, fireworks, a concert by the Athens Philharmonic Orchestra and a performance of Sophocles's *Antigone* (Cook, 1909; Mallon and Widland, 1998). The marathon, introduced for the first time despite its supposedly ancient origins, added spectacle, provided a link with tradition,[9] and supplied an important symbol. Spectators lined the route through the Greater Athens region and filled the stadium to see the finish. Its popularity, enhanced by the victory of a local man, Spiridon Louis, not only brought a new fixture to the athletics canon,[10] but also served to provide a focus that stressed the unity of city and Olympics.

Although small by contemporary standards, the 1896 Games showed that the modern Olympics had considerable potential as a coherent framework for a new international festival. By contrast, the two succeeding Games came perilously close both to derailing the Olympic movement and to downgrading the relationship between host city and Games to inconsequentiality. In both cases, the reason lay in the conflict between the nascent Games and what were then the larger and more important International Expositions (or World's Fairs).

Paris 1900 reflected a conscious, if misguided decision to associate the second Games with the 1900 Paris Exposition Universelle. Coubertin, assuming the role of IOC President in 1896, believed that the Olympics could capitalize on the Fair's many visitors and festive backdrop and, notably, wanted to build a replica of Olympia at the show, replete with temples, stadia, gymnasia and statues and an archaeological display.[11] The organizers, however, remained unmoved by this idea. Disputes over the control of the sporting element resulted in the Olympic movement effectively withdrawing, with a new committee appointed to plan the Exposition's Games (Mallon, 1998, p. 6). The Olympics became an International Games rather than a true Olympics. They were of indeterminate length given that they lacked Opening or Closing Ceremonies and that the organizers haphazardly added events to the programme, some of which, like fishing in the River Seine (Harlan, 1931, p. 88), did not conform to Olympic standards. Indeed, some competitors in tournaments connected with the Exposition never realized that they had entered Olympic competitions. For example, Michel Theato, the marathon winner, only learned in 1912 that he was the 'gold medallist' at the 1900 Olympics (Mallon, 1998, p. 9).

Compared with the considerable impact that the Exposition had on the city – with a 543-acre (219-hectare) fairground located in the heart of the city in the Avenue Alexandre III and the Bois de Vincennes – Paris 1900 scarcely registered a presence. Only thirteen nations competed and few bothered to send representative teams. The Games received no publicity as they were regarded as a sideshow to the Exposition, with competitors often outnumbering spectators (Rogan and Rogan, 2010, p. 27). There was no stadium or running track. The track and field events were held at the Racing Club of France's grounds in the Bois de Bologne, but the owners refused permission to remove any trees. As a result, discus and javelin throws often landed in wooded areas. The 500 metre grass running track sloped and undulated. Former telegraph poles served as unyielding hurdles. The organizers hastily constructed a grandstand, but a stand of trees obscured the track from spectators (Howell and Howell, 1996). Wholly overshadowed by the Exposition, the movement that had shown 'so much promise in 1896 seemed to have collapsed by 1900' (*ibid.*, p. 17).

St Louis 1904 proved equally inimical to the revival of the Olympics. The IOC had strongly backed selection of a North American city and chose Chicago in May 1901 to stage the 1904 Games. Spoiling tactics by the organizers of St Louis's Louisiana Purchase International Exposition, however, led the IOC reluctantly to rescind that decision and re-allocate the Games to St. Louis, even though it was feared that the Olympics would again inevitably 'only be a sideshow attraction to the much larger international exposition' (Barnett, 1996, p. 19). Their unease proved justified. The Exposition itself brought considerable kudos to St Louis, created an extensive fairground from the wooded Forest Park, and stimulated much needed improvement works to the erstwhile heavily polluted and flood-prone Des Peres River. By contrast, the Olympics left little trace. There was at least a stadium, capable of seating 10,000 spectators, although with a one-third mile (536 metres) track instead of the standard quarter-mile circuit of the time. There was also 'something approaching' an Opening Ceremony on 14 May 1904 (Mallon, 1999*a*, p. 11).

The programme, however, lacked any sense of continuity, with sporting competitions held at irregular intervals through to November and scarcely any distinction between 'Olympic' sports and other competitions. Moreover, the organizers added sports of their own choosing such as college football (gridiron), local cross-country championships, professional events, the national championships of the American Athletic Union of the United States, and 'automobiling' (Anon, 1904, pp. 3, 48). Perhaps most detrimental to the Games' reputation was the addition of the infamous 'Anthropology Days' (12–13 August 1904) to the programme. Here, African, Asian, and Native American competitors competed in racially motivated athletic contests designed to denigrate their performances and give succour to theories of white supremacy (Brownell, 2008*b*; Delsahut, 2014). Following hard on the heels of the 1900 debacle, St Louis 1904 threatened the continuance of the modern Olympics (Barnett, 1996, p. 23).

In the event, it took a sporting festival not usually reckoned as part of Olympic history – the *1906 Intercalated Games* or Mid-Olympics held in Athens – to secure the future (Young, 1996, p. 166; Mallon, 1999*b*, p. 5). This was the first, and only, product of a tactical compromise made in 1897 that offered Greece the opportunity to hold a series of Intercalated Games at four-yearly intervals in non-Olympic years. Greece's disastrous defeat in the first Greco–Turkish War (1897) had left the country bankrupt and unable to initiate the series in 1898 (Davenport, 1996, p. 10), but improved economic circumstances permitted the staging of an Intercalated Games in 1906. This returned to the Panathenian stadium, albeit with more extensive and eye-catching rituals and festivities than those staged in 1896. The sporting festival once more spilled over into the city, in a manner that contrasted with the experience of Paris and St Louis. The streets and buildings of Athens were again decorated, the city's squares staged evening concerts and there was a sustained programme of entertainments. The international press was more in evidence than at previous Games, although the eruption of Mount Vesuvius (4 April) and the San Francisco earthquake (18 April) detracted from the coverage that the Games received (Mallon, 1999*b*, p. 6).

The Intercalated Games created something of a dilemma for the nascent Olympic movement. As a proponent of the ambulatory principle, Coubertin was at best ambivalent towards the concept of staging regular Intercalated Games – a point underscored by his decision to call an IOC Congress in Paris on the role of the arts in sport at the same time as the event taking place in Athens. Nevertheless, there is little doubt that the latter effectively rescued the Olympics from its disastrous flirtation with the fairground and initiated a period in which host cities actively welcomed the Olympic Games as an esteemed sporting event that merited purpose-built facilities.

Consolidation

Olympics by Design (1908–1936)

London 1908 came about largely by chance. Just as Vesuvius's eruption detracted from the coverage of the Athens Intercalated Games so, arguably, did it put paid to its intended successor as the severe strains that recovery from the devastation placed on the Italian economy led to Rome abandoning its attempt to hold the 1908 Games.[12] In November 1906, the IOC formally confirmed their transfer to London (Mallon and Buchanan, 2000, p. 3). With just twenty months in which to prepare the Games, the OCOG decided to use existing venues in the London region wherever adequate facilities were available. Hence, the tennis competitions were held at Wimbledon, polo at Hurlingham, and shooting at Uxendon School Shooting Club and Bisley Rifle Range. Yet recognizing the advantages of a large central venue, the organizers also decided to seek a purpose-built stadium where most of the Olympic competitions and ceremonies could take place; a strategy that broke with the practice of the previous Games but was necessary for a celebration 'worthy of the Motherland of International Sport' (BOC, 1907, np).

Its construction was facilitated by developing a partnership with the Franco-British Exhibition of Science, Arts, and Industry, held to commemorate the recent Entente Cordiale between the two nations. Linkage to that Exhibition, which conveniently was due to open in the summer of 1908, seemed *prima facie* to pose precisely the same threat of eclipsing the Games as so recently witnessed at Paris 1900 and St. Louis 1904. That this did not happen was due largely to the 1908 Games being both organizationally and spatially separate from the International Exhibition. Organizationally, they were firmly under the control of sports interests, in the shape of the Council of the newly founded British Olympic Association. Spatially, they gained distinctiveness from having a separate stadium. The Franco-British Exhibition, then under construction on a 140-acre (56-hectare) plot of former agricultural land, orchards, brickfields, and rifle ranges at Shepherd's Bush (West London), had included plans for entertainments to be staged at a small stadium with spectators standing on a surrounding mound. Under the new agreement, the Exhibition Organizing Committee agreed to scale this venue up into a full-blown stadium in return for 75 per cent of the Olympics' proceeds.[13]

The largest stadium of its day, its enormous concrete bowl enclosed athletics and cycle tracks, a 100-metre swimming pool, platforms for wrestling and gymnastics and even archery. Dressing rooms, restaurants and emergency services were located under the stands (figure 2.4). The foundation stone of the White City stadium, so-called because the Exhibition Buildings were finished in gleaming white stucco, was laid on 2 August 1907 and the stadium was inaugurated on the opening day of the adjoining Exhibition (14 May 1908). It held 93,000 spectators, with 63,000 seated. A newly opened station at Wood Lane, on an extension of the Central London Railway from its terminus at Shepherd's Bush, supplied both the Exhibition and Olympics with direct connections to central London.

London 1908 bequeathed a considerable positive legacy to the Olympic Movement by developing the spectacle of the festival and supplying the basis for 'a compact and independent Olympic festival' (Wimmer, 1976, p. 22). Yet while it allowed the Games to prosper as an event in its own right, London 1908 also left the less desirable physical legacy of a huge and largely unwanted stadium. Although the initial intention was to demolish it and provide 'no permanent addition to the athletic grounds of London' (Anon, 1907), its continued existence after 1908 made it arguably the first instance of the

Figure 2.4. The White City stadium, Shepherd's Bush, London, 1908. (*Source*: Historic postcard)

'limping white elephants' associated with the Olympics (Mangan, 2008).[14] It remained scarcely used for two decades before passing to the Greyhound Racing Association in 1926. The stadium was then renovated, with its capacity reduced from 93,000 to 80,000, installation of a greyhound track over the existing running track, and removal of the cycling circuit and the defunct swimming tank (Hawthorne and Price, 2001, p. 7; Jenkins, 2008). In 1932, the reconfiguration of the running track to a new 440-yard circuit allowed the stadium's use for national and international athletics events. On occasions, White City staged large-scale sporting festivals, such as the 1934 British Empire Games and the 1935 International Games for the Deaf, and provided a base for British athletics from 1933 onwards. However, when the athletics events moved to their new home at Crystal Palace in 1971 the stadium languished before eventual demolition in 1985, initially to make way for housing and offices for the British Broadcasting Corporation and later reconfigured as a mixed residential, office and leisure complex.

Stockholm 1912 associated the Olympics with a far smaller city,[15] making it easier for the OCOG to create a festival that integrated city and stadium. The design of the latter, built in the grounds of Royal Djurgården (Zoological Gardens), assisted that aim. More modest than White City, it seated 22,000 people, with stands arranged around a 400-metre running track (figure 2.5). From the outset, it was intended to be multipurpose, a decision that Coubertin applauded:

> The Gothic Stadium ... seemed to be a model of its kind. You could see it turned into a banquet hall, a concert hall, or a dance hall, and yet on the following morning always ready once again for carrying on with the contests. You could see how in a single night it got covered with ready-made squares of lawn, how hurdles were being put up, and

how it decked itself with blossoming brushwood for the riding tournaments. All this was achieved without any ado, any delay, any blunder. While in London it had proved impossible for the life of the great city to be in any way affected by the proximity of the Olympic Games, Stockholm turned out to be thoroughly imbued with them. The entire city participated in its efforts to honour its foreign guests, and one had something like a vision of what the atmosphere must have been like in Olympia in the ancient days... (quoted in Wimmer, 1976, p. 27)

Figure 2.5. The American team entering the stadium during the Opening Ceremony of the Olympic Games, Stockholm, 1912. (*Source*: Historic postcard)

The stadium offered evening entertainments, which included military concerts, displays of Scandinavian sports, gymnastic displays, fireworks, and illuminations. The city provided street decorations, opera, theatre, a two-day aquatic festival, the usual round of receptions and banquets, and played reluctant host to the artistic competitions that were a cherished part of Coubertin's vision of linking sport and the arts. For the first time, too, the event was backed by a professional advertising campaign (Edvinsson, 2014). This both publicized the Games and conveyed messages about Swedish tourism internationally through the Olympic movement, the Swedish diplomatic service, and paid advertisements in the national newspapers of other countries. The makings of the promotional activity that typified later Olympic Games had started to emerge.

The next Games took place eight years later. Hidebound by its insistence on observing the four-year cycle of Olympiads despite the inconvenient reality of the First World War, the IOC retained the fiction of a sixth Olympiad in Berlin in 1916. In the still non-belligerent USA, six cities (Chicago,

Cleveland, Newark, New York, Philadelphia, and San Francisco) had offered to act as hosts to avoid disrupting the series, but the IOC maintained that it had nominated Berlin as host for the 1916 Olympics and could not withdraw a nomination without that city's agreement. As the German Olympic Committee remained adamant that Berlin held the nomination, the sixth Olympiad was never held and the Games resumed their four-year cycle with the seventh Olympiad in Antwerp in 1920.

Affirmed at an IOC meeting in Lausanne on 5 April 1919 just over a year before the Games opened and against a background of a global flu pandemic (Constandt and Willem, 2021), the award of the 1920 Olympics to Antwerp – newly liberated from German occupation – was as much a political act of moral support for Belgium as it was a sporting event. Notably, the defeated nations from the First World War (Germany, Austria-Hungary, the Ottoman Empire, and Bulgaria) were not invited to participate, with the Soviet Union also choosing not to compete. In pragmatic terms, the Games were spread widely to make use of available facilities – the first time that a model of locational dispersal had been applied. The main events for *Antwerp 1920* were accommodated at the quickly renovated Beerschot stadium, with the shooting contested at Beverloo in the northeast corner of Belgium, the cycling road races and rowing near Brussels, the polo and yachting at Ostende, and football at various locations throughout the nation (Mallon, 1992, p. 8). Amsterdam in the Netherlands even assisted by staging a yachting event that Ostende could not handle.

The most common adjective used to describe the Games was 'austere' (*ibid*., p. 5). Shortage of resources and materials meant that the standard of facilities was much poorer than at Stockholm. Constant rain left the main stadium's running track pitted and rutted. The canal at Willebroek near Brussels, used for the rowing events, provided an industrial setting so ugly that Coubertin called it 'anti-Olympic' (Renson, 1996, p. 57). There were few associated festivities in the city. Yet despite the austerity and retrenchment, Antwerp 1920 recorded a deficit of 626 million Belgian francs, prompting accusations of acute financial mismanagement and leaving the organizers accused of treating the event as 'a symbol of conspicuous consumption' (Renson, 1996, p. 59; also Renson and Hollander, 1997).

The responsibility of consolidating the progress made at London and Stockholm therefore defaulted to the OCOGs of the two ensuing Games. *Paris 1924* was the first occasion on which the growing prestige of the Olympics produced appreciable international competition among cities seeking to host the Games, with four American cities (Los Angeles, Atlantic City, Chicago, and Pasadena) and five European (Rome, Barcelona, Amsterdam, Lyons, and Paris) expressing interest (Welch, 1996, p. 61). Selected at the twentieth IOC session in Lausanne in 1921, the return to Paris proceeded with assurances that, unlike 1900, the organizers would treat the Olympics seriously as an important international event. Rather than employ the Pershing stadium near the Bois de Vincennes, which had staged the 1919 Inter-Allied Games,[16] the Organizing Committee decided in June 1922 to construct a purpose-built stadium at Colombes. The Stade Olympique Yves-du-Manoir had seating for 20,000 spectators, standing room for an additional 40,000 (*ibid.*, p. 64) and would remain the main venue for national soccer and rugby matches until the opening of the Parc des Princes in 1972. Paris 1924 saw the introduction of a proto-Olympic Village at Rocquencourt, although the barrack-like accommodation with few services had 'very little to do with what was to be the first Olympic village' at Los Angeles 1932 (Muñoz, 1997, p. 30; see also chapter 8).

Paris also witnessed the first significant dissatisfactions about the growing size of the Games. The scatter of the main Olympic sports around fifteen locations in the Paris region (Terret, 2008*a*) necessitated long bus journeys for most competitors (figure 2.6). Taken together with two sports that needed specialist facilities best provided elsewhere (sailing at Le Havre and trap shooting at Reims and Issy-les-Moulineaux), Paris 1924, like Antwerp, had adopted a dispersed rather than concentrated pattern of venue provision, with all the attendant advantages and drawbacks with which that pattern is associated. It effectively introduced a multifaceted debate about concentration versus dispersal that would recur continually in subsequent thinking about the organization of the Games (Brown, 2019).

For their part, the organizers of *Amsterdam 1928* favoured the clustered model. Although the athletes were housed on ships in the harbour rather than in a purpose-built Village (Goldstein, 1996), the Dutch embraced

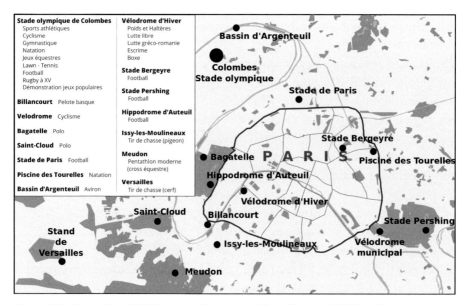

Figure 2.6. Map of the 1924 Summer Olympics in Paris. (*Source*: CC Shakki)

Pierre de Coubertin's cherished ideal of a 'Cité Olympique' to bring the stadium and associated facilities together in a sporting complex in which:

> all buildings are connected and architecturally embody the idea that the Games form one whole ... in agreement with and expressive of the grand fundamental idea of the Olympic Games. (Scharroo, 1928, p. 27)

The new athletics stadium, built on reclaimed marshland with the aid of 0.75 million cubic metres of sand (*ibid.*, p. 25), had seats for 40,000, with the other venues adding a further 30,000 capacity. A special adjacent belltower was belatedly built to hold the Olympic flame. The open-air swimming pool was adjacent to the main stadium (figure 2.7), along with gymnasia for boxing, wrestling, and fencing. Concerns were again expressed about the growing size of the Games, although the target was now the 'excessive festivities', with proposals that there should be reforms to allow only those that 'the reception of authorities and officials demanded' (Organizing Committee, 1928, p. 957).

The two final interwar Games completed the Summer Olympics' passage towards becoming a high-status international festival that would play an important part in the lives of host cities. *Los Angeles 1932* followed in the American boosterist tradition, resolutely serving to advance the city's economic and cultural interests against rivals (Siegel, 2019). Los Angeles had gained the right to stage the 1932 Olympics in 1923 but faced severe funding problems in the wake of the 1929 Wall Street Crash, with the federal

Figure 2.7. Water polo competition in progress, the Olympic Pool, Amsterdam, 1928. (*Source*: Historic postcard)

government refusing to contribute. The Games' survival rested on the city issuing bonds and capitalizing on connections with the private sector, most notably the film industry which actively promoted the Olympics. Yet the key to encouraging participation perhaps lay in making the Games affordable to competitors by assisting travel and in constructing the first true Olympic Village, an innovation that combined economy with the spirit of Olympism.[17] The Official Report of the Games (TOC, 1933, pp. 235, 237) waxed lyrically about the symbolism of the Village and intermixing of peoples, to the extent that the observers recommended the Organizing Committee for the Nobel Peace Prize for their work in promoting the fellowship of the Games through the nations' athletes living peacefully side-by-side (Stump, 1988, p. 199; White, 2005; see also chapter 8).

With the assistance of substantial subsidies for food and accommodation, 1,500 athletes from thirty-four nations competed at Los Angeles 1932 despite the parlous state of the international economy. Apart from the auditorium for the indoor competitions, most of the stadia were at Olympic Park (the former Exposition Park). The Memorial Stadium, the last Olympic arena to use the old-fashioned modified U-shape (Wimmer, 1976, p. 39), was created by refurbishing and enlarging the Coliseum into a venue with a seated capacity of 105,000. The swimming venue and the State Armoury, which staged the fencing competitions, were built nearby. Olympic Park also housed the Los Angeles Museum of History, Science and Art, which held more than 1,100 exhibits from the thirty-two countries that supplied entries for the Olympic Art Competition (TOC, 1932). The organizers added another important innovation by coordinating the decoration of the Olympic venues and the city using streamers and bunting in the official colours of blue, yellow, black, green and red. Flags of the competing nations, Olympic banners and large insignia hung across the main streets. The OCOG also encouraged the owners of businesses to buy specially manufactured materials to embellish their buildings.

Despite the economic climate, the Games achieved an enviable operating surplus, with 1.25 million people paying $1.5 million to watch events over the sixteen days of competitions, witnessing 'the metamorphosis of the Olympics from a relatively marginal and elitist event into an entertainment extravaganza with wide popular appeal' (Keys, 2006, p. 92). The Games offered an imagery far removed from unemployment lines and urban crisis (Dinces, 2018). Tourist agencies put together packages featuring the Olympics and the scenic attractions of southern California. Sixty-two conventions were attracted to Los Angeles, enabling their delegates to enjoy the Games and further boosting the local economy (TOC, 1933, p. 215). A visiting journalists' programme catered for several hundred reporters from around the world in the three years leading up to the Games (*ibid.*, p. 211); a strategy that maximized the possibility of favourable coverage. Not surprisingly, the 1932 Games left the city eager to repeat the exercise, with repeated candidacy before the Olympics next returned in 1984 (see below).

Berlin 1936, the final Summer Games before the Second World War, was a landmark in the political as well as sports history of the interwar period. Having bid unsuccessfully for both the 1908 and 1912 Games, Berlin had experienced the cancellation of the 1916 Games for which it held the nomination. Thereafter, its continuing ambitions were placed in abeyance until Germany was readmitted to the Olympic movement in time for Amsterdam 1928. In May 1931, the IOC awarded the 1936 Games to Berlin as an act of reconciliation, but the choice proved problematic with Hitler's rise to power. The Nazis' initial hostility to the financial burden and avowed internationalism of the Games seemed likely to bring rapid cancellation, but subsequent reappraisal of the classical origins of the Games to align them with National Socialist ideas of German origins[18] quickly brought enthusiastic support. This led to concern within the Olympic movement that the Games would be hijacked by the Nazi leadership for propaganda purposes (Hart Davis, 1986).[19]

Certainly, the creation of the stadium, the surrounding complex and other Olympic venues proceeded with wider ideological and propaganda goals in mind. The regime vetoed Werner March's original plans for expansion of the 1913 stadium, already approved by the IOC, favouring instead a proposal for a 110,000-seater stadium with a steel- and stone-clad structure. The stadium would lie at the heart of the Reichssportfeld, soon to become the world's largest sports complex, complete with swimming and diving pools (with seating for 18,000), facilities for lawn tennis, hockey, equestrian sports, the House of German Sports (Deutschland Halle) for boxing, fencing, weightlifting, wrestling, the Reich Academy of Physical Education, accommodation for female competitors and the Maifeld Parade Ground (figure 2.8). Located in a peripheral area of Berlin but well connected into the city's U-bahn rail system, the site became the focus of attention throughout Germany in the period leading up to and including the Games for a regime that relished opportunities for powerful spectacle. Berlin was specially decorated throughout the Games and codes of behaviour issued to present the best possible impression to visitors, with careful concealment of explicit aspects of racial policies. After the Games, the city and state gained the infrastructural legacy of a sports complex and parade ground that could be used for military purposes and for future National Socialist celebrations.

Austerity (1948–1956)

The bidding process after 1945 revived the pattern established in the interwar period. American cities, with their ingrained rivalries, featured prominently, with formal bids for the 1948 Games from Baltimore, Los

Figure 2.8. Aerial view of the Reichssportfeld, Berlin, 1936. (*Source*: Historic postcard)

Angeles, Minneapolis, and Philadelphia as well as informal interest from Chicago, Detroit, and several other potential US contenders. There was a feeling, however, that the United States was too far away for affordable travel in these cash-strapped years (Voeltz, 1996, p. 103). Therefore, after conducting postal inquiries, London emerged unopposed as the IOC's choice as host city for the Fourteenth Summer Olympics.[20]

London 1948 presented serious challenges for its organizers. Regrettably for the British, the next two years for preparation proved far more difficult economically than they had anticipated when agreeing to host the Games (Holt and Mason, 2000, pp. 27–29). Lack of resources brought speedy abandonment of any notions of laying on stunning spectacle or of constructing purpose-built stadia, especially given the competing urgent demands for repairing housing, industry, and infrastructure in the 'war weary and bomb scarred' city (Phillips, 2007, p. 1). Limited renovation of existing facilities, therefore, was the rule of the day when staging the Olympics. The Empire Stadium at Wembley, originally built for the 1924 British Empire Exhibition, became the Olympic Stadium, with the adjacent Empire Pool staging the swimming events. Although both venues needed conversion and repair, along with a new approach road to link the stadium to Wembley Park railway station, the costs were borne by Wembley Stadium Ltd rather than by the state. As with 1908, this was recouped from a share of the proceeds (Hampton, 2008, p. 29). Royal Air Force accommodation at Uxbridge, a convalescents' camp in Richmond Park, Southlands College in Wimbledon, and convenient school premises provided bargain basement substitutes for an Olympic Village. Other venues pressed into service included the Herne Hill Velodrome (cycling),

Bisley (shooting), Henley-on-Thames (rowing) and the more distant Torbay (yachting). The organizers borrowed sports equipment from the Armed Forces or from manufacturers on a lend-and-return basis. The Board of Trade adjusted rationing regulations for participants and new Tourist Voucher Books made it easier for foreign visitors to spend money in British shops.

Despite the difficulties, there were tangible and intangible non-sports legacies from London 1948. Although the city was not *en fête* as Berlin or Los Angeles had been, the Games undoubtedly lifted the mood of postwar Britain and recorded a modest profit of £30,000. The city's hotels enjoyed bumper visitor numbers (Holt and Mason, 2000, p. 31). The nation also received the morale-raising experience of hosting a premier international event and temporary respite from the greyness of Austerity. Yet the main legacy from London 1948 was again for sport. Admittedly, there were few tangible outcomes given the lack of purpose-built facilities or associated infrastructural improvement and the fact that very few of the venues used 'made any serious attempt at all to mark or commemorate their involvement in 1948, other than perhaps a brief mention buried somewhere in their histories' (Polley, 2011, 129).

By contrast, in intangible terms London 1948 successfully relaunched the Games after the traumas of war, drawing the highest-ever attendance figures for an Olympics. In return, the Games sowed the seeds of important change for British society through sports development. They eroded the long-established notion that participation in such sports was the preserve of gentleman amateurs (Hampton, 2008, p. 318). In addition, they indirectly played a catalytic role in encouraging disability sport. As chapter 5 shows, the archery competition held on the front lawns of Stoke Mandeville Hospital on 28 July 1948 – the same day as the Opening Ceremony of the London Olympics – is widely accepted as the first competitive sporting event for seriously disabled athletes. This symbolic event also marked the start of the process of convergence that would see London 2012, like other aspirant twenty-first century host cities, bidding to stage the Olympic *and* Paralympic Games rather than just the former.

The two succeeding Games mirrored London's low-key approach. *Helsinki 1952* had a history complicated by the Second World War and subsequent Cold War. The city held the nomination for the Twelfth Summer Olympics in 1940 after the Japanese voluntarily withdrew (Collins, 2007) and had built a stadium, swimming and diving arena, and a competitors' village in anticipation of that event. The organizers renovated and expanded the sporting facilities for the 1952 Games (figure 2.9), with the aid of a $1.25 million grant from the Finnish government but, as noted in chapter 8, the Olympic Village posed greater problems. The one originally constructed at Käpylä, 3.7 miles (6 kilometres) from the city centre, had long since been converted to public housing. The increased size of the Games required new

Figure 2.9. Olympic stadium, Helsinki, 1952. (*Source*: Historic postcard)

accommodation not just at Käpylä, but also at two new sites, Otaniemi and Töölö. The situation was further complicated by the Soviet Union's demands for a separate village for the socialist bloc's athletes (Hornbuckle, 1996, p. 117). In response, the organizers allocated the Otaniemi site to the USSR and its allies, placing competitors literally as well as figuratively into two ideological camps.

Melbourne 1956 was the last Summer Olympics developed under conditions of postwar financial stringency. The city's bid document for the Games (MIC, 1948) projected an image of a prosperous, developed, and well-equipped 'city of culture', with the promise of a new Olympic stadium complex on the banks of the Yarra River east of the Melbourne Cricket Ground (MCG). Once Melbourne had won the Games, the organizers decided to reduce costs by scrapping the proposed new stadium in favour of modifying the MCG. Construction of major new venues was confined to the swimming pool and velodrome. Available spaces at the local university, museum, art school, and public library were employed to display the four associated art exhibitions – on architecture, painting, graphics, and literature. The Olympic Village was built as a cheap housing project in the suburb of Heidelberg, using the existing system of government loans. These buildings, however, presented so many subsequent construction and social problems that the Games might well have been 'a force for urban degeneration rather than regeneration' (Essex and Chalkley, 1998, p. 194).

Reinvention

Catalyst (1960–1976)

Although important for their host nations, the financially straited 1948–1956 Games made little lasting impact on the development of thinking about Olympic cities. By contrast, the Olympic festivals held during the next six decades were increasingly hungry for land; demands that host cities most often met by means of clearance, often involving sizeable displacements of people and economic activities, or use of remediated ('brownfield') land. The process was partly due to the Games' tendency towards gigantism, with the spiralling numbers of events and participants having implications for venues and accommodation. Yet the thirst for development land also reflected new thinking once *Rome 1960* had pioneered the practice of attaching substantial urban restructuring to the Olympic project (Telesca, 2014; also chapter 12 *infra*).

Rome's Olympian aspirations stretched back many years (Frasca and Loriga, 2010, pp. 1–17). The city, as noted above, initially held the nomination for the 1908 Games and, under Mussolini, had lobbied hard for the right to stage the 1940 Olympics. Indeed, Rome 1960 effectively capitalized on two districts developed by the Fascist regime with international festivals in mind. The first, the Foro Italico in the north of the city, already offered two imposing arenas: the Stadio dei Marmi, built in 1932, and the Stadio Olimpico, built in 1936. The second district was EUR, so-called because it was initially designed to supply a spectacular setting for the cancelled 1942 Esposizione Universale di Roma – itself dubbed the *Olimpiade della Civiltà* (the Olympics of Civilization) (Casciato, 2015, p. 29). Located to the south of the city, it was only partially developed before the Second World War, but its monumental and spacious qualities made it an ideal place for the core of the Olympic facilities. These included the Palazzo dello Sport (Sport Palace), the Velodrome, the Piscana delle Rose (swimming pool) and the Fontane Sports Zone training area. Ten other venues were scattered throughout the city, with several using sites with classical associations to underline the Games' pedigree. The vaults of the Basilica of Maxentius built in 303 AD, for instance, housed the Greco-Roman and free wrestling contests, while the Caracalla Baths (217 AD) staged the gymnastics.

These 'Olympic areas' made a permanent contribution to the city's sporting and cultural life. The Village at Campo Paroli provided private sector housing (Wimmer, 1976, p. 202; see also Muñoz, 1997) and the city also gained from infrastructural improvements undertaken with the Games in mind. These included new roads and bridges built to connect the Village to the main Olympic sites, modernization of the airport, improvement of the telephone, telegraph and radio communication networks, and initiatives to expand hotel accommodation. The Rome Olympics also had a major impact on financing the Games. Core funding came from the Italian soccer pools, the Totocalcio, but now supplemented for the first time by sales of television rights. Broadcasters had refused to pay for rights at Melbourne, arguing that covering the Games was akin to televising news and should be similarly free to the broadcaster. The organizers of the Rome Olympics, however, managed to convince the major television companies that the Games were a proprietorial commodity for which payment was necessary (Wenn, 1993; 1995). The American Columbia Broadcasting System (CBS) paid $600,000 for US television rights, with Eurovision subscribing another $540,000. Grainy black-and-white pictures brought live coverage to a global audience. It marked a significant step towards realizing the economic potential of the Games and ensured that, when leaving aside wider infrastructural improvements, the Rome Olympics ran at a profit.

Tokyo 1964 took a leaf out of Rome's book by embarking on major redevelopment projects before the Games, merging the specific proposals for the Olympics into the city's ten-year development plan. As with Rome, there was historical context in terms of previous interest in staging mega-events, with a thread of connection between the 1964 Games and the never-staged 1940 Games, for which Tokyo held the nomination. The bid for the 1940 Olympics originated from wishing to rebuild the city, which continued to exhibit the impact of the 1923 Great Kanto earthquake. The bid for the 1964 Games still needed to address the aftermath of the wartime destruction of the 1940s (Ogura, 2018, p. 583), as well as tackling the city's needs for modern infrastructure.

The latter was particularly significant. Aiming to cater for Tokyo's infrastructural needs up to the year 2000, the combined works linked to the Olympic projects cost $2.7 billion. They provided for road improvements that included a remarkable system of grade-separated highways that employed verticality to maximize traffic flow within narrow spaces (c.f. Gold, 2012) and two notable rail developments – the Shinkansen high-speed 'bullet' trains and the monorail system that linked Haneda airport to central Tokyo. Beyond transport, there were improvements to housing, hotels, the harbour, water supply, sewage disposal and a public health programme (Essex and Chalkley, 1998, p. 195; see also chapter 21). The city had thirty Olympic sites, with thirteen major facilities concentrated in three districts: the Meiji Olympic Park, which contained the Olympic Stadium; the Yoyogi Sports Centre, which housed the swimming competitions; and the Komazawa Sports Park.

Accommodating participants in six Olympic Villages ensured, at least in principle, that competitors and officials had no more than a forty-minute journey to reach their venues (Organizing Committee, 1966, p. 114). Hoteliers received grants to remodel their premises for Western tourists, with a further 1,600 visitors lodged on ships in the harbour. Importantly, Tokyo saw the introduction of an approach concerned with the 'look' of a city during the period of the Olympic festival. This represented more than the old approach of simply decking the city in flags. Instead, conscious attempts were made to unify the disparate sporting and Olympic infrastructure into a cohesive whole through the design of signage, dressing the venues and decorating the streets. As a result of an open competition, the Japanese designer Yusaku Kamekura won a contract to provide visually consistent designs for all the ephemeral elements of the Games – symbols, signs, pamphlets, posters, tickets, decorations and even the colour scheme used for the city and at Olympic venues (Yew, 1996, p. 176).

Mexico City 1968 saw Latin America, and more specifically a developing nation, host the Olympics for the first time. The Games contributed to domestic unrest, most notoriously including a massacre of student protestors at Tlatelolco that left 325 dead (Lenskyj, 2000, pp. 109–110). It also stretched Mexico's resources, leading the organizers to use existing sports facilities wherever possible and blend them with new venues by means of a common 'look'. Yet despite its troubled beginnings and sports boycotts, Mexico City 1968 finished with a favourable balance sheet. Costing $175 million, much of which was spent on facilities with a lifespan that extended well beyond the festival, the Olympics were considered to have covered their costs. For some observers, the 1968 Games represented an important moment of achievement and harmony for the Mexican nation that fully justified the cost (e.g. Arbena, 1996). For others, the money diverted into the Olympics had exacerbated the divide between Mexico City's rich and poor. Before the Games, for example, the city chose to transfer $200 million from the social services budget to city improvement projects in an elaborate urban and national re-imaging campaign. Not only did this have a detrimental long-term impact on the city's provision for the poor, it had also triggered the protest demonstrations that culminated at Tlatelolco.

The ability of the Olympics to polarize opinion, already demonstrated by Mexico City, escalated steadily over the next decade. In their different ways, Munich 1972 and Montreal 1976 created crises for the Olympic movement: the former due to security problems and the latter over finance. Initial planning for both events, however, proceeded unproblematically with an upbeat view that emphasized the Olympics' apparently risk-free character; seemingly guaranteeing host cities advantageous international attention and endless prospects for undertaking urban development. Partly because of this mood, the 1970s Games were lavish affairs, with huge expenditure on iconic facilities and distinctive urban quarters.

The return of the Olympics to Germany at *Munich 1972* inevitably raised the spectre of 1936. The powerful militaristic and nationalist images still associated with that Olympics encouraged the Munich organizers to style theirs as a 'Carefree Games' (Organizing Committee, 1972, p. 28). Munich's bid to the IOC emphasized the city's claim to embrace international and modern cultures; a rich hearth of 'the arts and Muses' that offered four orchestras, twenty-three museums and seventeen theatres (*ibid*, pp. 24, 28). At the same time, Munich in the early 1970s was in the throes of rapid economic and demographic growth, with severe pressures on services and physical infrastructure. Preparation for the Games, therefore, also addressed the host city's broader planning goals, aligning Olympic developments with schemes designed to restore and pedestrianize Munich's historic centre, to improve and extend public transport, construct 145 miles (233 kilometres) of expressways, provide underground parking, and build new retail and hotel accommodation (Essex and Chalkley, 1998, p. 195).

The new Olympic Park was located in a derelict area in the north of the city long earmarked for redevelopment. Originally flat, its surface was bulldozed to produce a gently rolling landscape, with a hill created from wartime rubble and a small lake formed by damming the Nymphenburg Canal. The organizers then placed the athletes' warm-up facilities, the swimming pool and many smaller sports venues, a theatre, restaurants, the Olympic Village, press centre and stadium around the lake. The 80,000-seater Olympic stadium was an innovative tent-roofed structure designed by Gunter Behnisch and Frei Otto (figure 2.10). The Olympic Village, which housed 10,000 athletes, was designed for legacy conversion into a 'self-sustaining' community for single people and middle- and lower-income families – groups who found it difficult to find accommodation in the city (Essex and Chalkley, 1998, p. 195; Organizing Committee, 1972, p.

Figure 2.10. The Olympic stadium Munich 1972, with its tent-roofed structure designed by Gunter Behnisch and Frei Otto. The photograph shows the stadium with a ferris wheel in the foreground, as it was in August 2014. (*Source*: Tiia Monto)

125). Trams, an underground rail line and a rapid transit provided physical links between the complex and the city centre. Symbolic links were added by attention to the 'look' of the city. Coordinated by a German designer Otl Aicher, the city adopted a holistic design policy towards decorations for the city, venues and orientation of visitors. Besides choosing colours felt to resonate with Olympic values, the dominant colour of blue was chosen to symbolize peace with the 'aggressive' colour red deliberately avoided (Organizing Committee, 1972, p. 269; Yew, 1996, p. 213).

Viewed in organizational and financial terms, the Twentieth Summer Games were critically regarded as a success. They generated a working profit, with marketing and television rights producing over $12 million for the IOC and international federations. Munich and Bavaria gained lasting publicity benefit (Brichford, 1996, p. 151). Other aspects of their legacy proved more difficult. Despite the efforts to promote the 'carefree' theme, Munich 1972 brought the Olympics face-to-face with the realities of security. The massacre of Israeli athletes and officials on 5 September effectively destroyed the OCOG's attempts to stage a light-hearted, non-nationalistic Olympics. It also ensured that future host cities faced a bill for security measures of a wholly different dimension than previously, recognizing the Olympics' new, and unwanted, status as a prime target for international terrorism (see chapter 9).

The ensuing Games were a landmark for the extent to which they were ill conceived and badly prepared. Although intended as a 'modest Games', *Montreal 1976* produced a final shortfall of $1.2 billion, primarily caused by cost overruns on over-ambitious buildings. Admittedly, the times were not propitious. The Games took place against a background of severe world recession and inflation that profoundly affected costings, especially those concerning the surfeit of transport infrastructural projects associated with the Olympics. Nevertheless, a large measure of the blame rested with the counterproductive machinations of the mayoral regime led by Jean Drapeau and the flawed architectural design of the Olympic complex, particularly the Athletes' Village and the main stadium. Together they shared a substantial part of the responsibility for the severe cost overruns experienced at Montreal 1976.

The Village was not incorporated into the Games' original costings on the grounds that either a private developer or the city's public housing commission would develop the village with an eye to its post Games use as housing, thereby reducing the apparent budgetary requirements for the project (Patel *et al.*, 2013, p. 367). Extensive delays over choice of site, ground plan, building design and choice of contractors threatened the project's viability. In the final analysis, the OCOG were forced to step in and take over responsibility for the Village, especially after the IOC President Lord Killanin threatened in October 1974 that the Games might be moved to another city if progress was not forthcoming. At the insistence of the Drapeau regime, the chosen design comprised four architecturally innovative ziggurat structures, around nineteen storeys high at their tallest points. Given problems that included 'outrageous subcontracts, dangerous construction techniques, poor coordination, and theft' (*ibid.*), it was not surprising that it could only be completed on time with extensive overtime working and a tripling of the original budget. Thereafter, its exposed walkways – always likely to be ill-suited to a Montreal winter – and the servicing problems intrinsic to its structure would leave an unenviable legacy.

Similar difficulties but with an even larger cost overrun were encountered with the stadium. The organizers had rejected providing an orthodox open-air stadium in favour of a design that might be used all-year round. As the Olympic movement would not countenance a covered stadium for athletics, it was decided to build a new stadium with a retractable roof – understandably at much greater cost (Killanin, 1983, p. 123). The chosen design by the French architect Roger Taillibert, architect of the critically acclaimed Parc des Princes in Paris, exacerbated the problems by embracing

Figure 2.11. Olympic stadium, Montreal 1976 (architect Roger Taillibert). (*Source*: Photograph, John and Margaret Gold)

an unmistakeable monumentality. Most notably, it featured an innovative system for opening and closing the roof involving a 575-foot (190 metre) tower, inclined at 45 degrees, which supported the roof on twenty-six steel cables (figure 2.11).

Pursuit of this project clearly lay close to the hearts of both the architect and the mayor (Taillibert and Harmel, 2000), but its completion was plagued by labour disputes, construction problems and lack of financial and administrative control. Taillibert himself, who was removed from the project in 1975, later recounted:

> The construction of the Olympic Park and stadium showed me a level of organised corruption, theft, mediocrity, sabotage and indifference that I had never witnessed before and have never witnessed since. The system failed completely and every civil engineering firm involved knew they could just open this veritable cash register and serve themselves. (Cited in Todd, 2016)

Completion of the stadium in time for the Opening Ceremony was only achieved through the efforts of teams working in shifts around the clock. The radical conception that lay behind the roof design proved fatally flawed. In fact, the infamous roof was not completed until 1987 and quickly became unusable. It was an episode that eventually produced a seldom-used stadium with an impressive observation tower and a non-retractable roof.

Other buildings also contributed their share of problems. Difficulties with subsoil meant the velodrome needed new foundations to support its roof (Organizing Committee, 1976, pp. 16–17). The remote and expensive new international airport at Mirabel, built in defiance of traffic forecasts, closed three decades later without ever achieving any useful function. More generally, lack of proper operational planning and failure to sequence the construction process led to delays and bottlenecks. Plans drawn up in France to metric specifications repeatedly had to be redrawn for a construction industry that used British imperial measurements. In addition, labour problems caused the loss of 155 working days in the eighteen months leading up to the Games. Despite the round the clock working that was introduced at great expense to meet the Games deadline, it still proved impossible to complete all the facilities. In May 1976, emergency work began to erect temporary installations for several sports rather than continue with the intended venues. It all contributed to an event that inevitably presented a 'kaleidoscope of contradictory narratives and outcomes' (Kidd, 1996, p. 153). As Daniel Latouche (2007, p. 197) observed: 'Although Montrealers still retain a rather positive image of these three weeks in July, they remain convinced that in the short run the Games proved a catastrophe for the city's economy and its reputation, with very little to show except an over-sized and under-used stadium'.

Ideological Games (1980–1984)

The 1980 and 1984 Summer Games were staged by two superpowers as indicators of the superiority of their ideological systems, with each rebuffed by politically inspired boycotts orchestrated by their rivals. Political boycotts, of course, were nothing new. Montreal 1976 had been boycotted by a bloc of twenty-six African states protesting about New Zealand's participation in the Olympics given the continuation of that country's sporting links with South Africa (Hulme, 1990, p. 2). The boycotts of the 1980s, however, were essentially an extension of Cold War politics. The USA led a boycott of *Moscow 1980* as part of a package of measures taken in response to the Soviet intervention in Afghanistan in December 1979. This reduced participation to eighty competing nations compared with 121 at Munich and even ninety-two at Montreal, with many other nations sending weakened teams. Not surprisingly, a Soviet-led tit-for-tat boycott, ostensibly over the security of athletes and officials, saw fourteen socialist countries miss Los Angeles 1984. These gestures, however, only materialized in the final weeks before these Games and, therefore, did not materially impinge upon the plans made by the host cities for staging their respective Olympics.

With an eye to the lessons of the Montreal Games, both OCOGs made virtues out of economy and pragmatism. The OCOG for Moscow 1980 conspicuously rejected the recent trend towards gigantism that had left behind underused sports facilities that were prohibitively expensive to maintain. Rather they 'sought efficiency', building only 'essential' installations that would 'not remain monuments to vanity' but would be 'in constant use for the benefit of the Soviet People' (Organizing Committee, 1980, p. 43). They planned to use Moscow's existing sports facilities wherever possible, employing temporary grandstands and ensuring that any new structures would be designed as multi-purpose venues. The main ceremonies and the track and field competitions, for example, centred on the renovated Lenin Stadium (built originally in 1956).

Given the nature of the command economy, the authorities incorporated preparations for the Olympics into the city's planning strategy (the General Plan for the Development of Moscow 1971–1990) and the state's tenth Five-Year Plan of Economic and Social Development. The former adopted decentralist principles, dividing Moscow into eight functional zones, each with a population of between 600,000 and 1.2 million and their 'town public centres' and subsidiary centres, to achieve a 'balance between labour resources and employment opportunities' (Lappo *et al.*, 1976, pp. 138–140). The Olympics provided the opportunity to improve access to sporting, cultural, and entertainment facilities for those living within these zones by designing new venues for use once the Games were over (Promyslov, 1980, p. 230). The main Olympic facilities were distributed into six main areas, with the Village in a seventh. Located in the southwest of the city, the Village comprised eighteen blocks, each sixteen storeys high, arranged in groups of three with associated communal catering facilities, entertainment, shopping, and training facilities. After the Games, the Village would become a self-contained neighbourhood complete with cultural and sporting facilities (*ibid.*, pp. 245–246; see also chapter 8). This dispersal posed logistic problems, but there was little need for new road construction given the low levels of private car ownership at this time. Infrastructural improvement was primarily confined to building new media centres and renovating the city's three airports, with a new international terminal added to Sheremetyevo Airport. The authorities also renovated historic buildings (especially churches), planted trees, and commissioned new hotels, cafés, and restaurants. In a distant echo of Berlin 1936, Moscow was unusually free of banners expressing party slogans, posters and even the legendarily flinty guides working for Intourist desisted from propaganda during the Games (Binyon, 1980).

Notwithstanding the rhetoric of virtuous utilitarianism, the regime could not resist the urge to display Soviet technological expertise in designing large structures. This contributed to the organizers commissioning the world's largest indoor arena, known locally as the Olimpiisky, in north Moscow for the basketball and boxing competitions. Capable of seating up to 45,000 spectators, it could be used either as a single space or divided into two separate auditoria, allowing it to serve as a multipurpose space for sports, political, and cultural events after the Games (Promyslov, 1980, pp. 236–237).

Although not without expressions of boosterism – such as Peter Ueberroth's (1985) promise to make Moscow 1980 look like 'chopped liver' by comparison[21] – *Los Angeles 1984* sought economy in staging the Games, with the organizers' commitment to funding the Games without the public funds that had been available in the USSR. This resulted in an event that added fine-tuned commercialism to cost consciousness, using volunteers wherever possible and making maximum use of existing facilities. The Los Angeles Memorial Coliseum was refurbished as the Olympic stadium, with just four new venues required – for rowing, cycling, swimming, and shooting. Each attracted high levels of sponsorship. The McDonald's Swim Stadium, for example, was built in Olympic Park for the University of Southern California. The Southland Corporation, parent company of the 7-Eleven chain of convenience stores, funded the velodrome on the California State University site. Fuji Film sponsored the shooting range. The three Olympic Villages used sites on university campuses (University of California-Los Angeles, University of Southern California and the University of California-Santa Barbara), with the accommodation available later for students (Burbank *et al.*, 2001, pp. 76–77). This emphasis on named sponsorship and private finance introduced a measure of commercialism that the Olympic movement then felt powerless to resist. Rather more serious perhaps was the lack of intimacy caused by using existing facilities scattered around the sprawling, car-based Los Angeles city region rather than creating a nucleated Olympic Park. Some effort to create a sense of place came from decking the city in standardized colours to create a 'festive federalism' (Yew, 1996, p. 288), although it was recognized that only so much could be achieved by design.

Where Los Angeles 1984 excelled was in changing ideas about Olympic finance. The Games represented a 'transitional moment when the Olympic movement retreated from the idea of government-supported organization in favour of a new model of private–public partnerships, built heavily on corporate sponsorship' (Gruneau and Neubauer, 2012, p. 134). In doing so, it provided a formula that dramatically reduced the financial burdens for other prospective host cities. The Games made a profit of $225 million that was channelled into American sports bodies and programmes. Local universities gained major new facilities. The event injected an estimated $2.4 billion into the Southern Californian economy.[22] After the experience of the 1970s, the act of hosting the Olympics was fully restored as the pinnacle of ambition for cities with global aspirations.[23]

Shifting Horizons (1988–1996)

Seoul 1998 was less inspired by that thinking – which had yet to re-emerge when the city gained the nomination in 1981 – than by the success of Tokyo 1964, which the Koreans believed had altered perceptions of the Japanese and helped Japan join the ranks of the developed world in the cultural, social, diplomatic, and economic fields. The Games would provide a positive context for international scrutiny, show the economic transformation and political progress within Korea, and establish dialogue with Communist and non-aligned nations, even though there was a real risk of terrorism or international conflict arising from continuing tensions with North Korea – with which South Korea was still technically at war. It also provided an opportunity to regenerate Seoul. The South Korean capital faced severe environmental, economic, and demographic problems for which staging the Olympics seemed to offer a means to short-circuit the process of replanning and reconstruction.

The organizers concentrated the Olympic facilities in two locations: the Seoul Sports Complex, built in the Chamshil area on the south bank of the Han River around 13 kilometres south of central Seoul; and the Olympic Park, just over 3.5 kilometres to the east. The South Korean government had originally commissioned the Seoul Sports Complex in 1977 after recognizing that the country lacked the facilities even to host the Asian Games. The 145-acre (59-hectare) site contained a major stadium, which became the 100,000 capacity Olympic stadium, as well as a 50,000-seater venue for the exhibition sport of baseball. The complex was linked to the Olympic Expressway, which connected the airport with Seoul's downtown. The Olympic Park provided the venues for six events – cycling, weightlifting, fencing, tennis, gymnastics, and swimming. The Athletes' Village comprised blocks of flats of various heights (six to twenty-four storeys) clustered in groups around common open spaces. In total 5,540 units were built, which were sold after the Games as private housing for upper middle-income families (Kim and Choe, 1997, pp. 197–198). The discovery of the earthen walls of a fortress from the Baekje Kingdom (18 BC–660 AD) led to the designation of a historic park within the masterplan (*ibid.*, p. 208; also see Yoon, 2009).

Beyond the Olympic Park, the authorities conducted a programme of repairing historic monuments, including palaces and shrines, tree planting, and improvements to streets, drainage, and power supply. Two new urban motorways linked the airport to the Olympic sites and improved east–west traffic flows in the city. The authorities built new Metro lines and expanded the airport. Seoul's planners instigated the Han River Development Project, which combined anti-flood measures, water treatment for the heavily polluted river, habitat regeneration and the creation of a series of recreational areas. Temporary measures that applied for the duration of the Games included encouraging dust-producing firms along the marathon route and around Olympic venues to switch to shorter working hours or night-time operation, and advising public bath houses to take holidays on days of key events.

The strategies chosen to improve the city's built environment and infrastructure, however, drew international criticism for paying greater attention to urban form than to social cost. Ideas for improvement centred on the removal of slums and the creation of modernistic, often high-rise, developments for high-income residential or commercial use. Traditional walking-scale urban forms (*hanoks*), built at high density with narrow streets and passageways, were bulldozed for commercial redevelopment, with the displacements of an estimated 722,000 residents (COHRE, 2007*a*). Laws covering preservation and conservation were not introduced until 1983 and, even then, only the oldest historic buildings with connections to the Yi dynasty benefitted. Clearance continued in areas without that historic cachet (Kim and Choe, 1997, pp. 209, 212).

Barcelona 1992 would take the regeneration theme further, assimilating the experience of the Olympics into a programme that seemingly supplied a model of development through cultural strategy and urban design that could be readily applied elsewhere. Although still facing significant domestic security threats from Basque separatists and other groups (see chapter 9), the Games took place against a political background of brief-lived optimism about the world order, with no boycotts and fewer security problems. In conditions that allowed the potential of the Olympics to act as a vehicle for urban development to shine through, Barcelona launched a challenging package of regenerative measures that countered years of neglect under the Franco regime (Maloney, 1996, p. 192). This was not an entirely new strategy. The city had used earlier international festivals to address urban planning goals, with the 1888 Universal Exhibition in the Parc de la Ciutadella to the east of the old mediaeval centre and the International Exhibition of 1929 on Montjuic to the west both resulting in urban improvements and enhancements to the city's cultural institutions, open space and transport (Hughes, 1996).

The Olympics were seen in a similar light. Barcelona had previously bid to host the Games for 1924, 1936 and 1972. Selected at the IOC meeting in 1986 over Paris, the only other credible candidate, Barcelona's bid claimed that 88 per cent of the necessary facilities for the Games *per se* were already 'available'.[24] The Olympic Stadium was an updated and renovated version of that used for the 1929 International Exhibition. Ten other venues came from refurbishments to existing facilities, with forty-three other facilities used very much in their existing state (Essex and Chalkley, 1998, p. 198). The promoters emphasized that only fifteen new venues would be required. Altogether, only 17 per cent of the total expenditure for the 1992 Games went on sports facilities (Varley, 1992, p. 21), with the lion's share of the investment devoted instead to urban improvements. Barcelona's planners concentrated the Olympic facilities in four areas located in a ring around the city, roughly where the outer limits of the nineteenth-century city met the less structured developments of the second half of the twentieth century. These were: the Vall d'Hebron in the north (cycling, archery, and accommodation for journalists); the Diagonal (football, polo, and tennis); the Montjuic (the major Olympic site including the 60,000-seater stadium, the Sant Jordi Sports Palace, and the swimming and diving pools); and Parc de Mar, which housed the Olympic Village (figure 2.12). Large-scale investment in the city's transport systems, substantially stimulated by the Olympics, served to link sites together. The Metro system was extended, the coastal railway rerouted, the airport redesigned and expanded, and the telecommunications systems modernized (see also Brunet, 2009).

Barcelona 1992 changed the criteria by which to judge whether a Summer Games had been a success. The spectacle of the Games delighted the Olympic movement. Television audiences, for example, were captivated by images from the outdoor pool, showing divers performing against the panoramic backdrop of the city beyond. Environmentally, as chapter 7 suggests, it played a role in anchoring ideas developed at the Rio Earth Summit into the mainstream of Olympism (see also Aragón-Pérez, 2019). Economically, the Olympic festival *per se* performed less well. Cost overruns ate into the projected $350 million surplus such that the Games barely

Figure 2.12. The Olympic Village, Barcelona 1992, (*Source*: Photograph, John and Margaret Gold)

broke even (a mere $3.8 million surplus). The innovative Sant Jordi Sports Palace, for example, may have supplied stunning architecture but cost $89 million rather than the estimated $30 million. Construction costs on the ring road were 50 per cent more than the estimated $1 billion. The Cultural Olympiad also spawned heavy losses, despite trading on Barcelona's rich heritage in the arts and architecture (Hargreaves, 2000, p. 106).[25] Inflation and adverse movements in foreign currency rates also severely increased costs. Unemployment rose by 3 per cent in the city immediately after the Olympics, prices soared and business taxes rose 30 per cent (Maloney, 1996, p. 193).

Nevertheless, critical opinion remained highly positive with regard to the wider regenerative impact on Barcelona. The city had deployed the Games as part of a conscious long-term development strategy that existed before obtaining the nomination to stage the Olympics and continued afterwards. It represented a major transformation in the reputation of Olympic cities just sixteen years after the debacle of Montreal. Not surprisingly, therefore, Barcelona 1992 has had a lasting fascination for scholars and practitioners alike.[26]

Atlanta 1996, by contrast, would renew questions about staging the Games, particularly regarding commercialism. Unusually for Olympic practice, a private consortium undertook the organization, with heavy representation of and deference to business interests (Batuhan, 2015). Funding came from sponsorship, broadcasting rights and merchandising which, when combined with ticket sales, raised $1.72 billion (Burbank *et al.*, 2001, p. 94). In addition, the Federal government expended nearly $1 billion on infrastructure, housing, safety and security, with smaller amounts spent by the state of Georgia and the city (*ibid.*, p. 116).

Most of the spending on the Games and on infrastructure took place in central Atlanta's 'Olympic Ring' – an area around 3 miles (5 kilometres) in radius that contained sixteen of the twenty-five Olympic facilities and most of the urban improvements. The Atlanta Committee for the Olympic Games (ACOG) made use of existing facilities such as the Georgia Dome and Omni Arena, coupled with facilities at Atlanta's universities. The Georgia Institute of Technology, for example, provided sites for the Olympic Village, a new aquatic centre (swimming, diving, and water polo) and boxing. ACOG commissioned a new but temporary Olympic Stadium in the Summerhill district in the south of the Olympic Ring. This was tied in with a longer-term plan to develop baseball in the city. The Olympic Stadium was located next to the Atlanta Fulton County Stadium, which was used for the baseball competition. Built to seat 85,000 spectators, the Olympic Stadium was scheduled for partial demolition after the Games to create a new 47,000-seater stadium (Turner Field) for the Atlanta Braves, with the Fulton County Stadium demolished to provide parking space (Larson and Staley, 1998, p. 281). Neighbourhoods near Olympic sites experienced beautification, with projects designed to improve central city streets and upgrade twelve pedestrian corridors that linked the venues. This work included widening pavements, burying power lines, installing new street furniture, tree planting, history panels, signage, and the redesign of five parks and plazas.

Atlanta disappointed those who looked for more from a Games that marked the centenary of the modern Olympics (French and Disher, 1997). The conduct of the Games and the quality of ceremonial content led Tomlinson (1999, p. 69) to describe it as 'an elongated event of tattiness and tawdriness'. Concentrating so many facilities at the centre of the city placed pressure on the transport systems. Traffic congestion, slow journey times, and long queues to use the shuttle buses added to the difficulties for athletes, officials and spectators reaching venues (Larson and Staley, 1998, p. 278). The organizers' claims that Olympic sites were within walking distance of one another proved meaningless given the excessive summer temperatures. The repeated systems failures of the results service, the arrogance of officials, poor relations with the press, the large numbers of unauthorized street vendors, aggressive sponsorship, and unbridled commercialism undermined Atlanta's desire to stage a modern and efficient event.

The city's policy towards regeneration was deemed to perpetuate Atlanta's longstanding use of measures for spatial restructuring to perpetuate inequality. This applied notably to two areas close to the Olympic sites. One, the Techwood and Clark Howell public housing district to the south of the Georgia Institute of Technology, was demolished and replaced by a mixed gated community, effectively replacing poorer tenants with more affluent residents. The other, a rundown housing and industrial area near the Georgia World Congress Centre (GWCC), was cleared to create Centennial Park as an area where visitors and spectators could congregate during the Games and where entertainment could be provided (figure 2.13). Clearance here and in nearby Woodruffe Park removed more than 16,500 of Atlanta's poorest inhabitants to make way for the stadium. The additional loss of a hostel and three shelters displaced around 10 per cent of Atlanta's homeless (Burbank *et al.*, 2001, p. 112). Aggressive use of city ordinances that criminalized anti-social behaviour and measures to remove the homeless resulted in the physical eviction of 'undesirables' from the vicinity of the Games (Lenskyj, 2000, pp. 138–139).

The passage of time has eroded the force of some of these criticisms. For example, Atlanta's policy towards the stadium fully acknowledged the realities of post-Games use and spared the city from being saddled with expensive and underused venues, as was subsequently the case with Sydney, Athens, Beijing and, arguably, London. The Olympics raised Atlanta's profile as a sporting and conference destination, even if it failed to enhance its broader image as a cultural centre. Nonetheless, the distaste for the manner of its urban restructuring persists as has the disquiet for its rampant commercialism, with the IOC vowing that the Games would never again

Figure 2.13. Centennial Park, Atlanta 1996. (*Source*: Photograph, John and Margaret Gold)

be entrusted to an entirely privately-run organization (Whitelegg, 2000, p. 814; also Poynter and Roberts, 2009). Even a century after the revival of the modern Olympics, the formula for staging a successful event remained downright elusive.

Sustainability and Legacy (2000–2016)

The history of *Sydney 2000* stretches back almost four decades. Sydney had contemplated bidding for the Olympics since the early 1960s, following what Little (1997) described as a path from 'one brickpit to another'. A scheme originally designed in 1962 proposed developing large-scale stadia, an aquatics centre and indoor arena on 16 hectares of brickfield land at St Peter's in the north of the city. When that initiative foundered, the underlying principle of creating a site capable of staging an Olympics re-emerged when residents fiercely opposed a plan to redevelop the existing sports district at Centennial Park in readiness to bid for the 1988 Games. A specially appointed commission then scrutinized twenty possible sites in the metropolitan area before recommending Homebush Bay, 14 kilometres west of Sydney's city centre on the Parramatta River (Weirick, 1999).

Originally tidal wetlands and scrub, Homebush Bay at different times had housed Sydney's racecourse, the country's largest abattoir, a saltworks, the state brickworks and a naval munitions store. In the 1930s, the bay had regularly spawned algal blooms through contamination from waste products from the slaughterhouses and from depositing household and industrial waste in landfill sites. Work had begun in the 1980s to clean up the area and some rehabilitation had taken place to create a nucleus for Sydney's suburban expansion (Cashman, 2008, p. 28), but a successful Olympic bid would help regenerate the remainder of the site, tackle its severe environmental problems, supply the city with a replacement for the Royal Agricultural Society's outmoded Showground at Moore Park, and provide a cluster of modern world-class sports facilities. Any bid would involve the state and federal governments as funding agencies and as the owners of the land, as well as the city of Sydney.

Sydney gained the nomination for the 2000 Games in September 1993 against competition from Beijing, Manchester, Berlin, and Istanbul, with a key element in its candidacy being the promise to concentrate the Olympic venues in one central park, which would eventually have a built core surrounded by parkland. The main Olympic venue, named Stadium Australia, was built using public funds, sponsorship, and sale of corporate packages. Designed to hold 110,000 spectators during the Games, its capacity would be reduced to 80,000 for its subsequent life as a rugby and Australian Rules football stadium. The other major stadia at Homebush were the Hockey Centre, Superdome (basketball and artistic gymnastics),

International Athletics Centre (warm-up facilities), Tennis Centre, the Aquatic Centre (swimming and diving), and the Archery Park. The adjacent Olympic Village would accommodate all participants at a single centre for the first time. It comprised a mixed development of apartments and town houses, arranged in three precincts and designed to ecologically sustainable guidelines. Provision of a school and commercial precinct looked ahead to the area's post-Games future as a residential suburb of Sydney. The other Olympic facilities, particularly those associated with rowing and sailing, were located within the Sydney city-region at a maximum distance of 60 miles (100 kilometres) from Homebush Bay.

Planning for the Games embraced different agendas. First, responding to the growing mood of environmentalism, the bid claimed these would be a 'Green Games' expressing environmental responsibility in the use of resources and design of facilities. Secondly, the Sydney Games were a national project, celebrating the 'entire continent of Australia' rather than just the host city: a strategy also adopted at Melbourne 1956. Thirdly, capturing the Games would allow the organizers to highlight the profound changes that had taken place in the forty-four years since Melbourne, in particular the need for explicit recognition of the multicultural identity of Australia. The organizers of the Sydney Olympics in 2000, for example, were mindful of problems that arose at the Australian Bicentennial in 1988, when the celebration of European conquest had led to severe inter-communal frictions. Part of the adopted solution was to broaden the constituent basis of support for the Olympics, making efforts to gain the involvement of community leaders. Another element lay in seeking to change modes of representation, particularly with regard to tackling prevalent negative and stereotypic representations of Aboriginal peoples. Most notably, the Olympic Opening Ceremony commenced with an enacted encounter between indigenous and white Australians, emphasizing the antiquity of indigenous culture, its diversity, myths, legends, and spirituality. The Aborigines emerged as environmentally wise managers of the land, in contrast to the approach of what the Official Report described as the European period of 'vitality and violence' (SOCOG, 2000). Later in the ceremony, the Aboriginal athlete Cathy Freeman was selected to receive the relay-run Olympic torch and light the cauldron of the Olympic flame in the stadium.

One indication of the IOC's sense of relief at the success of the resulting Games came with the IOC President Juan Antonio Samaranch, resurrecting the statement that 'these have been the best Games ever', a description that he had pointedly omitted at the Closing Ceremony of Atlanta 1996. An early study of impact by the Australian Tourist Commission revealed that 75 per cent of the Americans surveyed had seen pictures and stories concerning Australia as a holiday destination as part of the Olympic coverage and half reported that they were now more interested in Australia as a destination

(Morse, 2001, p. 102). Locally, the Games passed off well. Potential demonstrations about homelessness, the plight of Aborigines, ticketing, and the claimed misuse of public funds did not occur. An economic analysis (Haynes, 2001) argued that the total cost of the Games at A\$6.5 billion was roughly neutral in that it was covered by an equivalent amount in extra economic activity in Australia between 1994–1995 and 2005–2006, of which A\$5.1 billion would accrue in New South Wales. For this price, Sydney had achieved the regeneration of a severely blighted industrial region, gained significant improvements to infrastructure, improved its tourist standing, and gained world-class sport facilities. For the Olympic movement, it again showed the value of a festival largely held at a central venue rather than the dispersal of Atlanta.

The experience of Sydney 2000 continues to influence subsequent OCOGs, albeit sometimes in complex ways (Cashman, 2009). The Sydney Games retain a positive aura in terms of organization, friendliness, and raising the profile of the city, but questions remain about aspects of the Olympic Park. Environmentalists question whether the decontamination of the toxic waste site had been fully tackled, criticizing burying 'so much toxicity beneath a metre of dirt and a mountain of public relations' (Chipperfield, 2000; also Berlin, 2003). Critics note the lack of the promised affordable housing. The main stadia have had a chequered history. The Superdome, rebranded first as the Acer Arena (2006–2011) and then as the Allphones Arena, had no pre-agreed legacy use and initially languished before developing into a thriving and internationally recognized entertainments venue on the basis of a successful private – public partnership.[27] By contrast, Stadium Australia, first renamed the Telstra Stadium (2002–2007) and then the ANZ Stadium, has laboured to shake off the 'white elephant' tag, and continues to struggle against competition from the pre-existing modern stadia clustered in the Moore Park area of east Sydney (Searle, 2002, p. 857).

Above all, there were criticisms about the delays in producing a viable legacy plan. The Sydney Olympic Park Authority (SOPA), established in 2001 to plan and manage the Olympic Park, struggled to take stock of the situation, producing a sequence of three master plans between 2002 and 2008. These progressively lengthened the development timeframe from seven to ten years to a more realistic twenty-two years, increased targets for the 'daily population' from 5,000 to 50,500; and raised target levels for employment and visitors. SOPA also started to change its frame of reference. Although still responsible for a delimited area of suburbia, it variously described the embryonic settlement as 'an active, vibrant town within metropolitan Sydney' and, more ambitiously, 'a unique, world-class urban centre' (SOPA, 2014). The new settlement, now known as Newington, would be 'responsive to its context' and further the Olympic Park's 'initiatives in energy and water management [and] green building design' (SOPA, 2009). Mixed land-use and densification policies would seek to create a blend of residential and business activities that would 'activate the precinct on a 24/7 basis' (*ibid.*). The new street networks would be 'pedestrian friendly', and use of public transport would be enhanced by full integration into the Sydney Metropolitan system.

With a population of 3.14 million in 1997 at the time when nominated to stage the Games, Athens would be the last medium-sized city to receive the Summer Games in the period considered in this chapter. Followed as it was by the nomination of cities with populations ranging from 7.46 million (London) to 37.16 million (Tokyo), it would be the last such host until the elapse of almost three decades and the Brisbane Games of 2032 (see chapter 21). As with any Games involving Greece, the history and development of *Athens 2004* inevitably involves circumstances unique to that country (D. Miller, 2003). As chapter 17 shows, the reconstruction of Athens and the return of the Olympics were parallel concerns for the Greek state during the nineteenth century and continued to have resonances even in the late twentieth century. The city's successful bid in 1997 for the 2004 Olympics claimed that most of the competition venues and almost all the training venues were already in place, with the makings of an Olympic Stadium and Park in the complex already constructed for the 1982 European Athletics Championships. The subsequent decision to revisit the plans and make drastic alterations, in particular exchanging the nucleated Olympic centres for a more dispersed approach, undermined the timetable to the point where completion on time hung in the balance.

The immediate impact of the Games was a profound psychological boost for the country and agreement that tourism had benefitted from transformation of the city centre, creation of pedestrianized routes interlinking Athens' major archaeological sites, and investment in the city's hotels, cultural sector and, especially, public transport. Yet, as with Sydney, wider questions about sustainability quickly surfaced. In the narrower sense, critics focused on the way in which the environmental guidelines for the Olympics were, at best, perfunctorily observed. In the more general sense of sustainable development, profound doubts surrounded the potential use of the Olympic facilities. Despite its architecturally sophisticated buildings being intended as a symbol of the new Athens, the Olympic Sports Complex at Maroussi remains heavily underused (figure 2.14), with the stadium only open to the public when events are being staged. The Faliro and Helleniki complexes also struggled to find alternative uses. Nevertheless, as chapter 14 indicates, there is at last progress in the long-awaited legacy in these areas which is beginning to counter the international perception of abandoned venues and a failed Games. Even so, the evidence continues to suggest that pre-Games plans for post-Games use of Olympic facilities in this city contained a strong dose of wish fulfilment: a product of a lingering desire

Figure 2.14. The Olympic Stadium and Park for the Athens 2004 Games, June 2009, (*Source*: Photograph, John and Margaret Gold)

to have a comprehensive set of facilities available whenever the opportunity might arise to stage further sporting mega-events.

The staging of *Beijing 2008* was the culmination of interests first kindled in the late 1980s and prompting a bid in 1993 for the Millennial Games. It was rebuffed on that occasion by just two votes at the IOC's Moscow meeting, largely due to the recent memories of the 1989 Tiananmen Square Massacre and concerns over environmental issues (Poast, 2007, p. 76; also Gartner and Shen, 1992). In November 1998, it was again decided to declare the city's candidacy, with the target being the 2008 Games. This time, its bid gained overwhelming support, achieving an absolute majority on just the second round of voting against opposition from Istanbul, Osaka, Paris, and Toronto. The ease of its victory partly reflected a carefully crafted message that recognized 'the importance of considering what others might think of China and making adjustments to be sure that nothing offended' (Guoqi, 2008, p. 243). The bid team deftly promised an environmentally friendly but 'high-tech' Games that would promote cultural exchange, act as 'a bridge of harmony' between peoples and embody the 'unique integration of sport and culture' intrinsic to Olympism (*ibid.*, pp. 243–244). It effectively addressed key areas of dissatisfaction with the first bid and allowed the attractions of the site plan and other elements of the proposal to shine through.

Within days of the city's success in the bidding process, Beijing's municipal government unveiled an ambitious five-year plan to modernize infrastructure, carry out urban regeneration and improve the environment (Broudehoux, 2004, pp. 200–201). While some of the estimated 180 billion yuan ($22 billion) expenditure would have been incurred anyway as part of the city's development plans, there is no doubt that the Olympics acted as a catalyst for a substantial part of this investment. In addition, a total of $14.25 billion was officially earmarked as funding for developing the sites for the Beijing Games, although as Brunet and Xinwen (2009, pp. 166, 169) note: 'the total investment catalysed by the Games is likely to be much larger – between $20 and $30 billion dollars – especially when the private sector contribution is added'. Modernization and development, however, rested substantially on urban clearance, with estimates in 2007 that at least 1.5 million people had been displaced to make way for Olympic-related developments (COHRE, 2007*a*).

In total, the Games required thirty-seven venues, of which thirty-one were in Beijing and the rest scattered elsewhere within the People's Republic of China (particularly for soccer and sailing) and Hong Kong (equestrianism). Of the venues within Beijing, twelve were newly built, eleven were renovated or extended from pre-existing structures, and eight were temporary sports facilities or related installations (such as the Media Centre). The main examples of architectural spectacle were among the seventeen venues clustered in and around the Olympic Park in the north of the city (He, 2008, pp. x–xiii). The new National Stadium served as the Olympic stadium and the setting for the Opening and Closing Ceremonies. Designed by a team that included the Swiss firm of Herzog and de Meuron, project architect Stefan Marbach, the artist Ai Weiwei, and the Chinese office of Arup Associates, this oval-shaped arena seated 91,000 during the Games, with post-Olympics reduction to 80,000. Its nickname, the 'Bird's Nest', derived from its open lattice structure of interwoven steel trusses, which exposed glimpses of the interior to the outside (*ibid*., pp. 2–7). The National Aquatics Centre, situated to the west of the 'Bird's Nest', provided an equal measure of spectacle. Widely known as the 'Water Cube', its exterior covering of 3,000 irregularly shaped, translucent, blue 'air pillows' provided a highly distinctive panorama when set against the background of the adjacent National Stadium (*ibid*., pp. 20–26).

In most respects, Beijing 2008 was a Games for the television audience, without the now customary carnival atmosphere in the streets provided by live entertainments and giant screens. The pre-Games Olympic torch relay proved a public relations disaster when it passed through countries willing to allow protests and occasional disruption by Free Tibet activists and other demonstrators. Once the relay came within the control of the Chinese authorities, however, such incidents disappeared. Viewers around the world joined the spectators in the stadia in witnessing the stunning and intricately choreographed Opening and Closing Ceremonies, albeit with television viewers of the former witnessing effects that were partly enhanced by overlaying computer graphics.[28] Summarizers and analysts routinely appeared against the backdrop of the Bird's Nest and Water Cube – two of the most iconic structures ever produced for an Olympic Games. After the Games, these facilities have remained very much on the tourist trail, even if the initial signs suggest that post-Games use of the Olympic Stadium is likely to be sparse enough to join the 'white elephant' category.

The legacy agenda in Beijing is overseen in part by the Beijing Olympic City Development Association (BODA) set up in 2009, this was more of an events and sports legacy body than a physical planning agency. While able to advise on 'city development policies and practices' (BOCOG, 2010, p. 300), it is not responsible for planning and directing development in the Olympic Park as in the case of comparable bodies for Sydney and London. Instead, planning is accomplished through the five-year Beijing plans[29] and the overarching Beijing Masterplan (2005–2020). These plans increasingly envisage the cultural and creative sector as an important pillar of the Beijing economy and seek to promote clusters of activity. As such, it aims to maximize the use of the Olympic venues, boost the construction of new cultural facilities, develop the museum economy and improve the tourism service environment with the aim of creating a centre for international cultural, sporting, and business events (NPC, 2011, p. 64).

Projects to realize these objectives began after the Games and still continue. The China National Convention Centre was fashioned out of the Fencing Hall, International Broadcasting Centre and Main Press Centre. The National Aquatics Centre accommodates public use alongside elite sport, along with convention, exhibition and theatrical spaces and retail, food, and drink outlets. Investment in new museum and arts facilities include the China Science and Technology Museum (opened 2009), the China National Arts and Crafts Museum (opened 2022) and plans for a new building for National Art Museum of China. An Olympic Park Observation Tower in the north of the Park opened to the public in 2014.

Official statements that paint a picture of a solid Olympic legacy and vibrant Olympic Park contrast with the Western media's emphasis on 'rotting' and 'abandoned' Olympic venues (BBC, 2012; Engel, 2012). Although the state of some facilities supported the latter narrative (for example the kayaking, rowing, beach volleyball, and baseball venues), the force of some of these sentiments have been ameliorated by the renovation and reuse of some of the major facilities for the 2022 Winter Games. Although the choice of host cities for that event was extremely limited (see chapter 3), the existence of the Olympic Green played a central role in Beijing's successful bid, with the 'Bird's Nest' staging the opening and closing ceremonies. To some extent, therefore, that validated the original concept that saw the Olympic Green as a focus that would allow Beijing to compete for international events.

London 2012 was the first Summer Olympics to be awarded after the twin elements of sustainability and legacy had been firmly embedded in IOC thinking (see chapter 7). That dispensation was clearly articulated in the bid documents and was a powerful factor behind proposing that the prime location for the Games would be in the Lower Lea Valley at Stratford (East London) rather than in the west of the city (as for 1908 and 1948). In many ways, the reasons this area being available resembled those that applied at Homebush Bay (Gold and Gold, 2020*b*). Long histories of accommodating noxious industries and acting as a dumping ground for toxic waste products had left substantial areas of dereliction and heavily contaminated brownfield land. Unlike Homebush, however, there were small but significant communities living in the future Olympic Park – 450 people at the Clay's Lane housing cooperative, around 400 students in university accommodation, and thirty-five families at two long-term gypsy and traveller sites. There were also 284 light manufacturing and waste disposal businesses, employing over 5,000 people primarily drawn from surrounding districts (Gardner, 2022, p. 174; see also Davies *et al.*, 2017), as well as significant clusters of arts studios in former factory premises.[30]

The presence of the existing populations and businesses, however, remained largely under the radar at the time when the bid was being formulated and presented. With eyes firmly fixed on remediating the dereliction almost as if the site was a *tabula rasa*, development planners and local politicians (e.g. Owens and Ward, 2022) recognized that site cleansing would be expensive but, if completed successfully, would allow the lower Lea Valley's positive attributes to emerge. These included the area's proximity to central London, its excellent transport links, and the possibility of meeting the IOC's preference for a compact Olympic Park that was integrated into the life of the city. The lower Lea Valley was also situated in the midst of predominantly multicultural districts that were ranked among the poorest urban areas in England (see chapter 16). The development of an Olympic Park there might then be presented not just as a way of fast-tracking decontamination and urban regeneration, but also as a way of promoting sustainability (Levett, 2004) and for using sports-driven change as a vehicle to overcome multiple deprivation and social inequality (Gold and Gold, 2008).

These ideas resonated with IOC members. Selecting London for 2012 would allow the Olympic Movement to show that staging its premier sporting and cultural festival could truly make a difference. Along with effective lobbying and bid presentation, it was a package that helped London to emerge victorious from the selection meeting in Singapore in July 2005 by the narrow margin of fifty-four votes to fifty over Paris, the long-term favourite. Once the bid was accepted in 2005, the Olympic Delivery Authority took charge of constructing the venues. Accelerating the process of land acquisition that had already begun in earnest *before* the bid was accepted (Owens and Ward, 2022), an Olympic Park of 607 acres (246 hectares) was created. This housed the main Stadium and Village, together with the Aquatic Centre, Hockey Centre, Velodrome, multipurpose arena (used for handball) and Media Centres. All were later destined to be permanent fixtures, with another temporary arena for basketball. Two other zones (River and Central) housed activities in existing venues, in temporary structures or in spaces occupied on a temporary basis (LOCOG, 2013*b*).

London was the first Olympic city to set up a legacy body before the staging of the Games. Established in 2009, the Olympic Park Legacy Company (OPLC) had responsibility bounded by the limits of what is now known as the Queen Elizabeth Olympic Park (QEOP). The OPLC was replaced in February 2012 by the London Legacy Development Corporation (LLDC), a body under the control of London's Mayor. The change was more than just a question of name since its remit stretched beyond the boundaries of the QEOP, with the stated purpose of planning the redevelopment of the QEOP and the surrounding area in partnership with the private sector (see chapter 16).

As originally formulated, the Legacy Master Plan laid down a framework for a new inner-city district (postcode E20). The Athletes' Village, redesignated as the East Village, would offer 2,818 homes with planning permission for a further 2,500. The QEOP would gain a further five neighbourhoods constructed after the Games providing over 6,000 new homes. Beyond housing, eleven schools and nurseries and three health centres would be supplied for what, it was envisaged, would be a young population. Employment comprising 7,000–8,000 new jobs would be supplied at three hubs: the Press and Broadcast Centre in the west (now known as Hear East); Stratford Waterfront in the east; and Pudding Mill in the south (OPLC, 2010). Provision of parkland was regarded as vital given the shortage of open space in adjacent boroughs. The northern part of the Park would be characterized by waterways and landscaped parklands with the emphasis on outdoor recreation and biodiversity; the southern area would be leisure- and events-oriented – intended to become an animated space along the lines of the Tivoli Gardens in Copenhagen or the South Bank in London.

After the Games, changes that arose directly from the Olympics took precedence. These included the removal of temporary arenas, carrying out landscaping and related works to restore access to the waterways, and the conversion of the Athletes' Village to market-rented, affordable, and social housing (figure 2.15). However, the process of delivering the urban legacy perforce takes place in an environment where little or nothing is available from the public purse. Regardless of the grand plan-making, the need for investment from the private sector can require compromises that challenge the integrity of the original Master Plan. In addition, by 2013, new ideas had crystallized that were not part of the initial mix. In particular, it was now proposed to create a Cultural and Educational Quarter on three pieces of land wrapping around the Aquatics Centre. This area was originally earmarked as part of Marshgate Wharf neighbourhood; the largest of the five new housing neighbourhoods planned for the Park. Revisiting this idea Mayor Boris Johnson argued that more ambitious plans were needed to capitalize on the success of the Games and the dynamism of the London economy particularly in the cultural and creative industries. He maintained that the Park needed to:

> move beyond the old preconceptions about the future of the park – essentially that we would build infill housing around the venues. It is now clear that this would be to miss a historic opportunity to accelerate the transformation of east London and to deliver a significant economic boost to the UK. (Anon, 2013)

Initially dubbed 'Olympicopolis' in tributary allusion to its predecessor 'Albertopolis', the South Kensington cultural quarter created from the

Figure 2.15. Social housing area in the East Village (formerly Athletes' Village), Queen Elizabeth Olympic Park, Stratford, London, May 2015. (*Source*: Photograph, John and Margaret Gold)

proceeds of the 1851 Great Exhibition (Hobhouse, 2002), this new quarter would exploit the 'natural movement of the city' as the 'artists, and the designers and the techies' spread east from Hoxton, Shoreditch, to Hackney, Newham, and Tower Hamlets. Later renamed East Bank, it would provide jobs and growth to match the housing already created, thus contributing to the convergence goals for East London (V&A, 2015).

The creation of East Bank effectively represented an approach to leveraging development that looks Janus-like to the past and future. The new Cultural and Education Quarter refers to the same marriage of science, education, and the arts that underpinned its South Kensington predecessor (Gold and Gold, 2017*b*). The city and nation as a whole would benefit from creating a critical mass of cultural attractions that would complement the area's retail and sporting offer. This would include the arts and theatre (linked to the Victoria and Albert Museum, the BBC, and Sadler's Wells) with education, research, and development through the presence of the universities that have moved or are moving to the development: University College London, Loughborough, and University of the Arts. Yet, the project also is framed in terms of culture-led urban regeneration that will create connections between East Bank institutions and local communities and businesses. Interestingly, the rhetoric surrounding this development revalorizes the East End by emphasizing its traditions in fashion, art, design, and craft industries along with the dynamism of its artists. For promotional purposes, this effectively replaces the trope of decline and deprivation while justifying the emphasis on cultural and creative industries. The vision is that of a development that will stimulate a positive legacy at several levels: encouraging innovation and entrepreneurship; raising aspirations and engaging local people through training and education; enhancing audiences for the arts; and boosting local participation in cultural projects. The fact that these putative benefits will be bought at the expense of providing housing – and especially housing for those unable to afford full market prices – is not made readily apparent.

Rio de Janeiro 2016 represented only the second Latin American city to bid successfully bid for the Olympics after Mexico City in 1968. The city had previously bid for the 2004 Games, but then failed to advance to the short-listing stage. Looking back on it, Carlos Roberto Osorio, the Secretary-General of the Brazilian Olympic Committee, recognized that the bid was deeply flawed (see Monteiro and Shropshire, 2010). He noted that:

> When we first tried to get the Olympic Games for the year 2004, we had a very basic project, and not a very deep understanding of the Olympic world and the requirements to host the Olympic Games.

Nevertheless, he argued that it was a vital initial step in two respects. First, it had inculcated an understanding of the broader context, demonstrating that the sports sector could not organize such events 'without the support of the public sector', especially given the associated demands for 'additional public services and additional infrastructure'. Secondly, it had underlined the need to gain experience in running large-scale sports festivals if the city was to gain the chance to stage the 'most complex and the largest event that exists on our planet during times of peace' (*ibid*.).

That process received a significant stimulus in August 2002 when Rio de Janeiro was awarded the right to stage the 2007 Pan American Games and Paralympic Pan American Games, followed in May 2007 by the International Military Sports Council nominating it as host city for the Fifth Military World Games. The former proved particularly important, as the Pan American Games has a multisport basis similar to the Olympics and also has an Athletes' Village. Staging the Pan American Games, therefore, not only showed the international community Brazilians could deliver a large sporting event, it also bequeathed facilities that might to some degree be reused. These included the 45,000-seater João Havelange Stadium (the Engenhão), which was used in 2007 for soccer, track, and field; the Maria Lenk Aquatic Park, used for swimming and diving events; and the Barra Velodrome. The revamped Maracanã Stadium, now reduced to around 90,000 seats, staged the Opening and Closing Ceremonies, with the associated Maracanãzinho Gymnasium housing volleyball events. The Athletes' Village, custom-built for the Games at Barra da Tijuca, covered an area of 91 acres (37 hectares) and comprised seventeen ten-storey buildings with a total of 1,480 apartments (Goulartt, 2007, p. 18). Noticeably, the venues were situated within four nodes that were all located within a span of 15 miles (25 kilometres) and have good connections to the city's motorway system. They provided an integrated core of facilities that might be used for any subsequent multi-sports festival.

Hence when applying for both the 2012 (unsuccessfully) and the 2016 Games, the bidding team essentially proposed a scaled-up version of what had been supplied for the Pan American project. The 2016 bid would proceed against rivals that, *prima facie*, might have seemed to have equal or better cases for the award of the Games. When, for example, the results of an eleven criteria first phase questionnaire (IOC, 2008*a*) were announced in June 2008, Rio de Janeiro ranked fifth with a score of 6.4, comfortably behind Tokyo (8.3), Madrid (8.1), Chicago (7.0) and Doha (6.9). Technically speaking, Rio should have been eliminated at this stage but received a reprieve because the IOC was not prepared to move Games to October – outside the normal time-frame – in order to avoid Doha's fierce summer temperatures.

This narrow escape from elimination at the shortlisting stage led the bidding team to recognize the relative weakness of their case and redouble efforts to improve the technical quality of the city's proposals. The basic locational plan then laid out by the Candidature File (ROCOG, 2009) outlined the ideas that, in the fulness of time, supplied the template for the 2016 Games. All sports apart from soccer were accommodated within the city within four main zones ('clusters'), namely, Barra da Tijuca, Copacabana, Deodoro, and Maracanã. The Barra contained the Olympic Park, which hosted nineteen Olympic and thirteen Paralympic sports. Some of the facilities were upgraded versions of those introduced for the Pan American Games, such as the Maria Lenk Aquatic Park and the Velodrome; others were new: the Olympic Village, Olympic Training Centre, and the International Broadcast Centre and the Main Press Centre. Copacabana, roughly 10 miles (16 kilometres) to the east housed some aquatic disciplines, triathlon, and beach volleyball. Deodoro, situated around five miles (8 kilometres) north of the Olympic Park, staged the BMX and mountain bikes, white-water canoeing, equestrianism, shooting, and pentathlon. Finally, the Maracanã cluster provided the Olympic Stadium (the Maracanã), used for soccer and the main ceremonies, with the João Havelange stadium staging track and field.

To the surprise of many observers, given that Chicago had been the bookmakers' clear favourite, the October 2009 IOC meeting in Copenhagen awarded the nomination to Rio de Janeiro after three rounds of voting. With the signing of the Host City Contract by the Brazilian Olympic Committee and the IOC, the city embarked on a path that replicated in reverse the feat of Mexico City in 1968–1970 by hosting the Summer Olympics as well as co-hosting the FIFA World Cup in just two years.

The preparation phase would not be confined to creation of the sporting venues and associated infrastructure. As outlined in chapter 17, an ambitious development programme had long been attached to the Games that, arguably, make the 2016 Games a highwater mark in the recent history of mega-event led urban regeneration. Besides sports and housing schemes directly linked to the four Olympic zones, there would be extensive regeneration schemes in the waterfront area at Porto Maravilha, introduction of a Bus Rapid Transport (BRT) system with four main routes, and expansion of the metro system. Large-scale clearances of the city's squatter settlements (*favelas*) always lurked in the background.

The path to preparation proceeded with the usual hiccoughs, which the world's press avidly reported. Items published before the event focused on incomplete facilities, the collapse of the sailing ramp, state-fostered drug abuse programmes, Brazil's economic doldrums, the Petrobras scandal, the potential impeachment of President Dilma Rousseff, and the Zika virus. During the Games the daily drip-feed continued. Notwithstanding abundant televisual images of a highly successful sporting festival staged in arenas framed by stunning scenery, there were shots of largely empty stadia juxtaposed with images of long queues at ticket booths, the diving pools that mysteriously changed colour, the volunteers who failed to materialize, the expensive express buses that ran empty, the pollution in Guanabara Bay, the ticketing scam involving the Olympic Council of Ireland, and the funding crisis facing the Paralympics.[31]

After the Games, familiar topics appeared. The Olympics were an extravagant party that diverted money from better causes. Rio has been left with sports venues with high maintenance costs but little legacy use. The infrastructural improvements, especially the metro extension, primarily serve those living in richer districts. Sports participation is unlikely to rise. Rio's structural problems will remain. Noticeably perhaps, most contemporary scholarship on the subject of legacy still centres on London 2012 and further back to Sydney 2000 rather than dwelling overmuch on the lessons of Rio 2016.

Tokyo 2020/2021

The success of the 1964 Olympics, both as an exercise in cultural diplomacy and in its lasting legacy for the rebuilding of Tokyo, had left the Japanese wanting to repeat the exercise. In 2009, a bid had been crafted for the 2016 Games, ultimately won by Rio. As with the previous event, the Games would be linked to a major urban planning exercise. The Olympic areas would deploy brownfield land to create an Olympic Park on the waterfront along with land reclaimed from Tokyo Bay that would afterwards leave a legacy of parkland, new housing, retailing, and entertainment venues. The event would also fit in with transportation and open space strategies to allow the creation of a green corridor to reconnect the city centre to the waterfront.

Generally felt to be lacklustre, the 2009 bid was eliminated in the second round of voting but, as with many predecessors, failed bids supply the basis for subsequent attempts. In 2009, the Tokyo team helped their cause by crafting a bid that fully incorporated the IOC's known preferences, particularly for compactness and for legacy. Briefly summarized, the bid proposed situating twenty-eight of the thirty-three competition venues within the city's boundaries in two loosely defined zones. One, the Tokyo Bay Zone, offered the possibility of building substantial numbers of new venues, including the Athletes' Village, on waterfront land that could be requisitioned or reclaimed. The other, the Heritage Zone, sought to capitalize on the physical legacy of the earlier Games. Notably the Kasumigaoka National Stadium, the Olympic stadium from 1964, would be rebuilt as the equivalent for 2020. The bid stressed integration of the Olympic projects into overall city planning and promised a rich legacy in terms of improvements to infrastructure and the urban fabric.

In an uncomfortably ironic echo of the past, the bid for the 2020 Olympic and Paralympic Games partly addressed the desire to recover from disaster, in this case the devastation inflicted by the Great East Japan Earthquake and tsunami of March 2011. The main goal, however, was not wholesale physical reconstruction for the host city as it had been in 1964 but to frame a national project that offered momentum for moving ahead again (Kirakosyan, 2022). As noted in chapter 18, the consensual view prioritized soft legacy, notably in terms of making Japan an attractive business and tourist destination, displaying Japanese technology to best advantage (e.g. Nagata, 2014), and focusing on cultural challenges connected with the ageing population, social inclusion, and disability.

Tokyo's comfortable success at the IOC's selection meeting in October 2013 set in train the long-term trajectory by which the Games are prepared, staged and their aftermath managed. The preparation period for *Tokyo 2020* would see a series of minor crises that briefly threatened to derail progress. One concerned the original design of the festival logo, which had to be scrapped after it was found to be plagiarized from that of the Théâtre de Liège in Belgium. Another arose from the difficulties of building a key access link due to delays in relocating Tokyo's historic Tsukiji fish market; difficulties only resolved after a mysterious fire removed the obstacle in August 2017. Perhaps the most significant problem related to the design for rebuilding the Olympic stadium. The decision to abandon the original spectacular sinuous design for the stadium, shaped like a giant cycling helmet, was attributed to construction cost, but had undertones of not wishing to give a prestige project to a non-Japanese practice – the London-based Zaha Hadid

Figure 2.16. Olympic Stadium, Tokyo 2020. (*Source*: Photo © Louise Claire Wagner)

Architects. Several years' preparation time were lost in the process before a new and more conventional design (figure 2.16), commissioned from the practice run by Japanese architect Kengo Kuma, was built in its place.

Despite these problems, the organizers did manage to deliver the stadia and infrastructure comfortably on time and in line with notions of Olympic legacy and sustainability. In July 2019 with a full year to go, the IOC voiced its approval at the progress of preparation works (Blair, 2019), with the city and nation more preoccupied with finding strategies to cope with excessive ticket demand and the anticipated tourist boom. The associated infrastructure was intended to display the advanced state of Japanese technology. Hydrogen energy powered both the Olympic Village and the fleets of vehicles used to transport participants between the competition venues. Manufacturers and suppliers would also be able to show off their products to visitors in fields such as 5G telecommunications, driverless vehicles, and robotics as part of the legacy possibilities of the event.

As it was, there were few to whom Japan's technological prowess could be flaunted. As described in the previous chapter, the outbreak of COVID-19 led quickly and reluctantly to the postponement of the Games and their replacement with a spectatorless format in 2021. Although currently still in the early phases of the legacy process, present assessments indicate a substantial gap between the expected and achieved economic impact gained by hosting of the Tokyo Summer Olympics and Paralympics. While the Games had had a clear positive economic impact at least prior to the event, with a boost in GDP accompanying infrastructure investments and other factors, the net economic impact during the event was extremely limited and may have even been negative (Toshihiro, 2022). Lack of spectators also meant that there was little opportunity to use the Games as a vehicle to showcase advanced Japanese technology to the world, particularly regarding hydrogen powered vehicles and electricity production. Although delayed for a year and facing difficult economic circumstances, most of the urban regenerative projects connected with Tokyo Bay have commenced or are in prospect. It may be that, as Faure (2023, p. 218) suggests: 'The success of the organization of the Games in the face of unprecedented constraints seems to hide the relative failure of an urban project that has become a simple pretext for supporting a series of shopping centres and leisure consumption zones that are struggling to find their place in the Tokyo landscape.' That style of criticism, however, is one routinely levelled at large-scale development projects and is by no means unique to Tokyo 2020.

Notes

1. Spoken by Prince George, later Duke of Clarence, in William Shakespeare (1593) 'Henry VI, part 3', ii, iii, 53.

2.   Although there was a nearby village called Andilalo – the name means 'village of the echo' – it is just as possible that the name simply relates to the spot where the remarkable reverberating echo found at Olympia occurs (see Leake, 1830, vol. 1, p. 31).

3.   Along with old school ties and royal jubilees, Bastille Day, the Daughters of the American Revolution, May Day, the Internationale, the Cup Final, and the Tour de France (Hobsbawm, 1983, p. 303).

4.   The event was mentioned in a letter dated 30 April 1679, written by Colonel Edward Cooke in London and addressed to the Duke of Ormond, Viceroy of Ireland, in Dublin. *Source: Notes and Queries*, Tenth Series, X (22 August 1908), p. 147.

5.   Baron Pierre de Coubertin (1863–1937), a French educational reformer, was the key figure behind the movement that founded the IOC (see note 7).

6.   The word 'traditional' needs to be emphasized here, since it can be argued that more recently the IOC's version of Olympic history has started to offer a more rounded picture of Brookes's contribution (e.g. see Heck, 2014).

7.   This came at the end of a speech made at a Jubilee event to celebrate the fifth anniversary of the founding of the Union of French Sports Associations.

8.   At the outset, the IOC was a small, conservative and entirely male-dominated body, heavily under the sway of Coubertin, comprising prominent sportsmen and titled individuals whose social status might lend weight to the embryonic organization. The first committee comprised fifteen members from twelve countries. By 1904, this had increased to thirty-two members, of whom seventeen had aristocratic or civil titles (eight counts, three barons, two princes, a knight, a professor, a general, and a bishop). To Coubertin, that social background seemed to suggest people whose impeccable pedigree and private means would insure their impartiality. To later commentators, it would provide the lasting recipe for cronyism and an unrepresentative self-perpetuating oligarchy (e.g. Simson and Jennings, 1992; Sheil, 1998; Lenskyj, 2000, 2008).

9.   The marathon made connection with ancient legend, with the story of the runner who brought news of the Greek victory over the Persians from Marathon to Athens in 490 BC. In reality, however, the race had no parallel in ancient Greek practice, where races rarely exceeded 5 kilometres (Lucas, 1976). For other suggestions as to the martial connotations of the original Games, see Rustin (2009, p. 11).

10.   Athletes returning from the Athens Games established the Boston Marathon the following year (Lovett, 1997, p. xii).

11.   Mallon (1998, p. 5) points out that Coubertin had previously suggested a recreation of Olympia for the 1889 Universal Exposition in Paris, with some sporting events.

12.   There may well have been an element of pretext here: it is now suggested that the Italians were preparing to withdraw from the Games before the eruption occurred (Mallon and Buchanan, 2000, p. xxxvii).

13.   British Olympic Association, Minutes of Council Meeting, A7/3, 18 February 1907.

14.   Martin Polley (2011, pp. 100–127), for instance, argued that the amount of use that the stadium had over the next seventy years was sufficient to absolve it from the accusation of being a 'white elephant'.

15.   With a population in 1900 of 300,624 compared with Greater London's 1901 figure of 6.5 million.

16.   Named after General John Pershing, the Commander-in-Chief of the American Expeditionary Force, the Pershing stadium was built by the Americans on land donated by the French.

17.   This prefabricated encampment was for male athletes and was demolished after the Games. Female athletes were housed in the Chapman Park Hotel as it was thought they required a rather more permanent type of residence (TOC, 1933, p. 292).

18. It was suggested, for example, that ancient Greece was partly settled by early Germanic migrants during the Neolithic period (Arnold, 1992, p. 32).

19. The lessons of the voluminous literature on the political and ideological controversies surrounding Berlin 1936 lie beyond the scope of this chapter. For more discussion, see: Guttmann (2006); Large and Large (2016); and Hilmes (2018). For an indication of how the Olympics became intertwined with issues of German identity, see Diem (1912, 1942).

20. The Games of the Twelfth and Thirteenth Olympiads were not celebrated because of the Second World War.

21. Peter Ueberroth, President of the Los Angeles Olympic Organizing Committee, was representative of a long line of business entrepreneurs who sought to promote Los Angeles through mega events and other high-profile activities (Reich, 1986).

22. Although accusations of commercial excesses galvanized the IOC into taking control of sponsorship through TOP (The Olympic Programme). For all the disdain of commercialism, the IOC now found itself in the position of inviting corporations to pay tens of millions of dollars to become worldwide Olympic sponsors.

23. Discussion of the televisual portrayals of the Games and their implications is found in MacAloon (1989).

24. *Financial Times*, 15 October 1986.

25. This was partly through facing the competing attractions of Expo 92 in Seville and having Madrid as 1992 European City of Culture.

26. The following comprise a selection from a large literature: Buchanan (1992); García (1993); Borja (1995); Moragas and Botella (1995); Esteban (1999); Calavita and Ferrer (2000); Monclús (2000, 2003); Marshall (2004); Capel (2005); Delgado (2005); Degen and García (2012); González and González (2015); Charnock *et al.* (2021); and Uzqueda *et al.* (2021).

27. In this respect, its history resembled that of London's O2 Arena.

28. Notably for a sequence that involved a set of twenty-nine footprints in the sky (Spencer, 2008).

29. The tenth Plan covered 2001–2005, the eleventh 2006–2010, the twelfth 2011–2015, and the thirteenth 2016–2020.

30. Carpenters Road Studios, situated on the site of the old Yardley's factory, was said to be the largest studio block in Europe with 140 studios on site. Managed by Acme Studios, they housed working spaces for around 500 artists between 1985 and 2001, including such luminaries as Rachel Whiteread, Fiona Rae, and Grayson Perry.

31. These items were catalogued in Gold, J.R. (2016) 'If you have to ask the price…', *Blogged Environment.* Online at: http://alexandrinepress.co.uk/olympic_cities_JRGold.

Chapter 3

THE WINTER OLYMPICS 1924–2026

Stephen Essex

The delay in establishing a separate Winter Olympic Games until 1924, almost 30 years after the revival of the modern Games, reflected the exclusion of winter sports in the original conception of the Olympics. Pierre de Coubertin objected to their inclusion partly because of Scandinavian fears that to do so would have possible detrimental effects on their traditional sports festivals, such as the Nordic Games and Holmenkollen Week.[1] However, as the popularity of winter sports spread, the movement to include them in the Olympic programme gathered pace. Some of the early Summer Games included figure skating (London 1908, Antwerp 1920) and ice hockey (Antwerp 1920) in their programmes. In 1924, a separate winter sports week was held at Chamonix six months before the Summer Games in Paris. Following the success of this winter sports week, the International Olympic Committee (IOC) amended its Charter in 1925 to establish the Winter Olympics, with Chamonix retrospectively designated as the first Winter Games. Until 1948, the country hosting the Summer Games (held every four years) also had the opportunity to stage the Winter Games. Thereafter, the selection of the host for the Winter Games was subject to a separate competition decided by a vote of IOC members, and the event continued to be staged in the same year as the Summer Games. From 1992, further change occurred, with the Summer and Winter Games being staged alternately every two years in order to maximize the profile of the Olympics and its television revenue (Borja, 1992).

As the Winter Olympics approaches its centenary in 2024, this chapter reviews the role of the Winter Olympics in changing and modernizing the built environment of its hosts, together with its long-term legacies. Certain features, of course, remain relatively fixed. The construction or refurbishment of sports facilities has been a constant requirement on hosts throughout the history of the Winter Games, albeit with different outcomes based on local circumstances. In addition, although the detailed specifications may change, the range of sports facilities required for the event is normally standard. The main sports venues for the Winter Olympics include a stadium, slopes for slalom and down-hill ski runs, cross-country ski-trails, bobsled and luge runs, and an indoor ice arena. The scale of provision of the associated infrastructure, such as the Olympic Village, Media Centre, hotels, and transport, reflect the increasing popularity and interest in the event. However, the impact on host cities involves greater degrees of variability. In this respect, there are inevitable comparisons to draw with the Summer Games, which have witnessed a progression from the minor impact of the early Games to a more substantial, wide-ranging approach to urban planning through Olympic-led development, encompassing economic, social, cultural, and environmental sustainability as well as legacy planning (see also Essex and Chalkley, 1998, 2002; Chalkley and Essex, 1999). The Winter Olympics are clearly different from the Summer Olympics in that they are staged on a smaller scale and in fragile landscapes, with less coherence in the types of venues required for the various competitions (mountains to urban ice rinks) and logistical challenges of transporting athletes and spectators to remote venues. The key questions addressed in this chapter are whether the Winter Olympics have had a similar trajectory of development impacts on host centres and the extent to which the aspirations for sustainability and legacy have been delivered in recent games.

To answer these questions, this chapter draws on the Official Reports of the Organizing Committees and identifies five sequential phases in the development of the event to offer a framework for organizing and understanding the experiences of the past twenty-four hosts of the Winter Olympic Games from 1924. These phases are characterized as: (1) minimal infrastructural investment (1924–1932); (2) emerging infrastructural demands (1936–1960); (3) tool of regional development (1964–1980); (4) large-scale transformations (1984–1998); and (5) sustainable development and legacy planning (2002–present). While business interests have consistently been instrumental in galvanizing a desire to stage the Games, the public sector has traditionally organized and funded much of the infrastructural investment for the Winter Olympics, as well as accumulating the main debts. Moreover, although private sources of capital, such as television rights and sponsorship, have emerged since 1984, the public sector remains pivotal for the organization and delivery of the event (Essex and Chalkley, 2004; Gaudette *et al.*, 2017; Brown, 2020).

Phase 1: Minimal Infrastructural Investment (1924–1932)

The first three Winter Olympics (see table 3.1 and figure 3.1) were characterized by relatively low levels of interest and participation. The events

Table 3.1. Host cities and candidate cities for the Winter Olympic Games, 1924–2026. (*Source*: Compiled by the author from Documentation files held at the IOC Olympic Studies Centre in Lausanne, Switzerland)

Games	Host City	Host nation	Other Candidate Cities
1924	Chamonix	France	–
1928	St. Moritz	Switzerland	Davos, Engelberg (Switzerland)
1932	Lake Placid	USA	Montreal (Canada), Bear Mountain, Yosemite Valley, Lake Tahoe, Duluth, Minneapolis, Denver (USA)
1936	Garmisch-Partenkirchen	Germany	St Moritz (Switzerland)
1948	St. Moritz	Switzerland	Lake Placid (USA)
1952	Oslo	Norway	Cortina (Italy), Lake Placid (USA)
1956	Cortina	Italy	Colorado Springs, Lake Placid (USA), Montreal (Canada)
1960	Squaw Valley	USA	Innsbruck (Austria), St Moritz (Switzerland), Garmisch-Partenkirchen (Germany)
1964	Innsbruck	Austria	Calgary (Canada), Lahti/Are (Sweden)
1968	Grenoble	France	Calgary (Canada), Lahti/Are (Sweden), Sapporo (Japan), Oslo (Norway), Lake Placid (USA)
1972	Sapporo	Japan	Banff (Canada), Lahti/Are (Sweden), Salt Lake City (USA)
1976	Innsbruck	Austria	Denver (USA), Sion (Switzerland), Tampere/Are (Finland), Vancouver (Canada)
1980	Lake Placid	USA	Vancouver-Garibaldi (Canada): withdrew before final vote
1984	Sarajevo	Yugoslavia	Sapporo (Japan), Falun/Göteborg (Sweden)
1988	Calgary	Canada	Falun (Switzerland), Cortina (Italy)
1992	Albertville	France	Anchorage (USA), Berchtesgaden (Germany), Cortina (Italy), Lillehammer (Norway), Falun (Sweden), Sofia (Bulgaria)
1994	Lillehammer	Norway	Anchorage (USA), Öestersund/Are (Sweden), Sofia (Bulgaria)
1998	Nagano	Japan	Aoste (Italy), Jaca (Spain), Öestersund (Sweden), Salt Lake City (USA)
2002	Salt Lake City	USA	Öestersund (Sweden), Quebec City (Canada), Sion (Switzerland)
2006	Turin	Italy	Helsinki (Finland), Klagenfurt (Austria), Poprad-Tatry (Slovakia), Sion (Switzerland), Zakopane (Poland)
2010	Vancouver	Canada	PyeongChang (South Korea), Salzburg (Austria)
2014	Sochi	Russia	PyeongChang (South Korea), Salzburg (Austria)
2018	Pyeongchang	South Korea	Annecy (France), Munich (Germany)
2022	Beijing	China	Almaty (Kazakhstan), Oslo (Norway)
2026	Milan-Cortina d'Ampezzo	Italy	Calgary (Canada), Stockholm-Åre (Sweden)

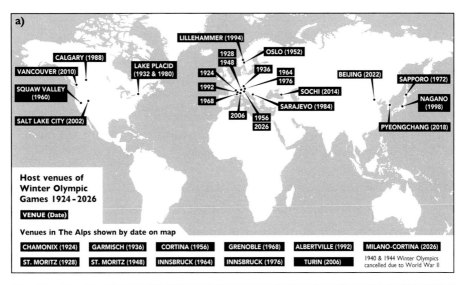

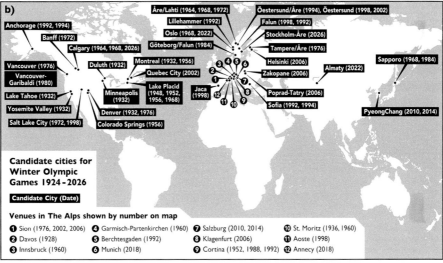

Figure 3.1. (*a*) Host venues for the Winter Olympic Games, 1924–2026; and (*b*) Candidate venues for the Winter Olympic Games, 1924–2026. (*Source*: IOC, 2015a; IOC OSC, 2022)

were staged in settlements with populations of about 3,000, with less than 500 athletes competing in each of the Games. Nevertheless, the motivations of the hosts in staging the Games allude to some interest in the development prospects, especially given the emerging interest in winter sports tourism. Chamonix, in the Haute-Savoie department of eastern France, appears to have been volunteered as the host by the French Olympic Committee, which was no doubt cognisant of the need to have world-class facilities to develop winter sports. Similarly, the local Chamber of Commerce was not slow to recognize the economic advantages for the town created by the popular interest in the Games (see figure 3.2). Funding of the first Winter Olympics

Figure 3.2. The stadium for the Winter Olympics in Chamonix in 1924. (*Source*: COF, 1924, p. 648; Photograph, Auguste Couttet)

appears to have been shared equally between the public and private sectors. In 1928, the Games in St Moritz were led by the local authority and assisted the consolidation of the resort as an international winter sports destination.

Although the initial idea to stage the Winter Olympics in Lake Placid (USA) in 1932 came from the American Olympic Committee in 1927, it was the Lake Placid Club, which owned existing sports facilities in the area, that had investigated the feasibility of the event. The decision to bid for the Games was made only after a representative of the Lake Placid Club had visited a number of European resorts and the St Moritz Olympics of 1928 to convince himself, on behalf of the community, that Lake Placid could match the highest standards abroad and secure longer-term benefits from the investment required. To support the bid, in July 1928, the Lake Placid Chamber of Commerce set up a guarantee fund of $50,000, but it was in fact New York State that provided the main funding for infrastructural requirements for the event (see figure 3.3). The State's involvement eased the concerns of some local residents about the magnitude and responsibility of the task (LPOOC, 1932, p. 43). The organization of the event was a partnership between New York State, Essex County Park Commission, North Elba Town Board, North Elba Park Committee and Lake Placid Village Board (*ibid.*, p. 74). In 1932, substantial funding from New York State led to the establishment of the New York State Olympic Winter Games

Commission to ensure that the money was spent wisely (*ibid.*, p. 60), which is a model that has been followed in subsequent Games.

Many of the hosts of the early Winter Olympics were especially aware of

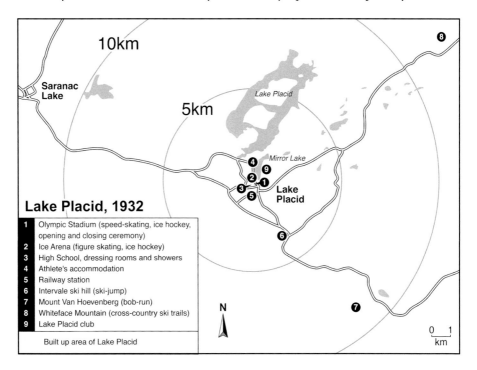

Lake Placid, 1932

1	Olympic Stadium (speed-skating, ice hockey, opening and closing ceremony)
2	Ice Arena (figure skating, ice hockey)
3	High School, dressing rooms and showers
4	Athlete's accommodation
5	Railway station
6	Intervale ski hill (ski-jump)
7	Mount Van Hoevenberg (bob-run)
8	Whiteface Mountain (cross-country ski trails)
9	Lake Placid club

Built up area of Lake Placid

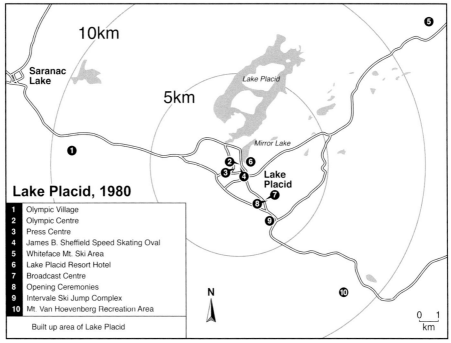

Lake Placid, 1980

1	Olympic Village
2	Olympic Centre
3	Press Centre
4	James B. Sheffield Speed Skating Oval
5	Whiteface Mt. Ski Area
6	Lake Placid Resort Hotel
7	Broadcast Centre
8	Opening Ceremonies
9	Intervale Ski Jump Complex
10	Mt. Van Hoevenberg Recreation Area

Built up area of Lake Placid

Figure 3.3. Comparison of the Olympic facilities provided for the Winter Olympic Games of 1932 and 1980 in Lake Placid, USA. (*Source*: LPOOC, 1932, 1980)

the long-term viability of facilities when deciding whether to stage the event, mainly because of the settlement's small size and limited capacity to sustain expensive, high-order facilities. For example, the skeleton[2] run constructed at the eastern Swiss resort of St Moritz for the 1928 Games proved to be an expensive and unviable legacy. Fewer than 30 people used the facility after the Games. As a result, the organizers of the subsequent Games at Lake Placid 1932 questioned whether the projected cost ($25,000) of a similar facility could be justified.[3] In light of the expected high costs and low post-use,[4] the event was eliminated from the programme at Lake Placid and was not re-introduced until Salt Lake City (Utah) in 2002.

By contrast with this prudence, the Lake Placid organizers were criticized for the extravagance of building an indoor ice rink very late in the preparations. The plan was not supported by the State of New York because of the proposed costs ($375,000). The organizers were responding to a suggestion by the IOC President that such a facility would provide an alternative venue for events in the case of bad weather (which had so badly disrupted the St Moritz Games 1928) and would also be a tangible and physical memorial to the event. The site for the rink was cleared and, with the prospect of a derelict site in the town centre, the authorities were forced to fund the construction via a bond issue (Ortloff and Ortloff, 1976, p. 77). According to the organizers, the indoor ice rink proved its worth by providing an alternative venue for skating events affected by the unseasonably warm weather and so prevented the programme from being disrupted (LPOOC, 1932, p. 154).

The construction of Olympic Villages or new hotels was certainly not justified in this first phase because of fears of over-provision. Instead, existing accommodation within a wide geographical catchment area were adapted and, if necessary, upgraded for winter occupation. Hotel and cottage owners in the vicinity of Lake Placid were urged to 'winterize' their summer accommodation by the organizers of the Games of 1932 in an effort to house the expected 10,000 visitors. As no additional accommodation capacity was developed near the venue, accommodation in Montreal, which was three and a half hours from Lake Placid, had to be used to cater for the demand (LPOOC, 1932, p. 112).

Despite the small-scale nature of the events in Phase 1, some Olympic-related developments proposed for early Winter Games raised environmental protests, marking an issue which was to become much more of a prominent concern in later phases. In March 1930, a local action group (the Association for the Protection of the Adirondacks) brought a successful legal action against a proposed Olympic bobsled run for the Lake Placid Games on environmental grounds and because building on state land was unconstitutional. As a result, a less sensitive site was found at South Meadows Mountain, later renamed Mount Van Hoevenberg (*ibid.*).

Phase 2: Emerging Infrastructural Demands (1936–1960)

The second phase bears many of the hallmarks of the first phase: host centres were generally small (normally less than 13,000 residents) and had been offered as hosts by a combination of National Olympic Committees, Sports Federations, and local authorities, with infrastructural investment funded predominantly by the public sector. The key difference was that, by 1936, there was substantial growth in the number of participating countries and athletes. Investment in Olympic-related infrastructure continued to be constrained by the same factors of long-term viability as in the first phase, but with the added pressures created by the temporary influx of larger numbers of competitors and spectators. Initial plans for an Olympic Village at Cortina d'Ampezzo in northern Italy for the Winter Games of 1956 were abandoned after opposition from local hoteliers who feared the effect of an increase in the town's accommodation capacity on their businesses (CONI, 1956, p. 267). The award of the 1960 Games to Squaw Valley, according to the organizers, had transformed a remote mountain valley into a 'throbbing city' (California Olympic Commission, 1960, p. 27). Although the development of the Olympic Village for Squaw Valley 1960 was out of scale with the small local community, it was considered necessary because of the number of athletes now requiring accommodation and because local hotel capacity was needed for officials and journalists (Chappelet, 1997, p. 83). Yet, it was only a temporary construction as the town's small population (*c.* 4,000) meant there was no viable post-Olympic use.

The main exception in this phase was the Norwegian capital Oslo, which hosted the Winter Olympics of 1952. With a resident population of 447,100, the city was by far the largest centre to have hosted the Games by that date. The larger population created new opportunities for the type of facilities provided, as the post-Olympic viability and future use was more assured. In the period before 1960, Oslo was also the only host to have built an Olympic Village, albeit dispersed in various locations around the city with planned post-Olympic uses, such as university halls of residence, a hospital and an old people's home (Organisasjonskomiteen, 1952, pp. 23, 42). However, new infrastructural requirements were also created by the increased size of the host settlements. For example, larger urban centres were often at some distance from competition sites. Large numbers of athletes and spectators required transport to cover considerable distances to isolated locations in difficult terrains and within limited timeframes, sometimes compounded by adverse weather conditions. Investment in transport infrastructure such as new roads, bridges, and ski-lifts, therefore, became essential to the operation of the Oslo 1952 and subsequent events.

Phase 3: Tool of Regional Development (1964–1980)

The third phase (1964–1980) was characterized by a number of definite shifts: an expansion of the number of athletes, appreciably larger host centres, and the emergence of regional development and modernization as a key motivation for staging the Games. Four of the five hosts during this period had populations of more than 100,000, with the other having more than one million. Only Lake Placid in 1980 had a population size that was similar to those of previous phases. Both private development companies and local authorities recognized the potential of the Winter Olympics for justifying major infrastructural investment as part of broader modernization programmes. Television revenue was also emerging and grew substantially as a source of income during this phase, although the local public sector remained central to the organization of the event. In 1964, the Innsbruck Games received $597,000 from television rights, while the 1980 Lake Placid Games received $15.5 million.

Partly because of their increased size, the Winter Olympics were recognized as a tool of regional development from the 1960s onwards. Innsbruck 1964 was used as a showcase for Austrian businesses, especially those related to ski equipment (Espy, 1979, p. 90). The modernization of the Isère Department was accelerated by the Grenoble Games of 1968 (Borja, 1992) and as a means of remodelling its planning system after a period of rapid growth (1946–1968) (COJO, 1968, p. 46). The Sapporo Games of 1972 were viewed by the Japanese government as a unique economic opportunity to invigorate the northern island of Hokkaido (Borja, 1992). Most of the spending was on investment in the urban infrastructure, with less than 5 per cent of capital improvements for these Games expended on sports facilities (Hall, 1992, p. 69).

With the choice of host centres with larger populations after 1960, the post-Games viability of a purpose-built Olympic Village became more assured, usually as a residential area of the host settlement or a student hall of residence for a local university or college. For example, the Olympic Village at Grenoble was built in a Priority Urbanization Zone and subsequently was used as an 800-room university hall, a 300-room hostel for young workers and a tower block with fifty-two apartments (COJO, 1968, p. 71). In Innsbruck, which staged the Games of both 1964 and 1976, the organizers were forced to build an Olympic Village for each event. The four apartment blocks built for the Winter Games of 1964 were not available for the Games of 1976 as they had become a residential suburb of the town in the interim. The second Olympic Village, consisting of nineteen apartment blocks, was therefore built on an adjacent site. The 1976 organizers later reported that having to build another Village was, perhaps, rather extravagant, as not all the athletes wished to stay there, with some preferring to be closer to event sites.

In retrospect, they felt that accommodating athletes in hotels might have been preferable from cost, security, and transport perspectives (HOOWI, 1967, p. 400). Nevertheless, the two Olympic Villages had created a new residential area at Neu-Arzl in East Innsbruck (Chappelet, 1997).

Olympic-related investment in transport infrastructure was often central to the regional development objectives. Road construction accounted for 20 per cent of the total investment for Grenoble 1968 in the French Alps (COJO, 1968, p. 46), and was designed to decentralize the region and facilitate economic growth. The investment included a motorway link from Grenoble to Geneva, which acted as a catalyst for the regional economy and transformed the host town into a major conference and university centre (Chappelet, 2002*a*, p. 11). The city's old airport at Grenoble-Eybens was closed to make way for the Olympic Village and was replaced by two new airports at Saint-Etienne-de-Saint-Geoirs and Versoud (COJO, 1968, p. 290). For Sapporo 1972, transport investments included extensions to two airports, improvements to the main railway station, forty-one new or improved roads (213 kilometres) and the construction of a rapid transit system (45 kilometres). This last project had already been started by the City of Sapporo but was completed for the Winter Games using government funding.

The risks associated with staging the Games became greater with the increasing scale of the Winter Olympics. First, warnings about the long-term limitations of the event as a tool of regional development began with the debt accumulated by the organizers of the Grenoble Games, which was eventually paid off by 1995 (Terret, 2008*b*, p. 1904), together with the abandonment or demolition of some of its venues. It was also during this third phase that the award of the Winter Olympics of 1976 to Denver had to be reassigned, which is the only time in Olympic history that this has happened (Olson, 1974). The reason was local concern about the rising cost of the event and how the organizers, led by business interests, were ignoring environmental considerations. An action group, 'Citizens for Colorado's Future' was successful in placing the issue on the State and City ballots in November 1972. The citizens then had a vote on whether the Games should be staged using state funding. The turnout was high (93.8 per cent) and 60 per cent voted against the Olympics, which meant that both state and federal funding for the event would not be forthcoming. Denver was therefore forced to withdraw its candidacy for the Winter Games of 1976, which were then staged in Innsbruck at short notice. Secondly, the changing scale of the event affected the character and operation of the Games. One of the consequences of the Winter Olympics being staged in larger cities and across whole regions was that the focus and impact of the event became dissipated. Critics claimed that the size and dispersed geography of the Games had detracted from the camaraderie of the event and increased transport problems.

In other hosts, efforts were made to mitigate the environmental impacts, though in different ways. For the 1972 Sapporo Games, the only mountain close to the host city and suitable for downhill ski events was Mount Eniwa, within the Shikotsu-Toya National Park. The National Park Council gave permission on condition that all related facilities were removed and the terrain in the affected area restored to its original state. A comparable instance concerned the 1980 Games at Lake Placid, where the town itself lay within Adirondack Park, designated in 1971 and regulated by Adirondack Park Agency. The park's public lands were directly administered by the State Department of Environmental Conservation, which also operated bobsled and luge runs, the biathlon and cross-country trails and the Whiteface Mountain Ski area (LPOOC, 1980, p. 18). The extensions of the ski jumps, originally built for the 1932 Games, had to comply with standards set by the Adirondack Park Agency and the Federal Environment Agency (*ibid.*, p. 38).

Phase 4: Large-Scale Transformations (1984–1998)

The fourth phase (1984–1998) is characterized by the most significant increase in participation in the Winter Games. By 1994, the ratio of support staff to athletes was 6.5 times bigger than in 1956. Numbers of athletes were also growing, with over 2,000 athletes at Nagano in 1998 (Chappelet, 2002*b*). The accommodation of athletes, media, and spectators became a substantial infrastructural challenge in itself. After 1988, two or more Olympic Villages became necessary to accommodate athletes closer to their event venues. Separate villages for the media were also necessary. These demands have favoured centres with larger populations. Perhaps more significantly, television revenue rose from $91.5 million in 1984 to $513 million in 1998, with the additional revenue partly funding ever larger and more ambitious urban redevelopment.

These various changes intensified the advantages of placing the Games in host centres with substantial populations. In this phase, the Games were staged in centres with an average population of about 298,000, although three of the five hosts have been considerably larger and two smaller. The role of the Winter Games as a means to secure major urban infrastructural change and modernization had intensified. The Games staged in Sarajevo in 1984, therefore, were taken as an opportunity to modernize the city by the government. The motivation for Calgary 1988 and Lillehammer 1994 was to act as a stimulus to revive the local economies (e.g. COWGOC, 1988, p. 5). At Calgary, the Organizing Committee moved some venues originally selected by the Calgary Olympic Development Association to make them more viable after the Games (*ibid.*) and the Games also caused some facilities to be provided much earlier than would otherwise have occurred.

For example, the construction of the Olympic Saddledome (20,000 seats, C$7 million), home for a professional ice hockey team established in 1980, was fast-tracked to show the city's commitment to its bid (Hiller, 1990, p. 124). Large investments required to stage the 1992 Albertville Games appear, however, to have made more difficulties for other northern French Alpine resorts seeking finance for restructuring (Tuppen, 2000, p. 330). This case shows that Olympic investment has 'opportunity costs' which may postpone or eliminate other forms of investment.

Given the changing circumstances, smaller hosts in this phase faced problems in justifying investment in permanent purpose-built Olympic Villages. In 1992, Albertville, which had a population of only 20,000 at the time, renovated a small spa at Brides-les-Bains as the Olympic Village rather than constructing a purpose-built facility. However, the village proved to be too far from the sports facilities, so seven smaller Olympic Villages were established in existing hotel accommodation closer to the event sites. After this experience, the IOC stated that it favoured the use of a single Olympic Village in future Games in order to promote contact between athletes from different countries (Charmetant, 1997, p. 115), although this aspiration has not proved possible in more recent events. At Lillehammer in 1994, which had a population of 23,000, a temporary Olympic Village consisting of 200 wooden chalets, was constructed. These examples were significant departures from the trajectory of large-scale infrastructural investment.

The increasing scale of the event has also necessitated more formal recognition of environmental issues in the planning and development of related infrastructure (May, 1995). The intrusion of built structures into fragile environments, as well as the use of chemicals to create the appropriate snow conditions, had become a major issue in the preparations for the Winter Olympics. Most notably, the preparations for the Lillehammer Games of 1994 incorporated, for the first time, the principles of sustainable development. The proposed location of one of the main indoor arenas was moved to protect a bird sanctuary, while its heat circulation was generated from excess heat from its refrigeration unit. Contracts with suppliers and contractors included environmental clauses. The approach influenced the IOC to add an environmental commitment to its Charter in 1996 (Cantelon and Letters, 2000), with the candidates for the Winter Games of 2002 being the first to be required to describe their environmental plans in their bid documents (IOC, 1999a, p. 5; Lesjø, 2000).

Phase 5: Sustainable development and legacy planning (2002 onwards)

During the fifth phase (2002 onwards), the trend for the event to require large-scale infrastructural investment continued, but with a greater emphasis on the protection of the environment, sustainable development, and legacy planning. As a consequence, the Games began to be staged by large metropolitan cities, together with clusters in the surrounding mountain communities, essentially making them multiple-centre events (Chappelet, 2008, p. 1897; Dichter and Teetzel, 2020, p. 1222). There have also been other significant pressures which have altered the character of the Winter Olympics, such as the threat from international terrorism and reforms to the host city selection process following corruption over the award of the 2002 event.

As noted earlier, Salt Lake City was the first host city to have been elected after having been required to outline their environmental plans in the bid process. However, the Winter Olympics of 2002 are likely to be better remembered for the corruption scandal that tainted the city's election as host and for the heightened security threat following the terrorist attacks in New York on 11 September 2001. In December 1998, an allegation emerged that the Salt Lake Bid Committee had made payments to IOC members in return for support in the selection process (Booth, 1999; Lenskyj, 2000; Toohey and Veal, 2000, p. 232). The official inquiries concluded that the IOC's lack of accountability had contributed directly to the gift-giving culture (Kettle, 1999; Sandomir, 1999), although six IOC members were excluded and a further ten were given warnings (IOC, 1999*b*). The controversy led to reforms in the host city selection process, including the elimination of member visits to candidate cities, the creation of a permanent Ethics Commission, and amendments to the composition of the IOC itself. These changes were relevant to the future selection and conduct of both the Summer and Winter Olympics.

Similarly, the 9/11 terrorist attacks on New York made the security risk associated with the Winter Olympics much greater. Salt Lake City was staging the Games only five months after the attacks, so the security measures were enhanced and placed centre stage. Strict constraints were introduced for local air space as well as access to zones within the city (Warren, 2002, p. 617). The organizers spent $200 million on security and public safety measures and deployed 9,750 security-related personnel during the Games (SLOC, 2002, pp. 490, 114). Although security had been a major concern and expenditure since the Munich Games of 1972, Salt Lake City 2002 set a new benchmark for the implementation of security plans and measures at the Olympic Games in an era of global terrorism.

The development of infrastructure and facilities for the Salt Lake City Games was based on three Master Plans: for Downtown, the University of Utah and Park City. A total of seven permanent venues were constructed, with only three requiring investments by the Organizing Committee itself. The other four venues were built by public-private partnerships, with a further twenty temporary venues or overlays (*ibid.*, p. 187).[5] There was significant investment in transport infrastructure, involving ten Olympic-related roads and highway projects and four non-Olympic related regional projects, including the reconstruction of two interstate routes and two light rail transit lines (*ibid.*, p. 179).

All Salt Lake City developments were subject to environmental management systems to minimize adverse environmental impacts. The Environmental Plan contained four 'aggressive objectives', which were all achieved. First, 95.6 per cent of all waste was recycled or composted to achieve the objective of 'zero waste' (*ibid.*, p. 26). Secondly, the Games succeeded in its goal of 'net zero emissions' by offsetting its carbon footprint of 122,936 metric tons of hazardous and greenhouse gas emissions as well as 243,840 metric tons of pollutants in Utah, the US and Canada (*ibid.*, p. 196). The event was certified as climate neutral by the Climate Neutral Network. Thirdly, the event's advocacy programme for urban forestry resulted in 100,000 trees being planted in Utah and fifteen million trees planted worldwide (*ibid.*, p. 26). Finally, zero tolerance for environmental and safety compliance errors was successful (*ibid.*, pp. 195–198). The environmental and sustainable development agenda has been clearly cemented as part of the organization of the Winter Olympic Games following those in Salt Lake City.

The award of the Winter Olympics of 2006 to Turin, with a population of 1.4 million, represented the use of the event as part of a strategy to transform an old industrial city into a modern post-industrial city, a scenario which is normally associated with the Summer Games. Turin as an industrial city had been almost totally dependent upon the motor car manufacturer Fiat for a century and had become known as the 'Italian Detroit' (Rosso, 2004, p. 5). With the contraction of Fiat in the city in the 1980s, involving the loss of 110,000 jobs by 2001 (Winkler, 2007, p. 16), there was a need to forge a new urban identity to attract tertiary businesses and improve its tourism potential.

In order to modernize the city's infrastructure, innovations were first required in the city's governance structures. When Fiat had been dominant in the city, a tradition of industrial conflicts and strong economic interests inside the Municipal Council had prevented the creation of an overall vision or strategy for the city (Pinson, 2002, p. 483). Instead, town-planning interventions had only been allowed to act in a pragmatic and opportunistic way. Following the corruption scandals that led to the collapse of both national and local government in Italy in 1992, national political reforms were introduced involving directly elected mayors with increased executive powers and resources (Winkler, 2007, pp. 18–19). In 1993, Valentino Castellani, Turin's first elected Mayor, emphasized the importance of the internationalization agenda to the city's revitalization and long-term future. This focus, assisted by over fifteen years of political continuity, created a space for dialogue and an opportunity for organizational and entrepreneurial capacity to develop. It placed the municipality at the centre of collective governance as facilitator with an emphasis on open regional partnership, collaboration, and networks rather than centralized secretive confrontation and conflict dominated by Fiat (Pinson, 2002, p. 489; Winkler, 2007, p. 23).

An Urban Master Plan had been prepared in 1995 to alter the city's urban structure and create opportunities for regeneration (figure 3.4).

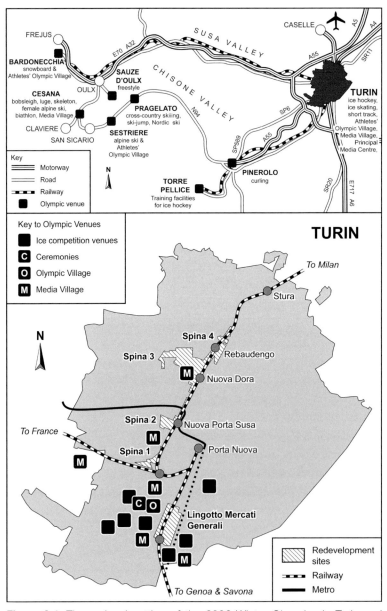

Figure 3.4. The regional setting of the 2006 Winter Olympics in Turin and the Urban Master Plan for the city's redevelopment devised in 1995. (Source: Winkler, 2007)

Figure 3.5. Redevelopment along the Spina Centrale in Turin, which reconnected the two halves of the city previously separated by a railway line, became part of the urban transformations associated with the Winter Olympics in 2006. The restored older buildings on the left were originally a prison (1870–1986), which now operates as a museum (Museo del Carcere Le Nuove). The tower (Il Nuovo Centro Direzionale di Torino) is the headquarters of the banking group Intesa, which accommodates 2,000 employees together with a 364-seater public hall at ground level and a restaurant on the roof. This building was opened in December 2014. (*Source*: Photograph, Christopher Balch)

The Plan focused on the improvement of transport access and private-led investment on brownfield sites within clear land-use zoning and regulation. The organizing principle of the plan was the 'Spina Centrale', which was a north–south avenue along the railway line, which had divided the city into two. The railway line was taken underground, which enabled an increase in service capacity, the physical reconnection of the two halves of the city on the surface and a new urban centrality along the central backbone (see figure 3.5). A new cross-rail system, the 'Passante Ferroviao', was introduced, and new mixed-use developments, including libraries, theatres, banks and regional government offices, were developed on brownfield sites adjacent to the railway stations, often in iconic buildings. A programme to improve the quality of neighbourhoods, public spaces and cultural and leisure attractions throughout the city was implemented (Falk, 2003).

The award of the Winter Olympics to Turin, on 19 June 1999, therefore enabled the scope and importance of the new vision for the city to be integrated (Rosso, 2004, p. 17), prioritized (Pinson, 2002, p. 485) and, above all, to be implemented. The Strategic Plan for Turin was formulated through a highly participatory process and signed by all relevant agencies in February 2000. It outlined six overall strategies focused around: the creation of a metropolitan government; integration into the international system; the development of training and research; the promotion of enterprise and employment; the promotion of Turin as a city of culture, tourism, commerce and sport; and the improvement of the overall quality of the city. Implementation of the corresponding twenty objectives was overseen by the Torino Internazionale Association, the 'Invest in Turin and Piedmont' inward investment agency, and Turismo Torino (Pinson, 2002, p. 485; Rosso, 2004, p. 18; Winkler, 2007, p. 28). The Olympics were perceived as an opportunity to modernize the city's infrastructure (Pinson, 2002, p. 485) and galvanize the longer-term vision for the city.

The staging of the Winter Olympics was also organized as a means of regional integration between the three urban centres (Turin, Grugliasco, and Pinerolo), which provided venues for the ice competitions, an Olympic Village, Media Village, Press Centre and International Broadcasting Centre, and the surrounding mountain communities, which provided venues for the snow competitions and two Olympic Villages (Torre Pellice, Pragelato, Bardonecchia, Sauze d'Oulx, Claviere, Cesana-San Sicario, Sestriere). The purpose of this strategy was to extend the benefits of Olympic investment beyond the city to the whole region through opportunities to upgrade ski facilities and structures and to extend the tourism season (Dansero et al., 2003). Substantial improvements were made to the local road networks to increase the area's tourism potential, as well as to benefit daily life for its citizens. The transformation of Turin as a European metropolis was also signalled with plans to connect to the high-speed rail lines to Milan (2009) and Lyon (2011), thus positioning the city in the dynamic Mediterranean arc of technopoles in southern France (Sophia-Antipolis and Montpellier) through to Barcelona (Falk, 2003, p. 213).

As with the other recent Winter Olympics, Turin 2006 was notable for its emphasis on environmental protection and sustainable development. A strategic evaluation assessment (the so-called 'Green Card') was adopted by the Environment Department of the Turin Organizing Committee (TOROC) to assess the environmental consequences of proposed developments and to monitor environmental impacts.[6] This environmental management system was awarded ISO14001 status. All plans and projects were assessed by the Consulta Ambientale (Environmental Council) before implementation so that recommendations about environmental sustainability could be implemented. An 'Ambiente 2006' logo was awarded to companies who manufactured goods for the Olympics in compliance with predetermined environmentally sustainable criteria (TOROC, 2006, p. 122), and local hotel accommodation was awarded an 'Ecolabel' for adopting sustainable practices (*ibid.*, p. 124; Bottero *et al.*, 2012; Bondonio and Guala, 2011). The Games themselves offset 100,000 metric tons of greenhouse gases through the HECTOR programme (Heritage Climate TORino) (TOROC, 2006, p.122). Indeed, Turin secured advances in the minimization of the environmental impact of the event for future Games to emulate. Turin 2006 was noteworthy for its achievements in transforming the city's structures for governance and in mobilizing the city's long-term redevelopment plan. In this respect, Turin is the closest that the Winter Olympics have come to matching the transformational effects of the 1992 Summer Olympics in Barcelona, although there were some questions about the long-term trajectory of the Olympic legacies following the 2008 recession (Vanolo, 2015).

The Winter Olympics in 2010 were held in Vancouver, Canada, which also emphasized its credentials in sustainable development (Holden *et al.*, 2008). The urban centre of Vancouver acted as the venue for the ice competitions and the neighbouring winter resort of Whistler provided the venues for the snow competitions. New and upgraded facilities were constructed, together with a rapid transit link between the airport and central Vancouver and an upgrade of the 'Sea-to-Sky' highway between Vancouver and Whistler. The 'performance goals' of the organizers focused on accountability, environmental stewardship and impact reduction, social inclusion and responsibility, aboriginal participation and collaboration, economic benefits from sustainable practices and sport for sustainable living (Chappelet, 2008, p. 1896). The provincial government set up an independent not-for-profit company called '2010 Legacies Now' to ensure that each region in British Columbia benefitted from the Games, through maximizing social and economic opportunities, building community capacity, and expanding volunteer resources (2010 Legacies Now, 2009). The agency was funded by grants from various levels of government, contributions by the private sector, and investment income and it undertook various programmes in school education, sport and recreation, the arts, volunteerism and literacy to achieve its goals (2010 Legacies Now, 2008). It created a new model for securing 'softer' Olympic legacies related to people, skills, and employability rather than simply the 'harder' legacies related to the built environment.

Despite the apparent concern for securing a positive post-Olympic legacy, the organizers in Vancouver faced criticisms. The onset of a worsening global recession in 2008 threatened to jeopardize the financial viability of many developments, including the Olympic Village where the city government had to subsidize the project in order to ensure its timely completion (O'Connor, 2009). Social impacts resulting from the effects of land speculation and reversals on promises of affordable housing produced substantial concerns about increasing homelessness in the city. During the pre-Olympic development boom, 1,400 low-income housing units were lost from the Downtown Eastside neighbourhood in order to create more space for tourists and corporate investors (Esparza and Price, 2015, p. 32). Rent increases or conversions into high-cost condominiums or boutique hotels resulted in increased evictions and homelessness.

Indeed, the concern of the authorities to present the best possible image of the city to the world led to various pieces of legislation (such as the Assistance to Shelter Act, 2009 which gave powers to local authorities to place the homeless into temporary shelters) and initiatives (such as the Project Civil City, 2006–08) to remove evidence of social inequality from the streets (Boyle and Haggerty, 2011). The PCC initiative involved increased CCTV surveillance; public realm improvements to beautify areas, encourage active use and design out crime; and deploy 'downtown ambassadors' to act as street concièrges for visitors and the 'eyes and ears' of the police on the ground (*ibid.*). Between 2008 and 2010, anti-poverty activists staged an annual 'Poverty Olympics' to draw attention (by employing irony) to the 'world class poverty' in Vancouver's Downtown Eastside, including events such as 'the poverty-line high jump', 'the welfare hurdles', and the 'broad jump over bedbug infested mattresses' (Esparza and Price, 2015, p. 32; Perry and Kang, 2012, p. 591).

Indigenous peoples objected to their political groups being co-opted onto the local Olympic organization as a means for their artists, cultural performance groups and symbols to be appropriated in Olympic events, while continuing to live in disadvantaged conditions and the Olympics being staged in unceded and non-surrendered indigenous lands (No Olympics on Stolen Native Land campaign) (O'Bonsawin, 2010, p. 148). Some groups considered the use of an Inutshuk as the symbol of the 2010 Olympics as disrespectful as it reduced, objectified, and dehumanized over 630 First Nation Aboriginal communities into a single 'culture', which reflected the dominant colonial view of Canadian nationhood (Perry and Kang, 2012, p. 584). Environmental protests against the construction of the 'Sea-to-Sky' highway through Eagleridge Bluffs resulted in twenty arrests and two jail sentences. The cost of the Vancouver Olympics rose to over $6 billion (O'Connor, 2009) at a time of severe cutbacks to health care, the arts, education, and social assistance (Perry and Kang, 2012, p. 579). Public displays of opposition against the Olympics were the first to employ 'convergence tactics', whereby activists are called to a particular location to protest using mobile/social media communications facilitated by the internet (Esparza and Price, 2015, p. 24). The staging of the Winter Olympics had become as contested as their summer equivalents.

The decision by the IOC in 2007 to award the 2014 Winter Olympics to Sochi in Russia appears to have been a political gesture and commercial opportunity to extend Olympism into the former communist world, along the lines of the Summer Olympics of 2008 in Beijing. For Russia and

President Putin in particular, the Olympics was to be a national project and symbolic of a resurgent Russia (Orttung and Zhemukhov, 2014). The bid proposed to develop the small mountain village of Krasnaya Polyana in the Caucasus Mountains from almost nothing into a new 'world class' winter sports resort to be used for the venues of the snow competitions, together with the existing seaside resort of Sochi as the venue for the ice competitions (figure 3.6). Sochi is located in a sub-tropical coastal region, while Krasnaya Polyana, 49 kilometres away, is part of an alpine mountain range. Besides eleven new Olympic sports facilities and over 19,000 new hotel rooms (IOC, 2007, pp. 18, 24), substantial investment was made in power and gas lines, telecommunications, water supplies, and transport. No less than seven power stations (some thermoelectric and hydroelectric) were constructed or refurbished to increase the capacity of the region's energy network by 2.5 times in order to secure a stable power supply for the event and beyond (SOOC, 2009). A new terminal was built at Sochi airport, together with a new offshore terminal at Sochi seaport. A light railway was constructed from the airport to the Olympic Park. Transport between Sochi and Krasnaya Polyana was enhanced by the reconstruction of the railway to a double track line and a new motorway (IOC, 2007, pp. 25–26). The total costs associated with these developments have been estimated at more than $50

Figure 3.6. The Bolshoy Ice Dome, which was one of the main pieces of sports infrastructure built for the Sochi Winter Olympics in 2014. It was emblematic of the government's use of the Olympics as a 'national' project and symbolic of a resurgent Russia. (*Source*: IOC/ Olympic Museum Collections. © 2013/Comité International Olympique (CIO)/MORATAL, Christophe)

billion (Trubina, 2014, p. 2) and so appeared to be at odds with the IOC's concern to reduce the cost and scale of Olympic events (Chappelet, 2008, p. 1897). One estimate equated the cost of this government investment to be about €60,000 per inhabitant of the region (Müller, 2012, p. 697).

Serious environmental concerns also existed over the preparations as some of the venues were located in the Sochi National Park and the Caucasus State Biosphere Reserve (an UNESCO World Heritage Area). Initially, the National Park was to be re-zoned to allow the construction of an Olympic Village in Krasnaya Polyana and the bobsleigh and luge runs in a buffer zone of the Reserve. In July 2008, Vladimir Putin, then the Russian Prime Minister, ordered the Olympic facilities noted above to be relocated. He is reported to have stated that 'in setting our priorities and choosing between money and the environment, we're choosing the environment' (Finn, 2008). It later emerged that the boundaries of the reserve were changed to accommodate the development (Alekseyeva, 2014, p. 165). An appeal by Greenpeace Russia to the Russian Supreme Court about these environmental concerns was rejected (IOC, 2007, p. 14; GamesBids.com, 2009). Müller (2013, p. 28) argues that the sustainability agenda for Sochi was framed by and for an international audience and so was out of tune with the realities of environmental politics in Russia and national conceptions of sustainable development and nature-society relationships.

Sochi 2014 was controversial in other ways, not least in relation to violations of human rights. During the land assembly for the Olympic infrastructure, concerns were raised about the expropriation of property and resettlement of residents with no right of appeal, together with the poor treatment of migrant construction workers who had to endure inadequate working and living conditions (Müller, 2014). Other issues arose, which raised the threat of international boycotts of the event, and included the discriminatory legislation against lesbian, gay, bisexual, and transgender groups; and a campaign by a diaspora of an indigenous group (Circassian) to recognize the genocide of its people by Tsarist forces in 1864 on the site of the Olympic facilities (Arnold and Foxall, 2014).

Security concerns were also voiced regarding the 2014 Winter Olympics because Sochi is located close to the disputed region of Abkhazia (Georgia). A website (RevoketheGames.com) was designed to draw attention to Russia's attack on Georgia in 2008 and to campaign for the 2014 event to be moved from Sochi to another host. Moreover, in November 2008, the Georgian National Olympic Committee requested that the IOC reconsider its decision to award an Olympics which would be staged close to a conflict zone. However, the IOC rejected Georgia's request, arguing that security was the responsibility of the Russian organizers and Sochi 2014 was, of course, staged as planned. Nevertheless, it is clear that the Games challenged the IOC's agenda about the scale, cost and environmental implications.

PyeongChang in the Kangwon province of South Korea hosted the Winter Olympics of 2018 and presented yet another set of challenges to the IOC's sustainability agenda. The city's two previous bids for the Games in 2010 and 2014 had been led by local institutions eager to stimulate regional development in a depressed area. South Korea's third and successful bid in 2011 for the 2018 Games, however, was a government-led project (Merkel and Kim, 2011, p. 2376). By this time, PyeongChang already possessed a number of venues, either completed or planned, all located within a '30-minute' radius. There was substantial financial support pledged by the national government and strong South Korean public support (93 per cent approval for hosting the Games) had been recorded. Its connectivity to the rest of the country was improved by a new high-speed rail line between Seoul and Gangneung, together with new national highways. In 2011, it won the IOC vote outright in the first round. Despite the formulation of PyeongChang's preparations over three bid periods that had enabled the organizers to establish well-developed legacy plans, these were never implemented due to changes in the leadership of the project, a lack of communication with Olympic stakeholders, and uncertainty over government support (Kim and Grix, 2021).

The Olympic Stadium had been planned to utilize the Alpensia Ski Jumping facilities (built in 2009) by increasing its capacity to 50,000 spectators. However, these plans were amended when a review identified critical problems related to spectator congestion at entry and exit points, athletes' training facilities, and risks posed in the event of heavy snow and severe cold. A new Olympic Stadium and Olympic Plaza were therefore built at Hoenggye, for which no budget had been included and no designated post-Games use was devised (POOC, 2019, p. 45). The Hockey Centre also changed locations from a temporary to a permanent structure, but also with no post-Games use (Kim and Grix, 2021). The original site for the Olympic Village was in the Mountain Cluster, but this location proved not to be viable. A new developer and location were offered at the Yongpyong Resort, one kilometre south of the original site, and was completed with government financial support (POOC, 2019, p. 87).

The construction of the Jeongseon Alpine Skiing Resort on Mount Gariwang (see figure 3.7) proved most controversial as it involved the clearance of part of a designated forest genetic resource. Although there were plans for the 'restoration' of the landscape and its vegetation, it seemed an ineffectual action once an original habitat had been destroyed. It has therefore been argued that the resort was clearly an economically motivated business and tourism project (Kim and Grix, 2021).

There were also political concerns about inter-Korean relations as the host region is situated close to the border with North Korea (Merkel, 2008). In the spirit of the Olympic Truce during the Games, the two Korean teams

Figure 3.7. The Jeongseon Alpine Centre on Mount Gariwang, which was developed for the PyeongChang Winter Olympics in 2018. The image shows the spectator viewing terraces and the media area at the end of the ski run. (*Source*: Olympic Museum Collections, Lausanne. © 2018 IOC/ LIVESEY, Alex)

paraded together at the opening ceremony and entered a unified women's ice hockey team. A series of inter-Korean summit meetings were subsequently held after the Games in the spirit of peace and reconciliation, although these ceased in 2020 (Lee and Tan, 2021, p. 2071).

The staging of the 2022 Winter Olympics was also problematic for the IOC. Having started with a good field of potential candidate cities (Krakow, Lviv, Munich, Oslo, St Moritz-Davos, Stockholm), only Almaty (Kazakhstan) and Beijing (China) remained as willing hosts by the time of the IOC selection vote (July 2015). Krakow, Munich and St Moritz-Davos all withdrew their bids because local residents had voted against staging the event in referendums. The city government in Stockholm declined to offer financial support and Lviv withdrew its bid because of political unrest in Ukraine (Associated Press, 2014). The cost of hosting the event, the damaging environmental impact in sensitive mountain areas, and uncertain post-event legacies represented significant concerns for the residents of the potential host cities (Chappelet, 2021*b*).

Beijing was awarded the event and became the first city to have the opportunity to stage both the Summer and Winter Games. The basis of the government's bid was the development of winter sports in China, involving a market of at least 300 million Chinese, valued at about $144 billion by 2025 (Lee and Tan, 2021). Three sites around Beijing hosted the events: the site of an obsolete steelworks in Beijing itself, an existing ski resort in

Zhangjiakou, and an undeveloped site in Yanqing (Xin and Kunzmann, 2020). Investment in improved transport connections between the three sites, including a high-speed railway line and three expressways were made by the Chinese Government. The high-speed railway line connected Beijing with Yanqing in 20 minutes and Zhangjiakou in 30 minutes (*ibid.*). Concerns were raised about the lack of a natural source of snow and the reliance on the large carbon footprint of artificial snow production; protests from human rights groups; and environmental impacts of deforestation and destruction of natural ecosystems (BBC News, 2015; IOC, 2015*b*; Lee and Tan, 2021). The staging of the event was affected by COVID-19 restrictions, which prohibited the general sale of tickets to the public. However, there was some allocation of tickets to targeted groups of people who were required to comply with strict prevention measures. Indeed, allocations were further extended during the event as control measures proved effective (Reuters, 2022; Zhang *et al.*, 2022).

The apparent increasing reluctance of cities willing to host the Olympic Games relates to the scale, cost and demands of staging the event. Reforms suggested by the Olympic Games Study Commission to control and limit the scale of investment in Olympic preparations at the start of Jacques Rogge's period of presidency of the IOC (IOC, 2003*b*) resurfaced at the start of Thomas Bach's term of office as IOC President (2013–). The Olympic Agenda 2020, agreed by the IOC in December 2014, revised the bid process to become an invitation and open dialogue between potential hosts and the IOC rather than a tender bid, so that the Olympic-related infrastructure can be negotiated to suit the city's long-term development needs rather than being imposed. The IOC also appears to be moving away from the concept of a 'compact games' by allowing greater flexibility in venue locations, which can be outside the host city or even the host country (IOC, 2014*a*; 2014*b*; 2015*b*; 2015*c*; 2018*d*; 2021*e*). The extent to which these reforms will increase the enthusiasm of host cities to stage the Olympic Games will become apparent over the next few years. Writing several years ago, some authors anticipated a future in which hosts in countries with a strong centralized state organization, substantial government funding, and a more top-down planning culture, combined with less concern for environmental issues and a greater push for modernization and urban transformation, might become the major players staging mega-events in the early twenty-first century (Müller, 2011; 2012; Trubina, 2014). In the years since such predictions were articulated in the literature, evidence has emerged that lends some support to the ideas that were expressed.

The first Winter Olympics to be affected fully by the Olympic 2020 Agenda is the 2026 event, which has been awarded to Milan-Cortina D'Ampezzo. As shown in figure 3.8, the geography of the proposed venues is spread over two urban centres and four regions (Lombardy, South Tyrol, Trentino,

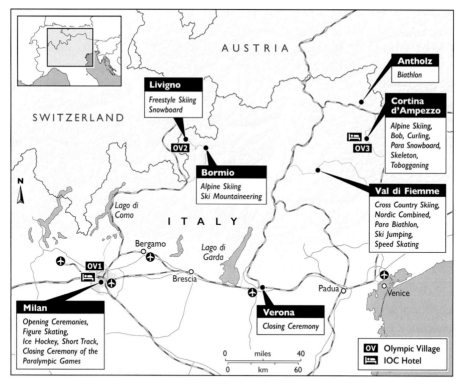

Figure 3.8. Planned Winter Olympic venues for Milan-Cortina D'Ampezzo in 2026. In addition to the Olympic-related infrastructure indicated on the map, the Medal Plaza 1 and International Broadcast Centre (IBC) will be based in Milan and the Medal Plaza 2 in Cortina D'Ampezzo. (*Source*: Adapted from material available on Milan Cortina 2026: https://milanocortina2026.olympics.com/en/places/)

and Veneto). While this dispersed model presents benefits in terms of cost reduction and sustainability, organizational challenges of coordination, cooperation and managing rivalries between regions competing for investment, external branding and legacies have been anticipated (Bazzanella *et al.*, 2022). Nevertheless, the plan indicates a possible benchmark for future Olympic legacies with venues spread over larger territories, more emphasis given to the host's long-term development strategies and less importance to iconic buildings (Schnitzer and Haizinger, 2019). The revival of interest in staging future Winter Olympics will be shaped by the success of this more decentralized model.

Discussion and Conclusions

In parallel with the evolving experience of staging the Summer Olympics, a marked growth in the scale, complexity, sophistication, and attendant controversy is discernible in the history of the Winter Games since the 1920s. The chronological sequence of phases adopted as the organizing framework of this chapter offers a means to understand both the broad changes in the scope and character of the Winter Olympics, and the specific circumstances that have affected the twenty-four past hosts of the event. The key characteristics of these urban transformations are summarized in table 3.2. Planning for the Winter Olympics (like the Summer Games) has built incrementally on the experience of past events, the gradual accumulation of knowledge and the desire to constantly raise the spectacle of the event. What emerges from this historical review is a number of clear trends and research themes.

First, the Winter Olympics have shifted from an event that has promoted

Table 3.2. Summary of key urban transformations of the Winter Olympic Games (Phases I–V). (*Source*: Compiled by the author)

Phase	Time	Broad Description	Characteristics of Urban Transformations
Phase I	1924–1932	Minimal infrastructural transformation, apart from sports facilities. Small host populations (*c.* 3,000)	Development prospects for winter sport tourism 'Winterization' of existing accommodation rather than over-provision of accommodation Event initiated by private interests, but funded jointly with public sector Environmental concerns raised
Phase II	1936–1960	Emerging infrastructural demands, especially transportation Small host populations (*c.* 13,000)	Growing volumes of participants and spectators requiring investment in transportation Limited basis for other permanent infrastructure
Phase III	1964–1980	Tool of regional development, especially transportation, Olympic Villages and economic development opportunities. Medium host populations (*c.* 100,000 or more)	Infrastructure investment as part of regional modernization and development Substantial public sector funding, but emerging television revenues Concern emerges about the increasing size of the event with regard to camaraderie, transport problems, debt and environmental damage

Table 3.2 continued on page 106

Table 3.2 continued from page 105

Phase	Time	Broad Description	Characteristics of Urban Transformations
Phase IV	1984–1998	Large-scale urban transformations, including multiple Olympic Villages Large host populations (*c.* 300,000)	Role of Winter Olympics as a means to secure major urban infrastructural change Higher television revenues More formal recognition of environmental issues in planning and development
Phase V	2002–2022	Sustainable development and legacy planning Large populations/ metropolitan areas (*c.* 1 million) Reluctance and opposition to host Olympic Games in developed economies related to scale, cost and demands of the event	Large-scale infrastructural investment and re-development reflecting global and political ambitions of host cities High television revenues Greater emphasis on environmental protection and sustainable development through environmental management systems Emergence of 'soft' legacies (social inclusion, human rights, integration of indigenous cultures), but also more international debate and controversy over adoption of international norms
The 'Future'	2026–onwards	Renewed emphasis on sustainable development and legacy planning through relaxation of 'compact games' concept	Reform of IOC expectations for the event: hard and soft legacies determined by dialogue rather than competitive bid

winter sports tourism in single mountain resorts to an event that has begun to emulate the Summer Olympics in its ability to modernize and stimulate urban regeneration. It is now usual for the host of the Winter Olympics to comprise both a large urban centre and surrounding mountain communities. Nevertheless, the scale of investment can still represent a challenge to the hosts in ensuring that the post-Olympic legacy is positive, and facilities are sustainable, for what are specialized facilities dispersed around remote and mountainous rural regions. Indeed, the increasing scale of the event has introduced new infrastructural demands, such as major improvements to transport systems, enhanced security measures and projects integrating sustainable development. In some cases, the athletes' demand to be closer to competition venues has required the Winter Olympic Villages to be fragmented into smaller and more dispersed units. Given such investments have associated opportunity costs, the extent to which the Winter Olympic Games therefore represents a cost effective and positive force for sustainable legacies and urban revitalization policies is much contested.

Second, in economic terms, legacies appear mixed and uncertain, with the impacts often experienced as an 'intermezzo', that is a short dramatic interlude yielding a poor long-term return on investment (Spilling, 1998). In Spilling's research into the effects of the Lillehammer Games of 1994, new business start-ups were substantial immediately after the Games were awarded, but many did not survive. The impact of the event can also be uneven across different sectors. During the Winter Olympics in Salt Lake City, hotels and restaurants prospered (experiencing a combined estimated $70.6 million net increase in taxable sales), while retailers suffered (with a larger net loss of $167.4 million) (Baade *et al.*, 2008). The tangible economic impacts might be short-lived but intangible impacts, such as the creation of new networks, skills and images, can have longer-term importance. Research into the effects of the 1988 Games on Calgary's image in twenty-two centres in America and Europe between 1986 and 1989 showed an increased awareness immediately before and after the event but tended to dissipate after a few years (Brent Ritchie and Smith, 1991).

Third, in social terms, it has proven extremely difficult to reconcile the demands of the Games with the kinds of built environment that might be suitable for residents of the locality after the Olympics have finished. Indeed, the host city's concern to use the Winter Olympics as a development and revitalization tool to create new spaces for inward investment and tourism as well as the best possible place marketing/branding have often led to insufficient public consultation over redevelopment plans, the displacement of former inhabitants (usually disadvantaged groups), and increased street security and surveillance. In the post-Olympic period, redeveloped areas become gentrified and obvious representations of social equality and exclusion. In some cases, such as Victoria Park following the Calgary Winter Olympics in 1988, a process of residential obsolescence was triggered, whereby uncertainty about future mega-events in a residential zone around a stadium impeded investment (Hiller and Moylan, 1999). Intertwined with these issues are human rights violations (related to land claims, treatment of migrant construction workers, and discrimination against minority groups) and the commodification of the symbols of indigenous people for Olympic marketing and external image. The emergence of local action groups opposing bids for Winter Games in several potential hosts has been indicative of some local perceptions of the negative impacts (for example,

Helsinki 2006 Anti-Olympic Committee; Olympics, Turin, 2006; No 2010 Network and Native Anti-2010 Resistance, Vancouver, 2010).

Fourth, given that the Winter Olympics are staged in much more fragile landscapes than their summer counterparts, the environmental implications of staging the event have been much more prominent and evident, even in the earliest hosts. Habitat destruction, heat generation from refrigeration units, chemical pollution, and unsuccessful restoration schemes have been common concerns in host settlements. Arguably, the sustainability agenda adopted by the IOC in 1996, and now ingrained in all Olympic events, albeit arguably a 'light green' form of corporate environmentalism (Lenskyj, 1998), was a direct outcome of the criticism of the Albertville Games in 1992 and the example set at Lillehammer in 1994. Each successive Olympic Games has subsequently claimed to be the most sustainable ever, although practices now appear to be relatively established in terms of recycling measures, low carbon emissions and/or offsetting, environmental procurement and compliance standards, and environmental management and monitoring. The extent to which the Sochi (2014) and Pyeongchang (2018) Olympics ran counter to the IOC's expectations in some of these areas has raised questions about the institution's ability to hold host cities accountable to their bid promises and accepted international norms. It is also sobering to consider that the ability of the nineteen previous hosts of the Winter Olympics between 1924 and 2014 to stage the event in the future will be significantly compromised by climate change. Only ten or eleven hosts will remain climatically suitable in low–high emission scenarios by the 2050s, which reduces to six in the high emission scenario by the 2080s (Scott *et al.*, 2015).

Fifth, despite more entrepreneurial approaches to the urban management of the Olympics, the role of the public sector appears to remain central to the organization and, to a certain extent, the funding of the event. The initial motivation to stage the Winter Olympics might emanate from business coalitions and the generation of income through corporate sponsorship and television revenue, but it is public-sector expenditure that is usually pivotal to the success of the event. The French government treated Grenoble 1968 as an *affaire nationale*, met 80 per cent of the basic sports installation costs and provided a subsidy of 20 million francs for operational expenses (COJO, 1968, p. 39). While the Albertville Games of 1992 were originally conceived as a means of regional modernization by local businessmen, it was the French government that funded the project. Similarly, the Norwegian government covered the huge costs and debts of Lillehammer 1994. The staging of Turin 2006 was pivotal in the city's transformation from an industrial to a post-industrial centre and Sochi 2014 represented a 'national project' to create a new ski and winter sports resort in Russia.

Sixth, the debate about the increasing size of the Winter Olympics has been a long-running affair. Preparations for Oslo 1952 included consideration of a proposal to reduce the number of events. It was feared that the increasing size of each Winter Games would detrimentally affect their character and make it impossible for any town to undertake the necessary arrangements.[7] There is no record of the response to this proposal but, in practice, the Games continued to grow. Avery Brundage, the IOC President from 1952 to 1972, criticized the huge expenditures at the Grenoble Games of 1968. He wrote: 'the French spent $240 million … and when you consider that this was for ten days of amateur sport, it seems to be somewhat out of proportion. With that kind of money involved there is bound to be commercialization of one kind or another' (quoted in Espy, 1979, p. 136). As a result of related controversies, Brundage hoped that the whole Winter Olympics would receive a 'decent burial' at Denver, the original host of the Winter Games of 1976 (Espy, 1979, p.135). Nonetheless, the Winter Games have survived and, in terms of scope and size, it has continued its upward trajectory. The risks of staging a Winter Olympics are now immeasurably greater as issues of financial debt, uncertainty over legacy, security and terrorism, political reputation, and corruption can potentially taint the best prepared of hosts. The limited field of finalist cities for the 2022 event is the clearest manifestation of these concerns and, depending on the outcomes from the IOC's Olympic Agenda 2020, a potential theme for the next phase in the trajectory of the Winter Olympics heralded by the Milan-Cortina d'Ampezzo Games in 2026.

Notes

1. The Nordic Games, founded in 1901, were organized by the Swedish Central Association for the Promotion of Sports. The Holmenkollen Week is a leading Norwegian winter sports event.

2. 'Skeleton' refers to a one-person sled which is driven by a competitor in a prone, head-first position down an ice track. The availability of the run at St Moritz meant that the event was held there as part of the 1948 Winter Olympics, although it was generally referred to as 'toboganning'.

3. Olympic Museum Archive, Lake Placid General file 1928–1991. Letter, G. Dewey, Chairman of Lake Placid, to M. Le Comte, President of the International Federation of Bobsleigh and Tobogganing, Paris, 9 November 1929.

4. Olympic Museum Archive, Lake Placid General file 1928–1991. Letter from IOC, 29 March 1930.

5. Overlays are temporary structures such as walkways, which are required for the Games, but might be removed after the event itself.

6. A quality benchmark, first published as a standard in 1996, specifies the requirements for an organization's environmental management system. It applies to those environmental aspects over which an organization has control and where it can be expected to have an influence (BAB, 2010).

7. Olympic Museum Archive, Oslo Correspondence COJO, 1947–1953. Undated draft of suggestion of the Special Committee regarding the reduction of the sports' programme of the Olympic Games, Jeux Olympiques de 1952 Oslo Correspondence COJO, 1947–1953.

Acknowledgements

The author wishes to acknowledge use of the IOC Archives, Olympic Studies Centre, Lausanne for some of the material presented in this chapter. Thanks also to Professor Brian Chalkley for his collaboration in previous Olympic-related papers and to Professor Mark Brayshay for his comments and advice on an earlier draft of this chapter. Credit also to Jamie Quinn for the cartography.

Chapter 4

THE CULTURAL OLYMPIADS

Beatriz García

The notion that the Olympic Games should complement the showcase of elite sport competitions with a programme of arts and cultural activity was central to the vision of Pierre de Coubertin. It was a principle inspired by his interpretations of the ancient Greek Games tradition, which involved the showcase of human excellence in a variety of forms, from athletics to music and poetry. However, the Olympic cultural programme or 'Cultural Olympiad' has a mixed history and is one of the least visible components within the Olympic Games hosting process. Within the Paralympic Games, the history of cultural and art contributions is much shorter but has rapidly evolved since the year 2000 and become a valuable platform for collaboration between the two Games.

This chapter starts with an overview of the evolution of the Games' cultural programme, from its original presentation in the form of Olympic Art Competitions to its latest incarnation as a four-year Cultural Olympiad and its rise in prominence within the Winter Games and Paralympic Games. It then discusses key trends and challenges and ends by touching on the new culture frameworks emerging in the aftermath of the *Agenda 2020* manifesto launched by the International Olympic Committee's (IOC) in 2014 with substantial later revisions and amendments.

A Brief History of Art in the Olympic Games

Origins: The Conference on Art, Letters and Sport, 1906

The principle of holding an arts festival in parallel with the celebration of sporting competitions is embedded in the foundations of the Olympic movement. The movement was founded in 1894 by Baron Pierre de Coubertin, a French pedagogue who sought to revive the ancient Greek tradition of quadrennial celebrations of athletics and the arts that had been held in Olympia from 776 BC to 393 AD (see also chapter 2). In the

Ancient Games, athletes were called to showcase their talents in parallel to philosophers, scholars, poets, musicians, sculptors, and high-profile leaders. Coubertin defined such gathering of talents as the 'spirit of Olympism', and Olympism was in turn defined as the simultaneous training of the human body and the cultivation of the intellect and spirit, together viewed as manifestations of the harmoniously educated man. On this basis, Coubertin's ambition was to create an environment in modern society where artists and athletes could, again, be mutually inspired. In support of this ambition, the Olympic Charter establishes that 'blending sport with culture and education' is a fundamental principle of Olympism (IOC, 2021*g*, p. 8).

As discussed in chapter 2, Coubertin's ability to coordinate and attract the attention of critical decision-makers around the world led to the re-birth of the Games in 1896 – Athens – and to their continuation in 1900 – Paris – and 1904 – St Louis. Nevertheless, none of these Games incorporated arts activities alongside the sporting events. To change this, Coubertin convened a 'Consultative conference on Art, Letters and Sport' at the Comedie Française in Paris in 1906. He invited artists, writers, and sports experts to discuss how the arts could be integrated into the modern Olympic Games. The invitation stated that the purpose of the meeting was to study 'to what extent and in what form the arts and letters could take part in the celebration of modern Olympic Games and become associated, in general, with the practice of sports, in order to profit from them and ennoble them' (Carl Diem Institute, 1966, p. 16).

The original proposal tabled at this first meeting established the following as a possible cultural programme to develop at each Games edition (table 4.1). As a result of the conference and in order to ensure a clear association of the arts with the modern Olympics sport programme, Coubertin proposed the creation of an arts competition and requested it to be a compulsory part of every Olympic Games celebration from that time (Coubertin, cited in

Table 4.1. Programme for the 1906 Conference, circulated by Pierre de Coubertin. The material in italics records the first indications of a possibility for 'competitions' to emerge. (*Source*: Müller (2000, pp. 609–620); author's emphasis)

Dramatic art	Outdoor productions; essential principles; recent writings; sports on stage
Choreography	Processions; parades; group and coordinated movements; dances
Decoration	Stands and enclosures; mats, badges, garlands, draperies, clusters; night festivals; torchlight sports
Literature	*Possibility of setting up Olympic literary competitions*; conditions for these competitions; sporting emotion, source of inspiration for the man of letters
Painting	Individual silhouettes and general views; *possibility of and conditions for an Olympic painting competition*; photography as aid to the artist
Sculpture	Athletic poses and movements and their relationship with art; interpretation of effort; objects given as prizes; statuettes and medals

IOC, 1997*b*, p. 92). This competition was called the 'Pentathlon of Muses' and involved the awarding of medals in five classic art categories: sculpture, painting, music, literature, and architecture.

The organization of the first 'Pentathlon of Muses' was designated to a special commission in the context of the London 1908 Olympic Games, the first Games after the 1906 Consultative Conference. Nevertheless, time constraints and disagreement over the programme contents led to its cancellation at the last minute (see Burnosky, 1994, pp. 21–22). Consequently, the first official Olympic arts competition did not take place until the Stockholm Games in 1912 (figure 4.1).

Figure 4.1. Original emblem for the Pentathlon of Muses, Stockholm 1912. (*Source*: Müller, 2000, p. 628)

From Stockholm until London 1948, arts competitions were organized in parallel to the sporting competitions and artists, like athletes, competed and won gold, silver and bronze medals (Stanton, 2000). However, regulations and contest parameters changed considerably due to difficulties in defining the different competition sections and disagreement in defining the most appropriate subject for the works presented. Over the years, the competition's sections changed from the five areas composing the 'Pentathlon of Muses' to a long list of sub-categories that tried to account for an ever-increasing range of art-form variations. The appropriate theme for Olympic artworks was also controversial, as there was disagreement over whether or not to restrict the entries to works inspired by or portraying sports activities exclusively. Initially, it was compulsory to present a sporting theme but, with the growth in abstraction as an international artistic trend, this proved difficult and limiting in areas other than architecture or design for sports buildings (Burnosky, 1994, p. 23).

Further problems stemmed from the dominant Western bias in the definition of cultural value and aesthetics, as most judges and competitors were European and, in consequence, it was rare that non-Western artists were awarded a medal. Other problems were of a logistical nature, in particular transport difficulties for large sculptural works which were accentuated due to the inconsistent funding and operational support received from respective Games Organizing Committees.

Another and, eventually, determining factor limiting the appeal and success of the cultural programme stemmed from the regulation of amateurism in the Olympic movement.[1] The 'amateur' regulation implied that, as in the case of athletes at the time, the participation of professional artists capable of making a living out of their art, could not be accepted as part of the official Olympic programme. In the context of the arts in the 1930s and 1940s this became even more problematic than in the sporting context. This was because most artists were considered 'professional in their devotion to their vocation' and high-quality artistic expression was equated with professionalism (IOC, 1949, cited by Burnosky, 1994, p. 34).

Most disappointing for Coubertin and his closest supporters was the poor audience participation attracted by the arts competitions. As noted by Hanna (1999, p. 108): '... cultural celebrations based on sport were increasingly irrelevant; while people ... watch[ed] competitive sport, their interest did not extend to sport in art'. This was a profound setback to the promotion of Coubertin's ideals, as a major reason for holding cultural events alongside the sports competitions was to inspire discussion and the promotion of ideas among all Olympic participants and spectators.

In this context, the Berlin 1936 Games edition stands out. In contrast to other host cities where Olympic arts manifestations had played a minor role, the so-called 'Nazi Games' presented a cultural festival of unprecedented dimensions for which a large scale national and international publicity campaign was created to ensure maximum recognition and participation. The Official Games report states:

> Because of the slight interest which the general public had hitherto evidenced in the Olympic Art Competition and Exhibition, it was necessary to emphasise their cultural significance to the Olympic Games through numerous articles in the professional and daily publications as well as radio lectures. (Organizing Committee, 1937, vol. 2)

The most ambitious example of Olympic art programming that Berlin

1936 offered has been seen by many as evidence of culture and the arts being used for propaganda purposes; a view that is hard to deny given that the Berlin Arts Committee programme was actually chaired by a representative of the Reich Ministry of Propaganda (*ibid.*). The Games had been identified by the local host as an opportunity to promote the ideals of Nazi Germany and cultural activity was seen as a good vehicle to represent the supremacy of the Arian race and Western civilization. This, in turn, meant that the cultural programme was taken as seriously as the sporting competition programme, and it thus secured high levels of investment and public visibility.

Cultural innovations introduced at the Berlin Games included the first Olympic torch relay, travelling from Ancient Olympia in Greece (symbolic cradle of the Olympic Games) to the Berlin stadium; and the first artist-led Olympic film, Leni Riefenstahl's *Olympia*. These cultural manifestations became as central to the Olympic experience as the sport competitions, both during the Games and in subsequent visual and broader narrative representations of the 1936 Olympic edition. Notably, the torch relay and the principle of producing an official Games film have become a key part of the Games staging process and its symbolic representation to this day.

The 1940 and 1944 Olympic Games and related arts programmes were not held because of the Second World War, but by the time of London 1948, the appointed Organizing Committee succeeded in paralleling the sports with arts competitions. After the cultural programme ended, the British Fine Arts Committee that had been set up in tandem with the Games compiled a 'report of jurors' suggestions for future arts contests' (Good, 1998, p. 33). This was intended for use as a guide to subsequent Organizing Committees since, until then, there had been no operational framework about how to produce an Olympic arts programme. Good (*ibid.*, p. 20) explained that 'the recommendations included reducing the number of arts categories' and concluded that the 'interest in the exhibitions would be greater if they were more closely linked up with the Games themselves and if a more intensive press campaign had been organised'.

By 1950, however, the problems and difficulties that had been common to most Games were perceived to be far greater than the benefits and achievements brought by hosting Olympic art competitions. To review the situation, extended discussion took place within the IOC from 1949 in Rome to 1952 in Helsinki. As a result of this process, which involved a detailed assessment of the 'amateur' nature of Olympic contributions, it was decided that from 1952 on, the presence of the arts in the Olympics would take the form of cultural exhibitions and festivals instead of competitions.

Olympic Art Exhibitions and Festivals (1956–1988)

The first official (and non-competitive) Olympic arts festival was held at

Melbourne 1956, after several rushed changes in focus for the cultural programme in Helsinki 1952. The Melbourne festival was coordinated first by a Fine Arts Subcommittee, elected in 1953, and then by a Festival Sub-Committee, created in 1955. The festival had two major components: one of visual arts and literature, and another of music and drama. Exhibitions and festivals were staged simultaneously in the weeks leading up to and during the Games and featured local, national, and international artists and performers. A special book on Australian arts was published after the Games, entitled *The Arts Festival: a Guide to the Exhibition with Introductory Commentaries on the Arts in Australia*. The Official Report of the Melbourne Games concluded that 'the change from a competition to a Festival was widely welcomed, since the Festival provided a significant commentary on Australia's contribution to the Arts' (cited in Good, 1998, p. 29).

This new stage in the Olympic cultural programme tradition brought opportunities as well as challenges for the integration of the arts and culture as a core dimension of staging the Olympics. On the one hand, Games organizers had greater freedoms to define the purpose of such programmes and determine who should be presenting what type of work. On the other, the effect of eliminating the competitive element completely divorced the programme from the patriotic rivalries and nationalistic edge that typically accompanied the sporting events. This situation accelerated the trend towards diminishing numbers of Games participants (particularly, athletes, but also sport fans) that were involved or interested in the cultural programme and also, during the next few Games, led to a loss in international focus. As highlighted by the Australian report, the programme was now mainly a platform for local cultural representation and directed according to the specific interests of the host authorities (mainly, Ministries of Culture or related bodies), with much less direct involvement and regulation from the top Olympic structures or other sporting bodies.

In this new context, some Olympic host countries saw the programme as an important opportunity to make a statement about their history, and as an opportunity to profile the host nation, above and beyond what was possible within the sporting arenas or the highly regulated Olympic ceremonies and protocol. Despite their disconnection from the sporting world, host cities became increasingly ambitious in their treatment of the arts festivals, progressively aligning them with the 'growing arts agenda' that developed after the Second World War including an aspiration to address 'audience development, access, and inclusion' in the arts (Gold and Revill, 2007, p. 73).

From Melbourne 1956 to Tokyo 1964, the focus was almost exclusively on the presentation of national heritage, but the late 1960s and 1970s saw an upsurge in contemporary cultural initiatives and some radical rethinking about the role and relevance of the arts as a component of the Games staging process and a key vehicle to project the Olympic city. Mexico in 1968 presented what remains, to this day, one of the most ambitious and innovative Olympic festivals. It spanned an entire year and featured the best of both Mexican heritage and folklore and also the best of Mexican contemporary arts. These were showcased alongside the works of leading international artists and art. The ambition and quality of the programme proved that while Mexico may have been considered a country that was economically part of a 'developing world' from an economic point of view, it was part of a 'first world' in terms of *avant-garde* art and culture. Crucially, Mexico viewed the Olympic cultural programme more holistically than other Games hosts and, beyond the arts, incorporated discussions about education and science as well as advertising, design, and communications that were, in turn, used to promote and explain the value of the Games (Organizing Committee, 1969).

Montreal 1976 also presented an innovative cultural programme, exploring the national identity of Quebec and Canada, but also attempting to recover the original Coubertin aspiration to explore the connections between art and sport, a topic that had become secondary since the end of the art competitions. The linkages between art and sport were presented not just as a theme, but also as a staging process, involving the introduction of arts activity within sporting venues, in particular, the main Olympic Park avenue and the areas surrounding the stadium.

Throughout the 1960s and 1970s, other areas where artists and related creative practitioners made major contributions were the design of banners and logos to dress the city and signpost Games venues – what is now termed 'the look of the Games'. The imageries for Mexico 1968, Tokyo 1964, and Munich 1972 are all exemplars of *avant-garde* visual design (see, for example, figure 4.2) rather than simple marketing and branding exercises; they can be viewed as leading examples of urban cultural policy innovations emerging out of the Games. These elements of the Games were, however, rarely treated as part of the official cultural programme (with Mexico City 1968 being a notable exception). Subsequent Games (apart from Barcelona 1992 and Turin 2006, see below) have also failed to use 'the look of the Games' as an expression of advanced and place-sensitive creative practice. Table 4.2. summarizes the key format variations and characteristics of Olympic cultural festivals in this period. As this makes abundantly clear, each Olympic host approached their cultural programming with different priorities and the length of activities varied significantly, from four weeks in Helsinki and Melbourne, to one year in Mexico City 1968.

Cultural Olympiads: Barcelona 1992 to Paris 2024

Another stage in Olympic cultural programming was initiated by Barcelona's

Figure 4.2. Cultural Olympiad pictograms complementing the sport pictograms, Mexico 1968. (*Source*: Organizing Committee, 1969; Courtesy of the IOC)

Table 4.2. Olympic arts festivals, Summer Games (1952–1988). (*Source*: Adapted from compilation by Gold and Revill (2007, p. 74) and from official reports of Organizing Committees.

Olympiad	Length	Content and Themes
Helsinki 1952	4 weeks	International exhibitions of architecture, painting, graphic arts, sculpture, literature, music
Melbourne 1956	4 weeks	National (Australian) culture
Rome 1960	6 months* 3 weeks	National (Italian) culture with an emphasis on history; sporting references in exhibition programme
Tokyo 1964	7 weeks	National (Japanese) high art and traditional culture
Mexico City 1968	1 year	International; high art and indigenous culture; nation-wide celebration of culture Overall title: Cultural Olympiad
Munich 1972	3 months* 6 weeks	International; high art and folk culture Overall title: Olympic Summer
Montreal 1976	4 weeks	National: showcase for Canadian provincial culture
Moscow 1980	1 year* 5 weeks	National: mass participation, high art and folk culture; national art of the peoples of the USSR
Los Angeles 1984	10 weeks 3 weeks	7 weeks: international festival for domestic consumption LA and US culture for international Olympic audience
Seoul 1988	7 weeks	Korean high culture and traditional culture for an international audience; international artists and companies; contemporary culture for a domestic audience

* Length of cultural festival including exhibition runs and pre-Games programme.

1992 Olympic bid, which proposed that the implementation of a Cultural Olympiad should take place during the four years of the Olympiad – from the end of one Games to the start of the next. Barcelona's Cultural Olympiad thus started in 1988, at the end of the Seoul Games, and evolved up to 1992 with a different thematic emphasis for each year. García (2012) noted how this decision stems from the organizers' vision for the Games as a platform to improve the city's urban landscape and assist in Barcelona's international projection far beyond the Olympic staging period. Indeed, Barcelona 1992 has come to be remembered as the first Games that placed the city at the heart of the Olympic experience (figure 4.3).

Figure 4.3. 'Art in the Street' programme, connecting the city and its waterfront, Barcelona 1992. (*Source*: Photograph, Beatriz García)

The four-year format was maintained in subsequent summer Games up to 2012. This stemmed from the initiative of respective host cities rather than any IOC directive, as there has never been a formal requirement to create a four-year cultural programme as a build-up to the Games competition fortnight. This stage in Olympic cultural programme development was characterized by two additional phenomena resulting in large part from the commitment to multi-annual cultural programming. On the one hand, there has been a clearer alignment of the Cultural Olympiad with local and national cultural policy ambitions than ever before; on the other, the programme has faced growing operational tensions.

The first phenomenon means that priority objectives for the Games have become more clearly aligned with established cultural, social, and economic agendas. From a cultural point of view, the Games period has been used not only to expand sport audiences but also cultural and arts audiences. Furthermore, besides being used to expand sporting facilities, the Games have served to advance broader local creative development aspirations (García, 2012). From a social perspective, it is now common for the Games and their Cultural Olympiad to aspire to improving community inclusion, expanding access to marginal or deprived communities, and strengthening local or national identity (García, 2004). Finally, from an economic perspective, it is increasingly widespread to present a Cultural Olympiad as a catalyst to advance urban regeneration, reposition the host city and grow cultural tourism (*ibid.*). This is further analysed in the ensuing section.

In parallel with the above, new tensions have also emerged, mainly due to the high professionalization and global mediatization of the Games (García, 2012). Most notably, the branding tension between 'official' Olympic arts events, sporting competitions and related Games activity became apparent in the 1990s and 2000s and led on to varied attempts at establishing separate Cultural Olympiad or Olympic Arts Festival brands (García, 2001, 2012). A common Cultural Olympiad feature in most Games between 1992 and 2008 was the design of annual thematic festivals, one for each year of the Olympiad. In Barcelona, the themes evolved from a 'Cultural Gateway' in 1988 to the 'Year of Culture and Sport' in 1989, the 'Year of the Arts' in 1990, the 'Year of the Future' in 1991 and the 'Olympic Art Festival' in 1992. Atlanta also covered a wide range of subjects during its four years of festivals, arranged into two main themes: 'Southern Connections' within the United States and 'International Connections'. Sydney offered a taste of the many and diverse Australian cultural communities through presenting an indigenous festival in 1997 ('Festival of the Dreaming'), a festival dedicated to multicultural groups and the waves of immigration in 1998 ('A Sea Change'), and international festivals in 1999 ('Reaching the World') and 2000 ('Olympic Arts Festival') (García, 2012). Finally, Athens reflected on major philosophical and humanistic principles by exploring the notions of

'Man and Space', 'Man and the Earth', 'Man and the Spirit', and 'Man and Man'.

By the time of Beijing 2008 and London 2012, however, this trend was changing yet again. Instead of annual thematic festivals, both Games opted for generic mass participation countdown events without any specific theme other than the aspiration to generate excitement around the Games build-up (e.g. the 'Open Weekend' initiative for London). It was not until their respective Games years that both Beijing and London presented a more ambitious 'Olympic Arts Festival' with a clearly curated and strong international focus (e.g. 'London 2012 Festival'; see García and Cox, 2013). Moreover, London went further than previous Games by also presenting the most extensive national cultural programme to date, with themed programming organized, not per year, but per UK region, resulting in twelve distinct Olympic regional cultural programmes (*ibid.*).

Table **4.3**. Cultural Olympiads, Summer Games (1992–2024). (*Source*: Compiled by the author)

Olympiad	Length and Format	Official Denominations	Location
Barcelona 1992	4 years; thematic	Cultural Olympiad; Individually branded (thematic) years	Host city, some nationwide events
Atlanta 1996	4 years; two main clusters	Olympic Arts Festivals	Host city
Sydney 2000	4 years, thematic	Olympic Arts Festivals; Individually branded years	Host city, some nationwide, some international
Athens 2004	4 years, thematic	Cultural Olympiad, Athens by Art, Individually branded years	Mainly host city, some nationwide
Beijing 2008	5 years, differing clusters	Olympic Cultural Festivals	Host city plus nationwide
London 2012	4 years, differing clusters	Cultural Olympiad, London 2012 Festival, Inspired by 2020, Open Weekends	Nationwide – extensive
Rio 2016	Launch 4 years prior, most activity over a few months in the Olympic year	Celebra	Host city, small profile
Tokyo 2020	Launch 4 years prior, most programming over 2 years	Nippon Festival, Cultural Olympiad	Host city, plus some national dimension
Paris 2024	Launch 4 years prior, most activity over 6 months in the Olympic year	Cultural Olympiad	Host city, plus some national dimension

Returning to the issue of overall duration, Rio de Janeiro 2016 was the first Summer Olympic Games since Seoul 1988 not to organize a four-year Cultural Olympiad. This is also the case with Tokyo 2020 and Paris 2024 which, while retaining the name 'Cultural Olympiad', have organized build-up events only in the one to two years prior to the Games and discontinued the tradition of presenting them as 'thematic' years. This opens what could become a new chapter in Olympic cultural programming, as the focus becomes less about the overall duration and more about the ways in which the cultural programme can shape or project the host city and be part of the 'Olympic experience' (table 4.3).

Art at the Winter Games: 1956 Onwards

The artistic programme of the Winter Games was not formally established until Cortina d'Ampezzo in 1956 and started at quite a small scale. More ambitious cultural programmes comparable to the Summer Games began with Grenoble 1968, the same year that Mexico City hosted their year-long international Cultural Olympiad. Since Salt Lake City 2002, the ambition of winter Olympic host cities to attract attention, building on a cultural discourse, has grown considerably and is aligning with broader urban cultural policy agendas.

Given the smaller scale of operations at the Winter Games, there are interesting nuances that allow for different kinds of cultural programming and have resulted in growing differences from Summer Games protocols. This differentiation has evolved since Salt Lake City in 2002. One of the most noticeable is the establishment of a 'medals plaza' as a distinct mixed venue within the host city centre. This is a space where medals are awarded to athletes, thus extending and changing the ceremony that would normally take place exclusively within sport venues. The justification for this extension has been that winter sports take place mainly within mountain resorts away from any urban centre and have thus a low capacity to generate a festival atmosphere.

The staging of a medals plaza as an additional Olympic venue has allowed organizers to intensify the experience of the winter Olympic city (figure 4.4). Integral to medal plaza ceremonies is the programming of cultural activities in addition to the presentation of the winning athletes. For instance, in Salt Lake City, Turin, Vancouver, and PyeongChang it was typical for medals ceremonies to be followed by feature performances by international singers and musicians. This is one example of how Winter Games hosting has impacted Olympic protocol in a way that could be seen as conducive to more effective and better integrated city programming. Another relevant winter development has been in the approach to dressing the city during the Games. In Turin 2006, the traditional *Look of the Games*

Figure 4.4. Medals Plaza, a way to connect sport with its city and cultural context, Turin 2006. (*Source*: Photograph, Beatriz García)

programme, dedicated to highlight sporting venues, was complemented by a comprehensive programme, dedicated to promoting the city's cultural assets in a manner reminiscent of Mexico 1968 (see García and Miah, 2007).

Other developments include the extension of cultural programming periods. For instance, the Cultural Olympiad of Vancouver 2010 lasted four years, a first for any Olympic Winter Games, and it became a visible element within the city's dressing strategy, with dedicated 'culture' flagpoles in the years leading to the Games and during the Games fortnight in 2010. Further, also in Vancouver, the launch of a Cultural Olympiad Digital Edition (CODE) allowed the profiling of new technologies that resulted in creative artform interventions as well as ways to engage dispersed communities throughout Canada. These communities were invited to reflect on their sense of identity via social media environments and share them within a dedicated online platform, Canada CODE, that became one of the most effective mechanisms to generate nationwide involvement in the Games (Klassen, 2012).

Following on Vancouver, Sochi 2014 also presented a four-year Olympiad and adopted the annual thematic focus approach that had been common for the Summer Games. At Sochi, the themes evolved from a 'Year of Cinema' in 2010, to 'Theatre' in 2011, 'Music' in 2012, 'Museums' in 2013 and a combined 'International Arts Festival' in 2014. PyeongChang 2018 presented an ambitious winter Cultural Olympiad from a contemporary art point of view. Some distinctive characteristics of the PyeongChang cultural offer included the launch of a Cultural Olympiad bus – which all Games-time visitors were welcome to use to explore cultural offerings throughout the Olympic city; a high-profile contemporary art biennale, K-pop concerts to appeal to a large international audience, and highly ambitious art and technology displays (García, 2021). Finally, Beijing 2022 offered an Olympic Cultural Festival that expanded on the already existing 'Meet in Beijing' international cultural festival, launched at the time of the 2008 Olympic bid in 2000.

Art and Culture at the Paralympic Games: Sydney 2000 Onwards

With regard to the Paralympic Games, cultural programming remained a low priority until the turn of the twenty-first century. Sydney 2000 was the first Games to work towards a high-profile Paralympic Cultural Olympiad and proposed a single team to manage both the official Olympic and Paralympic cultural programme. Further, in the wake of Sydney 2000, a series of agreements between the IOC and the International Paralympic Committee (IPC) resulted in closer synergies between the two Games, including the decision to establish a single Organizing Committee.

In the context of London 2012, the team responsible for the cultural programme committed to expanding organizational synergies into an all-encompassing Games cultural policy narrative, where there was no distinction between Olympic and Paralympic cultural activity. Indeed, the London 2012 Cultural Olympiad incorporated a celebration of long-established UK disability arts organizations as part of its four-year national programme and a range of regional cultural programmes placed an emphasis on presenting activity that questioned the notion of 'normality' as a way of bridging the gap between perceptions of 'abled' or 'disabled' bodies, be it in the realm of sports or arts. Further, the Games-time 'London 2012 Festival' spanned both Olympic and Paralympic fortnights without interruption, thus acting as a symbolic bridge between both events. To maximize visibility, London also created a distinct label and brand for its disability arts programme: 'Unlimited' (see García and Cox, 2013).

For Rio de Janeiro 2016, there was no capacity to host a four-year Cultural Olympiad and the Paralympic Games did not incorporate an official art and culture component beyond a collaboration between Brazilian and British disabled artists – initiated in 2012 as part of 'Unlimited', under the auspices of the British Council. Tokyo 2020 continued the tradition of a joint Olympic and Paralympic cultural programme and delivered 'ONE – Our New Episode', an inclusive festival hailed as a first for Japan in terms of its ambition to present artists of all genders and abilities to a mainstream audience in a country where this is not yet the norm.[2] Paris 2024 is also committed to a disability arts programme, but details are yet to be published at the time of writing.

Overall, the sharing of a common team and a single programme of activity places the Cultural Olympiad in a significant position to promote greater synergies between Olympic and Paralympic Games in years to come. This is because all other Games programmes, from the sport competitions to symbolic events such as the torch relay or the ceremonies, follow a different planning and delivery cycle. This could help assert the added value brought by a flexible approach to Games cultural programming.

Main Trends, Challenges, and Opportunities for Culture at the Games

The dynamic nature of the Cultural Olympiad is manifest in the diversity of formats, objectives and management structures put in place to implement it since it was formally launched in 1912. While the sports competitions and infrastructural dimensions of the Olympic and Paralympic sports programme have become extensively rationalized and standardized, the cultural programme has remained an area open to free interpretation. This section offers a brief summary of key programming and strategic trends over time.

Thematic Focus: From Sporting Heritage to Contemporary Fusions

The Olympic cultural programme has explored a wide range of art forms and thematic emphases. It started with an exclusive focus on classic art forms (fine arts) under a mainly Western (European) canon. Interestingly, during the time it operated as an art competition, rather than just focusing on the display of old masters and well-known works of art, it effectively encouraged the production of 'new' artworks that can be considered an important contribution to the development of Olympic cultural heritage. This is because the art on show had to be inspired by Olympic ideals as well as sporting achievement. The founding focus of the Olympic cultural programme thus resulted in the production of a series of distinct artworks, many of which form the permanent art collection at the Olympic Museum in Lausanne.

The move away from competitions into art exhibitions and festivals led to abandoning the production of new 'Olympic' artworks and instead prioritizing the showcase of the host's best-known national artists and cultural expressions. The focus continued to be on classic artforms, but the remit broadened into national folklore displays. Most hosts during this period opted to showcase almost exclusively their national artistic heritage.

From the 1960s to the 1980s, however, a majority of hosts placed a new emphasis on contemporary and often international art. The most outstanding examples within this period were Mexico 1968, Munich 1972, and Los Angeles 1984, all of which involved world-class artists and invested in new contemporary art commissions to be presented during Games time. Munich and Los Angeles went a step further in their attempts at linking contemporary art trends with the Olympic narrative by introducing the notion of an 'Olympic art poster' series. While the production of Olympic posters had started with the first modern Games in 1896, renowned artists had never been involved in their production. The point of distinction in Munich, Los Angeles and, subsequently, Sarajevo 1984 and Barcelona 1992 was that world-leading artists of the time were commissioned to produce a visual statement representing Olympic achievement without the need to produce a literal representation of sport (see figure 4.5).

From 2000 onwards, in line with global cultural policy trends, many hosts in Western countries expanded into what is commonly termed cultural fusion and innovation as part of their Cultural Olympiad programming. This

Figure 4.5. Art and Sport links, as represented via the tradition of Olympic art posters from London 2012. (*Source*: LOCOG; Courtesy of the IOC)

involved pioneering cross-sector collaborations between the arts, health, and technology fields, among others. Vancouver 2010 and London 2012 are two key exemples in this area. Nevertheless, the 'cultural fusion' narrative is mainly a Western construct that contrasts with the approach by most Eastern Games hosts. The latter have largely continued to prioritize the display of traditional arts and their most valued cultural heritage over cross-sectoral collaborations (e.g. Beijing 2008, Sochi 2014), but this has changed with PyeongChang 2018 and Tokyo 2020, both of which highlighted technology as a top priority within its cultural narrative.

Despite the broadening of topics and formats, the one area that has remained secondary since the demise of the art competitions has been the exploration of links between art and sport. While at every Games there are art communities that, on learning about the existence of an Olympic cultural programme, argue in favour of exploring such connections, examples of truly innovative and meaningful collaborations in this domain remain scarce, and most attempts at an art and sport fusion have been unsuccessful from an audience or media-attention point of view. The only exception to this has been the few examples of Olympic art poster series, a tradition recovered by London 2012 after the previous four editions in Munich, Los Angeles, Sarajevo, and Barcelona (figure 4.5). The Olympic poster tradition is now being coordinated with the assistance of a newly dedicated culture team at the IOC and it is expected that it will feature prominently in all future Games via the dedicated programme 'The Olympic Agora' (IOC, 2022c).

Vision and Priority Objectives

As indicated earlier, while the Cultural Olympiad has reached maturity, with Olympic cultural programming increasingly aligned with key strategic priorities within the Olympic host city and nation, most cities have focused on the opportunities for image projection, but there are some relevant examples of Games being used to advance broader economic, social, and creative agendas through their Olympic cultural programming. In many cases, the pressures emerging out of operating within an outward-facing context, with national – or indeed, global – audiences and stakeholders in mind, have played a defining role in pushing new (or more ambitious) cultural policy frameworks than those in place prior to the event.

An analysis of cultural programming choices and priority objectives by Olympic Organizing Committees since the 1960s[3] (the time when Olympic cities started to feel more empowered to develop a cultural narrative) suggests that the most dominant local agendas behind Olympic cultural programming could be summarized as follows:

1.   'Politics and identity': growing or reigniting national pride;

2. 'Economics and regeneration': city reimaging and tourism projection;
3. 'Entertainment, look and feel': crowd management, city animation and city dressing;
4. 'Cultural and social change': creative innovation and community empowerment.

To look at these in greater detail the first, *politics and identity*, occurs when the official cultural narrative intends to grow or reignite national pride. This was the most frequent priority for Games during the Cold War era from the 1960s to 1980s. Recognizable examples are Moscow 1980, which presented a large cultural programme celebrating Russian folklore as well as high culture icons in the areas of classical music and dance and Los Angeles' response in 1984, which focused on a celebration of the US 'way of life' through the lenses of postmodernism and popular culture as represented by the Hollywood film industry. Other Games with what could be interpreted as having a marked 'identity politics' angle include those taking place in cities aiming to project minority cultures or to showcase a cultural identity distinct from larger nation states: Montreal in 1976 and Barcelona in 1992 used the Games' cultural programme to present Quebecoise and Catalan culture and explain their differences in the context of Canada and Spain respectively. More recent examples – combining a national and regional focus – include nationwide choral singing and folklore dances presented in the lead up to Beijing 2008 and Sochi 2010. In both cases, these were celebrated by organizers as a first attempt at a nationwide cultural programme open to exploring the diversity of Chinese and Russian cultures respectively.

Economic impact and city regeneration became the most noticeable agenda in the 1990s, with Barcelona and Sydney being two outstanding cases. Their cultural programme was linked to a wider tourism strategy that saw the promotion of urban centres in opposition to outdated views of their host countries as loci exclusively for 'beach tourism' 'cheap food' and 'good weather'. The Cultural Olympiad thus emphasized activity that could highlight the most recognizable city skyline and iconic venues: la Sagrada Familia and Las Ramblas featured strongly in Barcelona, while the Sydney Opera House was the sole performing arts venue for the Olympic Arts Festival in 2000 (García, 2012). In more recent editions, tourism and 'place branding' strategies have extended beyond the host city, such as with the London 2012 Festival, used to promote iconic locations such as Stonehenge and Hadrian's Wall in parallel to the positioning of new city areas such as East London.

A broader emphasis on '*entertainment, look and feel*' has been common in Games where organizers understand cultural programming mainly as a tool to assist with crowd management and expand public engagement during the Games. Games that prioritize this over any other agendas have often relied on a generalist type of cultural offer, favouring standardized entertainment practices and design motifs that have done little to present a distinct view of the host and advance autochthonous cultural policies. However, as noted earlier, there are examples of innovative and internationally influential approaches in the 1960s and 1970s, when the Games showcased *avant-garde* trends in graphic design and advertising. Mexico 1968 and Munich 1972 are two of the best examples. In more recent editions, innovations were the now firmly established tradition of 'Live Sites' – and medal plazas at the Winter Games – as hubs of free activity and entertainment. Graphic design innovations were also noticeable in London 2012 and Tokyo 2020.

Finally, '*cultural and social change*' can be interpreted as the most ambitious and recent policy agenda, an area gaining prominence particularly since the Millennium. Sydney 2000 was ambitious in its plea to bring contemporary Aboriginal art troupes to the mainstream, and its dedicated Aboriginal Olympic arts festival ('Festival of the Dreaming') was pivotal in bringing Aboriginal work to the Sydney Opera House for the first time, as well as generating the expectation that emerging Aboriginal art should be showcased regularly within high profile festivals (García, 2012). Similarly, London 2012 contributed to the repositioning of disabled artists as world-class performers and creators through its nationwide programme 'Unlimited', which was supported by the British Council to inform work at the Rio 2016 Olympics (García and Cox, 2013). The London 2012 Cultural Olympiad also placed a strong emphasis on advancing the role of young people as producers – not only consumers – of art and culture and made this ambition manifest through its approach to programming design and production (García, 2015). Other examples of social focus included collaborations with homeless communities and the unemployed in the case of London 2012. In Tokyo 2020, the journey of the community-built puppet – Mocco – was a highlight of the official cultural programme and a platform to support and promote the recovery of the devastated region of Tohoku.

Taken together, there are many examples of progressive cultural policy being applied as part of the Cultural Olympiad and resulting in local, national and, occasionally, international advancements to position and expand the role of previously ignored or minority causes and actors. However, few of these examples have benefitted from the Games as a global communication platform. The next section discusses some of the possible reasons.

Delivery Formats

Despite the many advancements made when it comes to cultural programme objectives and thematic priorities, the underlying challenges in terms of visibility and linkage between artistic programming and other Games activity have remained practically the same throughout a century. As Masterton (1973) and García (2012) argue, these problems have been accentuated by the absence of an international cultural organization comparable to the international sports federations in its ability to coordinate and support Olympic arts initiatives. Subsequent attempts to address this gap, such as the proposal to establish a permanent Cultural Olympiad foundation in Greece (see below), have lacked sufficient international backing to become viable models. Instead, as is the case with other cultural event networks, transfer of knowledge regarding operational issues has relied on personal connections and informal word-of-mouth rather than being a thoroughly documented and transparent process. As a result, to date, there is no standard model of delivery for the Cultural Olympiad. Beyond the many variations in terms of duration and thematic emphasis, other key variations that have affected the consistency and ease of identification of the programme are its geographical spread and the approach to branding and communications – issues to which we now turn.

Geographical Spread

Most Olympic Games have concentrated their cultural programmes in the host city, mainly within central areas or within the Olympic Park and related Olympic venues. However, with the growth in duration of cultural

Table 4.4. Geographical locations for the Cultural Olympiad. (*Source*: Compiled by the author)

City centre – famous cultural venues:	The most common approach since 1912 and the most popular location of Cultural Olympiad events to this day.
City centre – public spaces/street:	This has grown since the 1960s and is an important area of development as a complement to the so-called Live Sites so that the street entertainment on offer showcases host cultures and/or explores innovative creative practices.
Olympic venues/ Olympic Park:	There are few good examples in this area. The scarce presence of cultural programming in Games venues has limited its impact and relevance for Olympic fans. Munich 1972, Montreal 1976 and PyeongChang 2018 presented ambitious artistic programming within the Park, but most editions offer generic entertainment instead, not related to the aspirations of their Cultural Olympiad. London 2012 was the first Games to present a contemporary public art programme within its Olympic Park embodying its vision for innovative, unusual, sustainable and locally representative art. PyeongChang 2018 presented the first high quality contemporary art gallery within an Olympic Park.
Host regions/nationwide/ internationally:	There has been a growing interest in nationwide programming since Barcelona 1992. The most accomplished example to date is London 2012. Paris 2024 is attempting to follow this lead with its nationwide programme 'Terre de Jeux'.

programming, a parallel ambition has been to involve communities beyond the host city to ensure that the Games are owned at a regional and national level – and, sometimes, internationally. This has brought an additional challenge, as the more dispersed the activity, the more difficult it is to ensure that the programme is widely visible and recognized – particularly from the perspective of media coverage.

The first nationwide cultural programme took place in Mexico 1968, with various attempts at following this trend seen in the lead up to Sydney 2000, Athens 2004, London 2012, Tokyo 2020, and Paris 2024. London set a precedent by supporting the creation of thirteen regional 'Creative Programmer' posts that coordinated and encouraged Olympic cultural activity in their respective regions, without depending directly on the Olympic Organizing Committee. This facilitated opportunities for legacy but also made it harder to establish a clear identity and brand. Table 4.4 summarizes the main types of Cultural Olympiad programming locations.

Promotional Frameworks

To date, the Cultural Olympiad has not been formally included as a clearly distinguished promotional asset within Olympic marketing guidelines. As a result, there have been noticeable variations in the way each succeeding Games refers to this programme. This includes variations in its written denomination (e.g. Cultural Olympiad, Olympic Arts Festival, Olympic Cultural Programme, to name just a few) and marked variations in its visual identity which, at times, presents no resemblance or apparent association with the visual identity of respective Olympic Games.

In many cases, the cultural programme has been represented by a visual icon that echoes the main Games iconography (figure 4.6). However, in some instances, the approach has been to create a different brand altogether. This was the case in Barcelona 1992 and Athens 2004. The Cultural Olympiad of Athens 2004 provides an example of the extremes that organizers have been ready to go to in order to establish a strong Olympic cultural programme identity and brand. The programme was given a prime position within the event hosting process, in which the city celebrated the contribution of Greece and Greek heritage as the cradle of European civilization and the birthplace of the Olympic Games. The Cultural Olympiad was thus utilized as a platform to convey ancient Olympic values and claim ownership of the Games in ways not accessible to other Olympic hosts. This involved the establishment of a Cultural Olympiad Foundation in 1998. The Foundation had backing from UNESCO, and it aimed to become a permanent institution to coordinate Olympic cultural programming in the same way that the IOC coordinates the sporting programme. However, by as early as 2008, the foundation was no longer in existence, providing yet another indication of

Figure 4.6. Cultural Olympiad visual icons (1984, 1992, 2000, 2004, 2012). (*Source*: Visual archive of respective Games editions by their Organizing Committees; Courtesy of the IOC)

the persistent challenges embedded within the Olympic cultural programme tradition (Panagiatopoulou, 2016).

Be it as a derivate icon or a distinct brand, the most common challenge for establishing a clear branding association between the cultural programme and the rest of the Games stems from the commercial restrictions imposed on the use of the Olympic rings. The Olympic rings are highly recognizable as the symbol of the Games and one of the most recognizable brands worldwide. However, Cultural Olympiad activity has rarely been granted access to this asset because global Olympic sponsors seldom play a part as funders of cultural programming or agree to be official presenters of artworks during Games time. Instead, most Cultural Olympiad activities are funded by alternative sources which, at times, include competing commercial sponsors.

The London 2012 culture team engaged in extensive Games branding discussions from the moment they were awarded the event. Their objective was to establish a Cultural Olympiad brand that did not conflict with Olympic sponsor interests but allowed cultural contributors to search alternative sources of funding or acknowledge their own long-term sponsors. This resulted in the establishment of an 'Inspired by 2012' mark, a visual icon that was clearly associated with the London 2012 Games but did not include the Olympic rings. The approach was deemed successful by many British cultural partners and also benefitted other types of Games-related programming, such as educational, volunteering, and business-oriented initiatives (see García and Cox, 2013). This has been an important development for the Cultural Olympiad programme, as it was the first time a reasonably flexible label was approved by the organizing committee, thus retaining a clear association with the Games, while being open to use by organizations other than exclusive-right Olympic sponsors and broadcasting partners.

Figure 4.7. 'Inspired by 2012', a London 2012 brand excluding the Olympic rings. (*Source*: LOCOG; Courtesy of the IOC)

Tokyo 2020 continued to explore the notion of a non-lucrative Games-associated label and as has Paris 2024, which devised a dedicated Cultural Olympiad label without including the Olympic rings. The International Olympic Committee has become increasingly supportive of this approach, which may open a new chapter for the Cultural Olympiad as a programme clearly associated with the Games but more porous and inclusive of non-Olympic corporate stakeholders.

The Future

Between 2014 and 2020, the IOC embarked on a comprehensive visioning exercise framed as *Agenda 2020* (IOC, 2014*a*; 2014*b*; IOC, 2021*e*; see also chapter 1 above). As part of this exercise, the IOC proposed to rethink the role of arts and culture within the Olympic Games hosting process to overcome the programme's traditional marginalization. This was in line with the expanding debate over the need for 'legacy', sustainability, and a '360 degree' Olympic experience (IOC, 2009, pp. 27, 62), a term that refers to the IOC's ambition to improve the integration of all Games programming dimensions and ensure that the sporting competitions embrace the local context within the Olympic cities where they take place (figure 4.8).

These new commitments by the IOC have already had an impact on Olympic cultural programming. First, *Agenda 2020* principles have had an effect on Candidate City bidding guidelines, discouraging the traditional relegation of 'cultural programming' to a separate chapter in the bid

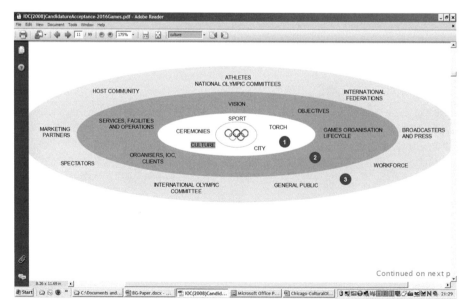

Figure 4.8. Visual representation of 'Olympic experience' components. (*Source*: IOC, 2008*b*, Author's emphasis)

proposal, but instead making it a core dimension of the Olympic city's and spectators' experience that is presented within the introductory sections to the bid. This suggests a push for organizers to think more creatively about ways to embed their cultural proposals within the Olympic Games hosting process rather than treating them as a separate programme of activity. It remains unclear, however, how this may translate into actual budgeting and operational changes that provide greater certainty for Cultural Olympiad operators (García, 2022).

Furthermore, in 2014 the IOC established the Olympic Foundation for Culture and Heritage, with staff working on a dedicated cultural strategy and policy framework to guide the way towards delivery of programming that contributes to the development of a distinct, values-led Olympic narrative. The Foundation has launched the aforementioned 'Olympic Agora' (IOC, 2022*c*) and supports an Olympic artists-in-residence programme during the Games. Since 2013, the Foundation and their culture-liaison counterparts at the IOC Games department are also contributing to ongoing discussions to ensure that Olympic branding and media relations guidelines are better attuned to the needs of the cultural programme, for example, by enabling the creation of non-lucrative Games-related labels.

Beyond the possibility for clearer and more strategic regulations from an IOC perspective, host cities have also become more effective and strategic in their profiling of culture around the Games hosting process. Whether as a political, economic, social, or broader cultural objective, local organizers have become well aware of the importance of contextualizing the Games as a global mega-event within a distinct and meaningful cultural programme in order to secure a sustainable legacy. This suggests that the role and relevance of future Cultural Olympiads will keep growing and that the demand for greater clarity and effectiveness in their delivery framework will also develop. This is already noticeable in the build up to Paris 2024, where local authorities in Games' competition hubs, notably, Seine Saint Denis – host for the Olympic Park and organizing committee headquarters – and major French cities such as Marseille – host of the sailing events and football preliminaries – have been working for years on dedicated Olympic cultural strategies and Cultural Olympiad spin-offs (see Seine Saint Denis, 2021).

As has been extensively argued by scholars for the last three decades, Olympic cities and nations may come to prominence through the opportunity to host sixteen days of international elite sport competitions. At the same time, they are best remembered, and differentiated from one another, by their ability to showcase their unique skylines, public spaces and approaches to celebration that are sensitive to their specific heritage and diverse community values, as well as engaging with emerging and globally relevant cultural and creative practices. For this, ambitious and meaningful Cultural Olympiads are key.

Notes

1. In the original conception of the Olympic Games, a key criterion for inclusion as an Olympic competitor was the need to be an amateur athlete, that is, not to be a full time professional and compete in sport for financial or commercial gain. This rule was also applied to the arts competition, and caused controversy as it became a challenge to attract artworks of the right quality if contributors could not be professional artists. Avery Brundage was elected as IOC president in 1952 and was strongly opposed to any form of professionalism in the Olympic Games. His views prevailed during the lengthy revision of Olympic Arts Competitions formats and priorities that took place between 1949 and 1952 and led to their replacement by Arts Exhibitions.

2. The impact of the COVID-19 pandemic forced practically all public space delivery of Cultural Olympiad activities to be cancelled. Although it had been originally conceived as a pioneering inclusive festival for Japan, bringing artists from all genders and abilities to high profile mainstream venues in Tokyo for the first time, the ONE festival was presented as an entirely digital event.

3. Analysis conducted by the author over documentation stored at the Olympic Museum – Olympic Studies Centre relating to every Olympic official cultural programme between Helsinki 1952 and Atlanta 1996, plus Cultural Olympiad materials and observations collated during fieldwork visits to Olympic Summer and Winter host cities from Sydney 2000 to PyeongChang 2018.

Chapter 5

THE PARALYMPIC GAMES

John R. Gold and *Margaret M. Gold*

The Paralympics is becoming a truly worldwide event …
we want it to be the same as the Olympic Games.
Tanni Grey-Thompson

Speaking to an academic audience, Dame Tanni Grey-Thompson (2006), then the leading medal winner in the history of the Paralympic Games, noted the remarkable convergence of the Paralympic and Olympic movements. From pragmatic beginnings as part of the treatment of spine-injured ex-servicemen towards the end of the Second World War, disability sport has developed so rapidly that it now supports sport-specific national squads of elite athletes participating in international competition. As the summit of disability sport, the Paralympic Games have played a major part in changing social attitudes by emphasizing achievement rather than impairment and by accelerating the agenda of inclusion. They have also forced changes in official attitudes in countries where disability was ideologically problematic if to accommodate international opinion when bidding for the Olympics (Gold and Gold, 2007). Yet Grey-Thompson's aspiration for the Paralympics to be the same as the Olympic Games remains some way off. The Paralympics are now the second part of a double-headed event that proceeds in the same host venue and within the same organizational framework as the Olympics, but the latter remains the senior event in all key aspects. In particular, it is the Olympics rather than the Paralympics that drives the urban legacy of the Games.

This chapter considers the development of the Paralympics from small beginnings as an archery competition for ex-servicemen and women in the grounds of Stoke Mandeville Hospital (England) to the present-day international festival held in Olympic cities immediately after the Summer or Winter Games. It traces their origins to the work of Dr (later Sir) Ludwig Guttmann at the National Spinal Injuries Unit at Stoke Mandeville Hospital in Buckinghamshire, who used sport as an integral part of the treatment of paraplegic patients. The sports competition held at the hospital to coincide with the Opening Ceremony of the London Games in July 1948 became an annual event attracting the first international participation in 1952, after which it became the International Stoke Mandeville Games. From 1960 onwards attempts were made to hold every fourth Games in the Olympic host city, although the path towards acceptance by host cities proved difficult. As will be seen, it was only from 1988 onwards that a process of convergence began that brought the Paralympics into the central arena of the Olympics, both literally and figuratively, leading to the host city being required to include a bid for the Paralympics as part of its candidacy for the Olympics.

The later parts of this chapter discuss the relatively modest ramifications of this requirement for prospective host cities, given that Paralympians make use of many of the same facilities as their Olympian counterparts. Although unlikely ever to drive major infrastructural or regeneration projects, the Paralympics have repercussions for the host city in the need to accommodate a group of athletes and officials with different requirements and in promoting the cause of a barrier-free urban environment. The implications of these provisions are discussed in relation to the Paralympics of the twenty-first century, particularly in relation to the emphasis placed on the disability agenda in the successful bid made by London for the 2012 Games and in the subsequent staging of the event. The final part discusses the continuing trajectory of the Paralympics in terms of provision for disability sport at the Summer and Winter Games from Sochi 2014 through to Tokyo 2020. Although the progress within this period proved less assured than previously – most notably with the near-cancellation of the 2016 Paralympics – it nevertheless shows how the goals of Paralympic sport closely meshed with growing awareness of the need for inclusiveness in society.

Origins

The first stirrings of disability sport emerged in the late nineteenth century, primarily through the work of activists in the deaf community. The first Sports Club for the Deaf was founded in Berlin in 1888 and by 1924 national sports federations for the deaf had emerged in Belgium, Czechoslovakia, France, Great Britain, Holland and Poland. Collectively, these six federations sent 140 athletes to Paris in 1924 to participate in the First International Silent Games – the gathering that marked the birth of a four-yearly cycle of 'World Games for the Deaf' (Séguillon, 2002, p. 119). Subsequently divided into Summer and Winter festivals after the pattern of the Olympics, these were later recognized by the International Olympic Committee (IOC) as the Deaflympics.

The Deaflympics were important as an indicator of possibilities, but the deaf community retained a separate existence as a disability group rather than participating in the movement that would create the Paralympics. Instead, the latter stemmed from the treatment of severely injured servicemen at the end of the Second World War and particularly the work of Ludwig Guttmann – a figure whose role is comparable to that of Baron Pierre de Coubertin in reviving the modern Olympics (see chapter 2). Guttmann, a prominent Jewish neurosurgeon, had arrived in Britain as a refugee from Nazi Germany in 1939. After appointment to a research post at Oxford University's Department of Neurosurgery and then at the Wingfield-Morris Orthopaedic Hospital, he became director of what would become the National Spinal Injuries Centre at Stoke Mandeville Hospital (Aylesbury, Buckinghamshire). Guttmann later commented that paraplegia was the 'most depressing and neglected subject in all medicine' at this time (quoted in Goodman, 1986, p. 96), characterized by poor patient survival rates, low morale amongst nursing staff, and difficulty in recruiting specialist physiotherapists. His approach instituted a programme of 'total care', having patients turned physically every two hours day and night to prevent pressure sores and improving standards of bladder hygiene to help tackle problems of infection. Physiotherapy assisted limb flexibility and, for some patients, increased mobility. A pre-vocational work regime and various forms of recreation including concerts, visits and *competitive* sports, designed to keep patients busy and create a sense of purpose, complemented the medical regime.

In this context, therefore, sport transcended mere leisure. Not only was it 'the most natural form of remedial exercise' restoring physical fitness, strength, coordination, speed, endurance and overcoming fatigue, but also had the psychological impact of restoring pleasure in life and contributing to social reintegration (Guttmann, 1976, p. 12). Developing these ideas, Guttmann formulated the idea of a sports festival that would promote contact with other patients and counter attitudes towards the capabilities of disabled people. On 28 July 1948, an archery competition took place on the front lawns of the hospital, involving sixteen competitors arranged into two teams: one from Stoke Mandeville and the other from the Star and Garter Home for disabled ex-servicemen in Richmond-on-Thames. The event was consciously chosen for its demonstration of potential, symbolized by being held on the same day as the Opening Ceremony of the London Olympics, with archery seen as second only to swimming in its 'physiotherapeutic value … for the paralysed' (Special Correspondent, 1948). In 1949, Stoke Mandeville hosted a larger competition, involving 60 competitors from five hospitals participating in what became a steadily widening group of sports (table 5.1). During the meeting, Guttmann gave a speech in which he hoped that the event would become international and achieve 'world fame as the

Table 5.1. Paralympic sports. (*Source*: Compiled by authors from IPC, 2006a, 2023)

Summer Games	*Year included in the Full Paralympic Programme*
Archery	1960
Athletics	1960
Basketball	1996–2000
Boccia	1984
Bowls (lawn)	1968–1988, 1996
Cycling	1984
Dartchery	1960–1980
Equestrian	1996
Football 5-a-side	2004
Football 7-a-side	1984–2016*
Goalball	1980
Judo	1988
Para badminton	2021
Para canoe	2016
Para triathlon	2016
Para taekwondo	2021
Powerlifting/Weightlifting	1964 men
Powerlifting/Weightlifting	2000 women
Rowing	2008
Sailing	2000–2016
Shooting	1976
Snooker	1960–1978, 1984–1988
Swimming	1960
Table Tennis	1960
Volleyball – standing	1976–1996
Volleyball – sitting	1980
Wheelchair basketball	1960
Wheelchair fencing	1960
Wheelchair rugby	2000
Wheelchair slalom	1964–1968
Wheelchair tennis	1992
Winter Games	
Alpine Skiing	1976
Ice Hockey	1994
Para Cross Country	1976
Para Biathlon	1994
Snowboard	2014
Wheelchair Curling	2006

* for athletes with cerebral palsy

disabled men and women's equivalent of the Olympic Games' (Goodman, 1986, p. 150).

The Stoke Mandeville Games quickly acquired an international dimension, particularly by drawing on institutional connections that the Hospital had developed through training visiting staff, through staff moving to other hospitals and spreading Stoke Mandeville's characteristic approach to sport, and through ex-patients who pioneered paraplegic sport in their own countries. In 1952, another Olympic year, the involvement of a group of Dutch war veterans presaged wider European participation. In 1953, teams from Finland, France, Israel and the Netherlands appeared, along with a Canadian team. The Americans first participated in 1955, followed by the Australians in 1957 – by which time the Stoke Mandeville Games had commonly gained the nickname 'Paralympics' (Carisbroke *et al.*, 1956; Brittain, 2010, pp. 24–25).[1] The word 'Paralympics' at this stage was clearly a pun combining 'paraplegic' and 'Olympic' (IPC, 2006*a*), effectively confronting Olympian traditions of celebrating excellence and the perfectly formed body with the realities of disability. It was only over time that reinterpretation occurred. In part, this was driven by the Games embracing participants with forms of disability other than paraplegia. Equally, it resulted from a process of convergence that closely allied the Paralympics with the Olympic movement. With an ingenious revision of the etymology, the approved version of the term asserted that the first syllable of 'Paralympics' derived from the Greek preposition 'para', meaning 'beside' or 'alongside'. Viewed in this way, the Paralympics constitute a festival that exists alongside and operates in parallel with the Olympic Games, while retaining a separate identity (*ibid.*).

Building Connections

As the Games grew, demands for greater professionalism towards the organization, funding, and management of international sport for disabled people saw the establishment in 1959 of the International Stoke Mandeville Games Committee (later Foundation, hence ISMGF). This ran and developed the annual Stoke Mandeville Games and oversaw the organization of a parallel four-yearly 'Olympic' competition until 1972 (see table 5.2).

The process of building links with the Olympics, however, proved long and torturous despite highly promising beginnings. In 1956, during ceremonies at the Melbourne Olympics, the IOC had awarded the Fearnley Cup to Guttmann for 'outstanding achievement in the service of Olympic ideals' (Goodman, 1986, p. 157), a remarkable degree of recognition less than a decade after the foundation of the Stoke Mandeville Games. The next stage was to take the Stoke Mandeville Games to the Olympic host city itself and, when the Games were held in Rome 1960 and Tokyo 1964, the convergence of the two sets of Games seemed assured. Such arrangements, however, depended on the goodwill of the host city, sponsorship and public funding to cover the cost. The Rome Games, for example, had the cooperation of the Spinal Unit at Ostia, gained sponsorship from INAIL (*Istituto nazionale per l'assicurazione contro gli infortuni sul lavoro* – the Italian National Insurance Institute Against Accidents at Work), and had the support of the Italian Olympic Committee (CONI). The 400 disabled athletes used the Olympic Pool and Village, but last minute changes meant that those parts of the Village equipped with lifts were unavailable. Moreover, withdrawal of an offer to use nearby Olympic facilities meant that

Table 5.2. Summer Paralympic Games. (*Sources*: Compiled by authors from various sources, with particular use of Scruton, 1998)

Year	Aegis	Location	Number of Countries	Number of Athletes	Number of Sports for which Medals Awarded	Disability Groups
1952	Stoke Mandeville Hospital	Stoke Mandeville*	2	130	6	SI
1960	ISMGC	Rome	23	400	8	SI
1964	ISMGC	Tokyo	21	357	9	SI
1968	ISMGC	Tel Aviv, Israel*	29	750	10	SI
1972	ISMGF	Heidelberg, West Germany*	43	984	10	SI
1976	ISMGF ISOD	Toronto, Canada*	38	1657	13	SI, A, VI, LA
1980	ISMGF ISOD	Arnhem, Holland*	42	1973	12	SI, A, VI, LA, CP
1984	ISMGF	Stoke Mandeville*	41	1100	10	SI
	ISOD	New York*	45	1800	14	A, VI, LA, CP
1988	ICC	Seoul	61	3013	18	SI, A, VI. LA, CP
1992	ICC	Barcelona	82	3021	16	SI, A, VI
		Madrid*	73	1400	5	ID
1996	IPC	Atlanta	103	3195	19	SI, A, VI, LA, CP, ID
2000	IPC	Sydney	122	3843	19	SI, A, VI, LA, CP, ID
2004	IPC	Athens	136	3806	19	SI, A, VI, LA, CP
2008	IPC	Beijing	146	3951	20	SI, A, VI, LA, CP
2012	IPC	London	160	4200	20	SI, A, VI, LA, CP, ID
2016	IPC	Rio de Janeiro	176 tbc	4350 tbc	23 tbc	SI, A, VI LA, CP, ID (tbc)
2020	IPC	Tokyo	tbc	tbc	22 tbc	SI, A, VI LA, CP, ID (tbc)

* Years in which the Paralympic Games did not take place in the Olympic location.

Guide to abbreviations: *SI* Spinal Injury; *A* Amputee; *VI* Visually Impaired; *LA* Les Autres; *CP* Cerebral Palsy; *ID* Intellectual Impairment.

competitors were perforce conveyed by a forty-minute bus ride to the Tre Fontane sports ground (Scruton, 1998, p. 308).

The Tokyo Games offered somewhat greater hospitality in contradistinction to aspects of official policy. As noted by Brittain (2022, p. 79), Japan had found notions of disability problematic. Measures introduced in the early 1940s and not repealed until 1996, for example, allowed for the forcible sterilization of disabled people; other policies in place until the 1980s routinely confined them to institutions. It was therefore notable that, following on from the Summer Olympics, competitors were accommodated in the Athletes' Village and shared facilities that were recently used by the Olympic athletes. Its Opening Ceremony, with the Crown Prince and Princess acting as patrons, attracted 5,000 spectators. Hence, despite the obvious contradictions, Tokyo 1964 earned a special place in Paralympic history by virtue of its welcoming and respectful attitude towards the fledgling Games.

From this apparently promising juncture, problems with the host city seriously affected further progress. Another twenty-four years passed before disabled athletes again competed in an Olympic host city (Seoul 1988), with a succession of cities refusing to host the Paralympics. The IOC, in its role of handling the bidding process for the Games, was only interested in the candidate cities' ability to meet the costs and needs of elite Olympians. There was no stipulation that the Olympic city must host parallel games for athletes with disabilities. Admittedly, the Paralympics became a greater challenge to hosts as they grew in size (see table 5.1), especially with admission of a wider range of disability groups after 1976. The increasing scale of the Games, coupled with prevailing building standards that failed to accommodate the disabled people, shortage of available funds and lack of any inclusive philosophy regarding athletes with disability proved obstacles for further collaboration with many Olympic cities.

For example, despite having sent three observers to Tokyo, Mexico City declined the Games in 1968 because of 'technical difficulties'. They were held instead at the sports centre of the Israel Foundation for Handicapped Children in Ramat Gan near Tel Aviv. In 1972, the University of Heidelberg staged the Games rather than Munich, as plans for the post-festival use of the Olympic Village had meant transferring the site to developers for conversion into private apartments immediately after the Olympic Closing Ceremony (Scruton, 1998, p. 320). Lack of suitable accommodation, real or claimed, plagued subsequent events. In 1976, Toronto acted as hosts rather than the Olympic city of Montreal, with the athletes housed at Toronto and York Universities. The two Paralympic Villages were located some distance from each other as well as from the competition venues. When the Moscow Olympic Organizing Committee failed even to respond to a request to stage the Games, the 1980 festival took place at Arnhem in the

Figure 5.1. Stoke Mandeville stadium (Aylesbury, Buckinghamshire). (*Source*: Photograph, John and Margaret Gold)

Netherlands. Here, too, the available accommodation (an army barracks) was inconveniently located for access to the sports venues. In 1984, the Americans agreed to host the Games for all disabilities, but not in the host Olympic city (Los Angeles). Instead, they were to be split between New York and the University of Illinois (Champaign); an arrangement that foundered when the latter withdrew through funding problems just four months before the Games. As a result, 1,800 amputee, cerebral palsy, visually impaired, and Les Autres[2] athletes competed at the Mitchel Park athletics complex in Uniondale, New York, with 1,200 athletes participating in the wheelchair events that were hurriedly rearranged at Stoke Mandeville (*ibid.*, pp. 184, 202). Ironically, these were the first Games that the IOC officially recognized as the Paralympics (figure 5.1) although the first full Games to use this title was in 1988 at Seoul.

The early Winter Paralympic Games fared little better (table 5.3). Established in 1976, initially they too did not take place at the Olympic venues or even in the same countries. The first Winter Games took place in Örnsköldsvik (Sweden) rather than at Innsbruck (Austria). These were followed in 1980 by Games at Geilo (Norway) rather than Lake Placid, at Innsbruck in 1984 rather than Sarajevo (although an exhibition event was held in the Winter Games there), and Innsbruck again in 1988 rather than Calgary, which declined to hold the Paralympics.

Table 5.3. Winter Paralympic Games. (*Sources*: Compiled by authors from various sources, with particular use of Scruton, 1998)

Year	Aegis	Location	Participating Countries	Number of Athletes	Number of Sports	Disability Groups
1976	ISOD	Örnsköldsvik Sweden*	17	250	2	VI, A
1980	ISOD ISMGF	Geilo Norway*	18	350	2	VI, A, SI, CP, LA
1984	ICC	Innsbruck Austria*	21	457	2	VI, A, SI CP, LA
1988	ICC	Innsbruck Austria*	22	397	2	VI, A, SI, CP, LA
1992	ICC	Albertville France	24	475	2	VI, A, SI, CP, LA
1994	IPC	Lillehammer Norway	31	492	3	VI, A, SI, CP, LA
1998	IPC	Nagano Japan	32	571	4	VI, A, SI, CP, LA
2002	IPC	Salt Lake City USA	36	416	3	VI, A, SI, CP, LA
2006	IPC	Turin Italy	39	474	4	VI, A, SI, CP, LA
2010	IPC	Vancouver Canada	44	502	5	VI, A, SI, CP, LA
2014	IPC	Sochi Russian Federation	45	547	5	VI, A, SI, CP, LA, ID (tbc)
2018	IPC	PyeongChang Korea	49	569	6	VI, A, SI, CP, LA, ID (tbc)

* Years in which the Paralympic Games did not take place in the Olympic location.
Guide to abbreviations: SI Spinal Injury; *A* Amputee; *VI* Visually Impaired; *LA* Les Autres; *CP* Cerebral Palsy; *ID* Intellectual Impairment.

This retreat from the positive pattern established in the early 1960s greatly disappointed the Paralympic movement. Guttmann (1976, p. 174) denounced the thinking that had prevented Mexico City 1968 or Munich 1972 holding the Games, commenting on 'the lamentable lack of appreciation of the place thousands of disabled sportsmen and women have earned for themselves in the field of international sport'. Chiefly as a result of this, a new complex of buildings was constructed at Stoke Mandeville (figure 5.2), comprising a venue first entitled the Stadium for the Paralysed and Other Disabled (opened in 1969 and later renamed the Ludwig Guttmann Sports Stadium for the Disabled) and an 'Olympic' Village in 1981 (Goodman, 1986, p. 164). Thus the sporting facilities were finally separated from the hospital itself and from the notion of 'illness', reflecting the fact that disabled athletes were now achieving elite status with an emphasis on performance.

Figure 5.2. Cauldron for the Paralympic flame, Paralympic Games, Stoke Mandeville, 1984. (*Source*: Photograph, John and Margaret Gold)

Organizational Convergence

The problem, however, was not simply the resistance of Olympic cities and their Organizing Committees, since the definition of disability and competing jurisdictions of relevant organizations also affected progress. The Stoke Mandeville Games originally confined entry to medically controlled paraplegics, but the organizers felt impelled to respond when other groups pressed for participation in internationally organized sports festivals. The foundation of the International Sports Organization for the Disabled (ISOD) in 1964 created opportunities for the blind, amputees and individuals with other locomotor disabilities (De Pauw and Gavron, 2005, p. 39). ISOD collaborated with ISMGF in broadening the scope of the 1976 Toronto Games to include amputees, visually impaired, and Les Autres. Competitors with cerebral palsy joined the 1980 Games.

The expanding scope of disability sport quickly generated new international disability organizations. The need to coordinate their activities and eliminate duplication of events required further organizational developments, leading in particular to the foundation of the ICC (International Coordinating Committee of the World Sports Organizations) in 1982. This brought together nominated senior representatives from the four major International Sports Organizations: ISMWSF (International Stoke Mandeville Wheelchair Sports

Federation, previously the ISMGF), ISOD (International Sports Federation of the Disabled), IBSA (the International Blind Sports Federation), and the CP-ISRA (Cerebral Palsy International Sport and Recreation Association). These were later joined by CISS (International Committee of Sports for the Deaf) and INAS-FID (International Sports Federation for Persons with Mental Handicap – later changed to Intellectual Disability). Thus constituted, the ICC gave the disabled sports movement a single voice for the first time. It also allowed greater clarity in developing relations with the IOC and Olympic Games Organizing Committees, which found immediate expression in the geographical convergence of the Summer Games at Seoul 1988 and the Winter Games at Albertville 1992.

The ICC oversaw the Games held in Olympic cities in 1988 and 1992, with the exception of the Winter Games in Calgary in 1988. The 1988 Seoul Olympics and Paralympics had separate Organizing Committees, but with sufficient coordination to allow the sharing of venues, equipment and key personnel. They also received the same spectacular Opening and Closing Ceremonies as the Summer Games, watched by capacity crowds of 75,000. This direct linkage with the Olympics marked the start of the Paralympics achieving 'significant global notice' (Darcy *et al.*, 2017, p. 4), but there was still a distance to travel along the road to parity. In particular, the Olympic Village at Seoul was unavailable after the Olympics, with a specially designed Village needing to be constructed for the Paralympians.

Barcelona pioneered the organizational integration of the two sets of Games by giving overall responsibility to the Organizing Committee of the Barcelona Games (COOB), with a separate Division charged with overall responsibility to plan the Paralympics. This ensured explicit attention to the needs of disabled athletes and comparable treatment with Olympians. The Paralympic Games now had their custom-designed Opening and Closing ceremonial spectacles (Rognoni, 1996, p. 264). Free admission to Paralympic events ensured large numbers of spectators and there was substantial television coverage. At the same time, COOB imposed its own decisions, cutting the number of sports to fifteen and refusing to allow the mentally impaired to participate in the Paralympics. Instead INAS-FID held an officially recognized Paralympic Games in Madrid in which 1,400 athletes from seventy-three countries competed. This took place after the Barcelona Paralympic Games.[3]

Atlanta 1996 showed even more than Barcelona that the new relationship between the Olympic and Paralympic Games was still *ad hoc* and 'vulnerable to the priorities of the local Organizing Committee' (Darcy *et al.*, 2017, p. 5). Problems over insensitive and patronizing media coverage were compounded by funding problems that contributed to the Village and the venues being left in a state of operational chaos after the Olympics (*ibid*). The poor condition of the venues and the Athletes' Village in particular almost led to a protest by participating athletes during the Paralympic Closing Ceremony (*ibid.*, see also Cashman and Darcy, 2008*b*, pp. 38–39). The need for improved liaison between the organizers of the two Games and better coordination of their actions was readily apparent (Heath, 1996; Gold and Gold, 2007).

The final stage in the evolution of the organizational basis for the Games came with the establishment of the International Paralympic Committee (IPC) in 1989: an organization similar in structure to the IOC itself. Based in Bonn (Federal Republic of Germany), it serves as the umbrella organization for 176 National Paralympic Committees, five regional bodies, seventeen international disability-specific sports federations, and four International Organizations of Sport for the Disabled (in the areas of cerebral palsy, the blind, intellectual disability, wheelchair and amputees). It also acts as the international federation for ten of the Paralympic sports (IPC, 2015*a*, p. 6; IPC, 2016). Its vision is to enable 'Paralympic athletes to achieve sporting excellence and inspire and excite the world' and it professes an eleven-point mission which includes sport development 'from initiation to elite level' (IPC, 2006*c*, p. 3; see also McNamee, 2017). Crucially, since 1992 it is now the sole coordinating body for Paralympic sport recognized by the IOC.

As the IOC and IPC moved closer together, there was identification of areas that had produced conflict, notably, the use of the term 'Olympics' (which the IOC regard as their copyright), and the Paralympic Logo. The IPC Logo, originally introduced at the Seoul Games, comprised five traditional Korean decorative motifs (Tae-Geuks) in the Olympic colours (blue, black, red, yellow and green). Given that the IOC felt this was too close to their five-ring symbol, the IPC reduced the five Tae-Geuks to three in 1994 and replaced them completely as part of a rebranding exercise in 2003. The new logo, comprising three 'agitos' (from the Latin *agito* meaning 'I move'), was first used at Athens 2004, along with the new motto 'Spirit in Motion' (IPC, 2005, p. 6; see also IPC, 2006*b*).

Four agreements between the IOC and IPC signed between 2000 and 2006 clarified the relationship between the two organizations, set out the principles for further cooperation and provided financial support for the IPC. An agreement in October 2000 brought the workings of the two organizations closer by co-opting the IPC President to the IOC and including an IPC representative on eleven of the IOC Commissions, including the Evaluation Commission – the body that examines the competing bids from cities seeking to host the Olympic Games. The IOC also undertook to pay an annual subvention towards IPC administration costs ($3 million per annum), annual sums for development projects, and specific assistance to help athletes from developing countries attend the 2002 Salt Lake City Winter Paralympic Games and the 2004 Athens Summer Paralympics (IOC, 2000). A second agreement in June 2001 elucidated the organization of the Paralympic Games, confirming that the location would always be the Olympic host city and would take place 'shortly after' the Olympic Games using the same facilities and venues. From the 2008 Summer Games and 2010 Winter Games onwards, there would be full integration of the two Organizing Committees (IOC, 2001*a*). The third agreement in August 2003 concerned revenues for broadcasting and marketing the Paralympics. This guaranteed IOC payments to the IPC of $9 million for the 2008 Games and $14 million for 2010 and 2012 (IOC, 2003*b*). The final agreement (June 2006) extended these arrangements through to 2014 and 2016, increased funding for the IPC and set out the respective roles of the IOC and IPC in the planning, organization and staging of the Paralympics, the use of technical manuals, the sports programme, and the number of accredited individuals (IOC, 2006). In 2012 the co-operation agreement signed in 2006 was extended further to 2020 and a new partnership between the IOC and IPC was implemented, identifying areas of IOC activity in which the IPC could participate. These included Olympic Solidarity, Knowledge Transfer, commercial activities and closer cooperation in the planning and delivery of the Games (IPC, 2012).

Accommodating the Disability Agenda

The move towards a 'one city, one bid' approach for selection of Olympic host cities was of vital importance to the IPC. It meant that the two festivals came into line as part of an overall package that prospective host cities would put together. Cities bidding for the Games in 2008, 2010 and beyond had to show complete organizational integration between the Olympic and Paralympic Games, with details of the Paralympic Games fully articulated in the bid documents. Indeed, the speed of integration was more rapid than these agreements stipulated, with both Salt Lake City 2002 and Athens 2004 establishing a single Organizing Committee (IOC, 2003*b*) and information on the Paralympic Games appearing in the official Reports of the Olympic Games since Sydney 2000 (e.g. SOCOG, 2000, pp. 47–49).

This development, of course, needs to be set in proper perspective. On the one hand, it was never likely that this smaller festival, held in the wake of the main events, would assume the same significance as the Olympics or preoccupy the thinking of city planners to the same extent. For many cities, the right to stage the Olympics is a prize aggressively won, whereas 'they inherit the Paralympic Games as an obligation' (Cashman, 2006, p. 247). As such, the Paralympics tend to be fitted into the package offered for the Olympics – a pragmatic strategy given that they produce little demand for additional facilities, other than for a few sports such as boccia and goalball that have special requirements[4] and for modifications to transport and stadia to allow barrier free access for competitors, officials, and spectators. It is also scarcely conceivable that the Paralympics *per se* would ever act as a catalyst for major infrastructural investment or urban regeneration.

Yet, on the other hand, their significance for the host city is far from negligible. A city's Olympic bid that features a lukewarm or ill-considered approach to the Paralympics may well suffer regardless of the strength of its proposals for the Olympics. In addition, the act of staging the Paralympics impacts on host cities through the way that they confront questions of disability, most notably with respect to creating a barrier-free environment.[5] Although, as noted, the requirement to integrate the two sets of Games only became binding with the 2008 Beijing Games, hosts with an established record of upholding disability rights and with legislation guaranteeing rights of access already in place have enjoyed an advantage in the bidding and preparation of the Games. Hence, cities such as Sydney, Turin and London could build on their existing practices which were already enshrined in legislation, whereas the Games in Athens and Beijing were the catalysts for initiating the disability agenda.

In terms of Games planning, Sydney set about addressing problems seen at Atlanta 1996, such as the lack of visibility of the Paralympic Games and poor coordination between them and the Olympics (Darcy, 2001, 2003). As host for the Eleventh Paralympic Games, the city achieved a good working relationship between the bodies responsible for the two Games (SOCOG and the Sydney Paralympic Organizing Committee), which shared departments, and with other Games-related organizations. The Games themselves took place in the Olympic Park, with the (Paralympic) Village home to 6,943 people, comprising 3,824 athletes, 2,315 team officials, and 804 technical officials (BPA, 2007). The design of the Olympic Park also represented a drastic improvement in accessibility over previous Paralympics, with Australia able to capitalize on the country's longstanding active involvement in disability sport. The improved access provided in the Olympic Park, however, was 'only as good as the city and suburban network which fed into it' (Cashman, 2006, p. 254). For example, only five per cent of railway stations facilitated easy access for wheelchair disabled, and relatively few buses had low-floor access (*ibid.*).

The Winter Games in Turin 2006 similarly sought to boost the visibility of the Paralympics. The Italians treated the staging of the Paralympic Games in Italy as a welcome reminder of history, given that Rome in 1960 had been the first Olympic city to welcome the Stoke Mandeville International Festival (BPA, 2007). Continuing the themes adopted by the Winter Olympics (e.g. as in figure 5.3), the Paralympics used the same accommodation and facilities (figure 5.4). The major innovation was worldwide coverage of all sports of the Paralympic Winter Games, with over 100 hours of content provided through an internet television channel owned by the IPC, (paralympicsport. TV), narrowcast free-to-air. Seen as a way of overcoming the resistance of the larger broadcasting networks, the service was relaunched in 2007 and provides coverage of all Paralympic sport in addition to full coverage of the Games themselves. Over 240 hours of Paralympic coverage was provided during the Beijing Games (IPC, 2009, p. 40) and with the use of YouTube and Facebook, the Games are using social networking sites to engage with a broader audience.

Figure 5.3. Welcoming slogan, Turin Airport, March 2006. (*Source*: Photograph, John and Margaret Gold)

Figure 5.4. Turin Esposizione, venue for the sledge hockey, Paralympic Games, Turin, March 2006. (*Source*: Photograph, John and Margaret Gold)

By contrast, there was little tradition of disabled sport in Greece. This was addressed in the years leading up to Athens 2004 by developing an accessible sports infrastructure for athletes with disability that could be used in the preparation of Greek athletes and to permit training by other Paralympic teams (ATHOC, 2005, p. 178). Eighty-five per cent of the venues used were the same as for the Olympics, with additional ones provided for the Paralympic-specific sports. Nevertheless, while it was possible to plan for disabled access in new Olympic investment (including public transport, venues, and the public spaces around venues), the wider environment posed challenges. The Official Report of the Games went so far as to call Athens 'unfriendly' to the disabled community and requiring 'drastic measures' to make the city accessible (*ibid.*, p. 177).

The Organizing Committee (ATHOC) produced design guidelines and accessibility information for the municipalities making up the Greater Athens area, where much of the Olympic infrastructure was located, to encourage them to upgrade their public spaces, particularly along key routes identified by ATHOC (see chapter 14). Furthermore, it urged private businesses to promote accessibility in their own premises and to raise awareness among their staff. To this end, ATHOC and the Chambers of Commerce of the four cities participating in the Olympics (Athens, Thessaloniki, Heraklio, and Volos) developed the Accessible Choice Programme (ERMIS). Businesses compliant with this programme earned the right to display a symbol indicating that they welcomed customers with disabilities and their details were included in a directory issued to all Paralympic delegations on arrival in Greece. Although attendances were less than at Sydney (850,000 compared with 1.1 million) and some venues were less than half-full, part of the value of the festival was considered to lie in its pedagogic impact. As in Australia, the organizers had developed an educational programme to promote greater understanding of the Paralympics and a large proportion of the audience were children. An accident that killed seven students who were travelling to watch the Paralympics cast a shadow over this strategy, leading to cancellation of the artistic and entertainment sections of the Closing Ceremony out of respect. The ceremony continued, but with only the protocol elements required for the completion of the Games (*ibid*, p. 511).

Beijing's plans for 2008 also reflected significant shifts in attitude. China's own participation in the Paralympic Movement is relatively recent. When invited to the Rome Games in 1960, the official statement declared there were no disabled in China (Lane, 2006). Relaxation of this ideological stance saw the establishment of the Chinese Sports Association for Disabled Athletes in 1983 (De Pauw and Gavron, 2005, pp. 127–128). Chinese athletes started to compete in international competition, with a small group entering the 1984 Games held in New York. The increasing seriousness with which the Chinese then took sport for the disabled is reflected in the spectacular improvement in the performance of their athletes – rising from ninth in the medal table in 1996, to sixth in 2000, and first place at Athens 2004 and Beijing 2008.

This new priority reflects China's characteristic use of sporting investment as an adjunct of foreign policy (see chapter 15), as much as any root-and-branch change in prevailing attitudes. Nevertheless, the requirements of provision for 2008 focused attention on the challenge of creating a barrier-free Games in a city where access has only been on the agenda for a short time and where much of the infrastructure was anything but barrier-free. The Beijing Municipal People's Congress adopted the country's first local legislation relating to physical accessibility when passing the 'Beijing Regulation on Construction and Management of the Barrier-free Facilities' in April 2004. The regulations applied to public transport, hospitals, banks, public toilets and parks. As a result, for instance, underground stations had ramps installed, disabled toilets, tactile paths for the visually impaired and public telephones for wheelchair users, with disabled seats provided on trains (CIIC, 2004).

However while reshaping the built environment proved relatively straightforward, the challenge of changing public attitudes towards the disabled was highlighted in May 2008 when the *Manual for being Olympic Volunteers* was published (BOGVWCG, 2008). Chapter 6 dealt with 'Volunteering Skills' and, in attempting to provide the volunteer with information on how to engage with visitors from different cultural backgrounds, revealed some disturbing attitudes towards people with disabilities. For example, section 2, on the 'physically disabled', stated the following:

> Physically disabled people are often mentally healthy. They show no differences in sensation, reaction, memorization and thinking mechanism from other people, but they might have unusual personalities because of disfigurement and disability. For example, some physically disabled are isolated, unsocial, and introspective; they usually do not volunteer to contact people. They can be stubborn and controlling; they may be sensitive and struggle with trust issues. Sometimes they are overly protective of themselves, especially when they are called 'crippled' or 'paralyzed'. It is not acceptable for others to hurt their dignity, so volunteers should make extra efforts to assist with due respect. (*ibid.*, pp. 6–7)

The guide was hastily withdrawn and 'poor translation' blamed. Dame Tanni Grey-Thompson's reaction to the guide was to observe that the Paralympics themselves would do more to change attitudes and Mike Brace, chair of the British Paralympic Association, called it 'a clumsy attempt to override years of limited awareness' and observed that this was in fact progress given that up to seven years before, disabled people were often not recognized at all (O'Connor, 2008).

London 2012

In the case of London's bid for the 2012 Games, there was no doubt that, perhaps for the first time, the quality of that portion of the Olympic bid which concerned the Paralympic Games was seen as constituting a major positive factor for the entire candidacy. The location of Stoke Mandeville in London's Home Counties meant that there was a sense of the Paralympics 'coming home'. From the outset, Paralympians were part of the group responsible for organizing and drafting the bid and attended the vital IOC meeting in Singapore in July 2005, where the outcome was decided.

Under the new rules agreed in 2001, the candidate cities for the final phase of the Olympic selection procedure had to complete a questionnaire with seventeen themes. Theme 9 related exclusively to the Paralympic Games and contained nine sets of questions covering the structural integration of the organization of the Paralympics within the Organizing Committee, the dates and the competition schedule, the venues, accommodation, transport operation, travel times, disability awareness (including staff and volunteer training), media facilities, vision for the Games, finance, and the Games' legacy (IOC, 2004*a*). In its bid, the London Committee capitalized on the heritage of disabled sport in the United Kingdom, a tradition of volunteering for Paralympic events, anti-disability discrimination in service provision dating back to the 1995 Disability Discrimination Act, and a good record in disability awareness training. The London Bid Book promulgated three goals: to strengthen the Paralympic Movement; to deliver accessible and inclusive designs for all facilities; and to maximize media coverage (London 2012, 2004, p. 173). The bid contained eight specific commitments for the Paralympics (*ibid.*, p. 191):

◆ Creating an Olympic Village that is fully accessible to all from the outset;
◆ Maximizing media coverage and exposure, as pioneered by the BBC;
◆ Integrating Olympic Games and Paralympic Games planning;
◆ Training all Games workforce in the principles of inclusion;
◆ Establishing operational policies that encompass Paralympic values;
◆ Recruiting suitably qualified disabled people;
◆ Promoting the Paralympic Games nationwide;
◆ Creating a cultural programme featuring disabled artists.

However, much of the subsequent documentation coming out of official agencies as they planned for the Games tended to concentrate on the legacy aims for the Olympics with scant reference to the specifics of the Paralympics (Keogh, 2009; Misener *et al.*, 2013). The five legacy promises for example were: to make the United Kingdom a world-leading sporting nation; transform the heart of East London; inspire a generation of young people to take part in local volunteering, cultural and physical activity; make the Olympic Park a blueprint for sustainable living; and demonstrate that the United Kingdom is a creative, inclusive and welcoming place to live, to visit and for business (DCMS, 2007*a*, 2007*b*). While projects for the disabled were being developed and were referred to in these documents the main thrust was the Olympics themselves. Even the 'inclusive' goals in the fifth promise were interpreted in the introductions to those documents as being about employment, skills, and workforce capacity – getting people into work and long-term employment rather than inclusion of the disabled people.

In December 2009, with 1,000 days to the opening of the London Paralympic Games, Tessa Jowell, the Minister with responsibility for London 2012, announced a sixth legacy promise for the London Games: 'to bring about lasting change to the life experiences of disabled people' (Office for Disability, 2009) This finally gave greater visibility to Paralympic outcomes and lent weight to claims that the two games are part of the same project. This was followed in March 2010 with a legacy document *London 2012: A Legacy for Disabled People* which finally set the Paralympic project in the context of the government's wider disability agenda: 'Our goal is not only to host the most accessible Games ever, but also to ensure that we harness the full power of London 2012 to help realize progress towards achieving equality for disabled people by 2025' (DCMS, 2010, p. 2).[6] The document identified three 'areas of change', within each of which were a further four objectives (see table 5.4).

This legacy document focused on people rather than physical places and spaces. The Olympic venues by this point had already been planned as

Table 5.4 Legacy vision for the Paralympic Games. (*Source*: DCMS, 2010, pp. 4–7)

	Aims	Objectives
1	Influence the attitudes and perceptions of people to change the way they think about disabled people	(*a*) Ensuring comprehensive media coverage (*b*) Providing an accessible and inclusive London 2012 Games (*c*) Connecting the UK with London 2012 (*d*) Engaging children at home and abroad
2	Increase the participation of disabled people in sport and physical activity	(*a*) Encouraging disabled people to be more active (*b*) Widening sports opportunities for disabled adults (*c*) Widening sports opportunities for disabled children and young people (*d*) Increasing the supply of accessible facilities
3	Promote and drive improvements in business, transport and employment opportunities for disabled people	(*a*) Opportunities for business (*b*) Access to jobs and skills (*c*) Accessible tourism (*d*) Improved public transport

barrier-free environments and the Olympic Delivery Authority had won a Royal Town Planning Institute Planning Award for their accessibility strategy (*ibid.*, p. 29). The hard legacy issues identified in this strategy related to 1,000 sports and leisure facilities to improve access (under objective 2b); to encourage more hotels to adopt improvements in accessibility (under 3c); improve infrastructure of London Transport's system (164 stations) and 145 main line stations by 2015 (although Olympic related stations within that group would be upgraded by the Games under 3d).

The real emphasis was on soft legacy. The first aim was about social attitudes (including the role media play in shaping those attitudes), support to participate in the Games and Cultural Olympiad as volunteers, employees, spectators or participants in the ceremonies and torch relay. The second aim concerned participation in sport for all age groups – within and beyond educational institutions covering leisure sport and elite participation. The third aim was about inclusion more generally in the economy for businesses owned by disabled people, access to employment and skills training, and greater customer provision and care in tourism and transport. The document also demonstrated how many of the existing Olympic programmes fed into these goals: Cultural Olympiad-Unlimited; Access to Volunteering Fund; Get Set Programme; Let's Get Moving; Be Active Be Healthy; Playground to Podium; Compete For; Access Now; and Personal Best. These national goals were ambitious targets for a one-off event even on the scale of a Paralympics.

The Games when they came were hailed as a great success. From the Opening Ceremony on 29 August through to 9 September they used the barrier-free, accessible facilities of the Olympic Park, River Zone and Weymouth (for sailing). Public transport was upgraded so that there were sixty-six underground stations and twenty-four overground stations boasting step-free access (although at 24 per cent and 31 per cent of their respective networks there was still some way to go). Nevertheless, LOCOG felt able to claim that 'London now has undoubtedly the most accessible transport system in the world' (LOCOG, *2013b*). More importantly, London raised the status of the Games, winning audiences in its own right, without recourse to issuing free tickets or bussing in school groups. 2.7 million tickets were sold, most events were full to capacity, and a cumulative global TV audience of 3.8 billion in 115 countries was achieved. It seemed that disability had become a mainstream topic of news and interest as a result of the Games.

Certainly the President of the International Paralympic Committee felt that the 2012 Games had impacted significantly on the movement. Sir Philip Craven talking at the London School of Economics in 2014 under the title 'The Paralympic Movement Takes Off', pointed to the 'commercial interest' generated by the London Games, leading to IPC success in securing contracts for Paralympic Games television rights and attracting sponsors (Craven, 2014). In particular he was referring to the two-Games deal signed between the IPC and NBC for significant increases in television coverage for Sochi and Rio de Janeiro (IPC, 2014*a*). BP became an international partner of the IPC in 2013, signing an agreement lasting to the end of 2016.

When assessing the impact of the 2012 Paralympic Games on London much of the literature has focused on the impact on public attitudes, disability sport participation, health and mobility issues (e.g. Mahtani *et al.*, 2013; Darcy *et al.*, 2014; Gilbert and Schantz, 2015; Kerr and Howe, 2015; Li, 2015). For attitudes in the United Kingdom, one of the most significant indicators of possible changes in attitude was the television coverage. Channel 4 was awarded the UK broadcasting rights in 2010. They set about recruiting and training disabled presenters and reporters, building audiences and marketing the Games – increasing public awareness of the Paralympics from 16 per cent at the end of July to 77 per cent by the start of the Games. They provided sixteen hours of coverage per day and 500 hours across all platforms during the Games. A peak audience of 11.6 million viewers watched the Opening Ceremony, and 25 per cent of viewers watched the daily live coverage. Post-Games research suggested that the coverage changed perceptions of disabled people, encouraged viewers to see past disability to the excitement of sporting performances and more importantly provided viewers with the vocabulary to talk about disability (Channel 4, 2012).

Further post-Games research suggested a positive effect of the Paralympics on attitudes to disability. An Ipsos MORI survey at the end of the Games indicated that 81 per cent of those surveyed believed that disabled people were now viewed more positively by the British public as a result of the Paralympic Games. Further, in a National Statistics Opinion Survey the following year, 53 per cent agreed that the Paralympics had affected their own perceptions of disabled people positively (HMG/ML 2013, p. 71).

The raising of sport participation rates for disabled people was a key goal and the evidence suggested that rates increased leading up to the Games (from 15.1 per cent of those over sixteen in 2004–2005 to 18.3 per cent in 2011–2012) but has since drifted downwards to 17.2 per cent in 2014–2015 (Sport England, 2016). These figures mask complex mechanisms at work upon which a single event can hardly be expected to provide lasting impact. Ongoing and new initiatives that aim to provide this longer-term support include Sports Fest, Projectability, Deloitte Parasport, and a National Paralympic Day in early September (initiated in 2013).[7]

For London, there have been both hard and soft legacies accruing from the Games in the Queen Elizabeth Olympic Park. These include the accessible sport facilities themselves and projects to boost participation such as Motivate East set up in 2013. Apart from meeting the targets for creating jobs for disabled people in the run-up to the Games, post-Games there have been positions for the impaired in park facilities. In addition there have been events to showcase disabled sport and the arts. Regular festivals include the Anniversary Games, which includes Paralympians, and the Mayor of London's Liberty Festival for disability arts, which now takes place alongside National Paralympic Day. Together these events attracted 30,000 visitors in 2014 (HMG/ML, 2015, p. 85). The inaugural five-day Invictus Games, an international competition for wounded, injured and sick servicemen and women, was held in the Queen Elizabeth Olympic Park in September 2014 (Invictus Foundation, 2016). Although for some it raised questions about the 'entanglement of parasport performance; conceptions of injury, illness, and disability; and the logics of nation-state and military' (Blair and Johnson, 2022, p. 96), this venture successfully added a new sequence of ambulatory events hosted by cities worldwide.[8] It also again underlined the growing acceptance of parasport as a regular part of the sporting calendar.

Unsteady Progress

A bubbling sense of new visibility and significance of the Paralympics permeated thinking about the Games after London 2012, partly because of the manifest development of the Paralympic movement and substantially also due to the wider agendas of issues linked to disability sport and social inclusion (Di Parma *et al.*, 2016; Ferez *et al.*, 2020). The return of Olympic events to Russian soil was a good index of this trend. Unlike Moscow 1980 when the Organizing Committee had snubbed the Paralympic movement (see above), Sochi 2014 made conscious strides to accommodate the Paralympics and to do so in a barrier-free environment. In October 2008, the Russian State Duma passed new legislation embedding IOC and IPC standards in Russian law in anticipation of Sochi's hosting of the 2014 Winter Games (IPC, 2008). Attention was given, for example, to modifying the transport infrastructure and correcting gaps in the path system being devised for the Winter Olympics to provide full accessibility for disabled people (Bukarov, 2018, p. 522). In doing so, the organizers took steps to align the Paralympics not just with the principles enumerated by the IPC's Accessibility Guide (IPC, 2013*a*) but also with its sense of 'a value-added understanding that the increased accessibility of the host city becomes an infrastructural legacy post-game' (Darcy, 2017, p. 53). For instance, funding was made available for the Paralympic Training Centre, created for the Games, to operate sustainably at least for the medium-term as legacy after the Games (Bukarov, 2018, p. 528).

The promised results for Paralympic legacy were enthusiastically trumpeted in advance of the Games by the IPC (2014*a*), claiming, without citing specific evidence, that the positive example set by Sochi was being felt throughout Russia:

Approximately 200 Russian cities have already adopted Sochi's best practice example and created a barrier-free environment that facilitates the adoption of an active lifestyle by people with an impairment.

Somewhat less contentiously, the statistics did show that Sochi 2014 continued to develop the Games' media profile. Figures published by the IPC heralded Sochi 2014 as the most watched Paralympic Winter Games thus far, attracting a cumulative global audience of 2.1 billion people across fifty-five countries, with the 316,200 tickets sold being 86,200 more than at the previous Winter Games in Vancouver (IPC, 2015*a*, p. 14; cited in Goggin and Hutchins, 2017, p. 233).

Yet for all the positive features, a non-sporting event linked to the aftermath of the break-up of the Soviet Union indicated that priorities substantially remained much as before. Bearing in mind the established wisdom that the ambition to stage the Olympic Games remains as the prime motive for prospective organizers (Darcy and Appleby, 2011), it was notable that the Russian military intervention in the Crimea was delayed until 2 March 2014. That would seem to have been sufficiently long after the Closing Ceremony of the Winter Olympics so as not to distract attention away from the event in which the Russians had invested so much money and prestige (see chapter 3). The fact that this date was also five days before the Opening Ceremony of the Winter Paralympics seemed to matter rather less. *Prima facie* at least, there seemed little doubt about the relative global significance of the two events in the minds of the media-conscious Putin regime.

If Sochi demonstrated the continued prevalence of awkward truths, the next Paralympics at Rio de Janeiro 2016 would see a real crisis that saw the cancellation of the Games only narrowly avoided. Much though had started well. Identified as a potential economic powerhouse due to the prevailing high commodity prices for primary resources,[9] Brazil notably expressed its growing self-confidence through successfully gaining the nominations to host such hallmark events as the 2014 FIFA World Cup and the 2016 Olympic and Paralympic Games. To the general promise that the resulting events would be well-funded was added specific measures that advantaged the disabled sporting community. The passage of The Inclusion of People with Disabilities Act in 2015 had promised to eliminate accessibility barriers for disabled people across education, transport, housing, services, and sport. The Brazilian Paralympic Committee also received 37.04 per cent of federal lottery sport revenue – an increase from 15 per cent previously (IPC, 2015*b*). One of its key activities was then to administer the Brazilian Paralympic Training Centre. Established in Sao Paulo in 2013 and funded by the federal and Sao Paulo State governments, its immediate purpose was to improve the nation's prospects at its home Paralympics, providing training facilities in fifteen Paralympic disciplines. Subsequently it would have legacy use, including hosting athletic competitions in its own right.

During the preparation phase, however, an ever-worsening economic and political crisis within Brazil radically changed matters (see chapter 17). One of three key aims of the Games had been to challenge negative attitudes to disability and thereby assist social inclusion, but this largely evaporated in favour of simply prioritizing a sporting legacy for the Paralympics (Brittain and Mataruna Dos Santos, 2018, p. 539) – an outcome that, as argued below, is always difficult to identify. More specifically, budget cuts and woefully short ticket sales meant that the Rio Paralympics came close to cancellation a few weeks before their Opening Ceremony, with threats to reduce the numbers of events, withdraw transport links, and shut facilities (Rumsby, 2016). Promised travel grants for participating teams had not been paid.

In the event, a determined round of negotiations produced the release of sufficient federal funds for the Paralympics to go ahead, but not without major adjustments. These included closure of sites in the Deodoro cluster (which was effectively dismantled), cuts to transport, and additional reductions in numbers of both paid and volunteer labour (Brittain and Mataruna Dos Santos, 2018, pp. 543–544). Adjustments to prices and a concerted publicity campaign managed to drive up ticket sales to 2.3 million, which was second only to the 2.7 million tickets for London 2012 (see above) but much less than the 3.3 million to which the organizers once aspired. Global television audiences of 4.1 billion for the Rio Paralympics, with 500 hours of coverage across mainstream media platforms, broke all previous records (Thorpe, 2017). As a result the extent of the crisis was not readily apparent and, in the final analysis, could allow the Paralympic movement to claim that the Rio de Janeiro Games were a great success, not least because of the continuing existence of the Paralympic Training Centre. Nevertheless, the nature of the late cuts and the fact that last minute cancellation could be seriously contemplated again underlined the continuing differences in the relative standings of the Olympics and Paralympics in the eyes of the host city's organizers (Brittain and Mataruna Dos Santos, 2018, p. 548).

The choice of PyeongChang in South Korea for 2018 saw the Games return to the country where, thirty years previously at Seoul, the Paralympics had made their breakthrough in terms of being the constant companion event to the Olympics (Park and Ok, 2018). On this occasion, the Paralympic community were spared the cliffhanging drama of cancellation threats that characterized the weeks immediately prior to Rio de Janeiro 2016. The Games attracted record participation with 567 athletes from forty-nine delegations, competing in eighty medal events across six sports. Spectator attendance and media coverage also recorded the highest levels in Paralympic history. Issues of legacy, however, provide a less positive picture. At the bid stage and during preparation, there were well-developed legacy plans that served as the target for post-Games adjustment. For the Paralympics these revolved around the 'Actualizing the Dream' strategy. Introduced with government funding in 2011 prior to winning the bid, 'Actualizing the Dream' comprised thirteen programmes under four different streams. These aimed at raising public awareness of the Games, increasing participation in para-sport, improving the profile of the Paralympic movement, and changing public awareness of disability (PyeongChang 2018, 2016). However, as with the Olympics, few of the formal legacy plans – especially those involving para-sport development and enhancement of sporting infrastructure – went ahead due to a mixture of organizational, funding, and political problems (see chapter 3). Other potential aspects of intangible legacy from PyeongChang 2018, particularly in the area of cultural acceptance and attitudinal change, remained difficult to pinpoint with any accuracy.

The evidence of the Paralympics held between 2014 and 2018 showed again the extent that the Games were still in the sway of external circumstances. That conclusion was amply compounded by the conditions surrounding Tokyo 2020 that, as noted elsewhere in this volume (see chapters 1 and 18), saw the COVID-19 pandemic cause a year's postponement of both Olympics and Paralympics and required their staging under strict testing and isolation conditions (figure 5.5). When it came to it, the Paralympics proceeded effectively as a televisual event. Globally the Tokyo 2020 Summer Paralympic Games had 4.25 billion viewers, continuing the upward trend

Figure 5.5. The Women's Wheelchair Marathon, staged through the city's streets, gives the general public a rare opportunity to view Paralympic events live at Tokyo 2020. (*Source*: CC Hetarllen Mumriken)

from 3.8 billion for the 2012 London Paralympic Games and 4.1 billion for Rio de Janeiro. To some extent, however, the proliferation of devoted internet channels and diffusion of enhanced information technology competencies due to the pandemic and lockdowns may have influenced these figures. Indeed the comparative figures for the Paralympics were considerably better than the viewing figures for the Olympics which, even allowing for time zone problems, were deemed to be disappointing in most regional markets (Berkeley, 2022*a*).

Tokyo, the city that was the first to host two Summer Paralympics, extended its respectful approach to the legacy of the Games, stressing the credentials of the Paralympics as a co-equal part of the occasion. The two key venue clusters, for example, are to be lastingly known as the Ariake Olympic and Paralympic Park and the Musashino Forest Olympic and Paralympic Park. Plaques, symbols, and murals will be physical expressions of Paralympic as well as Olympic memory in the urban environment (IPC, 2022). A similar inclusive approach was taken by the key early document on legacy, the 'Tokyo 2020 Action and Legacy Plan 2016' (TOCOPG, 2016). The approach throughout is commendably integrated. Paralympic legacy was framed around five 'pillars' – a term that echoes the vocabulary of the Olympic Charter. These were: sport and health; urban planning and sustainability; culture and education; economy and technology; and recovery from the Great Eastern Earthquake of 2011. At one level, to do so implies the equality of the two movements and supports one of the Report's key aims of 'placing particular emphasis on promoting awareness of and interest in the Paralympic Games' (*ibid.*, p. 10). Yet, at another level, the smaller Paralympics, which has relatively little urban impact in its own right and drives little of the key decision-making, gets somewhat lost in such legacy formulations.

When considering the course of debate over the Paralympic legacy, it is worth recalling that Tokyo 2020 was also the first Games to have had the opportunity to develop its legacy proposals from the outset in line with the IPC's Handbook (IPC, 2013*a*), which was introduced in 2013. Somewhat remarkably given that the IPC is a sports organization with a mission to 'enable Paralympic athletes to achieve sporting excellence and inspire and excite the world', only the second of the four broad legacy categories that were listed were exclusively about sport (*ibid.*, p. 37):

◆ Accessible infrastructure in sport facilities and in the overall urban development;

◆ Development of sport structures/organizations for people with an impairment, from grassroots to elite level;

◆   Attitudinal changes in the perception of the position and the capabilities of persons with an impairment as well as in the self-esteem of the people with a disability;

◆   Opportunities for people with an impairment to become fully integrated into social living and to reach their full potential in aspects of life beyond sports.

Measured against these criteria, the results thus far have been, at best, patchy (Kirakosyan, 2022). Certainly, performance with regard to the relatively small changes necessary in the built environment has achieved results that are better than many predecessors or potential successors. Tokyo had ensured that more than 95 per cent of metro stations were step-free in 2020. That compares with around a quarter of the stations on the London underground for 2012 and what is likely to be no more than 10 per cent in Paris for the 2024 Games (Ataman and Laborie, 2023). Greater difficulty, however, was found for those goals that reflect conditions found in the wider society. For instance, while good progress was made in integrating the major organizations responsible for the 2020 Games, rather less success was reported in achieving integration between disabled and non-disabled groups within the major Japanese sports federations (Ogura, 2018, p. 598). Even greater challenges have been encountered in finding ways to promote 'barrier-freedom in … the spiritual sense' as well as the physical 'in the minds of the general public' (*Ibid*., p. 597). Cultural values and societal norms do not change that quickly. In an analysis based on interviews, Brittain (2022) explored the high and explicit expectations of change that were attached to the 2020 project. After a somewhat discouraging picture of the treatment of disabled people that is still prevalent in Japan, he highlighted:

> a key issue when trying to plan for Paralympic legacies for disabled people living in the host city – that of non-disabled people assuming they know what is best for disabled people or implementing changes that are the easiest and most cost effective, so that they can appear to have made an effort towards change without actually changing too much. (*Ibid.*, p. 59)

Conclusion

That observation is not intended to single out Japanese society for criticism or to minimize the progress that has been made by the Paralympic movement. In the first place, other host societies have performed little better and often worse. French disability activists, for example, have castigated attitudes that disabled people perceive 'as social and medical cases, they are not considered as citizens' (Ataman and Laborie, 2023). Secondly, the current

Paralympic Games show remarkable development from the first competition between 130 British and Dutch athletes in 1952 to the position that they now occupy. Notwithstanding a chequered history and the characteristic dissonance between bid promises and final realities, the Paralympic Games have spread geographically, have moved into new sports, have encompassed a wider range of disabilities, and have helped give credence to the belief that access to sport is available to all. In the early years, the Paralympics went to places best able to accommodate athletes with disability and organizers worked round any shortcomings in the facilities or the wider city. Once the Paralympics started sharing host cities with the Summer Games in 1988 and the Winter Games in 1992, athletes were able to enjoy environments designed principally for the Olympics but adapted for Paralympic use. As the Games came progressively closer to the heart of the Olympic movement, the disabled community have been accommodated, figuratively and literally, within the planning, design, cultural, and educational programmes of Olympic cities.

All these are positive developments. However, it does not follow that the two festivals receive equal treatment throughout the planning and consultation stages, for it is still the Olympics that drives the desire to host the Games and the legacy agenda. For the Olympics, to date physical ('hard') legacy has generally been an important part of the equation. For the Paralympics, that is less significant than the attention focused on soft legacy and issues of access and discriminatory practices. When considered in relation to an Olympic host city at one point in time, the Paralympics have the potential to provide a demonstration effect that may well have implications for that city and wider host society – a property loudly heralded whenever possible by the IPC and various of its host cities. However, it can be argued that such considerations perhaps place a disproportionate responsibility on sport to drive disability agendas in wider society. Paralympic legacy, like any other form of legacy, can only materialize if it is nurtured, managed and funded in the longer term.

Notes

1. Nomenclature has varied. Other terms used in the 1940s and 1950s included 'Paraolympics' and 'Paraplegic Games' (Brittain, 2010, p. 15). The first use of the term Paralympic was traced by Brittain to the *Bucks Advertiser and Aylesbury News* in 1953. He also has found a number of newspapers from the *New York Times* to the Dublin *Evening Herald* using the term in 1960 (Brittain, 2008, pp. 21, 247).

2. Les Autres athletes have 'locomotor conditions such as Arthrogryposis, Arthrosis, cerebral palsy (some types), spinal cord conditions (e.g. polio), multiple sclerosis and muscular dystrophy [and] are allowed to participate in events under the Les Autres classification. Les Autres also incorporates dwarf athletes under its classification. The locomotor conditions may be congenital or as a result of an injury or accident' (BALASA, 2007).

3.   The subsequent inclusion of INAS-FID athletes in the Paralympic Games between 1996 and 2000 was ended abruptly after an investigation showed that ten of the twelve Spanish basketball team were not intellectually disabled. After two years of negotiations between INAS-FID and the IPC, the IPC General Council voted in November 2009 to admit athletes for the London 2012 Games in four disciplines: athletics, swimming, rowing, and table tennis. The aim was to progress further with inclusion in Sochi 2014 and extend the Rio de Janeiro participation to basketball and futsal (a form of indoor football). For a full discussion of the issues involved, see *inter alia* Howe (2008), Bailey (2008), Cashman and Darcy (2008*a*, 2008*b*) and Brittain (2010).

4.   'Boccia' is similar to petanque (French bowls) played individually or as a team game by people with cerebral palsy and other locomotor disabilities. 'Goalball' is a three-a-side gymnasium team game for the blind or visually impaired played on a special court of the same size as that used for volleyball. It involves trying to propel a heavy sound-enhanced ball past the backline of the opponents' half of the court.

5.   For more general thinking on planning and disability, see Imrie (1996), Gleeson (2001) and McCann (2005).

6.   See the Prime Minister's Strategy Unit's *Improving the Life Chances of Disabled People: Final Report* published January 2005, which sets out the strategy for independent living, support for families of young disabled children, transition to adulthood, support and incentives for getting and staying in employment (PMSU, 2005).

7.   For more on these initiatives, see BPA (2015).

8.   Subsequently celebrated at Orlando (2016) and Sydney (2018), and then, after an interruption caused by the COVID-19 pandemic, at The Hague (2022) and Düsseldorf (2023).

9.   This was reflected particularly by the inclusion of Brazil in the informal grouping known as the BRICS nations. The view circulated, particularly in the wake of the subprime banking crisis of 2008–2009, that Brazil, Russia, India, China and latterly South Africa would be likely to be the economic powerhouses of the future (Armijo, 2007).

PART 2

PLANNING AND MANAGEMENT

Chapter 6

OLYMPIC FINANCE

Holger Preuss

Each Olympic Games has wanted to be 'The best games ever!'. To host the most successful Games of all time has always been the unwritten aim of each organizer, but how can we measure this success? Should we refer to the financial, social, organizational, or sporting success? In addition, from whose perspective shall we measure the success – that of politicians, the construction industry, the medallists, the spectators, the human rights organizations, the citizens or only the International Olympic Committee (IOC) members? The question of who the real winners are remains open, but the fact remains that various stakeholder groups will benefit differently from hosting the Games and that, at each new edition of the Games, the benefits will be distributed differently.

This chapter provides an overview of the groups who benefit from staging the Olympic Games and identifies those that benefit most noticeably. The information is important because it is the basis on which decisions must be made about who should be involved in the Games, how much should be spent, and who will be held ethically responsible for the Games and their economic, environmental, and social outcomes. Many stakeholders, of course, are negatively affected by the Games, but they are not the topic of this chapter.

How much and which stakeholders benefit depends on a city's motives for hosting the Games, because the motive leads the distribution and amount of money invested. Table 6.1 shows that the host cities' aims, and consequently the impact on the stakeholders, vary widely. The primary goal of Los Angeles 2028, for example, is to prove that the Games can be organized without either any new construction or with a deficit. To do this, the event organizers will use the existing infrastructure. Barcelona 1992, on the other hand, made urban renewal the highest priority (Millet, 1995) and thus invested heavily in new infrastructure. Beijing 2008 had yet another set of priorities: it aimed to demonstrate China's increasing economic potential in what was regarded at that time as the beginning of a new world order and

Table 6.1. Motives for applying to host the Olympic Games. (*Source*: Adapted from Preuss (2015) and respective webpages of future hosts)

Motive for Applying	Examples of Host Cities with this Objective
Image enhancement	Munich 1972, Korea 1988, Sydney 2000, Beijing 2008
Urban development	Munich 1972, Montreal 1976, Seoul 1988, Barcelona 1992, Athens 2004, Turin 2006, Beijing 2008, London 2012; Sochi 2014, Rio 2016, Paris 2024
Regional Development	Paris 2024, Milan/Cortina 2026, Brisbane 2032
Demonstrating economic power	Berlin 1936, Tokyo 1964, Munich 1972, Seoul 1988, Beijing 2008; Sochi 2014
Demonstrating a political system	Berlin 1936, Moscow 1980, Los Angeles 1984
Increasing tourism	Innsbruck 1976, Barcelona 1992, Sydney 2000, Athens 2004, Sochi 2014, PyeongChang 2018, Brisbane 2032
Increasing city's importance in host country	Barcelona 1992, Atlanta 1996, Nagano 1998, Beijing 2008, Sochi 2014
Increasing inward investment	Grenoble 1968, Lillehammer 1994, Barcelona 1992, Atlanta 1996, Nagano 1998, Sochi 2014
Social impact of sport	Paris 2024, Los Angeles 2028, Brisbane 2032
Increasing domestic political stability and self-confidence	Seoul 1988, Beijing 2008, Sochi 2014
Sport structure development	Sochi 2014, PyeongChang 2018, Brisbane 2032

to foster patriotism among the Chinese people. The Games following Paris 2024 all put their focus mainly on the social impact.

The Olympic Games, being a mega-event, has to be financed by many stakeholder groups (Preuss *et al.*, 2019). Its costs and benefits cannot simply be assigned to certain target groups and often the group paying for the Games is not the one with the largest benefit. Hosting this event has numerous positive and negative external effects – almost the entire country is affected by the Games on grounds of efficiency and opportunity costs (Preuss, 2009). This chapter discusses 'profit', in the broad sense of a benefit to society. This profit is determined not only by the stakeholders that contribute directly to the economic benefits of the Olympic Games, but also by the stakeholders who primarily receive the benefits.

The stakeholder approach selected (Freeman and McVea, 2001) explains that the purpose in organizing the Olympic Games is not only that of creating value for the Olympic Family (the International Olympic Committee [IOC], National Olympic Committees [NOCs] and International Sports Federations [IFs]), but also for external groups (such as viewers, citizens, entrepreneurs, and politicians). This chapter intentionally dissociates itself from the shareholder value approach (Bea, 1997), because observation of the Olympic Family's financial gains reflects only a part of the benefit of such global and, broadly, public events. Although not all stakeholder groups have the same importance for the IOC, the latter generally does not want any influential interest group to bear higher financial burdens by hosting the Games, because that may cause an undesirable opposition to the Olympic Games.

A stakeholder is someone who has certain claims towards an organization (as here the IOC and Organizing Committee). From a managerial point of view, stakeholders are persons or groups that initiate certain claims on the organization regardless of whether these are legally sound. Stakeholders, then, are seen as 'interest groups' who want to persuade an organization to consider their interests. In terms of the Olympic Games these include, among others, environmental or anti-globalization groups (Lenskyj, 1996, 2000, 2002). On these grounds, the IOC and the Organizing Committee of the Olympic Games (OCOG) are regarded as coordinating bodies that try to meet the diverse requirements and sometimes conflicting interests of various claimants. The Olympic Organization is a social entity that wants, and should want, to satisfy the demands of diverse social groups.

Figure 6.1 shows a selection of Olympic Games stakeholders, without claiming to be exhaustive. Shareholders are distinguished from stakeholders. The main shareholders involved in the Olympic Games are the IOC with its members, who constitute the IOC sessions (the General Assembly). In contrast to the shareholders, the stakeholders consist of wider groups, such as the employees of the IOC, the NOCs and IFs, the athletes, the audience, the TV broadcasters, the sponsors, the suppliers, and the 'public' (represented by state institutions). A superficial consideration reveals that

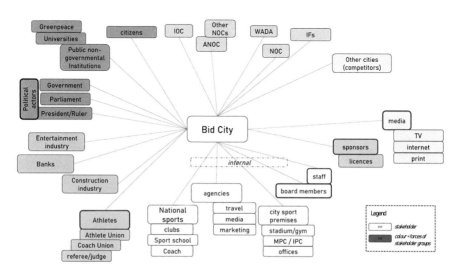

Figure 6.1. Stakeholder landscape for bid cities. (*Source*: Adapted from Preuss *et al.*, 2022, p. 25)

the interests of the stakeholders are quite different and often conflicting. In general, the shareholder commits to high profitability and wants to keep the power of his or her organization (here the IOC) by limiting the risk. In contrast, stakeholders as employees claim security of their workplace, pleasant working conditions and high wages. Athletes, another stakeholder group, want to ensure the best training conditions, prize money, voting power, concentrated support, and perfectly organized competitions. The spectators desire a vast, entertaining event with decent pricing and great competition; the broadcasters' aim is a product with high TV ratings; the sponsors claim the highest output for their advertising campaigns; the suppliers seek good business based on reliable and financially strong customers.

Finally, the public (the State) is interested in secure, entertaining, socially inclusive, environmentally friendly, and remarkable events that satisfy the population. These events, especially for the public, should also be inexpensive, and provide economic and social sustainability. Moreover, they should foster the development of the local and regional infrastructure, increase tax revenues, create additional jobs, and result in a positive image of the city. The dispute over alleged conflicts of interest between shareholders and stakeholders in the past often escalated into an emotional debate. In particular, when the stakeholders accuse the shareholders of unilateral maximization of material values, it is often spoken of as 'over-commercialization' in relation to the Olympic Games which frequently results in a greater demand from stakeholders benefitting of the Games (athletes, NOCs, IFs, host cities and other organizations). However more money also increases the potential for corruption. The counterargument of the shareholders is that their main concern is to offer the best possible organization of the Games to the athletes, citizens, and spectators. That is also the reason why the IOC initiated the Youth Olympic Games in 2010 to revive the values of the Olympic Movement and to make it more attractive to the younger generation.

The Development of the Games: An Economic Overview

Economic considerations have always been significant in the history of the modern Olympic Games. Dividing it into five periods, two aspects prevail: the growing importance of new markets and the changing patterns of the groups who profit by hosting the Games.

The first period, 1896–1968 was characterized by financial problems of the OCOG. In 1896, the first Games were held in Athens at a time when Greece had just declared bankruptcy. The staging of the Games was financially secured by the generosity of prosperous Greeks living abroad (Georgiardis, 2000). After the first five Olympic Games were hosted – all of them having major financial problems – Baron Pierre de Coubertin concluded that 'the question is not whether they [the Games] will be held but how they will be held, and at whose expense' (Coubertin, 1913, p. 183). Remarkably, during this first period of the Games, many new funding sources were developed to fulfil the considerable financial responsibilities; some have only been used for one Games while others developed into regularly used sources of finance, as in the case of postage stamps (Landry and Yerles, 1996, pp. 183–187).

In the second period, 1969–1980, the pressure of developing further financing sources increased due to the ongoing growth of the Olympic Games. Although private financing sources started to materialize, such as the sale of television broadcasting and sponsoring rights, the main source of income for the OCOG remained public subsidies. Munich 1972 was still predominatly financed by the public sector. If one excludes the OCOG's own revenue (approximately 19 per cent), the Games were financed by special funding from the government from surcharges for stamps, mintage and a lottery (50 per cent), and by tax revenues from the government, federal state and city (approximately 31 per cent). The deficit that occurred at the end of the Games was immense but was covered by the national government (50 per cent), the federal state of Bavaria (25 per cent), and 25 per cent by the cities of Munich and Kiel (Organizing Committee, 1972, pp. 53–54). For the Games in 1976, Canada did not provide financial backing to the city of Montreal. Due to a 'written guarantee that the government would not be called upon to absorb the deficit nor to assume interim financing for organization' (Organizing Committee, 1976, p. 55), the OCOG – supported only by the city of Montreal – had to finance the Games themselves. Ultimately, only 5 per cent of the necessary resources had been generated by sources from the private sector. The remaining 95 per cent was covered by special financing arrangements and by the public sector (*ibid.*, p. 59). The deficit was exclusively covered by the city of Montreal, the official guarantor. Montreal's taxpayers were paying the Olympic debt until 2006, ultimately in the form of a special tobacco tax. However, it should be stressed that the deficit was not the result of the host's low revenue in the first place but based on huge investments in the infrastructure, mismanagement, strikes on construction sites, and high fluctuations of currency exchange rates. As a result of Montreal's financial burdens other cities became reluctant to apply to host the next Games (in 1984) leaving the future undecided (Commission of Inquiry, 1977, vol. 1, p. 314). The cost of hosting the Olympic Games appeared no longer to be acceptable. Thus, there was a declining interest in bidding in this period.

Regarding Moscow 1980, no reliable information is available about finance, though it can be assumed that these Games were mainly financed by the state given the Soviet Union's intention to plead for the superiority of the communist system (Ueberroth *et al.*, 1986, pp. 55–59). Furthermore, in this period, the state-funded 'amateurs' of the Soviet bloc led the acting IOC

President Lord Killanin to connect the status of 'amateurs' in sport with the financing of the Games: 'The word amateur unfortunately no longer refers to a lover of sports but, possibly, a lack of proficiency' (Killanin, 1983, p. 43).

The third period, 1981–1996, started with the presidency of J.A. Samaranch. At the beginning of this period, the Olympic Games opened up to professional athletes in almost all sports. This was possible because the term 'amateur' was removed from the Olympic Charter at the end of Killanin's presidency. This change has contributed to the continuous and stable increase in revenue from the sale of sponsorships and media rights. The development of emerging markets and companies that operate globally opened the Games for sponsoring agreements worth millions of dollars. In addition, the pressure to finance the Games without public resources (IOC, 1978) led to the real beginning of commercializing the Olympic Games. Previously, sponsoring was understood as solely ensuring the visibility of company logos and brands. Henceforth, the IOC expected the sponsors to embrace a stronger partnership with the Olympic Movement, which allowed the sponsors broader advertising opportunities. As of 1984, the prospects of high marketing revenues increased the interest of cities to host Olympic Games. This fundamental change contributed to the financial independence of the Olympic Movement. Finally, it ensured the ending of the political crises and financial shortfalls that had beset the Olympic Games in the 1970s and 1980s (Hoberman, 1986).

The first Games of this period took place in Los Angeles in 1984. After the city's unsuccessful bid to host the 1976 and 1980 Olympic Games, there were no candidates other than Los Angeles to be elected at the IOC session in 1978. To cover the costs of the city's security, transportation, and other services, the OCOG took a surcharge of 0.5 per cent on hotel tax and 6 per cent on ticket sales (Ueberroth et al., 1986, pp. 121–122). The lack of other candidates and the absence of public subsidies enabled the OCOG to enforce contractual terms and conditions with the IOC, to which the latter would not have agreed had there been alternative candidates (Hall, 1992, pp. 159; Reich, 1986, p. 24; Ueberroth et al., 1986, p. 53). After long negotiations, the Olympic Charter was amended and the city of Los Angeles was allowed to disregard some financial requirements, which were usually associated with the organization of the Games. These Games were, for example, the first in history that were not associated with public stakeholders in the host city and the first fully financed by the private sector (Preuss et al., 2019). Therefore, it is not surprising that these Olympic Games did not leave any large physical Olympic legacy since there was little investment in urban infrastructure and sports facilities. The total costs of the Olympic Games were low and covered by the revenue of the OCOG. Moreover, there was an official surplus that was divided between the Olympic Committee of the United States (USOC), the Amateur Athletic Foundation, and the national institutions in order to support Olympic sport (Taylor and Gratton, 1988, p. 34). The Olympic Games in Los Angeles mark the turnaround from public funding to private financing.

Nevertheless, funding by the public sector remained important, particularly as nations other than the United States did not have the same potential for commercial financing. The growth of the Olympic Games and, above all, the promotion of national interests became the incentives to organize the Games (see table 6.1). This resulted in an increased involvement of governments. For instance, South Korea was very interested to use the Olympic Games in Seoul 1988 to display the rapid economic growth of the country globally, enhance its status in international sports, and improve diplomatic relations with Communist and non-aligned movement states. In addition, the government wanted to open the country for tourism and Korean exports (Park, 1991, pp. 2–5). However, 53 per cent of the costs of the Olympic Games were covered by the public sector (Kim *et al.*, 1989, p. 42), so that the alleged surplus of around $192 million needs to be treated with caution (Hill, 1992, p. 93).

Among others, the authorities in Barcelona took advantage of the Olympic Games to implement political aims. The re-urbanization of the city was intended to allow it to compete with Madrid as an internationally recognized industrial and tourist location. These goals justified the considerable governmental investments, and compensated for the disregard of long-term investments in socially meaningful areas like leisure, culture, sport, and transport (Millet, 1995, p. 191). Despite the public subsidies of $7 billion, the proportion of private funding increased due to marketing revenues of 38 per cent. The official revenue of the OCOG was low at $3.3 million (Brunet, 1993, p. 113; also Brunet, 1995). The increasing costs of the sponsors and television channels led to a situation in which the Winter Olympics would no longer be organized in the same year as the Summer Games. The goal was to create stronger attention on the Olympic Movement by spreading the budgets over several years. This was the main reason for shifting the Winter Olympic Games by a two-yearly alternation with the Summer Olympics starting in 1994.

As in the Los Angeles Games, the citizens of Atlanta rejected any financial obligation for the city from the 1996 Olympic Games. The OCOG had to rely mainly on the private sector, which developed the commercialization of the Olympic Games further. Therefore, at that time, the 1996 Atlanta Olympics counted as the most commercialized Games. Shortly after awarding the Games to Atlanta, the IOC President Samaranch stated that the commercialization of the Games helped to achieve the financial independence of the Olympic Movement. On the other hand, he warned against further commercialization. He proclaimed that the sport should be able to determine its own fate rather than being mainly directed by the interests of the sponsors (Samaranch, 1992). Nevertheless, compared to Seoul and Barcelona, the Olympic Games in 1996 had a very low budget with expenditures of $2.2 billion (ACOG, 1998, p. 222; French and Disher, 1997, p. 384). The city's infrastructure hardly changed, although a few new sport venues had been built. After the Olympic Games, the venues were adjusted to fit the necessities of the city's population and universities. Many establishments were modified by reducing the seating capacities, dismantling temporary venues, or moving them to different locations as in the case of the velodrome. With the exception of the publicly funded rowing course in Cumming (Georgia), all sports facilities were financed by the OCOG. The result was that the Games did not generate any surplus revenues. This counteracted the original intention of the IOC because Atlanta was chosen over Athens to host the 'Centennial Games' in the hope that the profits would have supported the Olympic Movement. Instead, the OCOG used it for financing Olympic facilities, in particular the Olympic Stadium. This must be seen as an ambivalent act as it became the ballpark of the Atlanta Braves immediately after the Olympics.

The fourth period, 1997–2016, began with the Olympics in Nagano 1998 and Sydney 2000 and ends with Rio de Janeiro 2016. After the negative experiences with Atlanta's OCOG, which was independently managed by the city, this period is characterized by stronger public financing. From this time onwards, the number of state guarantees requested by the IOC has been extended and each country is required to organize the Games in close cooperation with the OCOG. Key responsibilities for both stakeholder groups were defined. For the first time, the OCOG for Sydney 2000 had simply to organize the Olympic Games, while the state-run Olympic Co-ordination Authority was responsible for the development of infrastructure. The investments for the latter were approximately $1 billion (NSW Government, 2001, p. 6.5). The cost of the Games in Sydney was $4.8 billion (Audit Office, 1999, pp. 59, 161, 156, 157).

Based upon the Sydney model, Athens 2004 separated the organization of the Games from the provision of the necessary infrastructure. Due to massive investments in transport infrastructure, in security and (oversized) sports facilities, these Games were by then the most expensive. The information on the true costs of the Games vary greatly as in some cases non-Olympic projects such as the construction of the new airport have also been included in the 'Olympic costs'. The total expenditure of the OCOG was $2.4 billion whereas the infrastructure costs added $2.5–5 billion depending on what is included (ATHOC, 2005, p. 22; Preuss *et al.*, 2019, p. 66).

The development of infrastructure and sports venues for Beijing 2008 was also organized by public authorities. The Chinese central government and the Beijing municipality thus covered the expenses. The costs for the OCOG were around $2.8 billion in line with the expenses of former

Olympics. Nevertheless, the People's Republic of China initiated considerable infrastructure projects including projects to improve air quality and energy supply so that the estimated 'Olympic costs' came to $45 billion. The city, the region and the nation had carmarked a total investment of $33.7 billion before the Games but only $3.4 billion for building the Olympic venues (Lin, 2004; Preuss *et al.*, 2019, p. 80).

The cost of Vancouver 2010 was shared by three levels of government, Olympic and Paralympic sponsors, and the (VANOC). The city and VANOC were responsible for key aspects of the Games that took place in British Columbia (BC). The only exception was the Olympic Village, which was largely funded by the City of Vancouver (VANOC, 2010). The OCOG budget was C$2.1 billion (Preuss *et al.*, 2019, p. 84).

London 2012 intended to develop the east side of the city by hosting the Olympic Games. Money for the development of the necessary infrastructure came from public funds. New to this approach was that in the course of preparing for the Games priority was given to the long-term sustainability of investment. By following this strategy, redundant infrastructural projects were to be avoided. The Olympic Delivery Authority (ODA) was established in April 2006 by the London Olympic and Paralympic Games Act 2006 and was responsible for building the permanent venues and infrastructure needed for the Games (ODA, 2015). Overall, the public funding of the Games was £9,298 million (National Audit Office, 2012, p. 22), including all work on infrastructure, whereas in the post-Games period, the revenues from the sale of land in the Olympic Park or the sale of the Olympic Village reduced this funding severely (DCMS, 2012*a*, p. 16).

Information about the finance of Sochi 2014 is difficult to find (Preuss *et al.* 2019, p. 101) but, as for all Games in this period, the construction of venues and infrastructure was independent from the OCOG. The investment was very high as the entire city was restructured and many venues were built as high-performance winter sport facilities for their post-Games use. The financing system applied for Sochi was the complete opposite to Salt Lake City (*ibid.*). While Salt Lake City tried to use almost no public money to finance the sports venues, Sochi was mostly financed by public funds, and a large part of the cost of venues was significantly more expensive than actually planned.

Rio de Janeiro 2016 marks the end of this period as IOC president Thomas Bach launched *Agenda 2020* and later *2020+5*. This transformed the Games organization as the costs were reduced, legacy became more important, the concept of short distances between venues ended, and oversized and unnecessary infrastructure was avoided. Rio had already experienced several changes in master planning after the award of the Games. The main changes in relation to the original budget were among others (*a*) the inclusion of four new sports (golf, rugby, para-canoe and para-triathlon);

(*b*) new technologies; (*c*) Games security; and (*d*) spending on usage and retrofitting of the Olympic Village. There were protests over costs; while political unrest, a recession and environmental concerns drew attention to the vast construction undertaking, the cost of which made up a large portion of the overall Rio Games budget. All this marks the end of this period.

The fifth period started with PyeongChang and Tokyo. These Games experienced the first changes under Agenda 2020, but Paris 2024 will experience the first comprehensive impact of these changes. Dubinsky (2022) added an important observation in that Tokyo 2020 is the first in a series of the Games so far awarded that were either elected or hosted in an unprecedented way. Tokyo 2020 was the first postponed Olympic Games, almost without spectators and with restrictions on athletes and others regulated in a playbook (*ibid.*, TOCOPG, 2021). The Games were held under a state of emergency, and as the coronavirus was not being contained, Japanese people and Tokyo residents repeatedly showed their objection to the Games in a variety of surveys (Kuhn, 2021). The following Games in 2024 in Paris and 2028 in Los Angeles were awarded together for the first time after multiple cities withdrew from the 2024 bid due to lack of local or governmental support (Preuss *et al.*, 2020; Dubinsky, 2019). Thereafter, under Agenda 2020 and the New Norm, bidding regulations changed from competing bids to a consultancy bidding process with candidate cities. Under this new way of bidding, the IOC session in 2021 awarded the 2032 Olympic Games to Brisbane. Overall, as shown in figure 6.2, we can see that the number of bidding cities decreased in periods 4 and 5.

For more than forty years, commercialization has had a significant influence on the Olympic Movement. The danger of dependency on

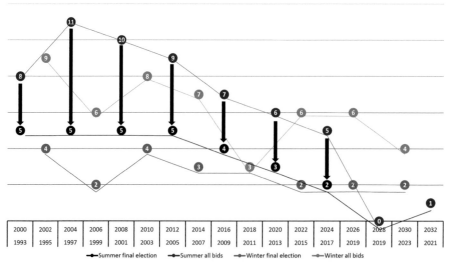

Figure 6.2. Number of bid cities and bid cities at final selection from 1993 to 2021. (*Sources*: Data from www.gamebids.com)

sponsors has forced the IOC to re-evaluate these relations. It tries, on the one hand, to avoid over-commercialization and, on the other hand, to intensify the promotion of Olympic Ideals. The IOC is doing this by instructing the sponsors how to make use of the Olympic Ideals in regards to commercialization without causing harm to the values upon which they are based. For this reason, Jacques Rogge, the former IOC President, launched the Youth Olympic Games and Thomas Bach the Agenda 2020+5. Similarly, the IOC intended to sign long-term contracts with sponsors and media corporations in order to strengthen the sense of responsibility towards the 'Olympic' brand, and chose sponsors that not only give money but also add value and services to the Olympic Games.

The fifth period started with financial security even though the COVID-19 pandemic caused considerable difficulties. The IOC has taken control of the negotiations with the sponsors and broadcasters while the marketing of the Olympic Games is run completely in-house. The power of the IOC has increased compared with the hosts, while the financial risk for the bidding cities has been reduced because the IOC provides a guaranteed IOC contribution of almost $2 billion for the host cities even before the selection of the future host city has been made.

Selected Winners through Hosting the Olympic Games

The range of those who benefit from the Olympic Games is large and varies from one host city to another. In this section, the stakeholders considered are those that are involved in the financing and/or organization of the Games. Table 6.2, which focuses on their interests, also necessarily considers the socio-cultural, political, and economic background of each host nation. However, it should be noted that the interests listed in table 6.2 relate solely to recurring patterns. They do not allow for generalization of the existing socio-cultural, political, historical, and economic characteristics and conditions of the individual host country.

IOC Members

The first stakeholder group are the IOC members. Their collective desire is to award the Games to cities that are able to develop them in the best way possible and secure their future through excellent organization. Successful Games will strengthen the power of the IOC and its members. This is essential, as one has to be aware that the IOC is the rights holder of just four products, the Olympic Games, Olympic Winter Games and the Youth Olympic Games and its winter edition. None are organized by the IOC itself but by host cities. Thus, it becomes a matter of fact that the more cities that bid to host Olympic Games in the future, the higher will be the commitment

Table 6.2. Stakeholders which profited from the Olympic Games. (*Source*: Adapted and extended from Preuss, 2005, pp. 421–422)

Stakeholders	Interest
IOC-members	Organization of best possible Games to maintain power/cultural or geographical location of Games; Bring Agenda 2020 in action
Host country	Improvement of international relations; Soft power; Nation building and national pride; Opportunity to show the world the changes in their own country (e.g. modernization)
Host city and its politicians	Increase tourism; Become a 'global city' and thus get more attention compared to similar large cities or receive more attention from the capital; Economic impact; Positive legacies; Accelerated urban development; Career opportunities and additional employment
Construction industry/Tourism industry	Additional demand for tourism and construction; Better chance in competing for international tourists and projects
Sponsors	Improved relations with customers, suppliers, partners, and employees; Global recognition; Image enhancement
Media Groups/ Networks	Increased ratings and more lucrative sales of advertising time; Data collection; Customer relations
NOCs	Additional funding through joint marketing programme and profit shares from OCOG (if the NOC belongs to the host country); Funding through the IOC sale of TOP marketing programme; Olympic Solidarity funding for NOCs; Sport promotion and funding from national governments
IFs	Funding through the IOC's sale of media rights

of the candidates competing with each other. Even though the competition in an auction-like bidding process increased the quality of the Games, at the end there are many losers and disappointed cities. This has caused refusals to bid again. Therefore, according to Agenda 2020 and the New Norm, the IOC changed its bidding process and now secures the quality of the bid by targeted dialogue. That reduced the costs of bidding significantly by ensuring that only well-suited cities bid. However, at the end of the process it is still the simple majority of votes among all IOC members that decide the next host. Among the IOC members there are sub-groups with different cultural, political, and geographical backgrounds whose interests play a role in the bidding process, as cultural studies prove that the phenomenon of cultural belonging is the reason that IOC members favour certain candidate cities and vote for them (Persson, 2000, pp. 157–161; Preuss, 2000).

Host Country

Government officials of the host country comprise another winning stakeholder. The IOC makes the state's involvement in financing all infrastructure necessary to stage the Olympic Games a requirement. All Games revenues have solely to be used for the organization of the Games, which so far has ensured that all Organizing Committees managed a more or less balanced account. Thus, the more Olympic-specific venue construction is needed, the more taxpayers' money is used, which is justified if there is an envisaged legacy for each venue.

The public sector directly and indirectly benefits from the Games. Directly, because the economic growth and infrastructure development of the Olympic city leads to additional employment and increased income. The stimulus, additional investments and timetable pressure of the Games as well as their global presence often allow for developments, which without an upcoming Olympics, would have been politically difficult to stimulate. Indirectly, the host country can benefit by improving its worldwide reputation and soft power through a perfectly organized Olympics, by maintaining international relations, by implementing domestic goals or by demonstrating the superiority of its economy or political system. Of course, several of these reasons increase the willingness of governments to finance the Olympics with public money. However, the exact effects of the state's contribution to the Olympics in terms of economic growth, job creation, or external effects are difficult to determine (Sterken, 2007; Preuss, 2009; Preuss, 2011). The reasons why governments refuse to support the Games financially are often due to lack of confidence in achieving the effects noted above, as well as the risk of possible public debt. Other explanations for non-funding can be a missing legacy for the needed infrastructure and the concern about any unintentional and socially unjust redistribution of public funds (Preuss and Solberg, 2006; Scheu *et al.*, 2021).

In general, the Olympic Games offer a city and a country the best opportunity to raise awareness and increase soft power. The sponsors start advertising their partnership with the Olympics several years before the event promoting the name of the host city in their advertising campaigns. In the months prior to the Opening Ceremony, the press gives preliminary reports about the hosting country and its citizens. In the run-up to the Olympics, the Olympic torch relay generates additional media interest.

Preuss and Alfs (2011, p. 65) analysed internet reports on the 2008 Olympic Games in Beijing in order to examine how the media from China, the USA, Europe, and the rest of the world reported the Olympics. Data were interpreted using common signalling theories (e.g. Connelly *et al.*, 2011), such as principal-agent theory with reference to 'adverse selection' and information asymmetries, as well as signalling by 'demonstrative consumption' to build up symbolic capital (see figure 6.3). Between 1 July and 30 September 2008, 740 messages or reports were collected using Google alerts and searching for the key words 'Olympic Games Beijing 2008'. The data were analysed using quantitative analysis of coding schemes.

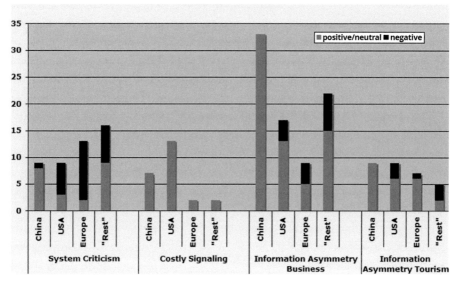

Figure 6.3. Distribution of Internet reports by category, origin and value. (*Source*: Preuss and Alfs, 2011, p. 65)

The findings show that China used the Olympic Games mainly to reduce information asymmetries, which were directly connected to China's active search for potential business partners and investors. Overall, the researchers found out that the four geographical areas studied showed different contents in the communication patterns regarding the Olympic Games. China's success in eliminating the information discrepancies in a positive way was overall an accomplishment, although it was also weakened by negative news coverage.

Host City and Its Politicians

The politicians of the host city are another stakeholder group. The economic impulse generated by the Olympics is much bigger for the host city in comparison with the rest of the host country. The investments in the city increase its attractiveness for tourists and international investors since many locational factors improve (Hall, 1992, p. 17; Weirick, 1999, p. 70). It is often observed that Olympic Games are used to solve urban problems.

However, problems in construction, with crime and delays such as in Rio 2016, can affect reputations in a manner not entirely positive. While cities such as Tokyo 2020, London 2012, Sydney 2000, and Barcelona 1992 improved their international images by hosting safe and efficient Games where the sports were the main story, Rio did not successfully capitalize on its image as a playground for tourists to enjoy themselves. The expected positive impact of promoting the city as a place for tourism and international business did not materialize (Burdett, 2017).

In contrast, a positive example is provided by Barcelona, which was able to build a ring road that significantly reduced the traffic within the city. After many years of ineffective municipal negotiations, this project came to life in the course of preparing for the Games of 1992. Other Olympic hosts like Athens built a new airport outside the city and a high-capacity metro system. Beijing afforested areas and relocated some industrial zones in order to improve the city's climate, London 2012 gentrified the east side of the city, and Rio 2016 improved its public transportation system. However, while these examples are initially positive for the host city, they become the opposite for the many residents who were relocated by municipal and governmental authorities from areas of Olympic-related development to the outskirts of the city.

An objective of local politicians is often to obtain prestige in their country, to achieve more attention and, ultimately, to acquire public subsidies for their city. For instance, Barcelona's desire to host the Olympic Games was also a result of striving for more autonomy from Spain, while Atlanta wanted to demonstrate the power and strength of the South *vis-à-vis* the northern United States. Beijing also took advantage of the Olympics in its rivalry with Shanghai. Thus, host cities are often interested not only in showing the world their productivity and ability as a whole but in signalling their success to their national rivals.

If a city cannot complete its planned infrastructure projects by the start of the Games it will be exposed to global criticism and its image will be severely damaged. This happened before the opening of the Olympics in Athens 2004, in Turin 2006 and in Rio 2016. After a city has been awarded the Olympic Games, time pressures keep urban development on track. It can often be observed that longstanding political stalemates in urban planning will be resolved as the fear of failure leads to accelerated urban development (Cox *et al.*, 1994, p. 35; Daume, 1976, p. 155; Garcia, 1993; Geipel *et al.*, 1993, p. 296) and higher costs (Preuss *et al.*, 2019). In Munich 1972, for example, urban development supposedly occurred ten years faster than would have happened without the Olympic Games. With the exceptions of the privately financed Olympic Games in Los Angeles and Atlanta, politicians made use of the Olympics to accelerate urban development and to implement projects that were already planned in the long term. In many cases, global attention on the host city also helped to overcome internal political differences between planners, politicians, and citizens concerning these important urban projects.

However, these trends also create the danger of inefficiency and corruption in construction before hosting the Olympic Games as the IOC demands tight deadlines, high quality venues and often overlooks the interests of minority groups. Hall (1992, p. 131) also suggested that pressures of time can result in the suspension of environmental directives or even the suppression of projects of high ecological value. Therefore, it is impossible to generalize by claiming that the best means to stimulate the economy of a region is to host the Olympic Games (Baade and Matheson, 2002, p. 145).

In this context, it seems worthwhile examining whether the necessary investment in infrastructure for the Olympic Games is the best use of financial resources for the city, as claimed by Szymanski (2002, p. 3). Of course, this depends on whether the necessity for infrastructure to organize

Table 6.3. Usage of brownfield land for the Olympic Games. (*Sources*: compiled from García, 1993, pp. 251–270); Geipel *et al.*, 1993, pp. 287–289; Lee, 1988, pp. 60–61; Levett, 2004, p. 82; Meyer-Künzel, 2001; Pyrgiotis, 2001; Preuss, 2005, p. 429; Burdett, 2017; TOCOG, 2021; Preuss *et al.*, 2021; Wolfe, 2022)

	Previous Usage of Selected Areas (ecological term), Examples	*Usage of Selected Areas after the Games (benefits to the population)*
Munich 1972	Set-aside property, debris, fallow land	Olympic Park, public transport, recreational area, housing space
Montreal 1976	Fallow land	Olympic Park, recreation area
Seoul 1988	Contaminated sites (Chamsil, Han River)	Olympic Park, leisure facilities (sports facilities), water treatment, recreational area
Barcelona 1992	Dilapidated industrial areas, old railway lines, underdeveloped harbours, fallow land	Housing space, docks, parks, complex of service providers, recreation area, sports facilities
Atlanta 1996	Derelict sites, underdeveloped residential area (city centre)	Office building, recreation area
Sydney 2000	Contaminated sites, fallow land, landfill	Olympic Park, residential area, recreation area, 100,000 trees and bushes have been planted
Athens 2004	Airport, military and industrial sites on the coastal region	Recreation area, wetland ecosystem, beach
Beijing 2008	Underdeveloped residential area	Recreation area, 1 million trees have been planted in the city
London 2012	Industrial sites (Lower Lea Valley)	Upgrade and stimulation of economic activity, housing, municipal facilities and infrastructure
Rio de Janeiro 2016	Barra, an undeveloped district and Deodoro, the rundown area of Porto Maravilha	All districts got large investments and gentrification took place, public transportation increased
Tokyo 2020	Water, non-used new land	Housing area near city centre
Paris 2024	Seine-Saint-Denis with many poor communes and Grand Paris with fractured landscape	New housing, two new areas close to new Grand Paris stations, the creation of an Olympic Aquatic Centre and the renovation of sports facilities to serve as practice centres

the Olympics coincides with the future structural needs of the city. In the final analysis, it depends on municipal decision-makers as to exactly what the city aims to 'produce'. Hospitals produce medical care, schools and universities produce education and the Olympic Games produce worldwide attention, soft power, and entertainment. The primary goal of the organizers of Paris 2024 is not only focused on productivity but also on the social and environmental sustainability of each activity and newly built or modified facility for the Olympics. For the 2012 Games, LOCOG tried to avoid and reduce the negative environmental impact as best it could, as did all other Games following London. In cases where this approach was not possible, organizers compensated with an 'appropriate' environmental performance (Levett, 2004, pp. 69–89). Since Paris 2024 this compensation will be by planting trees in the Olympic Forest in ninety villages in Senegal and Mali, where the IOC wants to achieve 200,000 tonnes of Plan Vivo certified carbon savings between 2021 and 2024 (IOC, 2022*d*).

The reconstruction of previous industrial wastelands is often very expensive but the benefits for the environment gained from the rehabilitation of the urban region could compensate for such costs over the long term. The removal of brownfield land indicates a revaluation of the city and, more importantly, it should be judged as a positive impact for the entire urban population.

The structural transformation of the city by hosting the Games also changes the relationship between public and non-public sites. It is not unusual for public space to be transferred into private hands after renovation, for the benefit of affluent buyers rather than being built as a habitat for children, elderly people, or for the wider public (Siebel, 1994, p. 18). As a result, the city loses a key element of its urbanity and welfare by leaving out these groups which represent important members of society. On the other hand, decision-makers think they improve the quality of the city by constructing pedestrian zones and public parks. However, pedestrian zones may become dominated by shops for the rich and events hosted in the parks are often based on entrance fees. The result is that social groups of lower income are excluded from various leisure activities or are left out by the overpriced market for apartments, as affordable housing no longer exists. The gentrification of housing areas creates exclusive residential areas near the city centre with an attractive and lively city experience (Roaf *et al*, 1996, p. 9). The middle and upper class, a stakeholder group in their own right, benefit considerably but only very indirectly from broader housing offers in the city and from the gentrified areas. However, such developments often have many disadvantages and even displacements (Müller *et al.*, 2021). Finally, the connection between the Olympics and the host municipality can improve the image of its politicians. The media frequently mention their names in the same breath with the Olympic Games. This allows them to profit from the allure of the Olympics with minimum effort (Snyder *et al.*, 1986).

Construction and Tourism Industry

If cost-benefit analysis is taken into consideration, the main goal of the public sector is the improvement of public welfare. In contrast, the private sector is driven by profit maximization and the growth of individual benefits. Many companies benefit from the investments in the host city during the preparation and while organizing the Olympic Games. This is particularly the case for both the construction and the tourism industries.

The construction industry benefits from the point when a city is awarded the Olympics. Until 2021, investment in infrastructure started seven years prior the Opening of the Games; with Los Angeles 2028 and Brisbane 2032 it is even earlier. During a (regional) economic boom, the price for construction work usually increases due to the additional demand. This means that companies gain more profit for the same amount of work than would have been the case without the Games. Moreover, in recession, companies are able to win additional contracts through the Olympics that would not otherwise have been available. It also increases awareness of construction companies, in particular if they are responsible for 'flagship projects' such as building the Olympic Stadium. These opportunities will diminish in future Games as the percentage of existing and temporary venues is 95 per cent for Paris 2024, 93 per cent for Milan/Cortina 2026, 100 per cent for Los Angeles 2028, and 84 per cent for Brisbane 2032 (IOC, 2022*f*).

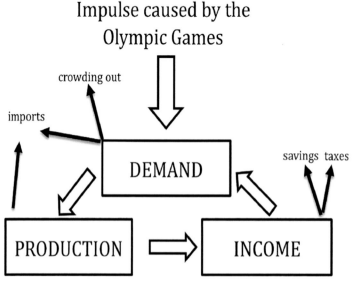

Figure 6.4. Keynesian model of consumption and income cycle. (*Source*: Preuss, 1999, p. 66)

Figure 6.4 shows the primary economic impulse caused by the Olympics in the Keynesian model of the consumption and income cycle. The impulse is provided by the autonomous consumption expenditures of tourists, as well as most expenditures of the OCOG because that money stems from sources outside the Olympic region. The autonomous money entering the region will always increase demand and thus has a positive effect on the regional economy. However, changes in stock, imports and crowding out effects reduce the impulse. The growing demand will directly increase production of goods or services and consequently lead to new jobs and income. After the deduction of taxes and marginal savings rate, the higher income induces additional demand, which in turn increases production further and likewise once more demand through the operation of the multiplier effect.

The economic benefit of the Olympic Games is much related to the economic strength of a country. For developing countries, the autonomous expenditures (i.e. the funds from outside the region spent in the region) are probably limited to the tourists, the Olympic Family and the OCOG and therefore the economic benefit can be very small. This happens because many of the required products and services are not domestically produced and therefore have to be imported. This example demonstrates well that the winners of the Olympic Games vary from host city to host city depending on economic strength.

Sponsors

Many major corporations see the Olympic Games as a unique opportunity to initiate business relations, to make new contacts and to improve their image. The worldwide recognition and the positive association that goes hand in hand with the symbol of the Olympic Rings, brings the Olympic Games to a higher level of advertising. The companies, the sponsors, the supporters, and the suppliers of the Games are therefore another group that benefits from the Olympics. Otherwise, they would not put so much money into being officially associated with the Games. Figure 6.5 shows an overview of how much money the Olympic Games generate from sponsors, ticketing, and broadcasting. The sponsoring is divided into two parts, the domestic sponsors, and the international sponsors (TOP sponsors).

The IOC holds all rights to the Olympic symbols. The NOCs have the right to use their own Olympic marketing logos free of charge but can include the Olympic Rings as well. The NOCs are allowed to market them exclusively in their territory. In addition, the OCOG holds exclusive rights to their specific emblems and mascots at national level as provided by the 'joint marketing agreement'. In order to protect the exclusivity of the sponsors, the agreement enables the OCOG to control all its relevant Olympic marketing matters for four years in the host country.

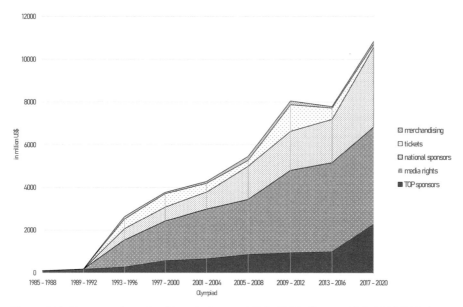

Figure 6.5. Revenues from the Olympic Games 1985–2020. (*Source*: IOC, 2020/2021)

Broadcast Partners

A further stakeholder group that profits from the Olympic Games is the media corporations. Broadcasting the Olympic Games is the key to the commercial success of the Olympics. The media corporation groups, including the new media, benefit from the Olympic Games by increasing their reputation as an official broadcaster. Yet more importantly, based on the high rating television figures, they can sell high-priced advertising space. The global television audience has slowly decreased (London 3.5 billion, Rio de Janeiro 3.2 billion and Tokyo 3.05 billion) but the digital unique users have increased (London 1.2 billion, Rio de Janeiro 1.3 billion, and Tokyo 2.24 billion). The Olympic media rights are sold in a bid contest. This usually consists of a single-sided, auction-like tender process, where various broadcasters, media agencies and, more recently, network operators try to acquire the television and internet rights to attractive sporting events. The tremendous increase in the value of these media packages sold by the IOC to the broadcasters is shown in the development of the cost for television rights (IOC, 2022*e*, p. 22). NBC bought the rights for the combined Winter and Summer Olympics from Sochi 2014 to Brisbane 2032 at a record breaking $7.75 billion (Timms, 2021). In 2015 another US channel, Discovery, bought the European media rights from 2018 to 2024 for US $1.6 billion (Berkeley, 2022*b*). Thus, the major share of the television broadcasting revenues come from the USA.

The growing importance of media coverage via the digital media should not be overlooked. In particular, changing leisure behaviour has a large influence on the demand for television because leisure activities compete with the time available to watch television. Tokyo 2020 achieved 10,200 hours of content produced by OBS (the IOC in-house broadcasting company) with a 139 per cent increase in digital video views when compared with Rio 2016 (IOC, 2022*a*, p. 135; 2022*b*).

National Olympic Committees and International Professional Associations

The last stakeholder group covered here is the Olympic Family (IOC, NOCs, and IFs). While media groups profit from high audience ratings and sponsors benefit from advertising opportunities with the Olympic rings, the Olympic Organization receives money from both. The distribution of the IOC's revenue generated from the sales of sponsoring and TV broadcasting rights is allocated according to fixed criteria. In the course of recent years, these criteria have been changed moderately but nevertheless continuously.

Figure 6.6 provides an overview of the distribution of the revenues the IOC takes. The IOC retains 10 per cent for its own administration and for its security reserves, while the vast majority of the revenue is distributed to the international sports federations (IFs) and the NOCs. Nevertheless, the largest amount of revenue goes to the OCOGs of the hosting countries. With seven and more years between the awarding and the hosting of the Olympic Games, an early launch of rights sales is guaranteed. This allows the IOC to provide a financial warranty to the host. While the warranty was linked to a percentage of the revenue in the past, it has been changed to a fixed amount to cover the organizational costs, the so-called IOC contribution (figure 6.7). Above all, the Olympic Family is benefitting from the increased

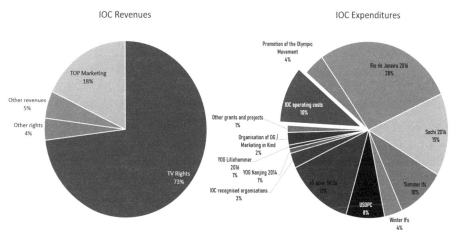

Figure 6.6. IOC revenues and expenditures for the Olympiad 2013–2016. (*Source*: IOC, 2019a)

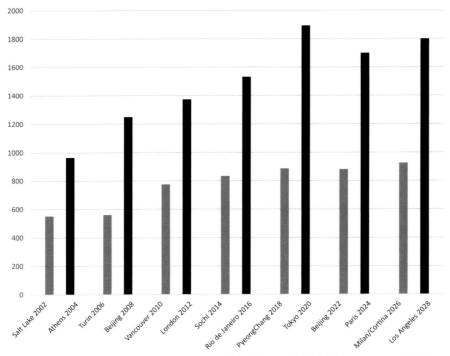

Figure 6.7. IOC contribution to the host city of the Games in US$. (*Sources*: compiled from Garcia, 1993, pp. 251–270; Geipel *et al.*, 1993, pp. 287–289; Lee, 1988 pp. 60–61; Levett, 2004, p. 82; Meyer-Künzel, 2002; Pyrgiotis, 2001; Preuss, 2005, p. 429; Burdett, 2017; TOCOG, 2021; Preuss *et al.*, 2021; Wolfe, 2023)

commercialization of the Games more than ever before. Fourteen per cent of all IOC revenues are given to the IFs and 21 per cent to NOCs also through Olympic Solidarity. It is worth pointing out that the revenues of the IOC in figure 6.6. may seem to contradict those in figure 6.5. However, the latter shows all revenues for each of the Games. Ticket revenues and national sponsors contribute solely to the OCOGs and from that 10 per cent is given to the IOC, seen in figure 6.6. under 'other revenues' (for more details, see Preuss, 2022).

Conclusions

This chapter has described the various beneficiaries of the Olympic Games. At each Games more or less the same groups benefit. We can sum them up as those which:

◆   benefit from the increased economic activity in the city (corporations, retail market, hotels, tourism industry, and construction industry);

◆   are capable of consuming the (expensive) products such as entertainment; and after the Games to use the gentrified infrastructure such as shopping malls, restaurants, concerts (middle- and upper-class citizens);

◆   benefit from the global media interest in the Games which results in increased (new) media attention. This includes TV broadcasters, media corporations, sponsors, politicians, and the host cities (through city marketing);

◆   get a share of the revenues made by the Olympic Games (IOC, NOCs, and IFs, OCOG, other organizations);

◆   use the newly created general urban infrastructure, in particular the transport infrastructure (households, companies); and

◆   use the newly created sports infrastructure (professional athletes, recreational sports, entertainment industry).

Chapter 7

OLYMPIC SUSTAINABILITY

John R. Gold and *Margaret M. Gold*

The IOC's role is: to encourage and support a
responsible concern for environmental issues,
to promote sustainable development in sport and to
require that the Olympic Games are held accordingly.[1]

As organizer of the world's largest mega-event, it was inevitable that the International Olympic Committee would need to address the environmental agenda which challenged the wisdom of huge expenditures, infrastructures, and impacts in order to accommodate a mere two weeks or so of sport. The adoption of the environment as the third pillar of Olympism at the centenary International Olympic Committee (IOC) meeting in Paris in 1994 recognized the growing significance of sustainability issues for the Olympic movement – a significance that went well beyond the staging of the Summer and Winter Games to include the regular activities of the IOC, its constituent bodies and sport in general. The environment was added to the Olympic charter in 1996, and from then onwards the Olympic Movement has evolved its environmental policies, actions, and thinking. In doing so, it has allied itself closely with the United Nations Environment Programme (UNEP) and has thereby sought to contribute to global programmes and goals through the realm of sport. At the same time, the movement is still challenged by environmental lobbyists and a sceptical public as environmental agendas and understanding evolve. The question of climate change in relation to winter sports, for example, poses particular issues for the IOC and has become an increasing concern as mountain environments face declining annual snowfall.

Against the background of these challenges, this chapter considers the concept of sustainability as it applies to the work and practice of the Olympic Movement and the staging of its mega-events. As such, it examines the origins and development of environmental policy in the thinking of the Olympic

Movement as it evolved over time, also touching on parallel concerns with sustainable legacy, and with the impact which the new approach has had on host cities as they respond to emerging policy. The final part offers an assessment of the IOC's engagement with sustainability and legacy.

The Rise of Environmentalism

For almost a century after its foundation, the IOC was comfortable in its self-proclaimed view that it contributed to 'the harmonious development of man' (*sic*) espousing values of peace, joy, and respect for 'universal fundamental ethical principles'. The version of the Olympic charter published in 1991, for example, stated that:

> The goal of the Olympic Movement is to contribute to building a peaceful and better world by educating youth through sport practised without discrimination of any kind and in the Olympic spirit, which requires mutual understanding with a spirit of friendship, solidarity and fair-play. (IOC, 1991, p. 7)

However, as the festivals of youth that were the Summer and Winter Olympics became ever larger and as cities became ever more ambitious in the ways in which they staged the Games, the movement found itself increasingly at odds with growing concerns of the impact which these mega-events were having on the local environment.

Although earlier antecedents exist, the beginning of concern about the environment as a global issue effectively dates back to the clarion calls issued in the 1960s and early 1970s. *Inter alia*, early works such as *Silent Spring* (Carson, 1962), the *Population Bomb* (Ehrlich and Ehrlich, 1968), *The Ecologist*'s *Blueprint for Survival* (1972) and the Club of Rome's report *Limits to Growth* (Meadows *et al.*, 1972) pointed, with varying emphases, to the damage that unfettered growth was having on the environment and warned that the rapid increase in resource use, industrialization, pollution, and population growth would result in the earth exceeding its carrying capacity.[2] In response to mounting concern, the United Nations (UN) declared the years 1960–1970 as its first Developmental Decade. Aiming to reduce global inequalities and address environmental degradation, the UN sought to shape environmental debate and action through its conferences and publications and to build infrastructures for targeted action.

The UN Conference on the Human Environment took place in Stockholm in 1972 as a first expression of this strategy, with a concrete outcome in the shape of UNEP. A follow-up conference in Nairobi a decade later led, in 1983, to the establishment of the World Commission on Environment and Development under the chairmanship of Dr Gro Harlem Brundtland, a former Norwegian Prime Minister. The task of the Commission was to find 'long-term environmental strategies for achieving sustainable development by the year 2000 and beyond' (Brundtland, 1987, p. ix). Their report was published in 1987 and is commonly taken as the starting point for any substantive discussion on sustainable development, which was defined as 'development that meets the needs of the present without compromising the ability of future generations to meet their own needs' (WCED, 1987, p. 43).

The Commission addressed the challenge of how to reduce poverty through increasing productive capacity in ways that ensured 'equitable opportunities for all' without compromising the environment in the short or long term (*ibid.*, p. 44). Thus, sustainability was conceived with triple and interlocked social, economic, and environmental dimensions, which required political will to ensure that development did not disadvantage the poor. While the report necessarily discussed issues that affected the developing world, it recognized the problem of urban inequality and the need for 'urban development' in 'relatively limited' areas of developed cities (the report did not use the term regeneration). However, in this instance it was felt that the resources and expertise at the command of such cities bestowed 'resilience and the potential for continuing recovery' provided that there was the political will to make social choices (*ibid.*, p. 243). One of the strategies used by such cities, of course, has been the staging of events to leverage funding and momentum for regeneration. However, the overriding message of the report was that society required the 'promotion of values' that would encourage consumption within the 'bounds of the ecologically possible' (*ibid.*, p. 44). To this end, one of the aims of the Commission was to 'raise understanding and commitment to action of individuals, voluntary organizations, businesses, institutes, and governments' (*ibid.*, p. 4).

The IOC and Sustainability

By this time, the IOC had reached a critical stage in its own relationship to the environment. There had been a number of occasions, particularly in relation to the Winter Games, when heated campaigns had been staged against the potential environmental consequences of planned venue construction. In several instances those campaigns had undermined the bid ambitions of candidate cities. This was the case with Banff which lost out to Sapporo for the 1972 Games after extensive protests about development in a Canadian National Park and with Denver which, despite having won the bid for the 1976 Games, was faced with such opposition to both the cost and the environmental impact that the event was ultimately hosted by Innsbruck (Gold and Gold, 2015, p. 144).

Indeed, public opinion and activist campaigns often seemed to be moving ahead of the IOC. In February 1992, just five months before the

Rio Conference, the Winter Games had taken place in Albertville, France. These were generally regarded as an environmental disaster despite the rhetoric used by the organizers or the congratulatory words of the IOC, with Samaranch even calling it a 'return to nature Games' (Cantelon and Letters, 2000, p. 301). In contrast, these Games were roundly condemned by both the Council of Europe and the European Union (Aragón-Pérez, 2017, p. 27). Even the Official Report of the Games admitted that mistakes had been made (Gold and Gold, 2015, p. 144). However, on a positive note, in 1988 the IOC had awarded the 1994 Winter Games to Lillehammer[3] when, somewhat fortuitously, the author of *Our Common Future*, Dr Gro Harlem Brundtland, was again Prime Minister of Norway. Brundtland spoke powerfully in Seoul in support of the Lillehammer bid, calling for a 'new global ethic' and 'an understanding of nature and an understanding of our role within it' (Cantelon and Letters, 2000, p. 303). As the 1992 Congress approached, therefore, the Olympic Movement saw a Games being organized along very new lines – embracing the new vocabulary of sustainability and implementing goals and procedures in a manner that went far beyond anything the Olympic Movement had seen from their host cities to date.

Drawing partly on that experience, the IOC could effectively represent itself as being aware of the rising concern over environmental issues and as having started to take a more serious stance in relation to the environment. An addition to the Olympic Charter in 1991 would state that one of the aims of the IOC was to see that 'the Olympic Games are held in conditions which demonstrate a responsible concern for environmental issues' (IOC, 1991, p. 9). Moreover, the 97th IOC session in Birmingham in June 1991 agreed that the Centenary Congress of the Olympic Movement planned for 1994 should examine the relationship between Olympic sport and the environment as one of its key themes.

The IOC at Rio

Along with other international organizations and NGOs, the IOC attended the United Nations Conference on Environment and Development in Rio de Janeiro in June 1992. Compared with the significance that the Olympic Movement retrospectively attached to this landmark conference – otherwise known as the 'Earth Summit' – the delegation at Rio was distinctly low key in its membership, notably not including the IOC President Samaranch or any of the members of the IOC Executive Board. The delegation's presentation, too, was uninspiring and somewhat soft in its approach to potential action on the environment. Entitled 'The Olympic Movement and the Environment', it offered little on past achievements, referring merely to planting trees in the Munich Olympic Park in 1972, building the new IOC headquarters and planning the new Olympic Museum in Lausanne without damaging or removing trees, and recalling instances of the movement's history of cooperation with other UN agencies that were also present in Rio. Looking ahead, the IOC announced that environmental criteria would be introduced to the next bidding round (for the 2000 Summer Games), and that the environment would be 'an additional topic' at the planned Centennial Congress in Paris in 1994 (Aragón-Pérez, 2017, p. 29).

After Rio, the available IOC minutes convey few signs of discussion of the Earth Summit, instead stressing that proper debate needed to be left to the 1994 Congress. However, the IOC did immediately adopt the Rio initiative of the Earth Pledge in time for athletes to sign at Barcelona 1992, as well as starting work on environmental specifications for bidding cities. In 1994, the IOC signed a cooperation agreement with the UNEP. This resulted in the first World Conference on Sport and the Environment, which was held in Lausanne in July 1994, with 120 delegates looking at the responsibility of government, the Olympic Movement, and industry towards the environment and towards the role of education (SEC, 1996, p. 164).

Furthermore, things had progressed behind the scenes. Richard 'Dick' Pound, an IOC Executive Board member, recalled writing to Samaranch in 1992 pointing out the need for the IOC to develop a formal position on the environment (Pound *et al.*, 2008, p. 21). At the next IOC Executive Board meeting, held in Acapulco in November 1992, Samaranch formally asked Pound to prepare a draft declaration on sport and the environment, saying that the IOC ought to have its own environmental policy in time for the Lillehammer Games. Pound did so and presented the results to the Executive Board in Lausanne in December, saying that he believed it was important 'to adopt such a policy statement as soon as possible, thereby taking the initiative rather than simply [responding] to pressures' (see table 7.1). Nine principles were formulated. They covered the IOCs own management activities, incorporating environmental assessments into host city selection and evaluation, awareness raising and leadership within the Olympic Movement, meeting international obligations and being proactive in adapting to new developments. They would also foreshadow much of what the IOC would be doing in the coming decades.

1994 Centenary Conference

The 1994 IOC Congress, which marked the centenary of Coubertin's first meeting in Paris, is often taken as a realistic starting point for IOC Environmental Policy (e.g. Langenbach and Kruger, 2017), especially given that the Lillehammer Winter Games had just taken place and exemplified what could and should be done in terms of Games planning. The Congress was organized around four themes, the first of which was the Olympic

Table 7.1. IOC and the Environment. Draft by Dick Pound presented to the Executive Board, Lausanne, December 1992. (*Source*: 'IOC and the Environment 1992', draft paper for discussion. Annex 14, pp. 156–157. Minutes of the meeting of the Executive Board, Lausanne 7–8 December 1992)

Principles	Environmentally Sound Policies, Programmes and Practices
1	To educate and raise awareness of environmental issues and the importance of environmental protection and preservation throughout the Olympic Movement through its leadership and through initiatives undertaken with all elements of the Olympic Family;
2	To provide leadership in educating, motivating and providing guidance for all elements of the Olympic Family on the relationship between sport, the Olympic Movement and the environment and in the application of sound environmental practices to all activities of the Olympic Movement;
3	To include environmental considerations and the need for environmental assessments in the evaluation of candidate cities to host the Olympic Games and in the formal documents awarding the Olympic Games to the winning candidate, including the regular monitoring of such matters by the appropriate authorities within the host country during the planning, preparation, management and operation of the Games and the reporting thereon by the Organizing Committee of the Olympic Games to the IOC Executive Board;
4	To contribute to international efforts to achieve the common worldwide goal of sustainable development by working together with governmental and non-governmental organizations and the private sector;
5	To continually seek new means of achieving sustainable development through the introduction of innovative economic, scientific, and technical advances or the creation of appropriate relationships with other organizations and institutions;
6	To meet and, wherever possible, exceed the environmental standards, regulations and legal requirements of the jurisdictions in which the IOC is located;
7	To establish environmentally sound management as a priority in the operations and activities of the IOC;
8	To integrate environmental considerations into IOC decision-making;
9	To regularly monitor and evaluate progress in the application of these principles to IOC policies, programmes and practices with the aim of continual improvement.

Movement's contribution to Modern Society within which was 'sub-theme B: Sport and the Environment'. The discussion on this subject was chaired by Dick Pound, with those contributing to the discussion including IOC members, representatives from NOCs, IFs, the media, environmental groups, academics, and Organizing Committees.

There was considerable diversity in the views expressed. At one extreme were those who claimed that environmental regulation would be counterproductive compared to a more circumspect approach through education and persuasion (IOC, 1994, pp. 103, 110) or that the IOC should restrict itself to calls to respect ecology (*ibid.*, p. 103), be environmentally friendly (*ibid.*, p. 105), or to simply minimize impact (*ibid.*, p. 108). At the other end of the spectrum were delegates who recognized the need for 'specific goals and rules' (*ibid.*, p. 110) to direct suitable courses of action. Suggestions included formulating an environment strategy (*ibid.*, p. 104), a Sustainable Development Charter for the Olympic Movement (*ibid.*, p. 107), a permanent environmental working group within the IOC organization (*ibid.*, p. 104), a Commission on the Environment to scrutinize host city bids (*ibid.*, p. 108), and strengthening the wording in the Olympic charter concerning the environment to incorporate the possibility of certain competitions being held in another city of the country hosting the Games if necessary on environmental grounds.

This all suggested that different groups within the Olympic movement were moving at various speeds and with contrasting levels of understanding about environmental issues, but various recommendations did emerge. Two were of general intent, namely: to contribute to environmental education in the sporting world; and to promote sustainable practices in the organization of sport in general and the Olympics in particular. Three were of a more immediate nature: to make environment the third pillar of the Olympic movement alongside sport and culture; to strengthen the Olympic Charter in the area of sustainability; and to set up an Environment Commission (Parienté, 1994, p. 395). The adoption of the environment as the third pillar was immediate. The revision of the Olympic charter took until 1996, when the new clause was inserted to state that the role of the IOC was to see that:

> the Olympic Games are held in conditions which demonstrate a responsible concern for environmental issues and encourages the Olympic Movement to demonstrate a responsible concern for environmental issues, takes measures to reflect such concern in its activities and educates all those connected with the Olympic Movement as to the importance of sustainable development. (IOC, 1996, p. 11)

A Sport and Environment Commission was set up in 1995 under the leadership of Pal Schmitt. Its remit was to provide:

> advice to the IOC Executive Board on matters relating to sport and the environment. It may provide advice to the IOC itself on the environmental policy, the policies to be encouraged for host cities of the Olympic Games and any other sporting events to which the IOC lends its patronage and general policies which the Olympic Movement should adopt with respect to the environment. In so doing, the IOC Commission on Sport and the Environment should consider the developments in environmental awareness in other fields of activity and make appropriate recommendations for sustainable development in sport, taking into account the activities in such fields. The IOC Commission on Sport

and the Environment should also consider and make recommendations on how best to create a responsible awareness, both within and outside the Olympic Movement, of the importance of the environment.[4]

This new Commission had its first annual meeting in March 1996 and presented its first report to the 105th IOC session in Atlanta in July that year. Thereafter it reported annually. It exuded an impressive dynamism, making nine proposals that covered the Olympic charter; minimum environment requirements; education and public awareness of environmental issues; and networking and cooperating with other organizations.[5] In order to promote global awareness of the IOC's new stance on the environmental agenda, the Commission took over the running of what now became a series of biennial World Conferences on Sport and the Environment. Ten were held between 1995 and 2013 – in Lausanne, Kuwait, Rio, Nagano, Turin, Nairobi, Beijing, Vancouver, Dohar, and Sochi – with each attracting around 300 delegates from NOCs, IFs and OCOGs. Additional smaller regional seminars were held each year for more localized discussions.

In parallel, the Sport and Environment Commission produced a series of publications which outlined what the IOC believed were the practicalities of organizing sport events while taking environmental considerations into account. The first of these was the *Manual on Sport and the Environment* (IOC, 1997*a*). This in the words of Jacques Rogge was to supply a 'useful tool to better learn and identify the environmental issues related to the practice of sport and thus to continue placing sport everywhere at the service of the harmonious development of humanity and our environment' (*ibid.*, p. 5). The report contained a strong pedagogic element. It presented a scientific underpinning of the actions which were being proposed, covering everything from event management, to building sports venues to what needed to be included in the bidding for the Games (*ibid.*, pp. 47–48). This report was updated and reissued in 2005.

A second item of particular note was the Olympic Movement's Agenda 2021 document, *Sport for Sustainable Development* (IOC, 1999*c*). The fulfilment of the IOC's Rio Earth Summit promises made seven years earlier, it expressed the IOC's commitment and integration into the international effort to protect the planet. It concentrated on three areas of activity: socio-economic conditions (including sport participation, health, and sport infrastructure); the conservation and management of resources for sustainable development (which included staging events, building facilities, and the Olympic movement incorporating sustainability practices into all aspects of its practices); and addressing the need for the social inclusion of women, youth, and indigenous peoples. A noteworthy feature of this document was perhaps the appearance of the logo of Shell International on its back cover. Its inclusion, along with a warm vote of thanks for its financial support in the preface (*ibid.*, p.14) reflected the decision to seek sponsors for the Commission's various activities and a specific suggestion that it would be beneficial to approach a 'major oil company' for help with the education work. Surprising as this might seem in line with current sensitivities, it is a salutary reminder of the steadily evolving context in which environmental policy was to be framed.

Further discussion in 1999 centred on the abiding question of the distinction between impact and legacy. The IOC was fully aware of environmental damage caused by staging the Games but argued that more positive messages about environmental legacy had been missed. A working group was charged with collecting examples of environmental benefit from the Games starting with Barcelona and Albertville in 1992. Its work would fit alongside the ongoing discussion of legacy (see chapter 1), complementing the thinking that lay behind the decision to hold the 2002 symposium and that underpinned its report *The Legacy of the Olympic Games 1984–2000* (IOC, 2003*a*).

The process of coming to terms with the outcomes of the Olympics was reinforced under Jacques Rogge's presidency of the IOC. One of his first actions was to set up an Olympic Games Study Commission, again chaired by Dick Pound. This body was charged with examining the issues of gigantism and the increasing costs of the Games, with a view to identifying ways in which they could be made more streamlined and efficient. The report also emphasized the notion of legacy and that 'the IOC also wants to ensure that the host cities and their residents are left with the most positive legacy of venues, infrastructure, expertise and experience' (IOC, 2003*b*, p. 5). The work of this Commission resulted in legacy being added to the Olympic Charter in 2003, with the specific requirement that:

> [The IOC] takes measures to promote a positive legacy from the Olympic Games to the host city and the host country, including a reasonable control of the size and cost of the Olympic Games, and encourages the Organizing Committees of the Olympic Games (OCOGs), public authorities in the host country and the persons or organizations belonging to the Olympic Movement to act accordingly.

Agenda 2020 and Onward

The following decade saw emphases on economic sustainability and legacy thinking being formally expressed in the regeneration agenda of London 2012 and Rio 2016 and embedded in the bidding, preparation, and staging of both Summer and Winter Games. However, a major shift towards a broader approach to sustainability came with the presidency of Thomas Bach in 2013 and a shift in IOC policymaking towards the environment. This started with the launch of *Agenda 2020* in December 2014 and the various initiatives that sprang from that. Although the IOC was financially in good shape and there remained sufficient cities keen to take on the burdens of staging both summer and winter games, Bach saw concerns that needed addressing with regard to the organization's credibility, the public trust that it enjoyed, the need for transparency, and the wish to ensure the Olympic Movement's continuing reputation. This is reflected in the three pillars that developed from this initiative: creditability, sustainability, and youth.

An extensive consultation ran throughout 2014. Working groups, including one on the environment and legacy, tackled key areas, and contributions from Olympic Movement stakeholders, organizations, and individuals were sought (IOC, 2014*a*, p. 3). For environment and legacy, it was felt that the IOC was under greater scrutiny than before. Notably, there was public disquiet about the cost and impact of the Games, and the IOC needed to take a more 'proactive approach' to embedding sustainability not only in the organization of the Games, but throughout the whole Olympic movement (IOC, 2014*b*, p. 22). The final document that was approved in December 2014 contained forty recommendations. Recommendations 4 and 5 related to the environment and legacy. As shown in table 7.2, these emphasized the major dimensions of sustainability and the requirement that

Table 7.2. Recommendations relating to the Environment and Legacy contained within Agenda 2020. (*Source*: IOC, 2014*b*, p. 120)

Recommendation 4: Include sustainability in all aspects of the Olympic Games

The IOC to take a more proactive position and leadership role with regard to sustainability and ensure that it is included in all aspects of the planning and staging of the Olympic Games.

1.   Develop a sustainability strategy to enable potential and actual Olympic Games organizers to integrate and implement sustainability measures that encompass economic, social and environmental spheres in all stages of their project;

2.   Assist newly elected Organizing Committees to establish the best possible governance for the integration of sustainability throughout the organization;

3.   The IOC to ensure post-Games monitoring of the Games legacy with the support of the NOC and external organizations such as the World Union of Olympic Cites (UMVO).

Recommendation 5. *Include sustainability within the Olympic Movement's daily operations.*

1.   The IOC to embrace sustainability principles:

◆   The IOC to include sustainability in its day-to-day operations,

◆   The IOC to include sustainability in its procurement of goods and services, as well as events organization (meetings, conferences, etc.),

◆   The IOC to reduce its travel impact and offset its carbon emissions,

◆   The IOC to apply the best possible sustainability standards for the consolidation of its Headquarters in Lausanne.

2.   The IOC to engage and assist Olympic Movement stakeholders in integrating sustainability within their own organization and operations by:

◆   developing recommendations,

Table 7.2 continued on page 202

Table 7.2 continued from page 201

- providing tools, e.g. best practices and scorecards,
- providing mechanisms to ensure the exchange of information between Olympic stakeholders,
- using existing channels, such as Olympic Solidarity, to help and assist in implementing initiatives.

3. To achieve the above, the IOC to cooperate with relevant expert organzations such as UNEP.

these dimensions should be embedded in all aspects of bidding, planning, staging, and post-games legacy. These objectives would be assisted by adoption of recommendations 1 and 2 which were concerned with the economic sustainability of the Games. They foresaw a bidding process which prioritized the use of existing venues, creating temporary venues for sports where no post-Games facilities were required, and staging sports outside the host city or even outside the host nation if sustainability considerations favoured doing so (*ibid.*, p. 9 and 10).

The final recommendation of Agenda 2020 envisaged reviewing the scope and composition of the IOC Commissions to align their operations with the goals of *Agenda 2020* (*ibid.*, p. 25). This immediately impacted on the Sport and Environment Commission, which was summarily replaced in 2015 by a Sustainability and Legacy Commission chaired by Prince Albert of Monaco (who had also chaired the Environment and Legacy working party for *Agenda 2020*). This new Commission's remit was pitched wider than its predecessor despite the reservations of the outgoing chair Pal Schmitt, who was concerned that attention would be spread too thinly to do justice to the environment.[6] Prince Albert, however, justified the new arrangements and the greater emphasis on social and economic sustainability in his first report to the IOC, arguing that there was a feeling that the IOC was falling behind in its approach to sustainability and that sustainability had to be implemented in all three areas within a common framework.[7]

Thinking was also influenced by developments taking place at a global level, with the UN moving ahead with several initiatives that impacted on the IOC. Its 2030 Agenda for sustainable Development, launched in 2015, had seventeen sustainable development goals to be met by 2030. In addition, the UN Climate Change Conference (COP21) led to the Paris Agreement to slow the rise in global average temperature to below 2°C above pre-industrial levels, while pursuing efforts to slow the rise to 1.5°C. Taken together, these specific institutional and contextual considerations shaped the way that the IOC's new Sustainability and Legacy Commission responded to its remit of fostering 'positive change and legacies in the social, economic and environmental spheres' through advising the IOC on sustainability and legacy strategy, reviewing progress in these areas and providing advice to the

Olympic movement to promote 'best practice' in all areas of activity.[8] The first steps towards implementing *Agenda 2020* comprised clarification of the two related areas of sustainability and legacy and then formulating a strategy for each. The *IOC Sustainability Strategy* (IOC, 2017*a*) was launched in October 2017 and the *Legacy Strategic Approach – Moving Forward* (IOC, 2017*b*) two months later.

The *IOC Sustainability Strategy* (IOC, 2017*a*) was organized around the three spheres of responsibility that had been identified in Recommendations 4 and 5 of *Agenda 2020*. These were the IOC's leadership role of promoting sustainability goals within the Olympic Movement as a whole; the IOC's role in guaranteeing the sustainability credentials of the Olympic Games in its summer, winter, and youth versions; and the need to ensure that its own daily operations met sustainable standards (IOC, 2017*c*, p. 3). Cutting across these themes were five focus areas which identified the main spheres of action required: infrastructure and natural sites; sourcing and resource management; mobility; workforce; and climate. Collectively, these emphasized the use of existing venues and infrastructure where possible, the protection of natural and cultural resources, sustainable sourcing, the sustainable transport of people goods and services, social justice for the workforce, and carbon reduction strategy to 'align' with the Paris Agreement on Climate Change (*ibid.*, p. 5). As shown in table 7.3, eighteen objectives were laid out to meet these ends (*ibid.*, pp. 42–43).

Table 7.3. Sustainability strategy 2017 – objectives and progress 2017–2021. (*Source*: Compiled by authors from IOC, 2021*d*, pp. 9–20)

Number	Sustainability Objective 2017–2020	Progress 2017–2021
IOC	As an Organization	
1	Design and construction of future Olympic House to be certified according to nationally and internationally recognized sustainability standards	Achieved and closed
2	Increase energy efficiency of our buildings	Achieved and closed
3	Integrate sustainability in the sourcing of goods and services, including those from TOP Partners and official licensees	Partially achieved
4	Achieve a measurable reduction in waste quantities	Achieved and closed
5	Reduce the IOC's travel impact (business travel for IOC staff, members and guests; vehicle fleet; staff commuting; freight)	Achieved and closed
6	Further increase staff diversity, in particular with regard to gender and geographical diversity	Achieved and closed
7	As part of IOC@work2020, further develop a wellness programme to promote healthy and active lifestyles at the IOC	Achieved and closed

Table 7.3 continued on page 204

Table 7.3 continued from page 203

8	Achieve carbon neutrality by reducing direct and indirect GHG emissions, and by compensating emissions as a last resort	Achieved and closed
9	Include sustainability in corporate events	Partially achieved
IOC	*As owner of the Olympic Games*	
10	Ensure sustainability is addressed as a strategic topic with cities as early as the invitation phase and throughout all phases of the Candidature Process	Achieved and closed
11	Reinforce sustainability commitments in the Host City Contract so that bidding for and hosting an Olympic Games edition can act as a catalyst for sustainable development within the host city and region	Achieved and closed
12	Strengthen support and monitoring of the OCOGs' implementation of sustainability-related bid commitments, Host City Contract requirements and IOC's recommendations, including through the provision of common methodologies and independent third-party assessments where appropriate	Achieved and closed
13	Facilitate exchanges between Olympic Games stakeholders (e.g. OCOGs, national partners, host city authorities, TOP partners) and build strategic partnerships with relevant expert organizations to develop innovative sustainable solutions for planning and staging of the Olympic Games (will remain a commitment)	Achieved and closed
IOC	*As leader of the Olympic Movement*	
14	Provide mechanisms to ensure exchange of information and best practices between Olympic Movement stakeholders	Achieved and closed
15	Facilitate access to relevant expert organizations to develop guidelines and innovative solutions	Achieved and closed
16	Leverage Olympic Solidarity to assist NOCs in implementing sustainability initiatives	Achieved and closed
17	Set up an ambassador programme including athletes, in order to raise awareness on sustainability in sport	Partially Achieved
18	Profile the role of the Olympic Movement in sustainability, through aggregation of information and collective reporting	Achieved and closed

The *Legacy Strategic Approach* document (IOC, 2017*b*) sought to define legacy and clarify the relationship between sustainability and legacy. The definition of legacy struck an ideologically positive note, emphasizing the benefits of the Games and attempting to balance the needs and desires of host cities with the interests of people and the Olympic Movement. It asserted:

Olympic legacy is the result of a vision. It encompasses all the tangible and intangible long-term benefits initiated or accelerated by the hosting of the Olympic Games/sport events for people, cities/territories and the Olympic Movement. (*Ibid.*, p. 13)

The conscious emphasis on the Olympic movement is noticeable. It sought to reposition the IOC at the heart of legacy planning after feeling somewhat sidelined by the spectacular city remodelling that had taken place with funding leveraged from staging the Games. To this end, the strategy itself aimed to embed legacy 'through the Olympic Games lifecycle' from the dialogue stage of exploring candidature to the final legacy delivery stage post-Games.

The strategy also tried to distinguish between sustainability and legacy, with legacy referring to 'long-term benefits, or outcomes' and sustainability 'the strategies and processes … to maximise positive impacts and minimise negative impacts in the social, economic and environmental spheres' (*ibid.*, p. 17). This echoed earlier concerns in the Olympic movement that discussion of sustainability was frequently juxtaposed with negative environmental impacts while the benefits were underestimated. The legacy strategy proposed that the movement should 'document, analyse and proactively communicate the legacy of the Olympic Games' not only for future hosts, but retrospectively to highlight and celebrate the positive achievements of the Olympic Movement on host cities, and to minimize the negative impacts. The IOC website, for example, now offers a section entitled 'Living Legacy', which provides a database of legacy in all Olympic host cities IOC (2023*b*). In the same vein, a major study entitled *Over 125 Years of Olympic Venues: Post-Games Use* (IOC, 2022*f*) presented a survey of 923 venues from fifty-one Games. Its conclusion, which sought to counter the trope of white elephants and wasted expenditure, was that 817 were permanent structures of which 85 per cent were still in use. Of the 124 venues not in use, eighty-eight had been dismantled or demolished for reasons that included age, wartime destruction, and regeneration programmes (*ibid.*, p. 11). Only thirty-six venues, it was asserted, were closed or abandoned.

The period following the launch of the sustainability and legacy strategies witnessed unprecedented publishing activity. This included a series of reports setting out sustainability principles, practical advice on how to implement them, and annual monitoring reports for the sustainability strategy. December 2021 saw the publication of the sustainability report (IOC, 2021*d*) that assessed the performance of the movement in reaching the objectives set out in the 2017 strategy (as seen in table 7.3). Most goals were deemed to have been met, but in the case of sustainability, efforts were recognized as inevitably ongoing. Table 7.4 provides an overview as to how these goals will continue in amended form for the period 2021 through to 2024.

Overall the IOC pronounced itself satisfied with the progress that had been achieved, stating that sustainability 'was now firmly embedded as an

Table 7.4. Sustainability objectives 2021–2024. (Source: IOC, 2021*d*, pp. 26–30)

Objective	Sustainability Objective
IOC	*As an organization*
1	Reduce our CO_2 emissions in line with the Paris Agreement, with a 30 per cent reduction in our travel emissions by 2024 and additional measures targeting our digital activities, buildings and catering
2	Create an Olympic Forest to support our climate positive objective while delivering long-term social and biodiversity benefits
3	Ensure that the IOC Sustainable Sourcing Guidelines are fully implemented across our supply chain while promoting respectful, sober, circular and regenerative models
4	Develop a comprehensive training programme, across all levels of responsibility, to increase staff competency in implementing the IOC Sustainability Strategy
IOC	*As owner of the Olympic Games*
5	Assist and accelerate the transition to climate positive Olympic Games through the development of guidance and expertise for Interested Parties, Preferred Hosts and OCOGs, and the revision of relevant existing operational requirements
6	Require that no permanent Olympic construction occurs in statutory nature and cultural protected areas and UNESCO World Heritage Sites and that the IOC, OCOGs and IFs work together to protect and enhance biodiversity within the host city/region and/or Games venues
7	Conduct a gap analysis across all the IOC's Olympic Games and Youth Olympic Games functional areas – and all Olympic Games phases – to identify areas where sustainability needs to be reinforced and formalized
8	Support OCOGs and their partners in developing monitoring oversight of Olympic Games supply chains and construction workers' rights as part of their human rights approach
9	Work with OCOGs and partners to promote sustainable tourism and responsible consumption for Olympic Games participants, spectators and visitors to educate, create awareness and incite action on the ground
IOC	*As leader of the Olympic Movement*
10	Work with IFs whose sports are on the Olympic programme to have a sustainability strategy in place by 2024 that sets goals, prioritizes actions and tracks progress
11	Develop a sustainability strategy template appropriate for all NOCs to use, and in collaboration with Olympic Solidarity support NOCs in the implementation of sustainable practices
12	Work with IFs whose sports are on the Olympic programme and NOCs for them to join the UN Sports for Climate Action Framework
13	Work with partners, including UNEP, to develop a framework that will enable the Olympic Movement, athletes and fans to contribute to the development of the Olympic Forest
14	Work with IFs whose sports are on the Olympic programme and NOCs for them to apply, as a minimum, the basic level within the IOC Sustainable Sourcing in Sport guidelines to all procurement associated with the Olympic Games and Youth Olympic Games
15	Develop an expert network and regular forum to showcase best practice in sustainable innovation in sport infrastructure to inspire the Olympic Movement

Table 7.4 continued on page 207

Table 7.4 continued from page 206

16	Work with and assist the Olympic Movement to leverage the information, best practices, guidelines and human capacity to implement sustainable actions through sport
17	Work with and support role models and influencers to raise awareness, educate and give visibility to sustainability through sport

Figure 7.1. International Olympic Committee Headquarters (Lausanne, Switzerland), March 2020. (*Source*: Photograph CC Gzzz)

executive priority' (*ibid.*, p. 6). These principles, for example, had been applied to the construction of the new IOC Headquarters at Vichy, on the western edge of Lausanne, which opened in 2019 (see figure 7.1). Designed by 3XN (Danish Architects) the building bought together some 500 staff previously housed in buildings scattered around Lausanne. It incorporated green roofs, solar energy panels and heat pumps (using lake water), and rainwater harvesting. It has met and exceeded international and national building standards, and achieved carbon neutral status, albeit by using carbon offsetting. Future plans are intended to reduce carbon emissions even further with the goal of becoming carbon positive by 2030 (taking more carbon from the atmosphere than is emitted), a goal to be achieved by using mechanisms such as the Olympic Forest project (see below).

Awkward Realities

Despite *Agenda 2020*'s apparent success and the new sustainability and legacy strategies, the last decade brought a fresh crisis for the Olympic Movement. *Agenda 2020* (IOC, 2014*b*, pp. 9–11) had tried to reshape the bidding process as an invitation rather than a competition and to reduce the cost of bidding. Nevertheless, for the new approach to work, there needed to be applicants. These were soon to be in short supply. The positive atmosphere that surrounded the Games after London 2012 had quickly dissipated. The Rio 2016 Games had run into financial crisis and the PyeongChang Winter Games 2018 were confronted with political issues relating to relations with North Korea. Cities had either become reluctant to bid for the Games or, if having started the bidding process, were prone to withdrawing their candidature. This had become an issue for both the Summer and Winter Games. In 2017, there were only two candidates for the 2024 Summer Games (Paris and Los Angeles). The IOC's decision to award the 2024 Games to Paris and the 2028 Games to Los Angeles effectively bought itself time by taking advantage of the willingness of two experienced host cities to take on the task. In 2019, a similar situation occurred when there were only two candidates left for the 2026 Winter Games – Stockholm-Åre (Sweden) and the chosen hosts Milan-Cortina d'Ampezzo.

Any lack of willing applicants will always be a source of weakness for the IOC in its relationship with potential host cities and can be seen as an undercurrent that lay behind the decision to publish two new documents. The first, best known by its sub-title *The New Norm* (IOC, 2018*d*), further developed the thinking of *Agenda 2020* in the areas of candidature, Games planning and legacy. In particular, there was further simplification of the Candidate phase. This comprised 'a non-committal Dialogue Stage' with the IOC assessing the 'benefits and requirements of hosting', followed by a phase of working with the IOC and its experts to develop the Candidature strategy. The IOC would carry out its own feasibility studies to present to the IOC Executive Board, who would then recommend whether the city should be invited to become a candidate city (*ibid.*, p. 14). Once identifying a candidate city as a preferred host, the documentation can then be finalized.[9] The new features of this approach would mean the end of the outright rejection of a potential host city and, given that the initial dialogue does not have any fixed time restrictions, discussions can continue until the city is deemed to be at the point of becoming a candidate city.

The second document was *Olympic Agenda 2020+5* (IOC, 2021*e*). In 2021 the IOC published its evaluation of *Agenda 2020* and launched *Agenda 2020+5* to take the Olympic Movement through to 2025. Recommendation 2 concerned sustainability and legacy. For legacy the IOC wanted to see key legacies achieved before the Games as well as governance and funding in place at an early stage to ensure that legacy commitments are achieved after the Games. The recommendation also calls for the monitoring of impact and legacy to consider how the city has contributed to the UN Sustainable Development goals. International Federations are encouraged to use Olympic venues for their meetings where possible and, going beyond the physical legacy of the Games, the plan calls for social, sport, education, and cultural programmes to continue after the Games. Linked to this, it advocates that the anniversary of the Games be celebrated on a continuing basis in each host city (*ibid.*, p. 6). Recommendation 2 also contains a strong message concerning climate change, committing the movement to staging climate positive Olympic Games 'at the latest' by 2030 (*ibid.*). As part of the effort to create carbon positive Games by 2030, the IOC has developed a number of 'mitigating measures' to offset unavoidable carbon emissions in order to attain carbon neutrality or positivity (*ibid.*, p, 30). These include a partnership with the IOC-DOW mitigation programme and the Olympic Forest Programme.

The Olympic Forest is being developed in Mali and Senegal in West Africa as part of the Great Green Wall project (*ibid.*, p. 31). This was originally set up by the African Union in 2007, with the intention of promoting climate resilience by creating a forest stretching 8,000 kilometres across the Sahel on degraded land through twenty-two countries. To date, 18 million hectares have been restored, and the project has been transformed into a 'comprehensive rural development project' including land restoration and natural ecosystem management, food security, renewable energy, skills, and employment. The project was given additional financial support at the One Planet Summit for Biodiversity in Paris (January 2021), with world leaders pledging $14.3 billion to launch the Great Wall Accelerator in order to maintain the momentum of the project. Later in 2021, the IOC announced its contribution to the project in the form of an Olympic Forest of some 2,120 hectares in Mali and Senegal, planting 355,000 trees and impacting on ninety village communities. The Olympic Forest is expected to remove 200,000 tonnes of CO_2 from the atmosphere between 2021 and 2024, and will contribute to the IOC achieving its carbon positive status by 2024.[10]

Assessment

Reference to sustainability has transformed much contemporary thinking about the environment and related thinking about social and economic issues. For the Olympic Movement, it has underpinned a transition from a soft approach of protecting the environment, to a green Games concept, and finally to envisaging a sustainable carbon positive event. The IOC was always aware that trying to set uniform goals for Games in different national and developmental contexts would be challenging and the results have been decidedly mixed. Hosts such as Lillehammer 1994 and Sydney 2000 pushed the IOC in its understanding of sustainability. Others failed to match the standards set, as was the case with Athens 2004 (see chapter 14). The IOC's insistence on environment impacted on Beijing's national and city environmental planning (see chapter 15). London 2012 provided an example of bringing together the legacy and environment agendas in a manner that fulfilled Jacques Rogge's ambition that lasting positive impacts

Figure 7.2. Velodrome for London 2012 by Hopkins Architects, Queen Elizabeth Olympic Park, Stratford. (*Source*: Photograph CC Martin Pettitt)

should be possible through an Olympics. Only five new permanent structures were built and these on brownfield sites. Each had legacy uses and several exhibited innovative architectural design, most famously in the case of the Velodrome, which was naturally ventilated, maximized the use of natural light, reduced heating requirements, and harvested rainwater (see figure 7.2).

For cities planning the Games after the publication of *Agenda 2020+5*, expectations of social, economic, and environmental sustainability are high. Legacy is to be planned from the start. Sustainability is to be embedded in all aspects of the planning, staging and delivery of the games – with particular attention paid to carbon footprint and the social agenda as well as considerations of cost and financial sustainability. Monitoring at the delivery stage as well as post Games is intended to ensure that sustainability and legacy plans are implemented as planned. Cities are no longer constrained by the demands for compact Olympic Parks with newly constructed venues intended to play a minor role. In the case of Los Angeles 2028, no new construction is planned. For Paris 2024 and Brisbane 2032, the Athletes' Villages are on brownfield sites and, additionally, both are part of regeneration programmes that seek to provide social housing.

The social dimension itself has grown in recent decades and represents one of the more politically charged areas for Olympic cities. As chapter 2 makes clear, population clearances, gentrification and broken promises in this area are frequent in Olympic history. Paris has taken a more proactive stance on social sustainability by creating a Paris2024 Social Charter to promote a socially responsible and sustainable Games around employment, diversity, and ethical business including attention to working conditions. The Charter aims: to ensure that young, unemployed, and vulnerable groups benefit from Olympic investment in the city; to promote good and stable working conditions; and to enable small- and medium-sized enterprises to access Olympic contracts. Particular attention is being paid to businesses in the social solidarity economy (those committed to ethical development, welfare, and environment). The programme covers training, apprenticeships, and schemes to help individuals integrate into the workforce. The intention is to continue this initiative post Games,[11] although experience elsewhere suggests that the retention of funding is often problematic.

This note of caution needs amplifying. On the one hand, there is no doubt that the Olympic Movement has made progress over the past three decades. The IOC's official websites are replete with triumphant tales of legacy, green sports venues, and reduced carbon footprints. It has finally got to grips with the range of actions needed to be taken to stage more sustainable sporting events and has disseminated this knowledge globally. Yet, on the other hand, criticism abounds outside the movement, from a broad coalition that includes the media, environmental groups, and the wider public.

Public opinion in particular has been responsible for a number of cities withdrawing from bidding competitions. Chappelet (2021*b*) examined the thirty-one local referenda that had taken place in candidate Winter Games cities from 1963 to 2018. Eighteen of these produced negative results overall but, notably, if just the more recent referenda are considered, then then the rejection rate is higher. Three of the four referenda held over staging the 2022 Winter Games went against the proposition that the city should bid for the event (St. Moritz, Munich, Krakow). In the case of the 2026 Games, all four of the cities that held referenda saw the idea of bidding rejected (St Moritz/Grisons, Innsbruck, Sion, Calgary) (*ibid.*, p. 1371). This supports the idea that notwithstanding *Agenda 2020* and the enhanced environmentalist rhetoric, local people still see the Olympics as too expensive, environmentally destructive, and wasteful in terms of the demand imposed on hosts by the IOC and sport federations. The deteriorating image of the IOC is particularly marked from 2004 onwards where Games in Athens, Beijing, Sochi, Rio, and PyeongChang were seen as failing in cost, environmental and legacy terms (*ibid.*, p. 1378). Notably too, staging the Olympics had been linked with displacement of the poor (Hillier, 2014, p. 130) and with exacerbating urban problems rather than solving them, bringing in their wake gentrification, tax increases, non-democratically allocated expenditure, and creation of elite sports venues at the expense of local infrastructure (Lenskyj, 2020, p. 188).

The IOC is clearly unable to enforce the standards and practices that it is espousing. Its greatest success has been in reshaping its own institutional activities in sustainable terms. Dictating to the wider Olympic family – the International Federations, National Olympic Committees, and other sports bodies – is rather more difficult (Bayle, 2016, p. 757). Persuasion has limited effectiveness. Admittedly when it comes to the Olympic Games, there are points at which the IOC can insist on environment and legacy commitments and action, particularly in the dialogue and candidacy phases of host selection. Poor environmental quality was at least a contributing reason for Beijing's failure to gain the nomination for the 2000 Summer Games (see chapter 15). Yet once the bid is won, there is less control over the OCOGs. The routine monitoring of stakeholder activity rests with the host city and its organizational structure. Even the OGIS (impact studies) are carried out by the host city or nation and so are not wholly independent. Moreover, lurking in the wings is invariably what Müller (2015*b*, p. 7) called mega-event syndrome, where cities overestimate the benefits, underestimate the necessary budget, and suspend normal procedures of governance in order to meet deadlines and keep costs down.

The recent history of the Winter Games (see also chapter 3) offers penetrating insight into many of these issues, particularly those relating to governance and accountability. The question arises as to who is to scrutinize the actions of hosts, especially once actions are cushioned from critical analysis by the extensive administrative powers and legal sanctions afforded to the agencies preparing the Games. There are few signs of the establishment of independent evaluating bodies that some would advocate (Müller, 2015*b*, Geeraert and Gauthier, 2018).

It has sometimes been left to NGOs and local environment groups to take on this role. Greenpeace, for example, challenged aspects of the Sochi bid in the Russian courts (Pound *et al.*, 2008, pp. 36–37) on the grounds that 'venue development around the Black Sea resort contravened Russia's environmental protection legislation' (Play the Game, 2006). By contrast, the IOC verdict on Sochi was that Olympic development would produce a lasting legacy for the mountain resorts, stating that:

> Previously, the limited infrastructure in the mountains of the Krasnaya Polyana region made it difficult for visitors to take advantage of the excellent skiing conditions... As a result of hosting the Winter Games, however, a high-speed train line has been built – linking the region with Sochi – while a new resort has also been developed in Rosa Khutor, with shops, restaurants and international hotel chains all due to open in the coming months. After the Games, it is hoped that Rosa Khutor will become a major ski destination for both Russian and overseas holidaymakers – providing another long-lasting legacy from the Games. (IOC, 2013*b*)

Yet until the law was changed in 2006 it would have been illegal to hold large sporting events in this area. Further legal changes in 2007 abolished the need for environmental assessment and oversight for construction projects and permitted the felling of trees in 2009. The dumping of waste, loss of habitat, and disruption of animal migration routes occurred as outcomes of the construction of the road and rail connections, venues and accommodation. Harassment of environmental activists and a three-year sentence for one of their leaders (Evgeny Vitishko) were part of a campaign to silence opponents of the Olympic construction. Promised rehabilitation works remained unbudgeted (Chestin, 2014). After the event Russia was left with overcapacity in the ski resorts and underused road and rail links. As Martin Müller (2014, p. 649) noted: 'As if the $55 billion of total costs were not enough, the government will have to subsidize the operation and maintenance of venues, tourist, and transport infrastructures in the order of $1.2 billion per year for the foreseeable future'. None of these considerations accords with Olympic values or sustainability principles.

A similar story of environmental challenges has seemingly occurred in Pyeongchang where the construction of venues was intended to create a winter sports resort in a remote area of Korea. The Games followed sustainability guidelines, made an operating profit and costs were lower than previous editions. However, as noted in chapter 3, the construction of the Alpine skiing facilities at Jeongseon on Mount Gariwang – the only site in the area that met the International Ski Federation requirement for alpine courses to be at a minimum of 800 metres above sea level – gave cause for concern. The project involved major engineering works, the clearance of 78 hectares of forest and the removal of the village of Sukam at the foot of the mountain where the resort facilities were to be built. These works were permitted as a result of legislation removing the area from the forest reserve. The aim was to dismantle the facilities at the end of the Games. With that proviso presumably in mind, as the closing ceremony took place the IOC (2018*d*) hailed the Games as a demonstration of sport as a positive agent for change, benefitting:

> both humanity and the environment across several areas. They include: reducing greenhouse gas emissions; embracing renewable energy; building sustainable venues; using an environmentally-friendly transport infrastructure; and conserving biodiversity and restoring nature.

To some extent, the comment was fair. The goal of promoting winter sports in the Pyeongchang area has been achieved and the facilities will be used in 2024 for the Youth Winter Olympic Games – very much in line with the desire of the IOC to see Olympic investment reused for other sporting events. Yet the finance for the forest restoration was unclear. A Gangwon official stated that the province needed:

> to restore the Alpine Centre to a forest genetic resource reserve. However, we invested more than 200 billion Won to build slopes, gondolas and roads. We don't have an exact budget yet to restore it, but it will cost us more than the cost of building the Alpine

Centre. So we think that if we leave a gondola and a road, we can use the view from Mountain Gariwang to create a great value added, such as mountain tourism and an eco-experience centre. (Cited in Kim and Grix, 2021, p. 160)

In 2021, the Korean government finally announced it would finance the restoration of the forest and that consultations with the environment ministry and the Korea Forest Service would start before the end of the year. Yet the cable cars remain a bone of contention, with opinion varying between those wanting to retain them as an attraction and those wanting them demolished as part of the restoration work. As an interim measure, they will remain at least to 2024 until a final decision is made (Korea Times, 2021). Similarly, it remains unclear what will happen to the 33.7-million-gallon reservoir constructed to feed the artificial snow operation required to create the ski runs (Hopewell, 2018). Although creating less extreme outcomes than those experienced at Sochi, it again suggests that even temporary facilities can cause environmental damage and create a significant carbon footprint in their construction and demolition.

The question of artificial snow and the need for snowmaking facilities are yet another feature that has created controversy at recent Winter Games. For Pyeongchang the mountains in this area have consistently low temperatures during the winter months but have habitually low snowfall. In other instances, Olympic hosts are facing changing climatic conditions and rely on the input of artificial snow to function effectively. For its part, the IOC seems to have been more accepting of this situation if presented with legacy plans to develop winter sports centres and develop winter sports participation.

In some respects, there is nothing new about this situation. The earliest use of artificial snow at a Winter Games was at Lake Placid in 1980 (De Guzman, 2022). Vancouver, normally blessed with plentiful snow, was forced to transport snow into competition sites from higher altitudes and make artificial snow after an unusually warm winter in 2009–2010. Since then, every winter Games has had to use artificial snow, with Sochi 2014 reliant on 80 per cent artificial snow to meet its needs, PyeongChang 2018 98 per cent, and Beijing 2022 100 per cent. It has also now become a regular feature of other International Ski Federation events and in resort management generally in winter sport areas. For elite athletes it provides fast and reliable surfaces, although there is concern that it may create more dangerous conditions (Scott *et al.*, 2023, p. 485). At the same time, artificial snow raises the carbon footprint, requiring large amounts of water and considerable energy to make the snow. The application of the artificial snow impacts on the natural vegetation below with moderate levels of chemical contamination also posing a problem.[12]

Beijing 2022 planned to use artificial snow *ab initio* as natural snowfall was insufficient in the chosen areas despite prevailing low winter temperatures. Here it was estimated that it took 200,000 gallons of water to cover one acre with a foot of snow, with a total demand for 49 million gallons of water in an area characterized by water shortages (Boyle, 2022). For some, the idea of selecting a winter sports venue without snow was preposterous. As Richard Butler (cited by Ungood-Thomas, 2021) noted:

> The 2022 Olympics shows clearly how misused and now useless the term sustainable really is. It is used for whatever anyone wants and has become meaningless. Clearly money, power, influence and politics came together to award the games to an area without sufficient snow.

BOCOPG, however, dismissed fears over the specific environmental impact. It pointed out that a system of reservoirs, water conservation and recycling was in place to ensure sufficient water for snow making and human consumption (Boyle, 2022). For its part the IOC expressed concern over the reliance on artificial snow, but characteristically focused on the general picture when arguing that:

> When organising the Games, both the hosts and the IOC weigh the environmental impact with the benefits and opportunities. In the case of Beijing 2022, the economic and social opportunities created by the Games have already helped reduce inequalities between rural and urban areas. They have boosted local economies and improved the livelihoods of many. (IOC, 2022*g*)

In short, for the IOC potential environmental cost was outweighed by the overall economic and social benefits associated with encouraging winter sports participation in China, promoting tourism, and developing resorts in Yanqing and Zhangiakou to assist the rural economy. After the Games, too, the OCOG's sustainability report (BOCOPG, 2023, p. 53) was at pains to downplay notions of environmental damage. It argued that Beijing 2022 was the first Games to implement *Agenda 2020* fully from bidding to legacy, that the event was certified as carbon neutral, and used 100 per cent renewable energy in its venues:

> Beijing 2022 carried out low-carbon management, explored the establishment of GHG emission reduction measures and carbon neutral mechanisms, implemented various emission reduction measures such as low-carbon energy, low-carbon venues and low-carbon transportation, significantly reduced GHG emissions and eventually achieved full carbon neutrality, providing a sample for climate change mitigation, adaptation and impact reduction through practical actions.

These controversies, however, will not go away. The problem of selecting winter hosts brings the IOC face to face with the issue of climate change. Scott *et al.* (2023, p. 492), for example, examined possible snow conditions at all twenty-one of the previous Winter Games' host cities under different global warming forecasts. Even if the Paris Agreement targets for temperature rises are met, only nine of these locations would have reliable snow conditions in the 2050s and eight in the 2080s. If the worst-case scenario occurs, then only four – Sapporo, Lillehammer, Oslo, and Lake Placid – would be reliable in the 2050s, with just Sapporo remaining reliable by the 2080s. Another aspect of rising temperatures is the shortening of the winter season. Typically lasting from seventy-six days in the 1950s, this would decline to fifty-six days in the 2050s if the Paris targets are met, but to twenty-seven days in the 2080s if, again, the worst-case scenario occurs (*ibid.*, p. 487). The implications for the Paralympic Games are especially challenging given that this event follows on in March from the Winter Olympics when conditions are likely to be warmer.

Conclusion

Some impression that this message is being recognized is seen in the IOC's decision to delay the announcement of its 2030 Winter Games host to the Paris IOC session in 2024 rather than announcing it as planned in 2023. The reason given was to ensure that climate issues can be considered in further detail. In December 2022, the Future Host Commission for the Olympic Winter Games had been charged with studying 'the landscape of winter sport with a view to the election of the host of the Olympic winter Games 2030 and beyond' (IOC, 2022*h*). At the time of writing, it is difficult to say more than that this study's analyses and commendations are intended to be used to inform future policy. It is mooted, however, that another double award – for 2030 and 2034 – is possible on the same lines as recently enacted for the Summer Games. With the idea of longer-term planning surfacing here, it is possible that thought might also be given to the Winter Games' specific problems of the maintenance of reliable sporting conditions, with suggestions that there should be a pool of cities, with existing facilities and proven track record from which to select future hosts. As such, this would prevent further environmental damage and unwanted specialist venues in mountain environments.

What is true for the Winter Games also applies more generally. Issues of sustainability are part of the fluidity of thinking that now surrounds the Olympic project. Many would argue that the notion of a sustainable Olympics is simply an impossibility. As mentioned at the outset, the expenditure of huge budgets to prepare facilities to assemble athletes and spectators for Games of just a few weeks' duration is hard to justify. Elements of this situation are, of course, recognized given that the Olympic Movement has been discussing and seeking measures to reduce the size of the Games and costs of hosting for over quarter of a century. Although neither goal has been realized, attempts to move the Games to a more sustainable model, or at least reducing its lack of sustainability, have shown greater progress. A series of carbon positive Games and a winter host in 2026 which has hosted the Winter Games previously, with Cortina d'Ampezzo being used for the snow events, give some grounds for optimism. However, as we have seen, having a model and ensuring its implementation are two different things.

Notes

1. IOC (2021*g*, p. 14).

2. A detailed discussion of the early phase of environmentalism lies beyond the scope of this chapter. For work that places issues in context, see: Pepper (1996); Seefried (2015); Harjian and Kashani (2021); and Club of Rome (2022).

3. The IOC in 1986 voted to change the timing of the Winter Games so that they intercalated the Summer Games rather than taking place in the same year. Lillehammer was the first Games to take place using the new schedule.

4. 'What form do issues of sport and the environment take and how do we resolve them?' Item 2 Annex 3 Minutes of the 7th Meeting Lausanne, 22nd November 1995, p. 32.

5. Report of the chairperson of the sport and environment commission, 105th session Atlanta 15–18 July 1996 Annex 16, pp. 164–168.

6. Minutes 126th IOC Session February 2014, p. 11.

7. Minutes, 129th IOC Session, August 2016.

8. IOC, Mission website. Available at: https://olympics.com/ioc/sustainability-and-legacy-commission#:~:text=The%20IOC%20Sustainability%20and%20Legacy,and%20legacies%20in%20the%20social%2C.

9. The full details of the new system can be found in IOC (2019*d*) *Future Host Commissions: Terms of Reference*. Lausanne: IOC.

10. IOC (2021*c*) IOC reveals details of its 'Olympic Forest' project. Available at: https://olympics.com/ioc/news/ioc-reveals-details-of-its-olympic-forest-project.

11. Paris2024 (2023*a*) *A Social Charter for Responsible Games*. Available at: https://www.paris2024.org/en/a-social-charter-for-responsible-games/.

12. Although newer snowmaking techniques have now reduced this problem.

Chapter 8

OLYMPIC VILLAGES

Tony Sainsbury

In 1996 the International Olympic Committee supported a major symposium on the subject of Olympic Villages.[1] The programme ranged over many subjects (see De Moragas *et al.*, 1997), but contained a particularly insightful overview by Francesc Manuel Muñoz (1997). He defined and grouped past Villages into specific categories dependent on factors such as location in the host city, the amenities provided, building types and planning issues. What is interesting in retrospect is that, while the location and planning issues and challenges remain similar even today, the nature of the athlete in that intervening period has radically changed.

In 1996 athletes presenting themselves for the Games still primarily held amateur status as far as International Olympic Committee (IOC) eligibility was concerned, although the cracks in that much defended characteristic had already appeared. Barcelona 1992 saw the 'Dream Team', the USA's professional basketball team, accepted as participants – a client group that was reluctant either personally or because of their team management to reside in the Olympic Village. The days of the 'youth of the world' living and competing together as an international family for the total period of the Games started to be openly challenged. Furthermore, while Muñoz's categorization of Village types is still applicable to the modern athletes' accommodation, its relevance is less marked as other factors have taken precedence in the preparation of sportsmen and women for Olympic competition. The services and amenities for amateur athletes were based on the understanding that accommodation was needed, that the host city providing it would save National Olympic Committees (NOCs) the trouble of making necessary separate arrangements in a foreign city. It was also generally felt that, as amateurs who had faced numerous daily challenges to be able to perform at the top level, they would be grateful for what was provided no matter how basic. In this regard, Barcelona 1992 and the succeeding Atlanta 1996 would prove to be watersheds in attitudinal change.

This chapter traces the development of Olympic Villages for the Summer

Games from the perspective of the athletes and provision of services. It also considers the role and interplay in that endeavour of the Organizing Committees (OCOGs) of the day, the Olympic host cities, and governments – local, regional, and national.

Beginnings

Initially, individuals and teams were left to their own devices when it came to accommodating athletes for the Games. People attending the Games, whether as participants or spectators, simply booked accommodation to suit their pockets as if they were tourists. There was no impetus then to supply a single accommodation space for all the athletes and their support teams. While the national coordination function was served by the respective NOCs, individual accommodation needs were determined by their national sports federations in a parochial way without any thought about multi-sport cohabitation. That would come later as the period over which the Games were staged became compressed and the accommodation became more difficult to secure for the numbers involved. In 1910 Pierre de Coubertin had promulgated the idea of a *Cité Olympique*, wherein sports facilities were concentrated in a particular area of the host city to help create an ambience of Olympism, sportsmanship, friendship, and internationalism. As part of that vision, he strongly favoured barracks to house the athletes during the Games (Müller, 2000, pp. 256–268).

Stockholm 1912 created a specific Committee to research and negotiate accommodation within the city, recognizing the ever-increasing numbers of participating athletes and nations and the resulting consequences of such involvement in terms of cost. There was no desire as yet to take up Coubertin's cry for a barracks to house the athletes during the Games, with the search centred on two categories: schools and other premises offering lodging only (with no food) that would be lower-priced; and higher-price range hotels and pensions. In order to understand the demand, the Accommodation Committee sent a detailed questionnaire to the nations seeking numbers, dates, and types of requirement with a final submission date of 1 October 1911.

The Games' Official Report (SOC, 1913, pp. 226–241) subsequently conveyed the major findings, providing a fascinating insight into the challenges of arranging accommodation for an event of this kind that remains relevant today. *Inter alia*, it pointed to the difficulty for NOCs to be specific about exact numbers before trials were held; their inability to state whether low-cost or high-cost accommodation because of funding uncertainties; and the conviction held by some nations that they could gain a better deal by turning up and negotiating separately from the OCOG. Stockholm was the first Olympic city to realize that, for the good of all concerned, it was essential to try to coordinate these affairs to avoid potential chaos. Three pages of the Official Report deal with where and under what conditions the various delegations used their accommodation. Probably the closest that teams came to the multisport communal living of an Olympic Village was those teams who travelled by sea and used their cruise ships as accommodation for the Games and those who decided to accommodate their whole team together using school premises. The Stockholm report also reflected one of the concerns of the developers and funders of purpose-built Villages, namely their nervousness about what condition they would be in after the departure of the athletes. However, in this case their worries were unrealized – which is nearly always the situation today:

> On our side it is a pleasant duty to state that the visitors deserve every acknowledgement for the gentlemanly way in which they behaved while in these quarters; with one or two unimportant exceptions there was absolutely no complaint made against our guests. The charges which the Committee had to pay against the damages after the premises had been inspected at the close of the Games … amounted to no more than a few shillings, a result which must be counted as satisfactory. (*Ibid.*, p. 236)

The outbreak of war meant that there were no further Olympic Games until Antwerp 1920 in war-torn Belgium. In some ways, the Village concept did not move on from the lessons of 1912. The Organizing Committee had hoped that the Allies would have made their refugee and other camps available for competitors, but eventually this option was withdrawn. Antwerp therefore established yet another Accommodation Committee tasked with the same research and negotiation undertaken in Stockholm just two years after the end of hostilities and in a much more challenging environment. Schools, barracks and hospitals were all on the lists for the nations to consider. The results might have been less than ideal, but it is interesting to note that the British Olympic Association would later comment that there was a growing feeling that the team should be together and remarked on the benefits of that togetherness for team morale at Antwerp 1920 even though the team was based in school premises (Renson, 2004, p. 73).

A further interesting aspect of the Antwerp Games and one which inevitably had an impact on later Games and athletes' accommodation was the circumstances surrounding Team USA's use of a questionable cruise-ship for their journey from the USA (as previously mentioned then a common practice). The ship, the USS Princess Matoika, was a last-minute replacement for the intended vessel, the USS Northern Pacific. The latter was a modern and fast-moving passenger liner that had been damaged on a voyage to New York, whereas Princess Matoika had been used as an Atlantic troop carrier during the War, then as a hospital ship, a vessel for repatriation of the dead and wounded from the Great War to the USA, and finally for transporting prisoners-of-war back to Europe through the port of Rotterdam. It had not been repaired or refurbished during the whole of that period but was the only available option if the US team was to compete in Antwerp.

The athletes only learned of the change of vessel hours before embarkation and were instructed to make the best of things by their team management. However, before the end of the trip, the majority had assembled a list of fundamental grievances and demands that were sent to the American Olympic Committee and distributed to the press. They castigated the ship for being dirty, vermin-ridden (especially rats), insufficient sanitary arrangements, poor service, inadequate quarters, and incompetent crew. Their action, known today as the 'Mutiny of the Matoika', was significant for being perhaps the first time that the voice of the athlete was heard. This moment of collective representation was unique in terms of athletes' concerns about their preparations, the accommodation offered, and the unacceptability of this state of affairs for those representing their country after years of dedicated commitment. This assertive action presaged important shifts in expectation that needed to be considered when providing accommodation at the Olympics (Phillips, 2015).

Pioneers

For Paris 1924, the organizers were able to develop something of Coubertin's notion of a *Cité Olympique* through the choice of the Stade de Colombes as the main Stadium. Ironically, this had not been the first choice. After being awarded the Games, the OCOG, supported by Coubertin, had initially argued for a new stadium in central Paris, clearly seeing how much easier it would be to galvanize the interest of spectators if within the city centre rather than in some remote location on the periphery. Having failed to develop such a stadium, however, they turned to the existing venue at Colombes, where the Committee concentrated track and field, aquatics, fencing, tennis, and training areas. At this point, the idea of 'accommodation' seems to have entered the organizers' thinking, given the large open spaces that surrounded the stadium. Paris, of course, was well endowed with hotels and commercial lodgings, but there was real concern that participants might be deterred if cheaper accommodation was not secured.

It was therefore decided that there would be a *Village Olympique*. Far from lavish, it comprised several hundred three-bedded wooden huts arranged in rows with earthen passageways, described by the Official Report of the 1924 Paris Games as: '*la construction à Colombes d'un camp de baraques en bois, aux allées de terre étroites et au confort sommaire*' (COJO, 1924, p. 59). Basic communal washing and toilet facilities and temperatures soaring to 45°C on some days would have made life uncomfortable in such a compact community.

An estimated 600 bed spaces were provided; clearly only sufficient to accommodate a small percentage of the 3,089 athletes taking part in Paris 1924. There is no record of precisely who took up the French offer to be accommodated in the Colombes Village but the proximity of a number of facilities, including swimming and track and field, suggests that some NOCs used the facility as a base for athletes involved in Colombes-based sports, albeit probably only at the critical periods of their competitions. In addition, the Village was not available for the team sports which preceded the Olympics proper. Diary entries for members of the USA rugby team indicate that they had heard about the provision of a Village prior to their arrival and may have intended to stay there, but were unable to do so because 'it will not be ready to receive the team for eight to ten days'. They therefore stayed on in their hotel (Ryan, 2009, p. 32).

Similarly, the deliberations of the officials of the Netherlands NOC clearly state that they decided to accommodate only their track and field team in the Village and secured other more centrally based accommodation for the other members of their team. The Dutch press duly reported their impression of this first Olympic Village:

> The organizers, who were scared that they didn't have enough room for all the people to stay, built a village nearby the Colombes Stadium. We have visited this extraordinary place. But it's not that spectacular. It's no more than some wooden barracks without comfort...
>
> At this time the area is filled with souvenir shops, potato fries and ice cream shops. We wonder how the athletes would have their rest before the matches. (Translated by author from Vugts, 1992, p. 46)

Whatever is said about the Village for Paris 1924, it was the catalyst for what is known today as the Olympic Village, with a palpable influence on the Games of Los Angeles 1932 and Berlin 1936, although not Amsterdam 1928. For their part, the frugal Dutch were unconvinced about the sustainability of such a model and reverted to the Antwerp approach of providing a range of accommodation options for NOCs to choose from for Amsterdam 1928: the USA choosing once again to cross the Atlantic by the boat that would be used as their base during the Games.

The Los Angeles Games were staged in the midst of the Great Depression in a location far away from the centres of performance sport in Australasia and Europe. Against the fear that nations might not be able to afford to attend,[2] the OCOG intelligently turned their thoughts to the athletes and their support teams. They set about making deals with steamship companies for reduced fares for teams and with the trans-continental railways from the eastern seaboard. They also recognized that cheap affordable accommodation was required, but Los Angeles faced the same challenge as previous cities (with the exception of Paris). The region was then insufficiently developed and hotels were in short supply for the numbers anticipated. From a starting point born out of necessity came thinking about the provision of a Village for athletes and their support teams (Muñoz, 1997).

This could have been done on a shoestring basis rather than providing what was later touted as a 'Village of the Universe' or the 'Village of Dreams'; a development as never before in an imposing location with superb facilities (TOC, 1933). However, William May Garland, the inspiration behind the Los Angeles bid (see chapter 2), understood that the performance of athletes relied on their needs being met. Mindful of the Mutiny of the Matoika and recognizing the pressures on American athletes, who frequently travelled considerable distances to meetings,[3] he realized that supplying them with a comfortable place to rest, good food, a pleasant location, training and entertainment amenities would be important for the success of the Village. It would allow athletes to concentrate on what they did best and not feel the need to embroil themselves in issues outside of their control.

Great care was taken with location. The OCOG, for example, realized that many of the athletes attending the Games came from the temperate regions and might find the potential heat of a Californian summer oppressive and impact negatively on their performance. 'The summer of 1931 (reinforced this concern) was one of the hottest ever experienced in Los Angeles' (TOC, 1933, p. 255). Thermometers were placed in a number of potential locations and eventually Baldwin Hills was chosen because it was 10 degrees cooler on average than any of the other potential sites. Here, a ground plan was prepared at an elevation of 130 metres above sea level to catch the breeze, with a perspective downhill to the centre of the city (25 minutes away) and views of the Stadium (10 minutes away) and of the Pacific Ocean.

The resulting Olympic Village (figure 8.1) consisted of around 500 huts, a total of 2,000 bed spaces – enough for the male athletes and team officials reported to have stayed there. The accommodation was uniformally laid out in spacious surroundings with dining facilities and bathhouses at convenient intervals. The residential buildings were made of timber in sections and erected on site. Each building could accommodate its four residents in two rooms with washing facilities. The dining facilities comprised a number of long and wide structures capable of division into various units to accommodate teams of specific size, who had their own kitchen and cooks to prepare meals according to their particular menus and tastes. The rationale to this dining solution was explained in the Official Report (*ibid.*):

> It was plainly out of the question to attempt to serve special food wanted by the various national groups, in a single dining hall and out of a single kitchen. Not even a Swiss hotel-keeper could achieve that feat.

Figure 8.1. Today's view of the Baldwin Hills 1932 Village location with Los Angeles in the distance. (*Source*: Photograph T. Sainsbury)

At this stage, as noted, the Village remained an all-male preserve. The official records state that 1,408 athletes from thirty-seven countries took part, of which 127 were woman. As the idea of a Village for athletes of both sexes was still a thing of the future, the female athletes were accommodated in downtown Los Angeles. The Official Report (*ibid.*, p. 292) went on to state:

> The Organizing Committee early abandoned any plans it might have had for housing the women contestants in the Olympic Village or in a village similar to the men. It was felt that feminine needs could be more completely met in some permanent type of residence.

Instead, the Chapman Park Hotel on Wilshire Boulevard was chosen and made available at the same price per diem as for the men, two dollars a day, with the additional cost being borne by the OCOG.

The athlete-centred approach, part of the DNA of the OCOG responsible for Los Angeles 1932, had important consequences. The creation of an exemplary Village, endorsed by the participants, would be telegraphed around the world, promoting the image of a city and society that knew how to deliver and giving support to promotional claims about Los Angeles' potential as a global city of the future. Moreover, the details contained in the Official Report together with all the illustrations and coloured photographs make it a handbook for anybody, even today, who wishes to understand what an Olympic Village at its best should deliver. But not all were convinced.

The resulting worldwide accolades were not lost on the hosts for Berlin 1936. Hitler was initially lukewarm about the idea of the Olympic Games and most certainly against spending vast resources on its delivery. However, as with his mind-set generally, once recognizing the opportunity to align the Games with Germany's political goals, he gave the project his full backing. The two architects of the Berlin bid were Theodor Lewald, President of the German NOC during the early preparations for the Games, and Carl Diem who had promoted the bid for Berlin 1916 that never occurred.

Both were close to the IOC leadership and had attended previous Games including Paris 1924 and Los Angeles 1932. They were particularly impressed with the 1932 Olympic Village and supported Coubertin's idea for a *Cité Olympique*. Much of their planning centred on the Reichssportfeld, a monumental Sport Park which fitted ideally into the regime's ideological sensitivities. Several locations were considered for the Village, before ultimately deciding to extend a military camp some 15 miles (24 kilometres) from Berlin. It would accommodate nearly 4,000 male athletes and their staff, with the female athletes accommodated in a hostel, the Friesenhaus, close to the Stadium. There were recreation facilities and training grounds, comprising a running track, sports halls and an indoor swimming pool. All this was laid out in 130 acres (52.5 hectares) of wooded landscape. Somewhat surprisingly given the fierceness of fighting in and around Berlin in the Second World War, a significant proportion of the Village estate remains today, albeit largely in a dilapidated state.[4]

Figure 8.2 shows a diagram of how the 140 buildings were laid out in the Village. Each bore the name of a German city, as part of a schema that saw the buildings laid out in the form of a map of Germany. The principal building, which represented the heart of Germany (the city of Berlin), was a huge central structure containing thirty-eight separate dining rooms – one for each nation with their own chefs and kitchen staff. Each house contained thirteen bedrooms with two athletes in twin beds. Showers and toilets were at one end of the building and a sitting room at the other. There was a substantial main entrance with facilities such as a bank, post office, camera store, travel agency, and sports shop. This was an extension of that provided in Los Angeles but with a variety of provision recognizable in any modern Games Village. These Games were also the first to have television broadcasts and the Village was equipped with its own receiver and set. Jesse Owens, for example, remarked how instead of attending the Opening Ceremony he watched it all on a very fuzzy television screen (Schaap, 2008).[5]

The success of the Village, assisted by able management,[6] was born out of a different set of values and perspectives than preceding Games. For Paris, Coubertin wanted to replicate in Colombes the *Cité Olympique* to which he had often referred, although the Paris organizers also saw this as a cheap solution and an encouragement for NOCs to attend. For Los Angeles, the

Figure 8.2. The outline of the Berlin 1936 Village displayed at the site today. (*Source*: Photograph T. Sainsbury)

city's promotional objectives made it important to avoid the poor press that the Paris Village achieved, with the 1932 Village translated into an athlete-centred space. Germany's Third Reich wished to make the Village an exceptional and equally athlete-centred location, but the location and the security which surrounded it also suited the darker forces in Hitler's entourage: those who worried about too much public exposure to their longer-term ambitions.

Since the award of the Games to Berlin there had been concerted efforts, particularly in the USA, to encourage NOCs to boycott the Games because of the regime's anti-Semitism and territorial ambitions (Bachrach, 2001). Notable athletes becoming involved in such matters might undo all the benefits that the Nazi leadership saw coming from staging the event. Hence, it can be argued that confinement and control was a key objective; managing the athletes' movements to and from the venues and making sure there was little reason for them to move away from the comforts of the Village.[7]

The three Villages at Paris 1924, Los Angeles 1932 and Berlin 1936 laid the foundation for all future Olympics, but the outbreak of the Second World War prevented further developments for the time being. Both London 1948 and Helsinki 1952 were marked by 'austerity'. Planning for London 1948 centred on completing the task in the best possible way with the resources available but without any thought of a future model. This was particularly the case with the athlete accommodation. Despite the global circumstances, the Olympic Movement demonstrated its enduring attraction with over 4,000 athletes from fifty-nine nations participating, a record attendance for the Games (Hampton, 2008).

Yet, as the Official Report noted, no Village was or could have been planned in such circumstances and there was no single location suitable to accommodate all the athletes (Organizing Committee, 1948). Eventually, two Royal Air Force camps, a hospital in Richmond and local schools housed the male athletes and their staff, with female athletes accommodated in the halls of residence of three London Colleges. This scattered approach meant significant amounts of time were spent travelling on buses to and from venues. However, the OCOG recognized that athletes' needs were more than bed and food and provided cinema, laundry, bank, and small shops wherever possible at each location. Food was the greater challenge because the country as a whole was still facing rationing in many basic commodities. Realizing that this was likely, many delegations either brought with them or acquired extra food supplies, which caused some friction with those who had more limited resources.

Helsinki had been awarded the Summer Games for 1940 when Tokyo withdrew (see chapter 2) and, with time in short supply, had pressed ahead with its planned Games building programme. This included the first purpose-built piece of permanent residential estate with dual use: hosting the Olympic athletes followed by post-Games community use. By 1940, twenty-three blocks of flats were already constructed for the expected 3,000 athletes, but towards the end of April the organizers accepted that the Games could not proceed given Finland's conflict with the Soviet Union. The IOC cancelled the Twelfth Olympiad some days later.

In 1947 Helsinki won the bid for the 1952 Summer Games against fierce competition from other nations even though, as with London, the country was still in a parlous state. Food was in short supply and rationed. Buildings were being reconstructed and there was a shortage of adequate housing. The previously constructed venues including the Village either needed significant repair or no longer existed for Games use. The Helsinki organizers therefore decided to build the Käpylä Olympic Village. Designed for 7,500 persons, it contained 565 apartments, a hospital, training areas, a cinema, saunas, and a huge dining facility. Yet while these numbers suggested that the Village could have accommodated all 5,000 athletes and their staff, this did not happen. A number of sub-Villages were commissioned in educational and war-invalid institutions for sports such as rowing, shooting, equestrian, and wrestling. Female athletes were lodged separately in the City's nursing school, which provided beds for more than 500 women from thirty-six countries.

For ideological reasons, the Soviet Union and its allies demanded that their teams and staff were billeted separately from the other competitors, with student residences and other facilities at the recently built University of Technology becoming an Eastern Bloc Village. The entire Finnish team was housed in the Cadet School at Santahimina (Organisasjonskomiteen, 1952). Thus, in spite of Helsinki being the first to venture into the realm of building a new residential estate for Games and permanent legacy use, it was impossible to deliver the scope required including the attendant Games overlay in a single location. As a consequence there was a mix of the pre-1928 athlete accommodation world with what would essentially become the modern Games mode, a multi-sport, multi-nation Village.

Major Steps Forward

In 1956, the Melbourne organizers first considered using the City's University facilities and municipal state schools before they decided to build a future area of family homes as the basis for the Village in the suburb of Heidelberg, with a canoeing and rowing sub-Village at Ballarat. If Los Angeles 1932 provided the catalyst for the possible and the essence of an athlete-centred service which can be seen today, Melbourne took the model a step further: indeed, including many elements that one now finds as IOC obligations.[8]

When deciding to build this new community with post-Games legacy, the OCOG received a government grant to construct a permanent estate of 851 units made up of apartments in two- to three-storey blocks and town houses. The problem was, yet again, that of knowing how many participants would attend. The main Village had accommodation for 6,500 participants but in the end only 4,285 athletes and officials resided there due primarily to various politically-inspired boycotts of the Games (see chapter 2) together with Australia's own decision to decline to host the equestrian events because of its own strict quarantine regulations.[9] Eventually the space not taken up was used to enable, first, the sub-Village team members to return to the main Village after competition; secondly, for all team judges and referees to be accommodated there too; and, thirdly, to provide beds for the 650-strong workforce who had to be drafted in (chefs and cooks recruited from Europe and Malaysia). Other features included were the first International Plaza[10] comprising a Press Centre and various shops and services, saunas, a cinema, recreation room, kiosks providing free drinks, a main dining area, medical centre, and multi-faith centre. For the first time, male and female athletes were housed in the same Village. Attention was given to privacy within the Village, the security arrangements protecting athletes from an inquisitive public (Organizing Committee, 1958, p. 129).

If one accepts Melbourne as the link between the old and the new, one can argue that it established in future hosts' minds the need for the Village to be a vibrant centre of communal living that gave primacy to the athletes' needs, even if the boycotts and the equestrian ban meant that these ideals could not be fully realized. By contrast, Rome 1960 ushered in the period of using the Olympic and Paralympic Games (see below) as the catalyst for major urban regeneration on a grand scale. The Rome Olympic Village was located on a piece of flat swampland at a bend in the Tiber. After the Second World War the area comprised a shanty town of old railcars, with rusting truck chassis and pitiful tin and cardboard shacks occupied by refugees still displaced from the fighting of more than a decade before. It was replaced by a new modernistic estate of 1,348 apartments in thirty-three yellow-brick buildings of two or four storeys that were raised on concrete stilts (*pilotis*), one storey high, to provide shaded areas beneath for cooling breezes from the intense Italian summer sun (Maraniss, 2008). Taken together, these provided beds for 8,000 participants. The accommodation was supported by amenities including banks, with recreation space and a security fence around the entire complex (CONI, 1963).

Two issues pertaining to the Olympic Village at Rome 1960 deserve further comment. The first concerned housing female participants. Although technically one Village, the women's and men's sections were divided by a fence and a highway that split the two residential areas. This separation certainly helped allay the fears of the anxious parents of young female athletes – there were swimmers who were just 13 years old. However, one American mother had to write urgently to her 15-year-old daughter exhorting her to close the curtains of her apartment at all times because the highway which overlooked the two Villages had become a gathering place for voyeurs armed with binoculars and telephoto lenses! This, at first, was problematic as curtains had not been provided, but was overcome by using bed sheets (Maraniss, 2008, p. 24).

The second issue stemmed from the architecture of the Village which, although in keeping with the new era, would also prove to have a negative aspect for any future use by physically impaired individuals in parts of the estate. As noted in chapter 5, 1960 was the first occasion when the Stoke Mandeville Games were moved to the Olympic city – a development that would anticipate the eventual convergence of the Olympics and Paralympics. It was an enterprise in which CONI (the Italian Olympic Committee) freely cooperated, making venues and the Village available to the International Stoke Mandeville Games Federation (ISMGF).[11] However, just prior to the arrival of the teams, the ISMGF was informed that the part of the Village with lifts was no longer available for use. They therefore provided other residences, built on concrete stilts with staircases and temporarily installed, extremely steep wooden ramps between floors (Scruton, 1998). Faced with this situation, the parallel Organizing Committee had no choice but to draft in helpers to move the 328 wheelchair athletes between the ground and their accommodation for the period of the Games (Brittain, 2008).

Tokyo 1964, the first occasion that the Games were held in Asia, provided an indication of the increased awareness of the importance of the Village as a key centre for the athletes' final preparations before the sports programme commenced. The Official Report, for example, devoted more than seventy pages to the genesis, planning, operation, and delivery of the Olympic Village (Organizing Committee, 1966, p. 281). When the Games were awarded to Tokyo in 1959, war reparations were still in force and, as part of these arrangements the United States military still retained and maintained large areas of land for US army personnel. Initially, therefore, available locations around Tokyo of suitable size and proportions for the Village were not under the control of the Japanese government. The OCOG was obliged to negotiate with the US military for the use of their preferred location. After months of failed negotiations, a compromise was reached which allowed an area known to the Americans as Washington Heights and as Yoyogi to the Japanese to be handed back permanently to the Japanese government.

Although it was more detached from the Games venues than might have been their first choice, the advantage of this location was that it had been the site of a military housing base containing 249 large two- and single-storey cottages and fourteen concrete apartment blocks. The area now forms the municipal Yoyogi Park, close to the Olympic and Paralympic venue of the same name at Tokyo 2020. One can still find the last preserved example of one of the cottages in the Park which was used by the Netherlands team in 1964. 'Rome was never like this' was the first impression of most of the more experienced visitors to the Village. Instead of the bleak, impersonal blocks of Rome 1960 (blocks which even now the Italians regard as something of a white elephant), the Tokyo village had hundreds of small, tired-looking little houses rather like chalets on a run-down holiday spa. The grass was faded and dusty. There was peace there, however, in valuable contrast with all the strain and stress of the training grounds (Allen, 1965).

While the OCOG was nervous about the final numbers who might attend, they eventually prepared 8,868 bed spaces, of which 1,100 were ultimately given over for delegation support services, offices, and medical spaces. In the end some 5,100 athletes attended from ninety-three nations. There were also a number of sub-Villages for cyclists, canoeists, sailors, and the three-day equestrian teams. All the usual services seen in modern Villages existed including a daily newspaper. To help orientation, the Village was divided into seven colour-coded areas.[12] Each of these areas as now had an Athlete Services Centre, which was broadly similar to the 'front of house' facilities one might see in a hotel dealing with general information, maintenance reports, special requests from residents, post and other message delivery, and equipment replacement.

For the first time, there was evidence of the growing complexity involved in allotting accommodation to the teams including, then as today: the separation of teams within buildings; the desire of sports within a team to be separate from other sports; and the separation of team support staff from athletes. The one variable not in the mix was that of gender since, as with previous Games, the women had their own quarters. The treatment of the Paralympic athletes also merits comment. These Games were the last for some time where the parallel 'wheelchair Olympics'[13] would be held in the same city using the same facilities. During the transition period between the two Tokyo Games in 1964, the Village was prepared thoroughly in terms of accessibility for its 378 athletes. Few of the traumas of Rome 1960 were repeated in that respect. The presence of the Imperial Family at the events and their visits to the Village during this second phase of its use ensured that the Games were a resounding success and, it can be argued, delivered for Japan and its people an understanding of the abilities and potential of people with impairments rather than a focus on their disabilities.

Regeneration

Mexico City 1968 had its distinctive features. The Village comprised twenty-nine blocks, varying between low- and high-rise, which contained 904 apartments. Of these, twenty-four blocks were used by the men, three by the women and the remaining two were allocated as accommodation for the world's press (albeit separated by fences). There were also two sub-Villages devoted, respectively, to participants in the sailing regatta and three-day eventing. Altogether, some 5,500 athletes from 112 countries attended the Games. The Main Village had six zonal dining facilities, with two dining rooms and kitchens in each zone. The users were themselves split into six groups: eastern European; western European; Africa and Asia; Latin; English-speaking; and International. Those, in short, were all the culinary tastes one finds in one place in the monstrous 5,000-seater dining facilities found in today's Villages.

Significantly, a pattern had now been established. Mexico 1968 joined the programme initiated by Rome 1960 of using the Olympic Village as part of a more general programme of local regeneration. Many of the Villages from Munich 1972 through Montreal 1976, Moscow 1980, Seoul 1988 and even to Beijing 2008 were focused on a model of a densely populated residential footprint, high-rise in many cases, with concrete and glass; a pattern of multi-storey regeneration of mass housing with overlay amenities to supplement whatever legacy provision could be utilized for the Villages' resident services. The Games' challenges then and now are always centred on the dining facility and the transport mall; two enormous pieces of temporary overlay without which the Village would not operate and the participants would not get to the venues. Even in London 2012 where 50 per cent of Olympic athletes and 75 per cent of Paralympic athletes could live and compete in the Olympic Park area, a transport mall was needed in excess of 25,000 square metres.

Of all Olympic Villages world-wide, people remember the horrific scene of the balaclava-clad terrorist keeping watch from the concrete balcony of the Munich Village. Post-Games the men's Village became part of a new community and the women's part University student accommodation (Reeve, 2001). For its part, Montreal 1976 was infamous for the cost overruns, in which the Village played its part and where only in recent years the debt has been totally eradicated. Moscow 1980, Seoul 1988, and Beijing 2008 all used the Games to create more housing for their growing populations. Placed side by side in terms of their architecture, the physical outcome could have been any city of this period – major multi-storey modernistic edifices. Even the separate Paralympic Village built in Seoul for the 1988 Paralympic Games followed the same model, coupled with a lack of understanding of the principles of inclusion in spite of all their well-intended and much appreciated enthusiasm. At least in the 1980s there was a growing recognition that landscaping and public space were important factors to soften the harsh edges of the residential massing.

In their inception and even now in legacy, these generally austere Villages were unremarkable as sets of buildings or urban environments. In their own ways, they had served the athletes well in a functional sense, but most had aimed to be *outstanding*. That was the mantra of all those planning and designing the Village as that temporary home for the athletes – the principal participants in this quadrennial summer festival. Some Villages, however, did offer important lessons for all future Village planners and developers, with individual characteristics that are worthy of note.

Figure 8.3. Montreal's 1976 Olympic Village. Built by a consortium of architects, it was massively over budget and a key factor in the Games' huge cost over runs. (*Source*: Photograph CC Taxiaorchos, 2008)

The Campus Model

First in this respect were the Villages for the 1984 and 1996 Games, both held in the USA. Briefly, the broader context was crucial to Los Angeles 1984. Montreal 1976 had overrun in costs leaving a massive debt which took thirty years to clear and suffered from boycotts over South Africa. The subsequent Games in Moscow 1980 suffered boycotts because of the Afghanistan invasion. With the IOC unsure of its future role and struggling financially, the Games and the Olympic Movement looked threatened. That these threats did not materialize is explained by many commentators in terms of three elements coming together to change the downward spiral, namely: the election of Juan Antonio Samaranch to President of the IOC; instigation of The Olympic Partner (TOP) programme; and Peter Ueberroth's role in delivering the 1984 Games in a memorable but frugal manner (Ueberroth *et al.*, 1986).

As noted in chapter 2, the OCOG for Los Angeles 1984 was essentially a private company receiving little or no capital resources from federal or state funds. The plan therefore was to operate on a revenue-generated basis and use existing facilities and services by begging, renting and borrowing with as minimal outlay as possible. This objective applied equally to the Village and therefore the solution was to use existing University campuses. There could not be a single Olympic Village because there were insufficient bed spaces on a single campus to accommodate the likely numbers. Interestingly perhaps, knowing the significance of the Athletes' Village as an entity and that he could not deliver a single location, Ueberroth always referred to that accommodation as 'Housing of the Olympic Athletes and Team Officials (Villages)'. In doing so, he laid down a principle, grasped by some and less by others, that the project needed to be a partnership of the possible (Baker and Esherick, 2013).

Three university locations were utilized: the University of Southern California (USC); the University of California-Los Angeles (UCLA); and 125 miles away at the University of California-Santa Barbara (UCSB), which coined the phrase 'satellite Village' (LAOOC, 1985). In each case, use of the student dormitories (halls of residence), existing dining, recreation and shopping facilities and public space proved a very successful combination. Simple use of scaffolding poles and the application of the Look of the Games transformed what might otherwise have been a visually sterile landscape. Of particular note was the creation at USC of what would now be known as the International Plaza, which compensated for limited space by extending the Plaza area on scaffolding directly over the bleachers of the training track.

The NOCs were given direct responsibility for allocating housing. Of the 139 NOCs that attended, seventy-nine were accommodated at USC and sixty at UCLA. Thirty-four of those same teams had members housed at UCSB for canoeing and rowing. Many elements found in the IOC's

Villages' Guide of today stem from recommendations from the 1984 Games report including guest pass quotas, office and medical space quotas, and that athletes should be accommodated two to a room wherever possible since larger, apartment-style 'facilities proved inefficient for team space allocations, despite the space they provided' (*ibid.*, p. 402). This indeed is the reality where the units are family houses offering ten or more bed-person spaces: allocating a small team of four can only be overcome by incorporating its office and medical space in the same unit. In the University model, the ability to subdivide units physically is limited generally by an unwillingness of University authorities to countenance radical alterations to the residences and by the time available for such conversions and retrofit before the beginning of the academic year.

Peter Ueberroth's model was for a private enterprise project driven by a genuine desire to see the Olympic Games maintained and developed in a new way, but the same resolve was not a feature of Atlanta 1996. General consensus on those Games testifies to a dysfunctionally-led project in which athletes' needs and the promotion of Olympism were secondary to delivering an event for the benefit of its instigators with minimal investment. No better example of the paucity of spirit can be provided than ACOG's lack of collaboration and support for the Paralympic Games which followed the Olympics. Apart from the endless battles over marketing and fundraising, in which the IOC had to intervene directly, the Village provided one of the worst examples of a lack of any sport ethos. To elaborate, the transition period between the Games is critical for the Paralympics. The ACOG insisted that removal of Olympic resources would occur before access was given to the APOC to prepare for its Paralympic guests. The ACOG stripped the Village so completely that on the first night no linen, pillows or blankets had been available to be off-loaded into the now Paralympic Village. Many of the new arrivals therefore spent the night solely on mattresses.

Despite those comments, University accommodation can be used successfully where the OCOG recognizes that it needs to start the dialogue as early as possible to convince the University authorities as to the benefits of its use and to establish the key relationships which will give confidence and assurances that all will be well during the Games and that the retrofit and return will not interfere unduly with the academic imperative of the institution. Use, for example, of facilities at Royal Holloway (University of London) for the London 2012 Rowing and Canoe Sprint Village indicated the mutual benefit of collaborative working.

Trend Setters

Barcelona 1992 saw the Village at the heart of the Games. It was built and incorporated into the old city in an area of reclaimed industrial land to the north of the Las Ramblas, a 10 minute walk away. While it lacked substantial green public space, it featured a new beach which was a private Village space during the Olympic Games. The Village services were located around a shopping precinct as a central core which, amongst other elements, now features a large supermarket and a multi-screen cinema at its heart (COOB, 1992). Barcelona was the first Games to embrace the inclusion agenda of the Paralympic Games, not only for the venues as in Seoul 1988 but also in terms of the accommodation. The design facilitated easy access for wheelchair users and persons with other disabilities: its flat topography and easy layout greatly enhanced that feeling of inclusion by design. Perhaps the only drawback was the use of the central shopping centre as dining facilities located on a basement level. While the stairs and two small escalators worked for the Olympic Games this was a challenge in the Paralympics which followed. Undaunted, the OCOG created a wide ramp down the central core. With the assistance of military volunteers, everyone could access the dining facilities. The Barcelona Village, in turn, has been the exemplar for many that followed (Muñoz, 2006).

The Sydney 2000 Village developed the 1992 model further in terms of service delivery (Gordon, 2003). The Village topographically had challenges in that it ran north–south on a hillside which sloped down west–east. It was very narrow and stretched in terms of footprint, which meant that principal facilities were based at either end of a 1,500 metres spinal road. Moreover, at the southern end roughly one-third of the Village was given over to beach type wooden bungalows (figure 8.4), which were later sold off. The main

Figure 8.4. The beach type bungalows from the Sydney Village. (*Source*: Photograph T. Sainsbury)

permanent residential provision was a combination of apartments and three- or four-bedroom townhouses. In the latter the garages were converted into two twin-bedded bedrooms with the adjacent utility room as a shower area. The gardens had a double metal temporary portacabin, with a twin bedroom at either end and a shared accessible bathroom in the middle of the unit. This configuration on one plot meant that as many as twenty people were accommodated; a nightmare for the allotment team as multiple-bedded plots meant potential for wastage when given to small teams (a feature previously observed at Los Angeles 1984).

If Barcelona 1992 and Sydney 2000 provided models of good practice for provision of Villages, sadly the Village for Athens 2004 was equally an exemplar of what not to do. The Village was 110 hectares in area, around double the size of most modern Villages and three times that for London 2012. The housing was low-rise apartments in small plots scattered across the whole site. All the main facilities were located at one end and the choice then was to either wait for the in-Village transport system to get around the site or walk in the height of the oppressive Greek summer heat. The NOCs located near the facilities were generally happy with their ability to create their own enclave remote from other NOCs and to service the needs of their own athletes. Those further away had a less positive experience. In addition, despite being an integral part of the Games structure, the Village was remote from the centre of Athens and all the associated events without any adjacent public transport infrastructure. The Village just about functioned for the Games, but it lacked cohesion. In addition, it has not fared well in terms of long-term legacy. Today, it is a wasteland of half empty properties, vandalism, and little one can call a community. These conditions and the lack of transport remain a problem for those still living there.

The Village for Beijing 2008 has already been mentioned above as exemplifying the model of a densely populated residential footprint, but it would be unfair to suggest that it only had concrete and overlay defunct facilities as its epitaph. The residential element was very well presented and reinforced the hugely positive impact that mature trees, bushes, plants, lawns, and sculptures can have on a development (figure 8.5). The appreciation of the athletes was evidenced by their use of these spaces to meet and mingle. These attributes also reinforced the sense of maturity of the estate and created goodwill among the residents in those early days. The old adage of first impressions was relevant here.

London 2012

Shortly after the end of the London Games, the President of the IOC declared the Olympic Village as one of the reasons the 2012 Games were outstanding. Carlos Nuzman, President of Rio de Janeiro 2016, declared that the London Village was the best Village ever (figure 8.6). These accolades, of course, were testimony to the thousands of individuals involved in the Olympic Delivery Authority, LOCOG, the contractors and volunteers. At the same time, the essence of the 2012 Village was not an accident but

Figure 8.5. Public art, Athletes' Village, Beijing style. (*Source*: Photograph T. Sainsbury

Figure 8.6. A bird's eye view of the London 2012 Village with temporary venue, bottom left. (*Source*: Courtesy of Mike O'Dwyer/Lendlease)

built on what the reader will have gleaned from all the previous narrative. As such, it is possible to identify six elements from the history of Olympic Villages to which tribute is due for the success of the London 2012 Olympic and Paralympic Villages.

The first tribute (T1) goes to Paris 1924 and Coubertin for seizing the opportunity to add the Village element to the plan for the event and in doing so creating a *Cité Olympique*, even if in basic form. London recognized this principle. *Cité Olympique Londres* was a bustling sport and globally focused place for weeks with the Olympic Games followed closely by the Paralympic Games. The athletes' accommodation was sufficiently close to the Olympic Park as to be immersed in what was happening there daily and hearing the sounds from the venues reminded everyone of their moment yet to come, in the same way that Coubertin envisaged the classical athletes' camp in Olympia.

The second tribute (T2) is due to the American athletes and the Mutiny on the Matoika, which strengthened Garland's resolve to avoid anything that might provoke a similar mutiny in the Baldwin Hills. Garland understood the needs of athletes and that an outstanding Village would also serve his other objectives related to the reputation of Los Angeles. He also wanted the athletes immersed in the excitement of the occasion and arranged for thousands of visitors a day to come to the Village (even though they could not enter). By doing so, he helped to create an atmosphere that made the athletes feel special and not like a valuable commodity locked away in a vault. Based on that principle, the Athletes' Committee at London 2012 made a number of recommendations to reflect the needs of modern participants.

The third tribute (T3) goes to the Village at Melbourne 1956. The organizers built on the 1932 model and created a truly service-driven culture where nothing was too much for the residents, allowing the athletes to prepare themselves for competition and to instil long-term memories of admiration for things Australian. There was genuine appreciation of what high performance athletes of the 1950s cherished most and how essential that understanding would be to supporting those travelling such long distances for the first time. There was no doubt in 2012 that the Games were in the UK and London where accessibility to the city and region was key for both the Olympics and Paralympic Games – reportedly the most barrier free Games to date.

The fourth tribute (T4) is due to Barcelona 1992 where the ability of its city life to make the Village outstanding was recognized, a perfect example of a *City Village*. However, their ambition went further, particularly with regard to the engagement between the Games, the city, and the region. London 2012 exploited the proximity of the Olympic Park and the ability for the athletes to walk there if they wished; the Westfield Shopping Centre served as a focus for friends, family meetings and meaningful distraction;

the ease of access to Central London allowed Village residents to imbibe the atmosphere of the host city; televisions in all apartments enhanced the sense of the moment by images from in and around the Games, the UK and beyond; and the crowds of enthusiastic and excited spectators invigorated both the Olympics and the Paralympics.

The fifth tribute (T5) is due to Sydney 2000 and the Village team led by the indomitable hotelier Maurice Holland. He was passionate about staff being proactive towards 'guests' and being delighted at the opportunity to add to residents' overall experience. This core team were able to convert volunteers and contractors to the same culture even in trying circumstances, which was much appreciated by both athletes and their support staff. Such skills and experience, however necessary to provide outstanding service to the highest level, are developed over years and not just in the few weeks of venue training at Games time. In the case of London 2012, the hospitality-trained professional managers from around the world employed by Holiday Inn were critically important at the core of the 8,000 workforce that served the Village.

Finally, a personal tribute by this author (T6) as a former secondee from London 2012 goes to Beijing 2008. Within the residential area, the organizers succeeded in reinforcing the importance of a well cultivated, open public green space with features and sculptures that spoke volumes to the athletes about the maturity of the whole estate and the genuine affection of the OCOG towards its guests. For the London Village, UK garden centres were busy cultivating trees, shrubs and flowers years in advance for that first day of athlete arrivals: something unfortunately too often an afterthought in modern developments.

Any study of past Athletes' Villages attempts to explain their evolution in terms of design, scope, and the ever-changing requirements of 'athlete services'. Unfortunately, 'reinventing the (Summer Village) wheel' syndrome Games-after-Games continues to exert a dramatic impact on host cities. This reinvention is compounded because, even at the earliest conceptual stage, a potential candidate city feels compelled to focus on the specific athlete requirements as defined in often outdated IOC Village Technical Manuals rather than according to a host's legacy ambitions. Over-attention with the issue of athletes' needs seriously inhibits a host's clarity of thought about what *it* will be fifty years in the future. This overthinking of athlete needs at such an early stage can have serious financial consequences: London 2012 for all its experience did not avoid this avoidable issue.

To be sustainable, the project demands a forensic needs and risks analysis of the legacy residential imperative. Adopting part of a potential host city or region's existing residential strategic plan offers the best chance for long-term viability and any Games' enhancement to that strategic plan comes later. Too often there is an overwhelming urge to 'tick the IOC box'. The other factor which drives this urge is the time required for implementation. Hosts need to be more assertive in those early years as to what will be provided to ensure compatibility with its own needs and long-term residential accommodation strategy. The major danger for this approach from an IOC needs' perspective is that if the land-grab for the built estate is boxed in and does not provide enough significant space for the Games' temporary overlay then essential overlay and access issues will be addressed too late in the process. This challenge can be overcome by early regular reviews in conjunction with the legacy design team with a Games Villages expert to ensure that the legacy plan is not totally dysfunctional in terms of the Game's needs. London 2012's east London plan benefitted greatly from the expertise of Alison Nimmo who had worked on major British regeneration schemes. Having become an integral part of the Bid team she went on to become a key cog in the Olympic Delivery Authority.

A further aspect which in the interests of completeness cannot be ignored is the impact on the traditional communities which become the focus of the new Games venues, including the Village. One can think of the *hutongs* of Beijing 2008 or Clays Lane development of London 2012. As with all matters of displacement or upheaval, engagement as early as possible is not only critical to the project but humane to those most impacted. In London, for example, one of the groups displaced to the north of the Village site at Clays Lane was a long-standing travellers' site with poor amenities. Following consultation, the group of families were reasonably content to move to a bespoke modern site nearby. The group's leaders designed the new site near the old site meaning that community connections were preserved. This issue of engagement is particularly relevant in the development of the Games infrastructure when one discusses Rio 2016 and those packed communities who had traditionally called some of the targeted *favela* locations home.

Taken together, the lessons of Villages over the previous eighty-eight years, good and bad, were the basis when planning the London 2012 Village. These were summarized by the author in his notes for the section of the Official Report that dealt with the Village (see LOCOG, 2013*b*, pp. 50–52). These are reproduced below, with added cross-reference to the points noted above:

> The Olympic village, and the satellite villages at Eton Dorney for rowing and canoe sprint and Portland for sailing, lay at the heart of London's vision of 'athlete-centred' Games. The goal was to ensure that the villages responded to the needs of athletes, prioritising optimum performance on the field of play.
>
> The Olympic Village was also an important element of the promise to use the Games to transform East London. Games operations and legacy were planned in tandem from the outset. Both were factors in the selection of the Stratford site, which offered excellent transport links being directly adjacent to the Olympic Park and could therefore

help drive the regeneration of the area with a commitment to deliver 2,800 new homes after the Games, 30 per cent of which would be classed as 'affordable housing'.

The Olympic Village site benefitted from natural boundaries and was designed with the aim of creating a quiet residential haven in the centre, with the athlete blocks organized around an area of landscaped parkland (T6), helping to create the feel of a traditional English village (T1). All the services were located on the periphery of the site, which had the additional benefit of making life easier for team managers. A bridge connecting the village to the Olympic Park offered many athletes the opportunity to walk to their venues (T3).

London's Village provided direct connectivity, not only with the venues and local communities but also with the wider city. This offered athletes the chance to enjoy the many festivals and activities taking place across London; to connect with their local or national communities in the city; and to visit friends and family staying elsewhere. Providing such access to external attractions helped ensure that the site remained a high-performance sport village, and not a party location, throughout the days of the One Event-Two Games (T4).

The goal was to ensure that the villages responded to the needs of athletes. Specific improvements were identified by the Athletes' Committee (T2), which played a large role in the development of the Olympic village, informing and validating all key decisions. Their recommendations included introducing:

◆ Soft furnishings in all lounge areas ensuring such comfort was not only the preserve of well-funded teams;

◆ Televisions in every apartment providing live Games feeds for every sport;

◆ 100 per cent blackout curtains;

◆ Grab-and-go food carts positioned across the site, catering for athletes who did not have time to go to the main dining hall;

◆ Free Wi-Fi internet access in every apartment and in dedicated hot spots and hubs to encourage athletes to come out of their accommodation and mingle.

The focus on individual needs was partly based on an understanding that modern Olympic Villages do not need to serve as 'homes-from-home', accommodating athletes for weeks at a time. That responsibility sits with the NOCs/NPCs but the obligation remains for the hosts to provide the wherewithal for that to happen. Our goal for the Villages was to provide a level of hotel service equivalent to that which today's world-class athletes commonly experience when they travel.

We worked with our LOCOG hotel partner IHG to recruit highly experienced hospitality professionals (over 100 multi-lingual senior managers) from around the world. The Village was run effectively as a 17,000-bed hotel with hotel-style staffing structures, operational processes and a service culture that allowed residents the freedom to be themselves (T5).

Significant emphasis was also placed on the development of the Village Plaza, which was designed to encourage residents to gather and socialize. Attractions included a replica of an athlete's room for showing to friends and family and a time-lapse DVD recording showcasing the development of the Olympic Park. But it was of a size and scope suitable for immediate privacy and resident needs but not comprehensively designed and funded as the IOC Technical Manual prescribes given the presence just metres away of one of the largest modern shopping complexes.

In the early stages of the project, with venue developers focused on legacy, the Village team faced a challenge in ensuring venue operations were accommodated at every stage. A 'one team' approach was generally adopted towards the project and in many cases Games' operational requirements contributed to the post-Games product – for example the accommodation was constructed to a higher sustainability, inclusive, and accessible standard than most new-builds in London, bringing amongst other benefits noise reduction and energy efficiency.

More than a decade after the Games, London can celebrate those years leading to, and the delivery of those fantastic days of 2012. Visitors to the Queen Elizabeth Olympic Park will marvel at what has been achieved and what continues to be delivered as legacy. The Olympic Village remains at its core with a thriving community including its own shops and cafés, the school and health centre of the Games. Moreover, thousands of new residences are joining those Olympic dwellings for an ever-expanding Stratford population.

London Stratford built on the experience of the opportunities that Barcelona 1992 had the foresight to envisage. Barcelona's industrial area, which acted as a barrier both to the coast and to any desire of future residents to locate north of it, meant that the city, bound by mountains to the west, was spreading inexorably to the south and to the affluent areas of the University sector and the airport. The Olympic Village opened up the opportunities, the attractiveness of the north and re-centred the heart of the city. It can be argued that the East London Project[14] as it is now known has had a similar impact. East London had its own infamous reputation – social, political, and economic – all associated with lack of investment, dilapidation, poverty, poor health, and education profiles. London East is now thriving as a place for employment, living, entertainment and commuting. London East is repositioning the City of London back centrally as the east now acquires something of the attraction that has been traditionally enjoyed by London West.

Rio 2016

In July 2009, Rio de Janeiro became the first South American country to win the right to host the Summer Olympics. But the city's glossy magazine image of breaking blue surf and endless beaches, stretching into the distance north and south, obscures the presence of the millions living in their own versions of that famous city – the *favelas*.

In terms of the Olympic and Paralympic project, both the IOC and IPC had no illusions about the plan to which Brazil had committed itself, including the nagging realization that it all had to be accomplished in a challenging social context with a complicated business model and tight timescale. Analysis of those years by many writers since 2016 has confirmed that the concerns even at that early stage had substance.

Barra da Tijuca, the site chosen for the Village, was situated north of the most popular tourist beaches (see chapter 17). It was part of the wider Games venue development project around the Jacaparegua Lagoon and alongside the Vila Autodroma – the *favela* was 'permitted' to remain within the circuit of the Nelson Piquet International motor-racing track when the latter was constructed in 1975. Despite numerous reassurances, this sizable community was regularly threatened by eviction even at the planning stage for the circuit. In 1994 around sixty families were granted property titles to protect their homes on the site, but that did not prevent the Prefecture, which already had Olympic development ambitions, reducing the community by 80 per cent through expropriations and eviction orders. In 2022 just twenty new homes, built adjacent to the *favela*'s original location, were the outcome. The rump of the community that remained living there in those years leading to the Games would face all the disruption, access problems, dirt and noise that could be envisaged for a development that was to yield a multi-venue Olympic Park and one million square metres of Village development.

The Rio 2016 Athletes' Village comprised a double series of high-rise residential blocks. These overlooked the lagoon, with views of the distant seafront. The internal oval created by these blocks had gardens, sports facilities, and quiet spaces in its central core, with a transport mall at its northern end near the main dining area. To the east, all the other ancillary facilities were located in the temporary overlay, including the polyclinic, NOC/NPC services, gymnasium, Chef de Mission Hall and casual dining. The Village's support services area was situated further east.

The numerous complaints of arriving teams were widely reported in the media with the most vociferous coming from the Australian delegation, which had chosen to be accommodated in one of the most northerly blocks. These, the last to be completed, were lambasted as having 'blocked toilets, leaking pipes, exposed wiring, unlit stairwells, infestation, and hazardous and dirty floors'. These issues, however, are not uncommon given the race to complete such a major project in such a short period of time. The solution is always to ensure close and honest collaboration between the developer and the Organizing Committee, including trust and truthfulness no matter how bad the 'news'! There were clearly questions concerning the degree of professional stakeholder oversight of the progress of this project even during the days immediately prior to the teams' arrivals.

Rio 2016 witnessed developments that would be significant for the future arising from delegations' ever-increasing demand for support activity space. Previous allocation of space for medical activities like physiotherapy and massage were based on team size, but the larger teams sought allocations for recovery, post-training, communal relaxation, and administrative space that far exceeded their entitlement, particularly to cater for the specialist demands of elite athletes. Rio saw teams exercise ingenuity in choosing plots that afforded sufficient space to create this recovery service with ice baths, stretching mat areas, equipment, and facilities for personnel. The need to cater for these requirements would become a recurring theme for Tokyo 2020.

Overall, the 2016 Village proved adequate as accommodation for the Olympic and Paralympic athletes but was isolated from city life and the internationally renowned attractions of its host city. Its legacy use, as chapter 17 shows, has proved problematic. In the years after the Games, only a small percentage of the accommodation had been converted and sold as expensive condominiums, with the shuttered state of many of the residences making the estate feel desolate. Perhaps most regrettably, what will emerge will always be a self-contained, gated community with no reference or integration into the local area.

Tokyo 2020

When Tokyo was chosen in 2013 to host the 2020 Olympic and Paralympic Games the world, as was noted in chapter 1, was a much different place. The organizers' decision to locate the Athletes' Village on the reclaimed peninsula at Harumi in Tokyo Bay, previously used as an exhibition site and the arrival point for international cruise ships, seemed to provide outstanding regeneration opportunities. It comprised thirty-four hectares of which the incineration, recycling plant and existing apartments in the north-eastern corner occupied nearly six hectares. A satellite area measuring two hectares was created on the eastern side of the new expressway to house the main entry, the international plaza and external waterside communal space.

Access would prove problematic. The athlete transport was allotted to the main internal legacy access route that would run east–west from the existing residential area into the new build. For all other purposes, access to the site was via two underpasses. Only the southern one, adjacent to the International Zone, would have sufficient clearance to take large vehicles during normal operating hours, with the second underpass to the north having a severe vehicle height restriction. The southern underpass was therefore extremely congested at times, with high-sided operational vehicles mixing with residents and visitors to the Village and a very limited pedestrian walkway. This area required supervision by personnel throughout the day to ensure separation as athletes are accustomed to vehicle-free movement in and around the Village.

In earlier planning rounds, measures had been suggested to avoid this problem. The southern part of the expressway over the water, for example, might have been used as the transport mall, with precedent for employing local roads established at previous Games such as Barcelona 1992 and Atlanta 1996. Certainly, the main entry and international zone would have been more convenient if located adjacent and connected to the residential zone on the site of what eventually became the transport mall. Another planning idea mooted before the Games but not adopted – probably due to the IOC's requirement for the dining facility to be located close to the bus transport mall – concerned the site for that main dining facility. Given the provision of grab-and-go food provision across modern Villages, the IOC's requirement for co-location has less relevance now than previously. Providing a spacious single-storey temporary dining facility close to the western end of the site, with its view across Tokyo Bay, particularly at night, would have been spectacular.

The temporary main entry building was an all-wood affair, with the beams having been provided by Prefectures throughout Japan. Each beam was marked with data of the Prefecture for it to be returned from whence it came for use in other local building projects post-Games – a wonderfully sustainable innovation for an eye-catching internal design. Due to the delay in Games-use, none of the public realm within the plots had been delivered apart from the green space near Tokyo Bay. Those other areas were covered with a green carpet which did little to enhance the surroundings. They were left soaking when it rained and were used as short cuts between buildings. However, given that athletes were only spending the minimum amount of time in the Village due to COVID restrictions, this was perhaps a sustainable solution for these strange times.

The Tokyo developers however did incorporate some interesting and novel ideas into the design and operations. Hydrogen energy was the power source within the residential apartments, as it was for many of the fleet cars and other transport used for the Games. What used to be called IVTS (the In-Village Transport System), for a time offered driverless cars. Initially seen as an excellent innovation they were subsequently used sparingly after a resident inadvertently walked into one. During the Paralympic Games, with so many visually impaired athletes in residence, they were largely withdrawn from service, apart from the odd exhibition display or driver-controlled use.

Other innovations reflected the Games' special circumstances with the whole project delayed for twelve months for its participants and their need to subscribe to COVID restrictions. The need for regular virus testing saw a COVID Centre added to the facilities. In the same vein, each building entrance used modern technology to identify the crowd levels at the principal athlete services around the Village. This innovation was welcomed by the residents and could well be repeated in the future.[15] It was a significantly different place, too, in terms of its atmosphere when compared with recent predecessors. Some teams discouraged their athletes from mixing even from within their own delegations. One team in the Paralympic Games chose to use a converted space as a dining room and kitchen and provided meals within the Village to enable their athletes to avoid the busy dining room. The interaction, socialization, collective relaxation, and an analogy for a harmonious example of world order as described by Muñoz (2006) in the term 'resort Village' was felt undesirable in the face of a world pandemic. Indeed, one might suggest that it resembled the barrack-type Villages of the early days – primarily a place to eat and sleep.

Reference was made above to the increasing demand for space within the Village by many of the larger teams. In Tokyo those teams began to think 'out of the box' and not see the Village and its limited space as the solution. In the 1990s teams had already started to look outside the Village for associated services – Heineken House being the most famous, a place for family and friends to meet up with their athlete relatives. Many delegations now have their national house. Similarly, holding camps, near or far from the host city are now commonplace, allowing professional athletes to enjoy a more nationally organized environment and one designed to meet their cultural and comfort needs. Tokyo 2020 saw the emergence of Athlete Centres away from the Village in which recovery activities and personnel were based, where media interviews could be undertaken, and even food provided. Of course, this had implications for transport, with fleets of self-managed cars and minibuses.

Conclusion

The final paragraph in the equivalent chapter of the previous edition of this book started with the question: 'What then of the Villages of the future?' (Sainsbury, 2017, p. 201). More than five years on, are we anywhere nearer the answer? For many the pandemic seems to have driven the thinking to a much more utilitarian and basic version with time-limited occupation by the athletes. Others would argue that this was an inevitability once the inclusion of professional athletes took place at Barcelona 1992. Perhaps therein lies the dilemma for the IOC, the IPC, and future hosts.

The essence of the Village of amateur days was that, with a few exceptions, it was a world community of men and women from a multitude of sports and disciplines living, communicating, socializing, and living their lives from Games start to Games finish in this respectful and peaceful bubble as an example of what the world could be like. For those who have worked on Villages for decades, however, this Coubertin vision has been slowly eroded as professional athletes see the Olympic and Paralympic Games as just one event, albeit a very important one, in their lifecycle career. They cannot afford the luxury of spending unproductive periods socializing for days or weeks on end as part of that old model of community living. While there are exceptions to this generalization, this temporary residential occupation by athletes occurs mainly within the numerically larger teams which contribute nearly 75 per cent of the Games' residents.

Moreover, as reported above, their leaders continue to respond to their athletes' feedback by creating homes-from-home in an ever more exclusive manner both inside the Village and outside and, by so doing, accelerate the erosion of what is regarded as the essence of an Olympic Village. The incidental and spontaneous mixing and socializing and making new friendships of the past has all but disappeared other than within their own multi-sport domestic teams and their own disciplines. For Paris 2024, the decision not to complete part of the legacy project prior to the Games means that a proportion of some teams' staff allocation will be housed in Paris hotels at the organizers' expense. Brisbane 2032 will have at least three (main) Villages located within Brisbane, Gold Coast, and Sunshine Coast. To reassure delegations that these locations will have the same level and quality of services, the two coastal Villages will not be referred to as satellite Villages as might have been the case in the past. There will be no automatic right for an athlete to have a second bed in the other main Brisbane Village. This approach provides a sensible sustainable solution. Yet it comes at a cost in terms of what makes the Olympic and Paralympic Games unique. The question then arises: does it matter?

Notes

1. The event was a collaboration between the Olympic Museum in Lausanne and the Centre d'Estudis Olyimpics i de l'Esport, Universitat Autònomea de Barcelona.

2. The fact the number of athletes who attended Los Angeles was only roughly 50 per cent of the numbers competing in Paris and Amsterdam shows their concerns were not unfounded.

3. The biographies of the likes of Jesse Owens (Schaap, 2008) and Louis Zamperini (Hillenbrand, 2014) indicate that even as students these athletes travelled the length and breadth of their country in pursuit of their athletic ambitions.

4. In 2021, the Mayor of Wustermark announced a major residential development scheme for the site that embraced sensitivity to the historical significance of the Games Village there and the artefacts that it contains.

5. Louis Zamperini also acknowledged watching his rivals and fellow track stars in their races back in the Village (Hillenbrand, 2014).

6. Much of this was due to the German army commandant, Captain Wolfgang Fürstner: he was in effect the Village General manager responsible for all the planning and delivery of the Village. Tragically just before the arrival of the athletes he was demoted to second-in-command when it was discovered he was a non-Aryan: he committed suicide immediately after the Games (Cohen, 1996).

7. If evidence is needed, it is found in a seemingly insignificant piece of display in Number 39 Darmstadt, one of the restored houses and now a small museum. On a bedroom wall are two frames – one with a handwritten letter and its envelope addressed to Jesse Owens and a formal letter from the German Secret State Police.

The letter is a plea from an American fan asking Owens not to boycott the races at the Games but simply to refuse to receive the medals he inevitably will win as a protest against Nazism. The second letter accompanied the first and stated that it had been intercepted by the German Post and 'reviewed' by the SS. It had been considered inappropriate for delivery prior to the Games but was now being returned to Owens as he left Germany for the USA (Dost, 2003).

8.   The obligations until recently were laid out in the *Technical Manual on Olympic Village* (IOC, 2005) now renamed *Olympic Games Guide on Olympic Village*.

9.   They were held instead in Stockholm.

10.   Although not known by that name.

11.   The ISMGF was the equivalent of the IOC and fore-runner of the International Paralympic Committee. For more about the organization and management of Paralympic sport, see Chapter 5.

12.   They painted the houses but the paint faded in the sun, so the aim was not realized. In modern Villages, this type of orientation tool is used by Look features such as flags and banners (see Chapter 2).

13.   Until 1976 only spinal cord injured, wheelchair users participated in the Paralympic Games, hence the oft quoted title, 'wheelchair Olympics' (see also Chapter 5).

14.   See Hill (2022).

15.   The data were also available via an app.

Chapter 9

SECURITY AND THE THREAT OF TERRORISM

Jon Coaffee and *Pete Fussey*

As a condition of staging the Games, the International Olympic Committee (IOC) places responsibility on host cities to provide a safe environment for the 'Olympic Family' (competitors, officials, and dignitaries), while ensuring that such securitization does not get in the way of the sporting activities or spirit of the Games. As Thompson (1999, p. 106) observed, 'the IOC has made clear that the Olympics are an international sporting event, not an international security event, and while Olympic security must be comprehensive it must also be unobtrusive'. However, given the escalation and changing nature of the terrorist threat since 2001, 'securing' the Olympics has been increasingly difficult and costly to achieve (Coaffee and Murakami Wood, 2006). Certainly, if the risk of terrorism remains at its present critical level, there is the possibility of seeing core notions of Olympic spectacle replaced by dystopian images of 'cities under siege' as host cities' security personnel attempt to deliver an Olympics with maximum safety but minimum disruption to the schedule (Coaffee and Johnston, 2007).

As has been well documented, as a result of increased fears of international terrorism catalysed by the events of 9/11 (11 September 2001), the cost of security operations surrounding, in particular, Summer Olympic Games has increased dramatically since Athens 2004 (*ibid.*) with a large proportion of this increased cost being attributed to extra security personal as well as an array of temporary security measures, especially those which are effective at stopping or minimizing the impact of vehicle-borne improvised explosive devices (Coaffee, 2009). For most Olympic organizers, preparations for the Games necessarily include attempts to equate spectacle with safety and to 'design-out' terrorism, often by relying on highly militarized tactics and expensive and detailed contingency planning.

This chapter outlines how, since 9/11, such practices have intensified in form and scale. Moreover, such intensification is set to continue as we move towards the XXXIII Olympiad in Paris, a city itself subjected to a terrorism-related state of emergency spanning the years following the November 2015 attacks; a situation that has seen an extensive security infrastructure embedded into the urban scene alongside the vast deployment of armed police. Added to this is the emergent health related *état d'urgence sanitaire* introduced in response to the COVID-19 pandemic and representing a broadening of security concerns from the mobility of terrorism to the mobility of viruses (see Coaffee, 2022).

The Olympic Games have become an iconic terrorist target that imposes a burden of security on host cities well beyond what they would otherwise face. Security planning is now a key requirement of bids submitted to the IOC by prospective host cities and has become a crucial factor in planning the Games. There is now a broadly accepted security management 'model' for Olympic Games, which is modified according to local circumstances of place and that comprises elements of governance and organization which seek to forge a relationship between the numerous public safety agencies and the local Organizing Committee. This follows the example almost thirty years ago by the successful use of a dedicated Olympic police force at the 1994 Winter Games in Lillehammer, Norway. As well as the planned deployment of police and military personnel, and the co-option of private security and safety volunteers, a typical Olympic security regime also deploys the latest technology in an attempt to plan for and deter terrorist attacks. For example, recent Olympiads (especially the Summer Games), as well as other major sporting and cultural events, have become highly militaristic at certain geographical locations through the construction of large-scale bunkers and barriers, secure fencing around the key sites, as well as almost ubiquitous closed circuit television camera coverage. Pre-Games and Games-time monitoring of key sites also commonly occurs, for example, using scuba divers, helicopters, and high-tech devices such as ID badges with computer chips, biometric identifiers and remote detection hardware.

Such exorbitant levels of security also transform the cityscape into a series of temporary 'spaces of exception' (Agamben, 2005) with displacement of the policing by consent as special regulatory regimes are brought to bear to control behaviour and maintain order. As Browning (2000) observed during the period immediately before the 2000 Games, 'Sydney in September will be under siege'. Likewise, for the duration of the 2004 Games, Athens became a 'panoptic fortress' to give assurances to the rest of the world that the city was safe and secure to host the world's greatest sporting spectacle (Samatas, 2004, p. 115).

Securing the Olympic Spectacle

In light of these circumstances, the scrutinizing committees and delegates of the IOC will carefully examine bids to ensure that host cities provide the necessary safety and security for the smooth running of the games. This is particularly the case regarding international terrorism, which since the early 1970s, has become a crucial factor in planning the Games.

The imperative to address the phenomenon of international terrorism began with the so-called 'Munich Massacre' in 1972 when members of the Israeli Olympic team were killed after being taken hostage by the Palestinian terrorist organization Black September. This event, widely considered to have launched a new era of international terrorism (Reeve, 2001), saw the security bill for future Games soar. In particular, the events at Munich stimulated a period of reactivity, continuing to this day, whereby organizers have prioritized security to avoid hosting a repeat tragedy.

Sharply contrasting with Munich's 'low-key' approach to security (reflecting then-contemporary German sensitivities over conspicuous public displays of social control), little expense was spared on securing the 1976 Olympiad in Montreal. The fallout from Munich and the global condemnation levelled at the IOC and German authorities also led protection from terrorism to become *the* key security concern for Montreal's Organizing Committee (COJO, 1976). This was manifested in the first of many 'total security' approaches alongside the inauguration of several core principles informing the protection of subsequent Olympiads. These incorporated a strong emphasis on preventative strategies, a conspicuous security force presence, enhanced integrative practices (a failure at Munich), and intensive surveillance measures. Within these general principles, specific measures included isolated secure transport corridors between sites, accommodation, and transportation hubs; enhanced accreditation requirements for site workers and probably the first widespread and systematic deployment of CCTV to feature at an Olympics (*ibid.*). Montreal's reaction to the Munich massacre became a blueprint for future Olympic security operations.

These themes were embraced and consolidated at the next Olympic event at the geographically proximate Lake Placid Winter Games in 1980. Augmenting the Olympic site's geographical isolation were several strategies aimed at strengthening and surveying its perimeters including 12-foot touch sensitive fencing, voice analysers, 'bio-sensor' dogs, ground radar, night vision and CCTV (LPOOC, 1980). Together, these measures drew from strategies deployed to secure military sites and airports. Such was the level of securitization, the post-Games legacy of the Olympic village saw its conversion into a correctional facility (*ibid.*). Also of note was the unprecedented scale of private security deployment, a feature that has since become central to almost all subsequent Olympic security operations.

Although seen by some as isolated and distinct from other Olympic operations (Sanan, 1996), the components of Moscow's Olympic security strategy illustrate how these standardized principles may cut across geographical and ideological barriers. For example, the deployment of US-made security apparatus including metal detectors and x-ray scanners used at previous Games, including at Lake Placid during the same year, demonstrates continuity between Moscow and its predecessors. Moreover, the extensive use of zero-tolerance style policing approaches and exclusion orders have also featured at subsequent games, notably Sydney (Lenskyj, 2004) and Beijing (Peng and Yu, 2008), albeit with variations of scale. Although the contemporary form and function of social control in Brezhnev's Russia may have allowed these strategies to be applied with an intensity unacceptable elsewhere, with Sanan (1996) estimating that 120,000 people were displaced by Moscow's security strategy, many of the underlying principles informed both previous and subsequent Olympic security programmes. According to the *Wall Street Journal*, the average cost of security at the Summer Olympics Games rose from around $80 million to $1.5 billion over twenty years between Los Angeles 1984 and Athens 2004. When viewed based on cost per athlete, this equates to a rise from $11,627 per capita to $142,857 per capita (see table 9.1).

Table 9.1. Security costs of Olympic Games 1984–2004. (*Source*: Adapted from the *Wall Street Journal*, 22 August 2004)

Games	Total Security Cost (US$)	Cost per Athlete (US$)
Los Angeles (1984)	79.4 million	11,627
Seoul (1988)	111.7 million	13,312
Barcelona (1992)	66.2 million	7,072
Atlanta (1996)	108.2 million	10,486
Sydney (2000)	179.6 million	16,062
Athens (2004)	1.5 billion	142,857

Security for Los Angeles 1984 was organized by the private sector, but successfully launched a relationship between the numerous public safety agencies and the Organizing Committee that has been adopted subsequently. At Los Angeles, the arguments to spend large amounts of finance on security were largely premised on heightened tensions emanating from the Cold War. Notably, less than three months before the Opening Ceremony, the Soviet Union announced that it was boycotting the Games, blaming not only the overt commercialization of the Olympic spectacle, but crucially a lack of adequate security measures. This, they argued, amounted to a violation of the Olympic Charter.

By contrast, Seoul 1988 witnessed the South Koreans engage in a large-scale security operation, with their major concern being North Korea's use of Japanese proxies to bomb Korean aviation in the run-up to 1988 and the spectre of further attacks on the Games. This involved over 100,000 security personnel drawn from the police, military, and private security forces – the largest in Games history at the time. The organizers also drafted thousands of volunteers in to help with security. The Korean question became further involved in Games' security when riot police were sent in to break up demonstrations by student protestors seeking unification of the two countries. In addition, North Korean hostility to the Seoul Olympiad led the IOC to adopt a new and unprecedented international diplomatic function. For many, the security operation is what captured the headlines in news media rather than sporting spectacle.

Barcelona 1992 saw the deployment of over 25,000 security personnel due to fears expressed over reprisal terror attacks linked to the recently ended 1991 Gulf War, coupled with action from the Basque separatist movement, ETA, Catalan separatists, Terra Lliure, and left wing extremists, Grupo de Resistencia Antifascista Primo Octobre. Although this operation used fewer security personnel than in Seoul, security was highly militaristic at certain sites. The security forces, for instance, constructed large-scale bunkers around the perimeter of the main Olympic Village, with tanks situated at strategic locations. This complemented secure fencing and numerous closed circuit television cameras within the village, as well as a highly visible police presence at the sporting locations.

Prior to Atlanta 1996, terrorism was not considered the major risk facing the Games despite serious terrorist attacks on American soil at the World Trade Centre (1993) and at Oklahoma City (1995). As the *Wall Street Journal* (2004) emphasized, terrorism ranked behind heat-related illness and the possibility of soccer violence on the official lists of 'potential worries'. That said, law enforcement agencies assigned more than 20,000 military and law enforcement personnel to monitor security measures, supplemented by 5,000 unarmed volunteer security personnel in an operation that, for some, was seen as the most hi-tech and measured in Olympic history. On the eve of the Games, for example, Macko (1996), argued that:

> When it comes to the security of these games, nothing has been left to chance in Atlanta and the other venues that will be used by the athletes. An army of law enforcement officers will outnumber the athletes themselves. The security for the 1996 games is said to be the tightest ever in history. Security planners for the Olympic Games have tried to cover every angle possible – from cops on patrol to scuba divers and helicopters and high-tech devices such as ID badges with computer chips.

Despite these intensive preparations, the small-scale bomb blast that occurred at an unsecured public space designed for the Olympics, killing one person and injuring over 100, re-ignited fears of further attacks.

Fears of the alternative spectacle of violence led to even tighter measures to protect the official Olympic spectacle at Sydney 2000. The cost and sophistication of security rose steeply from that incurred in Atlanta and involved nearly all Australia's Special Forces plus 30,000 security personnel (drawn from the police, private security, and volunteers) who were also called to duty. Even though the National Australian government considered, in public at least, that the risk of attack was unlikely, the media began highlighting connections between Osama Bin Laden, the most wanted on the CIA's terrorist hit list, and Australia.

Although no major terrorist incident took place during Sydney 2000, the spectre of terrorist violence took on unparalleled concern for Athens 2004, particularly in view of the security situation in both Greece and internationally. The cost of security increased dramatically. As table 9.1 reveals, despite being the smallest nation to host the Games since 1952, the Greek authorities spent well over five times more than the amount spent by the Sydney organizers and deployed over 70,000 specially trained police and soldiers as well as another 35,000 military personnel to patrol the streets. Military hardware used for security was the most expensive used for the Olympics. It included a network of 13,000 surveillance cameras, mobile surveillance vans, chemical detectors, several Patriot anti-aircraft missile sites, NATO troops specializing in responding to weapons of mass destruction, AWAC early warning surveillance planes, police helicopters, fighter jets, minesweepers, and monitoring airships (see Smith, 2004). The airships themselves became icons of the Games and attracted much media interest. Indeed, the Security Airship patrolling above the Olympic sites was joined by a second Skyship that broadcast images for US television networks and gave spectacular aerial footage of the Games.

The Olympic stadium in Athens, always likely to constitute the most spectacular target, received the heaviest fortification. According to Peek (2004, p. 6) Athens was 'supposed to be one of the most secure places on earth, impenetrable to terrorists plotting a possible attack on this summer's Olympics'. Significantly, the Olympics forced the Greek state to speed up the modernization of its state security system. For the duration of the games, Athens became a 'panoptic fortress' to give assurances to the rest of the world that the city was safe and secure to host the world's greatest sporting spectacle (Samatas, 2004, p. 115). However, the retrofitting of such security systems was envisioned as a long-term project that would be maintained after the Olympics and which critics have argued will become a menace to privacy and civil liberties (*ibid.*, p. 117). Moreover, the technological centrepiece of the strategy, Science Applications International Corporation's 'C4I' ('Command', 'Control', 'Coordination', 'Communications', and 'Integration') system was a colossal failure. Unable to host the large numbers of potential users, the fabled communications system never operated to capacity and, on still failing to establish the system in time for the Beijing Games, its manufacturers were forced by the Greek courts to compensate the Athenian authorities (Samatas, 2007).

As chapter 15 makes clear, the IOC's award of the XXIX Olympiad to Beijing in July 2001 stimulated large-scale development of the city. Coupled with China's hosting of the 2010 World Expo in Shanghai and the 2010 Asian Games in Guangzhou, the Beijing Games catalysed a monumental security programme across the country both within these epicentres of tourism and beyond. Embedded within this programme was a central emphasis on technological and surveillance-based approaches that included use of Radio Frequency Identification (RFID) tags in tickets to some Olympic events (such as the opening ceremonies) to enable their holders' movements to be monitored. Despite such headline-catching technologies, however, the principal emphasis was on developing and inaugurating CCTV networks. These included the 'Grand Beijing Safeguard Sphere' (developed between 2001 and the start of the Games) which, according to some claims, cost over $6 billion and invested the city with 300,000 networked and highly capable public CCTV cameras (*inter alia Los Angeles Times*, 2007). Nationally, China's hosting of sporting mega-events has also coincided with the 'Safe Cities' programme aimed to establish surveillance cameras in 600 cities (*New York Times*, 2007). As elsewhere, these technological approaches were combined with more traditional 'low-tech' forms of policing. In particular, the state's capacity to mobilize security manifested in the deployment of 100,000 personnel whilst policing strategies adopted 'sand-pile' techniques (Peng and Yu, 2008), vernacular interpretation of zero-tolerance strategies adopted at other Olympiads (notably Seoul and Sydney). Moreover, security hardware often found itself centre stage in television coverage. As Boyle and Heggerty (2009, p. 64) observed: '… the conspicuous placement of ground-to-air missile launchers near the Bird's Nest stadium formed a striking backdrop for the many televised reports from the Games beamed around the globe'.

Planning for the Worst: The Security Games 2012

Planning for the worst has become a mantra of contemporary urbanism as pre-emptive actions are increasingly mobilized to alleviate fears of potential catastrophe. Such pre-emption developed through the exercising of emergencies in table-top or scenario planning exercises that better allow future security challenges to be addressed, becomes very visible during mega-event hosting where a range of precautionary governance techniques are employed to consider and plan for unpredictable and high consequence 'what if' events. As Boyle and Haggerty (2012, p. 241) noted in their analysis of Olympic security, the 'expressive dimension of security at the Games provides a window into wider issues of how authorities "show" that they can deliver on the promise of maximum security under conditions of radical uncertainty [and] how officials emphasize that they have contemplated and planned for all possible security threats, especially catastrophic threats and worst-case scenarios'.

In the United Kingdom, the securitizing of sporting spectacles became increasingly prominent as London geared up to hosting the Olympic Games. Not only did security concerns and responses play a critical part in the bidding process, they also dominated media discussion immediately after the host city was announced. On 7 July 2005, the day after the announcement of London's successful bid, a series of co-ordinated terrorist bomb attacks took place on the city's transport network, prompting even more detailed security plans. The initial security bill quadrupled from £225 million to over £1 billion with the adoption of advanced smart surveillance systems both to monitor crowds and athletes and to track suspects across the city (Fussey *et al.*, 2011). In a global city famed for its policing and surveillance assets, such additions contributed significantly to the overall securitization of the city. Indeed, Olympic security initiatives were grafted over a pre-existing security infrastructure, one which had evolved over many years due to the threat of Irish Republican and other forms of terrorism. As noted by the Metropolitan Police Authority (2007):

> The 2012 Olympic and Paralympic Games will require the largest security operation ever conducted in the United Kingdom. The success of the Games will be ultimately dependant on the provision of a safe and secure environment free from a major incident resulting in loss of life. The challenge is demanding; the global security situation continues to be characterised by instability with international terrorism and organised crime being a key component.

Olympic Security Planning in Policy and Practice

Demonstrating the domestic influence on mega-event security planning, an updated *Olympic and Paralympic Safety and Security Strategy* (Home Office, 2011) was developed in March 2011 which set out the key aims and objectives for the Police and Government in delivering security for the Games. The strategy's overarching aim was 'to deliver a safe and secure Games, in keeping with the Olympic culture and spirit' (*ibid.*, p. 7). This strategy was in line with the latest revised UK National Security Strategy: *A Strong Britain in an Age of Uncertainty: The National Security Strategy* (October 2010) and was harmonized with the third iteration of the UK's overarching counter-terrorism strategy, CONTEST (HM Government, 2011). The CONTEST strategy itself specifically focused on the 2012 Games, noting that the UK had guaranteed the IOC that it would 'take all financial, planning and operational measures necessary to guarantee the safety and the peaceful celebration of the Games' (*ibid.*, p. 105). Thus, despite the range of threats and hazards facing Olympic planning, terrorism and its attendant implication of ineffective security became the principal focus of the Games' security planning, overshadowing all others.

As the preparations for the 2012 Olympics were finessed a range of diverse agencies were drawn into play. Here, security planning became managed by the UK Security Services, the Olympic Security Directorate, and the multi-stakeholder London Resilience Forum which developed detailed pre-emptive security plans to sit alongside pre-existing resilience strategies, seeking to plan out vulnerabilities in advance. Thus, broader and more disparate security planning became sharply focused on issues of terrorism and on the means of mitigation. In May 2012, three months before the Games were to begin, 'Operation Olympic Guardian' began – a pre-emptive scenario-planning exercise intended to test security and resilience preparedness ahead of the Games. Militarized features in this role-play included the testing of air missile defence systems, the responsiveness of Typhoon jet forces, and the establishment of 'No-fly' Zones over London. As one BBC correspondent noted, such an exercise has the potential both to alarm and reassure in equal measure:

> Exercise Olympic Guardian is an opportunity to fine-tune military plans. But it is also aimed at reassuring the public... The sound of fighter jets and military helicopters, along with the sight of the Royal Navy's largest warship, HMS Ocean, in the Thames may reassure many. But for some, just talk of this military hardware is causing alarm – most notably the plans to station ground-based air defence systems at six sites around the capital. (BBC News, 2012a)

At that time, campaign groups such as the 'Stop the War' coalition accused the government of causing unnecessary alarm and a 'climate of fear' in the capital (BBC News, 2012b). Such claims were exacerbated by related activity which sited anti-aircraft missiles on the top of East London tower blocks. Residents learned through leaflets that a high-velocity missile system could be placed on a nearby water tower at Bow Quarter offering a perfect view of the nearby Olympic Park (BBC News 2012c). This again connected with an enduring set of processes by which, slowly but surely, saw military-threat-response technologies and procedures being repurposed for use in the civic realm (Graham, 2010).

As 2012 drew near and interest in all aspects of Games preparation intensified, security-related stories were increasingly common in the print media both in the UK and worldwide. Particularly notable here was the media emphasis on military-carceral features of the overall Olympic security strategy. For example, many reports centred on the use of military hardware to control city spaces, airspace, or transport corridors. Headlines included: 'Ministry of Defence to control London airspace during Games for first time since Second World War' (*Daily Telegraph*); 'Anti-terrorism tool at forefront of 2012 London Olympic security' (*Alaska Dispatch*); 'Sonic device deployed in London during Olympics' (BBC News London); and 'Armoured cars drafted in as security tightens ahead of the Olympic Games' (*Daily Mirror*). Other reports highlighted a set of issues regarding policing of the Games, often described as an unprecedented UK peacetime operation, with up to 12,000 officers from fifty-two forces deployed at 'peak time', alongside private security staff, and the use of novel security technologies: 'Metropolitan police plastic bullets stockpile up to 10,000 after UK riots – Scotland Yard confirms August unrest has led to increase in stock of baton rounds as security measures upped before Olympics' (*The Guardian*); 'Metropolitan Police double officers around torch as crowds bigger than predicted' (*Daily Telegraph*, 2012); 'Metropolitan Police given 350 mobile fingerprint scanners in Olympics policing boost' (V3 News, see Coaffee, 2012); and 'Former Royal Marines to ferry around super-rich Games spectators' (*London Evening Standard*, 2012).

Yet such urban incursions were not universally welcomed. As the Games approached, the uneven impact both on Londoners and visitors to the capital became highlighted: 'Fish photographer caught in Olympics terror alert: A man taking photos of a fish tank was stopped by a security guard who was supposed to be alert for hostile reconnaissance amid pre-Olympics terrorism fears' (*Amateur Photographer*, 2012); 'Olympics welcome does not extend to all in London as police flex muscles; Dispersal zone at Olympic Park will target anti-social behaviour, and there are claims sex workers are being cleansed' (*The Guardian*, 2012a); and, 'Olympic crackdown: UK govt targets protests' (*Russia Today*, see Coaffee, 2012). 'Brand' exclusion zones around all Olympic venues were also established (Advertising and Street Trade Restrictions Venue Restriction Zone) so that the Olympic canvas could belong exclusively to key sponsors. This type of scrutiny also extended to the clothing of spectators which was screened for prominent displays of competing (non-Olympic) brands: 'Brand Police on Patrol to Enforce Sponsors' Exclusive Rights' (*International Business Times*, 2012).

As the Games drew near, activist activity intensified and became distinctly focused upon the intensive militarized security measures being ushered into East London. One of the highest profile campaigns was the Stop the Olympic Missiles campaign, driven by the Stop the War coalition, architects of the anti-Iraq War demonstrations in 2002–2003. This led to an unsuccessful yet high-profile High Court challenge by residents of Fred Wigg and John Walsh Towers in Leytonstone contesting the Army's right to deploy missiles at their place of residence. Anti-Olympic activism reached its zenith the day after the Opening Ceremony with the 'Whose Games? Whose City?' event where hundreds of activists representing more than thirty groups marched through Tower Hamlets in protest at the militarization, territorial enclosure and corporatization of the Games (Boykoff and Fussey, 2013).

Post-Games Olympic Security as Local Legacy

In the event, the 2012 Olympics passed off without any serious threat of terrorism being reported and with minimum disruption. The visual appearance of security was, in large part, restricted to the entrance to the venues where search procedures were carried out by the British Army. After the Games, missiles were dismantled and troops redeployed.

However, less well documented in the coverage of security planning has been post-games *legacy* that has been materially inscribed on the East London landscape, and improved organizational ways of working that have been learnt by the agencies involved in security planning. Legacy has become an Olympic watchword in recent years as host cities attempt to extract maximum value from the event as well as seeking a convenient rhetoric for diffusing difficult arguments. As Gold and Gold (2010, pp. 2–3) noted, legacy has now become 'the touchstone' by which politicians and municipal managers judge the cost and benefits of bidding to stage major sporting events. Moreover, as host cities are selected, and pre-Games preparation starts in earnest, the rhetoric of 'legacy' promises plays an important function as the justification for a range of disruptions and cost increases. Legacy, in this context is thus often asserted as 'fact' of what *will* happen, whereas in reality, it is based on a set of loose assumptions about what will *hopefully* occur many years in the future.

Legacy was always a key component of the overall London 2012 security plan and was at the forefront of police strategies. As the Chief Inspector of Metropolitan Police noted in 2006:

> we want the security legacy to be us leaving a safe and secure environment for the communities of East London after the Games, on issues such as safer neighbourhoods, lighting and crime prevention. We want a Games legacy that will reduce crime and the fear of crime. (cited in Fussey *et al.*, 2011)

In London, as the post-games period progresses, there is little sign that much of the hi-tech equipment purchased by police forces has been put away. The security infrastructure is embedded within transformative urban regeneration programmes and is promoted as central to long-term community safety. It is hoped that Olympic-related security will assist in developing safer neighbourhoods through measures such as improved lighting, and lead to a reduction in crime and the fear of crime. For example, the Olympic Village, repurposed as private housing, was granted a new level of 'Secure by Design' status set to inform the construction of future housing developments, presenting a permanent material security legacy to its residents and users.

The story of securitizing the 2012 Games did not start on 7/7 but evolved over many decades into protection of the Olympic spectacle. Nor did it end once the well-protected Olympic flame was extinguished at the Closing Ceremony. The security legacy in London is the most comprehensive plan seen for urban regeneration *and* security in modern Olympic history. While at previous Olympics these security features have largely been temporary and removed in the post-games period, in London *permanent* design and architectural features have been embedded within the material landscape. Likewise, a significant repository of knowledge and expertise has been retained in London-based networks regarding civil contingency planning for an array of disruptive challenges and for securitizing urban areas at home and abroad. In its development of secure regeneration spaces, London's security community has created a 'blueprint' for knowledge transfer across the globe for when mega-events come to town.

Rio's successful candidacy to host the 2016 Olympic Games also drew on these continuities of mega-event security. Its Candidate file (Rio 2016 Bid Committee, 2009) argued that the city was able to develop a suitable security infrastructure, facilitated by other mega-events it would host in advance of the Olympics:

> The Games will act as a major catalyst for long-term systemic improvements in safety and security systems in the City of Rio, representing a genuine opportunity for transformation, a process already commenced through the staging of the 2007 Pan American Games and evolving with the preparation for the 2014 FIFA World Cup.

Although security practices became prioritized towards long-term crime prevention programmes rather than international terrorism (*ibid.*, 2009), security remained a major concern for Rio's Organizing Committee (Coaffee and Fussey, 2010). The immediate concerns specifically related to the city's murder rate and fears of theft from tourists. Solutions to these problems coupled attention to required Olympic security standards with Rio's tradition of delineating 'high value' spaces from their urban context through crime prevention measures (Coy, 2006), reinforcing the risk of further splintering of Rio's divided landscape and providing a significant challenge to its regenerative aspirations and legacy. Indeed, visits to Brazil by the UK Foreign and Commonwealth Office, intended to allow the UK security industry 'to pursue commercial opportunities and become the partner of choice for sport security', reported that:

> Brazil sees a step change in the security situation in Rio as a legacy of the Olympic Games in 2016 in particular and is making progress on sustainable 'pacification' of favelas. (FCO, 2011)

As in London, security planning in Rio began in the aftermath of the decision to award the Games on 2 October 2009. Two weeks later (17 October), fire fights between rival drug gangs resulted in a police helicopter being shot down and eight buses set on fire. This led public authorities to promise enhanced security ahead of the Games (and the 2014 FIFA World Cup). As such, resources have been poured into programmes to reduce crime and to enhance emergency planning organization, with authorities prepared to mount an overwhelming security presence at the sporting events to ensure safety. Indeed, the Games themselves saw the deployment of 85,000 security personnel (*New York Times*, 2016). Such operations widened the security perimeter around Rio's residential and tourist area and notably led to the deployment of specially trained police pacification units (UPPs) in over thirty local areas to deal with communities which for years had been ruled by drug traffickers and paramilitary militias. Notably, the extra impetus and funding given to the *favela* 'pacification' programme as a result of the 2016 Games afforded policing units with more advanced surveillance equipment, with some local claims that *Rocinha*, the largest *favela* in Rio, had the most expansive CCTV surveillance in the world, with more cameras per resident than London (BBC News, 2013). Some also argued in advance of the Games (e.g. Freeman, 2012) that such pacification is having uneven spatial consequences and forcing the poorest *favela* dwellers out as gentrification takes hold – a type of neo-liberal revanchist strategy which is cleansing and purifying the Olympic city to allow colonization by the rich in areas once considered *terra incognita*.

Rio also invested in strategic level technologies to co-ordinate and control its various security and disaster management processes in the build-up to the Olympic Games. Opened in 2010 the IBM-built 'operations centre' served to integrate the vast majority of the city's management functions, including security, in what many are hailing as the model for 'smarter city' development (*New York Times*, 2012). At the time, though, not all were convinced and wondered 'if it is all for show, to reassure Olympic officials and foreign investors. Some worry that it will benefit well-off neighbourhoods more than the *favelas*. Others fear that all this surveillance has the potential to curb freedoms or invade privacy' (*ibid.*; also Freeman, 2014.).

Rio's overall security plan, however, was explicitly about 'legacy', not for the event organizers who might be able to market Rio as a safe 'event destination', but for citizens of the city and of Brazil more generally. As the Federal Police Chief observed in March 2013, the Rio Olympics sought to create a safety and security legacy following a history of gang-related violence. He noted that crime was falling, and the divided city image associated with Rio was diminishing:

> Before now, we have never had a chance to help people in the favelas and they have been very isolated… But now that we have the World Cup coming to Brazil in 2014 and

the Olympics coming to Rio in 2016, we have been able to change this… For so long Rio has been divided, but this is our chance to bridge the gap… We are already seeing huge success because crime rates have dropped and we are recovering areas that had never been part of society before. This is a legacy from the Olympic Games that is happening right now and after the Olympics are gone, it will leave legacy of safety and security after so many years of violence… Everything is better and that is the great legacy of the Olympics. (Cited by *Inside the Games*, 2012)

More critically, scholars also commented how the advanced and fast-paced globalization being experienced in Brazil has impacted on the likely legacy of the 2016 Olympics. As Gaffney (2010, p. 7) noted, the uneven geographies caused by mega-events are now a concrete part of the infrastructure planning that 'impose a neo-liberal "shock doctrine", installing temporary regimes of extra-legal governance that [will] permanently transform socio-space in Rio de Janeiro'. Of enormous consequence is how such security infrastructures gained additional purpose during shifts in the post-Olympic political landscape. The 2018 ascendency of far-right president Jair Bolsanaro led to widespread persecution and human rights abuses, particularly against minorities. In security actions redolent of Brazil's military dictatorship, a *junta* publicly admired by Bolsonaro himself, police killed 6,416 people during 2020 alone, more than half being young black men (Amnesty International, 2021). Heavy investment in advanced state security architectures for a three-week sporting event, therefore, can and does have grave implications for minoritized populations for years ahead.

Standardization and the Olympic Assemblage

The numerous security vernaculars which inevitably penetrate the IOC's governance, given the exceptionality of security needs experienced by hosts, enables standardized forms of security to prevail. Together, the exceptionality of Olympic security coupled with the transference of its strategies across time and place culminates in standardized approaches that map on to the uneven terrain of diverse host cities. Borrowing from Bauman (2000), such transferable paradigms operate as a form of 'liquid security' where a shared *lingua franca* of defensible motifs coalesce into spaces that become disassociated from their geographical contexts. In turn, these spaces of exception, once constructed, generate a particular vision of order, a dislocated uniformity owing to, as Bauman (*ibid.*, p. 103) suggested: 'the lack of overlap between the elegance of structure and the messiness of the world'.

What we can gauge from a study of securitization employed by Olympic host cities is a series of normalized event security features which combine temporary physical features and the officious management of spaces with the aim of projecting an air of safety and security both for visitors as well as potential investors (Coaffee *et al.*, 2008).

First, there is intense pre-planning involving the development of control zones around the site, procedures to deal with evacuation, contamination and decontamination, and major incident access. Technical information was also scrutinized for all structures and ventures so that any weakness and vulnerabilities could be planned-out in advance.

Secondly, there is the development of 'island security' involving the 'locking down' of vulnerable areas of host cities with large expanses of steel fencing and concrete blocks surrounding the sporting venues. This combines with a high visibility police presence, backed up by private security, the security services, and a vast array of permanent and temporary CCTV cameras and airport-style checkpoints to screen spectators. Often events, such as the Olympics, are used to field test 'new' technologies. Most recently, in the summer of 2021 many advanced surveillance technologies that made use of facial recognition (and increasingly the internet of things and artificial intelligence) were deployed at the delayed Tokyo 2020 Summer Games for disease prevention, risk assessment, and venue security, and in contributing to the legacy aim of making Tokyo an increasingly inclusive and 'smart' city.

Thirdly, to back up the intense 'island security', peripheral buffer zones are often set up in advance containing a significant visible police presence. This is commonly reinforced by the presence of law-enforcement tactics such as police helicopters, a blanket 'no-fly zone', fleets of mobile CCTV vehicles and road checks and stop and search procedures. The result of these measures is that often access to 'public' spaces is restricted on public roads and the use of public footpaths, because of 'security concerns' (Coaffee *et al.*, 2008).

Fourthly, the enhanced resilience that such security planning, in theory, delivers is actively utilized as a future selling point for urban competitiveness in that the ability to host such an event in a safe and secure fashion and without incident is significant in attracting future cultural activities and in branding a city as a major events venue.

Fifthly, there is increased evidence from major sporting events that a lasting benefit of hosting events is the opportunity to retrofit permanent security infrastructure linked to longer-term crime reduction strategies and 'legacy'. This post-event inheritance of security infrastructures is a common Olympic legacy. Indeed, the legacy of retained private policing following the Tokyo 1964 and Seoul 1988 Olympiads, and the continuation of zero-tolerance style exclusion laws after the Sydney 2000 games are cases in point. Likewise for Athens 2004, the retrofitting of such security systems was envisioned as a long-term project to be maintained after the Olympics which has been condemned by civil libertarians (Athens Indymedia, 2005).

In London 2012 the emphasis on a regeneration legacy for the people of East London also extended to the machinery of security. Indeed, in 2009 the tenders for Olympic Park security providers encouraged companies to supply 'security legacy', thus bequeathing substantial mechanisms and technologies of control to the post-event site. Here, questions remain over the security priorities of a high-profile international sporting event attended by millions of people and the degree of infrastructure that will remain to police a large urban parkland.

Bidding to host an Olympics is also, in many cases, considered a strong enough stimulus to develop robust security planning procedures. For example, the unsuccessful bid by Cape Town for the 2004 Games required the city to be seen as secure enough to host the Olympics. As a result an extensive security infrastructure was introduced into areas posited as likely venues and visitor accommodation centres (Minnaar, 2007). After their bid failed, the CCTV systems were not removed; instead, they were justified as part of a general programme to combat crime, which was thought to be discouraging foreign tourists, investors, and conference delegates (Coaffee and Murakami Wood, 2006).

Conclusion

In terms of the relationship between security and Olympic spectacle, the IOC regulations and guidance for host cities make clear that it is their responsibility to provide a safe environment for the 'Olympic Family' (competitors, officials, and dignitaries), while ensuring that such securitization does not get in the way of the sporting activities or spirit of the Games. This, increasingly, is a difficult balance to achieve. Certainly, if the risk of terrorism remains at its present level, there is the possibility of seeing core notions of Olympic spectacle to some extent replaced by dystopian images of cities under siege as organizers, security personnel, and the media attempt to deliver an Olympics in maximum safety and with minimum disruption to the schedule (Coaffee et al., 2011).

Chapter 10

URBAN REGENERATION

Andrew Smith

Urban regeneration is often cited as one of the main justifications for staging the Olympic Games (Smith, 2012). Barcelona 1992 highlighted the potential of the Olympics as a vehicle for regeneration, inspiring subsequent host cities – particularly London – to use the Games to regenerate disadvantaged urban areas. Regeneration legacies have been principally pursued by the hosts of Summer Games, but they are increasingly relevant to winter editions too, for example the Milan 2026 Games (Del Bianco, 2021). There are also examples where urban regeneration has resulted from losing Olympic bids (Oliver, 2011), further highlighting the way that the Olympics have become *regeneration games.*

The aims of this chapter are to explore how and why the Olympic Games are used as a vehicle for urban regeneration, to outline the outcomes of these initiatives, and to suggest how Olympic regeneration might evolve in the future. Through this analysis, the chapter draws some important conclusions about the Olympic Games, but also about urban regeneration processes in general. Regeneration can be understood as a practice and an outcome, but also a discourse, and this chapter analyses the commonly cited rhetoric that the Olympic Games provide 'flagship' projects and 'catalysts' for regeneration. Instead of using the Games to stimulate urban regeneration, it concludes that the best outcomes are achieved when the Olympic Games are integrated within ongoing regeneration plans. It also highlights the need for more emphasis on social regeneration and ecologically regenerative urbanism, rather than physical and economic regeneration. Relevant editions of the Olympic Games are used to illustrate the discussion but, rather than discussing cases in turn, the chapter is organized around themes that help clarify the complex relationship between the Olympics and urban regeneration.

Regeneration: Definition and Critique

Urban regeneration means reversing the cycle of decline which afflicts many urban areas. The term is directly linked to the post-industrial era (roughly since 1973), a period when many cities and citizens have struggled to adapt to new economic circumstances. In this context, urban regeneration encompasses policies, programmes and projects designed to help specific parts of cities recover from decline. Regeneration has become a rather generic term, but it can be differentiated from wider urban policy by its geographical focus: it involves targeted interventions in post-industrial, brownfield sites. To provide focus, this spatially limited interpretation is adopted here and, thus, initiatives to stimulate economic development at wider scales – for whole cities, regions, nations – are not addressed directly.

Leary and McCarthy (2013, p. 9) define urban regeneration as efforts 'to produce significant, sustainable improvements in the conditions of local people, communities and places suffering from aspects of deprivation'. This focus on long-term, broad-based ambitions reflects the most widely used definition of regeneration: 'to bring about a lasting improvement in the economic, social and environmental conditions of an area that has been subject to change' (Roberts, 2000, p. 17). Definitions such as these highlight that, in the contemporary era, the term refers to social and economic ambitions as well as those linked to physical improvement. This holistic approach represents a welcome reorientation towards the needs of people, although one drawback is that it means regeneration has come to mean almost anything to do with urban change. Regeneration is inherently linked to other processes such as renewal, remediation, and renaissance – producing an alliterative lexicon which causes confusion. These three terms are often used inter-changeably but are best understood as more specific phenomena than regeneration: remediation means the reclamation of land; renewal refers to physical change, and renaissance implies the revival of urban culture.

The definitions cited above make regeneration sound like a very laudable, if rather vague and optimistic, endeavour. However, there are critics of the concept who point to some of the inherent problems when it is practised rather than merely proposed. Allen and Cochrane (2014, p. 1611) describe regeneration as 'a troubled and troubling concept' because it involves making promises which are incompatible and therefore impossible to achieve. For example, making an area more economically productive may require radical change that does not assist the people who currently live there (*ibid.*). Too often we see the regeneration *of* communities rather than regeneration *for* communities, a trend which means that regeneration is now regarded as a negative phenomenon by many communities and commentators, for example, in the context of London's housing estates (Watt, 2021). There are other reasons to be sceptical about regeneration. Like other normative ideas (such as sustainability), the term has been appropriated by a range of interests for their own ends. For example, it is now part of the language of property developers who use it to add value to real estate. Even more worryingly, regeneration is often used as a euphemism for radical urban transformation; something that helps to justify the eviction of people and businesses.

The Olympic Games and Urban Regeneration

Staging the Olympic Games requires hosts to provide appropriate sports facilities, as well as suitable accommodation and transport provision. Therefore, it is unsurprising that post-industrial cities have decided to use the Games as an opportunity to improve amenities, housing, and infrastructure in areas which have suffered decline. The scale of facilities required for the contemporary Games, particularly the summer Olympiad, means that densely populated cities can only accommodate them within the existing urban fabric by using sites that were formerly occupied by industrial installations such as railway yards, docks, warehouses, and factories. Following this logic, regeneration is a practical requirement to stage the Games, rather than an overriding objective. However, cities have gone beyond what is necessary merely to host the event; using the Games as an opportunity to make more radical and more extensive improvements to specific urban areas. This adds to the costs of staging the Games and causes confusion over what is and what is not part of the Olympic budget when overall costs (and cost-benefit analyses) are calculated.

During the post-industrial era, two main regeneration strategies have been used by Olympic hosts. The first is to identify a large, peripheral site that requires regeneration and redevelop it as a new piece of city. For example, in Sydney (760 hectares) and London (250 hectares), large sites were assembled, reclaimed, and developed as Olympic Parks. In both cases, a large amount of toxic industrial land was decontaminated – something that might not have occurred without the impetus provided by the Games. Post-event these have been re-developed as multi-functional sites which are typical of a new breed of mixed-use mega-projects (Lehrer and Laidley, 2009). These include sports stadia, but also office space, housing, retail and cultural facilities and parklands. A second approach, adopted by cities such as Athens, Barcelona, Rio de Janeiro, and Vancouver, has been to regenerate a series of smaller sites close to the city centre. These often include converting port infrastructures into leisure-oriented waterfronts (Pinto and Lopes dos Santos, 2022). For example, Barcelona used the Games to regenerate its waterfront as one of four main Olympic sites used to host the Games. In a similar manner, former industrial land in the southeast corner of False Creek was remediated to build the Olympic Village for the Vancouver 2010 Games.

The idea of the Olympic Games as an agent that regenerates cities has become widely accepted, but this is an over-simplistic and problematic interpretation. The Olympic Games do not and cannot regenerate urban areas. Regeneration achievements are sometimes attributed to the Games when they are actually the result of parallel urban initiatives or macro-environmental factors. However, staging the Games does offer certain advantages for governments and urban regimes wishing to pursue regeneration ambitions. It may unlock funding that would otherwise be unavailable, help to generate civic support for large-scale public investment in urban districts, and it provides a clear narrative and justification for urban change (Smith, 2012). The high-profile nature of the event means that political actors are forced to undertake improvements that might not otherwise be delivered. Finally, and perhaps most importantly, staging the Olympic Games imposes a non-negotiable deadline for urban projects. These characteristics and associated issues are discussed further below.

The Olympic Games as a Flagship

One way that new Olympic venues and associated infrastructure have been linked to regeneration is via their role as 'flagship' projects that kick-start (re)development in ex-industrial sites. Urban flagships are designed as 'marshalling points for further investment' (Smyth, 1994, p. 5) to encourage a 'flotilla' of other developments in their wake (Bianchini *et al.*, 1992). This mode of regeneration involves a top-down, property driven approach that emerged in the 1980s. In such cases, regeneration represents an intervention that helps to address the failure of market forces to instigate post-industrial transformation. Staging the Olympic Games provides a good excuse to remediate land and provide new infrastructure and venues, on the basis that this will lead to future commercial investment and jobs. Sydney 2000 was a good example of this type of approach. Before the Games organizers had not planned the post-event era; they merely assumed that remediating a well-located site, providing new infrastructure (rail and road connections) and Olympic venues would encourage future growth.

The Olympic Games are seen as a particularly valuable flagship project because investors know that governments have to deliver so, unlike other regeneration projects, there is less chance that development will drift, stall, or collapse. The global financial crisis that began in 2008 demonstrated this. Private consortia were unable to deliver Olympic Villages in Vancouver and London, so the government stepped in and funded them. These bailouts would not have happened if these Villages had been conventional housing developments, but Olympic projects were deemed too important to fail. Government intervention and public funding reassured private sector companies, encouraging them to invest in these regeneration projects. This highlights the way the Games act as a tool that 'de-risks' urban areas for potential investors (Smith, 2014). Improvements to the area's image derived from Olympic symbolism help to achieve this effect, but the scale of public investment is a major factor too.

Using Olympic projects as flagship developments sounds like a practical solution that unlocks the unrealized potential of large derelict areas. However, there are several problems with this type of approach. Olympic regeneration tends to involve using large amounts of public money to lower risks for private investors. So, even if investment is attracted to Olympic sites, commentators have argued that this represents a dubious public subsidy (Scherer, 2011). For example, it is suggested that public investment in Vancouver's Olympic Village involved a socialization of risk and a privatization of benefits (Vanwynsberghe *et al.*, 2013). The same thing had happened a decade previously in Sydney (figure 10.1), where large state subsidies were needed to help 'offset the risk' for the consortium tasked with building and converting the Olympic Village (Searle, 2012, p. 198). This links to a wider concern about Olympic regeneration: it tends to serve the interests of the construction and property sectors, rather than the interests of local citizens (Smith, 2012).

Another problem with flagship-led regeneration is that further investment does not automatically follow, or that it takes longer than expected to materialize. For example, in Sydney there was a relative lack of building

Figure 10.1. Olympic Villages post-Games in: Barcelona (top left); Sydney (top right); Vancouver (bottom right): and London (bottom left). (*Source*: Photographs Andrew Smith)

activity post-2000 and urban densities remain very low in and around the city's Olympic Park (Yamawaki and Duarte, 2014). The area now competes for investment with other Sydney suburbs, so further development is at the expense of projects in surrounding districts like Parramatta (Searle, 2012). Even if Olympic facilities do stimulate further development, it is hard to control what types of investment follow. Types of development that are most commercially viable might not be appropriate for the area's wider environmental or social objectives. Moreover, aside from their symbolic value, it is unclear whether stadia, indoor arenas, swimming pools and the other Olympic facilities are effective flagship projects that help to attract private sector investment. In some examples of Olympic regeneration, parallel development or infrastructure are deemed to have had a more significant effect. For example, Thornley (2012) argues that the contribution of Olympic venues to urban regeneration in East London is minor compared to the adjacent shopping centre and transport improvements. Here, as in Sydney's Olympic Park, businesses are lured by the availability of infrastructure and parkland, rather than the proximity of sports facilities. However, Olympic structures and associations provide useful visibility for these sites that might otherwise seem rather bleak and anonymous. This symbolic function helps to justify the notion of Olympic projects as flagship developments.

The Olympic Games as a Catalyst

One of the noted advantages of incorporating the Olympic Games into urban regeneration is that it speeds the process up. Regeneration inherently involves long-term objectives, but these might be achieved more quickly in Olympic host cities. Hence Olympic projects are touted not merely as flagship urban developments, but as 'catalysts for urban change' (Essex and Chalkley, 1998). A catalyst increases the rate at which a reaction progresses and, using related metaphors, some accounts suggest the Olympic Games help to achieve 'fast-tracked' or even 'turbo-charged' regeneration. The imposition of an immovable deadline (the date of the Opening Ceremony) means projects have to be finished within a specified timeframe. This, along with the potential for global exposure of dereliction, provides the necessary impetus to deliver projects more quickly.

The increased 'speed' of regeneration attributed to the Olympic Games varies between cases. It is claimed that the project to regenerate Homebush Bay in Sydney was delivered in half the original timeframe because of the Olympic Games (Wilson, 1996; Cashman, 2006). In Munich, the pre-existing (1963) plan to regenerate the Olympic Park site was scheduled for fifteen to twenty years, but the 1972 Games meant it was delivered in five (Chalkley and Essex, 1999). Nevertheless, the gold medal for accelerated regeneration seemingly goes to London. Officials claim that the project to regenerate East London was accelerated by fifty years because of the 2012 Games. At the Emerging Host Cities conference in 2013 Tessa Jowell (formerly the UK Government's Olympic Minister) argued that a project that would have normally taken sixty years was delivered in less than ten. This accelerated development explains why a senior official from London's Olympic Delivery Authority referred to the project as 'regeneration on steroids' (Smith, 2014).

It is important to analyse in more detail how the Olympic Games speeds regeneration up. The imposition of a deadline creates a sense of urgency, but complex ambitions still need to be realized. One advantage of the Games is that it tends to focus the minds of politicians, which means decisions are made more quickly. Olympic projects also tend to achieve greater 'buy-in' from key stakeholders than conventional regeneration efforts, and this helps to achieve a faster rate of progress. Regeneration inevitably requires effective partnerships between different government departments, and between the public and private sectors, and staging the Olympics seems to make it easier to get a range of individuals and organizations to work together for a common cause. This joint working can persist after the event allowing long-term regeneration objectives to be addressed. In short, the Olympics helps to speed up regeneration processes via the 'resources, political will and institutional co-ordination' that are seemingly mobilized when the Games is awarded to a city (Raco and Tunney, 2010, p. 2020).

Any claims made for accelerated development need to be treated with caution – this rhetoric is part of the way Olympic projects are justified. Although the Olympic Games can speed up the initial phases of urban regeneration (such as land assembly and remediation), wider projects often remain incomplete long after the event. In Sydney, work is still being undertaken to redevelop the main site of the 2000 Olympic Games and the latest masterplan provides a vision for 2030 (Davidson and McNeill, 2012). Similarly, the 'legacy phase' work for London's 2012 Olympic Park is programmed to 2030. The need for redevelopment in the post-event era to transform event sites into functioning areas means that the risks of slow, or stalled, urban development persist. The Olympic Games may ensure ambitious urban regeneration projects reach a certain stage, but they do not guarantee completion.

Even if acceleration could be proven – which it cannot because it is impossible to quantify a counterfactual rate of development – speeding up the regeneration process is not necessarily that helpful. There are good reasons why some urban regeneration projects take so long. Shortened timescales restrict opportunities for consultation with the local population and other planning procedures may also be compromised. The pressure for timely delivery means organizers circumvent normal processes. During

Sydney's Olympic preparations, a new Environmental Planning Policy was created which exempted Olympic proposals from proper assessment (Kearins and Pavlovich, 2002). Several years earlier, Montalban (1992, p. 9) described how Barcelona's politicians 'sacrificed the ethical obligations of their office under the pressure of completing preparations on time'. Rushing to finish work may lead to a reduction in quality and extra payments for contractors are usually required to ensure timely completion, pushing budgets higher. As deadlines approach, the requirement for extended shifts can lead to injuries and fatalities amongst construction workers. In short, accelerated regeneration comes with considerable costs.

The need to speed up regeneration is also used as a justification for new governance models. Regeneration is predominantly something that is 'funded, initiated, supported or inspired' by the public sector (Leary and McCarthy, 2013, p. 9), but Olympic projects are used to usher in new 'entrepreneurial' forms of urban governance: public–private partnerships, and/or new dynamic public organizations that pursue commercial activities. Rather than using existing governance apparatus, Olympic regeneration projects are usually managed and delivered by specialist agencies through which public funds are channelled (Raco, 2014). Local authorities are often under-represented or bypassed, which undermines the democratic legitimacy of Olympic regeneration (Owen, 2002).

The problems with time pressures noted above are important, but they may be alleviated by recent changes to Olympic bidding processes which mean that hosts cities now have longer to prepare. Officials in Barcelona, Atlanta, Sydney, Athens, London, Rio, Tokyo, and Paris had seven years to prepare for the Games, but in the cases of Los Angeles 2028 and Brisbane 2032, the period between winning the candidature and staging the Games was extended to eleven years. These changes – driven by difficulties the International Olympic Committee (IOC) had in recruiting candidate cities for the 2022 Winter Games and the 2024 Summer Games – should allow Olympic hosts more time to plan and prepare, while still allowing them to benefit from the advantages of a fixed deadline.

Strategic and Integrated Olympic Regeneration

Relying on flagship developments as catalysts is a rather speculative and spurious approach to urban regeneration, but these approaches can be better justified if Olympic projects are integrated within an existing strategy. If a stimulus is required to advance established plans for a derelict area, then the Games can be used to kick-start or speed up the development process. This is where Olympic projects can perhaps play the most effective role in urban regeneration. The IOC has recognized this: following *Agenda 2020* and *Agenda 2020+5*, the IOC now encourages hosts to consider how the Games fit into wider plans for their cities (Wolfe, 2023). Barcelona is usually cited as the inspiration for and epitome of this approach. Plans to recover and reorient the waterfront area had existed for many decades (since 1966), but preparations for the Olympics (1986–1992) were used as the opportunity to undertake the work. This strategy was further strengthened because Barcelona's new waterfront district was linked into a wider urban plan. This helped to ensure that Barcelona's regeneration was not led by Olympic projects – instead Olympic projects were used to achieve Barcelona's plans. The Olympic Games provided funding, urgency and civic support for strategic projects that might have otherwise been difficult to achieve.

This strategy of using the Olympic Games to advance pre-existing plans was also deployed in London. The remediation and regeneration of the Olympic Park was originally justified on the basis that it contributed both to the 2004 London Plan (the city's statutory spatial plan), and to the wider regeneration of the Thames Gateway region. Famously, Ken Livingstone (London's Mayor 2000–2008) expressed his disinterest in hosting a major sport event, but supported a London Olympics because it would help to achieve his plans for East London. Over time the limitations of this strategy have been exposed. Whereas building the Olympic Park was originally conceived as a way to assist the wider regeneration of East London, regeneration post 2008 refocused on the Olympic Park as a project in and of itself. This was partly an inevitable consequence of the global financial crisis and the more focused ambitions that emerged, but it was also due to the political capital associated with the Olympics. More mundane regeneration ambitions were sidelined in the quest to deliver the Games. Resources were devoted to dealing with the legacy issues that generate most media attention – for example, the future of the stadium – rather than more significant ambitions for East London. This illustrates how Olympic projects can override, disrupt, or distort existing regeneration plans – something Müller (2018) has dubbed 'event seizure'. Even in Barcelona, much lauded as the acme of good practice, the Games are thought to have disrupted the city's record of impressive and progressive urban transformation (1976–1992) by ushering in an approach more focused on entrepreneurialism and place marketing (Degen and García, 2012).

Outcomes

Regeneration is often regarded as merely an objective or an intervention. However, it is also an outcome, and various researchers have tried to measure whether regeneration has been achieved. This type of research is notoriously difficult: regeneration involves multiple objectives and appropriate indicators are difficult to ascertain and measure. The timescales involved are usually long which makes it difficult to know when to assess outcomes. The scale at which we measure these is also difficult to pinpoint and it is hard to attribute any changes observed to specific interventions. In the case of Olympic regeneration this is even harder as it is not clear what is and is not part of the intervention. What constitutes regeneration is also highly subjective and contested: it varies according to 'different vocabularies and imaginations' (Raco and Tunney, 2010, p. 2087). This makes establishing the outcomes of Olympic regeneration even more difficult.

Hemphill *et al.* (2004) used a series of weighted indicators to measure 'sustainable urban regeneration performance'. Their research is particularly relevant here as one of the projects analysed was Barcelona's Olympic waterfront complex (Vila Olimpica). Of six developments analysed (in Barcelona, Belfast, and Dublin), Vila Olimpica scored highest, with the authors surmising that it was a notable example of good practice. As an example of urban design Vila Olimpica has undoubtedly been successful, with generous provision of open spaces and clever submergence of transport infrastructure. One interpretation of the project is to see it as a democratic one that returned the waterfront to its citizens (Rowe, 2006). Yet its contribution to the social dimension of regeneration is more controversial. The expropriation and clearance of working-class housing and industrial units to deliver expensive housing and a new yacht marina benefitted some people at the expense of others (Arbaci and Tapada-Berteli, 2012). It was always unlikely that former residents would be able to remain here as none of the new flats was offered as subsidized or social housing, 'despite promises made to the contrary when the project was first made public in 1986' (Montalban, 1992, p. 6). The wholesale redevelopment of this district had been resisted for many years, but the Olympic Games provided a vehicle with which to placate opposition. This case highlights that, when considering the Olympic Games as a *force majeure* that allows development barriers to be overcome (Evans, 2010), we need to acknowledge that this includes its capacity to nullify opposition from incumbent residents and businesses.

Concern about the contribution of Olympic projects to gentrification in Barcelona reflects a wider reappraisal of the city's transformation, which, according to Arbaci and Tapada-Berteli (2012, p. 307):

> cannot be considered a successful case of regeneration since it has not fully addressed the needs of the long-term (low-income and more vulnerable) residents. Rather than tackle the main sources of deprivation, it has instead increased issues of neighbourhood affordability and housing affordability.

Barcelona's project was one that was successful physically, but not necessarily socially, and this reflects longer term assessments of other Olympic regeneration projects – for example, in London (Bernstock, 2020). The contribution to land remediation and physical regeneration is generally

Figure 10.2. A note fixed to fences surrounding the latest phase of development in London's Queen Elizabeth Olympic Park. (*Source*: Photograph Andrew Smith)

impressive (notwithstanding issues with redundant venues discussed elsewhere in this volume), but it is harder to find Olympic regeneration projects that have helped to improve the lives of disadvantaged people. This relates to difficulties reconciling physical and social regeneration. Olympic regeneration tends to be funded through property sales: the public or private (or public–private) organizations involved hope that Olympic interventions will raise land values allowing them to recoup investment via the sale of assets. This provides an in-built incentive to build the most lucrative housing which, rather than assisting disadvantaged citizens, tends to displace them (see figure 10.2). Analysed through a social lens, rather than a physical one, Olympic urbanism promotes gentrification not regeneration.

Complex issues such as gentrification highlight the contested nature of regeneration objectives and outcomes. For many of the professionals involved, gentrification is not an unfortunate by-product of regeneration projects, it is the specific aim. East London's Olympic transformation provides a useful illustration. There has been much debate about why, given London's shortage of affordable housing, more extensive social housing provision was not prioritized as an Olympic legacy (Bernstock, 2022). Of the 2,818 units available in the converted Athletes Village (now renamed East Village), just under half were made available at subsidized rates (675 social rent, 356 intermediate rent, 269 shared ownership, 79 shared equity). Cost was one obvious factor which prevented more generous provision, but another consideration was that key stakeholders (including local housing officials) wanted to use the new accommodation to change the composition of the local population. They wanted more middle-class families to rebalance both the socio-demographic profile and the composition of new development – which was dominated by flats for young professionals (Smith, 2014). Gentrification was envisaged as a vehicle for positive change, not a negative outcome. This approach was opposed by citizen groups who felt that housing existing residents should be the priority, not targeting new ones. The case underlines that regeneration is a political process, not a purely technical one, with any assessment of outcomes also politicized (Raco and Tunney, 2011).

Towards a More People-Oriented and Regenerative Approach

The limitations of regeneration projects that rely too heavily on physical transformations are now increasingly acknowledged. These tend to deal with the symptoms of decline – dereliction – rather than more fundamental issues and problems faced by local people. Accordingly, organizers of recent editions of the Games have tried to implement social programmes aimed at disadvantaged citizens in deprived areas. These programmes seek to provide more opportunities for local people, or at least to restrict the negative impacts of Olympic regeneration.

During the build-up to the 2010 Winter Games, Vancouver developed a series of social regeneration initiatives. The Organizing Committee initially committed to an Inner City Inclusivity Commitment Statement (ICICS) to protect the interests of low-income communities (Vanwynsberghe *et al.*, 2013). Employment initiatives were also formulated for those who faced obstacles preventing them from accessing 'traditional employment' (*ibid.*). The company awarded the contract to develop the Olympic Village on False Creek signed a Community Benefit Agreement that required them to provide 250 social housing units (Scherer, 2011). However, during the course of the city's Olympic preparations these commitments unravelled (see figure 10.3). This was partly due to economic circumstances, but it was also because there was little genuine commitment to these initiatives – they were designed to get community groups on side during the early stages of Olympic regeneration. As this example shows, when Olympic projects go over budget – as they invariably do – social regeneration ambitions tend to be watered down or abandoned completely. These initiatives are more vulnerable to political and economic shifts because there is less political consensus regarding the social dimension of regeneration. Within the prevailing neoliberal political philosophy, regeneration is about providing [physical] 'platforms' for growth – not about direct assistance for people on low incomes. In this context,

Figure 10.3. A banner protesting against the changes made to Vancouver's Olympic Village project on False Creek. (*Source*: Photograph Andrew Smith)

progressive projects which 'leverage' social inclusion and social development remain an underdeveloped aspect of Olympic regeneration.

Alongside a more people-oriented approach, the climate emergency and acute environmental issues also mean there is an urgent need for an approach which is *regenerative*, rather than merely one that seeks urban regeneration (Foth *et al.*, 2021). As Thomson and Newman (2020) noted, regenerative cities are those which are ecologically restorative, and pursuing regenerative urbanism requires urban planners to recognize that cities are part of their local bioregion and a global ecosystem. Only by adopting this approach can cities be sustainable and liveable (*ibid.*). In the context of the Olympic Games this means restricting the development of new buildings, minimizing carbon intensive travel, and reducing levels of extractive consumption, but also planning the Games to advance the host city's sustainability. This might be by promoting active travel, by converting brownfield sites into green spaces, or by nurturing pro-environmental behaviours amongst citizens. In this context, future Games precincts can only be justified if they are exemplars of, or experiments in, sustainable living (Mair and Smith, 2021). Future Olympic regeneration needs to be less focused on restoring the economic functionality of post-industrial cities, and more focused on restoring the ecological processes that will allow cities to remain liveable (Foth *et al.*, 2021). This is best summarized as a shift from urban regeneration to regenerative urbanism.

Conclusions

This chapter has discussed the various advantages and disadvantages of regeneration associated with the Olympic Games. Staging the Games can help to unlock the potential of areas which have stubbornly resisted regeneration through market forces or more modest interventions. The deadlines and political commitment involved can speed development processes up; especially in early stages – land assembly, remediation, and infrastructure provision. However, the discussion has also introduced a series of problematic aspects of Olympic regeneration. These include an over-emphasis on the physical and economic dimensions of regeneration (at the expense of the social and the ecological), the way the Games are used to make wholesale (rather than incremental) urban transformations, and the dubious use of public funds to subsidize private enterprise.

It is unfair to suggest the various issues noted here are uniquely Olympic problems, as these tend to feature in large-scale urban regeneration projects generally. For example, in a comprehensive review of European examples, Swyngedouw *et al.* (2002) suggest these tend to neglect social issues, create segregated islands of wealth, ignore local democracies, and direct capital from the public to private sectors. This chapter has outlined how Olympic projects neglect incumbent populations and contribute to gentrification, but these are problems with regeneration generally and are linked to the incompatible objectives of many regeneration projects (Allen and Cochrane, 2014). It is unrealistic to expect Olympic projects to surmount these problems or buck the trend for urban development that exacerbates socio-economic polarization and ecological damage. The failings of Olympic regeneration reflect the failings of large-scale urban regeneration projects generally. However, there are some reasons to be optimistic. There is now increased recognition of the need to give social aspects more attention within regeneration projects generally and within Olympic regeneration in particular. A new emphasis on the social dimension provides an opportunity to link regeneration to some of the other legacies sought by host cities: sports participation, education, and cultural activity. This trend may be assisted by the IOC's new insistence that host cities should use more temporary and existing venues and avoid building expensive, carbon-intensive, new ones. Paris 2024 is an interesting example of economic efficiency and eco-realism, with 79 per cent of venues existing or temporary structures (Wolfe, 2023). Spending less time and money building venues provides more scope to implement programmes that lever the Games for social development (Smith, 2012), but also for ecological restoration (Foth *et al.*, 2021). Ultimately, the aim should be regeneration *for* disadvantaged communities, rather than the regeneration *of* disadvantaged communities; combined with a new emphasis on regenerative urbanism, rather than urban regeneration.

Adopting an integrated and strategic approach has helped to achieve more positive outcomes in some host cites. In Barcelona, the Olympic Games were used to advance long-held regeneration ambitions, an approach recently emulated by Paris, where 2024 Olympic Games projects in north Paris are being used to help implement the longstanding Grand Paris plan (Wolfe, 2023). This enlightened approach is, however, rarely employed, since most cities decide to stage the Games and then think how it might be used to assist regeneration, rather than *vice versa*. Political, economic, and symbolic motivations – not assistance for socially and ecologically deprived areas – tend to explain why most urban regimes want to stage the Games. In these cases, rather than a strategic objective, regeneration is best understood as part of the way in which Olympic Games are justified. Regeneration rhetoric is particularly valuable in early stages of the process when it is used to get the media and public onside. The relationship between the Olympic Games and urban regeneration should not be merely understood as what the Games can do for regeneration, it is also about what regeneration can do for the Games.

Chapter 11

OLYMPIC TOURISM

Mike Weed

Hosting the Olympic and Paralympic Games is regularly justified by the argument that Olympic cities can generate considerable inward tourism, both as tourism destinations in their own right, and as gateways to wider regions surrounding the host city. This chapter examines the role of Olympic cities in the generation of tourism. In providing the context for this analysis, the early part of the chapter outlines a range of Olympic tourism products, before summarizing the ways in which the Olympic and Paralympic Games might be leveraged to generate tourism. The two substantive parts of the chapter then examine, first, the ways in which Winter Olympic Cities can be tourism gateways to the wider region surrounding the host city and, secondly, the contribution of the Summer Olympic Games to the development of the host city's tourism product and image.

Olympic Tourism Products

Fifteen years ago, Weed (2008) identified six Olympic tourism products, five of which related to sports tourism, and one to more general tourism. The following year, Weed and Bull (2009) further examined the five sports tourism products featured in Weed's (2008) analysis of Olympic tourism and this suggested that the earlier analysis might be updated as outlined below:

Event Sports Tourism. This refers to the provision of event sports tourism opportunities, both for participants and spectators. Clearly, it will include the Olympic and Paralympic Games themselves, but also the myriad of other events that take place in the years before and after the Games in and around Olympic cities. In this respect, even previously inconsequential competitions can become significant international events as athletes seek to experience and acclimatize to local conditions, providing an increased media and spectator sports tourism attraction.

Sports Participation Tourism. The most obvious sports tourism product, this refers to active participation in sports tourism activities, such as skiing, cycling, golf or sailing, or at multi-activity centres such as Center Parcs or various outdoor activity and education centres. For some activities, participating in Olympic venues can be an attraction, or at Olympic winter sports resorts.

Sports Training Tourism. Sports training camps are often talked about as being a generator of Olympic tourism, but the sports training tourism product also incorporates 'learn to play' courses and elements of advanced instruction. As such, it can overlap considerably with sports participation tourism in Olympic sports such as sailing and skiing.

Luxury Sports Tourism. Uniquely, this product type is not defined by reference to the sports tourism activity, but to the wider aspects of the experience relating to the luxury nature of the attendant facilities and services. It therefore overlaps with the other product types and may often use associations with the Olympic and Paralympic Games to add to the feeling of a premium product.

Supplementary Sports Tourism. The broadest of the sport tourism products, supplementary sports tourism refers to the provision of sports tourism activities as a supplement to the providers' main product. Examples include the provision of a range of water sports on beach holidays or the opportunity to hire a cycle for a day. It may also include trips to past or prospective Olympic sites, venues or museums as a supplementary part of a broader city visit.

Generic Tourism. The Olympic Games can be used as part of strategies to generate future non-sports tourism related visits. Such tourism may be generated among those who have visited the Olympic city for sports tourism related products, but who later return for a more general tourism trip, or among those who have been exposed to the city though various Olympic-related written and audio-visual media and as a result, believe it may be a nice place to visit.

Drawing on the range of Olympic tourism products outlined above, Weed (2008, p. 22) suggests that Olympic tourism should be defined as, 'tourism behaviour motivated or generated by Olympic-related activities'. This definition covers both pre- and post-Games tourism activity, including *aversion tourism*, in which people leave or avoid Olympic cities as a result of the Olympic Games or Olympic-related activities. It also covers the generation of generic tourism to Olympic cities and their surrounding regions stimulated by exposure to either corporeal (live) or mediated Olympic-related activities.

Strategies for Leveraging the Olympic Games for Tourism Outcomes

The Olympic Games is the resource with which to leverage the six Olympic tourism products outlined above. However, the potential impacts of the Olympic Games do not just occur during the Games period, but for several years before and after. As such, the Olympic Games as a leverageable resource provide a wide range of potential opportunities to develop Olympic tourism products, potentially over a fifteen-year period in the run up to and beyond the Games.

Table 11.1. Strategies for leveraging the Olympic Games for tourism. (*Source*: Weed, 2008, adapted from Chalip, 2004)

Leveraging Opportunities to Stimulate Olympic Tourism Trips	*Leveraging Olympic-Related Media Coverage to Raise Awareness of the Host City as a Tourism Destination*
Entice Olympic Tourism Spending	Benefit from Olympic-Related Reporting and Event Coverage
Retain Local Resident Spending	
	Use of Olympics in Host Destination Advertising and Promotion
Lengthen Olympic-Related Visits	
Maximize Olympic-Related Visits	

Two 'opportunities' are identified in table 11.1 for leveraging the Olympic Games. First, direct Olympic tourism trips may be leveraged by the Olympic Games. Secondly, Olympic media may be leveraged, either by capitalizing on Olympic-related media coverage of the host city, surrounding region or country, or by incorporating Olympic-related material into host city, region or country advertising and promotion. The strategic objective in leveraging Olympic media is to enhance the image of the Olympic host destination, which in turn will help to generate further future tourism business. As the strategic objective of leveraging Olympic tourism is to optimize Olympic-related tourism benefits, the opportunities to leverage Olympic tourism and Olympic media have very similar long-term goals. Perhaps a crude way of looking at the two leveraging opportunities is to view the leveraging of Olympic tourism as referring to immediate strategies to generate tourism business related to the Olympics, whereas the leveraging of Olympic media is part of a longer-term strategy for host destination image enhancement that is aimed at stimulating more generic tourism business in the future.

The Role of the City in Olympic Tourism

Unlike some other sport mega-events, such as the football, rugby or cricket

World Cups, the host for an Olympic and Paralympic Games is a city rather than a country. This presents a range of challenges for the country in which the host city is located, one of which is the way in which the Games can be leveraged for tourism, not only for the host city, but also for the surrounding regions and the country as a whole. In this respect, a useful way to analyse Olympic tourism is to regard Olympic cities as tourism generators. Olympic cities can be divided into those that largely act as a gateway for tourism to the wider region in which they are situated, and those that largely generate Games-related tourism to the Olympic city itself. While these two areas are obviously not mutually exclusive, the respective structures, histories, and requirements of the Winter and Summer Olympic and Paralympic Games mean that Winter Olympic cities, although destinations in their own right, can also act as tourism gateways, whereas tourism generated by Summer Olympic cities tends largely to be to the Olympic city itself.

Olympic Cities as Gateways to Tourism Regions: The Winter Games

Unlike the Summer Games that are discussed later in this chapter, Olympic tourism generated by the Winter Games is not dominated by any one Olympic tourism product. Given that the Winter Games focus on skiing and a range of other winter sports, it can be very effective in generating sports participation tourism. However, it can also contribute to the generation of event sports tourism related to winter sports, to luxury sports tourism products associated with the après ski experience, and, of course, to sports training tourism in relation to learning the basic skills for winter sports, to advanced instruction to improve technique, and to the provision of training opportunities for performance athletes.

Given that Winter Olympic tourism opportunities are spread across the sports tourism-related Olympic tourism products, it would appear that the greatest leveraging opportunities for tourism in relation to the Winter Games are those that are associated with the direct stimulation of Olympic tourism trips, rather than long-term image enhancements for general tourism. To a certain extent this is because Winter Games host cities are dwarfed by the size of hosts for the Summer Olympics. Despite the trend towards major city hosts, Winter Games hosts still need to be located near mountainous terrain to provide for the ski events. Therefore, although there has been a continuous growth in the size of Winter Games hosts, the average population size of Winter Olympic cities is still less than one tenth (236,000) of the average size of Summer Games hosts (2,840,000).

A number of implications emerge from this. While the cost of the Summer Games since 1984 has always been higher than that for the winter event, the

Table 11.2. Respective costs of Summer and Winter Games. (*Source*: Preuss, 2004)

Olympiad	Host Cities		Total Cost (US$ million)	Cost per Capita (US$)
XIV	WINTER:	Sarajevo, 1984	179	400
	SUMMER:	Los Angeles, 1984	412	121
XV	WINTER:	Calgary, 1988	628	981
	SUMMER:	Seoul, 1988	3,297	326
XVI	WINTER:	Albertville, 1992	767	38,350
	SUMMER:	Barcelona, 1992	9,165	5,578
XVII	WINTER:	Lillehammer, 1994	1,511	65,695
	SUMMER:	Atlanta, 1996	2,021	5,129
XVIII	WINTER:	Nagano, 1998	3,412	9,451
	SUMMER:	Sydney, 2000	3,438	929
XIX	WINTER:	Salt Lake City, 2002	1,330	7,628
	SUMMER:	Athens, 2004	–	–

latter are far more costly on a per-capita basis (Preuss, 2004; see table 11.2). Furthermore, because Winter Games host cities, notwithstanding their growth over time, tend to be smaller with less capacity to attract commercial funding for development (Essex and Chalkey, 2002), the burden of investment tends to fall on the public-sector (although as noted below, there is a long-standing link with the ski industry). While the Summer Games have increasingly attempted to follow the commercial model adopted by Los Angeles 1984, only the Calgary Winter Games of 1988 has had any success in following this approach.

The staging, therefore, of a Winter Olympics can yield varying benefits, with gains often being specific to host cities and to the stage of development of the city and region at the time. Preuss (2004) reinforces this, noting that a city's unique characteristics and the economic conditions at the time are largely responsible for relative successes. However, that is not to downplay the potential opportunities of the Winter Games for which, as they are hosted in much smaller cities than the Summer Games, 'effects can be proven much more easily because the economic impact to the host city is comparatively larger' (*ibid.*).

Chappelet (2002*a*) singled out Calgary 1988 as the point where the emphasis shifted from tourism promotion to economic development. The fact that Calgary was able to follow the Los Angeles model can be attributed to the fact that the petrochemical industry in Alberta subsidized the Games in an effort to attract inward investment, and the city grew to a population of almost 700,000. Notwithstanding the continued presence of tourism promotion as a goal of the Winter Games, not least at Lillehammer 1994 where the coverage of the small Norwegian ski resorts in the region on the world stage as worthy competitors with Alpine countries was significant, such promotion is now but one among a number of goals for Winter Olympic host cities.

1. *Salt Lake City 2002*

Prior to the XIX Winter Olympic Games in 2002, Salt Lake City and Utah were very much domestic tourism destinations; of the 17.8 million visitors to Utah in 2000, 96 per cent were US residents (IVC, 2002), and Travel Utah's 1,000-day plan reflects this. The plan, seen as long-term at the time, covered the 150 days leading up to the Games and the 850 days after the Games. In doing so, it appears that opportunities to capitalize on the Olympics in the pre-Games period may have been missed as Travel Utah considered that the 'window of opportunity' was only two years. One of the main goals of the 1,000-day plan was to capitalize on the 'awareness bonus' of the Winter Olympics and, whilst trying to improve awareness among Europeans, to focus on the link between Utah's brand values of 'Discovery and Recovery' with Olympic values and memories among the core American market.

Salt Lake City attempted to draw on lessons from Calgary in building a strategy for Olympic-related economic development and tourism. In taking this and the experiences of other past Winter Olympics, Travel Utah (2002) discussed the six key lessons that they had drawn from former Olympic hosts:

◆ *Context*: Each Games is unique and has its own political, social, and economic circumstances which, combined with external events, greatly influence future tourism activity in an Olympic region.

◆ *Post-Games Marketing*: Increases in tourism are not a direct function of hosting the Games or of Olympic media – such increases need to be effectively leveraged.

◆ *Economic Returns are Uneven*: Tourism growth is most likely in areas directly involved with the Games – outlying areas should consider ways in which they can associate themselves with an Olympic area.

◆ *Focus Strategies*: Leveraging strategies are most likely to be successful if they are targeted – holistic approaches can dilute resources and messages.

◆ *Sustainable Development*: Normal (i.e. 'without Olympic') growth patterns should guide expectations and development to avoid excess capacity which can destabilize the host region in the post-Games period.

◆ *Preserve Networks*: The people and organizations responsible for the presentation of the Games should also be those involved in leveraging the post-Games environment.

Table 11.3. Winners and losers from the Salt Lake City Winter Games. (*Source*: Travel Utah, 2002)

Winners	*Losers*
• Hotels	• Business Services
• Restaurants	• Finance, Insurance and Real Estate
• Retailers (particularly Olympic Vendors and 'Made in Utah' products)	• Ski resorts
	• Transportation
• Olympic Travellers	• Construction
	• Business and Ski Travellers

Hotspots: Olympic Venues, Park City and Downtown Olympic District

Empty: Businesses outside Downtown Olympic District

In seeking to examine how useful these lessons had been, Travel Utah (2002) conducted an immediate post-Games analysis of the winners and losers in the Olympic year (see table 11.3).

In relation to the impact of Olympic media, Travel Utah (2002) estimated that the value of print media that focused on tourism related themes during the Games was $22.9 million. This comprised:

$22 million – National and syndicated stories

$89,100   – Features from Sports Illustrated 'dailies'

$89,800   – *USA Today* Stories

$420,300 – US daily Newspapers from major markets

$367,600 – Southern Utah stories

Given the Travel Utah strategy of focusing on the US tourism market, this represents a very useful return. What is not clear, however, from the Travel Utah report, is what leveraging strategies (if any) were employed to generate these stories, and how 'tourism-related themes' are defined. Nevertheless, the generation of $22.9 million worth of print media alone is a significant achievement given the problems of attempting to get tourism destination themes into media coverage (Chalip and Leyns, 2002).

2. Turin 2006

A clear feature of Olympic host cities in the twenty-first century is a desire to learn from previous hosts. Turin attempted to apply more recent knowledge from both Summer and Winter Olympic cities to its specific modern European city context. Table 11.4 shows the complex range of lessons that Turismo Torino (2004) had attempted to draw from previous Olympic Games, both summer and winter, in the bidding, pre-Games, Games, and Post-Games periods. In fact, if there was a 'role model' for Turin, it was

Table 11.4. Turin 2006 – lessons regarding impacts and benefits for tourism. (*Source*: Turismo Torino, 2004)

	Bidding	*Pre-Games*	*Games*	*Post-Games*
Investments	Advertising	Infrastructure Media Interest	Visitor services	Promotion and avoiding the 'intermediate effect'
Effects	Image positioning Increase in popularity	Peak in market interest Creating new 'cathedrals' Increase in infrastructures	Customer satisfaction Media publicity Increase in number of tourists	Avoiding drop in occupation Increase in business tourism Long-term image growth
Examples	Sion 2006 Andorra 2010 Saltzburg 2010 Beijing 2008	Salt Lake City 2002 Sydney 2000	Sydney 2000	Barcelona 1992 Sydney 2000

Barcelona 1992 (Bondonia and Campaniello, 2006). Like Barcelona, Turin sought to improve its standing as a tourist destination on the world stage as well as within its own country:

> [Turin] … envisions a tourist mecca that would finally marry its historic centre – and all of its elegant cafes and museums – with the rustic Alps. 'When people think about northern Italy, they think Milan,' said Cosmo Perrello, a manager of the Amadeus Hotel, a 26-room local fixture just off the grand Piazza Vittorio Veneto. 'Torino has been a last stop in Italy. It has always been a town of working people. We hope now that it will become a first stop for Italy.' (*USA Today*, 2006)

Given that Turin, like many other major city Winter Games, was a two-centre Games: with Turin itself only able to host the 'arena' ice events, many venues were located outside the city in the 'Olympic Valleys' at distances of up to 60 miles (97 km) away. This generated high costs for transport, road construction, communications networks, and two Olympic Villages in the valleys (Bondonio and Campaniello, 2006), but it has also left an infrastructure that links the Alpine areas with the city, and thus allows the city to develop as a gateway for not only winter sports tourism, but also for summer sports such as canoeing, rafting, cycling and hiking, and for general 'lakes and rivers' tourism.

Turismo Torino, unlike Travel Utah which developed only a 1,000-day plan for tourism, considered the tourism impacts of its Winter Olympic Games from bidding until well into the post-Games period. In doing so it noted that, particularly in the pre-Games period, there was potential to displace and crowd out tourism, and that strategies were needed to address this, both in terms of general tourists, who may have felt that the city would be a 'building site' and business tourism organizers, who may have felt that the Olympic Games would cause price rises for conferences and meetings (Turismo Torino, 2004). This is reflected in the objectives for the Turin Games as laid out in their Olympic tourism strategy, which covered the pre-Games (2002–2005), Games (2006), and post-Games (2006–2008) periods:

◆   Avoiding a decrease in the tourist flow in the years preceding the celebration of the Olympic Games;
◆   Projecting the image of a city and an area under transformation that are evolving thanks to the Olympic Games;
◆   Achieving perfect co-ordination to promote both the Turin 2006 Olympic Games and Turin before, during and after the Games;
◆   Promoting the Olympic Games of Turin 2006 so as to create internal support and awareness, attracting the widest audience and the support of the tourist sector.

Among the strategies that Turin employed was an 'Olympic Turin' promotion programme that focused on generating positive stories about Turin in the non-sports media in the pre-Games period, thus seeking to leverage the image benefits of Olympic media. While the success of this programme does not appear to have been evaluated, it is a clear attempt to move towards the leveraging approach outlined in the early part of this chapter.

In February 2007, Turismo Torino reported on 'Turin 2006: One Year On' in which they noted that Turin's Olympic facilities have already hosted twenty sports events, including the Winter University Games and the World Fencing Championships (showing that Winter Olympic arenas need not exclusively be used for winter sports) as well as over forty non-sporting events (rock concerts and exhibitions). Turismo Torino's estimated figures claim an increase of 100,000 to 150,000 tourists per year to the Olympic area following the Games. A special guidebook for such visitors, *Turin: A Local's Guide to the Olympic City*, was a nice touch in leveraging the post-Games Olympic effect. Organizationally, the Fondazione XX Marzo Foundation has been established to run seven of the former Olympic sites and to optimize the legacy of the Games; an indication that Turin recognizes that legacy benefits, like most other Olympic impacts, need to be leveraged.

3. *Vancouver 2010*

A leveraging focus was a key part of Vancouver's preparations for the 2010 Winter Games from the outset. Eight years before the Games, Inter Vistas Consulting (IVC) were commissioned by British Columbia to report on the economic impacts of hosting the 2010 Winter Olympics in Vancouver, and a central part of this study was a recognition that:

> In order to achieve the higher tourism growth scenarios and capitalize on long-term opportunities, British Columbia's tourism industry will require significant marketing resources and a co-ordinated effort. (IVC, 2002)

Vancouver was fortunate in that it could draw on the recent experiences of Salt Lake City 2002, another North American Winter Games. However, like Turin 2006, Vancouver considered that the potential tourism impact of the Games extended beyond the 'two-year window of opportunity' on which Salt Lake City sought to capitalize. The IVC study (*ibid.*) for Vancouver 2010 set out four 'visitation scenarios': low, medium, medium/high, and high. In all but the high scenario, pre-Games Olympic tourism was assumed to commence in 2008 and the 'tail' of post-Games tourism was assumed to end in 2015. Nevertheless, in recognizing that the lessons from Salt Lake City did not 'represent the best outcome that British Columbia can achieve', largely because Salt Lake City's marketing efforts did not commence until five months before the Games, the 'high visitation' scenario assumed that pre-Games Olympic tourism would be introduced prior to 2008, but noted that this would be dependent on pre-Games marketing efforts commencing seven years in advance of the Games. Similarly, the 'high visitation' scenario for post-Games tourism included post-Games tourism through to 2020, but once again this assumed that tourism marketing organizations would use the Olympics as part of a long-term growth strategy and, more importantly, that the funds and determination existed to develop a marketing programme that had a positive impact on international visitors both before and after the Games. IVC's scenarios for incremental (i.e. additional) economic impact of Games visitors and tourists were:

Low	C$920 million	(*c.* $787 million)
Medium	C$1,295 million	(*c.* $1,108 million)
Medium/High	C$2,228 million	(*c.* $1,906 million)
High	C$3,145 million	(*c.* $2,690 million)

In providing a composite estimate of these numbers for the more concentrated two-years-before and two-years-after period, Jane Burns, the Director of British Columbia 2010, claimed that there would be approximately 1.1 million additional international (including USA and overseas) visitors to British Columbia across 2008–2012 (Burns, 2005). Burns's estimate was given to a US Senate sub-committee hearing on the potential impact of Vancouver 2010 on Oregon and the Pacific North West. Submissions to these hearings demonstrated that regions around British Columbia (in this case, those in another country) had been considering the range of Olympic tourism products they could offer and the nature of Olympic tourism flows. Todd Davidson, the Director of the Oregon Tourism Commission identified four opportunities arising from Vancouver 2010 for Oregon:

◆   Acting as a training site for Olympic athletes seeking to acclimatize;
◆   Reaching out to non-accredited media that attend Olympic Games to generate lifestyle stories;
◆   Exploring the potential to develop travel packages to bring athletes and spectators through Oregon and to encourage the extension of visits to include time in Oregon;
◆   Promoting Oregon at Olympic venues to build awareness.

Similarly, Dave Riley, the General Manager of Mount Hood Meadows Ski Resort in Portland (Oregon), but only 75 miles (120 km) from Vancouver, noted that a key opportunity for his resort, and for Oregon more generally, would be to capitalize on the numbers of skiers and snowboarders who would be avoiding Vancouver and Whistler in the run up to and during the 2010 Games. He identified the key opportunity as 'taking advantage of the displaced visitors who would otherwise have gone to Whistler by developing the amenities on Mount Hood between now and 2010 that are necessary to influence their destination choice' (Riley, 2005).

In terms of the understanding of the nature of Olympic tourism, planning for Olympic tourism in and around Vancouver was far in advance of that of the Winter Games that preceded it. In terms of tourism in particular, the explicit recognition that investment and co-ordination in marketing were key to leveraging the tourism potential of the Games was a core part of the planning process even before the Games were awarded to Vancouver. The recognition of this in the IVC study commissioned by British Columbia is a lesson for all future Olympic hosts: '[Tourism] benefits will not materialize automatically. They must be earned by a focussed, adequately funded and skilfully executed marketing programme' (IVC, 2002).

4. Sochi 2014

In contrast to the trend for twenty-first century Winter and Summer Olympic Games to learn from their predecessors and to plan to leverage tourism and image benefits, the Sochi Winter Games showed little sign of building on experiences of previous Games, or recognizing the need to develop and invest in strategies to leverage the Games for tourism. This was against an explicit and stated aim to develop Sochi not just for tourism, but to become a major tourism player on the world stage, something that was a key part of the pitch of the Russian President, Vladimir Putin, to the International Olympic Committee (IOC) in 2007: 'Sochi is going to become a new world class resort for the new Russia. And the whole world!' (Putin, 2007). This statement also encapsulated the second major goal for the Sochi Games. Like the Summer Games in Beijing in 2008 (see below), Sochi 2014 was envisaged as presenting the image of a 'new Russia' as an open and modern country attractive for tourism, investment, and geo-political partnerships. Sochi 2014 posters proclaimed: 'Russia – Great, New, Open'.

Unfortunately, the lasting image impacts of the Sochi Games were those relating to legislation passed 'against the propaganda of non-traditional sexual orientation to minors', which received widespread international coverage and condemnation (Van Rheenen, 2014; Lenskyj, 2014), and Russian intervention, largely seen internationally as aggression, in Ukraine. Economically, Sochi 2014 arguably has the dubious honour of being the most expensive Olympic Games in history, be it Summer or Winter. Unusually, particularly for a Winter Games, virtually all facilities and infrastructure had to be constructed from scratch, which led to estimates for the cost of the Games of between $51.4 billion and $55 billion (Müller, 2015a). Local organizers have argued that the vast majority of these costs should not be seen as attributable to the Games as they were part of a wider infrastructure investment in the region that would have taken place anyway. Certainly, there was a 'Federal Target Programme' for the Sochi region that pre-dates the awarding of the Winter Games, and this led them to claim that the true cost of the Games was $7.1 billion (*ibid.*).

However, the scale of investment in infrastructure projects undoubtedly increased as a result of the Games. For example, a combined road and rail link, costing over $10 billion, between the main coastal resort area and the mountain area was built to serve 20,000 passengers an hour, a capacity that exceeds many times the number of rooms available in the Krasnaya Polyana resort (*ibid.*). This is clearly a much larger investment than that required to service even the most optimistic estimates of enhanced tourism. Müller's (*ibid.*) estimate of the 'sport-related' costs of the Sochi Games is $11.8 billion, which is second only to London 2012's costs of $14.8 billion but he argued that costs should be normalized for the size of the Games into a cost per sports event. By that measure, Sochi spent an average of $120 million on each of ninety-eight events, which was two and a half times that of the next most expensive Games.

In excluding the wider infrastructural investment from the cost of Sochi 2014, the organizers claimed an operating profit of $261 million (*ibid.*), and this became a key part of the IOC's success story of the Games, with IOC President Thomas Bach noting that:

The extra tens of billions of dollars [are] part of Russia's long-term investment to turn the area from a faded summer resort into a year-round destination and winter sports complex for the whole country... The Games are serving as the catalyst. (Quoted in Wilson, 2014)

In this narrative, the additional capital and infrastructure costs are seen as a positive, with the claim that the Games has catalysed a wider investment in the region's tourism development, which somewhat contradicts the organizers' claim that this investment would have happened anyway.

Sochi was formerly the leading spa resort in Soviet Russia (Scharr *et al.*, 2011), but experienced considerable decay in the post-Soviet era, something that the 2014 Games were planned to arrest, re-invigorating summer tourism, and creating a new winter tourism market. The key supporting strategy to achieve this was to upgrade accommodation standards from those in 2007, where only about 1,700 of Sochi's 31,000 rooms had international star-rating classifications (Petrova, 2014). Investment to satisfy accommodation requirements for the Games almost doubled the number of rooms to 58,000, with 50 per cent of additional rooms at 3* standard, 40 per cent at 4* and 10 per cent at 5* (SOOC, 2014). As a result, Sochi's room capacity became roughly equivalent to that of major international established resorts such as Cancun in Mexico (Puls *et al.*, 2013).

Doubling the number of rooms meant that to maintain pre-Games occupancy rates, overnight stays would have needed to double. As such, a post-Games increase of 22 per cent in tourist arrivals in the 2014 summer peak season only delivered an occupancy rate of 40 per cent compared to occupancies of 70–90 per cent before the Games-related rooms expansion (Müller, 2015*a*). Unfortunately, increased arrivals were also driven by the domestic market, with a depreciation of Russia's currency, the rouble, almost doubling the cost of international holidays for Russians. Furthermore, international political tensions led to a ban on almost five million Russian citizens, mostly government employees, from travelling abroad (Ryzhkov, 2014), and a feeling among many Russians still at liberty to travel that a Europe largely antagonistic to their government was not a comfortable place to visit (Müller, 2015*a*). While these circumstances helped tourist arrivals, the preference of domestic tourists remained for the cheaper hotels and bed-and-breakfasts that characterized Sochi's pre-Games room stock (*ibid.*), with occupancy rates in some of the new hotels being as low as 8 per cent at some times in the year (Weaver, 2014). Longer-term prospects for international arrivals were also not positive as, despite the Games, Sochi is not an attractive destination for ski-tourists because its ski-trails are relatively small by international standards, lack of any direct flights, and Russia's demanding visa process.

Unsurprisingly given the lack of any strategy to leverage the Games for tourism, there was virtually no co-ordination of Sochi's post-Games tourism offer. The initial post-Games plan was to use venues for exhibitions, conventions, concerts and shows, but post-Games the Olympic Park did not have an overarching management organization, resulting in venues developing unilateral strategies for use and events, which attracted few tourists due to the lack of any major attractions and its remoteness from the city centre and beaches. The Olympic Stadium was re-constructed as a venue for matches during the 2018 Football World Cup, but Sochi did not have a football club that could take on the tenancy of a stadium of that size post-2018. In the mountain areas, the largest of the four ski resorts had a total trail length of only 77 kilometres, meaning that they cannot individually sustain more than two or three days of skiing, and while linking these areas would have created a much more attractive larger resort, this was not considered in pre-games planning. There was no funding available for the c.US$25 million investment required (Müller, 2015a), an amount that could probably have been accommodated within the Games budget had it been considered at the planning stage. More broadly, the public and private tourism sectors in Sochi estimated that it would take an investment equivalent to roughly 10–15 per cent of that made so far, and two or three years of further development, to re-purpose Sochi from an Olympic venue to a tourism resort. However, the local sector lacked the funds for such an investment and the Russian government refused all requests for additional funding.

Olympic Cities as Tourism Destinations: The Summer Games

As noted earlier, while the Winter Games generate tourism volumes across Olympic tourism products, sports tourism related to the Summer Games is most significant in relation to events sports tourism. While governments may attempt to claim that sports training tourism (training camps), sports participation tourism and supplementary sports tourism (particularly post-Games) are important products, events sports tourism is undoubtedly the major Olympic sports tourism product. However, the major tourism-related justification for investing in the Summer Olympic and Paralympic Games is the image benefits that hosting the Games bring, and the related future generic tourism numbers that such an enhanced image are likely to generate. As such, the greatest leveraging opportunity to develop tourism from the Summer Games is the leveraging of Olympic media for tourism image benefits. Due to the much more concentrated focus of the Summer Games, such image benefits are often reaped by the city itself, rather than by surrounding regions, or by the country in which the host city is situated, although London 2012 showed that country-wide benefits can be achieved. The generation of tourism to Summer Olympic cities is next explored in relation to the first four Summer Games of the twenty-first century.

1. *Sydney 2000*[1]

While successive Olympic cities since 2000 have been keen to draw lessons from previous Games, tourism planning for the Olympics in Sydney had to be developed without the benefit of prior experience as, at the time, there were few examples of how Olympic cities had previously planned for tourism. A review by the Australian Tourism Commission (ATC) concluded that the Seoul 1998 had left a legacy of new railways and an upgraded airport, but public relations had been oriented internally to Korea's domestic population, rather than to a global audience. The development of tourism infrastructure and Barcelona's enhanced credibility as an international tourist destination were noted as outcomes of the 1992 Games in the Catalan capital (ATC, 1998). Tourism impacts in Barcelona have been recognized to a greater extent more recently, as certain trends have become more apparent. A review by the Director General of Turisme de Barcelona concluded that the Games 'provided the impulse for Barcelona to become a leader in many respects, but especially in tourism' (Duran, 2005, p. 89). He noted that Barcelona had been named as the best world urban tourism destination in 2001 by *Condé Nast Traveller* magazine and described the dramatic growth in the number of cruise ships that now called at the port and of product launches, particularly for new car models, that had been held in the city. These developments were attributed to the way Barcelona's image had been positively affected by the Games (*ibid.*).

In contrast to the benefits gained by Barcelona, an assessment of Atlanta's performance judged that 'the city missed out on a golden opportunity for future tourism. Local attractions suffered substantial downturns in visitors, day trips were non-existent, and regional areas suffered. Neighbouring states took out advertisements telling people to stay away from Atlanta and the city suffered' (ATC, 1998). These findings served to reinforce what needed to be done in Sydney to ensure different outcomes.

Within the city of Sydney, proximity to certain routes and sites that attracted the largest number of Olympic visitors determined the type of impacts that were experienced (Brown, 2001). Some of the impact spread beyond Sydney to other areas of the state of New South Wales (NSW) which were able to host Olympic visitors. However, some areas experienced a decline in tourism demand. The dominance of the Games served to capture the attention and resources of visitors to the detriment of attractions that were effectively competing with the event. This situation was compounded when tour operators were unable to offer their normal services in the absence of buses that had been committed to the Games.

A desire to present the 2000 Olympics as a national event, for the whole of Australia, was contingent upon a sense of engagement by people throughout the country. Thus, strategies to spread tourism benefits were developed.

These included attempts to encourage visits by international teams for pre-Games training and to stage events, as celebrations, to coincide with the arrival of the Olympic torch.

Accurate post-Games measures of the impact of Sydney 2000 on tourism are not available as little research specifically examined this issue. As is the case with most major events, considerable effort was spent on gaining support for and justifying the bid and in ensuring that the event could be staged successfully. As such, while considerable research informed the planning stages, post-Games impact analysis received less attention as people with relevant knowledge moved on to work on the next event.

Research was conducted by the ATC, however, to track awareness of the Olympics in overseas markets and to monitor community attitudes towards the Games in Australia (ATC, 2000). In 1999, the highest level of awareness of the Games was recorded in New Zealand (92 per cent) followed by China (75 per cent), Korea (71 per cent), Germany (70 per cent) and England (58 per cent). Significant increases in awareness had occurred between 1998 and 1999 in Korea (from 47 per cent to 71 per cent), Malaysia (from 34 per cent to 43 per cent), Taiwan (from 28 per cent to 38 per cent) and England (from 38 per cent to 58 per cent). Nearly half of potential travellers in India (45 per cent) were found to be more likely to consider going to Australia as a result of the Games. The likelihood in China and Malaysia had increased between 1998 and 1999; from 30 per cent to 37 per cent and from 33 per cent to 41 per cent, respectively. Between 1998 and 2000 there was a steady increase in the perception of the host population that the Olympics would boost the image of Australia (1998: 25 per cent: 1999: 27 per cent; 2000: 29 per cent). However, there had also been a fall in the perception that the Games would bring economic benefits to the country (from 25 per cent in 1998 to 19 per cent in 2000).

Data from the Australian Bureau of Statistics reveal that there was a 15 per cent increase in the number of international arrivals to Australia in September 2000, the month of the Games, compared to the previous year with changes from markets closely associated with the Olympics being particularly noticeable. The number of tourists from the USA nearly doubled. Within the city, locations that housed 'Live Sites', such as Darling Harbour, were crowded throughout the Games and retail sales for businesses in the Harbourside complex increased considerably. This contrasted with the situation in regional areas of Australia where a 10–15 per cent decrease in normal visitation levels was recorded (Brown, 2001).

Indications immediately after the Games suggested that Australia would gain the anticipated tourism benefits. There was a 9.7 per cent increase in visitor arrivals in October 2000 compared with October 1999 and tour operators throughout Europe and North America were reporting un-precedented interest in and bookings to Australia (*ibid*.). A record 565,700 international visitors arrived in December 2000, a 23 per cent increase on 1999, the highest number ever for a single month (ATC, 2001). These increases helped arrivals for the year 2000 to reach a record 4.9 million but everything changed in 2001. The combined impact on demand from the terrorist attacks in New York in September 2001, the outbreak of severe acute respiratory syndrome (SARS) in Asia and the collapse of the airline group Ansett Australia meant that visitor numbers to Australia declined for the next two years. This was the first time that this had happened in Australia. Visitor numbers to the country have increased since 2003 but it is now impossible to determine the role played by any residual Olympic effect. This is disappointing but it does not minimize the lessons that are offered to other host countries by the strategies developed by the tourism industry in Australia that sought to maximize the benefits offered by the Sydney Olympic Games.

2. Athens 2004

Like many other Olympic cities, Athens wished to follow the Barcelona model in its development planning (Poulios, 2006). However, Beriatos and Gospodini (2004) claim that the Athens approach was very different to that used in Barcelona, and that it lacked focus in terms of a coherent urban development strategy. In fact, there were a number of worries among local businesses and policy-makers not only about the escalating costs of the Games (not unusual for Olympic cities), but also about the lack of planning. In 2002, *Sports Business* interviewed the President of the Athens Hotel Owners Association, Sypros Divanis, who claimed that while local hotel owners had invested over €500 million ($437 million) in modernizing and expanding hotels, they were being let down by the government which had failed to produce a plan for tourism linked to the Games. Divanis claimed that:

> The Olympics are the most positive event that could happen to the Greek tourism industry, but while there's over-activity on the part of the hotel community, the state … seeks sloppy solutions which will not offer the infrastructure needed. (Cited in Weed, 2008, p. 164)

One such 'sloppy solution' proposed by Gianna Angelopoulos, the head of the Athens 2004 Organizing Committee for the Olympic Games (ATHOC), was to accommodate visitors on islands or other tourist hotspots and to watch events on day trips to Athens. The lack of tourism planning for the Games was further highlighted in 2003, when the formal co-operation agreement between ATHOC, the government, and private enterprises was launched. At the launch in August 2003, it was claimed that the focus needed to be on the development of business and tourism after, rather than during or before, the Athens 2004 Games (Yannopoulos, 2003). However, this approached was severely criticized by George Drakopoulos, Managing Director of the Greek Association of Tourism Enterprises (SETE), who stated:

> Tourism is the principal sector where the economic benefits from hosting the Olympics are obvious, even to a child. And yet, neither the government nor EOT [the National Tourism Organization] have done anything all these years to formulate a marketing strategy that would make the Olympics the pole of attraction for millions of foreign visitors to Greece. Let's face it, we have forsaken the chance to make the Olympic theme the linchpin of our tourist publicity drive prior to the Games.

While Athens is by far Greece's most important city, Petrakos and Economou (1999) noted that within the wider European context, Athens represents a large peripheral city with low-level influence in the region. This is due to a range of spatial disadvantages, including unplanned residential areas on the outskirts, obsolete infrastructure, degraded built fabric, traffic congestion and environmental pollution, caused by unregulated rapid economic and physical growth as a result of rural immigration between 1950 and 1980 (CEC, 1992). Consequently, the 2004 Olympic Games presented a major opportunity to re-develop and re-brand the city. However, despite the city's expressed aim to follow the 'Barcelona Model' (Poulios, 2006), the development of Athens bore little resemblance to Barcelona's approach, and this might be seen as a planning shortcoming that has failed to leave the city with an infrastructure legacy that best provides for future tourism and inward investment. Specifically, some of the planning failings were:

◆   Lack of integrated planning – partial spatial interventions were not integrated into a strategic plan for Athens as a whole, especially in relation to the post-Games period (Beriatos and Gospodini, 2004).

◆   Failure to re-develop brownfield areas – Barcelona focused on the re-development of run-down areas whereas Athens largely developed green spaces on the outskirts or undeveloped sites in the city. Beriatos and Gospodini (*ibid*., p. 198) expressed surprise that Eleones, 'a large declined area with light industrial uses centrally located in Athens' was not considered for development.

◆   Architects and urban designers not given a central role – Barcelona incorporated architects and urban designers on the bidding and organizing committees for the 1992 Games, whereas Athens only consulted a few 'big name' architects, and did so much later in the process.

◆   Lack of spatial concentration – perhaps the key failing in creating a long-term legacy for urban tourism was the failure to concentrate spatial interventions and landscape transformations in a limited number of strategic sites. Unlike the approach taken in Barcelona, development and re-development projects in Athens were scattered 'all over the plan of the city without a focus' (*ibid.*, p. 192).

Despite these planning failings, there was a clear intention to create an urban legacy as around 95 per cent of Olympic projects were not temporary, but permanent spatial structures. There were also projects that sought to enhance the city's historic sites, in particular those carried out by the Agency for the Unification of the Archaeological Sites of Athens, which sought to link together a geographically disparate range of historical sites and to enhance the city's 'historic physiognomy' (*ibid*, p. 199; see also chapter 14). The intention, therefore, to link the historic local with the modern global existed, but was poorly implemented in practice.

Business File reported at the end of 2004 that tourism to Athens and Greece was 'lacklustre' during the Games and in the Olympic year, and that Olympic ticket sales were much lower than expected. However, there remained hope in the Athens tourism sector that the tourism benefit would occur in the post-Games period, with a gallery owner in Athens oldest neighbourhood commenting that despite lower-than-expected tourism in 2004, 'Next year will be better. We don't know, we just hope. It happened in other places and we think it will happen here too' (Business File, 2004).

Evidence in the time since the Games suggests that, despite the *laissez faire* approach to planning for Olympic tourism, the Athens Games have had a positive effect. A study by Alpha Bank, published at the end of 2004, estimated that the Games added €9 billion to Greece's Gross Domestic Product between 2000 and 2004 (against a total GDP of €163 billion in 2003). Nevertheless, the most optimistic estimates remained predictions: namely that foreign visitors to Greece 'may reach 19–20 million by the end of the decade', from around 13 million in 2004 (Alpha Bank, 2004). It is perhaps worth noting, though, that Alpha Bank was a major sponsor of the Athens Games, and thus had a vested interest in demonstrating a positive outcome from the Games.

3. Beijing 2008

A key goal of both Beijing's municipal government and the national Chinese government for the 2008 Games as stated in the Beijing Olympic Action Plan (2003) was to harness aspects of traditional Chinese culture in presenting the city and the country to the world in the run up to and during the Beijing Olympics. Elsewhere in the plan, the role of traditional Chinese culture in such an 'opening-up' strategy, as part of the humanistic 'people's Olympics' promotional theme, was clearly stated:

… we will take the hosting of the Olympic Games as an opportunity to … promote the traditional Chinese culture, showcase the history and development of Beijing as well as the friendliness and hospitality of its citizens. We will also take the Games as a bridge for cultural exchanges in order to deepen the understanding and enhance the trust and friendship among the peoples of different countries. (BOCOG, 2003, p. 2)

Yet there was no discussion of the strategies by which this would be achieved, and there was certainly no stated plan to leverage Olympic media, which was a key requirement for Beijing's Olympic tourism strategy. Furthermore, the lack of such a strategy cannot be blamed on the need to concentrate on ensuring that the facilities and infrastructure were ready as, four years before the Games, Ritchard (2004, p. 2) noted that:

Beijing will be supported by world-class facilities and logistics planning. The city is well underway in developing its Olympic-related facilities, including a new airport, magnificent stadia, convention centre and a much-improved transport network. Construction is reported to be on time and, in some cases, ahead of schedule.

Such efficiency in construction might be expected in a country that has only relatively recently undergone a transition from a planned 'state socialist' political system to what is still characterized as a 'socialist market economy'. However, as construction and infrastructure projects were well ahead of schedule, the need to turn attention to media concerns might be seen as even more pressing. Ritchard (*ibid.*, p. 3) claimed that the efficiency of infrastructure development and construction provided Beijing with a world-class tourism product to serve the 2008 Olympics and as such:

… the greatest potential of the Beijing Games will be the marketing opportunity which will instantly create global consumer awareness of 'China – the brand'… Beijing – like no other previous Olympic city – has a fascinating extra dimension: the unveiling of what China really is and what it can achieve, showcased to a global audience which, generally, knows little about the country. Beijing 2008 will be the source of many 'first impressions'. The Games will be the most comprehensive [and nicely packaged] up-close look at China in half a century, and history will judge the event as the vehicle for demystifying the world's image of the country.

The key question, though, was whether the 2008 Games, and the coverage of the city and country in the years before the Games, would be sufficient to 'convert public curiosity into travel bookings for conferences, leisure tours, city breaks, and business' (*ibid.*). In this respect, China did not have such an easy ride, and it was not really the case that an Olympic media leveraging strategy was all that was required. Despite reforms, politically Beijing remained located in a society strikingly at odds with Western liberalism (Wei and Yu, 2006). Furthermore, one of the key aspects of this difference was the Chinese state's perceived attitude to, and record on, human rights, with organizations such as Amnesty International, Human Rights Watch, and the Centre of Housing Rights and Evictions commenting both on the state's previous record and on alleged human rights violations specifically linked to the preparations for Beijing 2008.

The existence and coverage of such issues can increase perceptions of difference and distance from China and Beijing as a desirable tourist destination and, consequently, reduce travel propensities in the key Olympic tourist markets, virtually all of which are liberal democracies with a distaste for human rights violations. Specifically, it was alleged that, alongside censorship of the press, the 2008 Games led to the exploitation of construction workers, the use of child labour and the enforced displacement of families and communities from their homes, which have been demolished to make way for Olympic infrastructure developments. Against this background, Ritchard's 2004 comments that 'China is absolutely committed to ensuring the success of the Olympic Games – whatever it takes' (p. 2) and that the Games will be 'nicely packaged' (p. 3) become much more insidious. Of course, displacement of residents to facilitate Olympic development is not new. Many of the criticisms of Barcelona 1992 – often held up as the best example of the positive effects of the Olympics on long-term trade and tourism development (Sanahuja, 2002) – highlighted the displacement of 624 families (approximately 2,500 people) to facilitate the re-development of the waterfront area (COHRE, 2007a). However, this is a mere drop in the ocean against estimates that almost 1.25 million people were displaced in Beijing by 2007, and that this figure was set to rise to 1.5 million by the time the Games commenced in 2008 (*ibid.*).

With the glare of the global Olympic media spotlight concentrated on Beijing and China in the run up to 2008, these issues continued to feature in Olympic (and other) media and could not be addressed by a media strategy without addressing the underlying human rights issues themselves. As the Beijing 2008 torch relay progressed around the globe in the months preceding the Games in 2008, there was considerable disruption by protesters seeking to highlight a range of human rights issues in China. This became a major global story in the run up to the Games, although its long-term impact on 'China – the brand', given that Beijing undoubtedly hosted a largely successful and spectacular Games in 2008, appears to have faded in the post-Games period.

4. London 2012

Even before they had begun, the London 2012 Olympic and Paralympic Games were already being touted as the most planned for Games in history.

As a result, they faced considerable scrutiny across a range of legacy areas, as it was widely recognized that the London Games had benefitted from a decade of research and knowledge transfer in relation to the opportunities that an Olympic Games can present. In terms of tourism, the UK government, like previous national hosts, tried to buck the general trend of Summer Olympic cities as destinations rather than gateways in order to extend Olympic tourism benefits throughout the UK.

The possibility that a London Games might have an impact on tourism was first recognized even before London was awarded the Games, with the 2004 national tourism strategy, 'Tomorrow's Tourism Today', recognizing the benefits that London's bid might bring in terms of 'spotlighting the world-class visitor attractions of the capital, and stimulating further improvements in the visitor infrastructure' (DCMS, 2004, p. 14). Key issues were identified as: the need to consider the accommodation requirements of the Games; the need to plan for anticipated tourism activities in the years running up to the Games linked to the Cultural Olympiad; the need to plan Olympic-themed marketing activities within Visit Britain's overall 'brand architecture'; and the need to review the tourism opportunities arising from Olympic activities outside London (*ibid.*).

When London was announced as the winning bidder in July 2005, there were varying predictions for its impact on tourism, including that of a '£2bn tourist boost' and a 'million more international visitors' (BBC, 2005). However, much of the detailed discussion focused on dealing with the challenges the Games would bring, with VisitBritain and its industry partners noting that 'there will be a fight for the estimated 200,000 hotel beds available in London in 2012' and that 'July and August are already peak months for tourism' (*ibid.*). The twelve months following the award of the Games to London were similar to the twelve months preceding it, with much debate focusing on how the tourism implications of the Games would be managed. However, in July 2006, the government's consultation on a tourism strategy for the 2012 Games, 'Welcome>Legacy' (DCMS, 2006), was published. This acknowledged that there were some shortcomings in the British tourism product, and identified the need to 'put the UK's tourism industry in a position to successfully welcome the world in 2012' (*ibid.*, p.4). The document also discussed the 'policy and operational levers necessary to deliver outcomes', thus hinting at a change in emphasis towards capitalizing on the tourism opportunities presented by the Games rather than simply managing its consequences.

In terms of improving the quality of the British tourism product, 'Welcome>Legacy' provided the impetus for important changes, with a transition to quality being viewed in terms of value provided and an emphasis on the quality of the welcome, rather than focusing solely on physical infrastructure quality. Nevertheless, in terms of marketing Britain for tourism through the Olympic Games, it was the publication four years later of the 'Britain Marketing and 2012 Games Global Strategy' (Visit Britain, 2010) that marked a step change. This saw the launch of a holistic 'Britain Brand Proposition', supported by a 'You're Invited' strapline and a 'Britain Now' brand narrative:

> Britain is a stimulating and exciting place to be. A place of constant reinvention where castles host music festivals, museums hold fashion shows, country houses are transformed into spa hotels and where you'll find world renowned historic landmarks right next door to modern art galleries and restaurants. Not just one country but three, each with their own character and traditions, but connected by a common spirit and people who are genuine, down to earth, interesting and quirky. A country that will host the Olympic and Paralympic Games in London in 2012 and also invites you to experience the character and charm of the whole of Britain, right now. (*Ibid.*)

The Britain Brand Proposition, particularly the 'You're Invited' strapline, was employed within a wider GREAT campaign (using the word 'Great' from Great Britain) to generate exposure for UK business and tourism and claimed to be 'one of the most ambitious and far reaching marketing campaigns ever developed by the UK government' (DCMS, 2012*a*, p. 42), expected to generate £1billion in extra business for UK firms (*ibid.*, p. 39) and '£2billion additional spend by visitors to the UK in four years after the Games' (*ibid.*, p. 41). In terms of the tourism spend prediction, three widely available models were developed in the years before the Games that estimated its tourism impact (Blake, 2005; Oxford Economics, 2007; Lloyds Banking Group, 2012), two of which were developed before the economic downturn. Even the most optimistic of these (Blake, 2005) fell someway short of the government's £2 billion prediction for post-Games tourism impact.

After London 2012, these three models and their assumptions were consolidated in a meta-analysis (Weed, 2012) which provided an estimate (at 2011 prices) that the Games would generate additional tourism value of £1.6 billion, of which £972 million would be in the five post-Games years. However, Weed (*ibid.*) also used his meta-analysis to demonstrate that the largest modifiable tourism flows resulting from the Games would be the combined inward flows to London and the UK in the post-Games period. This was because effective marketing campaigns have significant potential to affect these flows, and as Weed *et al.* (2011) noted, a significant legacy of the 2012 Games for tourism was likely to be the way in which the British tourism policy community came together to embed the Games within the broad 'You're Invited' tourism marketing campaign, which itself was part of the wider GREAT campaign. However, there is no evidence to suggest these campaigns led to post-Games tourism flows more than twice the size of those estimated by Weed's (2012) meta-analysis (Weed, 2014).

The lessons from London 2012 for Olympic tourism, therefore, appear to be that long-term planning to leverage the Games for tourism, particularly embedding Olympic themes within a wider general tourism and business investment campaign, can lead to significant tourism impacts. At the same time, London 2012 also showed that, even when there was clear evidence of success, governments will still over-claim on the scale of the tourism impacts delivered.

Conclusions

A theme running throughout the discussions of the eight Olympic cities in the first fifteen years of the twenty-first century has been their stated desire to learn from the experiences of previous cities. However, the discussions often note planning failings in relation to the way in which the various Olympic cities have attempted to generate tourism. Such failings serve to highlight the very different contexts of the Games hosted by the Olympic cities discussed. The differences between the potential tourism implications of, and the resultant strategies that might be employed in, Winter and Summer Olympic cities have been highlighted. In particular, notwithstanding the ambitions and aspirations of national governments responsible for Summer Olympic cities, Winter Olympic cities appear to have a much greater potential to act as a tourism gateway to the wider regions in which they are situated as a result of the resource needs of the Winter Games (i.e. ski and other winter sports provision) that cannot be provided in cities. Summer Olympic cities, however, have a much greater potential to capitalize on the image benefits that the Games can bring as they are much larger cities than their Winter counterparts, and therefore have an infrastructure and a range of city resources and icons that can be leveraged for tourism image benefits through Olympic-related media.

However, the later editions of the Games discussed in this chapter appear to contradict these more general conclusions. London 2012's GREAT campaign was clearly focused on country-wide tourism benefits, which Weed's (2012, 2014) analyses suggest were delivered, while Sochi 2014 showed that even the largest infrastructure investment in Olympic history will not deliver expected tourism impacts, either for the city, or the wider surrounding region without clear planning and leveraging strategies.

Looking beyond the cities discussed in this chapter, the Rio 2016 Summer Games, like those in Beijing 2008 and Sochi 2014, took place in a turbulent political context and an unsupportive local environment, with major political protests against alleged corruption, and a considerable backlash against hosting the Games that went some way beyond the protests that are routinely associated with mega sport events (Weed, 2017). This significantly compromised any potential for a tourism legacy, and limited the lessons that could be learned, other than reinforcing the notion that legacies of any kind are almost impossible to leverage amid political instability and protest.

The realization of long-term tourism benefits from both Winter and Summer Games since Rio 2016 has, of course, been impacted by the global COVID-19 pandemic, which significantly curtailed global travel from the early months of 2020, and from which the global tourism industry is still projected to take a considerable time to recover fully (Weed, 2021). While the Winter Games in PyeongChang 2018 took place before the pandemic, the Games' tourism strategy focused on the post-Games use of venues for future sport event and conference tourism (Byun and Leopkey, 2021), which ceased completely when the pandemic took hold less than two years after the Games. The subsequent Summer and Winter Games, the year-delayed Tokyo 2020 and Beijing 2022 were held amidst travel restrictions before, during and after the Games, which meant that the tourism element was severely limited, if not entirely absent.

Looking forward to the next Summer Games in Paris (2024), and Winter Games in Milan/Cortina d'Ampezzo (2026), one sees traditional city and winter tourism destinations. As such, they are likely to be interesting and important tests of the continuing ability of the Olympic Games to generate tourism impacts, and of whether the strategies discussed in this chapter that pre-date the COVID-19 pandemic remain effective in a post COVID-19 world.

Note

1.   The discussions of Sydney 2000 are drawn from material contributed by Graham Brown to *Olympic Tourism* (Weed, 2008).

PART 3

CITY PORTRAITS

Chapter 12

ROME 1960

Giuseppe Telesca

In 1960 Rome organized a largely successful Summer Olympics. After the austerity Games that had followed the Second World War and the somewhat peripheral Melbourne 1956, the 1960 Games represented both the accomplishment of Pierre de Coubertin's dream of the return of the Olympics to its classic origins and a move towards a new dimension of the Games. Rome 1960 represented a first, crucial step in the direction of the Olympics as mega-event whether considered from the angle of urban change, where significant and unprecedented capital was invested in sporting venues and supportive infrastructure, or from the point of view of the impact of media where the Games were televised live for the first time to twelve European countries via Eurovision and only hours later in the United States, Canada and Japan. The final balance of the 1960 Games was positive when it comes to the organization of the event, the sale of Olympic tickets, the technical innovations introduced, and the interest that the event raised internationally. The foreign press was forced to abandon the easy *cliché* of Rome as a city gifted with beauty and history but flawed with disorganization and improvization.[1] Even in the events, the results of the Italian team were very positive and, with a total of thirty-six medals, Italy ended the Games in fourth place after the Soviet Union, the US, and a 'unified' Germany (Jacomuzzi, 1976, pp. 263–314).

Due to these successes, Rome 1960 was superficially celebrated for nearly fifty years as the symbol of the Italian 'economic miracle' and as the last Olympics 'with a human face', before the surrender of the Games to commodification and gigantism (Ministero del Turismo e Spettacolo, 1960; CONI, 1963; De Juliis, 2001). Then, over the last two decades, scholars from different disciplines finally overcame academic contempt towards the Olympic phenomenon and towards sports in general – an attitude particularly resilient in Italian academia (Giuntini, 2020). As a result, a body of literature has been growing around the 1960 Olympics, drawing a nuanced picture of this event, which has been reassessed in terms of its diplomatic (Sbetti,

2012, pp. 133–139; Forcellese, 2013, pp. 220–239), economic (Cassar and Creaco, 2012; Strangio 2013); political (Telesca, 2007; Giuntini, 2010; Bonini, 2011; Tondelli, 2011; Martin, 2017) and urban (Telesca, 2006; Modrey, 2008; Porro, 2010; Insolera, 2011; Fiadino, 2013; Telesca, 2014) significance. While these studies have filled many gaps, what seems to be missing is an overview of the Rome Olympics seen both in their connection with Italian history[2] and links with the evolution of the Summer Games.

This chapter addresses these gaps and, for this reason, starts with looking at the state of art of the research, and linking the Rome Olympics to the context in which they took place. It then reflects on the role that the 1960 Olympics played in heralding new opportunities for cities willing to bid to host the Summer Games. When considered under this light, the image of Rome 1960 as the last Games 'with a human face' appears inadequate. More appropriate, for a correct understanding of Rome 1960, is the image of the 'frontier edition', one capable of optimistically prefiguring new opportunities for future Olympic host cities.

The optimism surrounding the event had partly to do with the fact that the Games happened while Italy was – somehow unexpectedly – in the middle of an 'economic miracle' and the tensions related to the Cold War were subsiding after a decade of confrontation between the USA and the Soviet Union. If the 'economic miracle' and the international *détente* were crucial ingredients of the climate surrounding the Games, these latter also benefitted from the fact that the trajectory of the Summer Olympics as a mega-event was in its infancy and there was a widespread lack of awareness of the negative implications connected with hosting the Games that are noted elsewhere in this volume (see chapters 1 and 2). Certainly, the organizers of the 1960 Olympics, and the large public that took – directly or indirectly – part in it, did not give a lot of thought to the pitfalls that partially marred the Games of Rome. More than epitomizing the Italian 'economic miracle' Rome 1960 benefitted from it, as the buoyant context in which the Olympics took place made its shortcomings seem trivial. In 1960, a country with a great faith in its own potential, staged a bold and innovative Olympics that marked in many respects a new era for the Summer Games. However, Rome – unlike other big cities such as London, Los Angeles, Paris, and Tokyo – has not hosted the Olympics again and withdrew its bid for the 2020 and the 2024 Games. That experience is testament to the city's loss of vision, courage, and confidence in its own means and, at the same time, epitomizes the loss of 'innocence' of sports mega-events. It is to these themes that the conclusion returns.

The 1960 Games in Historical Context

Rome was awarded the organization of the XVII Olympic Games during the fifty-first session of the International Olympic Committee (IOC), held in Lausanne on 16 June 1955 (Sbetti, 2012, p. 133). At that time, the Italian economy had recovered from the scars of the Second World War and the 'miracle' was moving its first steps. It was from the late 1950s, and against the backdrop of the so-called 'golden age' of the Western international economy, that Italy was able to achieve its economic policy goals – usually against the odds (Felice, 2015, pp. 229–242). During the 1960s, Italian GDP increased by 6.5 per cent, labour productivity grew by 6.9 per cent, and exports increased by 11.8 per cent on a yearly basis. Yet the annual rate of inflation remained at 3.9 per cent.[3] A major contribution to this alchemy came from the process of gradual internationalization and liberalization of the Italian economy, epitomized by the first steps Italy took towards European integration.

Sport played its own (minor) role in this process. After the Second World War, the IOC started offering defeated or isolated nations the opportunity to complement their return to the international community through hosting big events. Italy entered the Northern Atlantic Treaty Organization in 1949, the United Nations six years later, and was among the founding countries of the European Economic Community in 1957 (Varsori, 1998, pp. 64–74). In the meantime, the IOC granted Cortina the possibility of hosting the 1956 Winter Olympics. Rome 1960 thus became a 'passport' to definitive re-entry into the international community.

The Italian economy did not only grow through export. The brilliant sporting results obtained on the field and recalled above were also an indirect consequence of the internal growth, as Italian society was moving towards affluence which, in turn, brought about better nutrition, the discovery of sporting activity and new forms of consumption (Crainz, 2001, pp. 132–42). A prominent place among these latter was occupied by tourism, which restarted slowly after the Second World War, both internally and internationally. The Catholic Jubilee, celebrated in Rome in 1950, marked the definitive ascent of a phenomenon that ceased to be the privilege of an élite and became the affordable dream of a growing middle class. International tourism – which increased nearly fourfold during the 1950s[4] – became one of the secret ingredients of the 'economic miracle', thanks to its positive contribution to the Italian balance of payments.

It is against this background that the Rome Olympics as a catalyst for tourism should be measured. The first thing to say is that, on the eve of the Games, Rome significantly reinforced its offer in terms of hospitality. The number of new hotels, which had grown at the (slow) pace of 15 per year in the first half of the 1950s, and 40 per year in the period 1955–1958, went from 712 tourist accommodation facilities, providing a total of 27,710 beds at the end of 1958, to 826 hotels and guesthouses, providing a total of 31,166 beds on the eve of the Games. This increase concerned mainly medium- to low-category establishments (Cassar and Creaco, 2012, pp. 170–171). During the period of the Games, the city of Rome hosted almost 200,000 tourists – with roughly three-quarters of them coming from abroad (table 12.1).

Unfortunately, there are no monthly surveys of tourist arrivals, so it is impossible to provide specific details of the Olympic weeks' figures compared to the general trend. Nevertheless, the data on the arrivals and the presence of tourists in Rome for the years 1959–1962 show that the 'Olympic effect' on tourism did not significantly influence a trend of constant growth of this phenomenon (table 12.2). Yet if it did not change the trend, Rome 1960 probably reinforced it. Moreover, during the Games the length of stay in Rome nearly doubled from a little more than three nights on average (see table 12.2) to more than six (see table 12.1).

Turning attention to the international context. David Maraniss, a former associate editor of the *Washington Post*, narrated the 1960 Olympics through the lens of the Cold War political, diplomatic, and ideological confrontation between the USA and the Soviet Union.[5] In reality, towards the end of the 1950s the consolidation of the 'reformist' leadership of Nikita Khrushchev in the Soviet Union and the moderation of the USA were conducive to a détente between the two blocs. As had already happened in 1956, the Federal Republic of Germany and the German Democratic Republic decided to take part in the competition together, under the Olympic flag. At the same time, the Games were not incident free. The trial of the American pilot Francis Gary Powers, accused of espionage after his U2 reconnaissance plane had been shot down in Soviet territory, was held in Moscow one week before the Games' Opening Ceremony (Maraniss, 2008, pp. 30–31).

Table 12.1. Movement of tourists to Rome from 25 August to 11 September 1960. (*Source*: Merlo, 1961)

	Arrivals	Present
Italy	49,243	188,553
Abroad	147,743	1,046,419
Total	196,986	1,243,972

Table 12.2. Movement of tourists to Rome 1959–1962. (*Source*: ISTAT, 1962)

	Arrivals	Present
1959	1,920,545	6,171,475
1960	2,117,161	6,757,372
1961	2,300,459	7,278,996
1962	2,305,832	7,461,899

Moreover, to appease Communist China, Taiwan was not allowed by the IOC to compete under the denomination of the Republic of China, forced instead to use the name of Formosa (Milza, 2002, p. 307). Powers's trial and the block on Taiwan's participation as the Republic of China fostered the internal Communist/anti-Communist cleavage. Indeed, the very celebration of the Games provided new ammunition to the advocates of the 'American way of life' on the one hand, and the devotees of the Soviet Union on the other – both ready to read into the athletes' results on the track the signs of superiority of one system over the other (Telesca, 2004, pp. 190–194; Martin, 2017, pp. 62–63).[6]

Relatedly, the Communist/anti-Communist cleavage was one of several political issues that divided Italian society. Another – the Fascist/anti-Fascist cleavage – also played a significant role in a country that had only recently freed itself from Benito Mussolini's regime and re-embraced democracy. Two episodes, which happened immediately before the Games, exacerbated the Fascist/anti-Fascist divide. In June 1960 the Italian government – led by Fernando Tambroni, an important figure of the senior majority party, the Christian Democratic Party (DC) – authorized the holding of the Italian neo-Fascist Party's national congress in Genoa, a city that had distinguished itself in the fight against the Fascist regime. The decision, probably related to Tambroni's need to enlarge his tiny parliamentary majority, moved the DC to the right of the political spectrum. Not surprisingly, a wave of demonstrations against Tambroni's decision took place in many Italian cities, and when the protests turned into riots the government's harsh response caused the deaths of ten demonstrators. As the one responsible for this tragic escalation, he was obliged to resign in July 1960 (Lepre, 1999, pp. 191–193). His place at the helm of the government was taken by Amintore Fanfani, a leader coming from the same party as Tambroni, but willing to prepare the ground for a new political majority supported by the Italian Socialist Party – a centre-left perspective that would eventually materialize in 1963 (Mammarella, 1993, pp. 265–269).

Immediately after Tambroni's resignation, another conflict risked producing harmful consequences, this time inside Rome City Council. The clash originated because of the presence of Fascist inscriptions at the entrance of the *Foro Italico* – a location built between 1928 and 1938 and formerly known as *Foro Mussolini* – which was at the heart of the Olympics. These inscriptions, *inter alia* celebrating the 'successes' of Italian imperialism under Mussolini, represented embarrassing memories of the Fascist regime. For this reason, a petition had been presented to Rome City Council at the end of 1959 asking for the removal of the inscriptions: they were considered a disgrace for a city that wanted to present itself in a new light while making use, in a rather contradictory way, of existing architectural symbols to highlight its connections with Ancient Rome (figure 12.1).[7]

Figure 12.1. Wrestling programme at the Basilica of Maxentius. (*Source*: CC photographer unknown)

The discussion over the inscriptions reached a crescendo in the wake of Tambroni's resignation when the left-wing parties campaigned with energy for the removal of the Fascist inscriptions. The government's decision to remove only the most controversial inscriptions disappointed both anti-Fascists and neo-Fascists. Since the 1956 municipal election, the DC and its allies had failed to obtain a majority in Rome City Council. This situation, combined with the Vatican's veto on a potential cooperation of the DC with the Socialists at local level (Vidotto, 2006, p. 278), had resulted in a series of centrist administrations surreptitiously supported by the neo-Fascist Party (Avarello, 2000, p. 370). The ambiguities on the issue of the Fascist inscriptions were, then, the consequence of the local government's political fragility, which also helps to explain why the significant investments for the urban renewal of Rome produced contradictory results. It is now time to look at this crucial aspect of the 1960 Games.

The 1960 Games and Olympic History

It was noted above that the 1960 Games indicated new avenues to be pursued by future host cities, the most prominent of which was urban renewal.

Unprecedented infrastructural investments were realized on the occasion of Rome 1960, providing 'the first indication of the Olympics' potential role as a trigger for major urban development and improvement well beyond the construction of sports facilities' (Chalkley and Essex, 1998, p. 195). In 1961 Rome's population was 2,188,160 inhabitants, a figure that had increased by more than a third in a decade. The presence of a fast growing, young population – where the over-65 category represented only 7 per cent of the total – underpinned a sustained demand for housing that, combined with a buoyant economy, opened a phase of urban expansion which started with the Catholic Jubilee and ended with the Olympic Games (Porro, 2010).

The juridical context of this expansion was the Fascist city plan of 1931, which had been repeatedly violated in different ways (Insolera, 2001, pp. 125–140). The need to put an end to this urban change *à la carte*, which was promoted nearly exclusively through private initiative, stimulated the debate over a new city plan. This was eventually sketched in the mid-1950s and elaborated by a technical committee (CET). As such, the plan recommended expanding the city eastwards and suggested either concentrating the sporting facilities in the north of Rome, or distributing them in the east of the city. The first option would make it possible to contain the costs of the Olympics and eliminate any logistical problems for the athletes; the second, complemented by a new main road (the so-called *asse attrezzato*), would contribute to improving living conditions in the poorest and most crowded areas of the city (Avarello, 2000, pp. 173–176; Insolera, 2001, pp. 220–227). The CET city plan conflicted with the interests of major real estate players – the Società Generale Immobiliare (SGI) above all[8] – whose properties were mainly located in the west of Rome and in the EUR area (south). These circumstances contributed to pressures that help to explain why the CET plan was rejected in November 1957 (Telesca, 2014, pp. 24–25).

The main Olympic sporting venues were then located in the northern area of the city and in the EUR area (see also chapter 2). A 15-kilometre Olympic road, the so-called 'Via Olimpica', was devised to provide a connection between the *Foro Italico* and the EUR zone. The *Foro Italico*, in the north of the city, hosted numerous sporting venues such as the Olympic Stadium (inaugurated in 1953), the *Stadio dei Marmi* and the newly built Olympic swimming pool (figure 12.2). The *Foro* was complemented by other facilities in that area, such as a new indoor sports arena and the refurbishment of the former national stadium, then renamed the *Stadio Flaminio*. The EUR, located in the south of Rome, had been planned to host Rome's universal exhibition in 1942, which was meant to mark twenty years of Fascism in Italy. This area hosted *ex novo* sporting venues such as the velodrome (figure 12.3), and a second indoor sports arena and Olympic swimming pool (Fiadino, 2013, pp. 189–214).

Rome was not the first city to build remarkable sporting venues for the

Figure 12.2. Aerial view of the Stadio Olimpico. (*Source*: CC photographer unknown)

Figure 12.3. The Olympic velodrome in the EUR area. (*Source*: CC photographer unknown)

Olympics. The facilities for the 1936 Berlin Games, for instance, were as impressive as in Rome, and were conceived to epitomize the Third Reich's ambitions. Yet, the Berlin sporting venues had only a modest impact on the city (Chalkley and Essex, 1998, p. 193). By contrast, in Rome significant expenditure was undertaken to build supportive urban infrastructure, starting with a new airport (Fiumicino), which was considered essential for the future of Rome beyond the Games – even if it was not completed on time for the Opening Ceremony.[9] The Italian government spent 64 billion lire on the Olympics, mainly through the Infrastructure Department, to promote Rome's overall urban renewal. The contribution of the Municipality of Rome to the Olympic investment was reckoned at approximately 14 billion lire, even though it must be said that, since 1953, the Italian state had provided special funding to the capital in support of infrastructure investment (Strangio, 2013, pp. 231–232). As for the sporting venues, they were built or refurbished at the National Olympic Committee (CONI)'s expenses. CONI invested roughly 21 billion lire to endow Rome with a modern array of stadia, swimming pools, indoor and outdoor training structures of every kind (Ministero del Turismo e Spettacolo, 1960, pp. 65–70).

Apart from the Fiumicino episode, the investment of roughly 100 billion lire for the event provided Rome with sporting facilities and supportive infrastructures that, taken singularly, in many cases were at the cutting edge of innovation (Dietschy and Pivato, 2019, pp. 148–149). The Olympic Village, for instance, cost 6.5 billion lire and was realized by an institution created during the interwar years with the task of providing affordable housing for civil servants. Apart from representing one of the most interesting examples of high-standard construction, the Olympic Village was by far the most important initiative realized by state-owned companies, and indeed one of the few of its kind. After the Games, its 1,800 apartments were allocated to civil servants (Vidotto, 2006, p. 292). Yet the overall outcome of urban interventions for the 1960 Olympics was disappointing. It could be argued that was this result of a fundamental lack of systematic vision or, alternatively, a consequence of the interests of powerful actors being prioritized over the needs of Rome's inhabitants (Telesca, 2006; Insolera, 2011). This point will be discussed further in the concluding remarks.

Two other innovations – the first relating to the funding of the Games and the second linked to the revenues generated by them – are worth discussing here, as they illustrate the groundbreaking character of the 1960 Olympics. First, with the exception of Berlin 1936, the modern Olympics had hitherto been a relatively low-cost affair. Rome inaugurated a series of 'costly' Games – Tokyo (1964), Munich (1972) and Montreal (1976) – which, in line with the Keynesian consensus of the 1960s and 1970s, were funded nearly exclusively with public money. The discussion on how to share the burden of the 1960 Olympics – entrusted to an inter-ministerial committee

established in May 1957 – proved to be a source of tensions between
the Italian government (and the Municipality of Rome) and CONI. The
former, while funding the supportive infrastructure needed for the Games,
was adamant about CONI's duty to finance the sporting venues (Telesca,
2004, pp. 103–106). The latter, anticipating a solution often adopted in
the following decades, decided to finance its share of Olympic investment
partially through the *Totocalcio*: a lottery linked to the Italian professional
soccer league (Davis, 1996, p. 132).

Since its re-establishment in 1944 CONI, under the guidance of Giulio
Onesti, had been seeking legitimation within international sports institutions.
While carrying out this ambitious agenda, Onesti tried to defend CONI's
autonomy from political interference based on a slogan – 'sport to the
sportsmen' – which behind its apparent clarity disguised an ambiguous
relationship with the political world (Giuntini, 2019). Onesti was particularly
close to Giulio Andreotti, another DC grandee who was appointed chairman
of the 1960 Olympics Organizing Committee in November 1958 while
being simultaneously Secretary of State to the Finance.[10] It was in this double
capacity that Andreotti had to reassure Onesti who had asked for a four-
year rebate of 25 per cent of the taxes that CONI paid on the *Totocalcio*'s
revenues at the end of 1957, in order to face the extraordinary expenses
envisaged for the Games. After a complicated discussion which also featured
the imminent launch of a new lottery, the *Enalotto*, the government refused
Onesti's proposal for a 25 per cent rebate to CONI. It was decided instead
that the government would intervene in support of CONI if the *Enalotto*
significantly reduced the revenues generated by the *Totocalcio*. Through an
extraordinary loan the Banca Nazionale del Lavoro (BNL) – an institution
directly controlled by the government and one of the largest Italian banks
– offered CONI a buffer to tackle the exceptional, Olympic-related financial
effort (Telesca, 2007, pp. 160–167).

CONI also asked the BNL to assist the New York agency Gardner
Advertising Company in its negotiation, on behalf of CONI, with the
American network Columbia Broadcasting System (CBS) for the exclusive
Games' broadcasting rights relative to the United States, Canada, Bermuda,
Cuba, and Mexico. This element represents the third novelty of the 1960
Olympics, in that Rome marked the true beginning of the synergy between
Olympics and television. Helsinki 1952 had not been televised, while only a
few pre-recorded events had been made available for the US channels of the
1956 Melbourne Olympics (Whannel, 2012, p. 263).

The negotiation between CBS and CONI, represented by Gardner, was
successfully concluded on 8 June 1959. The BNL historical archive holds
the dossier relative to this negotiation, which ended with the payment of
$425,000 by CBS, an amount that included the commission fees for Gardner
(table 12.3).[11] Besides the final figure,[12] the dossier relative to the Gardner-

Table 12.3. US network payments for Olympics television rights (in $ million) (*Source*: Whannel, 2012, p. 264)

	Summer	*Winter*
1960	0.39*	0.05
1964	1.5	0.59
1968	4.5	2.5
1972	7.5	6.4
1976	25	10
1980	87	15.5
1984	225	91.5
1988	300	309

Note: * Here there is a slight discrepancy with the figure of the BNL historical archive. More evident is the difference with Davis (1996, p. 132), who argues that CBS paid CONI $660,000.

CBS negotiation illustrates the first, uncertain, moves of the relationship between Olympics and television, which would become one of the pillars of the Olympics growth from 1960 onwards. To keep the price low, CBS argued that the summer was not a good time for broadcasters, as people were on holiday and distracted by factors such as the Democratic and Republican conventions that preceded the November Presidential elections and by the forthcoming September baseball World Series. To these questionable claims, CBS added a real disadvantage: not being able to broadcast the events live.[13] In spite of this constraint, the 1960 Olympics represented a success for CBS, which reported a 36 per cent audience share for the event. This success – combined with the new communication satellites which enabled the first intercontinental live broadcast for Tokyo 1964 – heralded, and partially triggered, the growth of broadcasting rights in the following decades.

From Rome 1960 to the (Vanished) Dream of New Olympics

Unlike those cities that have now hosted the Olympics on multiple occasions, Rome has still held just one despite three bids for the Summer Games. A new Olympic bid for Rome was next conceived and implemented in the 1990s. Since 1993, large Italian cities had been directly electing their own mayors. Rome elected Francesco Rutelli, a left of centre politician who was re-elected in 1997. Rutelli launched an Olympic bid for the 2004 Games building on the sporting venues that were already available thanks to the 1960 Olympics, in particular with the Olympic stadium that had been upgraded for the 1990 soccer World Cup, and for the 2000 Catholic Jubilee, which was expected to attract millions of visitors and stimulate urban transformations in strategic parts of the city (Fiadino, 2013, p. 214). After winning the 'internal' ballot against Milan – another city willing to put forward its Olympic candidacy – Rome launched a candidature bid in the mid-1990s. This was strongly supported by the newly elected left of centre government but countered, at both local and national level, by the opposition and a few media outlets, especially the influential *Corriere della Sera* and *La Stampa*, traditional newspapers of the north-Italian bourgeoisie. These divisions, combined with the IOC's determination to repair the 1996 snub, when Athens had been denied the organization of the 'centennial' edition of the modern Olympics, settled the destiny of Rome (Forcellese, 2013, pp. 244–246).

It is crucial, however, to bear in mind the experience of the Greek capital, another southern European city, in order to understand the context in which the next two attempts by Rome to bid to host the summer Games would fade away. Athens 2004 cost the Greeks taxpayers roughly €10 billion – a figure that appeared even more profligate in the light of the economic crisis which hit the country from 2009 onwards (Kissoudi, 2008). There was deep concern within Italy that this huge investment failed to pay off either in terms of job creation or in terms of economic and a touristic boost. Moreover, the results were poor when it came to urban renewal, producing many under-utilized infrastructure and sporting facilities.

The newly elected Roman mayor, the right-wing Gianni Alemanno, launched a bid for the 2020 Olympics, building on the committed support of the right-wing central government, local entrepreneurs, and the bipartisan backing of the other local authorities (Forcellese, 2013, pp. 248–251). However, the new Prime Minister, the economist Mario Monti, withdrew the government's financial support for Rome's bid in February 2012 (*Repubblica*, 2012). The so-called spread – the difference in yields to maturity of ten-year Italian bonds relative to Germany's ten-year *bund* – was at that time attested to 400 basis points, after a period of dramatic surge that, at the end of 2011, had triggered the previous government's dismissal and its substitution with a technocratic alternative. Monti's decision was aimed at sending a message of commitment to economic austerity to the international markets. There was no question of the quality and credibility of the project for Rome 2020, yet Monti wanted to avoid any potential risk of profligacy hidden behind the apparently unquestionable figures contained in the review of the Olympic proposal that the economist Marco Fortis (2011) had conducted on behalf of the Italian government.

The final bid, this time for Rome 2024, was launched through the combined effort of CONI's president, Giovanni Malagò, supported by local entrepreneurs, and Prime Minister Matteo Renzi, a young and ambitious left of centre leader. This time, Rome City Council and the Mayor, Ignazio Marino, took a back seat. The city was going through a prolonged period of crisis – with allegations of generalized corruption and soaring debt – that neither the previous, not the current administration, seemed to be able to end. The growing turmoil obliged Rome's Mayor to resign and call for a new election, which saw Virginia Raggi, local leader of the populist Five

Stars Movement, win a convincing majority in 2016. Raggi campaigned, *inter alia*, on a platform of refusal of the 2024 Olympics, claiming that part of the Rome debt, amounting to €13 billion, was linked the 1960 Games (Menicucci, 2016). This was a baseless claim, but one that highlighted Raggi's ability to use the Olympic bid as a polarizing campaign issue. With the 'official' media supporting the 2024 Rome candidature and her skilful use of the social media, Raggi burnished her credentials as an insurgent and mobilized large sectors of the city against the Olympics, depicted as a trojan horse to advance the economic interests of the few against the interests of the many (Bourbillères *et al.*, 2023).

Monti's and Raggi's decisions epitomized the waning interest in hosting the Games – a phenomenon already experienced elsewhere in recent Olympic history. Admittedly, their refusal to pursue the bids for 2020 and 2024 were rooted in different ideological perspectives: austerity and the need to contain public spending for the former; aversion to big events and infrastructure megaprojects for the latter. Nevertheless, while criticized by CONI and local entrepreneurs, both refusals, were supported by public opinion and both shared the same mistrust for politics and its capacity to conceive and implement long-term projects. This distrust was far from unjustified. Monti had been appointed at the helm of a technocratic government to deal with the wrecked legacy of an ineffective and conflictual political majority which had nearly failed the country. Raggi had been elected – despite her unimpressive personality and poor grasp of Rome's problems – after the voters of the Italian capital had been confronted with two dysfunctional administrations at the opposite ends of the political spectrum. Moreover, the waste and failures produced by mega-sports events, such as the aforementioned 1990 FIFA soccer World Cup, had left bitter memories in Rome and the rest of the country (Porro *et al.*, 2016).

In 1960, a city with many limitations, but great potential, was able to organize a bold and creative Olympics which, like the Italian economic 'miracle', were far from perfect. In the 1980s–1990s the Italian 'miracle' was well over, but the ephemeral economic revival of the 1980s inspired a new boldness that resulted in the FIFA World Cup and in Rome's bid for the 2004 Games. The aborted 2020 and 2024 Olympic bids are, on the one hand, symbols of the current fragility of Rome, which seems to have lost the ability to envision its future, and reflect, on the other, the loss of innocence of sports mega-events – more complicated affairs now than they were in 1960.

Conclusion

In a previous work devoted to the 1960 Games' shortcomings and in particular with regard to the urban transformation of the city, I made use of regime theory, a framework generally applied to the mega-event strategy pursued since the late 1980s in American cities (Telesca, 2014). As business leaders have a privileged position in local politics because of their command of economic resources and because local political decisions affect business leaders' opportunities, regime theory assumes that co-operation between local elected officials, bureaucrats, and business leaders is needed for a 'growth regime' to work properly. The composition and goals of a 'growth regime', as well as its effectiveness and the strength of the opposition against it, depend on economic conditions, the nature of local government and local business, and the existence of political cleavages (Andranovich *et al.*, 2001, pp. 4–29; Stone, 1989). I argued that, in 1960, Rome's 'growth regime' consisted of weak and divided local political actors, conditioned by influential exogenous agents (e.g. the Vatican) and powerful property developers (e.g. the SGI). Political opposition seemed unable to stop, or improve, the most controversial urban changes pursued by Rome's 'growth regime' through the Olympics. In 1960 the 'slow growth' or 'no growth' coalitions of environmentalists, neighbourhoods, activists, and others – which opposed growth regimes and played a role in Rome's most recent attempt to host the Olympics – were in their infancy. There was little awareness that hosting such an event could entail risks, and not simply bring benefits.

The very fact that, in order to explain the main weakness of an otherwise successful edition of the Games, it is necessary to make use of regime theory, hence incurring the risk of anachronism – the worst sin for a historian – represents the ultimate proof of the groundbreaking nature of the Rome Olympics. More than the last Games 'with a human face', Rome 1960 deserves to be remembered as a 'frontier edition' which, on the one hand, opened the door to new ways of interpreting the Olympics and new goals to be pursued by host cities through the Games, and, on the other, anticipated problems linked to hosting the Olympic Games that emerged more clearly in the following decades.

Notes

1. The comments of the foreign press were particularly appreciative both in relation to the Opening and Closing Ceremonies of the Games and in relation to the sporting venues and accompanying infrastructure realized for the Games.

2. Some of the essays mentioned above are included in two overview collections written – in Italian – on, or around, the fiftieth anniversary of the 1960 Olympics (see the 2010 special issue of *Lancillotto e Nausica*, **27**(1/2) and the edited collection *Le Olimpiadi del 'miracolo' cinquant'anni dopo*. Milano: Franco Angeli).

3. Elaboration from Ameco dataset.

4. Foreign visitors were officially 5,405,863 in 1951. Their number jumped to 18,010,111 in 1960 (ENIT, 1962, p. 4).

5. Maraniss's account of Rome 1960 is among the few written, in English, by non-Italian observers.

6.   Opposing examples of this rhetoric are two leaders dedicated to the Olympics: the first published in the official newspaper of the Italian Christian Democratic Party on 4 September (*Il Popolo*, 1960), the second published in the official newspaper of the Italian Communist Party on 11 September (*L'Unità*, 1960).

7.   The Rome Olympic Organizing Committee emphasized continuity with the past by celebrating some of the sports events in symbolic venues of Ancient Rome such as the Caracalla Baths (gymnastics programme), the Basilica of Maxentius (wrestling programme) and the Arch of Constantine, where the finishing line of the marathon was set. This choice was not without risks, since continuity with the Roman Empire was one of the main traits of the Fascist regime (Modrey, 2008).

8.   The SGI's prominent position among real estate players in Rome was granted by the possession of 6,750,000 square metres of the Eternal City's land and a board of directors in which the élite of Italian capitalism sat together with financial interests related to the Vatican. Moreover, the SGI could count on a successful business model which benefitted from the spinoff realized immediately after the war, with the creation of Sogene – the operative arm of the parent company SGI operating in Italy and abroad (Giannini, 2003, pp. 117–118).

9.   A Parliamentary Commission, appointed in May 1961 to inquire into this major delay, issued a final report stressing misconduct and negligence on the part of both the Infra-structure Department and the Department of Defence (Telesca, 2004, pp. 159–164).

10.   On Onesti's political links and, in particular, on his relationship with Andreotti, see Mazzarini (2010) and Tondelli (2011).

11.   Archivio Storico Banca Nazionale del Lavoro (ASBNL), Fondo Servizio Enti (FSE), fasc. 509, Contract CBS-Gardner, 8 June 1959.

12.   Of which there are different versions, see note to table 12.3.

13.   ASBNL, FSE, fasc. 509, Memorandum relativo alla cessione del diritto esclusivo di trasmissione della XVII Olimpiade alla CBS inviato dalla filiale BNL di New York alla direzione centrale della BNL, 6 June 1959.

Chapter 13

SYDNEY 2000

Robert Freestone

The Sydney Olympic Games, more formally known as the Games of the XXVII Olympiad, were staged between 15 September and 1 October 2000. In total, 10,651 athletes from nearly 200 countries competed in 300 events across twenty-eight sports. Sydney 2000 marked only the second time an Australian city had hosted the Summer Olympic Games, and the second time that the Games had been held in the southern hemisphere. Rio de Janeiro (2016) was the third and the 2032 Games will be hosted by Brisbane. The Sydney Games also celebrated 100 years of women's participation in the modern Olympic Games, as well as the debut of two new Olympic sports: taekwondo and the triathlon. The total cost of staging the Games has been estimated at A$6.6 billion (Davidson and McNeill, 2012), of which approximately two-thirds were paid for by the public sector, representing 0.6 per cent of the country's GDP in 1990–2000 (Cashman, 2006).

Sydney was awarded the right to host the Games on 23 September 1993 beating six other contenders: Beijing, Berlin, Brasilia, Istanbul, Manchester, and Milan. The bid process was managed by the Sydney Olympic Organizing Committee (SOCOG) with support from the New South Wales (NSW) State Government which made three crucial commitments: to provide venues and facilities; to ensure key support services such as health, security and transport; and to underwrite the costs of staging the event (OCA, 1998).

This chapter focuses on the physical planning and transformation of the main site at Homebush Bay.[1] The Sydney Olympic Park (SOP) precinct on what has latterly been termed the Olympic Peninsula was developed as the major venue with nine permanent facilities constructed including the main Olympic Stadium ('Stadium Australia') now known as Accor Stadium. The events held there included athletics, tennis, swimming, field hockey, table tennis, taekwondo, basketball, and gymnastics. The 640-hectare Sydney Olympic Park (SOP) precinct – which includes 430 hectares of parkland – is approximately 14 kilometres west of the Sydney CBD and south of the Parramatta River (Burramattagal). The site is almost entirely in public ownership. Managed by a state government entity, the Sydney Olympic Park Authority (SOPA) it is located within the local government area of the City of Parramatta. Other suburbs had world class sporting facilities constructed for the Games and these also continue to serve the community for sporting events all year round, including the Dunc Gray Velodrome at Bankstown and the Whitewater Stadium and International Regatta Centre in Penrith.

This chapter is framed around the notion of legacy and planning for it. Legacy, as noted in chapter 1, gained popularity once it was officially recognized as a necessary component for an Olympic bid, with the study of legacy becoming increasingly important as securing sustainable and equitable long-term benefits become paramount (Leopkey and Parent, 2012). The concept is briefly expanded upon in the next section before identifying a chronology of thinking which frames a narrative around four main stages to characterize the Sydney experience. This concludes with some reflections on the broader implications of this planning history. The analysis draws on previous research on the planning processes surrounding Sydney 2000 and the Sydney Olympic site (see for example: Lochhead, 2005; Preuss, 2007; Toohey, 2008; Cashman, 2011; Dickson *et al.*, 2011; Kassens-Noor, 2012; Leopkey and Parent, 2012; Cox, 2012; Davidson and McNeill, 2012; Searle, 2012; Davidson, 2013; Yamawaki and Duarte, 2014; Mulley and Moutou, 2015; Mussi, 2017). It also makes use of information gained by undertaking a series of interviews with key stakeholders involved in the planning and development of Sydney Olympic Park.[2]

Legacy

Legacy has a long history in mega-event planning and delivery with mixed results (Chalkley and Essex, 1999; see also chapter 1), but the underlying principles for Games preparation were especially evident from Barcelona 1992. A key value of mega-events is their potential to be a positive driver for urban development, particularly in infrastructure improvements, urban regeneration, and city branding (Johnson, 2008). However, it was not until 2002 that the International Olympic Committee (IOC) made a formal acknowledgement of the importance of legacy. In 2003, legacy was included in the charters of both the International Olympic Committee and the International Paralympic Committee (De Moragas *et al.*, 2003; Andranovich and Burbank, 2011; Leopkey and Parent, 2012). Scheu *et al.* (2021) identify six main categories: urban development; environmental enhancement; policy and governance; skills, knowledge and networks; intellectual property; and new or revised beliefs and behavioural changes.

Discussion of legacy can be fraught, because the construction of legacy is contestable in the eyes of different stakeholders, cumulative impacts colour expectations, and the time elapsed before coming to fruition is not always agreed (Toohey, 2008). Over two decades have passed since the 2000 Games to gain a better overall appreciation but this still remains a live story. From the start, planning in Sydney paid attention to legacy, notably by emphasizing sustainability as a dominant theme (Cashman, 2011; Dickson *et al.*, 2011; Kassens-Noor, 2012). This was largely aspirational at the beginning, attaining greater form and substance, and in time challenged by the demands of event planning, resource constraints, and stakeholder interests.

There have been claims and counter-claims regarding the legacy of the Sydney Olympics. Notwithstanding conspicuous successes, such as the introduction of sophisticated environmental management systems and the development of regional parklands, the legacy is tinged by significant lost opportunities (Cox, 2012; Kassens-Noor, 2012). Most forward thinking has come post-Games and ironically has had to address the spatial and functional constraints within the SOP precinct. The legacy agenda thus took years to solidify through a succession of master planning exercises (Sanchez and Essex, 2018) but continues to evolve in response to challenges and opportunities posed by the shifting metropolitan context of SOP.

The appreciation and development of legacy for the Sydney Games can be interpreted historically through four stages (table 13.1). Stage one, dubbed *Reactive Engagement*, refers to *ad hoc* legacy gestures responding to immediate infrastructure requirements through the processes of site selection and scoping of site remediation works preparatory to the official bid. A focus was on short-term financial responsibility. Conflicting goals between the short- and longer-term were ignored or managed out. Stage two, *Articulated Development*, the post-bid phase, saw more attention

Table 13.1. Planning for the legacy of the Sydney 2000 Games. (*Source*: Adapted from Freestone and Gunesekara, 2017)

Stage 1 (Pre-bid) Reactive Engagement	Stage 2 (Post-bid) Articulated Development	Stage 3 (Post-games) Consequential Legacy Planning	Stage 4 (New horizon) Metropolitan Integration
• Site selection (population growth, transport, environmental issues, cost)	• Site remediation and environmental management measures	• Finding a viable future	• Connectedness and role in sub-regional and metropolitan contexts
• Scoping site remediation (brownfield)	• Venue and facility development	• Stakeholder consultation and market interest	• Addressing old and new legacies
	• Transport infrastructure	• Upscaling residential development	
	• Parkland creation	• Town centre activation	

devoted to legacy, although still largely within a site-specific, short-term and reactive framework. Nevertheless, the range of planning activities increased significantly, with a strong 'green games' theme and infrastructure investment geared to event planning. Stage three, *Consequential Legacy Planning*, started immediately after the Games and continued with a more explicit future focus centred on new development, in particular with attention given to large-scale commercial and increasingly community development. Stage four, *Metropolitan Integration*, overlaps but extends this process ito the present-day, with investment priorities and responses more explicitly framed within a broader metropolitan context.

Pre-bid: Imagining an Olympic-Standard Sporting Precinct

Homebush Bay locality forms part of the traditional lands of the Wangal people who were among the first to encounter British settlers in the late eighteenth century. Early colonial activities included cattle grazing, timber gathering, commercial salt pans, and armaments storage. State government land resumptions in the early 1900s brought new noxious industries including a major abattoir and brickworks. By the 1960s, heavy industry was deserting Homebush, creating brownfield opportunities but leaving the area seriously polluted, degraded, and contaminated (figure 13.1). The site which

Figure 13.1. Homebush Bay from the air, late 1960s. The site of the state abattoirs and saleyards, government brickworks and Royal Australian Navy Armament depot. View north-east towards the Parramatta River. (*Source*: State Library of New South Wales, 25 September 1969)

was controlled by the state and federal governments boasted a number of positive opportunities including its location near the geographic centre of the metropolitan area, its ability to connect with existing transport networks, and prospects for environmental remediation.

The first stage of legacy planning covers the period from 1973 to 1992. The Homebush Bay area had been the subject of planning investigation since the 1970s. With a view to attracting the 1988 Olympics to Sydney, leading planner-architect Walter Bunning was engaged by the state government to consider the siting and development of a major new sports complex and to evaluate twenty possible sites across the metropolitan area in terms of four main criteria: location in relation to both the city's recreational needs and possible international requirements; accessibility to public and private transport; effect on the environment, visually and in terms of noise pollution; and cost factors. Bunning's 1973 report advocated development of surplus government-owned land at Homebush Bay (figure 13.2). This pleased community groups campaigning against projected redevelopment of Centennial Park in Sydney's eastern suburbs. This recommendation initiated a debate on urban regeneration which was subsequently played out through a succession of competing development plans produced by various state agencies.

In 1979 the state government made a formal submission to the Australian Olympic Federation to host the 1988 Olympics in Sydney centred on Homebush Bay but changed its mind, perhaps concerned that, by its own admission, there was 'not one existing venue for any of the 21 sports that could be used for Olympic Games competition without modification

Figure 13.2. Early vision of an international-standard sporting complex at Homebush Bay. 'Before taking the first step of defining the actual site, a great deal of exploratory work needs to be undertaken'. (*Source*: Bunning, 1973)

and upgrading' (NSW Government, 1979). The following year a joint Commonwealth and State Task Force established the feasibility of the site to host an international exposition to commemorate the bicentenary of British colonization, but this also did not proceed. Nevertheless, some key development decisions were made in the early- to mid-1980s: the NSW State Sports Centre (1984) followed by the Australia Centre business park were to be built on long-term leasehold land (Cashman, 2011). Later came the opening of Bicentennial Park (1988).

With a bid for the 2000 Olympics in the offing, in December 1990 the federal government announced that it would make 84 hectares of land at Homebush Bay available in what became the core Olympic site. In the lead up to the bid, Olympic responsibilities at the state level were shared by several agencies contributing to a lack of clarity about the direction of the project and degree of private sector involvement (*ibid.*). This led to the establishment in 1992 of the Homebush Bay Development Corporation (HBDC), an archetypal project-specific delivery agency to promote, coordinate, manage, and secure the orderly and economic development of the 'growth centre' at Homebush in anticipation of a successful Games bid. Its first masterplan in 1992 retained flexibility to proceed with redevelopment even if the bid was not successful, and alongside the sporting facilities was the prospect of more hi-tech business reflecting the rise of the knowledge economy. The masterplan established an urban core surrounded by extensive parklands. The orthogonal grid of the former abattoir pens was inscribed on the site and transected by a major new north–south boulevard (Johnson, 1999).

Initially, it was intended that Homebush Bay would serve two immediate purposes: not only a world class sporting hub but also a new permanent home for the Royal Easter Show (an annual town-country fair) relocated from the inner city to make way for a controversial movie studios development associated with Australian media entrepreneur Rupert Murdoch (Williams, 1997). Most attention was given to conceptualizing the venue as a facility for the Games. Writing at the time, Myer (1996, p. 2) commented: 'the primary motivation for most of the current activity at Homebush Bay is meeting the requirements of the 2000 Olympics – and longer-term planning issues generally appear to receive a lower priority'.

However, the 'green promise' was emerging as a hallmark of Sydney's bid for the Games (McGeoch with Korporaal, 1994). The bid coincided with a move by the IOC to recognize the environment as a core principle of Olympism. The IOC was influenced by the increasing global prominence of environmental management strategies in the wake of the 1987 Brundtland Report (see chapter 7). An environmental clause was added to the Olympic Charter in 1991 and an environmental theme was inserted into the bid manual for aspirant Olympic cities. In 1995, the environment was formally confirmed as the third dimension of Olympism, after sport and culture. The

Sydney bid's Environmental Guidelines were drafted soon after the 1992 United Nations Earth Summit and contained more than 100 commitments (Darkovich, 2020). Sydney's green programme engaged with two major agendas: emergent global concerns surrounding depletion of resources and the adverse impacts of non-renewable energy sources; and an array of site-specific conservation and remediation challenges far beyond what Bunning (1973) had comprehended. Homebush Bay was beset by a range of environmental constraints. There were significant areas of low-lying flood-prone land, poor geotechnical conditions, and extensive landfill that had been inadequately supervised and included dioxin, asbestos, and other hazardous materials.

Homebush Bay was envisaged as a unique venue combining sports and environmental legacies with commercial development. The design of venues and accompanying facilities would facilitate future use through flexible seating structures, relocation, and greater public use post-Games. However, the bid for the Games was not explicitly connected to a wider urban regeneration planning framework. This helps explain why links to regional planning frameworks were weak from the outset.

Post Bid: Articulating Development between 1993 and 2000

This second stage covers the period from the successful bid to the actual staging of the Games. Despite good intentions to balance short and longer-term planning agendas, the pressing demands of the Games' preparation dominated the agenda. Cashman and Hughes (1999) highlighted the pressure to focus on short-term imperatives coming from the top echelons of the state government to ensure that there was minimal risk that the Games would fail, be delayed, or run significantly over budget. This occupied much of the time and energy of planning and design teams, and marginalized forward thinking.

In September 1993 the HBDC was invested with Olympic responsibilities. Key tasks involved environmental management and renewal; provision of transport and infrastructure; master planning and urban design; asset management; and facilities maintenance. Importantly, it had to deliver most of the Olympic facilities including the stadium; the tennis, baseball, and archery centres; and the athlete and media villages (Cox *et al.*, 1994). There was still concern that Olympic responsibilities were fragmented across government and, with the design and construction programme falling behind schedule, a new Olympic Coordination Authority (OCA) came into being in 1995 with fresh leadership to drive development (Davidson and McNeill, 2012). Creation of the OCA publicly signalled that high-level coordination was a major priority of the state government (Cashman, 2011). A new ministerial portfolio was created to help rationalize governance and bring the costs associated with Games investment into one structure. The appointment of a state government Minister for the Olympics, who was also the president of the board of SOCOG, was a crucial and beneficial decision.

While legacy took a back seat, it was not forgotten and was injected through four main elements: site remediation and environmental management measures; venue development; transport infrastructure; and creation of perimeter parklands. Each of these is elaborated briefly below.

Significant funding was invested in site remediation and development of sophisticated environmental management measures in response to the 'green' promises that were part of the successful bid. This went on treatment and containment of waste to reduce exposure to contamination; stormwater capture and water recycling to re-use and conserve resources; cultivation of new wetlands to reduce flood levels and provide habitat, irrigation, aesthetics and restore creek catchment function; and development of green building guidelines for the entire lifecycle of materials, waste management and the use of energy (Cashman, 2011). Particular attention was paid to energy conservation, use of renewable energy, passive solar buildings, appropriate building materials selection, density of development, and appliance and equipment selections. WRAMS (Water Reclamation and Management Scheme), one of the world's largest wastewater recycling systems, was installed. Design of facilities was intended to maximize opportunities for energy conservation and recycling of resources.

While Sydney's credentials as the 'Green Games' were assisted by a partnership with Greenpeace Australia, the realities of delivering on bid claims proved more challenging than first recognized (Lenskyj, 2002) and the outcomes were mixed. The green utopianism of the original Athletes' Village was moderated by more pragmatic commercial considerations (Thalis and Cantrill, 1994), although solar panels and water recycling features were installed.

Chemical remediation of the site faced challenges. The OCA opted for compacting contaminated soil into large landscaped mounds, some of which doubled as observation points. Gold and Gold (2020*b*, p. 9) noted that some of these 'short-cuts … rebounded, necessitating further work to correct abiding problems'.

The OCA developed a revised and final masterplan in 1996, dividing the site into four main areas: an urban core (sporting, entertainment, commercial facilities, plus the new Showground); the Newington residential district based on the Athletes' Village; a major metropolitan park; and waterfront development. George Hargreaves, a renowned American landscape architect, further shaped the public domain creating more space between venues, paving, mature trees, and water features. A design review panel was set up to consider major public works including venues. In retrospect, the late 1990s emerges as a remarkably fertile and innovative period which helped establish sustainability and design excellence as touchstones for new architectural and urban design standards in Sydney (Weirick, 1999). A notable event in 1994 was a week-long design charrette, involving global names such as Deyan Sudjic and Jean Nouvel, which was intended to model strategies and concepts to guide long-term development (Anon, 1994). The Olympic enterprise employed a Who's Who of Sydney's most eminent architects, landscape architects, and urban designers (Bingham Hall, 1999). A consortium headed by Multiplex and Hambros Australia was chosen to design, construct, and operate the flagship A$463 million stadium with a Games capacity of 110,000 and post-Games of 80,000. It was always intended that the venues and facilities would be developed for multi-purpose use that would outlast the Games event itself.

During this stage in development a critical decision was made regarding transport infrastructure with profound downstream implications (Kassens-Noor, 2012). Establishment of the Olympic Roads and Transport Authority (ORTA) was a positive action, whereby all statutory decisions regarding Games transport were made by a powerful single agency (Owen, 2002; Mulley and Moutou, 2015). However, even this underscored an approach dominated almost exclusively by the event itself with its completely immovable deadline (Kassens-Noor, 2012). Several options were considered for transport connections, including exclusive bus transport, light and heavy rail (e.g. Deloitte Australia, 2015; O'Sullivan, 2015). The government's preferred option was to construct a rail loop off the main western railway line into a new station, along with a ferry wharf and an extensive internal road network accompanied by cycling and walking paths. The rail loop was the critical decision. While it served Games needs well, it has enshrined Sydney Olympic Park as a dead-end network destination (Owen, 2001). Further, the additional roads constructed to support access alongside the creation of 10,000 car parking spaces have promoted car-dependency.

The creation of one of the largest metropolitan parklands in Australia providing over 400 hectares of ecologically significant wetlands, woodlands and remediated lands and a network of over 40 kilometres of pedestrian and cycle paths is an enduring legacy. The parklands, extending Bicentennial Park, have a very clear set of management principles, enshrined in various pieces of legislation, including a statutory plan of management (2003, revised in 2010). Each of seventeen management precincts has a detailed, legislatively regulated set of characteristics with regard to planting, ecosystems, and human use (Davidson and McNeill, 2012). Ironically, construction of the Parklands still met heavy resistance in the 1990s and required determination by the OCA to proceed.

While Sydney Olympic Park took shape through the 1990s as a major outcome of public enterprise, it was difficult to attract the interest of private investors with an eye to the future because the site was seen as too far away from the CBD and carrying too many commercial risks. Two Accor hotels were opened in 2000, initially to house essential Games personnel, but the early resistance in the market only increased the pressure on the government to ensure that the short-term imperative of staging a successful Games event was achieved.

Post Games: Legacy Planning 2000–2022

The third stage of more explicit legacy planning began at the end of the Sydney Olympics, or more correctly the Summer Paralympics staged in October 2000. SOPA, created under a special Act of Parliament in 2001, was vested with the responsibility to develop and manage Sydney Olympic Park, including adjacent lands formerly under the custodianship the Bicentennial Park Trust, as a place of special metropolitan significance for sporting, recreational, educational, and business activities for the benefit of the community (Cashman, 2011). There was early media criticism regarding the lack of activity and seeming absence of long-range planning for future development. Prominent design commentator Elizabeth Farrelly (2002) wrote that 'you don't often find places quite as lonesome as Sydney Olympic Park'. This sentiment was expressed more directly by others: 'ghost town'.

There was a need for a switch in thinking from the operation of events to strategic land development to ensure the return on investment with the main focus on residential and commercial development, but there was still uncertainty as to what the precinct could best become – an office zone, a new urban village, an educational centre, a hi-tech node, a leisure and culture complex, or an amalgam of mixed land uses. The realities of adapting a low-density complex of elite sporting venues into a more sustainable urban precinct were inescapably confronted. The central dilemma has been balancing an Olympic Games-standard capacity to accommodate periodic major sporting, leisure, and exhibition events with more quotidian living-employment opportunities to deliver an ongoing return on major public and private investment. Planning rhetoric has consistently revolved around creation of a vibrant mixed-use precinct with strong urban design and environmental management practices. Driven by new development imperatives and transport infrastructure investments, the planning process has been virtually continuous for over a decade (figure 13.3).

SOPA inherited three key ingredients from OCA's post-Games vision: new development to attract more people on a daily basis; building on the carnival and festival atmosphere as a premier venue for major sporting and entertainment attractions; and cultivating a green oasis through progressive development of the Parklands. Five main precincts were envisaged: the town centre (transport hub, commercial and tourism); the core sporting and recreation precinct; south-west (campus development and IT); east

Figure 13.3. Planning for Sydney Olympic Park 2010–2022. (*Source*: SOPA, 2022*a*)

(commercial and residential); and a relict brick pit (ecological significance). In the first decade after 2000 a series of formal planning documents was prepared to guide precinct-based development, notably the *Sydney Olympic Park Vision for Beyond 2000* (2001), *Draft Master Plan* (2001), *Master Plan* (2002), and *Vision 2025* (2004) leading to the *Master Plan 2030* (2010). The accent was on a finer-grained urbanism with progressive renewal in time of older sites such as the Australia Centre and higher density infill (Sanchez and Essex, 2018).

In 2005 a major collaborative design initiative was undertaken by international and local multidisciplinary experts in the areas of planning, urban design, development, environmental sustainability, and transport planning, with the findings reported in Vision 2025 (Lochhead, 2005). This document was an important step towards looking at the potential of what Sydney Olympic Park could be with regard to land use, layout and integration with the surrounding area. The visioning document provided details down to the height of buildings within different precincts and transition to a more intimate scale supporting a variety of uses. *Vision 2025* also provided the structure for *Master Plan 2030* (Cashman, 2011) (see figure 13.4). The latter document through several revisions, notably in 2018, remained the long-term planning document for Sydney Olympic Park until early 2023. It aimed to make the town centre more liveable through higher-density, fine-grain, mixed-use precincts with greater permeability (Cashman, 2011). Critics highlighted a tension between the sustainability legacy and a pro-development neo-liberal ideology (Davidson, 2013).

A five-yearly review of *Master Plan 2030* (2010) by the state planning department highlighted challenging new influences facing SOP (DPE, 2016). These included the changing metropolitan and sub-regional context regarding transport, employment, and governance; the rise of the knowledge economy as a growth driver; the emergence of Wentworth Point and Carter Street as two contiguous residential precincts; and the need to move towards a more intensive urban morphology with significant floorspace and building height increases. Around the same time, the legacy of sporting facilities and

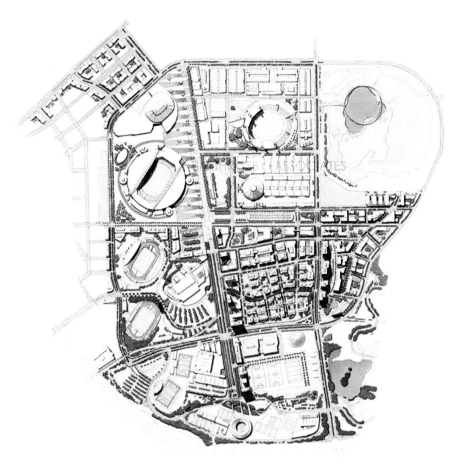

Figure 13.4. Master Plan 2030 illustration prepared by Tim Throsby (2006). The large block sections reflect the ten precincts described in the plan ranging from sporting, residential, commercial, educational and stadia uses. (*Source*: Tim Throsby & Associates)

green infrastructure shaped a future perception as a 'lifestyle super precinct' (GSC, 2016*b*). These considerations fed into a revised 2030 Plan which appeared in 2018 after a delay attributed to the finalization of transport plans (Saulwick, 2018). It still sought the same ongoing balance between SOP as both a major event destination and a robust and resilient community, indeed 'one of the world's greatest contemporary places' (SOPA, 2018, p. vii). A further review in 2021 considered changes to the street pattern and public domain, through site links and built form in the core of the town centre to accommodate a projected metro line and station (DPIE, 2021).

   Against this backdrop of strategic positioning, development of the town centre has continued incrementally. The Olympic Games failed to generate a surge in post-2000 economic development and this slowed progress of post-Games legacy planning. Searle (2012) claims that the Games actually generated a loss in Australian real, private and public consumption of $2.1 billion. Nevertheless, at SOP commercial precincts did emerge in the town centre. The Commonwealth Bank's Sydney headquarters employing 3,500 people came and went but SOP houses major private sector (including the National Roads and Motorists' Association, Royal Agricultural Society, and Samsung), government (including NSW Police, Rural Fire Service, and NSW Ambulance) and peak sporting (such as GWS Giants Australian Rules Football and Sydney Thunder Cricket) entities. In late 2021 the commercial vacancy rate had dropped to under 2 per cent with a total workforce estimated at over 19,000, though significantly reduced on-site by COVID work from home. Sydney Olympic Park has continued to be recognized as a premier destination for sporting and entertainment events. In 2020–2021 approximately seven million people visited, and over 3,500 events were held, both figures diminished from preceding years by COVID restrictions.

Housing development also accelerated through the 2000s. After the Games, the Athletes' Village was integrated into the new residential suburb of Newington, planned at above-average suburban densities along new urbanist lines with a population of around 6,000 (Sanchez *et al.*, 2022). Just outside the SOP boundary are Wentworth Point, an evolving dense waterfront high-rise precinct and the Carter Street Priority Precinct, a high-density regeneration of older industrial sites. In Sydney Olympic Park proper the turn has also been to vertical living, fuelled by the state government's urban consolidation (compact city) policies and the growing community acceptance of high-rise living underpinned by changing demographic and lifestyle trends. Land tenure is leasehold negotiated by SOPA. The current population is around 8,000 people with a median age of around thirty, dominated by millennials and a middle-class mix of Anglo, Korean, Chinese and Indian cultures (SOPA, 2022*b*).

Notwithstanding the demonstrable evolution and maturation of the town centre over more than two decades, there is a palpable sense of mission not yet accomplished. The town centre lags in activities and vibrancy. The Royal Agricultural Society's complex is a walled enclave. The town centre and parklands remain separate domains. International-standard sporting facilities are not readily available to the general public. Large surface car parks are a dominant land use while public transport access is limited. The extent of local community infrastructure is significantly underdeveloped (Mussi, 2017). Some recent criticisms have been harsh: a 'white elephant' (Davis, 2020) and testimony to 'decadal inaction and urban decay' (CWS, 2022, p. 38). Even SOPA (2022*a*, p. 46) itself acknowledges that the suburb lacks 'connectivity, activity and identity'. SOP thus still presents primarily as an events destination with a peripheral community of high-rise apartment dwellers. A new consensus among key stakeholders is to leaven the Olympic legacy, a chance that could be seen as threatening the staging of a future mega event. There is a realization in SOPA itself that it cannot be 'stuck in 2000'. This requires a shift from the privileging of an 'events precinct' culture to fostering a genuine community that stages events. The *Vision & Strategy* for SOP in 2050 released early in 2022 provides a first step towards that future.

Based on extensive consultation, *Vision & Strategy* interlaces numerous themes, actions, 'place pillars', 'step changes' and 'moves' to re-imagine SOP as 'Sydney's beating green heart'. Broken apart, this aspirational vision attempts to capture its contribution to broader planning issues including pop-up experimentation; a dynamism at both the everyday and events levels; the legacy of environmental awareness, amenity and management; and its geographic centrality to metropolitan Sydney. Ten strategic directions are identified to form the basis of a detailed spatial master plan to be prepared by mid-2023 (figure 13.5). The transformative long-term shift is towards an activated 'five-minute city' of around 30,000 organized into vertical neighbourhoods well-connected internally and externally (Parismon, 2022).

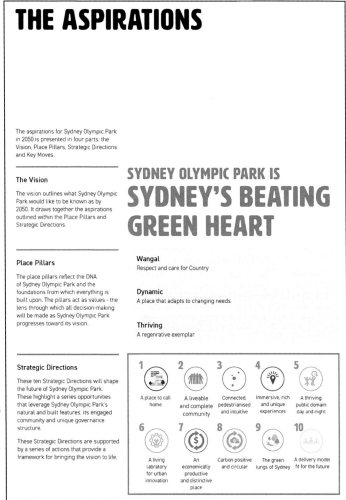

Figure 13.5. Strategic Directions in planning for Sydney Olympic Park 'to bring the place to life' by 2050. (*Source*: SOPA, 2022*a*)

New Horizon: Integrating Sydney Olympic Park into the Metropolitan Region

The course of town centre development reflects a neoliberal policy agenda in moves to make SOP self-sustaining and to promote commercial development, while continuing to exploit the sustainability narrative (Davidson, 2013). This captures the struggle faced by governments, who typically bankroll mega events well ahead of realized benefits, to recover their costs through value-uplifting private infill and redevelopment. Running parallel but now increasingly interdependent has been an incremental process of integrating development decisions within broader metropolitan planning agendas (Davidson and McNeill, 2012). SOP planning increasingly requires alignment with a phalanx of state, district, local and place-based controls, policies and strategies.

Vision 2025 (2004) was used by SOPA to convince the state government to recognize the area for the first time as a specialized centre within the metropolitan planning framework. A 2013 Draft Metropolitan Strategy for Sydney to 2031 made first mention of an 'urban activation precinct'. The 2014 metropolitan strategy *A Plan for Growing Sydney* identified SOP as a strategic centre positioned within the so-called Global Economic Corridor arching from the airport through the CBD to the western regional centre of Parramatta. The Greater Sydney Commission, a new strategic metropolitan agency established in late 2015, produced a new plan in 2018 which called for 'a metropolis of three cities' largely to rebalance employment location and commuting patterns in favour of western Sydney (Freestone and Pinnegar, 2021). Within this new spatial imaginary, the 'Eastern Harbour City', structured around the traditional CBD, is complemented by a new 'Western Parkland City', organized around a new international airport, and lying in-between is the 'Central River City' focused on Paramatta (GSC, 2016*a*).

SOP is one of four key major activity nodes within the Central River City critical to an integrated regional process of urban revitalization. A 2016 government report scoping the future identified it as an 'economic anchor offering inner-city style living' focusing on elite sports but with an appealing environmental quality making it a 'lifestyle super precinct' (GSC, 2016*b*). To ensure that aspirations match with development realities, a new place-based approach to support infrastructure needs has been put in place by the state government to try and ensure the effective financing and collaboration to make 'a complex strategic space' work (Pham, 2020, p. 110).

In this context, transport and accessibility have become major planning issues. Access into Sydney Olympic Park has always been a point of contention. Entry and egress via the motorway network can prove problematic during major events. For public transport, the rail loop built for the

Olympics has proved an 'Achilles heel' in restraining development prospects by not providing direct connection to the main line. The state government has committed to a future extension of the initial light rail line serving Greater Parramatta to SOP and Wentworth Point, with construction due to start in 2024. In the meantime, initial construction work towards a new 'Metro West' line serving Greater Parramatta and the Sydney CBD has commenced with an underground SOP station to be accommodated in the town centre and operational by 2030. The subject of detailed planning and environmental studies, this is a major development that will not only catalyse redesign of the town centre but significantly enhance regional accessibility and connectivity through reducing the relative isolation of SOP. The current strategic and structure planning work is substantially predicated on this major infrastructural move. The future emphasis on community-orientated rather than large-scale commercial development recognizes SOP's comparative advantage as a planned major residential precinct that will be minutes away from major local employment hubs such as Parramatta CBD and the Westmead Health and Innovation District.

Figure 13.6. Sydney Olympic Park from the air, *c.*2019. The grand Olympic Boulevard connects most of the major sporting facilities with the tennis complex in the foreground. To the right is the town centre area with a mix of commercial, accommodation, high-rise residential and retail uses. Extensive parklands border development to the top (north) and right (east). (*Source*: Reproduced with permission of the Sydney Olympic Park Authority)

Conclusion

The legacy of the 2000 Games at Sydney Olympic Park (figure 13.6) is still being assessed and written. Five conclusions arise from this analysis.

First, the conceptualization of legacy emerged gradually. There was no firm foundational formula as to what it represented in the larger scheme of things. Only as planning for the Games itself took shape was thought focused on legacy and, even then, it was largely subsumed by immediate priorities, timelines, and resource constraints. Moreover, a critical path dependency arose from the implications of early choices that constrained future scenarios. Sanchez and Essex (2018, p. 285) highlighted the disjointed retrofitting process followed in Sydney.

Secondly, the creation of a development authority to guide post-Games development from 2001 was a major step forward. The London Games in 2012 saw an admission that organizers there had 'shamelessly used' Sydney Olympic Park as a reference point for post-Games planning (Kimmorley, 2014). The challenge facing post-Games governance is not simply to wind down the Olympic infrastructure and to avoid ongoing costs, but to access new investment opportunities (Cashman, 2006). This has been achieved at SOP. However, the ongoing role for SOPA is to be determined. It has had a migratory existence through the state government bureaucracy and latterly a changing cast of CEOs impeding management continuity. The shared local governance with Parramatta City Council is still a work in progress and nearby development hotspots such as Wentworth Point undercut the rationale of a standalone entity only partially responsible for the Olympic Peninsula.

Thirdly, the standout legacy alongside an infrastructure of outstanding sporting venues is in site remediation and environmental planning. While now regarded as commonplace, at the time the so-called 'green promise' was both aspirational and experimental. It was aspirational because of the scope and scale of environmental measures that were undertaken, and experimental given the range of stakeholders whose interests needed to be aligned, notably, local authorities, Commonwealth and state governments, developers, and other private investors. While the discourse of sustainability can trend to a benign truism (Glasson, 2022), the 2000 Games began what is now regarded as a 100-year project to restore ecosystems, protect threatened species, and enhance biodiversity of flora and fauna (Darcovich, 2020). There is thus unfinished business including pockets of contaminated land still awaiting remediation (Hawken, 2014) and opportunities to build upon the Green Games legacy into the mid twenty-first century.

Fourthly, a new legacy of respect for First Nations people has developed. The Sydney Games was arguably the first global event to communicate the significance of Aboriginal culture in Australian society. Over time, this awareness has widened and deepened. The *Vision & Strategy* documentation developed in part through listening to and learning from First Nations leaders to embed a respectful connection with Country into the processes of strategic planning and placemaking. Future decision-making about SOP will more explicitly acknowledge Wangal Country in fundamental ways that were not evident in the 1990s.

Finally, a process is now in train to re-evaluate the Olympic legacy as it has been understood for over two decades. SOP could possibly be 'the most studied urban precinct in Australia' (SOPA, 2022*a*, p. 29), yet this has not readily resolved problems or avoided serious issues of economic, social, and environmental sustainability. The awareness now taking shape is that the Olympic legacy has been a double-edged sword in delivering infrastructure that is world class yet also problematized 'the shift towards a more diversified suburb' (*ibid.*, p. 48). The 2000 Games helped catapult Sydney into global city status (Vogel *et al.*, 2020). The challenge now is to choreograph a future for Sydney Olympic Park that more fully capitalizes on the benefits of that promise across community, regional, and metropolitan scales.

Notes

1.   This chapter is distinguished from the earlier 'Sydney 2000' chapter authored by Beatriz García (2007) which focused on the interpretation of Sydney's cultural discourse through the Olympic experience. It also revises a chapter with the same title by Freestone and Gunesekara (2017) covering the period to 2015.

2.   *2022 Interviews*: S. Skoudas, Director, Place Management, Sydney Olympic Park Authority, 28 September 2022; J. Gill, Executive Director, SGS Economics and Planning, 20 October 2022; J. Knapp, Director, SJB, 20 October 2022.

2015 Interviews: D. Van Der Breggen, Executive Manager, Development and Planning, Sydney Olympic Park Authority, 22 June 2015; C. Bagley, Executive Manager, Major Projects, Sydney Olympic Park Authority, 9 October 2015; K. Grega, CEO, Sydney Olympic Park Business Association, 9 October 2015.

2013 Interviews by S. Gunesekara: C. Johnson, CEO, Urban Taskforce, 27 September 2013; D. Richmond, former CEO, Olympic Co-ordination Authority, 4 October 2013; M. Knight, former NSW Government Minister for the Olympics, 21 October 2013.

My thanks to all respondents and Simon Gunesekara for their valuable insights but responsibility for the findings reported is mine alone.

Chapter 14

ATHENS 2004

Margaret M. Gold

In 2004 the Olympics will return to the place where
they were born, where they were revived and where
they will be renewed. The ATHENS 2004 Olympic Games
are more than an opportunity to participate in the greatest
celebration of humanity. They are an opportunity to be part of
a story as old as history itself. And when it comes to making
history, there is really no place like home.
ATHOC (2004, p. 31)

The relationship between Greece and the Olympic Games is like no other.
The slogan 'There's no Place like Home', used in all the advertising for
the 2004 Games, resonated with Greek identity, collective memory, and
historical experience. As home to the classical Olympics, the Games go to
the very heart of Greek culture. Indeed, from the point at which Greece
regained its independence in 1830, the possibility of reviving the Games,
along with the drive to rebuild Athens as a worthy successor of the grand
city of Antiquity, became key themes for those seeking to restore Greek
values and identity. While not inseparable, there would always be a close link
between staging the Olympics and the regeneration of Athens – the most
likely host city whenever the Games returned to Greece.

   This chapter looks at the 2004 Summer Olympic Games against this
background. Its early sections briefly chart the growth of the Olympic movement in Athens alongside attempts to regenerate the city, a period that
culminated in the first Olympiad of 1896 and the 1906 Intercalated Games.
The subsequent sections analyse the failed attempt to bid for the centenary
1996 Games and then the successful bid made in 1997 to stage the 2004
Games, coupled with the urban planning strategy associated with that event.
Finally, there is an assessment of the urban legacy bequeathed by Athens 2004.

An Immature Metropolis

Athens at the start of the nineteenth century was far from the grand city of classical imagining, as 'filtered through European scholarship and imagination' (Waterfield, 2004, p. 29). The handful of more adventurous visitors that made their way to this corner of the Ottoman Empire were confronted by a small provincial centre with a population of around 10,000. The upper town on the Acropolis contained the Turkish garrison with barracks, housing, shops, and a mosque intermingled with the remains of the Parthenon and other classical structures. A lower town on the northern and eastern slopes of the Acropolis housed the Greek, Albanian, and Turkish civilian populations. The city itself fared badly in the fight for independence (1821–1830). Although Greece gained its independence after the signing of the London Protocol in February 1830, the Turkish garrison did not leave until 1833. By this time the population had fallen to 6,000 and the city was described by the traveller Christopher Wordsworth in 1832 as: 'lying in ruins. The streets are almost deserted: nearly all the houses are without roofs. The churches are reduced to bare walls and heaps of stones and mortar. There is but one church in which the service is performed' (cited in Bastéa, 2000, p. 10). At this time, it was not even the Greek capital, with Nauplion, a strategic Venetian fortress on the east coast of the Peloponnesus, serving that function until 1833 (Georgiadis, 2000).

Understandably, thinking soon turned to finding readily recognizable symbolic strategies through which to reassert a sense of nationhood, of which the two that most readily came to the fore were the reconstruction of Athens and the revival of the Olympics. Two German-trained architects Stamatios Kleanthes and Eduard Schaubert, for example, had visited Athens in 1830–1831 and produced a plan for a city of 35,000–40,000 people. It featured a baroque-inspired layout based on radial axes (meeting at present day Omonia Square) where the Royal Palace, Parliament and Senate would be placed, and a series of grids creating nodal points for other key buildings (Travlos, 1981, pp. 393–394). The opposition to the necessary demolitions to implement the plan, the lack of resources to carry it through, and the immediate pressure of population influx as the functions of government were established in Athens and exiles returned, meant that the plan needed almost immediate amendment. Instead, the new Athens developed gradually rather than by radical reconstruction, with an approach that sought to respect the classical archaeology, while creating a new neo-classical townscape. There were later attempts to rectify this, with plans commissioned from foreign architects and planners, but none were adopted in the face of military conflict, and political and economic problems (Sonne, 2003, p. 146).

The idea for the revival of the Olympic Games emerged around the same time as the initial schemes for replanning Athens, although not without fierce debate between those that believed their restoration was essential for reviving Greek culture, values, and identity and those who saw the Games as a cultural irrelevance and practical impossibility. The Greek poet Panagiotos Soutsos, for instance, launched a campaign in 1835 based around a series of poems that featured figures from the past calling on present-day Greeks to reinstate the Olympic Games. As early as January 1837, a Royal Decree established a 'national gathering' with competitions in agriculture, industry, and athletics, with the specified athletic events being those associated with the ancient Games: discus, javelin, long jump, foot races, wrestling, and chariot racing (Young, 1987, p. 273; 2004, p. 141). The ancient Panathenian Stadium formed a natural focus for such activity and was restored to serve as the setting for two of the three Zappas Games (1870 and 1875; see chapter 2).[1] Various attempts were made to revive that series, notably in 1892, but they were thwarted by financial difficulties. The initiative of the Coubertin-led International Olympic Committee (IOC) in reviving the Olympics and choosing Athens as the site for the 1896 Games, therefore, served the interests of both Greece and the Olympic movement. Athens gained a new Olympic Games with international recognition and participation, whereas the revived Games benefitted from the imprimatur of being held on Greek soil. However, the IOC's preference for an ambulatory festival and fierce resistance to giving the Games a permanent home in Greece meant that, apart from the Intercalated Games of 1906, Athens would not receive another Olympic festival until the twenty-first century.

Bidding

By 1990, when Athens next formally sought the Games, the city was a byword for the problems characteristic of many Mediterranean cities (Wynn, 1984; Leontidou, 1990). Athens had experienced rapid growth in the 1960s and 1970s, driven by industrial investment, rural–urban migration, a building boom, and spontaneous development at the urban fringe – much of which was illegal and unplanned. Public transport was poor, and the city suffered severe environmental pollution and congestion. Although a capital city, Athens could not compete with other major centres in Europe (Leontidou, 1990, p. 263) and was unable to offer inducements to counteract its relatively isolated position. Certainly, the idea of seeking the modern Olympic Games, with its inevitable financial burden, appeared implausible before Los Angeles 1984 established the new financial model.

Athens's first, and unsuccessful, bid campaign for the return of the Games between 1987 and 1990 should be seen against this background. The city's reasons for bidding reflected a mixture of the general and specific. Like most potential host cities, there was a broad-based promotional message that sought to offset negative features (such as stereotypes about the Greek economy and culture) with positive images of a 'new face for Greece, outward looking and ready to take-up the challenges of globalization'.[2] The city looked to the mega-event to make Athens competitive in the world market for jobs and investment, while simultaneously enhancing Greek sporting infrastructure and helping to solve urban problems. As Vissilis Harissis, Director of the Organization for Athens, the body responsible for coordinating the Athens city plan, noted forcefully: 'Getting the Olympics is the best chance we'll ever have to save Athens. It'll be like fighting a war: there will be money and an incentive' (Hope, 1990).

Yet behind these broader objectives lay another set of ambitions that emanated from Greece's special relationship with the Olympics. The Greeks looked to the Olympics to help the nation recapture its soul: linking the ancient and modern in a meaningful and contemporary way for the twenty-first century. At the same time the Greeks wanted to reassert traditional values, especially as a reaction to the politicized and commercialized Games of the 1970s and 1980s when calls periodically surfaced that the Games might be able to regain their core values by returning to their geographical roots (Pound, 2004, p. 4). There was a strong sense that Greece wanted to 'correct the course' of the Modern Olympic Movement (ATHOC, 2005, I, p. 63). While talk of a permanent home for the Games had subsided, there seemed an incontestable logic in a Greek bid to host the Twenty-Sixth Olympiad in 1996 to celebrate the centenary of the revival.

The bid achieved Parliamentary approval in April 1986, with the Bid Committee presenting Athens's candidacy to the IOC in 1988 and the final Bid File in March 1990 for the IOC meeting in Tokyo the following September. The case was put that 70 per cent of the sports facilities were already in place or would be completed for the planned Eleventh Mediterranean Games in 1991. The documentation trumpeted Athens's experience in organizing international sporting competitions, listing twelve events hosted between the European Athletics Championships of 1982 and the Men's World and European Weightlifting Championship in 1989. Three of these, it was noted, had won awards from the International Press Association for the best organized press facilities. However, its publicity tactically overlooked the twin disasters of 1982 – the IAAF Golden Marathon when police failed to close the last five kilometres of the course to traffic, with runners encountering rush hour traffic, or the fact that the track in the new Olympic Stadium had not been laid by the time athletes were arriving for the European Athletics Championships (Payne, 2006, p. 258).

The strategic plan sought to concentrate the sports facilities in two centres. The first, the Athens Olympic Sports Complex (AOSC), at Maroussi, a suburban municipality nine kilometres north-east of central Athens. This would build on existing facilities, most notably the stadium constructed between 1980 and 1982 for the European Athletic Championships, with the intention of providing Athens with the means to bid for future major international events. AOSC would also feature the velodrome, swimming complex, multi-purpose sports hall, an indoor hall and tennis centre, the Press Village, Main Press Centre, and International Broadcasting Centre. The second complex, on the coast south of Athens at Faliro Bay and the nearby Karaiskaki Stadium,[3] would make use of the existing Stadio Erinis end Filias (Peace and Friendship Stadium) and new facilities to accommodate basketball, wrestling, judo, boxing, handball, baseball, and yachting. Existing facilities in Athens would be used for sports such as archery and shooting, while the city centre would be the focus of the cultural festivities, making use of the classical legacy such as the Panathenian Stadium and Herodeion. The centre would house IOC members, the Olympic Family and official guests, with the Olympic Village scheduled for construction on the northern fringes of the Athens Metropolitan Area on the slopes of Mount Parnitha. The Olympic Ring Road promised travel times of only 12 minutes between the Olympic Village and stadium and 18 minutes to Faliro Bay. Road projects, new metro lines, a new tram line, improvements to the existing Helleniki International Airport on the coast east of Faliro Bay and a new international airport at Sparta were also planned.[4]

The eventual decision to award the centenary Games to Atlanta came as a shock. Melina Mercouri, the Greek Culture Minister, protested that 'Coca Cola won over the Parthenon' and the Prime Minister, Andreas Papandreou, called it 'an injustice against Greece' committed by the international community (Senn, 1999, p. 250). Years later, the official Report from Athens 2004 (ATHOC, 2005, I, p. 65) admitted that part of the blame for the bid's failure lay in the perception of political instability created by the three general elections that occurred in the eight months leading up to the IOC decision – a factor noted in the IOC Evaluation Commission's report. While the Athens team was also accused of taking an arrogant approach towards endorsement, the real stumbling block was the size of the task needed to provide the required infrastructure and setting for the Games. Even the Mayor of Athens had recognized in 1987 that a radical transformation was required to deal with the city's atmospheric pollution, traffic congestion, noise, lack of parking, shortage of open space and new sports facilities, outmoded media facilities and deficiencies in the public transport network. Such was the scale of the problems that although he supported the government's plan to host the Games, he stated that 'if we are in danger of looking ridiculous, I will not go along with it, and I will stand up and tell the public the truth' (quoted in Anon, 1987).

Greece's wish to stage the Games quickly resurfaced after the disappointment of the award to Atlanta. In 1995, the government toyed with the idea of seeking the 2008 Games outside the customary bidding procedure by requesting 'a direct award' of the Games as 'an honour' recognizing the special status of Athens. This was pursued for a while but the impracticality of obtaining the support of two-thirds of the IOC for the necessary change in the IOC Charter led the Hellenic Olympic Committee, in December 1995, to canvass vigorously for a conventional bid for the 2004 Games. Athens's candidature was submitted on 6 January 1996, five days before the official deadline, joining a group of cities already well ahead with their preparations. These comprised Rome, regarded as the favourite, along with Buenos Aires, Cape Town, Istanbul, Lille, Rio de Janeiro, St Petersburg, San Juan (Puerto Rico), Seville, and Stockholm (ATHOC, 2005, I, pp. 67–68).

Not wholly surprisingly, Athens's final bid document for the 1997 IOC decision bore similarities to the failed 1990 bid, but with a less strident tone in the presentation (AOBC, 1997). The accompanying statements from politicians and officials now stressed the profound economic changes in Greece and Athens, particularly in the context of membership of the European Union. The Mayor, Dimitris Avramopoulos, wrote about the need to:

> give renewed impetus to the Olympic Ideal and to help the Olympic Movement start afresh at the beginning of a new century. Athens is ready, and we Athenians – all of us – are sensible of the responsibility that stems from the supreme and noble honour that, we hope, awaits us.

The Minister of Sport, Andreas Fouras, assured the IOC that:

> The long-term programme of construction and installation of equipment which will ensure that long before 2000 – and regardless of whether Athens is awarded the Games – the city will have made good the few shortcomings it still displays in the facilities necessary for all the Olympic sports.

The Master Plan sought to concentrate the Games in a small number of locations while making use of existing sports infrastructure. Indeed, the bid claimed that 75 per cent of the competition venues and 92 per cent of the training venues were already in place. The backbone of the strategy remained the four clusters identified in the earlier bid – the Olympic Village on the slopes of Mount Parnitha; AOSC at Maroussi to host seven events (athletics, basketball, cycling, football, gymnastics, swimming, and tennis); central Athens (Cultural Olympiad and accommodation for Official Visitors); and the Faliro Coastal Zone, designated as a major regeneration project for Athens's 'Riviera', which would house baseball, boxing, fencing, handball, hockey, judo, wrestling, softball, taekwondo, and volleyball.

The plan envisaged four further sites within the Athens conurbation – the Nikaia indoor hall for weightlifting and the Peristeri indoor hall for badminton (both in the west); in the north the Galatsi gymnasium for table tennis; and in the east, Goudi for the modern pentathlon. Beyond the conurbation, the equestrian and archery events were located at Tatoi in the north on Mount Parnitha; rowing, canoeing, and kayaking at Schinas on the coast north-east of Athens near the ancient battlefield of Marathon; shooting at Markopoulo south-east of Athens; and sailing and the triathlon along the coast at, respectively, Kosmas and Glyfada. The Olympic Ring Road project remained as before to link the conurbation sporting venues. Investment in roads and in metro, tram lines and suburban railways would improve movement throughout the metropolis and provide access to the other venues. A new international airport at Sparta had become a central part of the planning strategy, although for the period up to and including the Games it would work in conjunction with the existing airport at Helliniki. The latter was proposed for closure in late 2004 (AOBC, 1997). A four-year Cultural Olympiad was planned, with events taking place in Greece and abroad to 'restore the Olympic Ideal' in the opening years of the new Millennium. The estimated budget was $1.607 billion with the principal sources of income being television rights, sponsorship, licensing, official suppliers, donations, ticket sales, and lotteries (*ibid.*, p. 162). The non-OCOG budget, however, was $7.35 billion, which included expenditure on roads, airport construction and landscaping.

Planning Athens 2004

The IOC's decision in September 1997 to award the 2004 Games to Athens reflected the quality of the campaign run by the Greek bidding team led by Gianna Angelopoulos-Daskalaki. Despite assurances that the same team would lead the planning and organization of the Games, they were replaced on return to Athens (Payne, 2006, p. 259). Moreover, instead of immediate implementation of the Master Plan, the government instigated a review in early 1998 'to eliminate potential problems that might arise during the implementation phase due to the existing zoning and town planning legislation' (ATHOC, 2005, I, p. 143). These considerations, coupled with community views on site decisions and rethinking about the logistics of the festival, led to considerable and time-consuming changes to the original strategy.

The final scheme that emerged retained the AOSC complex at its heart, but the government decided to concentrate less activity in the Faliro area while retaining it as a 'pole' of the Games and maintaining the goal of urban regeneration for the area. After exploring the idea of moving some events to Aspropyrgos, west of the Athens conurbation – which proved unacceptable to both the IOC and the International Federations (*ibid.*, p. 144) – it was decided to use the site of the much criticized Athens International Airport at Helleniki.[5] Faliro was now to stage only four rather than eleven sports (volleyball, beach volleyball, handball and taekwando), Helleniki would handle baseball, fencing, hockey, softball, basketball, some of the handball matches from Faliro and, after a court case (see below), the canoe and kayak slalom centre (*ibid.*). Boxing and badminton were moved to, respectively, Peristeri and the Goudi complex. Two sports were moved to sites with classical connotations to assert the sense of Greek ownership of the Games: archery to the Panathenian Stadium and the shot put to Olympia. The decision on Olympia was controversial. The first suggestion was to stage the javelin or discus there because these were events that featured in the Ancient Games. This encountered opposition from archaeologists due to potential damage to the site (see chapter 2). The shot put was finally selected as likely to create fewer problems, but the Archaeological Service insisted that no electronic equipment could be used, the throwing circle was to be portable, and that 15,000 free tickets could be issued for spectators to sit on the grass, obviating the need to build a temporary grandstand.[6]

These changes to the original strategy set back the timetable. Some locations needed planning from scratch, with the transport strategy requiring revision to take into consideration the new sites and relocated sports. The process of rethinking, with associated debates, contributed to the now infamous delays in the completion of venues and infrastructure that Payne (2006, p. 261) called the 'three lost years'. Although it was claimed that 75 per cent of the venues already existed, the renovation work envisaged for some was ambitious: for example, the demolition and rebuilding of the swimming complex and tennis centre at AOSC. Additional problems arose from the presence of multiple and often conflicting agencies (Beriatos and Gospodini, 2004, p. 193), the difficulties of gaining cooperation from officials from different political parties, the bureaucratic planning system, and from archaeological discoveries made during construction that required excavation and recording before work could continue. In some instances plans had to be adjusted in order to preserve structures, such as the re-siting of the Olympic Village site to avoid archaeological remains (see below). Matters were not helped by the increased security concerns that inflated costs and caused a review of the layout of sports facilities.

The resulting delays caused alarm at the IOC, with Samaranch warning Greece in April 2000 that they might lose the Games if action was not forthcoming. The sense of crisis was fanned by the press, although some observers (e.g. Waterfield, 2004, p. 372) felt that there was insufficient recognition of the complexities of operating in an ancient city such as Athens. The government reacted by bringing Gianna Angelopoulos-Daskalaki back to the development team (Payne, 2006, pp. 261–262), making available emergency funds, and introducing new legislation and mechanisms to speed up the development process (Pyrgiotis, 2003, p. 417). This all added substantially to the cost of the Games, with 'speed bonuses' offered by government as an incentive to meet deadlines, coupled with threats of loss of licences to contractors that failed to complete on time.

The final plan for the Games was described by Beriatos and Gospodini (2004, p. 197) as a 'scattered model' suggestive of a strategy for promoting 'multi-nucleus urban regeneration and development' (*ibid.*, p. 192), in contrast to cities like Barcelona which focused investment on a few key locations. The plan diluted the original logic of concentrating development in major nodes by spreading the benefits of Olympic investment geographically to include poorer neighbourhoods lacking leisure facilities. The plan, however, contained apparent contradictions. Despite espousing the desire to protect and create open space, development focused primarily on greenfield sites and overlooked possible brownfield locations. Emphasis was placed on gaining spectacular buildings and monuments to create a sense of place and to signify the 2004 Games, yet these structures were outside the main tourist areas.

Broadly speaking, the plan proposed three approaches to preparing the city for the Games. The first concerned the permanent structures: the sports venues, transport infrastructure, city renovation, and arts infrastructure that were designed to be a physical legacy for the city. The second involved a series of temporary interventions designed to house additional sports capacity, visitor accommodation, and traffic movements. These also included measures to shape the 'look' of the city in order to provide it with a festive atmosphere that clearly identified it with the Olympics. The third comprised attempts to encourage volunteering and change the behaviour of the population by tackling issues such as litter and smoking.

Olympic Facilities

AOSC was the spectacular centrepiece of the Olympics, eventually developing into a focus that went far beyond simple renovation of the complex created for the 1982 European Athletic Championships. Having decided that it wanted an 'architectural landmark of international recognition', the Ministry of Culture approached the Spanish architect Santiago Calatrava in March 2001 to submit a Master Plan. The result was a series of projects, including equipping the Olympic stadium with an innovative two leaf, laminated glass roof to protect spectators from the fierce sunlight, roofing the velodrome, bringing about the aesthetic unification of the various structures and plazas of the site by means of landscaping and an installation – the sinuous 'Wall of Nations' – that could also double as a giant video screen (Tzonis, 2005). The stadium roof in particular was a complex design and was only moved into position on the day that the IOC set as a deadline for the project to be either in place or abandoned (Payne, 2006, p. 269). Even so, shortage of time meant that only 9,000 of the projected 17,000 trees were planted around the stadium.

In the original plan, Faliro Bay was recognized as a prime candidate for regeneration. This area had developed in the 1870s as an elegant resort serving the Athenian middle class but a century later, cut off from adjacent residential districts by the coastal highway, it had declined into a virtual no man's land, degraded, polluted, and an illegal dumping ground. The nearby low-lying housing districts of Moschato and Kallithea were also subject to flooding. The Olympics provided a unique occasion for upgrading this area, again opening Athens to the sea, and supplying much needed public open space. The downgrading of Faliro from the second most important Games complex to one staging just four events, none of which had any great importance within Greek sporting culture, meant there would be no legacy of specialized sports facilities here. Most construction work involved renovation of the two existing stadia – the Peace and Friendship Stadium for volleyball and the Karaiskaki for part of the football competition.

Having said this, the area did receive a moderate amount of remodelling. The racecourse at the east end of the site was moved and the land cleared. The Illissos River was canalized as part of the flood protection works, a marina was constructed in the east of the site and the area landscaped. An 800-metre-long esplanade was built from the old racetrack over the coastal highway to the new indoor sports hall and marinas. This connected the residential area with the renovated coastal zone, with walkways radiating westwards towards the beach volleyball arena. Improvements to roads and a new tram network linked the site to the centre of Athens and to the other Olympic venues. This was to be a prelude to planned post-Games projects intended to continue the anti-flooding work and move the coastal highway into a cutting allowing new bridges to the park beyond. Of the two new buildings constructed for the Olympics, the beach volleyball centre was intended to become an open-air theatre, and the indoor sports hall for handball and taekwando was to be converted into a Metropolitan Convention Centre taking advantage of its proximity to major hotels, the city centre and the coast (Romanos *et al.*, 2005, p. 6). Further landscaping of the area post Games was intended but initially nothing further happened.

The principle of coastal revitalization was continued further south with the redevelopment of the airport site at Helleniki. This entailed conversion of hangars to create indoor halls for fencing and basketball as well as provision of facilities for softball, baseball, hockey, canoeing, and kayaking (ATHOC, 2005, p. 144). Not surprisingly, conversion of this site tended to produce a sports centre with a ground plan dominated by the exciting geometry of the airport. Suggestions for post-Games usage hazily envisaged the conversion of the East Airport Terminal, designed by Eero Saarinen in 1960, into a Conference and Exhibition Centre and luxury hotel, with the surrounding area touted as the largest metropolitan park in Europe. The question of how many Convention Centres Athens actually required scarcely entered the equation.

Perhaps the most contentious location was the Schinas Rowing Centre, which attracted international controversy. Originally a wetland area, this coastal site had been partly drained for agriculture in the 1920s and had been used for civil and military aviation since the 1950s. The official view was that this was a degraded wetland in need of protection and the removal of existing installations. The 2.25-kilometre rowing course would be on the line of the old runway, along with practice facilities, an adjacent 400-metre slalom course for canoes and kayaks, grandstands for 10,000 spectators with space for 40,000 more along the course, associated start and finish towers, car parks, boathouses, and visitor facilities. In contrast, environmentalists saw it as a rare ecological habitat with a delicate freshwater wetland habitat used by 176 bird species, and with a rare stone pine forest on the coastal dunes. Archaeologists and historians saw it as the site of the battle of Marathon and an important cultural landscape. The Greek government was criticized for removing the area from a list of sites to be submitted for Natura 2000 status – the European Union's initiative to guarantee the maintenance, or reestablishment, of important habitats (Metera et al., 2005, p. 7).

When the Greek government ignored the European Commission's request for it to be reinstated, four environmental groups took the government to court.[7] Archaeological and heritage groups joined the protest, arguing that the Battle of Marathon had raged through the area and the development was akin to building a sports complex on the battlefield at Gettysburg. The government countered by saying that the area was previously under the sea and that there was no evidence of archaeological importance. The outcome did not prevent use of the site for the Olympics but did produce concessions. The area received National Park status, the facilities were moved to the western end of the site, provision of visitor facilities were curtailed, and the slalom course was re-sited at Helleniki (see above). There was also a commitment to restore the wetlands and create an environmental zone and archaeological park.

The site of the Olympic Village was chosen partly because the government already owned half of the land thereby reducing the need for compulsory purchase, and partly because the development, with its associated services, would 'upgrade the neglected area of the north-west section of the Greater Athens area' (AOBC, 1997, p. 26). The bid document had claimed the housing would be built to the highest environmental standards using solar energy, water management systems, planting of indigenous species and landscaping to create an ecological park. It was designed to accommodate 17,428 participants, with the maximum occupation level during the Olympics being 14,243 and 7,166 during the Paralympics (ATHOC, 2005,

II, p. 49). In addition, the Village development was intended to be self-financing, with the accommodation sold after the Games to middle-income families (*ibid.*, p. 26).

From the outset, the authorities were criticized for lack of progress, although discovery of the remains of Hadrian's aqueduct on the site caused delay for excavation and redesign to protect the archaeology. Rather more criticism came from environmentalists, initially because the development encroached into an environmentally sensitive area and later due to the failure to implement the planned environmental elements. The World Wildlife Fund, for example, criticized the lack of inbuilt water-saving measures, the irrigation of plantings in the surrounding areas from tap water, the lack of photovoltaic cells or solar heating systems in the design, and the failure to use environmentally friendly materials such as certified timber or ozone-friendly cooling systems (WWF, 2004, pp. 8, 9).

Infrastructure

The Olympics provided an opportunity to take a fresh and comprehensive look at transport within Greater Athens, with its attendant problems of congestion, parking, slow travel times, pollution, and the unpopularity of the public transport system (comprising bus, trolley bus, metro, and suburban railway networks). The metro consisted of a single line dating back to the 1860s which by 1957 ran from Piraeus to Kifissia. By this time, however, the city had long since expanded into Attica, with large swathes reliant on trams (until 1961), trolleybuses (from 1949), diesel buses and the private car. Investment in improving public transport and creating an integrated transport system for the first time was, therefore, paramount.

A proportion of the investment was scheduled before gaining the Games: for example, contracts for two new metro lines were signed in 1991. Nevertheless, early progress was extremely slow due to bureaucratic problems, geological difficulties, and delays for archaeological excavations ahead of station construction. Lack of progress on line 3, which connected with the airport, particularly concerned the IOC, with one observer commenting in 2002 that 'there are plans to extend this line all the way to the airport, but work has yet to start on this' (Dubin *et al.*, 2002). It remained incomplete at the time of the Games but, in reaching Doukaissia Plakentias by July 2004, it was possible to run services to the airport using a suburban rail line. Concerns over pollution led to replacement of the aged bus fleet, with environmentally friendly vehicles that also offered greater accessibility for disabled people. Developments specifically for the Games included a new tram network that connected central Athens with the coastal Olympic venues – with one branch serving the Faliro Coastal Zone and the other heading south to Helleniki, Agios Kosmas and ending at Glyfada. The route was not a rapid mode of transport however, given that traffic lights, frequent stops and vehicles obstructing the lines caused it to be 'strangely sluggish' (Sales, 2005, p. 29). The road network received investment to improve connections between Athens and other major centres and to create an outer ring road interlinking the Olympic venues, the international airport, and the city. AOSC gained a ring road that operated during the Games as a clockwise one-way system reserved for Olympic traffic (ATHOC, 2005, p. 173). Elsewhere, a new Traffic Management System meant that traffic flows could be managed to prioritize Olympic traffic, with appropriate signage and dedicated lanes. In the final event, the free-moving traffic was a public relations coup for a city where congestion and traffic jams were regarded as endemic.

Cultural infrastructure also benefitted from the Olympics. Major Athenian museums such as the National Archaeological Museum, Byzantine Museum, and the National Gallery were renovated for the Games, although in the case of the National Archaeological Museum the task was made more challenging by damage from the 1999 earthquake (it was not fully opened until 2005). The Olympics were also a vehicle for developing contemporary art. This led to the foundation of two complexes, both housed in former industrial premises: Technopolis, an arts and performance space that also houses a small Maria Callas Museum; and the Athinais, a restored silk factory that contains a theatre, cinema, music space, art museum, restaurants, bars and cafés, and conference facilities. These have acted as exemplars for further developments, most notably the National Museum of Contemporary Art, which opened in 2005 in a converted brewery and the new City of Athens Art Gallery, in a converted silk factory in Metaxourgio, which opened in 2010.

Beautification

As was seen with the examples of Mexico City 1968 and Atlanta 1996 (chapter 2), beautification of a city is a contentious issue, prioritizing impressing visitors over the interests of the poor, whether through redistribution of resources or displacement of previous residents. These issues arose in the case of Athens, but in the context of the longstanding desire to remake it as a city in keeping with the splendours of its august past. The return of the Games in 2004 witnessed a flurry of activity to beautify the city centre – the focus of the festivities and cultural activities that accompanied the Games, as well as the stage for the cycling road race and the finish of the marathon at the Panathenian Stadium (Sykianaki, 2003, p. 11). Perhaps the most important of the measures taken in relation to the Games was the unification of archaeological sites – a project that dated back to the 1832 plan which suggested that, when cleared and planted, the 'whole would be a museum of ancient building-art second to none in the world' (quoted in Bastéa, 2000, p. 219). The idea of a unified cultural-historic area had resurfaced periodically over the next century and a half, but financial and practical problems hindered progress (Papageorgiou-Ventas, 1994, p. 28). In 1993, a formal scheme to link the key classical sites by landscaped pedestrian routes and green open spaces received European Union funding. Its rationale rested in part on romantic nationalism, partly on a wish to marry together the old and the new into a functional whole, and partly on creating a unique tourist amenity that could compete with the great European tourist cities (*ibid.*, p. 398).

The city's planners considered it imperative to complete a major part of this project in time both to receive Olympic visitors and accommodate the road race which was planned to use the newly pedestrianized streets around the Acropolis. By the Games, for instance, it was possible to walk from the Panathenian Stadium to the ancient cemetery at Kerameikos, via the Olympieion, the south side of the Acropolis, the Theatre of Dionysus and the ancient agora (see figure 14.1). By contrast, other projects such as the restoration of the Parthenon and the development of the new Acropolis Museum proved impossible to complete before the Games, due particularly to archaeological and conservation issues. The Acropolis Museum finally opened in 2009.

Figure 14.1. Pedestrianized street beneath the Acropolis; part of the project unifying the archaeological sites. (*Source*: Photograph, John and Margaret Gold, June 2009)

The programme for improving central Athens also included improvements to street lighting, the refurbishment of city squares, restoration of façades, floodlighting monuments and key buildings, planting and landscaping, renewal of street furniture, repaving roads and improving pavements. Work was also carried out to upgrade the waste management systems of the city. The staging of the Paralympic Games had an important impact in moving towards a barrier-free city, with installation of more than 7,000 wheelchair ramps (Bokoyannis, 2006, p. 6), modifications to public transport, and encouragement from ATHOC for businesses to cater for the needs of disabled people (see chapter 5).

Besides the regeneration schemes and other projects that made a permanent contribution to the quality of life of residents and visitors, there were also the temporary measures that announced that the city was *en fête*. The notion of giving the city a distinctive 'look' during the Olympic festival, a recurrent theme since Tokyo 1964 (see chapter 2), was again observed at Athens. Like its predecessors, this involved the careful selection of colours (symbolizing summertime, landscape, the sea and sky), with the creation of a Kit of Parts that could be applied to all the venues and arranged so that athletes, visitors and television audiences could see the legend 'ATHENS 2004' and the Olympic Rings at all venues and along significant routes (ATHOC, 2005, I, p. 331). Construction sites and ugly buildings disappeared behind large building wraps, with images of ancient Olympia and photographs by Greek artists. Conscious of the over-commercialism of Atlanta 1996 – about which the Greeks had made considerable reference when bidding for the Games – attempts were made to control advertising displays throughout the city. By the summer of 2004, 5,000 billboards had been removed and official sites given over to sponsors and used for messages promoting the Olympic ideal. In the process, the Organizing Committee effectively enhanced the value of the investment made by sponsors in offering them 'a whole new level of protection against ambush marketing', comprising 'the most tightly controlled' marketplace to date (Payne, 2006, pp. 262-63, 266).

Legacy

The Games themselves were a triumph for the city, despite the scepticism of journalists who, only weeks earlier, described the rubble on building sites and listed the work still outstanding. What visitors and television viewers saw was a city 'transformed' (the most common adjective used) from a 'smoggy Aegean backwater' into a city of beautiful boulevards, clear and azure skies, a growing number of art centres, a vibrant and cutting-edge spirit, and the finest metro in Europe (Correspondent, 2004). The consensus was that the Games had been well run, with spectacular opening and closing ceremonies, smooth event scheduling, excellent transport, and first-rate athletes' facilities.

Evaluating the legacy of these Games, however, has proved complex. The lack of a coherent legacy plan for the Olympic sites, the economic crisis that enveloped Greece in 2008–2009, the inability to find immediate uses for many of the Olympic venues taken together, created a trope of a failed Games and a failed legacy. With nearly twenty years hindsight, the picture is more nuanced.

The Official Report (ATHOC, 2005, II, p. 525) outlined the legacy in terms of transport improvements, reduced pollution, land reclamation, sports facilities, beautification of the city, a culture of cooperation, civic spirit, and job training, concluding:

> The Games were a 17-day advertisement for our competence and sophistication, potential investors discovered that Greece has the talent, attitude and infrastructure – and the EU membership – to compete internationally. Finally we Greeks proved to ourselves that we can do whatever we set ourselves to doing, under extraordinary pressure, with a global audience. After the Olympic Games, we know we can compete with anybody.

The Director for the Organization for the Planning and Environmental Protection of Athens, Catherine Sykianaki and her colleague Sakis Psihogias (2006, p. 11) maintained that the physical legacy of the Games in terms of 'renewal and regeneration' represented a 'catching up process after some decades of inertia had eroded the competitiveness and quality of life of Athens'. The city now had an infrastructure conducive to economic growth. IOC marketing specialist Michael Payne (2006, p. 271) believed that the Games helped 're-brand Greece as a country' and that they had successfully managed to combine the mythological and traditional images with modern, dynamic designs. The Athens communication team even talked of 'just in time delivery' as if 'it was something that had been planned all the time so that the country could showcase its efficiency and ingenuity at the last minute' (*ibid.*, p. 269) to counteract the press view that it was in fact a 'last minute approach' (Smith, 2003). Yet, notwithstanding such promotional gloss, there is no doubt that corners were cut, plans cancelled, and tasks left incomplete; issues which impacted on post-Games planning.

Popular tourist literature applauded the changes made in connection with the Games that transformed Athens into a more attractive tourist destination:

> Major urban renewal has breathed new life into Athens' historic centre, spectacularly reconciling its ancient and modern faces with charming car-free streets that wind along well-trodden ancient paths, making it feel like you're walking through a giant archaeological park... The city's radical pre-Olympics makeover went well beyond new infrastructure. There's a newfound confidence and creative energy, particularly in emerging arts, dining and entertainment hotspots in newly hip, urban neighbourhoods. (Kyriakopoulos 2009, p. 7)

Tourism numbers in the years after the Games suggested success in this area as international tourist arrivals increased year on year from 2004 (3.1 million arrivals) to 2007 (3.9 million arrivals) after which the global financial crisis and the problems of the Greek economy hit Greece's tourism sector (Panagiotopoulou, 2014, p. 181).

Environmentalists, as mentioned previously, were particularly critical that the rules laid down in the tender for the Olympic Village were largely ignored when reducing construction costs became the priority. In more measured tones, commentators from the United Nations Environment Programme noted that while there had been undoubted achievements in the areas of transport, coastal rehabilitation and improvements in public awareness of environmental issues, in the matter of energy consumption and the building of eco-friendly facilities standards had fallen 'below expectations'. They regretted that there had not been more consultation at the preparation stages with 'key stakeholders, particularly environmental NGOs'.[8] For its part, the environmental assessment of the Games by the World Wildlife Fund (WWF) in July 2004 evaluated eighteen environmental performance indicators with a score from 0 (very disappointing) to 4 (very positive). As table 14.1 shows, Athens's average was just 0.77, scoring zero on no less than eleven of the criteria, including protection of natural habitats, protection of open spaces, siting of Olympic venues, use of green technologies, green energy, water saving, integrated waste management and recycling, and respect for environmental legislation. The highest scores were for public awareness (4), improvement of the built environment (3) and public transport (3). The WWF's assessment was that there had been no effort to integrate the environment into the planning of the Games and that opportunities were missed to improve environmental management in areas where Athens is vulnerable, such as water supply, energy provision and waste disposal. Indeed, nothing was done to promote renewable energy or water conservation or to tackle waste management other than to purchase a new fleet of dust carts.

Finding worthwhile uses for Games' facilities once the festival is over is

Table 14.1. Olympic environmental assessment, Athens 2004. (*Source*: Compiled from WWF, 2004)

Issue	Score	Highlighted Examples
Overall Planning		
Environmental planning	0	Principles of the Environmental Policy of ATHOC published 2001 – more a communications tool than an environmental strategy
Environmental assessment	0	Absence of concrete and measurable environmental commitments

(*continued on page 357*)

(*continued from page 356*)

Natural Environment

Protection of natural habitats	0	Schinas Rowing and canoeing centre; fragile environmental areas trapped by the expansion of the urban web

Urban Environment

Protection of open spaces	0	Use of open space for venues: Galatsi, Maroussi Press facilities, Olympic Village; failure to complete the ecological park at Faliro
Increase of urban green	0	Failure to plant Mediterranean species; planting out of season and requiring irrigation
Improvement of the built environment	3	Façades, removal of billboards, pedestrian network, unification of archaeological sites, street cleaning

Transport

Public transport	3	Metro, gas powered buses, urban rail and tram network, public awareness campaign to reduce car usage; no cycle facilities.

Construction

Siting of Olympic venues	0	Lack of public consultation over sites
Use of existing infrastructure	1	Olympic Stadium and Peace and Friendship Stadium used
Use of green technologies	0	Failed to include environmental obligations in the contracts for the Olympic Village: use of solar power, water saving systems, ozone-friendly cooling systems, certified timber; debris abandoned at constructions sites

Energy

Green energy	0	Solar and wind energy options not considered for the Olympic sites

Water

Water saving scheme	0	Tap water used for irrigation of Olympic Village site; 16 km pipeline supplies tap water to Schinais competition reservoirs in dry periods

Waste

Integrated waste management and recycling	0	No integrated waste management strategy, recycling bins provided at Olympic venues

Public Participation

Social consultation	1	No stakeholder consultation; opposition to the sites for Schinas Rowing Centre, Galatsi, Olympic Village, Press Centre
Transparency	1	Poor information; NGOs with an international base had more success in obtaining information than other groups
Public information	1	Website used as a promotional rather than an information tool; central role therefore played by the press in highlighting issues

General Issues

Respect for environmental legislation	0	Existing legislation bypassed, for example in the case of the Press Village Maroussi
Public awareness	4	Good environmental education and awareness to reduce car usage and water consumption
Total Score	0.77	

(4 = very positive; 3 = positive; 2 = fair; 1 = disappointing; 0 = very disappointing)

another canon of sustainable Olympic development. This question is the one that has come to bedevil the final reputation of these Games with press coverage that has been relentlessly negative. The summer of 2008 saw a spate of articles as the Beijing Games loomed, looking back to Athens as an example of how not to plan an Olympics. The same stories were repeated six years later to mark the tenth anniversary of the Games. Picking just three headlines gives the flavour of the coverage: from the *Daily Telegraph* in 2008 came 'Athens' deserted Games sites a warning to London Olympics' (Moore, 2008); the *Chicago Tribune* reported 'Testament to progress atrophies after Games – Athens Olympic venues suffer from lack of long-range planning. Chicago should take note' (Hersh, 2008); and the Daily Mail (Evans, 2014) 'The new ruins of Athens: rusting and decaying 10 years on, how Greece's Olympics turned into a £7 billion white elephant'. Whichever decade the coverage came from it repeated the same trope: photographs of dirty, graffiti-covered, seemingly abandoned facilities in a sea of derelict open space, locked away behind high fences or, in the case of the coastal facilities at Faliro, surrounded by gypsy encampments.[9] The former Olympic Village did not escape press censure with descriptions of abandoned and deteriorating homes, failing businesses, and unusable leisure facilities (Anon., 2011).

Legacy had already become a political issue in Greece, with the two major national political parties accusing one another over which bore more blame for the lack of post-Games strategy. The New Democracy Party, coming to power in March 2004 claimed that PASOK, their Socialist predecessors, had no proper business plans for the Olympic sites. PASOK countered that facilities were being allowed to deteriorate.[10] The New Democracy government established a state-owned holding company, Hellenic Olympic Properties (HOP), to which it transferred twenty-two venues. These included all the Athens sports facilities, the Media Press Centre and the International Broadcasting Centre but not the AOSC complex, the Olympic Village or Press Villages. AOSC remained an international sports complex and the Villages had post-Games plans in place. HOP's brief was to achieve 'sustainable commercial development' in areas of activity compatible with government strategy, with a general framework of permitted uses laid down in legislation passed in 2005–2006 (HOP, 2006). HOP was to manage the sites until leaseholders could be found in the form of foreign or domestic investors or public–private partnerships, thus helping to recoup building costs, avoid the expense of maintaining the venues (estimated at $100 million per annum), and benefit local communities in terms of cultural amenity and jobs.

Understandably, HOP faced the problem that the locations of the venues reflected political, landownership, and pragmatic considerations rather than planning for post-Games commercial use. A stated aim for the free-standing venues was to improve the infrastructure of the unplanned suburbs, but the municipalities could not afford to maintain them (MSNBC, 2004). The Faliro and Helleniki complexes were meant to generate critical mass since they contain a number of attractions, but it was estimated back in 2005, for example, that the cost of running Faliro was €5–7 million as against an income from the Marina and Indoor Hall of €2–4 million (Romanos *et al.*, 2005, p. 6).

Therefore, progress towards realizing a new life for the venues was patchy (see Kissoudi, 2008). Tenders were invited for the Badminton Hall at Goudi, the International Broadcasting Centre, the canoe-kayak slalom course at Helleniki, the sailing centre at Agio Kosmas, and the Galatsi Olympic Indoor Hall in 2005. In March 2006, further tenders were invited for the beach volleyball centre at Faliro. Initially only two of these venues attracted interest. In May 2006, a consortium signed a 25-year lease on the Badminton Hall for €12.5 million.[11] The Badminton Theatre opened in 2007 as a 2,500-seater auditorium – the largest in Greece – and capable of staging large-scale productions of opera, ballet, theatre, and popular concerts from 'Evita' to Matthew Bourne's 'Swan Lake'. Conference facilities were added in 2012 to allow it to host events.

At the International Broadcasting Centre (IBC) site, the Golden Hall, a luxury shopping mall, opened in November 2008 (Bouras, 2007). With 131 shops and 1,400 parking spaces, it was advertised as being the 'ultimate fashion destination for the northern suburbs of Athens'. It was expected to attract between seven and nine million visits in its first full year of operation (Michaelidou, 2009, p. 58). Two museums were planned for the remaining part of the IBC building which abuts the Olympic Stadium. One was a national project, the Museum of the Greek Olympic Games, and the other an International Museum of Athletics and an associated Hall of Fame. An agreement relating to the latter was even signed with the International Association of Athletics Federations (since 2019 World Athletics) in 2005 (IAAF, 2005). Neither museum materialized, but the idea of an Olympic Museum was very much part of Lamda Development's plans for the expansion of the Golden Hall following their purchase in 2013 of a 90-year lease for the whole site (Lamda Development, 2016). The Athens Olympic Museum finally opened in May 2021 on the second floor of the Golden Hall with views over the adjacent stadium and AOCC complex (AOM, 2021). This museum not only covers the Greek relationship to the Olympics ancient and modern but also the evolution of the modern Olympic movement and Olympism.[12] This initiative should play a major role in drawing visitors north of the city centre to the AOSC sports centre which until now has not been a significant attraction for tourists. Its slow development also illustrates the point that legacy plans can take a considerable time to materialize.

Nevertheless, even where potential investors were eventually found for Olympic venues, legal problems over property titles, and licensing (for rebuilding or operating conditions) could cause delays of up to six years in some cases, with investors resorting to the courts to recoup costs (Panagiotopoulou, 2016, p. 48). A number of the sites acquired public uses. Three were transferred to Sports Federations: the Faliro Marina to the National Sailing Federation as a National Sailing Centre, the Markopolou Equestrian Centre to the Hellenic Equestrian Federation, and Schinias Rowing Centre to the Greek Rowing Association as a national and international Rowing Centre. The Markopolou Shooting Centre became a police shooting academy and headquarters of Police Special Forces. The Nikea weightlifting arena was given to the University of Piraeus as its second campus (*ibid.*, pp. 56–59).

Economic Crisis

The global economic crisis of 2008 hit Greece particularly hard and had a two-fold effect on the Olympic legacy. In the first place the worsening economic situation meant that the opportunities to capitalize on the possibilities created by the Games were largely wasted (Ziakas and Boukas, 2012, p. 301; see also Correspondent, 2010). It would have been difficult to rectify the situation at the best of times, but with the financial crisis, any appropriate conditions 'for the effective management of the Olympic legacy' were lost (Boukas *et al.*, 2013, p. 220). The result was that the notion of legacy evaporated in the face of a trope of 'burden' (Papanikolaou, 2013, p. 4). The sight of the Taekwondo Stadium at Faliro, the hockey facility in Hellinikon, and the Galatsi Hall being used as reception centres for migrants arriving in Greece from Turkey and the Macedonain border in 2014 and 2015 seemed to symbolize the failure of strategic legacy planning in Athens (HRGSMC, 2015; Taylor, 2015; Strickland, 2015)

The second issue related to the conditions imposed on Greece by the international bailouts of 2010, 2012, and 2015, where Greece was expected to generate income by asset sales. In 2011, Hellenic Olympic Properties (HOP) along with the Hellenic Tourist Properties and the Hellenic Public Real-Estate Corporation combined to form a new body, the Public Properties Company. This now had a nationwide portfolio of over 70,000 properties from ports, airports, banks, utilities, and hotels and the remaining twelve Olympic properties (PPC, 2015). Its role was to manage the development and sales of assets. The body charged with the actual sale of land, properties, businesses, and leases was the Hellenic Republic Asset Development Fund (HRADF) also established in 2011 as part of the privatization strategy intended to re-establish credibility as a 'prerequisite for Greece to return to global capital markets' (HRADF, 2016). This process was intended to raise cash for the state to offset negotiated bailout loans and attract direct investment into undercapitalized assets and encourage the development of unexploited assets with the view ultimately of promoting economic growth (*ibid.*).

For many the story of the Athens Games ends at this point, seeing only underused and apparently abandoned venues. Yet as the Greek economy emerged from the economic crisis, investment opportunities started to pick up and the efforts to capitalize on the Olympic investment resumed. Three projects in particular have attracted investment. The two coastal regeneration areas of Faliro Bay and the Hellinikon have finally received funding and the grand vision of creating the 'Athens Riviera' seems to be underway. To the north of the city centre the athletic complex in Maroussi (AOSC) is being renovated to create a sustainable mixed-use sport and leisure space.

The Faliro Zone

The post-Olympic vision for the regeneration of Faliro Bay envisaged a coastal path and park with flood protection and access to the residential areas cut off from the coastal strip by Posidonos Avenue – a six-lane urban motorway running parallel with the coast. Four Olympic venues were to have provided sport, leisure, and cultural activities. The two stadia in the west of the zone: the Karaiskalis Stadium, rebuilt for the 2004 Games, is home to Olympiacos football team to 2052; and the Peace and Friendship Stadium, renovated for Athens 2004, continues its role as home to the Olympiacos basketball team. As mentioned above, the other two Olympic venues – the beach volleyball and Faliron indoor hall (Taekwondo Stadium) – have fared less well. In 2016, a short-lived proposal gained parliamentary approval to transfer the beach volleyball stadium to the Ministry of Justice for development as a courtroom to assuage the shortage of judicial space and reduce the backlog of high-profile court cases (Ekaterini.com, 2016). This met with considerable opposition and was dropped.

However, the whole narrative of this area changed with the building of the Stavros Niarchos Foundation Cultural Centre (SNFCC).[13] The Centre was built as a public–private partnership with a grant from the foundation of €608 million; the largest such grant ever given. The idea for the Foundation making a major cultural investment in Athens dates back to 1998 but the project was not set in motion until 2006, when the site of the old Athens racecourse, which had been cleared as part of the Olympic project, was chosen. The site was already linked by a promenade across the motorway to the coastal Olympic Zone by the Taekwondo Stadium (SNF, 2023*a*; see figure 14.2). This project, designed by Renzo Piano, houses the National Library of Greece, linked by an agora (a covered main square) to the Greek National Opera (figure 14.3). Completed in 2016, it was handed over to the Greek government in 2017. Although intended to be financially self-reliant, the foundation has provided ongoing grants, with a new grant of

Figure 14.2. Pedestrian promenade over the coastal motorway built for Athens 2004, linking the Taekwando Arena with the site for the Stavros Niarchos Foundation Centre, which will house the National Library and National Opera in a landscaped park. (*Source*: Photograph, John and Margaret Gold, June 2009)

Figure 14.3. Aerial view of the Stavros Niarchos Foundation Cultural Center. (*Source*: CC Strange Traveller)

€30 million announced in 2023 to cover five years' funding for cultural programming (SNF, 2023b).

The centre offers opera, music, dance, exhibitions, screenings, an education programme serving all ages and abilities, and family activities. The library provides a lending service as well as a reference collection. The Centre is set on an artificial hill giving views over the coast and towards the city, so that the architecture, views, gastronomy, and parkland make it an attractive visitor destination in its own right. The surrounding 42-acre park (17 hectares) including a 400-metre canal with dancing fountains provides opportunities for sport (both for organized groups and individuals) including kayaking, jogging, and cycling, and space for outdoor events from cinema screenings to seasonal festivals. All are free of charge.

Visitor numbers have far exceeded expectations. The target for 2019 of 700,000 visitors was exceeded by 5.6 million (BCG, 2022, p. 79) and the complex had received a total of 23.8 million visits up to February 2023. It has become the third most popular international tourist monument in Athens after the Acropolis Museum and the National Archaeological Museum, with 16 per cent of international tourists visiting (ibid., p. 19). As such, the centre has 'helped to remap the cultural face of Athens', drawing tourists away from the centre towards the coast and, in doing so, changing perceptions of Athens's cultural offer to include iconic modern architecture and contemporary culture (ibid., pp. 11, 19).

When the SNFCC opened, the contrast with the rest of the Faliro Bay area was stark, with 'barren' open spaces and difficulty in accessing the coastal strip across Poseidonos Avenue from the neighbouring residential areas (Markou, 2015). However, plans are afoot to complete the park project, with a project designed by Renzo Piano covering the area from the Peace and Friendship Stadium to the SNFCC. In the process, this will create a 220-acre (90-hectare) public park which, coupled with improved access, will finally produce an area similar to that envisaged in the original Olympic legacy thinking.

Hellinikon

The Hellinikon airport site, to the east of Faliro Bay, was the other coastal cluster of Olympic venues. This 1,530-acre (620-hectare) site became one of the largest properties transferred to the HRADF in 2011 and initially seemed one of the most intractable. With its concentration of arenas for sports not popular in Greece, there had been particular challenges in finding users for the venues. The baseball ground was leased to Ethnikos Football SA and occasional trade shows had been held in the old fencing hall. The canoe-kayak slalom centre was intended to become a water park, but this never materialized. The old arrivals, departure, and charter buildings became the

Hellenikon Exhibition Centre, but the envisaged Hellenikon Metropolitan Park never materialized. The original 2005 plans for a Metropolitan Park would have provided much needed public open space and recreation facilities including museums, but were superseded by ambitious plans drawn up by Norman Foster and Partners, for a new urban quarter that would be a 'landmark of national importance and international visibility' and reposition Athens as a destination city (Hellenikon SA, 2016, p. 2). This 'new vibrant city within Athens' would provide 11,000 homes for a residential population of between 33,000 and 44,000 people, leisure and recreation including museums, sports and recreational facilities, a marina, entertainment, a business park, convention centre, hotel, shopping mall, a major hospital, education, research, and innovation clusters (Pollalis *et al.*, 2013, pp. 2, 13–14). The site was initially put up for tender in 2011 and a deal worth €915 million was agreed in 2014 (Tagaris, 2014). This was for a 99-year lease with a consortium led by Lamda Development (from Greece), with Fosun (China) and Al Maabar (Abu Dhabi).[14]

In response, opposition groups described this as 'the most valuable real estate asset in Europe' being offered at 'an unacceptably low price'. They believed that the proposed development would not benefit surrounding communities and instead wanted something closer to the 2005 vision which prioritized public access, recreation space, and sustainability. Public incursions on to the site to remove fencing, plant trees or the 2011 Festival of Resistance and Creativity were ways in which local communities indicated their frustration with the proposals (City of Hellinikon-Argyroupoli, 2013). The bureaucratic, legal and political challenges continued until the land was finally transferred to Lamda in June 2021 with a down payment of €300 million of the €915 million transaction agreed in 2014 (see above). For the Greek government this deal was symbolic of Greece being ready for business, a good place for investment and a chance to finally put the negative images of failed development and the financial crisis in the past (Anon, 2021).

The scale of the project is impressive. Now named Ellinikon, it is an €8 billion project over twenty-five years, covering an area of 620 hectares (1,530 acres) comprising the old airport area, the coastal strip and the Agios Kosmos Marina (the site of the Olympic sailing in 2004). This is claimed as 'the largest urban regeneration project in Europe' representing three times the area of Monaco and promising to set 'new benchmarks for … sustainable living; for iconic placemaking; for smart-infrastructure; and for its broad base of business potential, from tourism to innovative commercial properties to ground-breaking destination retail'.[15] After all the delays, it was with some triumph that Lamda announced that, 'just six months after the contract for the Ellinikon was signed', it was opening a 70-acre (28-hectare) Experience Park to the public for Christmas 2021.[16] This newly landscaped area of walks, a fitness area, Zen Garden, children's playground, and interactive fountains was followed four months later by the opening of an interactive Experience Centre in a restored air force hangar where visitors were invited to 'discover the magnitude of the Ellinikon'.[17]

Construction on the first phase of the masterplan began in earnest in February 2022 with three projects. The first was to create a 1.3-kilometre tunnel for Posidonos Avenue with the rest being sunk below ground level so that the parkland and new residential districts have uninterrupted access to the waterfront and beaches. The second project was the disability hub in the northwest of the development, which provides care facilities and accommodation surrounded by landscape gardens for voluntary organizations working in the disability sector. Third the Norman Foster-designed Riviera Tower is currently being built on the seafront. Two hundred metres high with fifty floors and 169 apartments, it is Greece's tallest building as well as boasting that it is 'the tallest green skyscaper in the Mediterranean'. Green plantings on each floor are intended to create a park-like feel enveloping the building while, underground parking for electric vehicles removes cars from the surrounding landscaping. The fourth major project, due to start in 2023, is the commercial hub in the north of the park comprising retail, entertainment, and business accommodation. This first phase of the development is due for completion in 2026.[18]

However, the property prices in this development attract wealthier Greek and foreign buyers but are out of reach of most of the population. Demand was described as 'strong', with options being taken out on houses and apartments as soon as the land transfer in June 2021 empowered Lamda to take deposits on properties.[19] The promised quality of the project, the location and growing accessibility as plans for extending Metro Line 2 come to fruition, and the Greece's Golden Visa Programme which promises a five-year residency permit and visa-free travel in the Schengen area with the purchase of property worth €250,000 have proved attractive. Even when the threshold rises to €500,000, this should still make investment in Ellinikion an attractive proposition.[20] The scheme is also designed to attract tourists, with the international luxury market particularly targeted, with provision of mega-yacht berths in the marina, luxury hotels and high-end retailing in the form of the Riviera Galleria. Designed by the Japanese starchitect Kengo Kuma, it has a roof inspired by the rippling waves of the Mediterranean.[21]

With the rejuvenation of plans for Faliro Bay and the start of work on the Ellinikon project, there have been efforts to resurrect the vision for the Athens Riviera – a plan to treat the 70 kilometres of coastline south of Athens from Pireaus to Cape Sounion as a coherent entity. This project's long pedigree stretches back to the 1950s but has been reinvigorated by the availability of finance from the European Union's Recovery and Resilience Fund, established to help member states recover from the impact of COVID-19. With the aid of additional public funds, plans are mooted for a pedestrian and cycle path along the full stretch of coastline – no easy matter given the ownership patterns along the coast and the tradition of private beaches (Innocenti, 2021).

AOSC

Greece's sports complex at Maroussi (AOSC) has been compared un-favourably to the busy Olympic parks of Sydney, London and Beijing. The complex raised a familiar problem for Olympic cities, namely, the future of a large white elephant stadium that is scarcely used on any regular basis. The aim was to retain the facilities for sporting purposes. As elsewhere, there has been usage for football, with the ground initially shared by Panathinaikos and AEK Athens, but stadia essentially built for athletics rarely provide ideal conditions for football.

Panathinaikos had the long-term aim of developing its own stadium complex, a plan backed by the Municipality, which saw this development as spearheading the regeneration of the Alexandros Avenue area in the west of Athens to provide open space, cultural, sporting, and commercial facilities in a part of the city lacking good infrastructure (Bokoyannis, 2006, p. 18). The club's financial difficulties, the economic crisis, and local opposition initially put this plan on hold. Instead, Panathinaikos refurbished its old stadium (Apostolos Nikolaidis) and moved back in 2020 (Ioannou, 2014). In 2023 work started on a multi-sports complex on a new site in the Votanikos area. This will include a 40,000-seater stadium, 12,500-seater basketball stadium, a volleyball stadium, and an Olympic size swimming pool. This is due to be completed in 2026, with the site of the old stadium redeveloped as a park.[22] For their part, AEK Athens had moved to the Olympic stadium in 2004 when their Nikos Goumas Stadium at Nea Filadelfia in the northwest of the city was demolished. They, however, always intended to rebuild the stadium on that site. After legal and financial delays, work finally began in 2017 and the team moved into their new stadium in September 2022.[23] The familiar pattern of football teams keen to vacate Olympic stadia in favour of purpose-built football stadia – as seen before in Munich and Barcelona amongst others – has once more asserted itself.

Deprived of an anchor tenant, the stadium's main usage is for occasional rock concerts – usually between fifteen and twenty a year. Inbetween these events, the site can look bleak (figure 14.4). The Olympic Park covers a large area that easily absorbs the sports participants and visitors using the indoor sports hall and aquatic centre. Visitors do come to see the iconic architecture, but there are no visitor facilities or stadium tours. At the same time, persistent reports of the site being locked are untrue.

By 2020 plans had emerged to renovate and reconfigure AOSC. The site was 'decrepit' according to Professor Konstantinos Serraos, a spatial planning

Figure 14.4. The Athens Olympic Sports complex, Maroussi, Athens. (*Source*: Photograph, John and Margaret Gold, June 2009)

expert, and expensive to maintain in relation to the income generated. A number of the venues needed repairs and upgrades. Notably, the roofs of the Olympic Stadium and velodrome needed serious attention, while the poor energy efficiency of the venues and the inflexibility of their spaces were further areas to address. Reconfiguring buildings to accommodate non-sports events and uses would generate more usage and income, while attention to the outdoor spaces would make them more welcoming and greener. These changes, combined with better visitor facilities and a hotel, were seen as an essential part of plans to turn the area into a leisure destination that might attract up to 40,000 daily visitors. Resources for this would again come partly from the European Union's Recovery and Resilience Fund for Greece (Lialios, 2021). Given the residential nature of the area surrounding the Olympic complex and its excellent transport connections this could well transform visitor patterns to the area.

Conclusion

For Greece, Athens 2004 was about more than acquiring a set of Olympic venues; the Games were also seen as a means of achieving place promotion goals and the 'soft legacy' of support services, training, employment, attitudinal changes, and organizational knowledge that comes from the successful planning and management of a hallmark event (METREX, 2006, p. 6). In the case of Athens, this included the 'positive climate of opinion within which continued progress could be made' (*ibid.*, p. 7). Greek politicians quickly latched on to these ideas. Prime Minister Costas Karamanlis, for example, stated at the start of the Games that 'Greece will be a more experienced, a more optimistic and self-confident country' (Beard, 2004). In attempting to learn what such assertions meant in practice, Sykianaki and Psihogias (2006, p. 13) identified four important areas in which Athens 2004 created new working practices that might profoundly affect the city's future development. The first was in pioneering private–public partnerships as a new way of generating development funds. The government introduced legislation in 2005 to provide a framework for such partnerships, then new to Greek practice. This was seen as central to economic policy, something that would support entrepreneurship and make the Greek economy internationally oriented and competitive.[24] Secondly, it was argued that the Games had highlighted the problems of bureaucracy and encouraged a more flexible approach to problem solving. Thirdly, the Games were seen as a vehicle that showed how the city could use major events to lever investment, modernize the built environment, and expand Athens's international role. Finally, the Olympics were felt to have mobilized and involved citizens in the affairs of the city.

Any such improvements, however, have been put under strain by the economic crisis, and here it must be stressed that calculating the costs and benefits of an Olympic Games is a daunting task given the powerful indirect as well as direct effects of staging the Games for the domestic economy and society. They also depend on political viewpoint. Radical critics on the Left argue that they have been used as a 'pretext and the excuse' for accelerating the growth of neoliberal ideology in the Greek state through the use of private capital, the relaxation of planning and labour laws, the growth of a surveillance society, and removing the homeless and addicts (and stray animals) from the streets. Moreover, quite apart from the impact on civil liberties, the long-term consequences of the staging of the Games included reinforcement of trends towards the militarization of urban space, environmental damage, and destruction of heritage. Each could have costs for society beyond those that can be imputed in economic terms. Moreover, assessments of costs also depend on the accounting procedures adopted, particularly judgments as to whether or not investment was purely related to the Games or would have happened anyway (e.g. transport improvements and urban beautification). At the end of 2004, for example, the Economy and Finance Minister George Alogoskoufis assessed the cost of the Games as €8.95 million but consciously omitted the costs of the airport and metro, even though their development was expedited for the Games, and the continuing costs of maintaining venues until occupiers can be found.[25]

When looked at in narrow economic terms, ATHOC balanced its books and is eventually expected to declare a profit thanks to a larger-than-expected contribution from IOC broadcast and sponsorship revenues. Games spending helped the sluggish Greek economy to record a 4 per cent annual increase (Payne, 2006, p. 271), but most of the revenue benefitted the Athens region. Regional politicians argue that Athens sucked in investment at the expense of other regions, reinforcing the city's primacy and undoing 'past tendencies for decentralisation' (Coccossis *et al.*, 2003, p. 3). There is, however, consensus that the Games were expensive and over-budget, with infrastructural projects costing 37 per cent more than in the original plan. Greece was the smallest nation to host the Games since Finland in 1952, and there is no doubt that the scale of expenditure expected by the start of the twenty-first century was a strain for a small economy. In Greece's case, European Union membership and access to its funds were of central importance – in particular the Cohesion Fund (from which Greece was one of the major beneficiaries) and the access to loans from the European Investment Bank. European ties, however, also impose costs. The conditions attached to membership of the European Economic and Monetary Union (EEMU) meant that steps were needed to lower Greece's deficit, which, at 6.1 per cent of Gross Domestic Product in 2004, was more than double the limit set by the terms of the EEMU. This resulted in Greece requiring increased taxes, cuts in public spending, and wage restraint measures to realign its economy.[26]

The economic crisis that engulfed Greece in 2008 added to the cost of the Games by making the legacy goals of the government more difficult to attain. Yet notwithstanding the cost calculations, Athens 2004 is popularly remembered within Greece as a success that confounded journalist critics and came as a relief to those with any measure of responsibility for staging the Games. A study published in 2016 found that there was still nationwide support for the Olympic project with 72.8 per cent of respondents believing the Games benefitted from infrastructure development, and 70 per cent that they had reinforced national confidence and national pride (Georgiadis and Theodonkako, 2016).

There is no doubt that the city gained a tangible legacy of infrastructure that is providing the basis for the hoped-for cultural, convention, and business tourism trade. The centre of Athens is pedestrian-friendly and guidebooks wax lyrical on the transformation of the city. The cultural sector has benefitted from new performance spaces, exhibition spaces, and renovated museums. Certainly tourist numbers to Greece increased in the years following the Games (Cartalis, 2015, p. 195) and despite the recession tourism has started to grow again rekindling headlines such as 'Greek tourism bounces back' (Kotogiannis and Hope, 2014). The Games undoubtedly accelerated urban renewal and brought investment in transport and telecommunications. In turn, as Sykianaki and Psihogias (2006, p. 11) argued, these developments produced a more 'conducive environment for economic growth'. This has been borne out by the continued investment in transport infrastructure and the major cultural projects at Faliro Bay and the Ellinikon. Whatever costs have been incurred, it is scarcely plausible that the range of changes experienced would have occurred without being driven by the approach of an Olympic Opening Ceremony. Certainly, most Greek politicians would have settled for this outcome if they had been offered it before the event.

Notes

1. The first Zappas Games of 1859 were held in Loudovikou Square (Plateia Eleftheris).

2. Yannis Pyrgiotis, Executive Director of the Organizing Committee for the Olympic Games (Pyrgiotis, 2003, p. 414).

3   It was built on the site of the velodrome constructed for the 1896 Games.

4. Information from a brochure entitled 'Athens 96: Return to the Future', produced by the Executive Committee for the Candidacy of Athens for the 1996 Olympic Games.

5. In the bid document this airport was to be replaced by the new Elefthenos Venizelos International Airport near Sparta, and Helliniki was to continue in operation until the Games were over. Under the new plan it was closed in 2001.

6. Even so the site manager Xenia Arapogianni was quoted as saying 'We still have misgivings about the sanctuary being used in this way. Ancient Olympia isn't a film or television set', but the local mayor hoped that the television coverage would spur tourist development (Special Correspondent, 2004). Olympia also benefitted from renovation and three new museums.

7. These were the World Wildlife Fund Hellas; Greek Society for the Protection of the Environment and Cultural Heritage; Hellenic Society for the Protection of Nature; and Hellenic Ornithological Society.

8. UNEP Press Release 2004/37, August. Available at: http://www.unep.org, accessed 26 September 2006.

9. Alexandridis (2007, p. 13), in his study of the housing impact of the 2004 Games, estimated that 2,700 Roma were affected by the Games either through evictions or the abandonment of relocation projects.

10. Hellenic Republic Embassy of Greece, press releases, 12 October and 13 November 2004.

11. Three companies were involved: Adam Productions (event organizers); Half Note Jazz Club (club owners and event organizers); and Allou Fun Park (Greece's largest amusement park). Information from Hellenic Republic Embassy of Greece, press release, 16 May 2006.

12. As such, it is one of only 32 museums that are part of the Olympic Museums Network run from the Olympic Museum in Lausanne (IOC, 2023d).

13. The Stavros Niarchos Foundation was established in 1996 on the death of Greek shipping magnet Stravros Spyros Niarchos. Its remit is to fund projects in the arts, culture, education, health, sport, and social welfare. It has headquarters in Athens, Monaco, and New York and has a global reach.

14. Lamda bought out its partners in 2019 due to the 'demanding timetable' and the 'national character' of the project see: GPT Headlines 'Lamda Development Undertakes 100% of Hellinikon Mega Project'. Available at: https://news.gtp.gr/2019/09/20/lamda-development-undertakes-100-of-hellinikon-mega-project/.

15. The Ellinikon (2023) 'About the Ellinikon'. Available at: https://theellinikon.com.gr/en/about/.

16.   The Ellinikon (2021) Lamda Development opens to the public the first project of The Ellinikon, earlier than expected. Available at: https://experiencepark.theellinikon.com.gr/en/2021/12/13/est-dignissimos-consequatur-et-voluptas/.

17.   The Ellinikon (2023) Experience the future of living innovation. Available at: https://experiencecentre.theellinikon.com.gr/.

18.   The Ellinikon (2023) The development of projects at the Ellinikon. Available at: https://theellinikon.com.gr/; see also Hospitalitynet (2023) 'The Ellinnikon, one of the world's largest urban projects, breaks ground on Riviera Tower, Greece's tallest building'. Available at: https://www.hospitalitynet.org/news/4114867.html.

19.   Ekathimerini.com (2021) Elliniko homes selling fast. Available at: https://www.eka thimerini.com/economy/1163542/elliniko-homes-selling-fast/.

20.   Schengenvisa (2023) Greece Golden Visa – how to get permanent residency and citizenship, https://www.schengenvisainfo.com/eu-golden-visas/greece-golden-visa/.

21.   The Ellinikon (2023) In harmony with the sea. Available at: https://www.rivieragalleria.theellinikon.com.gr/en/the-design/.

22.   GTP (Greek Travel Pages) 2022 Athens: Votanikos Park and Panathiniakos Stadium Projects enter phase 2. Available at: https://news.gtp.gr/2022/05/23/athens-votanikos-park-and-panathinaikos-stadium-projects-enter-phase-2/.

23.   AEK (2016), AEKFC (2023).

24.   Information from Ministry of Economics, press release, 4 August 2006.

25.   Information from Hellenic Republic Embassy of Greece, press release, 14 November 2004.

26.   The aim was to get it down to three per cent by the end of 2006 (Church, 2005).

Chapter 15

BEIJING 2008

Ian G. Cook, Steven Miles and *Giorgos Chatzinakos*

It would be difficult indeed not to be impressed with the scale and majesty of the Beijing Olympics in 2008. From the spectacular opening ceremony to the almost as impressive closing ceremony, the Games were run effectively and efficiently. At the time the Beijing Olympics was claimed to be 'the most-watched Olympic Games ever' and 'probably the most-watched event in human history' with about 4.7 billion television viewers and 32,278 journalists reporting it around the world (Brownell, 2013, p. 67). There were some hitches and glitches, but as a modern mega-event the Beijing Olympics set a high bar for the subsequent London Olympics and later successors to live up to, not least because of the economic recession that has gripped the globe from 2008 to 2009. As Lord Sebastian Coe, Chair and CEO of the London 2012 Games, stated to the delight of Xinhua, the Chinese State-Run News Agency, in July 2009 at an African Olympic meeting in Abuja, Nigeria:

> Beijing was fantastic, the venues were superb, the planning was superb, the athletes were well looked after, and they performed well because they were well looked after.

Although Coe suggested that he was excited rather than 'challenged' by the success of Beijing, this was exactly what the Chinese authorities wanted to hear. After all the concerns expressed beforehand concerning human rights, social costs, atmospheric pollution and other issues, the People's Republic of China had achieved their objectives – to impress a respected Olympian such as Lord Coe and to develop a model for future Olympics. As social scientists, however, it behoves the authors to take a more critical perspective, to note the successes that did occur, but also the problems that arose, and to consider both the pluses and minuses of Beijing's legacy and the longer-term implications of the Olympics for the reinvention of China as a participant in the global economy.

Beijing itself is a city that has undergone significant transformation in recent decades. Anyone who has travelled to Beijing since the early 1990s will have witnessed enormous changes, with the city rapidly metamorphosing into an 'internationalized metropolis' (Cook, 2006). This period has seen Beijing make not one, but two, bids to host the Summer Olympics. The first bid was submitted in 1992–1993 and was eventually rejected, with Sydney winning the race to host the 2000 Olympics. 'Human rights' were cited as a major reason for the rejection of this bid, unsurprising given that Tiananmen was fresh in the memory, with the tanks having been sent in to clear the square on 4 June 1989. Environmental issues, however, were also a major factor. Beijing had already hosted the Asian Games by that date, and so the city had by then spent a considerable sum on stadia, a Games Village, and on transport infrastructure. Foreign observers noted how most schoolchildren in Beijing in 1992 seemed to sport the bright yellow baseball cap bearing the Asian Games logo. There was an air of expectancy that China would be awarded the 2000 Summer Olympic Games. The disappointment at rejection was palpable.

By contrast, the announcement in June 2001 that Beijing would host the Olympics in 2008 was greeted by mass rejoicing. Even Shanghai, often cast as a rival to Beijing, witnessed warm celebrations when the result was announced, not least because Shanghai was due to co-host the soccer tournament (figure 15.1). The announcement provided a sense of

Figure 15.1. Shanghai joins in the celebrations: Sofitel Hotel, central Shanghai after the announcement of the successful bid. (*Source*: Photograph, Ian G. Cook)

vindication of China's improved standing in the world. When the People's Republic of China was founded on 1 October 1949, Mao Zedong said in his address to the new nation that China had stood up and would never be humiliated again. After many years of effort, of marked successes and notable failures, the opportunity to host the 2008 Olympics was proof that China had not only stood up, but also that it was no longer a pariah state and was ready to take its rightful place as one of the leading countries on earth. To analyse the Beijing Olympics, therefore, is not only to analyse the specific urban dimension of this Olympic City, but also to contextualize Beijing's successful bid within the rise of the New China, a China that is proud of its past and increasingly proud of its present.

This wider contextualization highlights negatives as well as positives concerning the Beijing Olympics. This chapter, therefore, first examines China's uneven transformation, before considering Beijing's development path. The ensuing sections consider the bidding process, the relationship between the Olympics and urban regeneration and the controversies that beset the pre-Olympic period, including the environment, resettlement, human rights, corruption, and obesity. The Games themselves are then examined in terms of their impact and how they were organized, before the legacy is considered in terms of international prestige, environmental effects within Beijing, the social and cultural dimension within the city and beyond, and how the massive Olympic site is to be funded in future.

China's Uneven Transformation

The dramatic changes in China that took place in the second half of the twentieth century are well known (Cannon, 2000; Cook and Murray, 2001). The establishment of the People's Republic of China as a communist state led by the Chinese Communist Party (CCP) gave rise to three alternative models of development: first the Soviet model in which centralization and heavy industry were key features; then the Maoist model in which the decentralized commune was a major element; and finally, the Dengist model of market socialism, or 'socialism with Chinese characteristics'. The Dengist model took China, probably irrevocably, down the capitalist road – albeit under strong direction from the Chinese state. It was based on an Open Door for foreign direct investment (FDI), with the objective of modernizing China's agriculture, industry, defence, science, and technology. Under the market reforms unleashed by Deng and his successors, China's 'Gold Coast' has been opened up to global connections and China is now in rapid transition from being a closed, poverty-stricken rural society towards one that is open, wealthy and, for many, urban. In brief, the Chinese state sets the preconditions for investment to enter, the local state (at province, city, or town level) provides the infrastructure, and foreign companies provide the necessary investment through which China's resources of land and labour can be fully exploited. The scale and pace of change are phenomenal, especially in China's emerging cities, where the processes of globalization and urbanization interlock so dramatically (Cook, 2020; Gu and Cook 2018; Wu, 2006, 2007). The emergence of China as an economic superpower has been built on the apparently limitless potential of cheap labour and an aspirational population that, in the aftermath of Tiananmen, accepted a social contract in which they were given the freedoms associated with a consumer society in exchange for the maintenance of the political and human rights *status quo*.

China has twenty-nine provinces, plus four cities run directly via central government (Beijing, Shanghai, Tianjin, and Chongqing). Initially, most FDI flowed via Hong Kong into the neighbouring Guangdong Province. In 1997, Guangdong experienced $12.6 billion of actually utilized FDI. Although the annual total dropped slightly in 1998–1999 due to the combined effects of the Asian financial crisis plus a degree of investment saturation in the Pearl River Delta, by 2003 FDI in Guangdong was still high at $7.8 billion (National Bureau of Statistics, 1999, 2006). Shanghai and neighbouring provinces in the 'arrowhead' of the Yangtze River Delta are fast developing as an alternative attraction for FDI, with the corresponding figures for actually utilized FDI in Shanghai in 1997 and 2003 being $4.2 billion and $5.5 billion respectively. As for Beijing itself, the corresponding data show that by 1997 $1.6 billion FDI was utilized, rising to $2.2 billion in 2003. Part of the 'China miracle', this type of investment is ploughed into export-oriented manufacturing, the property market, the retail sector, and other activities, fuelling the dramatic transformation noted above. Multinational and transnational companies such as Volkswagen, Renault, McDonalds, KFC, Motorola, Nokia, Microsoft, BP, B&Q, and many more are engaged in this continuing struggle to enter the lucrative China market.

This investment, however, is spatially uneven. It is clear that the cycle of circular and cumulative causation, to use the old terminology associated with Gunnar Myrdal (1968), is very much oriented towards the coast. Chai (1996, p. 57), for instance, in his analysis of east–west income differentials from 1978 to 1991, found that regional income disparity had increased significantly. The trend of concentration of investment resources along the eastern seaboard was reinforced by the export-led growth and FDI policies adopted during this period. The eastern seaboard had ports facilitating the imports of raw materials and exports of manufacturing. Consequently, most of the export processing facilities tended to concentrate in the coastal areas. Furthermore, its proximity to the potential foreign investors as well as the special investment incentives created by the central government had attracted most of China's foreign investments into these areas.

Many other studies have similarly indicated the deeply embedded nature of these spatial contrasts (see Cook and Murray, 2001). They are also found with regards to urban-rural differentials and can also vary at the local scale within provinces, for example, perhaps reflecting upland-lowland contrasts. In recent years the Chinese leadership has seemed particularly concerned to tackle such disparities, emphasizing the importance of investment in the Western provinces, and of tackling rural deprivation. The huge stimulus package of 4 trillion yuan announced early in 2009 had a significant rural dimension, designed not only to support rural growth *in situ*, but also to slow down the exodus to China's cities and thus reduce spatial imbalances. Whether government can effectively redress these imbalances remains to be seen, however, in the light of the massive attraction of development in the Eastern seaboard (Zhang, 2014). China's Gini coefficient, a measure of inequality, now outstrips the USA and has increased by one-third in the last thirty-five years (Garst, 2015). Investment in the Beijing Olympics, of course, added still further to this uneven development, and thus to the imbalance at the national scale.

Beijing's Development Path

Despite a long and distinguished history, under communism Beijing became an austere, drab producer city, full of steel mills and petrochemical works (Cook, 2006). It was heavily influenced by the Soviet style of planning with wide thoroughfares, mid-rise flats on a large scale, occasional grand buildings, and the expansion of Tiananmen Square to become the new heart of the city. The population of 1.2 million in 1949 within the old boundaries, by the early 1980s was probably 4.14 million within its expanded boundaries, including 1.76 million specifically classified as 'urban' (Dong, 1985). In the western outskirts, the Shihjingshan Iron and Steel Works (also known as Shougang, or the Capital Iron and Steel Works) became one of China's largest. The city was worthy but dull, and by the 1970s an increasing proportion of its population was beginning to complain of the endless diet of revolutionary dramas and operas. The average family would aspire to own a radio, watch, and bicycle and there was little in the way of luxury available to the mass of the population. As for externalities, Zhou (1992, p. 30) observed that:

> over a rather long period, Beijing put undue emphasis on heavy industry at the expense of light industry, which was underdeveloped. The excessive heavy industry created a shortage of water, electricity and transport capacity, and worsened environmental pollution. Little attention was paid to housing and public facilities... The urban population expanded while the commercial service network decreased.

Today, Beijing is worlds apart from this brief sketch. The reform period has ushered in a period of massive urban change, with new hotels, banks, high-rise residences, ring roads, new subway lines, the largest shopping mall in Asia (Oriental Plaza) and the whole paraphernalia of a city that is seeking to internationalize and have a presence on a global scale (Cook, 2006; Gu and Cook, 2011). The total population was officially estimated at 14.93 million in 2004, which includes the *liudong renkou*, or 'floating population', who do not have resident status (Lin, 2004). These are the migrants who are usually tolerated by the authorities, if not by the long-term residents themselves who see the newcomers as 'new urban outcasts' (Solinger, 1995), and supply, for instance, the cheap labour on which the rapid pace of construction is based, work which is '3D' – difficult, demanding, and dangerous (Shen, 2002). Urban migrants or 'floaters' are often either exploited by their employers or self-exploited insofar as they work exceptionally long hours, more so given the intensity of the building programme and the tight deadlines associated with the Olympics, often below the minimum wage and often not receiving pay until weeks after its due. As Friedman (2005) puts it, the urban migrants are 'the cannon fodder of China's industrial revolution'.

Contemporary Beijing often seems to resemble a giant building site. All around, huge new buildings are in various stages of construction, often cloaked in huge nets to prevent tools falling on passers-by. The streets are hazardous due to the trenches which have been dug for pipes and cables, the pavements which are being laid, the trees that have been knocked down or are being replanted, and the trucks and workers' buses which cut across the flows of pedestrians and bicycles into the corrugated iron fortresses which surround the sites. By early 1999, with the advent of the fiftieth anniversary of the People's Republic of China, there were an estimated 5,000 building sites in the city (Cook, 2000).

Adoption of the trappings of modern consumer society accompanied this transformation of the built environment. Supermarkets carry Western-style red wines and beer, bread and cakes. The streets have American fast-food chains such as McDonalds, Kentucky Fried Chicken and Dunkin' Donut. Chinese tastes now extend to Western motor vehicles (BMW, Cherokee Jeep, Audi, Volkswagen, Mercedes and even Ferrari), clothing (Benetton, Adidas, or Wranglers), perfumes (Estée Lauder or Nina Ricci), electrical goods (Sony, Phillips, and Panasonic), and housing, with executive-style estates of detached houses complete with nearby golf courses and private schools, perhaps within the complex itself. For the growing middle class, material goods are in plentiful supply, although these are often more expensive than in Western countries. For the working class, too, the department stores are rapidly expanding their size and product range. A night out is increasingly to a Hard Rock Cafe, pub, or disco, usually featuring Western music, and a holiday is often taken overseas in such cities as London, Paris, New York, or Tokyo. It was in the light of such changes that Beijing made its bids for the Olympics.

The Bidding Process

As in other communist societies, sport became an important element in promoting the nation and patriotism. The annual *China Statistical Yearbook* on 'Culture, Sports and Public Health' routinely tabulates such outputs as 'Visits between Chinese and Foreign Sports Delegations', 'Activities of Mass Sports', 'World Records Chalked up by Chinese Athletes by Event' and 'World Championships won by Chinese Athletes'. Dong (2005, p. 533) shows that 'Chinese political and sports officials openly acknowledged that they viewed sport as an instrument for the promotion of national pride and identity... Contemporary competitive sport in China is motivated by nationalism and in turn contributes to the enhancement of patriotism'. From the mid-1980s, a strategy was developed to maximize gold medals, with an interesting feature being the success of female athletes, and the high proportion of females relative to males in the Chinese team. This has not always been unproblematic. There have been well publicized defections of top athletes plus question marks over the training methods and unprecedented success of 'Ma's Barmy Army' (after their trainer) of female marathon runners as well as the Chinese swimming team, with questions raised as to whether such athletes were 'chemically enhanced'. Dong shows that the first time that the question as to when China could actually host the Olympics was raised as far back as 1908 in the *Tianjin Youth Magazine*, but it was at the end of the successful Asian Games in 1990 that a huge banner was unfurled, stating 'With the success of the Asiad, we look forward to hosting the Olympic Games' (cited by Dong, 2005, p. 538).

As noted above, Beijing failed on that occasion, but only losing to Sydney by two votes for the right to host the Millennial Olympics in 2000. There were suggestions (e.g. GamesBids.com, 2007) that there was a vote scandal at this time, but there was also strong opposition from Human Rights groups and the 'Free Tibet' movement, who were vehemently opposed to a successful bid from China. Although the Asian Games had been successful, the shadow of Tiananmen still loomed large as far as many Western governments were concerned (see Broudehoux, 2004), and Beijing was still a severely polluted city at that time, with a relatively poor infrastructure. It was certainly no surprise to most observers that the 1990s bid was unsuccessful.

By 2001, however, much had changed. China had decided to bid once more, primarily as part of the drive to modernize and internationalize Beijing. The city, one of five shortlisted, prepared for the final visit of the bidding panel in February 2001 with great care. *Inter alia*, the short- and longer-term measures taken included investment into awareness of the 2008 bid, for example, illuminations in Olympic colours, billboards, magazines in taxis, the Millennium Museum showing Olympic films and displays, street signs in English, investment in infrastructure (notably the fourth and fifth ring roads), and development of new hotels. Older buildings were painted to improve appearances and grass was sprayed green. Parks were established, green and silver bins were introduced to increase awareness of environment through waste recycling. Air quality was improved by banning older cars and use of domestic coal, and closing the Shougang steel plant.

The bid adopted the overarching slogan of 'New Beijing: Great Olympics', with subsidiary themes of delivering a 'high-tech Olympics', a 'green Olympics' and a 'people's Olympics'. It featured a plan to construct an Olympic Park and strategies to address the serious environmental issues faced by the Chinese capital. The commitments included:

◆   An Olympic Park covering an area of 1,215 hectares. It would include an 80,000 seat stadium, 14 gymnasia, an Athletes' Village and an international exhibition centre, surrounded by a 760-hectare forest and greenbelt.

◆   During the tenth Five-Year Plan period (2001–2005) Beijing would build three green ecological belts, aiming to raise its green coverage to 48 per cent. By 2005, 'the city will realize the complete and safe disposal of treated waste and 96 percent waste waster will also be treated'.

◆   If Beijing gained the nomination 'there will be 5,750 sports venues by 2008 with 23 major stadiums to hold events. And last year a new airport was opened that can move three million passengers a month. Beijing will have 72,000 rooms in 241 quality hotels and there are plans to build a $500 million national theatre on the edge of Tiananmen Square, to hold cultural events during the Games'.

◆   The government plans to spend the equivalent of $15 billion on anti-pollution efforts through 2008, roughly nine times what China's Olympic committee organizers estimate the Games would cost.

Beijing's long-term plan for environmental protection to 2010 had its time-scale reduced to ensure readiness for the 2008 games. From 1998 to 2007, the plan envisaged such features as:

◆   Total expenditure of $12.2 billion on protection and enhancement of the ecological environment;

◆   Fourteen new wastewater treatment plants to be built to improve the sewage treatment rates to 90 per cent from 42 per cent;

◆   240 square kilometres of trees and grass to be planted around Beijing to create a 'green coverage' area of more than 50 per cent;

◆   200 industrial enterprises to change production or be shifted out of the downtown area altogether to reduce pollution levels;

◆   Completion of the fourth and fifth ring roads, five new subway lines, 90 per cent of buses and 70 per cent of taxis to use natural gas.

In all, it was forecast at the time that 280 billion yuan ($33.8 billion) of investment would be made in the period to 2008, mainly in stadia and gymnasia, increasing China's annual GNP growth by 0.3–0.4 per cent and Beijing's by 2.5 per cent (Xin, 2001). With these and other activities, the potential impact of the Olympics would be enormous, adding further to China's growing power and prestige on the international stage, and contributing significantly to Beijing's urban development *per se*. The city would move away from being a producer city towards being a city of consumption, of knowledge-based activities, and a city with an enhanced international profile.

For their part, the visiting panel were impressed by these and other evidence not just by the commitment of Beijing's residents to the Olympic ideal but also that of the nation as a whole. By May 2001 the Olympic Evaluation Commission Report was summarized as:

> This is a government-driven bid with considerable assistance of the NOC (National Olympic Committee). The combination of a good sports concept with complete Government support results in a high quality bid.
>
> The Commission notes the process and pace of change taking place in China and Beijing and the possible challenges caused by population and economic growth in the period leading up to 2008 but is confident that these challenges can be met.
>
> There is an environmental challenge but the strong government actions and investment in this area should resolve this and improve the city.
>
> It is the Commission's belief that a Beijing Games would leave a unique legacy to China and to sport and the Commission is confident that Beijing could organize an excellent Games. (IOC, 2001*b*)

Beijing's success soon afterwards (13 July 2001) was the climax of a series of celebrations, beginning with the return of Hong Kong in 1997, Macao in 1999, the fiftieth Anniversary of the People's Republic of China in 1999, and the eightieth Anniversary of the founding of the CCP in July 2001. Later, China unsuccessfully bid for the 2010 FIFA World Cup but successfully for a World Exposition in Shanghai in 2010. It is difficult to underestimate the symbolic nature of these successes for China's people, the CCP, and the leadership of the nation. It is indeed fair to say that the

Olympics in particular, and the associated city marketing implicitly had a strong ideological purpose, not least insofar as it used the city and its consumption as a focal point for the naturalization of power (Broudehoux, 2004).

Urban Regeneration

The assignment of the 2008 Olympic Games accelerated the course of Beijing's urban change and decisively contributed to its transformation from an impersonal capital into a modern and cultural metropolis (Wang and Bao, 2018). In the years following the bid's success, Beijing saw considerable work and investment towards realizing the Olympic dream, embarking on a massive urban redevelopment plan. In many respects, the Olympics were a national rather than just a city-based event. Key elements of the Olympics were staged away from Beijing, notably, sailing (Qingdao, Shandong Province), equestrian (Hong Kong), and football (Tianjin, Shanghai, Shenyang, and Qinhuangdao). In the case of Qingdao, Shanghai, and Hong Kong these cities are located hundreds, one thousand, and two thousand miles respectively from Beijing itself. Most of the effort and investment, however, was expended in Beijing itself. In 2003, work started on four Olympic venues, with a further eleven begun in 2004. By mid-2006, forty-four major projects were underway. The Olympic Village lay due north of the central city on the main north–south axis, and the now famous main stadium, with its lattice-work structure in the shape of a 'bird's nest'. Its environs for several years had the inevitable sheets of corrugated iron surrounding related construction activities. Beijing International Airport was considerably modernized and expanded through the building of the enormous new Terminal 3. Many new subway lines were built for the Olympics, while a new loop line was opened to the north of the city in 2002.

The Beijing Organizing Committee for the Games of the XXIX Olympiad (BOCOG) held its first plenary session in January 2004 at which it was announced that the first phase of development was complete (Cook, 2006). The second phase would run from 2004 to 2006, leaving the time from 2007 until the Games' Opening Ceremony for test events and fine-tuning. Construction of new hotels, road infrastructure and other essential facilities continued apace, including parks and water recycling centres. The new Opera House (Beijing National Theatre) behind the Great Hall of the People was also completed, notwithstanding the controversies over its huge cost and 'jelly-fish' or 'blob' architectural design (see Broudehoux, 2004; Cook, 2020). On the symbolic side, the new Beijing Olympic logo – 'Chinese Seal, Dancing Beijing' – was unveiled in August 2003, combining 'elements of engraving, calligraphy, painting and poetry' and bringing together elements of the ancient and the modern.

BOCOG, it was announced, was 'requiring all proprietors … to follow "green" environmental guidelines in the construction of Olympic venues' (Lei, 2004). Sustainable development was a key element with the main tasks identified by the executive vice-president of BOCOG as 'controlling air pollution, especially reducing the coal and industrial pollution and vehicle discharges, effective disposal of municipal sewage and municipal refuse, raising the green land acreage to 50 per cent' (*ibid.*). As an indication of success in these endeavours, in March 2006 Chaoyang District became the first urban area in Beijing to be named a 'model ecological zone', following three suburban districts of Yanqing, Pinggu, and Miyun (Li, 2006). Over 60 square kilometres of green zones were created between 2004 and 2008, and according to the municipal authorities: 'Greenbelts cover 43.5 per cent of the district, and green public space has reached an average of 15 square metres per person. Meanwhile, air and water quality has improved' (*ibid.*). The Capital Iron and Steel Works was gradually relocated to a coastal location some distance from the capital in Shandong Province. In the early 2000s it seemed that Beijing's environmental quality was becoming better than it was, with more blue sky days (one of the set targets), more tree planting, more green spaces, increased use of LPG in buses, and greater restrictions on pollution from industry or vehicles. Nevertheless, there were still many concerns before the Games as to the pollution impact upon Olympic athletes, while a number of other concerns also raised disquiet in some quarters.

Pre-Games Controversies

Despite the environmental focus of the Olympic plans and the improvements noted above, data from the European Satellite Agency in October 2005 stressed that Beijing remained the most polluted city in the world, while it and neighbouring provinces have the world's worst levels of nitrogen dioxide (Watts, 2005). Despite the huge volume of tree planting in recent years, China's Olympic plans were disrupted by a huge sandstorm that hit the city on 16 April 2006. Around 330,000 tons of dust were estimated to have fallen on Beijing that day, while the next saw most of north and northwest China enveloped in sandstorms. This was chastening for the authorities, given that it coincided with the Sixth National Conference on Environmental Protection. Addressing the conference, then Premier Wen Jiabao commented: 'Repeated sandstorms should send a warning to us all, we should feel heavy loads on our shoulders while meeting here to discuss environmental problems'. Yet while the government claims to take environmental issues seriously, the pace of social and economic change often outstrips the ability to regulate and control environmental pollution. For example, in 2003 the level of car ownership in Beijing reached the level anticipated for 2010. Much higher taxation rates were announced for large vehicles with rates on small-engine cars being reduced, but in a society with such a fast rate of wealth creation and where social status is increasingly a product of conspicuous consumption, it is probable that most people would not be deterred from buying larger vehicles unless punitive measures were taken. The authorities promised to respond by severely restricting vehicle use while the Olympics took place which meant that since Beijing is a city the size of Los Angeles the impact of any restrictions would be considerable.

Another controversial aspect of the Olympics schedule was demolition to make way for the new structures associated with the Olympics. The set target was 9 million square metres of 'dilapidated housing', replaced by new houses that would supply a living area of 18 square metres per capita (Xin, 2001). This was part of an ongoing process of demolition across the whole city, which particularly threatened the old *hutong* and *siheyuan* areas (Cook, 2000, 2006; Cook and Murray, 2001). Replacement of old neighbourhoods by high-rise apartments, shopping centres, and office towers, led to the dislocation of 'untold thousands of people, to make room for the thousands of development projects swallowing the city' (Yardley, 2005). Notably, just before the Games, the local authorities tried to cloak part of the city, shadowing its real image, through a 'beautification' campaign that aimed to make the city look clean for the duration of the Games. Densely populated, working-class, and ethnic neighbourhoods, south of Tiananmen Square, were 'disguised', keeping them out of tourist and public view. Officials put up green plastic nets, fences, and brick walls to hide slums from passers-by or to block the view of dilapidated buildings (Hooker, 2008). Some argued that the Olympics were built on the ruins of the lives of ordinary and mainly working-class people, followed by the violent displacement of internal migrants, property seizures, and land dispossession (DeLisle, 2008).

In brief, these old, often dilapidated, single-storey houses arranged along narrow lanes, originally with access to the 'Hong Tong' or water well, are in areas that ill befit the dreams of planners and developers concerned with creating the grand structures of an internationalized Olympic metropolis. From 1991 to 2003, 1.5 million people were relocated from such areas out to the high-rise residential blocks in the suburbs (COHRE, 2007*c*). The previous mayor admitted that the difficult problem of resettlement of families affected by this demolition process 'remains to be solved'. The new mayor, Wang Qishan, while admitting that some of these relocation projects violated the law, stated that older parts of the city would still continue to be demolished to make way for the Olympics projects (cited in Cook, 2006). Some estimates suggest that approximately 300,000 people were evicted specifically because of the Olympics, although the Government of the People's Republic of China denied this (Acharya, 2005). Certainly, the main Olympic site is far from the city centre, and in the early 1990s when Cook visited the Geographical Institute of the Chinese Academy of Sciences in that area much of the journey passed fields rather than housing so he finds it hard to see that much of the total urban displacement was due to the Olympics *per se*. Further, some were displaced temporarily while the Olympic area was under construction, with local roads considerably widened at the expense of pre-existing apartment blocks, rebuilt beside narrowed roads after the Olympics.

Nevertheless, the question of population displacement is a reminder that the issue of human rights refuses to disappear. Organizations such as Amnesty International or Human Rights Watch Asia continue to deplore human rights violations by the Chinese authorities. These crystallize around a number of broad themes, such as the overall lack of democracy, use of the death penalty, the occupation of Tibet, Uighur (Muslim) insurgency in Xinjiang Province, and the treatment of the Falun Gong (a Buddhist sect). Security in China, including internet security, is tight so the likelihood of violence marring the Olympics in 2008 was low, but there remained the possibility of public protests concerning these and other potential issues. Indeed, as in other countries previously, the upheaval created by the Games could in fact contribute to protest and dissent. For their part, the Chinese authorities retaliated by defending their human rights record by pointing to the lack of basic rights in countries such as the United States and maintained that the ongoing war on terrorism and the involvement of the USA and UK in Iraq at that time, complete with examples of human rights abuse by US and British soldiers, showed the operation of double standards. In fact, the points made by Cook (2007) proved to be prescient, for the Olympic Torch was beset by protests from Free Tibet activists in many countries and cities, particularly Paris, London, San Francisco, and Athens. This in turn led to counter-protests from People's Republic of China supporters in Hong Kong and China itself. Meanwhile, the Chinese government continued to condemn Western critiques of China's human rights record on the basis that they amount to an imposition of Western cultural values and constitute a fundamental misunderstanding of Chinese culture and the fact that cultural change occurs in China not overnight but over the course of development of a civilization.

Corruption constituted another thorny issue for the Chinese authorities. As shown above, vast sums of foreign investment have entered the country in recent years. Perhaps inevitably, corruption has become a problem for the Chinese government, and some would point to the lack of democratic controls as rendering it very difficult to root out corruption among officials and CCP members. Current President Xi Jinping is leading the internal struggle against corruption in high places. Reports of the first Beijing Olympic official to be sacked over corruption surfaced two years before the

Games (Watts, 2006). According to these reports, Liu Zhihua, a vice-mayor of Beijing responsible for overseeing construction of sporting venues for the Olympics was removed by the Standing Committee of the Beijing Municipal People's Congress for 'corruption and dissoluteness'. He was liable to face the death penalty for financial crimes if found guilty of taking an alleged 10 million yuan as a bribe from developers. The huge amount of money that has been budgeted for the various events and venues means that this may well not be the last such case to come to light. Reporting on the case was suppressed before the Olympics to avoid tarnishing China's image but after the Games in October 2008 Liu did in fact receive a death sentence, suspended for two years to allow his potential 'good behaviour' to commute the sentence to imprisonment.[1]

A final pre-Games concern was the contradictions that apply to the Beijing Olympics in particular (Dickson and Schofield, 2005). The main sponsors for the event include 'calorie-dense beverages (Coca-Cola) and food (McDonalds) as well as motorized transportation (Volkswagen)' (*ibid.*, p. 170). Such sponsorship ran the risk of exacerbating China's growing obesity problem. Other sponsors such as Samsung or Panasonic produce goods that further contribute to a sedentary lifestyle. They argue that 'the world's most populous nation is at the beginning of an explosion in lifestyle-related disease' (*ibid.*, p. 177), a point supported by Cook and Dummer (2004) who observed that the first 'fat camp' was opened in Beijing in 1994. This, they argued, reflected 'a growing problem of obesity as Western 'junk food' becomes increasingly popular in the cities … obesity in young children increasing by over 50% from 1989 to 1997' (*ibid.*, p. 338). Although the Olympics would help to encourage a proportion of China's population to take more exercise, as has happened in previous Olympic cities, Dickson and Schofield (2005, p. 177) maintained that this would be insufficient to offset 'the opportunities for massive multinational globalization and ultimately, globesity'. This would surely be the ultimate irony that the Beijing Olympics might contribute to the couch potato syndrome in China and the rest of the globe.

It is also important to recognize the fact that the Games came at the cost of significant human losses of the workforce which worked throughout the Olympic construction sites. The Chinese Committee itself, declared that six workers were killed during the preparation of the Games. The Chinese apparently had no intention of officially announcing this number, but they were heavily pressured by a report in *The Times* of London that stated 'China hushes up Olympic deaths' (Special Correspondent, 2008; see also Yardley, 2008), which reported ten deaths at the construction site of the new Beijing Olympic Stadium alone. Understandably, the outcry and reaction of international labour unions led those in charge to issue a statement claiming that six people had died in preparations for the Olympics. Moreover, it is reported that the bodies of the dead workers were swiftly removed by the police, while the people in charge of the works and eyewitnesses were reportedly warned that they should not report anything to anyone. The families of the victims were given compensation packages amounting up to £13,000 pounds (about €20,000) – culturally huge when recalling that salaries in construction barely reach €5 per day. The significant human cost of the Games and the desire to minimize the impact of such losses would impact on the image of a global Beijing.

The Games Themselves

There are perhaps two abiding images of the 2008 Beijing Olympics: the sheer awe-inspiring scale and richness of the Games' Opening Ceremony and the vision of Usain Bolt smashing the world record whilst de-accelerating long before the finish of the men's 100 metres. The Opening Ceremony offered a spectacular vision of a city steeped in its own history and yet one that was ready for the challenges facing a nation ready to declare itself a major player in the global economy. Directed by the high-profile film director Zhang Yimou, the ceremony featured over 15,000 performers and cost around $100 million to produce. Perhaps most memorable were the mass participation set pieces that offered a timely symbolic reminder of the sheer power of the Communist ideal. The sense of co-operation and united endeavour was undoubtedly reflective of broader social norms in China and also represented a statement of global intent on the part of the Chinese Communist Party. The ceremony was in part a physical manifestation of the Games' slogan 'One World, One Dream', of a world united by the Olympic ideal of peace and harmony. Equally, however, such a notion reaffirmed China's membership of a world united by the possibilities of consumer capitalism, and by the promise that China was now a fully paid-up member of the global economy.

In many respects then, the Opening Ceremony was more than just a ceremony in constituting a carefully choreographed (in more ways than one) statement of intent and of an arrival on the world stage that mixed Communist images of the obedient masses with the technological wizardry of advanced capitalism. The Opening Ceremony, and indeed the Games as a whole, served to present the Chinese way to the rest of the world and indeed the inherent belief amongst the Chinese people that the Chinese way is the best. This was questioned subsequently, however, when it was revealed that a young girl singer was replaced by another who lip-synched behind the scenes on behalf of her prettier colleague. Similarly, the ubiquitously youthful Olympic volunteers fed into the vision of a youthful newly emerging country and one that was blessed by the riches of hundreds of years of unsurpassed civilization, providing 'an almost picture-perfect blend of idealized chinoiserie and ultra-modern convenience' (Setzekorn, 2008). Even here, however, 'real progress in terms of language fluency and cross-cultural understanding was slight due to the controlled and directed nature of foreigner to volunteer interaction' (*ibid.*)

Although for the rest of the world the efforts of Usain Bolt will perhaps stay longest in the memory, the Chinese people were no doubt most affected by Lou Xiang's Olympic experience. Lou Xiang was literally the face of the Olympics and the fact he was forced to pull out through injury was a devastating blow not only to the people of China but to the CCP itself who were no doubt more than happy to promote Lou Xiang as a symbol of an internationally competitive China and less than happy at his demise. As it happened China topped the Olympic Games medal table achieving 50 gold medals in a total of 100 medals in all; this justified the massive investment on the part of the Communist Party to ensure that China was seen to succeed not only as a host, but, at least for now, as the greatest sporting nation on earth.

The Environmental Impact

As mentioned above, the Beijing city government issued a series of environmental policies to improve environmental standards and air quality. Among others these policies included the closure of factories, the relocation of heavily pollutant enterprises to neighbouring provinces (e.g. Hebei), the suspension of manufacturing production during the Olympics, coal desulfurization in coalfired power plants, and restrictions on the use of polluting vehicles (Wang and Bao, 2018; Zhang *et al.*, 2016). It would seem that the claim that the Beijing Olympics have, despite the negative environmental impact of the construction process itself, left a positive environmental legacy is a questionable one. On the positive side, new green areas were created, including the 'Olympic Green' as a resource for Beijing's citizens, while Watts (2009) reported that restrictions on car use proved to be so successful in reducing air pollution that these restrictions were extended for a further 12 months. This means that, according to the Beijing Traffic Management Bureau, one fifth of the city's 3.6 million private vehicles and a third of official cars continue to be barred from the roads every weekday, thus reducing emissions by 10 per cent, while plans to widen a ban on high-polluting cars and trucks from the centre to cover the whole city will save a similar amount. Such claims were supported by a report by the United Nations Environment Programme (UNEP), published in February 2009.[2] It stated that Beijing had 'raised the environmental bar and the Games left a lasting legacy for the city'. Positive elements included increased awareness of environmental issues across China but especially in Beijing, among residents and businesses alike; the introduction of Euro IV emission standards for cars instead of the Euro II; creation of '8,800 hectares of green space … using more than 30 million trees and rose bushes'; and a rise in blue sky days from 'less than 180 in 2000 to 274 days in 2008'. Lesser improvements were also recorded in waste disposal and recycling.

This positive 'big tick' for the Olympic environmental improvements was not, however, supported by an analysis of particulate matter in an eight-week period around the Games. The analysis, involving US and Chinese environmental scientists, caused some controversy in China, and led to the Chinese author backtracking on the article's conclusions.[3] The study, by scientists from Oregon State University and Peking University, funded by the National Science Foundations of the USA and China, found that the level of particulate pollution in Beijing was twice as bad as in Athens, Greece; three times as bad as in Atlanta, Georgia; and 3.5 times as bad as in Sydney, Australia. The authors suggested that some pollution was due to the movement of regional air mass from polluted regions beyond the city, but also that good weather on other occasions was responsible for reduction in air pollution to a greater extent than anti-pollution policies. Wang *et al.* (2010) found similarly that weather conditions in the wider Beijing area were also important, with variation in pollution being partly dependent on whether the airflow came from dirtier or cleaner regions and how much rainfall there was to dampen down air pollution, but that policies also had a significant influence. Cook had conducted regular field courses in Beijing over a twenty-year period from 1992 to 2012 and could bear witness to the fact that Beijing air quality improved around the time of the Olympics. By 2010, however, the problem of dust storms had reappeared, and by the time of a research visit to Tsinghua University in Beijing in 2013 air pollution in the city had once again reached crisis proportions, especially in the downtown area. This is not least due to the expansion in car ownership in the city, with 800,000 being sold in 2010 alone (Zhang, 2014, p. 155).

The 'Green Olympics' advocated environmental protection through the reduction of carbon emissions in the city. The policies adopted would supposedly have led to the increase of environmental efficiency, to resource and ecological balance, and finally to the promotion of sustainable development and green lifestyle (Long *et al.*, 2018). However, various authors illustrate the fact that the effects of these policies were quite unsustainable, did not have a long-term effect, and lacked continuity. This is the case, especially, when it comes to Beijing's air quality. For example, Long *et al.* (*ibid.*) found that even if the environmental efficiency of Beijing was positively affected during and after the Olympic Games, it negatively affected neighbouring cities, revealing that 'pollution-intensive industries might transfer from Beijing to its neighbour provinces' (*ibid*, p. 1431). Chen *et al.* (2013) compared how the air quality of Beijing changed before, during and after the Olympics. Even if they sought a significant improvement, the latter eroded one year later by approximately 60 per cent. In a similar vein, Zhang *et al.* (2016) agreed that Beijing's air quality improved remarkably between 2008 and 2010, with the average annual air pollution days reduced by 25 days. However, in the long-term these effects gradually disappeared after 2010. In fact, in 2012 the air quality returned to the level last seen before the Olympics. This is related to the fact that energy use and consumption varies throughout the seasons. It is no coincidence that any improvement related to any season other than winter, which accounts for about half the pollution days of a single year. This suggests that the overall improvement in the air quality of the city was very small overall. According to Zhang *et al.* (*ibid.*, pp. 37–38):

> the reason why Olympics could not bring long-term improvements to the air quality in Beijing was that many policy measures were short-term provisions. For example, the environmental policies like high polluting enterprises reduce capacity and driving restriction were cancelled after the Olympic Games, thus environmental policy lack of persistence... Therefore, to achieve lasting effort for environmental policies, the policy itself must keep continuity.

The Bird's Nest as White Elephant

As for the longer-term legacy of Beijing 2008, the physical impact of the Games is clear in terms of the massive programme of building work and infrastructural improvements and most notably perhaps the new Olympic subway line reflecting what Li *et al.* (2008, p. 261) described as the emergence of a 'hybrid global megacity'. Yet the smog soon returned to the city and the key sporting venues have largely stood unused. A key area of concern regarding the legacy of Beijing 2008 is one that is also found elsewhere with other Olympics, namely, who will pay for and utilize the new Olympic facilities, in particular the spectacular Bird's Nest. During field work in Beijing in March 2009, Cook first became aware that, at least for some, there were concerns that the Bird's Nest might become a White Elephant with very expensive upkeep. The construction cost of this magnificent stadium has been reported as 3.5 billion RMB or Renminbi (approximately $427 million) and the maintenance cost 170 million RMB. There are also loan costs to pay, as well as maintenance. One suggested solution was that the biggest football (soccer) team in Beijing, Beijing Guo An, would take over the stadium but, although football is increasingly popular in China, it is highly unlikely that support for this team would be sufficient to maintain such a huge stadium, while there are also high costs involved in preparing the pitch for each match (see also chapter 14). Sponsorship for the stadium by the likes of Adidas was also considered but rejected due to the national importance of the venue. Instead, it would seem that a combination of

Figure 15.2. The Bird's Nest: Beijing National Stadium, September 2022. (*Source*: Photograph, CC N509FZ)

visitor numbers (thousands pay 50 RMB to enter the stadium) and cultural events including a 'Charm of China' summer concert series involving such celebrities as Placido Domingo and Jackie Chan will be used to raise the funds required to keep this enormous stadium going. Another possibility is that the stadium is reinvented as a shopping and entertainment complex. Since then, it became a central feature in the 2022 Winter Olympics, albeit with the same problems likely to emerge.

The Bird's Nest does not, of course, exist in glorious iconic isolation. It sits beside the Beijing National Aquatic Centre 'The Water Cube', which is just as architecturally striking. The maintenance of such buildings is excessively expensive whilst the long-term use of facilities is questionable. For example, there appears to be limited need for a public swimming facility of this kind, and it is more likely to be used in the long term as a venue for elite aquatic sports. Some of the other facilities available on Olympic Park will no doubt in time be demolished. What remains is most likely to offer some kind of private haven: a space of elite consumption founded upon the memories of three weeks in the summer of 2008. This reflects a broader concern that the primary long-term impact of the Olympic Games is to redefine Beijing as a space for consumption so that the Olympic Green area in particular becomes a glitzy space for privatized public pleasures. As Marvin (2008, p. 249) put it:

> The official version of post-Olympic commercial, exhibition, sports, and entertainment spaces on the Green and elsewhere paints a civic picture of obedient consumers attuned more to immediate gratification than politics. In Lefebvrian terms the Green is a wholly new conceived space, a cagey gamble by a new generation of rulers who are betting that stripping national space of overt political content will diffuse its potential for 'lived' protest. They are likely to be encouraged by nearly two decades of public response to commercial malls and nighttime strips.

The concern here is that while the Olympics has transformed the city of Beijing, it has done so at considerable cost by adopting a model that is all about developing leisure enclaves for the rich that have simply served to impoverish the public life of the city. The primary role of the Olympics, as we suggested above, is a symbolic one that is concerned with portraying a confident harmonious China, but the problem is that China is more harmonious for some than for others, with the *fu-erdai* or scions of the rich being seen as a problem today (Garst, 2015). Indeed, the costs of the Olympics inevitably falls on those who least benefit from them. In quoting the pertinent figures, the Beijing municipal government, for example, spent over $10 billion on transport and infrastructure. Broudehoux (2004) argues that such investment blindly disregards local needs, there being no hard evidence that the local population actually benefits from the anticipated economic boom that would result (which in turn was belied by the effects of a world economic downturn). For Broudehoux (*ibid.*) the winners in such a scenario are always the multinational businesses involved in sport through sports, tourism, and property whilst the locals are left to deal with increased taxation, soaring rents, and restricted civil liberties.

Branding

Beijing 2008 is best conceptualized as a concerted and choreographed attempt to enhance China's cultural soft power and brand-building process to the rest of the world (Grix and Brannagan, 2016). For many commentators (e.g. Brownell, 2013), the Games were the appropriate occasion for China to improve its national image worldwide. Li (2017) explored the role of the Olympics in branding China while exercising its soft power. In his view, China utilized the Games to market its cultural attraction, rather than its economic modernization, to the foreign markets. This strategy managed to build the emotional side of China's brand characterized by Olympic Spirit, innovation, and cooperation, integrating the concept of soft power with the national branding process through the sectors of export brands and culture. In part, this discussion concerns the different levels of branding to which different institutions and actors at different levels are exposed. At the national level, the People's Republic of China has to a great extent overcome many negative external perceptions of China as a rather severe, autocratic, dictatorial society in which dissent is not tolerated, giving an impression of 'a peaceful China, a civilized China, and a progressive China' according to Te (2009, p. 84).

The International Olympic Committee (IOC) agreed with this view, insisting that 'lasting legacies' were produced for Beijing and its people, and that as regards criticisms of human rights, 'the games have elevated international dialogue on such issues' as the leader of the IOC evaluation commission put it (CBS News, 2009). Others may be less sanguine, including those who welcomed the alternative Tibetan Freedom Torch that was carried through more than fifty cities before completing its journey near the Tibet border in Ladakh, India, or the 149 people who applied for permission to protest at the three officially designated protest zones – all seventy-seven applications were withdrawn or rejected (Radio Free Asia, 2008) 'and in one case two elderly women who had applied to protest were initially sentenced to re-education by labour, though this sentence was later cancelled' (Fahey, 2009, p. 384). Chinese citizens, nonetheless, 'displayed new standards of national quality development', of 'civilization', 'passion' and 'smile' (Te, 2009, pp. 88–89).

Such contrasting perspectives are also shown in the survey conducted by Zhang and Zhao (2009) in different locations in Beijing, Tiananmen, Sanlitun, and Houhai, with 100 respondents. There were high ratings of Beijing's position and power in international affairs and of the cultural significance of the city. 'In ranking, the respondents considered the tangible, eye-catching indigenous liberal arts and ancient architectures as the foremost representative cultural symbols of Beijing' (*ibid.*, p. 250). In contrast were low scores on 'liveability', with low ratings for 'ecological conditions, the provision of public amenities, the standard of public services, and urban governance' (*ibid.*). The sustainability of environmental improvements via the Games was questioned, while there were also concerns about rising property prices, notwithstanding the global recession. Despite successes during the Games:

> the respondents were sceptical about the introduction of a new quality of life and the common good by the Beijing Olympics. While official branding tried to sell the friendly, smiling and comfortable city, people generally thought that a one-time event could not help to satisfy material needs of the economically and socially marginalized groups (including the city's laid-off workers and rural low-skilled migrants working in the city). (*Ibid.*, pp. 251–252).

Conclusion

There is no doubt that in many ways the Beijing Olympics were an enormous success and that they succeeded in portraying a new confident China to the global audience and China expanded its 'soft power' overseas (Gu and Cook, 2011, p. 124). The human rights issue never went away, images of protestors interrupting the Olympic torch procession were undoubtedly damaging to the CCP, but the image of a revitalized China largely won through, not least as a result of the awe-inspiring opening ceremony.

For Brownell (2008*a*), the greatest bequest of the Beijing Games will be its human and cultural legacy and in particular the way in which the Games provided an opportunity to train Chinese people for a globalizing world. As far as the future of China is concerned the Games have of course played an important role in ensuring China's role as a key player on the world stage: its unrelenting enthusiasm and commitment to the Games reflecting its commitment to not only being a full member of the global community but a leading player in the drive towards the construction of a global society (Close *et al.*, 2007). A key concern in this respect is the degree to which the China that emerged from the 2008 Olympics reflected and reinforced a particular set of values broadly described as those associated with global consumer capitalism; a set of values that are more attainable in theory than in practice for many social groups including the migrant population discussed above. The concern here is the 'one World, one Dream' to which the Games so vocally referred turns out to be a world in which only some components of Chinese society can actually partake.

The abiding question remains: how far were the Beijing Olympics able to change global perceptions of China and its international status? On the one hand, China has undoubtedly asserted itself as a global economic, cultural, and political power since 2008 and the Games played a key role in speeding up this process. However, recent controversies over Beijing's hosting of the Winter Olympics in 2022, and the fact that countries including the USA, United Kingdom, Canada, and Australia announced a diplomatic boycott on these Games in protest against human rights abuses, suggested two things. First, the Olympic Games can and did provide a significant foundation for asserting a country's global presence but are nonetheless incapable of comprehensively 'sportswashing' the realities of human rights abuses on the ground. Secondly, the impact of the Olympic Games and of China's rise to power since 2008 demonstrates that the trajectory of China is such that other nations continue to recoil in horror. Clearly, what scares these nations is not China's sporting prowess, but rather the relentless drive towards global influence and power that the Beijing Olympics uncompromisingly unleashed.

Notes

1. http://www.telegraph.co.uk/news/worldnews/asia/china/3227533/Corrupt-Beijing-vice-mayor-gets-death-sentence.html.

2. http://china.org.cn/environment/report_review/2009-02/19/content_17300306.htm.

3. http://www.usnews.com/articles/science/2009/06/21/study-beijings-air-worse-than-at-past-olympics.html.

Chapter 16

London 2012

Graeme Evans and *Özlem Edizel-Tasci*

The London 2012 Summer Olympics were born out of failure. First came the failure of preceding English cities, Birmingham (1992) and Manchester (1996 and 2000), to bid successfully for this mega-event. The accumulating support for London was therefore fuelled by the realization that only the capital had the capacity, capability, and cachet to compete on a world stage. Secondly, a more domestic failure also stalked London 2012; the ill-fated Millennium Festival centred on the Millennium Dome in London's Greenwich peninsula, which was perceived to be a failure in terms of confused purpose and content, high cost, lower-than-predicted visitor numbers, and critically, the legacy of the iconic building itself (Evans, 1996a). Could London do it better this time – in spectator numbers, experience, media opinion, cost, and legacy uses? On Wednesday 6 July 2005, the International Olympic Committee's meeting in Singapore voted to award the 2012 Summer Olympics to London. The decision represented a combination of Eurovision-style partisanship, tactical voting global schmoozing, and notably the failure of its direct competitors and the long-term favourites.[1] London's *coup de théâtre* was a multicultural-faced group of excited East End children in contrast to the sombre-suited Parisian *messieurs*. These failures therefore informed the strategy for the London 2012 Games and shaped the narratives which have accompanied it across changing political regime.

However, as celebrations began the next day in Stratford, the heart of the prospective Olympic Park, four suicide bombers killed fifty-six people including themselves in attacks on underground trains and a bus in central London. The 2012 award celebration party was cut short and thinking inevitably started to focus on the size of the task ahead, with all its attendant problems. These started with the security concerns, the need to face the renewed terror threat, and the woefully underestimated capital budget used in the successful bid. This not only excluded the extra security costs, but also VAT and other taxes on construction that together added £1.5 billion on to the original £4 billion bid estimate. By March 2007, the publicly funded

Olympic infrastructure budget stood at £9.375 billion, excluding the costs of staging the event, land acquisition, and wider regeneration and transport investment, including the legacy conversion of Olympic facilities themselves.

This chapter provides a critique of the London 2012 Olympic project from the bid period to the post-award development, delivery, and 'post-event' legacy phase ten years on. Earlier editions of this chapter on London 2012 (Evans, 2007, 2010; Evans and Edizel, 2017) focused particularly on the bidding, build up, finances, and aspirations of the 2012 Games, while we have also written in depth elsewhere on how London 'Dressed Up' for the Games (Edizel *et al.*, 2013), the design and master-planning process (Evans, 2015), and historical comparisons (Evans, 2020). London 2012 has also spawned a healthy attention to evaluation, including official meta-evaluation studies, and a wide range of academic perspectives which provide a rich source of material, including many doctoral theses. This chapter will therefore not attempt to synthesize or select but will offer a particular reflection on the event process, its legacy and future planning of the Olympic site, including perspectives from local surveys and resident engagement through follow up research studies undertaken by the authors.

Regeneration Games

In discussing the rationale for hosting hallmark events – whether site, area or sub-regional in scale – (Hall, 1992, p. 29) developed a chronology that identified the period from the early 1960s as 'the city of renewal'. Over fifty years on, it was surprising to note that a review of literature on the Olympics found only nine out of over 2,000 entries specifically on 'regeneration' or 'renewal' (Veal and Toohey, 2012). Articles and reports, and a growing number of edited collections, were dominated by 'impacts' – economic, physical, political (urban regimes and globalization), and tourism – and themes of marketing, image, and place-making. In contrast, analyses of long-term regeneration effects were notable by their absence, despite Barcelona's status as 'exemplar' in this respect. London 2012, however, marked a turning point (preceded perhaps by the urban Beijing Olympics), with regeneration and legacy dominating the Olympic rationale and literature, although Olympic effects tend to be subsumed into wider redevelopment and competitive city narratives. This makes it problematic to measure the true impact and cost of the Games (and similar large-scale, event-based regeneration projects).

In the case of London, this event phase also represents the 'unfinished business' of the precursor London Docklands Development Corporation, which had presided over the development of Canary Wharf and other inner docklands areas between 1979 and 1993, and the London Thames Gateway Development Corporation that had taken over planning powers

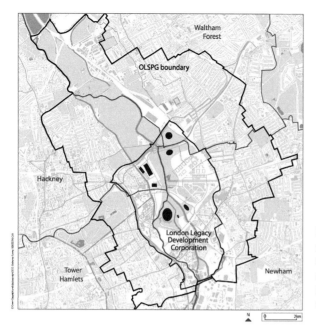

Figure 16.1. LLDC Area map: Olympic Legacy Supplementary Planning Guidance (OLSPG) and LLDC boundaries. (*Source*: GLA, 2012)

from incumbent local authorities in 2005 until it was wound up in 2012 in the spirit of 'localism'. In the decade before London's Olympics bid, successive schemes of area-based regeneration had continued in this area while strategically the Lower Lea Valley, within which the Olympic site is situated, had been designated as a key sub-regional regeneration area in successive London Plans crossing borough boundaries. The mayor's special-purpose Olympic legacy authority, the London Legacy Development Corporation (LLDC) – also with extended land-use planning powers – now operates within these designated areas of the London Boroughs of Hackney, Newham, Tower Hamlets, and Waltham Forest (figure 16.1) until at least 2024.

In London's bid, the greatest emphasis has been placed on the legacy and after-effects of the Olympic leverage opportunity, rather than the event, its content, and purpose. As Allen (2006, p. 3) percipiently indicated: 'Talk of the "Olympic Legacy" is so common that it has started to sound like a tautology; shorthand for the perceived wisdom that the Olympics has everything to do with urban regeneration and only a passing concern with patriotism, athletics or public spectacle'. This presents a fundamental problem to the national Olympic and city regeneration delivery agencies. The financial, land ownership and usage, construction, and related infrastructural and promotional efforts are of necessity dominated by the event delivery objectives and cost pressures and targets. National performance in the competition itself, i.e. in the final medal league table, is the test of sporting success.[2] It is here that compromises in community benefits (social, local economy and procurement), design quality, and after-use, are most likely to be made:

it's now becoming clear that the idea is something of a smokescreen. In practice, it's becoming apparent that this legacy involves putting the narrowly technical demands of the (27) days of the games above everything else, and then trying to adapt the site for long-term use afterwards. (Sudjic, 2006)

The visionary masterplans, artists' impressions and promises at the bidding and consultation stage are just that – promises. Barcelona's Olympic Village housing, for example, was privately sold but not 'affordably' as promised (Nel-lo, 1997), as was also the case in London. The final form and function of the Olympic site is therefore dictated by budget and contractual realities, political stamina, and consensus, as it was in other regenerating Olympic cities.

Following the host city award in 2005, the Olympic Delivery Authority (ODA) and the Mayor's London Development Agency (LDA) hastily took over compulsory land purchase and strategic planning powers in place of the locally elected authorities. The LDA's initial responsibility for land acquisition and preparation was only a transitory role, however, since another unelected body, the Olympic Park Legacy Company (OPLC) was formed in 2009 by the Mayor with national government Communities (DCLG) and Olympics (DCMS) ministers, to further develop and dispose of land and facilities post-event. This new body was itself wound up to be replaced by a Mayoral development corporation, the London Legacy Development Corporation (LLDC) in April 2012 under the central government's 2011 Localism Act. This also transferred land-use planning powers previously held by the London Thames Gateway Development Corporation and ODA to the LLDC, including local authority land within the Olympic zone (figure 16.1).

This fragmented and temporal governance structure contrasts with inner-city regeneration organizations in other countries where a long-term agency is established to see through redevelopment, such as in La Défense (*Établissement public pour l'aménagement de la région de la Défense* – EPAD) in Paris and *Euromediteranée* in Marseilles. This international experience and the lessons from London Docklands in terms of governance, distributive effects, and gentrification (Butler, 2007) do not appear to feature in London 2012 Olympic planning, organizational structures, and evaluation efforts. Rather, the current approach can be seen to mirror this earlier regeneration trajectory of which London 2012 is in many senses an extension both spatially and chronologically, with the Olympic opportunity the new *force majeure* required to remove the barriers to the exceptional levels of public sector investment and top-down land-use development. Historically this also represents the goal of readdressing convergence strategies to tackle the imbalance between west and east London through successive waves of regeneration and the creation of a new 'destination'. This has echoes of earlier

London Olympics and World's Fairs centred on White City in west London (e.g. 1908), where the promotion of electrified railway and underground routes gave access to and from the newly developed outer London suburbs. The reassertion of London via Olympic branding and massive public re-generation investment – inevitably diverting funding away from the regions and regional cities – was enabled, again, by an erstwhile national event.

Olympic Visions

The preceding 'national' public project with sub-regional regeneration goals was the Millennium Dome across the river from Canary Wharf on the Greenwich peninsula. The Greenwich site had been selected as the location for the national Millennium celebration. Part of a £4 billion regeneration of the wider Greenwich peninsula, like the Olympic Park, the site required toxic waste and contaminated soil to be removed prior to construction.[3] Built as the centre of the nation's celebration of the new Millennium in 2000, its vague purpose and escalating capital cost cast a cloud over such *grands projets* in Britain. The four themes of the Millennium Exhibition (The Environment; Art; Culture and Community Activity; and Improved Access to the Natural and Technological World) were intended to deliver 'the best event of its kind in the world'[4] and were echoed in the Olympic visions and delivery programmes promoted by both national and London city governments, as well as host boroughs (table 16.1).

Financing London 2012

The design and development of the London 2012 Olympic project took place during an extreme cycle of economic boom and bust. The bid and cost estimates were produced in an unprecedented period of global consumption and construction growth and in the UK particularly growth in residential development. This boom had been fuelled by further liberalization and availability of credit following the dot.com crash (2000–2001). Low borrowing rates leading to speculation and what became known in the USA as 'sub-prime' lending, led to the downfall of several financial institutions in the USA including Lehmans, the country's fourth largest investment bank, and in the UK, Northern Rock, a demutualized building society. London's capital bid estimates were quickly exposed, as the award made the project a reality. Construction costs rose rapidly as decisions over venue design looked to high-profile developers and star architects to produce the required Olympic effect. History confirms that architects of ambitious schemes – from Koolhaas to Hadid – seldom come in anywhere near their original budget, while global demand for materials and consultants made this 'a suppliers' market'. By the time the global credit crunch and ensuing economic crisis

Table 16.1. London 2012 Olympic and legacy visions. (Source: Evans, 2010, 2015)

London 2012 Olympic Objectives (2005) and Legacy (DCMS, 2007)	London 2012 Olympic Legacy Programmes (LDA, 2009)	UK Government Legacy Commitments (DCMS, 2010)	London Mayor Olympic Legacy Commitments	London 2012 Host Borough Legacy Framework	London Legacy Development Corporation 10 Year Plan (LLDC) (2014)
'Green', sustainable games, Lower Lea Valley regeneration *Making the Olympic Park a blueprint for sustainable living*	Olympic Park & Land delivery	Sustainable communities: Promoting community engagement and achieving participation across all groups in society through the Games	Delivering a sustainable Games and developing sustainable communities	Nexus with physical regeneration	Park – A successful and accessible Park with world-class sporting venues, leisure space for local people
Cultural Legacy, Olympic festivals, Creative Hub *Demonstrating that the UK is a creative, inclusive and welcoming place to live in, visit and for business*	Culture; Tourism and Business	Tourism and Business opportunities: Exploiting to the full the opportunities for economic growth offered by hosting the Games	Showcasing London as a diverse, inclusive, creative and welcoming city	Visitor economy	Place – A new heart for east London securing investment, nurturing talent to create, design and make world-beating twentieth century goods and services
Participation in Sport and Culture *Making the UK a world leading sporting nation; inspiring a generation of young people to take part in volunteering, cultural and physical activity*	Sports participation (including Healthy & Active Workplace)	Harnessing the UK's passion for sport to increase grass roots participation, particularly by young people	Increasing opportunities for Londoners to become involved in sport	Sporting legacy; Culture	People – Park offering leisure space for local people, arenas for thrilling sport, enticing visitor entertainment and a busy programme of sporting, cultural and community events to attract visitors
Park, environmental and transport improvements, Olympic Institute and Media Centre *Transforming the heart of East London*	Tourism & Business; London Employment & Skills Taskforce (LEST)	Ensuring that the Olympic Park can be developed after the Games as one of the principal drivers of regeneration in East London	Ensuring Londoners benefit from new jobs, business and volunteering opportunities; Transforming the heart of East London	Nexus with physical regeneration	Opportunities and transformational change for local people, opening up access to education and jobs, connecting communities and bridging the gap between east London and the rest of the capital

took effect in the United Kingdom during 2007/2008, the Olympic budget overruns were established and unrecoverable. To make things worse, the recession and the drying up of credit limited commercial sponsorship interest and the financing by commercial developers of the Olympic Village, necessitating further public funding and increases to the core budget.

Not surprisingly, the issues of capital and running cost overruns were the main concerns in the development phase, as well as planning for exceptional security and terrorism risks. Like the Millennium Dome, the Olympics were reliant on National Lottery ticket sales – £2.175 billion, up from £1.5 billion in the original budget, via a special Olympic lottery, and ticket revenue of £300 million. A total of 9.6 million tickets were to be available, with 75 per cent of all Olympic Games tickets costing £48, but 25 per cent priced above this level. The diversion of National Lottery funds to the Olympics was controversial in terms of the negative impact on other UK regions and the established beneficiaries of the state lottery (including the arts, heritage, sports, community, charity, education, science, and technology). However, this was expedient as it comprised a 'soft' source of 'off-balance sheet' funding for the government which was technically not public funding or spending. The Lottery had been established by the previous Conservative government in 1994 to provide funding for Good Causes which were to be 'additional' to government's own spending on public services and provision (Evans, 1996a). It was not designed to meet either a shortfall in public sector spending projects or programmes, or be directed by government, but to respond to applicants based on need. Lottery funded projects are also required to meet a public accessibility test. It is doubtful however if either additionality or public benefit tests were adhered to in the Lottery contributions to the Olympic development costs or whether any of the contribution will be repaid from subsequent post-event asset sales, given the ongoing capital spend on the Olympic Park.

While the British public at large could choose whether or not to buy lottery tickets or attend the Olympics, London rate payers had no choice but to pay an extra £20 per annum tax levied to raise a further £625 million towards the Games. The then Labour London Mayor, Ken Livingstone, pledged that Londoners would pay no more than £240 each towards the Games, despite the rising costs. Overspend by the Mayor's development agency (LDA) on land acquisition and other unfunded commitments inevitably had to be recovered via Londoners – whether through direct tax receipts, or reductions in London services (for instance on culture, transport, and regeneration). So it is no surprise that in a 2006 BBC London poll of the public's attitude towards the London Olympics, nearly 80 per cent believed that the Games would end up costing Londoners more than this levy, which turned out to be prescient. Only one bidder emerged for the main London 2012 stadium development and the ODA had difficulty in generating competitive bids for the other venues, as a lack of free market competition drove up prices and placed contractors in an unhealthily strong position (Raco, 2014). When combined with major transport and regeneration projects, the capital risk multiplies. In the case of the Olympics, this risk is ultimately underwritten by the state and municipal authorities, with the most direct and acute impacts falling on local communities and businesses.

Comparing and attributing Olympic Games and related regeneration expenditure is as much of an art as a science (see chapter 6; also Preuss, 2004). When major transport improvements, site clearance and security considerations are considered, total investment rises substantially. In the case of Beijing, an estimated $40 billion was the cost of getting the Chinese capital's infrastructure ready for 2008, with $23 billion for the Games themselves (BBC Sport, 2008). The spectre of the Athens 2004 Games also hovered over London. This eventually required expenditure of $12 billion, more than double the budget, with security costs (post-9/11) and poor ticket sales adding to the deficit. This was in addition to $16 billion in transport and other infrastructure development. Before that, Sydney 2000 cost over $2.8 billion against an initial budget of $1 billion (Cashman, 2006) and Rio's most costly 2016 summer games totalled nearly $14 billion. London 2012 is no exception to this credibility gap between bid estimates, promises and naïve assumptions, and the realities of the land acquisition, construction, and delivery package. The line between Olympics and regeneration and renewal becomes impossible to detect. The twenty-first century capital city Olympic Games have proved to be the most expensive to date. Ironically this was the reason in the previous century (after Tokyo 1964), that these cities became wary of hosting the event, but their interest has returned despite this trend, with major cities, like London, hosting the Games more than once.

The London 2012 Olympic budget quickly increased from the bid stage, with the £1.5 billion operating budget re-estimated at £2 billion; compulsory land purchases and compensation rising from £478 million to over £1 billion; and with construction inflation that was running at 7 per cent (versus 3 per cent in the original budget). The £2.375 billion capital cost of the sports venues alone was forecast by late-2006 to have risen by £900 million to £3.3 billion. In March 2007 the government announced its revised budget of £9.235 billion for the construction and security costs – £5.3 billion higher than at the bid stage – which excludes the event staging costs, land acquisition, and other government Olympic-related programmes (sports and culture programmes) and wider transport and infrastructure investment in and around the Olympic catchment area (Gold and Gold, 2009; see figure 16.2). The cost of individual facility budgets such as the main stadium increased by 20 per cent; and the aquatics centre originally budgeted at £75 million eventually cost £244 million, despite design changes (including the roof span) imposed early on to reduce costs. The Athletes' Village increased

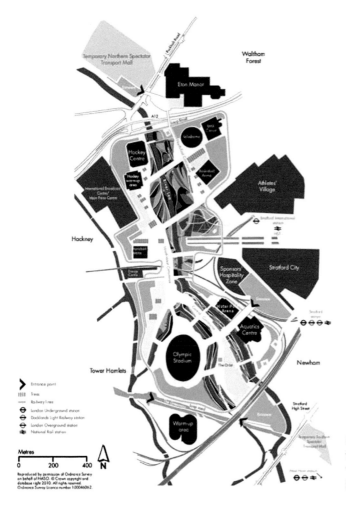

Figure 16.2. Map of the Olympic Park at 'Games time'. (*Source*: LOCOG, 2011)

in cost by over 60 per cent and, with private sector financing unable to be delivered by Lend Lease as the credit crunch hit, the government had to put in an additional £324m of public funding (Evans, 2010).

Frustratingly, a line-by-line comparison between London 2012 budget estimates is difficult to do as the UK government's Public Accounts Committee observed: 'despite the £5.9 billion increase in the public funding for the Games, the department has not specified what will be delivered in return for this expenditure and the current budget cannot be reconciled to the commitments in the original bid' (HCCPA, 2008, p. 5). This opaque reporting of public spending continues with the 'final' outturn figures, where expenditure is grouped under different headings from those used in the bid and revised capital budgets (Grant Thornton *et al.*, 2013) making variance analysis impossible. So, while lead contractors and government claimed that the Olympics were 'delivered on time and on budget', this is based on a 'final' adjusted budget which had already been increased by over 100 per cent, and included substantial contingency in order that this higher budget would not be breached. Despite this, there was overspending on venues, operations, the media centre, Athletes' Village, and ODA programmes.

Good Sports

Britain is a keen sport spectating nation: its spectators were highly visible at team events at Athens 2004 and regulars at other international sporting events such as the FIFA World Cup. Football and major sporting events regularly draw large crowds, albeit with ticket prices for premier events outside of the reach of lower income groups. The Olympics is, of course, a known quantity, and ticket sales for London 2012 were enthusiastically promoted and taken up and wildly oversubscribed online.

An 82 per cent ticket yield was forecast but in fact 11 million tickets (97 per cent) were sold out of a total 11.3 million available. Of these, 8.21 million tickets were Olympic Games tickets and 2.78 million were for the Paralympics. A total of £659 million was raised for LOCOG's operating budget to stage the Games. 319,000 tickets (263,000 Olympic and 55,000 Paralympic) were unsold, the majority of these being early rounds for Olympic Football. However, empty seats were a feature of several events, with a significant proportion of tickets allocated to members of the so-called 'Olympic family' and sponsors, who did not take up their seats. On the sailing finals day, of 851 tickets only one was available to the public, the rest went to sponsors while for Danny Boyle's iconic opening ceremony – one of the most in-demand tickets of the fortnight – only 44 per cent of the tickets were available to the public while 56 per cent went to the 'Olympic family'. On the day in the velodrome when Sir Chris Hoy, Jason Kenny, Phillip Hindes won the men's sprint final, only 43 per cent of tickets were available to the public.

In addition to sports related events, the IOC-designated Cultural Olympiad,[5] an ambitious four-year national cultural programme was held (García, 2013). This included the World Shakespeare Festival, a museums' project 'Stories of the World', 'Unlimited' a festival of deaf and disabled artists, and Artists Taking the Lead which commissioned regional projects. In the case of London, this included 'Bus Tops' – video screens on the top of bus shelters on which artists and the public could create messages and images to be viewed by passengers on the top of double-decker buses. The culmination of the Cultural Olympiad was the London 2012 Festival held from 21 June to 9 September, with a curated programme of 'high quality artistic animations, events, installations and interventions across live performance, film and visual arts' (LOCOG, 2013a). It took place in town centres, squares, and parks across the thirty-three London boroughs and throughout the UK. The London 2012 Festival series of branded events engaged more than 25,000 artists creating 33,631 different cultural activities. There were 11.3 million public attendances at free events and 4.8 million at charged-for events (García, 2013, pp. 17, 68).

Legacy Costs

Public investment does not of course cease at the event stage. Capital and revenue spending continues in the Legacy phase with an estimated spend of over £500 million for the planning, development, and post-Games transformation of the Olympic Park between 2012 and 2016. Most of this was to fall in the three years 2014–2017 after the reopening of the Park, with spending on LLDC Park Operations and Corporate services totalling £80 million (LLDC, 2014). In the latest LLDC plan, further capital spending was budgeted at £383m between 2021 and 2025, with £115m in revenue expenditure over this final period (LLDC, 2021).

A large element in this ongoing capital spend was the conversion of the main stadium to a football ground for West Ham Football Club, costing an additional £274 million, which was unforeseen when the stadium was first designed and built. This 54,000-seater stadium cost £760 million, far more than if it had been designed for this purpose in the first place. Despite the largesse available to a premier league football club, West Ham FC paid only £15 million of these conversion costs and remarkably only £2.5 million p.a. to lease the stadium for ninety-nine years (this sum would be reduced if the club were relegated from the Premier League). There is a fifty-year agreement that sets aside a one-month slot per year to stage athletics at a cost of £3 million p.a. to convert the stadium each year. Cutting the use for athletics would save this sum and turn the stadium into a fulltime football ground, albeit one which currently suffers from poor acoustics, sight lines and atmosphere for football. This one-sided deal with the Premier League club has meant that the LLDC would pay £10 million a year to manage the site, including security on match days. Between 2015 and 2020 the stadium had accumulated £450 million in losses. Not surprisingly, UK Athletics have recently been offered £15 million by the LLDC to cut ties with the stadium in order to reduce these ongoing costs, although this would effectively sever the athletics legacy from the 2012 Games.

Further retrofitting has also been carried out at the nearby ArcelorMittal Orbit tower with a giant slide installed in an attempt to make this attraction more popular; however, it lost £540,000 in 2014–2015 from 120,000 visitors against a business plan forecast of £1.2 million profit from 350,000 visitors. The attraction slid (*sic*) into over £13 million in debt due also to interest charged on the £9 million loan from the 'sponsor', Mittal, an Indian steelmaker. Finally, the lack of a legacy plan for the Aquatic Centre has meant that its internal design and operation is less than ideal (and no substitute for traditional municipal pools, several of which have closed in

Newham and other host boroughs). User access to this centre – best viewed from a distance – is also awkward and illegible. A blue-coloured film has had to be retrofitted to the exterior windows to reduce the glare which had meant that lifeguards could not see swimmers underwater (Evans, 2015).

Local Impacts

London and, more so, the outside world never expected the city to win the 2012 bid. Land acquisition and relocations had, not surprisingly, been taken less than seriously. The planning, IOC review visit, and press support built up a momentum in the last few months, as credibility and confidence grew but second place was regarded as the 'best' outcome. The regeneration legacy was not reliant upon the Olympics; this would be the icing on the cake and provide the international cachet, even to an established world city and cultural capital. London's bid therefore rested pragmatically on both broader regeneration and legacy plans, including explicit 'with' and 'without' the Games scenarios. This formed the consultation roadshow that was rolled out to the East London communities who would be most affected by the regeneration games. The master-planning team, led by the US firm of AECOM (formerly EDAW), with stadium architects Populous (formerly HOK) and urban designers Allies and Morrison, also employed a firm of community architects, Fluid, to undertake the community consultation on the Olympic and Legacy plans (Fluid, 2003). Community Engagement included over thirty public events, the distribution of 400,000 public information leaflets to incumbent households and the requisite (temporary) website.

LOCOG also organized several community meetings and drop-in sessions in the London 2012 host boroughs. Parking restrictions, security issues and additional signage that were to be in place during the Games were introduced during these meetings. An estimated 5,000 people participated in the event programme held in various community venues in the six Olympic boroughs. Local businesses (around 300 firms) and 'hard to reach' groups were also targeted to ensure their voice was at least heard. The firm undertaking the consultation worked with the Lea Valley Matrix Group, but this group had been established and led by the London Development Agency itself, comprising businesses, boroughs, and local regeneration partnerships. It was not a representative or independent community organization (Van Harskamp, 2006). Closer to the Games, the DCMS undertook a host borough survey – a one-off, area-specific survey – that covered the six Olympic host boroughs of Barking & Dagenham, Greenwich, Hackney, Newham, Tower Hamlets and Waltham Forest, in addition to the annual DCMS *Taking Part* Survey[6] which covered the whole of England. We have also incorporated survey data based on focus group meetings held by the authors with local residents living in the four host boroughs immediately bordering the Olympic Park – Hackney, Newham, Tower Hamlets and Waltham Forest (Edizel, 2014; Evans and Edizel, 2021).

Although the importance of local engagement in decision-making through government initiatives had been highlighted (ODPM, 2004) – in order to have strong, empowered and active communities – locals complained that the meetings organized by the Olympic organizations and local authorities were more informative than participative and felt that they were not involved in the decision-making. More than half of the respondents of the Host Borough Survey said that they were not informed about any action or meeting towards community consultation and the ones who *were* engaged with these meetings mentioned that the plans were already set, and the officials were not genuinely asking for the residents' ideas. During a Tower Hamlets focus group, a resident observed: 'they have been holding meetings, but whether the meetings are effective is a different thing … they are holding meetings to tick the boxes, obviously, I don't think they actually impart any information to us', while a Hackney resident said: 'having a meeting is one thing, having people actively participating in the decisions being made is something totally different. I mean, anybody can hold a meeting, but are they really involving groups locally?'.

There were two main reasons for locating the Olympic Park in this area of east London. The first, which needs little emphasis, was the availability of so-called brownfield, or previously developed, land and existing transport extensions to rail and underground systems, including Eurostar and the Jubilee Line Extension (Evans and Shaw, 2001). Given that the Olympic zone, located in the Lower Lee Valley had been the site for industry, waterways, marsh, and farmland for several centuries, this ignored the reality that much of the land developed for the Olympics was open and green space, albeit with neglected canals and a legacy of polluted land and water. As the master planner from developer Lendlease noted:

> Lee Valley and marshes are often described as abandoned, but in fact there were significant and much-loved places there too, some amazing moments of loved use like the beautiful little allotments right by the river and the cycling track, moments of intense activity, but somewhat hidden. It is not really a neighbourhood yet – still more outpost than back garden. It's that feeling of normalness that still isn't quite here yet. (Quoted in Murray, 2020)

While the 'new' Park is promoted as the key additional amenity for this part of London, in fact the Olympic development has produced much new hardscape and reduced the amount of open and green space (figure 16.3). Snaith (2014) also observed that local ethnic minority groups (in a borough that is majority 'non-white') are under-represented in the north of the Park

Figure 16.3. Olympic
development area, 2003
aerial view and 2030 plan.
(*Source*: LLDC, in Evans,
2015)

with 'natural', wide open spaces, while the more urban south attracts a
more locally representative ratio of users, with aesthetic and programmatic
characteristics of the North Park appealing to a more white British user
group than from other groups in the area.

Housing

Housing development was already under way in Stratford and in a number
of canalside developments prior to the Games, so the Athletes' Village (now
renamed East Village) represents the first non-sports legacy, providing 2,800
homes with a mix of private and affordable (50:50) housing, an academy
junior school and health clinic. However, the catchment for these new

community facilities was much wider than the local area. Cost and timing have meant that compromises to the original masterplan had to be made from the planned four to eight-storey blocks to standardized blocks of six to twelve storeys and finally to eight to ten. Housing affordability is a serious misnomer in this case, since for property purchase, the value of a one-bed apartment would require borrowing of five times the average earnings of a Newham resident, while affordable rent can represent 80 per cent of market rates under current government guidelines. Legacy and plan promises of 35 per cent affordable housing in Olympic legacy housing was made up of affordable rent, shared ownership and social rent. This target has already been reduced in the case of Chobham Manor opened in 2016 to 30 per cent (from 40 per cent target) in the new canalside urban villages (1,500 dwellings) of East Wick and Sweetwater. Even here, the affordable housing is funded by the public sector via the LLDC, and according to Bernstock (2014, p. 135): 'another development that is likely to make a relatively negligible impact on the urgent need for genuinely affordable housing in the area'.

At the outset, 30–40,000 new homes were promised by the Local Organizing Committee (LOCOG) much of which were to be affordable and available to key workers such as nurses and teachers. However, ten years on, only 13,000 homes have been built of which only 11 per cent are genuinely affordable. Whilst the LLDC insists that 64 per cent of all homes will consist of 'family housing', this includes two-bedroom flats. As an indication of the high-end housing developed, 'Luxury Living' in East London includes two new tower blocks which welcomes residents to its gated 'village green' – where no dogs, ball games, or unsupervised children are allowed. Built by a development arm of the Qatari Royal family, neither includes a single affordable home, with rents starting at £1,750 per month rising to £4,000 for a penthouse.

A further 1,000 planned homes had already been cut from the revised Legacy plan to accommodate a new 'cultural hub', necessitating additional government capital funding to compensate for the proceeds that the LLDC would previously have received from its delivery of residential developments. This new complex of arts and educational buildings will house the relocated London College of Fashion (University of the Arts London), two new galleries of the Victoria & Albert (V&A) museum, a 500-seat dance venue run by Sadlers Wells Theatre, and the BBC's Orchestra and Music Studios (figure 16.4), with separate facilities for outposts of Loughborough University (London) and University College London (UCL East) nearby. In the words of then-Mayor Boris Johnson: 'the idea behind Olympicopolis is simple and draws on the extraordinary foresight of our Victorian ancestors. We want to use Queen Elizabeth Olympic Park as a catalyst for the industries and technologies in which London now leads the world' (LLDC, 2013).

Figure 16.4. East Bank design showing V&A East, London College of Fashion, BBC Music Studios and Sadlers Wells East. (*Source*: Evans, 2020)

Over 3,000 jobs were claimed to be generated from this development, which was forecast to attract 1.5 million additional visitors to London and generate £2.8 billion of economic value to Stratford. In the words of the then Chancellor, George Osborne: 'this will secure the legacy of our wonderful Olympic Games, as well as creating thousands of jobs and boosting London's economy by an estimated £95m each year'. Olympicopolis, modelled on Albertopolis,[7] a legacy from the 1851 Great Exhibition, was renamed 'East Bank' by the (Labour) Mayor in 2018, pairing the project with London's South Bank cultural quarter and site of the 1951 Festival of Britain. Johnson's rationale for this was also that it would lead to more homes being built in the future in the surrounding area. However, combined costs of this development have increased by over 60 per cent, from £385 million to £628 million, with the LLDC (i.e. the taxpayer) picking up both the risk and majority of these cost increases. While UAL and the BBC are covering two-thirds and a half of their building costs respectively, the V&A and Sadlers Wells Theatre are only paying for the internal fit-outs, not the construction costs.

The attraction of the Olympic zone served by new transport links to central London, Canary Wharf, and the suburbs had already seen the borough of Newham produce the highest increases in average house prices in the UK between 1999 and 2020; up 750 per cent compared with the national average of 200 per cent. At the same time there have been above-average rises in the neighbouring Olympic host borough of Hackney (1,000 per cent) over the same period. This has occurred despite the house price and credit crunch following the banking crisis of 2007/2008.

The Olympics has therefore provided an investment leverage opportunity to accelerate development, with 25 per cent of London's entire housing growth predicated on developments within the Olympic zone. Those respondents who lived in Newham generally agreed that the Games has increased numbers of people moving (63 per cent), while a Hackney resident said of the new accommodation in the Park: 'if they're gonna regenerate the flats into super-duper flats, we're not gonna get the same sort of atmosphere that we have if they're ordinary people living in them. They're gonna send us away since normal people won't be able to afford them'. As a result of improvements in facilities and infrastructure, the area has become more attractive for middle- and high-income groups, and social division remains a challenge. As experienced in other Olympic cities, residents, environmentalists, businesses, creatives, and others were anxious about the negative impacts, spiralling costs and displacement arising from the development. The re-opening of the Park (renamed the Queen Elizabeth Olympic Park after the Games and in celebration of the Queen's Diamond Jubilee), the arrival of new communities and new housing developments and new schools were, not surprisingly, expected to have a significant impact on property prices.

Community Cohesion

Of those host borough residents surveyed, 72 per cent believed that they belong to their local area and 41 per cent that people from different backgrounds get on well in their neighbourhood. However, the views differed when questioned about the effect of the Games on feelings of belonging and community cohesion. It is fair to say that residents did not believe that hosting the Games contributed to community spirit. As a Hackney resident noted: 'I can't see any community spirit generated from hosting the Olympic Games'. Against that, a respondent from Tower Hamlets believed that the Games would strengthen community spirit: 'I think the Olympics have brought the positive side to the East End of London, because it's a once in a lifetime event that is happening in the East End of London. So I don't want to knock the Olympics down in that sense, and I think yes, it will encourage community spirit'.

Opposition to the Olympics was also evident locally, particularly from local housing interests, businesses, and artist groups in the face of displacement (Powell and Marrero-Guillamon, 2012). Ideological resistance was also apparent (Cohen, 2013), but the Olympic good news story and the outsider status of the London bid lessened the negative press. Most observers did not expect the city to win and so opposition was not coordinated. Following the award in July 2005, organized resistance focused on monitoring the development process and legacy promises[8] and on campaigning against land

and premises relocation as the pace of issuing compulsory purchase orders intensified. Three years after the 2004 bid feasibility plan the Olympic Park Masterplan was approved by central and local government. With construction commencing, an infamous and impervious blue wall was erected around the Olympic site cutting off access to and through the area for local people, which intensified local dissatisfaction and exclusion. Despite the Olympic Park development and new access routes, bridges, and pathways, the east–west divide (Stratford, Newham-Hackney Wick), which was master planned to be 'stitched together', persists and communities are still largely territorial in their horizons (Evans, 2015). This divide is exaggerated by the existing canals and river, and from our local community consultations, issues of safety, traffic (e.g. cyclists versus pedestrians), and lack of amenities limit interaction between these neighbourhood communities which effectively face away from the area, despite the new attractions in the Park and on the 'other side'. What remains of local cultural heritage, in terms of industrial and waterside buildings and natural environment, continues to be valued by locals, but again this is undermined by problems of pollution, safety, access, and intrusive management control of the Olympic Park itself (Evans and Edizel, 2017).

Employment

When designated, the area presented a wholly different picture on the ground. Criss-crossed by a maze of river channels and canals, it contained a mosaic of undeveloped flood plain and industrial land. Some of the latter was long derelict, but other sites involved manufacturing facilities and other employment activity which needed to be relocated. Within months of the award to London, Compulsory Purchase Orders were sent to nearly 300 businesses within the Olympic Park zone. These employed over 5,000 in the Marshgate Lane industrial area and several hundred in other sites. Compensation offered to firms who had benefitted from cheap industrial premises in proximity to central London and national transport access was reported to be 20 per cent to 30 per cent less than the original prices paid by owners: 'the Marshgate Lane Business Group argued that the LDA had allocated £450 million to relocate all the businesses when professional advisers to the businesses estimated that the real cost will be more than £1.5 billion' (COHRE, 2007*b*, p. 14). The LDA spent £1.3 billion on this exercise, leaving an excess debt of £500 million after intermediate land sales. Over the course of the land acquisition and clearance of the Lower Lea Valley area, businesses employing nearly 15,000 workers were reportedly forced to move with some firms offered alternative locations over 50 miles (80 km) away. Reluctantly most firms settled or had their appeals turned down at Inquiry. There has been surprisingly little follow up or monitoring of the impact of the enforced relocation of businesses by the LDA or other local authorities, and the direct and indirect loss of employment arising is again not reflected in the headline employment figures predicted for the new leisure-retail economy.

Over 30 per cent of the firms that were relocated to make way for the Olympic development had closed down by 2015. The loss of firms through relocation or cessation obviously has an impact on local employment and multiplier effects on the local economy, but the nature of production also suffers. This included artists and designer–makers located in Acme Studios on Carpenters Road, premises housing 140 studios that are now demolished. New studios have been incorporated in mixed-use developments in Stratford, but these have only replaced a fraction of this provision and the studio community will never be replaced at the previous scale and concentration. It is estimated that over 25 per cent of the UK's total artist studio provision (6,000 artists in 135 buildings) were located in the Olympic host boroughs, occupying genuinely affordable and supportive studio premises. This cultural asset has therefore been at threat, and the gentrification effect continues with the further development of the Hackney Wick and Fish Island industrial buildings for housing. As Millington (2009) observed: 'The irony is that, while London's vibrant, diverse and influential culture has been promoted as a significant aspect of London 2012, the very studio complexes that have contributed to that vitality, along with other supporting businesses such as materials suppliers, are under threat and some have disappeared altogether'.

Ten Years After

A decade on from the 2012 Games, there have been several press features, government reports, and in the case of the Legacy Corporation (LLDC) low key celebrations and events in the Park. Meanwhile the prospective new arts and education residents of the East Bank development (above) look forward to their delayed move in 2023 to the new facilities currently under construction, with Loughborough University (London) and University College London's outposts already occupying part of the Here East building (formerly the Olympic Media Centre). A challenging fact is that the borough of Newham in which this cultural quarter is located has the lowest arts attendance and engagement levels in the entire United Kingdom, so a key measure of success for these organizations is the extent to which they will attract and benefit local communities in the future.

Over the next three years the LLDC, which has controlled the post-event development of the Park and sports facilities, is due to come to an end and hand over planning responsibilities to incumbent local boroughs by the end of 2024: to the east the London Borough of Newham; to the south Tower Hamlets; and to the west and north Hackney and Waltham Forest (see

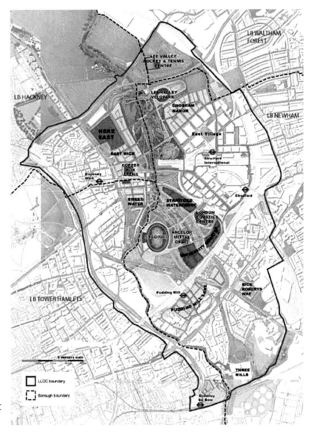

Figure 16.5. Olympic
Park Special Planning
Guidance area and housing/
development zones. (*Source*:
Evans, 2015)

figure 16.5). This administrative geography also underlines the complexity
of land and community stakeholding involved in the regeneration of this
sub-region, although non-local appointees have held the majority on the key
LLDC planning committee, ensuring development approvals despite local
rejection of proposed schemes. This key power will revert to the incumbent
boroughs from 2025, but the management of the Park and estate (e.g. East
Bank, sports facilities, housing, schools etc.) is likely to require a separate
joint coordinating body in the absence of the LLDC (assuming that the
Mayor does not extend the life of the LLDC itself).

The legacy body inherited the Vision and targets set by previous regimes
(see table 16.1) which had already been amended to meet both political and
economic expediencies, notably capital and income budgets and housing
targets, as discussed above. The last ten-year plan to take the Corporation to
handover in 2025 again revisited and revised the key Vision themes. This is
a pattern throughout the London 2012 Olympic regeneration governance
– the superseding of promises, strategic aims, and targets in order to meet
deficits in delivery and cost overruns. The result has been a continuing need
to look to government and the London Mayor for additional public funding
to plug repeated shortfalls in income from land sales and Park events and

facilities and from major overspends in capital projects, notably on the Olympic Stadium and East Bank development.

The 2016–2025 Plan (LLDC, 2016) reframed the three earlier Visions of *Park*, *Place* and *People* into three strategic outcomes: *Opportunity*, *Community* and *Destination*. This new set of 'purposes' has an explicit economic turn. *Opportunity* seeks to stimulate economic growth, attract investment and new jobs while raising perceptions of the area and local engagement. In 2021 yet another Queen Elizabeth Park strategy outlined the key activities the LLDC will take forward to the transition in 2025 in order to support delivery of the 2030 Vision, with '*Opportunity*' recoined as '*Inclusive Growth*' (LLDC, 2021). '*Place*' has morphed into *Community*, using the current terminology of urban place-making and the clustering of new housing neighbourhoods, education, culture, businesses and leisure facilities. Again 'exemplary community engagement' is referred to, but the reality of the development decision-making process makes this goal tokenistic at best. For example, approval was given in 2022 by the LLDC and Mayor to the MSG Dome project, despite over 800 objections.[9] Finally, and ironically, *Destination* replaces '*People*' with a combination of place branding, tourism, and a long-standing aspiration but elusive goal, to link the Park better with the surrounding area. Priority themes to support this revisionist Vision include Convergence, Equalities and Inclusion and ensuring High Quality Design and Environmental Sustainability.

However, the government's official Pre-Games OGIS report using some sixty indicator sets had found 'below average performance for the environmental outcomes indicators', as well as social outcomes indicators, with gains yet to be measured from Olympic facility life-cycle and energy consumption analysis (UEL/TGIS, 2010, p. 25). As Bernstock (2014, p. 202) concluded: 'the real risk is that the area will be regenerated, but with very little benefit to those existing communities.' From the survey of host borough residents carried out just prior to the Games, only a minority thought that preparations had a positive impact on improved housing (28 per cent), education, health, and community facilities (26 per cent), with more agreeing that parks and green spaces (39 per cent) and the image of area (49 per cent) had improved. Respondents also thought that crime, pollution, pressures on local amenities, as well as 'churn' would *increase* over the longer term – hardly an endorsement of the legacy of a 'sustainable community' that the project had promised (see table 16.1).

The 'post-Games' Impact Study (OGIS), the last to be required under the IOC regime, reported three years on from the Games (UEL, 2015), using secondary data on which a selected group of sixty-seven socio-economic and environmental indicators and performance are calculated in addressing these targets and themes. Most of these indicators are not measurable at the local area level, so cannot reasonably be attributed to any Olympic Games effect. The reality, of course, is that with natural turnover of households in this dynamic area of London, with high levels of both international and internal migration and gentrification, including direct effects of Olympic regeneration, the profile of this sub-region has not surprisingly improved (or rather, the population has changed). Across most selected social, economic and environmental indicators the OGIS reports an improvement over the pre- and Games-time impact studies, the latter underpinned by the massive clean-up and transport infrastructure investment both prior to and as part of the Games development.

What this exercise confirms, but also masks, is the extent of gentrification from the development stage to this post-event milestone. Not only an influx of wealthier households and the displacement of the previous population due to increasing unaffordability of rent and local services, but the breakup of established communities and social networks. In the period prior to the Games to this reporting point (2010–2016) the Olympic regeneration area had the highest gentrification index value in London as a whole, and the highest of all in the Olympic Village housing itself (Trust for London, 2016). The OGIS did not select these particular indicators or smaller area statistics in its methodology. Perhaps the most Games-specific indicator which even the OGIS could not ignore, was participation in sport, which the 2015 report confirmed, did not provide evidence for a step change in London or the host boroughs as was expected of the London 2012 Games. This was confirmed by primary research undertaken locally by the Olympic Regeneration in East London (ORiEL) study of physical and mental health. This longitudinal cohort study of adolescents and their parents in the host borough areas found limited evidence that the London 2012 Olympic and Paralympic Games had a positive effect on adolescent or parental physical activity, mental health, or wellbeing (Cummins *et al.*, 2018).

Conclusion

The Queen Elizabeth Olympic Park – the word park being a misnomer given the amount of hardscape, buildings and roads – is the main tangible amenity the Games provided, with new and converted housing literally populating what was a low-density group of urban neighbourhoods. However, it is the economic regeneration and consequent social benefits – given the association of poor housing, health, education and crime, poverty, and lack of work – that have been used to justify the sustainability of London 2012, and ultimately the longer-term benefits to offset the explicitly stated and indeterminate direct and indirect costs. For the long-term financial sustainability of the Olympic zone, beyond the transition from the current legacy operation, the LLDC look to completion of current developments – which are not due to be finished until the early- to mid-2030s – before dependency on public-sector subsidy can be avoided, and even in this case this will not include the ongoing costs of supporting the London Stadium. Therefore, twenty-five years on from London 2012 public funding is still likely to be needed to maintain the Park legacy.

Meanwhile, ten years on, major building work is still underway, with delays caused by the COVID-19 pandemic putting back the completion of the cultural and education East Bank Quarter and the International Quarter by two years. Both of these capital projects highlight the ongoing public rather than private investment which represents a costly legacy to the public purse. Cost overruns on the East Bank buildings are largely underwritten by the LLDC or, in other words, London taxpayers, while the new tenants of the Stratford International Quarter tower block developed by Lendlease reveals the reliance on public and charitable bodies – Transport for London, HMRC (tax authority), the Financial Conduct Authority, UNICEF, Cancer Research and the British Council.

In terms of regeneration, the overarching rationale for hosting the Games, one has to ask: would you start from here? Basing the scale of regeneration envisaged on the premise of an Olympic Games with all the attendant structures and assemblages (governance, physical, financial), the answer would probably be: no. This explains in part the schizophrenic nature of the building and landscaping, the zonal separations that are being created, and the substantial efforts that design and engineering teams have made at all levels to maintain both the master planned vision and legacy aspirations. It seems that once the project turned from area regeneration to one of destination and placemaking, designers are challenged in working with confidence over who or what they are designing for. This grand piece of urban design strains to keep its coherence as exigencies and political imperatives take over, with the Olympian visions necessary to maintain this trajectory continuing to rely on hyperbole and over-optimistic forecasts of jobs, investment, homes, and community (Evans, 2015).

From the outset, the prime reason for locating this extreme example of event-led regeneration was to accelerate house-building and social and economic development in the sub-region or, to use a more recent political phrase, to 'level up' the area. Yet with the Legacy Corporation's own projections still looking to the 2030s, it will be twenty-five years or more from the Games before the vision and public investment is complete. The legacy is a Park that is not really a park (little green space or shelter/trees, no ball games, no dogs) with new housing that struggles to establish real neighbourhoods or community; in truth an event space within which sit fragmented apartment blocks, amenities, and isolated sports venues.

The counterfactual – what would have happened without the Olympics in terms of regeneration and what were the opportunity costs from the public investment – can never be answered. Yet these are the most important questions underlying the Olympic regeneration's rationale, on which the London bid rested. As Hall (1992, p. 83) suggested:

it should be recognised that social impact evaluation will ask the difficult question of who benefits? A question which goes to the very heart of why cities host hallmark events in order to improve or rejuvenate their image and attract tourism and investment.

Notes

1. A misplaced vote might have helped London win the 2012 Olympics. Moscow and New York were eliminated in the first two rounds. An IOC member (President of the Greek Olympic Committee) had then mistakenly voted for Paris rather than Madrid in the third round. Paris received thirty-three votes to Madrid's thirty-one in that round, eliminating the Spanish capital. Had Madrid received the vote rather than Paris, the cities would have tied with 32 each, seven fewer than London, and entered a tiebreaker. London beat Paris 54–50 in the final round. In the run up to the IOC vote in Singapore, London was still ranked third after Paris, the clear favourite, and Madrid. No city had hosted the Games more than twice (London and Paris) and London had never won by competition, only hosting by default in 1908 and 1948.

2. According to the Chief Executive of the British Olympic Association: 'The sole measurement of the Games won't be on how efficient the organizing committee is, or how beautifully architectured the design of the stadiums are – it'll be decided on how many British athletes stand on the podium and collect medals' (http://ukolympics.org.uk, accessed 1 December 2006). The official target was to improve the place in the Olympic medal table from tenth in 2004 to fourth in 2012 and the results went beyond expectations. Great Britain moved to third place in the 2012 Summer Olympics Medal Table, and up to second in Rio 2016, but fell to fourth place in Tokyo 2020(21). However, even at this Games, 35 per cent of British medal winners were private school-educated – up from 32 per cent at Rio 2016 – nearly 50 per cent if boxing and BMX (which was added as an Olympic sport in 2008), are excluded.

3. The Olympic site located in this part of East London had traditionally been the dumping ground for toxic waste, including mustard gas stored during World War I, as well as engineering and manufacturing that produced pollutants resulting in poisoned soil and water.

4. The main criticisms of the Millennium project were the escalating cost and unclear purpose and content, as well as the problem of promoting the event as a national celebration in a non-central London location (Evans, 1996*b*, 1999). Despite this, the experience of visitors was generally positive with 88 per cent saying that they had a 'fun day' (BBC 'Vote on the Dome'). The final cost of the Dome was £790 million, of which £600 million was funded by the National Lottery and the balance from ticket sales. This was £200 million or 50 per cent over the original budget estimate, due to a shortfall in visitor numbers – around 6.5 million people came, compared with 12–18 million in the original business plan (Price Waterhouse, 1994; Evans, 1996*a*). The situation was exacerbated by the failure to secure its after-use and disposal. By 2005 the costs of annual insurance and security costs for the vacant facility were put at £1 million. The site had been sold following the year-long 'Millennium Experience' exhibition in December 2001 to Meridian Delta Ltd, a subsidiary of Quintain Estates & Development and Lend Lease (backed by Philip Anschutz, American billionaire oil, rail, sport and telecoms entrepreneur) with unfulfilled plans for a 20,000 seat sports and entertainment venue, and a housing and office development on the surrounding 150 acres (60.7 ha). Lendlease, an Australian property development company was also the

developer of the Olympic Village, housing athletes and providing a mix of social and private housing after the 2012 games. The Chief Executive (CEO) of the Olympic Delivery Authority (ODA) David Higgins was also CEO of the Lendlease Group from 1995. In May 2005 Anschutz sold the rights to the Dome to O2, a mobile phone company. The refurbished Dome with 20,000 seats and rebranded the O2, was reopened to the public on 24 June 2007 with naming rights extended to 2027. A bid for the O2 to host the UK's first 'super casino' failed in 2007 when the government awarded this licence to Manchester. For the 2012 Olympics, the Dome and adjoining temporary arenas were designated for use as venues for the artistic gymnastics, trampolining, and basketball finals. Due to IOC sponsorship regulations however, it was to be officially known as the 'North Greenwich Arena' during the Games.

5.   The Cultural Olympiad is an IOC 'branded' event, encompassing the opening, medal and closing ceremonies, torch relay and a national event programme delivered for London 2012 regionally by the Arts Council, the BBC and Royal Philharmonic Orchestra with local events promoted by the Greater London Authority, local and regional authorities. The London Legacy Development Corporation is also responsible for public art, installations and related events as well as other cultural aspects of the Park design and heritage, including supporting The Yard, a local theatre in Hackney Wick.

6.   *Taking Part* is a survey undertaken by DCMS which collects data on many aspects of leisure, culture and sport participation in England, as well as an in-depth range of socio-demographic information on respondents. The Host Borough Survey was a one-off, area-specific survey commissioned to inform the Meta-Evaluation of London 2012 Olympics and gathered information of the views, behaviours, and attitudes of the residents in the six Olympic host boroughs. The raw data from the Host Borough Survey have been analysed together with the focus group meetings with local residents to have more realistic and in-depth results on what people thought about the London 2012 related regeneration and their involvement in the decision-making process. These two data sets were collected around the same time periods and targeted to understand similar issues; therefore, they were easily integrated in this analysis, using a mixed method to gain an understanding of the community approach (Edizel, 2014; see also Host Boroughs, 2011).

7.   A key difference between Albertopolis and Olympicopolis is that the latter has been predominately publicly funded by the state (i.e. tax payers), albeit for substantial private benefit to commercial developers, landlords/holders and investors. The Great Exhibition and subsequent exhibitions had in contrast been financed by private subscription, whilst entrepreneurs and industrialists had developed much of the infrastructure (Evans, 2020).

8.   Games Monitor: debunking the Olympic myths (www.gamesmonitor.org/uk) and see Blowe (2004).

9.   Developed by Madison Square Garden (MSG) Entertainment Corp, the Dome is a large entertainment venue next to Stratford station, designed as a gigantic glowing ball as tall as Big Ben, with 36 million LED lights and seating for up to 21,500 people. Opposed by every local council, nonetheless it was approved by the unelected majority on the LLDC Planning Committee. As local MP Lyn Brown complained: 'This monstrous glowing orb makes a mockery of east London's Olympic Legacy (quoted in Wainwright, 2021, p. 8). Meanwhile, the demountable hexagon of the Abba Journey Arena will host the virtual concert residency at the southern end of the Olympic Park for five years (Moore, 2022, p. 30).

Chapter 17

Rio de Janeiro 2016

Gabriel Silvestre and *Erick Omena de Melo*

The Rio de Janeiro 2016 Olympic Games may well be the last chapter in the expansionist cycle of aligning large-scale urban development projects with the hosting of mega-events (Flyvbjerg *et al.*, 2021; also chapter 10 above). According to the plans presented in the candidature and further expanded once Rio was granted the hosting rights by the International Olympic Committee (IOC) in Copenhagen in October 2009, it included not only building and refurbishing new and existing sports facilities in the city, but also an ambitious package of infrastructural projects with improvements to the transport network (metro lines, light railway, bus rapid transit, cycling lanes, roads, tunnels, flyovers), public spaces (parkland, waterfront regeneration), museums, environmental programmes, and utilities infrastructure among others. As a result, the expectation was that the city and the population would benefit from the legacies of venues built for the Olympics and repurposed for wider uses as well as from the leverage of infrastructural projects tied with the event deadline that would address urban development targets (Lauermann, 2019). However, the track record of host cities following this 'mega-event strategy' (Andranovich *et al.*, 2001) has been contested and marked by cost overruns, corruption scandals, social impacts, and democratic deficits. In addition, the increased gigantism of the Olympic competitions and the specialist requirements have recently been accompanied by diminishing interest in hosting them and by public scepticism. This has led to claims that mega-events may well have reached their 'peak event' and have now entered a period of decline (Müller *et al.*, 2021).

In this chapter, we analyse how the urban interventions carried out in Rio de Janeiro for the 2016 Olympic Games can be understood through a multi-scalar process involving the Olympic governance system, the mega-event global complex, governments, and private interests at different levels as well as the host population. Rather than a particular episode of Olympic hosting, we argue that the successful bid for the 2016 Games exemplifies the contemporary phase of mega-event hosting as a way to promote urban development. The first section examines the history of Olympic bids presented in the name of Brazilian cities since the early 1990s alongside the development of a mega-event industry. The continuous refinement and changes in the strategy to attain hosting rights were reflexive to the changes in the candidature process and to the structuring of a network of consultants, experts, forums, and suppliers. The following section provides an analysis of the different areas of the city that were significantly affected by the programme of works associated with the event, including the Olympic Park and Village, other Olympic clusters, the Maracanã stadium, the docklands area, and the transport network. We consider both the history of these places as well as the Games' impacts six years after the event. Finally, we conclude by considering what the Olympics represented to Rio and Brazil as well as to the IOC.

Rio de Janeiro as a Model Olympic City

Between the early 1990s and the late 2000s, four candidatures were presented for the Olympic Games to take place in Brazil. First, the unrealistic proposal for the 2000 Games to be held in the federal capital of Brasília and then three bids to host the event in Rio de Janeiro for the Games of 2004, 2012 and 2016. Except for bids presented by Spain and Turkey, no other nation was so persistent in seeking to organize the world's greatest event. During these decades, the bidding for sports and cultural events evolved into a global industry leading to the formation of a mega-event complex. In reference to the Olympic Games, this comprised, among others, international consultants and specialist service providers (e.g. venue architects, planners, security specialists, and media strategists), as well as new organizations (e.g. the World Union of Olympic Cities) and forums for aspirant hosts (such as industry fairs specific to mega-events); in addition to the existing Olympic governance system including the IOC, National Olympic Committees (NOCs), and International Sports Federations (IFs), among several others (Chappelet, 2016). An analysis of the Brazilian bids presented provides a window on how the restructuring of the candidature process led by the IOC was accompanied by the evolution of this industry and by corresponding changes in the tactics by candidate cities to increase their chances of being awarded with the hosting rights. Ultimately, we argue that the Rio de Janeiro bid for the 2016 Games was exemplary in incorporating lessons of what it takes to be successfully nominated and to play to the rules of the mega-event complex.

After a period of low interest to host Olympic events, the number of candidatures increased again from the mid-1980s culminating with the 1992 Olympic Games in Barcelona, an important marker in terms of city marketing and urban development besides the organization of the mega-event. Until the candidature process to the 2000 Olympic Games, the bidding consisted of interested hosts announcing their intentions, paying a registration fee and providing information to the IOC about their plans. They would then be visited by IOC members and the candidatures would be voted on by delegates. In this context, a group of local business leaders articulated a bid in 1990 to organize the 2000 Olympic Games in Brasília to mark the five-hundredth anniversary of the arrival of the Portuguese explorers to Brazil, gaining timid presidential support and the tacit assistance of the Brazilian NOC. A masterplan was commissioned from renowned architects Oscar Niemeyer and Ruy Ohtake and promoted by figures such as the footballer Pelé and FIFA president João Havelange. However, after visiting Brasília and seeing the limited sports infrastructure in place, the then IOC president Juan Antonio Samaranch advised the bid to be withdrawn. The IOC Enquiry Commission (1993, p. 49) diplomatically noted the minimal planning in place while trying to be positive for future aspirations: 'Brasília's plans have the basic elements for a good Olympic Bid for the future. However, the bid could be vastly improved with earlier planning and the involvement of sports experts within the Bid Committee'.

Just as the Brasília candidature faltered, politicians and business figures in the city of Rio de Janeiro embarked on a more concerted enterprise to bid for the event. The project emerged from the policy exchange taking place between policy actors from Barcelona and Rio in the context of drafting a city strategic plan (Silvestre, 2020). The event was favoured as a catalyst to achieve political support and funding for urban interventions in Rio. Catalan experts involved in the organization of the 1992 event prepared the studies and led the proposal to use the Olympics to facilitate the development of neglected areas in the city's North End and the docklands. Influenced by what was achieved in Barcelona, it was expected that the proposed urban interventions would 'produce balsamic effects over the urban tissue with processes of regeneration and redevelopment' (Lluis Millet in Silvestre, 2017). At this stage, due to the increased number of candidatures and speculative bids exemplified by Brasília 2000, the IOC introduced a two-stage bidding process with a more structured evaluation visit and shortlisting of credible plans. The first Rio de Janeiro bid did not make the shortlist, with questions raised around the issues of security and transport.

A change of direction to the aspiration of hosting the Games in Rio was taken by the new president of the Brazilian NOC, former Olympic volleyball player Carlos Arthur Nuzman, with the support of Rio de Janeiro's mayor, Cesar Maia. Nuzman skilfully positioned himself as an intermediary between the Olympic governance system and the Rio and Brazilian political class, boosted by his appointment as an IOC member and increased levels of federal grants to the Brazilian Olympic Committee (BOC) to support elite sports.

Both the mayor and the BOC president dismissed the previous developmental approach taken in the 2004 bid to argue that it was influenced by political interests and that 'gone were the days in which the hosting of the Olympics was synonymous with the salvation of all the problems of a city. Today, the IOC understands that the city needs to meet basic requirements in the first place' (Nuzman, 2002, in Silvestre, 2020, p. 137). They argued that the event should be organized in the prosperous region of Barra da Tijuca, an urban frontier for middle-class housing, as it would be possible to build '70 per cent to 80 per cent of Olympic facilities' (*ibid.*). In addition, quoting the advice of Samaranch, chances would be increased if attention was given to hosting the Pan American Games instead, as a way of demonstrating the seriousness and credibility of Rio de Janeiro's ambitions. As a result, the 2007 Pan American Games was organized in Rio with new venues built within the Jacarepaguá motor racing track and a new 45,000-seat stadium in the North End, claiming to follow 'Olympic standards' beyond the requirements for the regional event.

In the process of the preparations for the 2007 Pan American Games, a new bid was submitted for the 2012 Games. This time, specialist expertise was sought from Australian consultants involved in the 2000 Sydney Games, a group that leveraged opportunities with the development of the mega-event industry to assist the IOC with knowledge transfer services and private consultancy (Cashman and Harris, 2012). The approach was to concentrate facilities within a large Olympic Park, as in Sydney's Homebush Bay, and make mediatic use of the natural surroundings. The bid was unsuccessful once again, failing to make it to the shortlist announced in 2004. However, the organization of the Pan American Games was explored by Nuzman and Maia as a demonstration of successful hosting of an international event and of having an appropriate sports infrastructure in place.

A new bid was submitted for the 2016 Olympic Games. This time, the context was very different to the previous attempts with Brazil rising as a global economic force as a member of the BRICS group and the mega-event identified as soft capital. The project gained full political and economic support from the federal government presided over by Lula da Silva, who used his international visibility to promote not only the intention to host the Olympics but also the FIFA World Cup (Horne and Silvestre, 2017). The candidature helped to cement a multi-scalar political coalition involving the federal government, the regional government of Governor Sergio Cabral and the newly elected mayor of Rio, Eduardo Paes. Nuzman once again acted as the key link in translating the requirements and expectations from the Olympic governance system. The group formed, in the opinion of a former IOC director, 'like a tightly knit team, at a level that the IOC rarely saw' (Payne, 2014; see also Payne, 2009).

In order to improve their chances of success, several international

consultants were hired including former IOC employees and experts involved in other successful bids and Olympic Organizing Committees
(Silvestre, 2012). The new strategy explored every opportunity to promote
the bid at IF meetings, chief of state meetings and media coverage. It
also included illicit tactics unveiled years later with the bribing of IOC
delegates voting in the final round, a reminder of previous scandals such
as the 2002 Salt Lake City Winter Olympic Games (Savarese, 2019). Amid
positive international media coverage, economic growth, and exhausting all
the strategies available, the city of Rio de Janeiro finally made it onto the
shortlist and was selected as the host for the 2016 Olympic Games ahead of
Madrid, Tokyo, and Chicago.

   The candidature to the 2016 Games was a successful product of the
mega-event complex that developed in the two previous decades since
Brazil started to bid for the sports event. It required insider knowledge, full
political backing to meet IOC demands, international consultants providing
specialist knowledge as well as lobbying within key networks, and the buying
of votes. Plans for interventions in the city were constantly adapted and
changed, and the planning rationale shifted from developmental to *ad hoc*.
The following section examines how the programme for the 2016 Games
attempted to conciliate different agendas while providing an opportunity for
a new political and economic coalition to be formed.

Before and After the Rio 2016 Urban Interventions

The Masterplan and the Budget for Rio 2016

The masterplan for the 2016 Games featured in the candidature file took
the venues and proposals of the Pan American Games 2007 and the bid for
the 2012 Games as a baseline. It presented the organization of competitions
in four cluster areas around the city (Barra, Deodoro, Copacabana, and
Maracanã) suggesting a balanced territorial distribution (figure 17.1).
However, the concentration of competitions and the extent of urban
interventions varied considerably between the clusters as we discuss next.
The proposals were framed around the notion of 'legacy' facilitated by the
staging of the event: both of venues and associated facilities required for the
staging of competitions as well as urban development programmes aligned
with the event deadlines, such as improvements in the infrastructure and
the regeneration of brownfield sites. The total budget estimated for the
event was $13.4 billion (table 17.1). The governance of the preparatory
works involved a complex arrangement of governmental institutions at three
different levels (federal, regional, and local) and Olympic bodies (Organizing
Committee, 2018), as well as multiple private partners, development
authorities, and relevant stakeholders. Each group of interventions brought

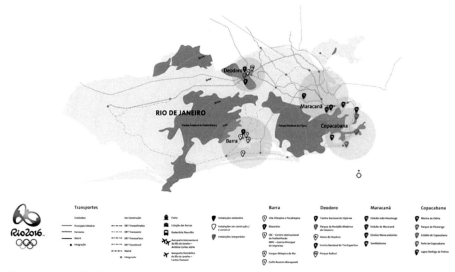

Figure 17.1. The Olympic clusters of the Rio 2016 Games. (*Source*: Rio de Janeiro City Council)

Table 17.1. Rio 2016 budget estimates (BRL million).* (*Sources*: APO (Olympic Public Authority), 2017; Brito and Wade, 2017)

Expenditure	Estimates 2017	Source of Funding
OCOG Budget	*9,200*	*Self-Financed*
Responsibility Matrix	*7,232*	
Olympic Village	2,909.5	Private
Olympic Park (PPP)	1,685	Public–Private Partnership
Olympic Park (Public)	1,330	Federal and Municipal
Deodoro sports complex	951.2	Federal
Sambodromo	65.0	Private and Municipal
Golf course	60.0	Public–Private Partnership
Marina da Gloria	60.0	Private
Olympic stadium	45.5	Municipal
Athlete's park	40.3	Municipal
Power/Electricity Infrastructure	60.1	Federal
Rowing stadium	7.6	Regional
Other facilities	18.1	Federal and Municipal
Legacy Plan	*27,273*	
Metro Line 4	9,700	State
Porto Maravilha	10,000	Public–Private Partnership
BRT	2,395	Municipal
Environmental programmes	1,604	State, Municipal and Private
Light railway	1,189	Federal and Private
Roads	972	Municipal
Urban renewal	758	Federal and Municipal
Upgrade rail stations	260	State
Guanabara Bay cleaning programme	125	State
Doping control laboratory	164	Federal
Social programmes	31	Federal
Total	*43,705.6*	

* 1 million BRL = ~US$204,000.

together a particular set of interested actors facilitating the delivery of works and benefitting from their later use. It resulted in the coordination of multiple coalitions of public and private interests that shaped the design and implementation of interventions, as well as helping to explain their sustained use or neglect in the post-event phase. The next sections review some of the main urban interventions associated with the 2016 Olympic Games considering the history of the area, the plans proposed, the governance arrangements, the social and environmental impacts, and the delivery of works and their legacy in the six years that followed the event.

The Olympic Park and the Olympic Village

The Olympic Park and the Olympic Village were built at the Barra cluster, which was the main games hub. This locational decision was part of a long history of development policies that privileged that region. Since the 1970s, Barra da Tijuca had become a special target for real estate and land speculation as municipal and state governments invested public funds to build new landmarks and infrastructure in a mostly greenfield and marshland area, including the city's major conventions centre and the Jacarepaguá motor racing track, both inaugurated in 1977. One particular local developer, Carlos Carvalho, pioneered directing attention to the area and acquired a very substantial amount of what was then low-value land. As the owner of the increasingly coveted plots, he waited for the implementation of new urban infrastructure over the following decades to build luxury gated communities and corporate towers (Guimarães, 2015).

The bid book for the 2016 Olympic Games presented the future Olympic Park on the site of the racing track, which was next to some of the small amount of vacant land in Barra belonging to Carvalho's company. In 2012, his company formed a consortium with two major Brazilian construction companies – Odebrecht and Andrade Gutierrez – to win the tender to build the sports venues in the Olympic Park. As part of the public–private partnership contract, the consortium was not only paid with public money, but also with the land on the western side of the future Olympic Park, where companies in the consortium planned to build new luxury housing in future years (figure 17.2). Additionally, Carvalho's company was also responsible for delivering the Olympic Village nearby, also on his land. The clear channelling of public funds and assets for the benefit of Carvalho and his partners has to be seen in the light of his major donations to the mayoral campaigns won by Mayor Paes in 2008 and 2012 (Correa et al., 2022). Therefore, millionaire public–private partnership contracts, land speculation coupled with public investments and private campaign funding were some of the most evident ties holding together the development coalition behind the Olympic Park and Olympic Village projects.

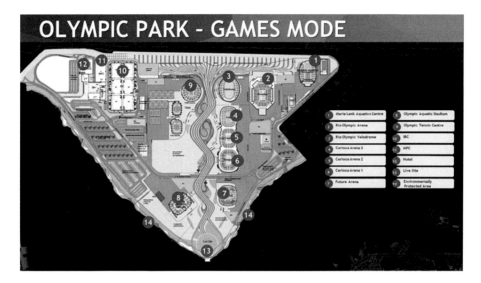

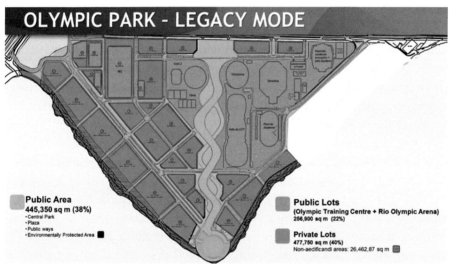

Figure 17.2. Master Plans of the Olympic Park for the Games and for the post-event phase. (*Source*: Rio de Janeiro City Council)

Nevertheless, others excluded from the coalition, who had had their interests particularly affected, openly opposed the plan. The more obvious ones were the users and employees of the motor racing track. However, since the venue had already lost importance due to the transfer of the Brazilian Formula 1 Grand Prix from Rio to São Paulo in 1990 and to the impact of the facilities built for the 2007 Pan American Games on the course, the local Motor Sports Federation had no real political clout left to stand against the proposed plan. However, to counter any possible resistance, the city government promised to build a new motor sports venue 20 kilometres away after the Games.

This was not the only obstacle in the way of the development coalition.

Vila Autódromo, a *favela* comprising nearly 550 self-built low-income houses next to the racing track, was targeted for eviction and demolition (Silvestre and Oliveira, 2012). However, this only happened after a slow and dramatic struggle between residents supported by local NGOs and universities, and developers backed by the city government. The persistent resistance of thousands of organized *favela* dwellers resulted in much-improved financial compensation than originally offered, the relocation of some residents to a new housing estate 1.5 kilometres away from the original site and even the reconstruction *in situ* of twenty houses for those who opposed the relocation programme. Given the usual aggressive treatment of *favelas* targeted for eviction by local authorities, these outcomes were rather exceptional (Keivani *et al.*, 2020).

By mid-2015, all the previously existing facilities and houses had been bulldozed. In addition to the venues built for the 2007 Pan American Games and renovated for the Olympics – i.e. the Maria Lenk aquatics centre and the multi-purpose Rio Arena – most of the new permanent infrastructure was built on the eastern side of the park. This included a tennis centre, a velodrome and three new sports arenas of varied sizes. On the other hand, most of the western side was filled with temporary facilities, with the exception of a new hotel and a car park. The layout corresponded to the demands of the construction companies to later convert the western side into luxury developments.

Six years after the Olympic Games, the outcome is still a far cry from what was originally planned. Firstly, the western side remains undeveloped and is only occasionally used for events and music festivals, such as the Rock in Rio festival (figure 17.3). Economic and political crises have hit the real estate market and developers hard, and they have opted to wait for a new expansionist period (discussed later in the chapter). Developers have had difficulty trying to sell the former Olympic Village apartments that hosted 18,000 athletes in thirty-one towers of seventeen storeys each totalling 3,604 units (Cerqueira and Pessoa, 2017). The site is known as the gated community *Ilha Pura* and was promoted as a new 'neighbourhood committed to good taste, luxury and sophistication' (Ilha Pura, 2015). However, only one third of the units have been occupied since 2016 (Loureiro *et al.*, 2021). Additionally, two temporary facilities that should have been dismantled and transformed into four new municipal primary schools – the handball arena and the Olympic aquatics centre – only started to be dismantled as this text was being written.

In addition, the new venues of the eastern side are considerably underused, despite promises from the federal government to make it an Olympic Training Centre for elite sports and of the city government to convert one of the arenas into a new primary school (Regueira, 2021*a*). On top of that, the city government has not kept its promise to build a new racing track

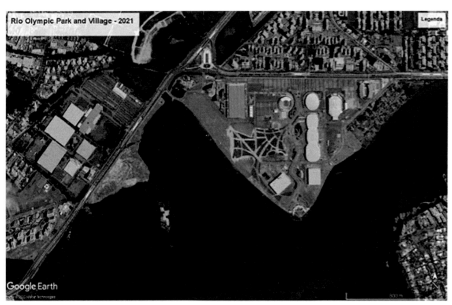

Figure 17.3. Aerial view of the Olympic Park in 2008 and 2021. Permanent and temporary venues can be found on the eastern side while the western side remains undeveloped. At the top left of the peninsula it is possible to see the significant reduction of Vila Autódromo. On the left is the group of buildings of the Rio Centre convention centre and next to it a section of Ilha Pura, the former Olympic Village. (*Source*: Google Earth)

as compensation to the Motor Sports Federation (Vecchioli, 2021) while some of the former residents of Vila Autódromo complain about the dire conditions of the housing estate to which they have been moved (Regueira, 2021*b*). All in all, the legacy of the Olympic Park has been one of halted projects, social cleansing, and a general sense of dissatisfaction for those involved.

The Deodoro Sports Complex

Among the four clusters of the 2016 Games, Deodoro in the city's West End was the least known area for visitors and many residents alike. Located in a region with a lower Human Development Index compared with the wealthy areas of Barra or Copacabana, the planned interventions were presented as a means of bringing infrastructure, services, and opportunities to residents and thus 'provide strong social and sport development legacy and opportunities' (RBC, 2009*a*, p.39). As such, the organization of the mega-event would potentially bring infrastructural improvements to the working-class neighbourhoods of Realengo, Magalhães Bastos or Ricardo Albuquerque. However, interventions in Deodoro were essentially *ad hoc*. In fact, most Olympic facilities were located within Vila Militar, an existing military enclave of the Brazilian Army.

The Deodoro Sports Complex was created for the 2007 Pan American Games with the modernization and expansion of military training grounds. Existing military facilities were subsequently remodelled for the 2016 Games to be used in the shooting, equestrian, and pentathlon competitions while temporary structures were built for rugby and mountain biking. New venues were built for field hockey matches – now part of the National Hockey Centre – as well as a sports pavilion that hosted fencing and basketball competitions, that since then have hosted martial arts competitions. Given the location of these venues on military grounds, they did not produce major changes to the surrounding neighbourhoods. As Davies recognized, 'all sports grounds in Deodoro – except for the X park – benefitted exclusively the Brazilian Army … since [the 2016 Olympic Games] the army manages the sports facilities as well as the residential projects built for the competitions' (Davies, 2017, p. 109; see also Davies, 2014). The Brazilian Army (Exército Brasileiro, 2016, p. 63) confirms that it received 'a considerable and important legacy, especially in Vila Militar' and adds that interventions in the area 'provided a significant increase in the quality of life for the military family'.

In contrast, nearby land belonging to the Brazilian Army was purchased by the municipality and transformed into the X Park, where new parkland dedicated to the practice of extreme sports was planned. The site made use of the BMX tracks and the canoe slalom facility built for the Games. Having to deliver a specialist facility with questions over its post-event use, Mayor Paes was quick to identify a political opportunity after a few youngsters climbed the fences to take a swim while it was under construction (Filipo, 2015). He exploited the occasion to announce that it would be open to the public as a new park with open-air swimming pools. Despite reported problems with maintenance and its closure during the COVID-19 pandemic, the area became popular with local residents (Regueira, 2021*a*).

The Maracanã Sports Complex

The refurbishment of the Maracanã sports complex was planned to cater for the requirements of both the 2016 Olympic Games and the 2014 FIFA World Cup. The venue belonged to the state government of Rio that tendered a contract of BRL 1.2 billion to a consortium of three large companies – Odebrecht, Andrade Gutierrez, and Delta Engenharia – for the nearly total reconstruction of the football stadium, which hosted the opening and closing Olympic ceremonies and the World Cup final match. A third of this amount was provided by a federal development bank – the BNDES – through subsidized lower interest rates whilst the other two-thirds came from the state government finances. Additionally, the state and city government invested BRL 287 million to regenerate the surrounding area. As the sharp differences between the budgets for internal and external works indicate, the Maracanã project was less about the revitalization of a dense neighbourhood and more about changes in the use of public assets. This became clear in the proposed plans for post-event uses.

The state government used a public–private partnership to lease the management of the venue to another consortium formed, again, by Odebrecht, the multinational entertainment company AEG, and IMX, a company owned by the emerging local tycoon Eike Batista. The consortium was expected to pay a total of BRL 181 million to the state government within thirty-five years. In exchange, the consortium would be able to exploit sport and entertainment events in the stadium and build new commercial facilities such as cinemas, restaurants and car parks commercially. These would physically replace existing sports and educational facilities within the Maracanã complex, such as the Célio de Barros athletics stadium, the Julio Delamare aquatics centre, and the Friedenreich municipal primary school. Additionally, a nineteenth-century building that was previously used as the first national indigenous museum would be demolished. The total relocation costs of BRL 594 million would be covered by the state government as well.

Given the great symbolic and functional importance of the Maracanã stadium to the Rio de Janeiro population and the negative reaction to previous attempts, both the refurbishment and the concession projects generated considerable discontent. The building of the stadium itself for the 1950 FIFA World Cup, provoked heated debates about costs and construction options (Omena de Melo, 2010). Its unique grandiose design, originally thought of as a symbol of the nation's urban development (Moura, 1998), quickly became a major reference for *Cariocas* (natives of Rio) from all walks of life who attended key sports, music, political, and religious events that marked the city's history (Gaffney, 2008). It was an important democratic space in a city marked by deep socio-spatial divisions.

As most of the other sports and educational facilities were added around the stadium between the 1950s and 1970s, they also became city references. Hundreds of athletes and beneficiaries of social projects – such as elderly and disabled people as well as children from lower income groups – had used the Maracanãzinho indoor arena, the athletics stadium and the aquatics centre for competitions, training, and classes. Furthermore, around 300 children studied at the primary school and a few dozen indigenous people had been squatting in the former museum building since 2006 demanding its reactivation as an indigenous cultural centre (WCOPCRJ, 2015).

From the early 2010s, two major groups with opposing views openly disputed the planned uses for Maracanã. On the one hand, Odebrecht, Andrade Gutierrez, Delta, AEG and IMX established business partnerships among themselves and with the state government, with the support of federal and city governments. This development coalition intended to optimize the commercial exploitation of a public asset through management and physical changes. On the other hand, groups negatively affected by these proposals, particularly the users of the Maracanã stadium and its surrounding facilities, sought support from public defenders, NGOs, social movements, and academics to build an anti-eviction coalition.

The outcome of the disputes was far from positive for most of the parties involved. First, the business and political coalition suffered a setback in 2012 when the construction company Delta abandoned the development consortium, with its owner arrested a few years later on charges of fraud and embezzlement. After the budget had nearly doubled in four years, police investigations unveiled overpricing practices and the consortium faced charges in the courts. Again in 2015, it was the marketing and entertainment company IMX that left the project, also due to its owner's involvement in corruption scandals. Second, Odebrecht, a company with interests on both the construction and management consortia, could not deliver all the planned interventions after the successful campaign by the anti-eviction coalition to reverse the bulldozing of the sports, educational, and cultural facilities. Nevertheless, the athletics stadium had its track destroyed through its use as a storage facility; activities for the elderly and low-income groups were discontinued; and the indigenous squatters were permanently evicted (see figure 17.4). Due to the consequent non-viability of the original business plan, Odebrecht entered into judicial disputes with the state government in the aftermath of the Olympics before it decided to cancel the management contract in 2019. Since then, two major local football clubs have taken over the management of the stadium on a short-term contract. However, the state government still intends to run another tender for a long-term public–

Figure 17.4. Aerial view of the Maracanã stadium in 2008 and in 2021. On the right is the Júlio Delamare aquatics centre (*top*) and the Maracanãzinho arena (*bottom*). On the left is the concreted track of the Célio de Barros athletics stadium. (Source: Google Earth)

private partnerhsip, thus again conceding the sports complex management to the private sector.

The Porto Maravilha Regeneration Programme

The largest regeneration project linked with the Olympics is located 18 miles (30 kilometres) away from the Olympic Park at the port area next to the city centre. Porto Maravilha is a megaproject intended to regenerate five million square metres of the city's derelict port area into a new mixed-use neighbourhood of office towers, luxury housing, and tourism and entertainment. Since launching in the aftermath of the Olympic announcement in 2009, signature buildings by renowned architects such as Santiago Calatrava and Norman Foster have profoundly changed the waterfront landscape. Despite not featuring any prominent Olympic facility, the programme was heralded as one of the main legacies of the Games (Organizing Committee, 2018).

The euphoric run-up to the sports mega-events in Brazil gave a significant boost to the port regeneration idea. Due to the large scale of the development, the very intricate ownership structure – as this is one of the oldest urban territories in the country dating back to the sixteenth century – the different public and private agents involved and the scale of resources required, the project only began to become a reality in the late 2000s, after decades of failed proposals (Correa *et al.*, 2022). Based on the promise of an Olympic legacy in a deprived area, the bid file originally proposed the construction of a 'Port Village' which would accommodate part of the event workforce and later be converted into housing for low-income groups (RBC, 2009*a*, Vol III, p. 49). After Rio was selected as Olympic host city, it was announced that referee accommodation would be developed in the area. However, in the wake of a few controversies between the city administration and the Organizing Committee, the IOC decided to not use the port area for official accommodation.

Whereas previous plans failed to progress from the study phase or produced only minor interventions, the announcement of Porto Maravilha took place in very favourable circumstances (Silvestre, 2022). First, political alignments facilitated negotiations and in this case the release of land belonging to the three levels of government. Secondly, the strong growth of the Brazilian economy in the latter half of the 2000s, and of Rio in particular, created a strong demand for office space. The growth of the oil and gas industry with the discovery of new deep-sea basins was an important factor pushing corporate demand for new office space in central Rio. Thirdly, new planning instruments introduced in 2001 enabled the implementation of self-financed regeneration schemes. The Urban Operation instrument foresees land value capture through selling certificates for additional building rights to erect taller buildings to developers with funds re-invested in the regeneration of the area. Fourthly, there was the interest and lobbying of three of the largest Brazilian construction companies which produced the feasibility plan for the regeneration programme and won the bid for engineering works and provision of services. Fifthly, there was the momentum given by the hosting of the mega-events, which further enhanced Rio's visibility and pushed for the fast-track approval of by-laws and planning permissions.

Despite presenting plans to be developed independently of the Olympic project, the association with the Games was strategic in a number of ways. In aligning the project with the Olympic deadline, it reassured investors about the completion of infrastructural works that included the demolition of an elevated expressway and its substitution with an underground tunnel, the upgrading of electricity, sanitation, and telecommunications structures, new roads and renewed pavements and urban furniture. It also enabled the city government to leverage federal funding to implement a new light railway system. Finally, the scale of the project supported the discourse of profound urban change facilitated by the Games while boosting the evidence of an urban legacy.

Nevertheless, three Brazilian construction companies – OAS, Odebrecht, and Carioca Engenharia – played a key role in sustaining the political and economic coalition behind the arrangements that enabled the implementation of the project. As already mentioned, they authored the original feasibility study that proposed the complex institutional design for the project and later underpinned the public–private partnership tendering process in which they were the sole contestants – due to the inability of other bidders to meet the rules they had been set – and thus the winners. They formed the consortium Porto Novo, which was due to be paid BRL 8 billion to deliver the programme of works and public services in the area, such as street lighting, rubbish collection, and road maintenance, for a period of fifteen years. In addition, police investigations (discussed later in the conclusion) indicated that the CEOs of these companies not only influenced the design and delivery of public policies but also carried this out via informal and illicit channels. Featuring as some of the major donors in Brazilian political campaigns, they were able to lobby in favour of the project at different government and legislative levels, including paying bribes to influence the executive decisions at the Federal Savings Bank to guarantee the delivery of the project by way of purchasing all the building rights certificates. However, up to September 2020 less than 10 per cent of the certificates were negotiated, indicating the slow real estate activity for high-rise developments. This has affected the cash flow of the operation and in 2018 the bank announced the illiquidity of its investment fund and stopped making payments to the private partner, bringing maintenance works and services to a halt and forcing the city government to resume the delivery.

At the end of the day, however, the urban landscape has changed substantially (figure 17.5) with a revamped street network and public spaces, a modern transport system, new museums, renovated warehouses used as event venues, and corporate towers interspersed with empty plots and old industrial structures. All this was trumpeted as one of the main Olympic legacies in Rio, even though there was no Olympic facility in the port area – except for being used as one of the main Fan Fest sites and displaying the

Figure 17.5. Aerial view of the port area of Rio de Janeiro in 2016 with the Museum of Tomorrow at the centre and renovated warehouses in the background. (*Source*: Bruno Bartholini/CDURP)

Olympic flame and cauldron for the duration of the event. The same cannot be said about the ongoing gentrification in the area, as the socioeconomic profile of locals has changed. At least a hundred low-income households were evicted from the Favela da Providência, situated within the Porto Maravilha limits, while the promises of developing up to 5,000 social housing units in the area – which arguably would be in line with the original Olympic bid pledges – never materialized (Keivani *et al.*, 2020).

Transport Systems

Rio's natural landscape has always presented significant challenges to the city's urban expansion and the development of the transport network played a vital part in pushing the city limits. Just as electric tramways opened the seafront of the South End for the local elite in the first half of the twentieth century, working-class neighbourhoods were established along the railways cutting through the North End and the Baixada Fluminense regions. In the 1970s the marshlands of Barra da Tijuca represented a new urban frontier after the gradual development of the coastal areas of Copacabana, Ipanema, Leblon, and São Conrado. Consistent with the planning rationale developed for Brasília, planner Lucio Costa envisioned the organization of new neighbourhoods in Barra along expressways that privileged the use of individual motor vehicles.

Between 1991 and 2010 the population residing in the Barra region grew from 526,302 to 909,955 (IPP, 2011). Encircled by mountains, access to the rest of the city was only possible via the roads along the coastline and through the valley passage north of Jacarepaguá, but by the 1990s traffic flow was already saturated. The 2016 bid promised the creation of a 'High Performance Transport Ring' and introduced the concept of the Bus Rapid Transport (BRT) system as a feasible way to connect the four Olympic clusters and deliver a new transport network in time for the event, in addition to the expansion of the metro system, a light railway in the port area, duplication of roads and the construction of bridges and tunnels (RBC, 2009b). In fact, mobility programmes accounted for more than 50 per cent of the 'legacy plan' budget destined for urban interventions or a third of all the costs associated with the 2016 Games (see table 17.1).

Barra was situated as the nodal point of the new BRT system totalling 117 kilometres and consisting of three segregated bus corridors: the Transoeste corridor linking Barra to the West End and to a new metro station; the Transcarioca line winding through the North End towards the international airport; and the Transolimpica, linking the Olympic Park with Deodoro - a fourth one would be added, Transbrasil but not aligned with the Games and due to be completed by the end of 2023 after several delays. Proponents of the BRT system (figure 17.6) such as former Bogotá Mayor Enrique Peñalosa, who became a global advocate of the policy, argue that it presents the only viable transport solution in terms of scale and cost for large cities in the Global South (Peñalosa, 2013). It is shown as a compromise between the lower costs of surface systems and the operation and comfort of the

Figure 17.6. The new BRT system of segregated bus lanes was devised to connect the Olympic clusters and the international airport and serve as the transport legacy of the 2016 Games. (*Source*: Renato Sette Camara/Rio de Janeiro City Council).

underground. Critics on the other hand, point to the marginalization of metro and rail expansion and that the system only gives temporary results as it can become saturated quickly. The experience of the Transoeste and Transcarioca lines after their first years of operation corroborated the latter argument. Press coverage of the systems inaugurated in 2012 and 2014 respectively documented overcrowding and safety worries as routine occurrences (França, 2015). Nevertheless, the potential benefit of easing the travel over long distances and speeding commuting time was offset by the reorganization of conventional bus lines in 2015 to accommodate the BRT system and was followed by a reduction in services in the following years due to the economic recession (Pereira, 2018). It was reported that from the initial fleet of 375 buses in operation in 2016, this number was reduced to 180 by 2021 (Loureiro *et al.*, 2021). According to a study by Pereira (*ibid.*), the accessibility level accrued to lower-income groups living in peripheral areas deteriorated while there were marginal improvements for higher-income groups.

The mobility programme also included the expansion of metro lines and upgraded rail services. The construction of the metro line 4 was the most expensive project associated with the Games consuming 23 per cent of the total budget at a 2017 cost of BRL 9.7 billion (Brito and Wade, 2017). It extended the service running along the South End coastline for 10 miles (16 km) with six new stations reaching Barra da Tijuca at its eastern point. It was also emphasized that the rail system would be completely renovated in order to deliver a 'world-class' service to the densely populated working-class areas in the north and west regions (RBC, 2009*a*). After reaching a peak of one million daily passengers at the beginning of the 1980s, the rail service was carrying around 620,000 passengers every day with frequent problems of disrupted services and overcrowding (Souza, 2014). Olympic-related investments promised to 'drastically focus on changing both the image and the effectiveness of the railway, upgrading stations, fully modernizing the rolling stock, upgrading infrastructure and systems, and improving maintenance works' (RBC, 2009*a*, p. 26).

However, only the refurbishment of six rail stations serving Olympic venues were included in the 'Legacy Plan' with the remainder of the upgrading works transferred to the private operator. A change in the terms of the contract transferred the refurbishment of the stations to the private operator and was followed by a reduction in the number of carriages to be purchased (Nogueira, 2015). The revised agreement shows how the Olympic mobility programme reinforced spatial and social inequalities. On the one hand, the new BRT corridors and the expanded metro network significantly improved transport connections in the region of Barra, where according to Rodrigues (2015) it accounted for only 4 per cent of existing jobs within the metropolitan region. On the other hand, minimal improvements were

made to the daily commute of more than one million people living in the
Baixada Fluminense area within the metropolitan region travelling to areas
such as the city centre that accounts for 35 per cent of jobs. According to
the author, despite the rhetoric of a 'revolution' in mass transport services,
an opportunity was wasted to articulate transport plans bearing in mind the
needs of the wider 12 million inhabitants at the metropolitan scale.

Final and more explicit evidence of social polarization was the eviction of

Figure 17.7. The *favela* of Vila do Recreio II was cleared to give way to a BRT corridor. The houses in the background belong to the few residents still resisting eviction in May 2011. (*Source*: Nelma Gusmão de Oliveira)

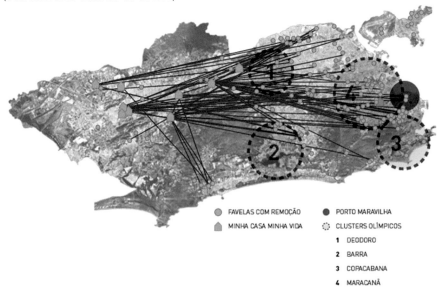

Figure 17.8. The map presents the location of *favelas* expropriated between 2009 and 2013 (in circles) and the destination of those accepting relocation to the Minha Casa Minha Vida social housing programme, largely concentrated in the West End. (*Source*: Lucas Faulhaber)

popular settlements from areas claimed to be needed for the improvement of the transport system (figures 17.7 and 17.8). The construction of the BRT corridors displaced some 5,000 families from the areas where they were settled, some for two or three decades (WCOPCRJ, 2015). As was documented in the cases of settlements in the West End displaced by the construction of the Transoeste line, many families were reallocated to social housing projects further away in the peripheral areas of the city lacking adequate infrastructure and posing greater difficulties to access jobs, schools, and health clinics (Silvestre and Oliveira, 2012). Further, disinformation and intimidation also rendered other families homeless or without financial compensation.

Conclusion

When hosting the 2016 Olympic Games was awarded to Rio de Janeiro in October 2009, the prospects for the organization of the mega-event seemed favourable from the perspective of the IOC. While many of the economies in the Global North were impacted by the Great Recession that started in 2007, the Brazilian bid explored the strength of the country's economic growth and made assurances that the budget would draw from the federal government's $240 billion package for infrastructural development (RBC, 2009b).

Politically, as mentioned earlier in the chapter, the hosting of the event helped to cement a political coalition among three government levels to overcome the red tape for the concerted action in urban interventions and in the organization of the event. The Games, alongside the 2014 FIFA World Cup and other large-scale projects in the country during the period, also strengthened the proximity between the political class and big national corporations. As demonstrated, a small group of construction companies were behind most of the stadia, transport, and infrastructural projects related to the mega-events of the 2014–2016 period. This articulation also had to be combined with interests operating at a more local scale, from the landowner monopolizing access to much of available land in Barra to the Brazilian Army owning a military enclave in Deodoro. It seemed then that all key interests with a stake in the mega-events were aligned and that their plans were on track.

However, this context reversed significantly just before the start of the first mega-event and would continue in the years of the post-event period. Starting in 2013, on the eve of the Confederations Cup – a test event for the FIFA World Cup – public demonstrations took to the streets of more than 100 Brazilian cities to protest against the political order (Omena de Melo, 2020). It covered a large spectrum of grievances that varied locally but centred on issues concerning the quality of public services and corruption scandals. The protests were the start of the fall of the political coalition at the national government level led by Lula da Silva's successor, Dilma Rousseff. Although there is no space to examine the complexity of the political crisis that led to the coup and impeachment of the president in 2016, it had an important impact in dominating much of the public's attention just as the mega-events were being held. As we saw, the 2013 protests in Rio were successful in countering the demolition of public areas and popular sports facilities surrounding the Maracanã stadium, as well as mounting pressure on Governor Sergio Cabral who resigned from office in 2014 and was imprisoned in 2016. His imprisonment was part of the major criminal investigation 'Operation Car Wash' that unveiled an extensive kickback scheme involving major political parties and construction companies. Large public contracts were systematically tendered at inflated prices with the companies returning the favour with campaign donations. Representatives of the construction companies discussed above confessed having paid bribes to financial decisions that secured the delivery of the Porto Maravilha project. Although Mayor Paes's government was less damaged by the scandals, his successor failed to be elected and marked the end of a period of twenty-three years in which actors from the same political group were in power and championed the hosting of mega-events as a strategy for economic growth and social benefits. This was compounded by an economic recession starting in 2015 that resulted in delays and major reviews in the organization and final delivery of works.

The political and economic crises had an important impact on the plans and governance of the legacy of the Rio 2016 Olympic Games. Definitions regarding management and funding for the maintenance and operation of facilities remained undefined for many years after the event. The intention that private companies play a part in operating the venues in the Olympic Park was unsuccessful following the lack of interest when tendering calls were announced in 2016. The federal government took on the management of these facilities that since then have been used for the training of elite athletes and sports competitions although access to the Olympic Park has been routinely closed to the public.

The 2016 Games was also identified as the end of the cycle of mega-event hosting and large-scale urban regeneration programmes. Accordingly, this was the last step to mounting criticism from the general public and international organizations of the waste of public funds, corruption, evictions, violation of human rights, and environmental degradation. In the last decade, a series of bids to host mega-events have been withdrawn following public referenda and protests. On the face of diminishing interest to an ever-expanding and expensive event, the IOC has sought reforms to its hosting requirements approved in 2021 while securing the viability of the Games in the short-term by awarding hosting rights directly and in advance for the 2024, 2028 and 2032 Olympic Games to Paris, Los Angeles and Brisbane, respectively.

The experiences of the city of Rio de Janeiro with the bidding and hosting of mega-events was part and parcel of a period in which the mega-event industry was structured at a global scale forming an Olympic complex moving enormous amounts of money while satisfying political and economic interests. It allows us to understand how international sports organizations were keen to stimulate competition and encourage bids seeking to leverage mega-event hosting as a strategy for large-scale urban transformation of their cities. Intermediaries in the chain of power and knowledge flows between these organizations and host nations and cities positioned themselves in licit and illicit ways to translate information in the race for hosting nominations. In the process, the 'Olympic city' of state-of-the-art sports venues and infrastructure catering for athletes and tourists was expected to stimulate private investment while also serving the needs of the residents of host cities, which as we saw were negatively affected. In this sense, Rio 2016 can be seen as the model city of the global mega-event industry.

Chapter 18

TOKYO 2020

Yasushi Aoyama

Tokyo 2020 was postponed for a year due to the COVID-19 pandemic and was held with almost no spectators, even though Tokyo was able to provide venues for athletes around the world who had been practising every day for this special event. Although there was strong opposition in Japan towards hosting the Olympics during a global pandemic, athletes from around the world actively participated. The Games began on 23 July 2021 and lasted until 8 August 2021. In total, 11,000 athletes from 205 countries and regions as well as a refugee team participated in thirty-three competitions and 339 events, with the number of participating countries and regions equal to the highest number in past Olympics. The Paralympics were held from 24 August to 5 September 2021, and about 4,400 athletes from 162 countries and regions and a refugee team participated in twenty-two competitions and 539 events. The number of participating athletes for the Paralympics was the highest ever.

This chapter discusses the kinds of conflicts in opinion that existed in the process leading up to the hosting of the Olympics during the COVID-19 pandemic, what the venue plans and costs were, and what the future image of the Tokyo Bay Area, where many venues were arranged, will be. It then discusses the legacy that should be left behind.

Tokyo 2020 and the COVID-19 Pandemic

The 2020 Tokyo Olympics were postponed for a year due to the global COVID-19 pandemic, and most of the games were held without spectators, making it a unique event in the history of the Olympics. The world's awareness of the pandemic began to rise at the beginning of 2020, and it spread rapidly. In March 2020, therefore, the then Prime Minister Abe held a phone call with International Olympic Committee (IOC) President Bach, accompanied by Tokyo Governor Koike and other related people, and decided to postpone the games for one year. A few days later, the IOC

decided to hold the Olympics for seventeen days from 23 July 2021, with
the Paralympics lasting for thirteen days from 24 August 2021 (see also
chapter 1).

A year later, however, the pandemic had not subsided, but rather it had
gained momentum. The Japanese Government had declared the fourth state
of emergency for the host city of Tokyo on 12 July 2021. Around this time,
Tokyo Governor Yuriko Koike and the other key people involved began to
declare publicly that the Games could be held without spectators, and in
the end, most of the Games were held on that basis. There was little choice.
A further postponement was not an option for the host city of Tokyo and
the Japanese Government. Given that athletes had limited time to prepare
to make this happen, a bubble system was devised to prevent them from
coming into contact with the general public at the various international
competitions. It was accepted that the significance of the Olympics is the
interaction between the athletes and spectators from around the world
and the people of the host country, but the excitement of the Games is
conveyed through media such as television even during normal times. The
Japanese Government and Tokyo Metropolitan Government believed that
even if most of the games were held without spectators, the excitement of
the Olympics would be conveyed.

Some Japanese felt uneasy about the spread of the pandemic as people
from many countries and regions around the world gathered for the
Olympics. However, as can be seen in figure 18.1, Japan's fourth wave of
the coronavirus did not spread during the period of the Olympics, but
rather began to subside. Leading up to the hosting of the Olympics, there

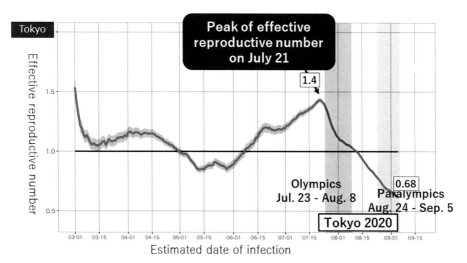

Figure 18.1. Change in effective reproductive number of COVID-19 in Tokyo during the
Olympics. (*Source*: Tokyo Metropolitan Government, from materials of the advisory board
meeting of the Ministry of Health, Labour and Welfare)

were also serious conflicts between the host city of Tokyo and the Japanese Government, and between Tokyo and the IOC over costs and the placement of facilities. However, there was no conflict over a one-year postponement amid the pandemic and the banning of spectators.

Games without Spectators

The question arises as to how the memories of the 2020 Olympics should be engraved in the history of Japan in the future. What will be the lasting significance of the rescheduled Games and near empty stadia?

It should be appreciated that Tokyo was able to provide safe venues and accommodation for the Olympic and Paralympic athletes whose preparation had already been interrupted by COVID-19 and whose practice schedules had necessarily been extended by twelve months. The appearance of the athletes competing hard and in good spirit brought considerable excitement to the people of the world. For example, in skateboarding, there was a scene where all the rivals hugged the female athlete who had fallen after attempting a difficult trick. It can be argued that the efforts and friendships of the competitors have been transmitted to the world.

There were cases of COVID-19 infections among athletes and other people involved in the Olympics, but no large clusters occurred. Some people involved in the Olympics were criticized for going shopping and sightseeing in violation of the rules, but it did not develop into a major incident. It was assumed that there would be a positive rate of 0.2 per cent in airport quarantines for athletes and Olympic Games officials, but in was in fact only 0.1 per cent. It was also assumed that the number of athletes hospitalized would be eight or more at its peak, but the result was just two. In addition to the lack of planned revenue such as admission fee income, expenses increased due to the COVID-19 control measures. However, there were also expenses that could be significantly reduced because of the lack of spectators.

While it is sad that the event had to be held without spectators and that the athletes had to compete without live spectator participation, the television spectacle of the athletes competing clearly impressed the world. Figure 18.2, for example, shows changes in water usage on the night of Friday, 23 June 2021, a public holiday when the Olympic Opening Ceremony was held. Official figures show that the water usage skyrocketed as soon as the ceremony was over. It can be reasonably inferred that many Tokyo residents were watching the games on television. Another significant figure was that sales of skateboards in Japan increased dramatically after the Olympics: evidence perhaps that the policy of trying to convey the appeal of sports to young people through the Olympics had been effective in skateboarding at least.

The notions of disaster and recovery were always part of this Olympics.

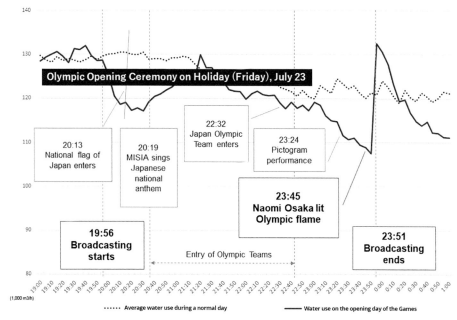

Figure 18.2. Change in amount of water distribution during the Games. The dashed line in the figure indicates the amount of water distributed on a typical day. The solid line indicates the amount of water distributed on the day of the opening ceremony of the Tokyo Olympics. The vertical axis shows the amount of water distributed, and the horizontal axis shows the change over time every 10 minutes. (*Source*: Bureau of Waterworks of the Tokyo Metropolitan Government)

Reconstruction from the Great East Japan Earthquake was from the outset a theme behind these Games and the response to the circumstances imposed by the Coronavirus pandemic dominated its staging. Although the Olympics did not serve as a testimony to overcoming COVID-19, it is important to reassess the significance of the Olympics while dealing with the coronavirus. While there have been trial-and-error and delayed responses to the world's COVID-19 countermeasures, it would behove the next generation to record frank reflections on these matters. It is also to be hoped that the willingness of citizens to cooperate internationally to respond to various disasters will be strengthened around the world.

Games Finances

The estimated cost of the Tokyo 2020 Olympics in the 2013 bidding file was $6,673 million, but there was always a fear that the actual cost would be several times higher than this figure. In the event, it cost about twice as much as originally planned. According to the final financial results announced by the Tokyo Organizing Committee of the Olympic and Paralympic Games in June 2022, the total cost of the Games to be borne by the national government, Tokyo Metropolitan Government, and the Tokyo Organizing

Committee was $12,944 million dollars[1] – a figure that includes $1,376 million for the Paralympic Games). The breakdown was as follows:

◆ $7,863 million for 'venue related expenses' such as permanent facilities and temporary facilities;

◆ $4,760 million, for 'competitions related' such as operation, transportation and security, as well as competition management and venue management;

◆ $321 million for COVID-19 countermeasures.

The total cost of the Games at $12,944 million is actually a reduction of $2,002 million from the $14,945 million figure presented in version 5 of the Games costings presented in December 2020. The breakdown of the $12,944 million in total expenses for the Games was as follows:

◆ $1,699 million for the national government;

◆ $5,422 million for Tokyo Metropolitan Government;

◆ $5,822 million for the Tokyo Organizing Committee.

The main income breakdown for the Tokyo Organizing Committee was as follows:

◆ $789 million from the IOC, International Olympic Committee;

◆ $3,929 million from sponsors;

◆ $455 million in insurance money due to the postponement.

In turn, the main expenditure breakdown of the $5,822 million spent by the Tokyo 2020 Organizing Committee was:

◆ $1,777 million related to venues (of which $948 million was for temporary construction);

◆ $4,045 million related to the Games (with $1,433 million for operations and related activities).

As a result, it was possible to balance the budget, but the problem of the scale of expenditure required for the Olympics leaves questions for the future of the Games. Many people agree with the Olympic spirit and recognize the significance of the Games, but the criticism that the Olympics are too costly has developed into a political problem in Japan – a point that is worth developing further.

The New National Stadium

A competition was held for the design of the New National Stadium, the main stadium for the Tokyo 2020 Olympics, by a judging committee chaired by architect Tadao Ando. As a result, in July 2012, a design by the British architectural practice led by Zaha Hadid was selected for the Grand Prize. After that, the discussion in Japan over this design became extremely confusing and contentious.

The selected design was neo-futuristic, with Zaha Hadid's unique streamlined building floating like a spaceship in Meiji Jingu Gaien against the backdrop of the Shinjuku subcentre buildings (figure 18.3). The design made a strong statement of Japan's enthusiasm for Tokyo, which at the time was competing with other leading cities as a candidate city for the 2020 Summer Olympics. However, there were various objections to this design in Japan most notably, first, that it was inappropriate for the history and tradition of Meiji Jingu Gaien, and secondly, that it was too expensive. In July 2013, the design company reported that the construction cost for this design would be $3,115 million. The cost would prove the biggest point of contention when it was reported to a group of developers advising the Japanese government. This sum amounted to nearly half of the total cost of the Tokyo Olympics as planned in the Olympic bid file.

Controversy also arose over Tokyo Metropolitan Government's contri-

Figure 18.3. Zaha Hadid's design proposal for Japan's National Olympic Stadium. (*Source*: Tokyo 2020 Olympic and Paralympic Games Bid Committee Candidature File, 2013)

bution to the new National Stadium. After the IOC decided in September 2013 to award the host city for 2020 Olympics to Tokyo, the Tokyo Governor Yōichi Masuzoe summoned the Ministers of Education, Culture, Sports, Science and Technology to Tokyo Metropolitan Government in July 2015 to ask questions publicly about the cost sharing of the new National Stadium. The discussion became even more heated and, as a result, the Prime Minister Shinzo Abe announced withdrawal of his support. The competition was then restarted, and Kengo Kuma's design proposal was adopted. The Tokyo Metropolitan Government agreed to bear a certain amount of expenses and Zaha Hadid's design effectively ended up being used only to show Tokyo's enthusiasm in the competition between the candidate cities.

The newly selected design (figure 18.4), which is now blending into the forest of Meiji Jingu Gaien, has a Japanese style, with eaves made of Japanese cedar on the second to fifth floors above the ground, and the use of wood as well as iron for the roof. The building is devised to allow air to flow between the stand and the roof, and to reduce glare by planting trees on the fifth floor. A total of 68,000 seats were prepared for the Olympic and Paralympic Games. There would be 456 wheelchair-accessible seats for the Olympics and 703 wheelchair-accessible seats for the Paralympics. However, the dispute over the stadium had a broader impact. The situation in which Governor Masuzoe, who was elected with the support of the central

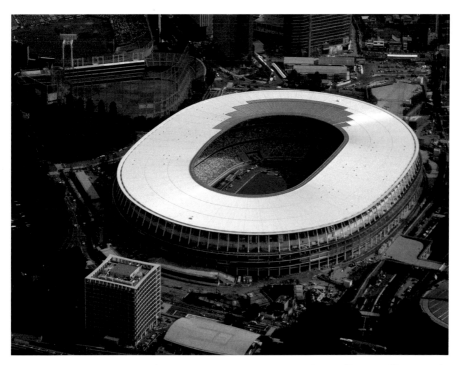

Figure 18.4. New National Stadium designed by Kengo Kuma. (*Source*: Photograph, Yasushi Aoyama, 2018)

government, was now at odds with the central government, gave the public a strong impression that the Olympics were too expensive.

The 'Koike Theatre' and Olympic Expenditure

In June 2016 Masuzoe, who had served as governor of Tokyo for two years, resigned after being criticized for the use of political funds before becoming governor. In the Tokyo governor election held in July, Yuriko Koike, who does not support a specific political party, was elected over a candidate supported by the central government. As noted elsewhere (Aoyama, 2022), Governor Koike fought aggressively not only against the government but also the IOC regarding the cost burden of the Tokyo Olympics and some of the venue locations. Until then, Koike had been a member of the Liberal Democratic Party's House of Representatives, but in the Tokyo gubernatorial election, she sharply criticized the policies of the city and the country, including the issue of Olympic expenses, and won the support of the people of Tokyo.

After being elected governor of Tokyo, Governor Koike began reviewing the venue plan and budget for the Olympics. She pointed out that construction costs were particularly high for three facilities (figures 18.5 and 18.6): the Ariake Arena (volleyball), the Olympic Aquatics Centre

Figure 18.5. Olympic Aquatics Centre (swimming). (*Source*: Photograph, Yasushi Aoyama, 2020)

Figure 18.6. Sea Forest Waterway (rowing and canoe course). (*Source*: Photograph, Yasushi Aoyama, 2020)

(swimming), and the Sea Forest Waterway (rowing and canoe course). Koike insisted on a drastic review of these three facilities, including the withdrawal of construction plans. Japan's sports associations, the central government, the IOC, and the Tokyo Organizing Committee strongly opposed this. In October 2016, IOC President Thomas Bach visited Japan and Governor Koike negotiated directly with him, with Japanese television and newspapers reporting the negotiations in detail. It was around this time that the term 'Koike Theatre' was coined. In December 2016, it was agreed that all three facilities would be built according to the existing policy but that every facility would be reviewed to lower the expense, which Koike explained saved the sum of $364 million.

Since then, Japan's prime ministers have changed several times, but Koike is still the governor of Tokyo. In the 2017 Tokyo Metropolitan Assembly election, her Tomin First political party became the leading party in the Tokyo Metropolitan Assembly. Koike was re-elected as Tokyo governor in 2020. In the 2021 Tokyo Metropolitan Assembly election, Tomin First's seats were reduced, but is the second largest party in the Tokyo Metropolitan Assembly. Tokyo Governor Koike's fierce confrontation with the central government and the IOC over the cost of the Olympics in 2016 remains a vivid image for Tokyo residents. Koike spoke for the people's doubts, which is still one of the strengths of her power as a politician.

The specific cost reduction effect of the Koike Theatre was not large, but it was significant from the perspective of democratic politics that the people's dissatisfaction with the cost of the Olympics was expressed through the conflict. In September 2016, when Koike was discussing Olympic costs with the central government and the IOC, she demanded that the Tokyo Organizing Committee of the 2020 Olympic and Paralympic Games be made an 'organization supervised by Tokyo Metropolitan Government'. She further insisted that: 'We will check whether Tokyo residents are being forced to bear unreasonably high expenses due to concessions or fraud, and make improvements'. If implemented, it will be a step towards 'transparency of tournament management.' The Tokyo Metropolitan Information Disclosure Ordinance stipulates that corporations and other bodies in which Tokyo Metropolitan Government invests are to disclose information voluntarily on a par with that practised by Tokyo Metropolitan Government. For its part, however, the Organizing Committee showed reluctance to create a supervising organization for Tokyo, citing the fact that the IOC was already strongly involved, and did not respond to negotiations. After the end of the 2020 Tokyo Olympics, a corruption case against a director of the Organizing Committee over a sponsorship contract became a problem. It can be seen, therefore, that there was a reason for Governor Koike's assertion in 2016.

The Venue Layout Plan and Athletes' Village Concept

Some of the venues for the 2020 Olympics Games, such as those for soccer, baseball, and sailing, were located outside Tokyo, but basically the Olympic venues were located in or near the centre of Tokyo (figure 18.7). As such, the venues in Tokyo were divided into the Heritage Zone and the Tokyo Bay Zone. The Heritage Zone continues the legacy of the Tokyo 1964 Games, with its centrepiece being the rebuilt New National Stadium. The Tokyo Bay Zone is a newly developed area that symbolizes the future of the city. New facilities such as the Ariake Arena, the Sea Forest Waterway, and the Tokyo Tatsumi International Swimming Centre are located here. The Athletes' Village (Harumi) and the Press Centre (Tokyo Big Sight) are also located in the Tokyo Bay Zone. Notably, the Athletes' Village is located where both the rings of the Heritage Zone and the Tokyo Bay Zone overlap. The ring of two zones (∞) itself makes us imagine the symbol of Infinite Excitement – a symbol embodies the boundless passion, commitment and inspiration of the world's elite athletes, the limitless potential of future generations, and the lasting legacy that will be passed on to the people of Tokyo, Japan and the world.

As for the Athletes' Village, Tokyo Metropolitan Government contracted with a group of eleven private companies to hand over about 113,000 square metres of land in Harumi, which was originally owned by the city. The

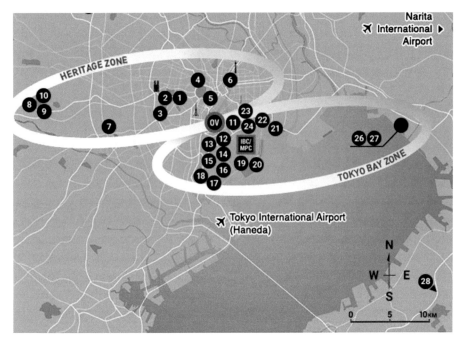

Figure 18.7. Map of the competition venues. Key points: *1* Olympic Stadium; *8* Musashino Forest Sport Plaza; *11* Ariake Arena; *20* Sea Forest Waterway; *23* Tokyo Aquatics Centre; *OV* Olympic/Paralympic Village; *IBC/MPC* Tokyo International Exhibition Centre (Tokyo Big Sight) (*Source*: Tokyo Metropolitan Government)

companies would build the Athletes' Village, renovate it after the Olympics, and sell or rent about 5,650 housing units. Two residential buildings (high-rise towers) would also be built after the Games. At Games-time, twenty-one residential buildings were temporarily used as lodging facilities for athletes with 18,000 beds for the Olympic Games, and 8,000 beds for the Paralympic Games. In this area, a sports gymnasium, general clinic, dining hall, and official store were temporarily installed and used as facilities for the Village.

After the Games, these facilities would become commercial buildings and schools, with housing for sale also being developed – mainly for families raising children. In addition, there would be rented accommodation and rental housing to suit a variety of needs, including smaller households, serviced furnished apartments, SOHOs (small office/home office), shared units and housing for the elderly with appropriate services (figure 18.8). The intention is that this area should become a model of an environmentally advanced city by utilizing new technologies to establish independence in the event of a disaster, and to achieve both comfort and eco-friendly living. Therefore, in addition to grid power and city gas, the aim is to realize low-carbon, energy-saving, and enhanced urban resilience by using a multi-layered combination of hydrogen and heat. Specifically, hydrogen will be supplied through pipelines within the district.

Figure 18.8. Image of the Athletes' Village converted into housing after the Games. (Source: Tokyo Metropolitan Government)

The Future of Tokyo Bay Area

In March 2022, Tokyo Metropolitan Government announced the Tokyo Bay eSG Urban Development Strategy 2022, which provides a defining image of the future of the Tokyo Bay Area, where most of the Olympic venues are located (figure 18.9). The letters 'eSG' in the title stand for Environment, Social, and Governance, where the letter 'e' also carries the meaning of ecology, economy, and epoch-making. The reason why the 'S' and 'G' are capitalized is that 'S' stands for Shibusawa Eiichi and 'G' stands for Goto Shinpei – two individuals who led the city and economy of Tokyo through the Meiji and Taisho eras, and who laid the foundation for the modern city.

When announcing the plan, Governor Koike declared that, despite having to overcome many difficulties, the successful completion of the 2020 Games, had greatly enhanced the maturity of Tokyo as a city and had given the opportunity for the Bay Area, which had had a role in hosting the Olympic Games, to be developed. The various results produced through the Games would become a city legacy, and the Bay Area would develop into a city that will be desired by future generations. Wider issues were also considered. It was declared that the Bay Area, which is close to the sea, would be developed into a city where everyone can play an active role by preventing sea level rise and the frequent and severe storm and flood damage caused by climate change. The COVID-19 crisis, which had such an impact on the Games, had also affected the economy and society through the growth in remote

Figure 18.9. Tokyo Bay eSG Urban Development Strategy 2022. (*Source*: Tokyo Metropolitan Government)

working and the progress of digitalization, and has perhaps changed people's awareness of their lives. While taking advantage of the city's agglomeration advantages, it is promoting urban development based on the concept of sustainable recovery that can respond to the new patterns of daily living.

In response, Tokyo Metropolitan Government in future will solicit advanced projects in three cutting-edge technologies – renewable energy, next-generation mobility, and environmental improvement and resource recycling – with the aim of putting such technologies into practical use in the Bay Area. This is a policy consciously to develop the legacy of Tokyo 2020. If these are realized, this will be the greatest legacy of the Olympics, both in the city and in society.

Transportation in the Tokyo Bay Area

Immediately after the Olympics, plans to extend subway lines related to the Bay Area took shape. First, the extension of Tokyo Metro Line 8 (Yurakucho Line) from Toyosu, located in the northern part of the Bay Area at the junction of various subway lines, to Sumiyoshi, which has been an issue for many years, has been virtually decided. This is expected to alleviate some of the congestion on the Tozai Line, said to be the most congested in Japan, which runs from Chiba Prefecture to the west of Tokyo along Tokyo Bay.

Second, the Shirokane–Takanawa–Shinagawa extension of the Tokyo

Metro Namboku Line has also been decided. Shinagawa, a major station on the west side of the Bay Area, is currently under construction for the Linear Chuo Shinkansen, which will connect to Nagoya in forty minutes. By connecting Shinagawa Station and Shirokane–Takanawa Station, it will be possible to go to Saitama Prefecture, in the north or Yokohama in the south by subway from Shinagawa.

Third, the construction of a new airport line (Kama-Kama Line) has been decided, and the direct connection between the Tokyu Tamagawa Line from the Yokohama area and the Haneda Airport Line of the Keihin Express will increase the accessibility of Haneda Airport.

Fourth, JR East's Haneda Airport access lines project is also underway. In addition to the direct connection between JR Tokyo Station and Haneda Airport, connections between Haneda Airport and Chiba and Shinjuku will be dramatically improved.

Fifth, as a result of the above-mentioned construction plans for each line, which had been pending before the Olympics, the TX (Tsukuba Express) will run from Akihabara through the Yaesu Exit of Tokyo Station, turning at Ginza and passing through the site of the Athletes' Village in Harumi. Momentum is finally building to advance discussions on the concept of a subway that goes to Tokyo Big Sight in the Bay Area.

As discussed elsewhere (Aoyama, 2016), Tokyo has been trying to expand its urban structure to the Kanto Plain since it began to improve the ring road and railway structure of the city at the time of the 1964 Olympics (figure 18.10). For this strategy the Bay Area is very important since realization of this concept is essential both to take advantage of the Olympic Village in Harumi and various Olympic facilities in the Bay Area, and to develop the Bay Area into a mecca of advanced information technology.

Haneda Airport is closely related to the development of the Bay Area. In 1999, the airport had 234,000 slots a year, but in 2020, this almost doubled to 486,000 slots a year – the result of the construction of a fourth runway and other improvements. Looking at the details of the increase in flights over the past twenty years, the number of international flights has risen significantly from four to 130, while the number of domestic flights has only grown from 316 to 465. Even now, there is a pressing need to increase the number of flights to Haneda from regional cities in Japan. Demand for increased international flights is also expected to increase, with a similar pattern expected in demand for air cargo. This is because there has been a shift to aviation due to international disputes affecting maritime transport disruptions in recent years, and also the demand for transporting electronic parts and high-end consumer goods.

The rise in passengers and the number of flights in recent years has been supported by improved access to the airport, which was completed in 2012 by improving the convenience of bus transport through the Keikyu

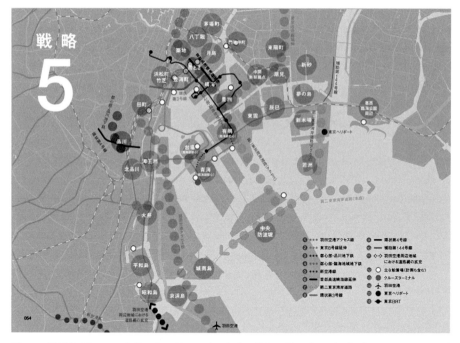

Figure 18.10. Transportation functions plan in the Tokyo Bay Area, indicating concepts and plans for new transportation functions. (*Source*: Tokyo Metropolitan Government)

Main Line/Haneda Airport Line continuous grade separation project. In the future, it is planned to increase the number of flights by increasing the number of trains operated by the JR East Haneda Airport Access Line and the Haneda Airport Terminal 1 and 2 underground tunnel construction of the Keikyu Airport Line. The dramatic enhancement of transportation network in the Tokyo Bay Area helps to encourage further development of the area and creates a synergistic effect. The legacy of the 2020 Tokyo Olympics is therefore evidenced in the Tokyo Bay Area; an influence which will continue to develop into the future.

Conclusion

The emblem that was first adopted for the 2020 Tokyo Olympics was withdrawn because of claims of plagiarism, which became a subject of international comment (see chapter 2). Its replacement (figure 18.11) was a design that showed how different cultures and ideas are interconnected. As such, the new 2020 Tokyo emblem conveyed the message of 'Diversity and Harmony', itself the ideal of the Olympic and Paralympic Games. If Tokyo, the host city of the 2022 Olympics, can show the world this aspect after the Olympics, it will be a great legacy.

At these Games, the number of athletes who revealed that they were part of sexual minorities was 182 at the Olympics and twenty-eight at the

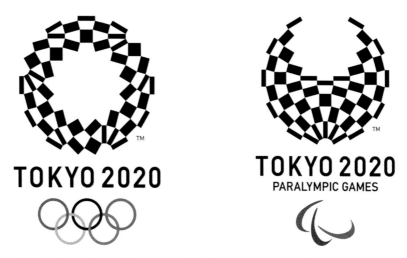

Figure 18.11. The emblem of the Tokyo 2020 Olympics. (*Source*: Materials released by the Tokyo Organizing Committee of the Olympic and Paralympic Games, 2016)

Paralympics. These were both record highs. In the past, Japan had many inadequacies in terms of how many sports amenities, public transportation, hotels, inns, restaurants, and similar facilities were barrier-free. In preparation for the Olympic and Paralympic Games, the 'TOKYO 2020 Accessibility Guidelines' were drawn up with the participation of many stakeholders, and considerable improvements were made. In 2018, the city of Tokyo enacted an ordinance aimed at realizing the principle of respecting human rights enshrined in the Tokyo Olympic Charter. Throughout the Games, there were a series of incidents in which the chairman of the Organizing Committee and other executives and managers were removed from duties and positions related to the Olympics due to discriminatory remarks against women.

This was an important moment. If it were not for the Olympics, this might not have been talked about. If understanding the importance of mutually recognizing diversity is deepened among Japanese, this will be the greatest legacy of the Olympics. As the present author previously noted (Aoyama, 2017), the legacy of the Olympics includes social evolution. The Tokyo Bay Area, where many Olympic facilities are located, will continue to take on the challenge of becoming a future city. The city of the future should not only be a place where dreams of cutting-edge technology can be realized, but also a city where the people who live and work there can feel 'Diversity and Harmony'.

Note

1.   The committee's budget and results have been announced in Japanese yen, but these have been converted here using the rate of 1 US dollar = Japanese 110 yen, which is close to the average rate over the past few years.

Chapter 19

PARIS 2024

Cécile Doustaly

In 2017, after three consecutive failed attempts, Paris won the bid to host the XXXIII Olympic and Paralympic Games at the International Olympic Committee's 131st session, held in Lima, Peru. Running from 26 July to 11 August and from 28 August to 8 September 2024 respectively, this will be the biggest event ever organized in the country. These ambitious and 'democratic Games' have been articulated around the French Republic's values of freedom, equality, and fraternity, symbolized by the mascots representing the Phrygian caps worn by French revolutionaries. Competitions will be mainly located in Greater Paris, but also in twelve *departements*, and will 'engage the whole of France … with a useful long-lasting legacy for all'. Besides the multifarious sports legacy (from amateur and professional practice and infrastructure, to parity, health, and Paralympics), the main legacy of the Games will involve soft power, tourism, cultural, social, economic, and urban impacts: notably showcasing French heritage (mainly Central Paris), and transforming its northern suburbs through transport, mixed infrastructure, and new neighbourhoods (Paris 2024, 2023*b*).

This chapter provides an overview of the challenges, opportunities, and innovations associated with Paris 2024 which entered full operational mode at the beginning of 2023, following a series of assessments and some organizational setbacks. Potential threats have now been clearly identified around issues connected with security, transport, funding, and sustainability. Like all Olympic cities, Paris voted through exceptional legislation, causing controversies and opposition (Braconnier, 2018).[1] As yet, however, the Paris Olympiad has understandably attracted little scientific publication but, like other Olympiads, the media are covering the project closely, relaying support and opposition, hopes and threats. French public opinion has generally been relatively positive, but the economic and political context is uncertain. This chapter relies on mixed research methods, from data collection and content analysis of scientific and grey literature to empirical research with actors of Paris 2024, drawing comparative analysis of literature from cultural policy studies, urban studies, heritage studies, and emerging Olympic studies. It also questions how this 'mega-eventization' of cities changes the way we think about the city (Iosa *et al.*, 2020). After a presentation of the bid, its context, and governance, this chapter focuses on the urban dimension of the event and concludes with its urban legacy.

The First 'New Norm' Olympic Games?

Once a prize coveted by bidding cities, hosting the Olympic and Paralympic Games has lost its appeal in the last decade due to concerns about corruption, lack of cost efficiency, dysfunctional governance, transparency, and disconnection with local priorities. As a result, an increasing number of citizens, civic groups, and authorities have opposed the organization of the Olympics in their city. Withdrawals in 2022, 2024 and 2026 because of fear of anti-Olympic movements or negative referendums (Boston, Rome), led to a situation where there were just two candidates for the 2024 and 2028 Games (Transparency International, 2016; Bourbillères and Koebel, 2020).

In this context, the Paris Games have deployed increased 'policy attachment', using the Olympics as a lever for development in varied sectors, from the environment, jobs and training to social cohesion and urban renewal. Such shifts can be traced back to the London 2012 Olympics' successes regarding the Paralympics (Richard *et al.*, 2020), the environment, and the cultural Olympiads, while democratic governance and social justice were questioned (Poynter *et al.*, 2016; Doustaly and Zembri-Mary, 2019; Doustaly, 2023). Organizing Committees, in turn, have conceived Olympics as glocal events that articulate global, national, and local impacts, with the associated governance aimed at pulling in resources and strengthening 'actors' coalitions' (Andranovich and Burbank, 2011). Such a collaborative and multi-scalar approach has been recommended in urban and cultural policy since the 2000s as best practice, from Cities of Culture to heritage management (Doustaly, 2019; also see Chapter 4).

Drawing on expertise from previous attempts (Lauermann, 2016), the Paris 2024 bid introduced new orientations reflecting questioning of the Olympic model. In 2017, in an unprecedented gesture, fifty cities signed a support letter for Paris 2024, launched by the Mayor of Montreal, saying that Paris had 'the assets and the will to give new life to the Olympic values, [organize] shared, useful and joyful [Games], trigger social and environmental progress, and be a lever of transformation for the whole of its metropolis' (author's translation, Mairie de Paris, 2017). Eventually, Paris and Los Angeles remained as the only candidates for 2024 and 2028, and Paris's continued interest in welcoming the Games, combined with reflexive commitments in favour of sustainable Games and improved governance, convinced the jury of the city's suitability to stage the Games (Faure, 2020).

Paris won its nomination in September 2017. The French candidacy committee and now the Olympic Committee have been co-led and led respectively by Tony Estanguet, a young (born in 1978), regionally based, triple Canoe Olympic champion (2000, 2004, 2012). This was a break from the previous two French failed candidacies in 2008 and 2012, personified by less charismatic, non-sports leaders. However, Estanguet also had a strong track record in sports administration, being elected to the International Olympic Committee's Athletes Commission (2012), Vice-President for the International Canoe Federation (2014) and subsequently particularly active in the IOC's Sustainability and Legacy Commission. Drawing on this experience to win the bid, Estanguet and the stakeholders involved (the sports movement, civil society, public and private sectors) managed multilevel lobbying, adapting their rhetoric to five types of crucial supporters to convince: the IOC, the sports, political and media spheres and public opinion with their own respective agendas.

After gaining the nomination and now president of the Paris 2024 Organizing Committee for the Olympic and Paralympic Games (*Comité d'Organisation des Jeux Olympiques et Paralympiques* – COJOP) Estanguet confirmed his aim 'to bring together all the communities and organizations that want to take part in the Olympic and Paralympic adventure to showcase France at its finest and tender a new model for more spectacular, more responsible and more open Games'.[2] The legacy dimension was strongly emphasized. If the spectacular seemingly contradicts the notion of responsibility, they both reflected public expectations (Gignon *et al.*, 2022; Le Monde, 2023*b*). The Olympic Committee defended its role as an organization, introducing positive multi-scalar change through sport and professional standards of ethics through its 'New Norm' (IOC, 2018*d*). The regulated and hierarchical Olympic governance, until then led by state and market-based organizations, shifted to meet main stakeholders' expectations, and as Chappelet (2021*a*) noted: 'failing to collaborate would risk losing the support of two essential stakeholders in ensuring the Games are a success: public opinion (through civic groups and NGOs) and, consequently, local, regional and national host governments'. The subsequent IOC Olympic Agenda 2020 (IOC, 2021*e*) was based on three pillars: credibility, sustainability, and youth, and recommended games answering city planning needs to improve cost-benefit.

The COJOP

Established in January 2018, COJOP is responsible for planning, organizing, financing, and delivering the Olympic and Paralympic Games in accordance with the Host City Contract signed by the IOC and the CNOSF (*Comité National Olympique et Sportif Français*). Illustrating the new 'collaborative

Olympic governance', Paris 2024 has sought to enlarge the involvement and variety of stakeholders (elite athletes, cultural and civic groups, education actors, sponsors, media, as well as local, regional, and national government). In effect, Paris 2024 is steered by a 'committee of partners' led by the inter-ministerial delegation for the Olympics (*Délégué Interministériel aux Jeux Olympiques et Paralympiques* – DIJOP) whose delegate is Michel Cadot (Cadot, 2020) with the City of Paris (taking second place), the Olympic Delivery Authority (*Société de Livraison des Ouvrages Olympiques* – SOLIDEO),[3] COJOP, Île de France Region, Greater Paris Metropolis, and the Seine-Saint-Denis Department.[4] Leaders Anne Hidalgo (Paris), Stéphane Troussel (Seine-Saint-Denis), Mathieu Hanotin (leader of Plaine commune and Saint-Denis mayor), from a currently fragile socialist party, have managed to work with centre-right government and parliament and Île de France region.

In 2023, the national public evaluation body (*Cour des Comptes* – CC) reported that the Olympic strategic planning phase and governance were satisfactory and that no major irregularities were found on public procurement. Eighteen months before the Games, however, it recommended:

◆ increased coordination between the COJOP and the SOLIDEO under the DIJOP;

◆ increased financial and operational clarity from all partners;

◆ stringent financial ethics and overspend controls; and

◆ risk mitigation on security and transport to deal with 7 million visitors, 800,000 per day – despite both facing dire recruitment issues. (CC, 2023)

Estanguet's collectivist approach can also be traced to his decision to broaden the existing model for the Athletes' commission to involve eighteen French athletes that were representative of sporting and Olympic values, with an expanded remit to:

◆ consult peers to allow representation from around the world to feed into the project;

◆ approve the athletes' living conditions during the Games, co-designing the Olympic Village, the Athletes' House and celebrations (Paris 2024, 2020);

◆ support engagement projects (schools' Olympic week; Olympic run day) and encourage sports practice as a tool for social inclusion and environmental protection. (Paris 2024, 2020; interviews)

The COJOP employs athletes, event managers, experts from public administration and civil society, and business leaders. Its diverse skills and profile were hailed to reflect the ambition for reformed Games, paving the way for the 'construction of the France of tomorrow'. From 2021, as a symbolic gesture, the COJOP offices were moved from the Boulevard Haussmann in central Paris to the northern suburb of Plaine Commune. 'Pulse', a recent constructed building rented until 2024, was chosen to reflect Paris Olympic identity and ambitions: it neutralizes its carbon footprint with a garden on the roof top and sustainable food and focuses on local recruitment for its activities and the Games in relation to construction, hospitality, catering, cleaning, and green spaces. In 2022, Paris 2024 employed over 800 people from ten different countries, 3,000 were expected in 2023, 4,000 in 2024. Confirming candidacy commitments, a Director for Impact and Legacy was appointed from the outset (Paris 2024, 2023*a*).

Theoretically, all was in place for effective governance. Until recently, however, the organization was characterized by instability. On some issues, meetings with partners have been organized by more than a dozen different people, leading to organizational confusion and delays. At ease with the Olympic Movement (in a majority on his Board) and with his sponsors, Estanguet has attracted criticism for centralizing decisions within his trusted circle, feeding internal strife, and keeping politicians, civil servants, and others especially close to Paris Mayor Anne Hidalgo at bay (Le Monde, 2023*b*; interviews 2022). The *Cour des Comptes* noted some improvements in 2023 and admits that the COJOP has had to work in a complex context, with CNOSF leadership in crisis in April 2023, and the state and local authorities coming from opposite sides of the political spectrum (Le Monde, 2022; CC, 2023).

Paris 2024 Intertwined Sport and Territorial Legacy

In terms of local authority steering, Paris initially headed the way as host city, with a strong and transparent investment in 2020 from Mayor Hidalgo. Her allies, however, had gradually been ousted from the COJOP as she lost her national standing. Collaboration with the Seine-Saint-Denis Department, also politically left-wing, turned out to be more productive. Despite having responsibilities in these two territories and initially contributing a similar budget to Paris funding in the Olympic budget, the centre-right Île-de-France region has surprisingly no Olympic blueprint. The region co-finances rather than initiates, and only makes contracts in relation to its main missions: transport (with serious concerns over adequate delivery in 2024), training (new international Sport Lycée in St Denis), job policies, and sport infrastructure (Le Monde, 2023*a*; CC, 2023; Le Parisien, 2022; interviews).

The COJOP and SOLIDEO have objectives which converge in many fields. Social and health objectives will be met more easily with improved infrastructure. Opportunities to win more medals will be provided by reforming an outdated French professional sports federation's model, based on associations and in need of professionalization and attraction. Paris 2024 will leave its imprint on the territory and modify urban life in the long term in diverse ways, impacting security and surveillance (potential negatives), professional and amateur sports legacy (with huge positive potential for the economy, health and wellbeing), Paralympics and inclusivity, transport and territorial justice, economic development, innovation and sustainable building expertise.

The *Terre de Jeux* (Land of the Games) 2024 programme launched in 2019 was designed by the COJOP to turn the Olympics into a national event and achieve its objectives by involving the rest of France in celebration, engagement, and sports legacy[5]. All twelve French regions and *departements* have paid to obtain the label, as well as a number of embassies, and over 3,000 towns. For the COJOP, it is a way to share and outsource while keeping some control and steering its objectives. It does not finance the activities of the labelled entities but, thanks to partnerships with institutions, helps to respond to calls for projects. Like most labels, it provides support and networked best practice, a distinct *Terre de Jeux* brand identity, communication, and event planning toolkit. The main advantage for local authorities is that it makes them eligible to apply to become a Preparation Centre for the Games for the 206 delegations and French teams, to be included in the Torch Relay itinerary (for an extra cost), and to create public sports itineraries very easily on an App and advertise them.

Mega events are structurally unsound environmentally, if only because they rely in their current model on an influx of visitors from around the globe. However, sustainability has been integrated in most parts of the Paris 2024 event and its physical legacy. From the candidacy phase, steps were taken to control the impact on climate of the event and its legacy, halving greenhouse gas emissions to 1.5 million tons (compared to London 2012 and Rio 2016) by employing low-carbon structures, renewable energy, and sustainable catering and using 95 per cent of existing or temporary buildings. The COJOP set up an expert committee for the Ecological Transformation of the Games and devised a new model (figure 19.1) to support the implementation of a climate and environmental strategy respecting the Paris agreement and offsetting 100 per cent of residual emissions (travel by spectators). Paris could rely on its many existing facilities and new building for the Olympics has been planned ready for repurposing and therefore considered as opportunity investment (i.e. needed investment). Rather than assessing the impact, the model now identifies an initial carbon budget.

Showcasing France, from Iconic Heritage to Inclusive Creativity

The spectacle taking place … will go down in history and Paris will be the centre of the world – the world of sport and so much more. The Games are a popular, multicultural

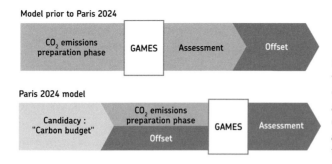

Figure 19.1. Changing the model: from a post-Games assessment to a pre-Games target. (*Source*: Cécile Doustaly, adapted and expanded from Paris 2024, 2023b)

festival, a celebration to share with the rest of the world. They represent a new adventure that will embark France on an experience unlike anything it has seen before. (Paris 2024, 2023a)

As indicated in table 19.1, the COJOP plans to welcome 12.6 million spectators from all over the world to watch almost 900 competitions. Around 200 delegations and 15,000 athletes will be housed in the Athletes' Village. It is a source of pride that there will be an increased presence for the Paralympics and inclusion of four new sports for the Olympics – break dancing, rock-climbing, skateboarding, and surfing – that address the expectations of young people. These are all sports that are characterized by being urban, outdoor, easy to practice, have an active social media presence, and allow the showcasing of Paris and the French Overseas Territories (Tahiti). The number of expected volunteers has been raised from 31,500 to 45,000 (COJOP, 2023). Although consolidated data is lacking, two surveys showed that public opinion was overall favourable towards the Games, with few expressing outright rejection. Expressions of anxiety focused on higher financial and environmental costs than anticipated and scepticism towards the promised positive socio-economic and urban impacts (Collinet *et al.*, 2020; Gignon *et al.*, 2022).

Table 19.1. Main data for the Paris 2024 Olympics. (*Source*: Compiled by the author from Paris 2024 official statistics, 12 March 2023)

Planned Figures for:	Olympic Games	Paralympic Games
Spectators	9.3 million	3.3 million
Sites and Competitions	41/329	19/549
Athletes	10,500 (parity women/men)	4,400
National Delegations	206	182
Sports	28 sports and 4 new ones	22 sports
Volunteers	30,000	15,000
Expected Media Exposure (based on Rio)	6,000 accredited journalists; 4bn. TV viewers; 350,000 hours of broadcast	3,000 accredited journalists

The COJOP's communication that this would be a democratic Games, a 'People's Festival', created high expectations towards ticketing. Of 10 million tickets, 20 per cent will be for official partners. From the remaining 80 per cent destined for the public, half will cost under €50 with one million tickets at the lowest price of €24. Ticketing is important to balance the budget (see below) and it was considered positive that all the one-third of tickets for the competitions offered in the first sale phase were sold. Two-thirds of these were bought by French people, regardless of huge outcry regarding the total costs. To balance bad publicity, the COJOP accelerated communication on future single ticket sales and its outreach programme. 100,000 and 300,000 seats for the Olympics and Paralympics respectively will be bought by the government at a cost of €11 million. These tickets will be distributed for the use of poorer families and educational outings (notably for disabled people), but also to thank essential workers and sports volunteers. This is a first in Olympic history and a logistics challenge as distribution will concern all France. Local authorities will also obtain and buy 600,000 tickets. The financial implications are not yet known (Le Monde, 2023c).

The ceremonies in Central Paris aim to be 'memorable, festive and popular', while some of Paris's most iconic and familiar heritage sites will be turned into sporting venues, providing impressive settings for the competitions. A programme of activities has been developed to engage people in central Paris, as in 2019 with a 2,024-metres run in the Place de la Concorde. The Organizing Committee is keen to point out that for the first time in Olympic history, the public will be able to take part in the same competitions as the athletes in the 'Marathon for all', where amateurs will run along the same historical Paris route as athletes, or in the Seine-Saint-Denis cycling road event whose itinerary is also devised to valorize the heritage of this little-known *departement*.

The historical heart of Paris will be on show globally throughout the competitions being hosted, providing continuity through thirty-five venues as well as showcasing the best-known iconic heritage landmarks, transformed as sporting arenas (figure 19.2). These are: archery on the Esplanade des Invalides; beach volleyball on the Champs de Mars; cycling on the Champs-Élysées; beach volleyball under the Eiffel Tower; swimming in open water; marathon and the paratriathlon starting at Pont d'Iéna; fencing and taekwondo in the Grand Palais; and wrestlers and judokas at the Grand Palais Ephémère on the Champ de Mars. The Place de la Concorde will be turned into an open arena for new urban disciplines (skateboarding, BMX freestyle, breakdance, and basketball 3x3). These disciplines, often overlooked because of their origins, were put forward as democratic, but were also chosen strategically for their popularity with young people and on social media. This choice of location supports their institutionalization and respectability, while also presenting the advantage of modernizing Paris's historical centre. The

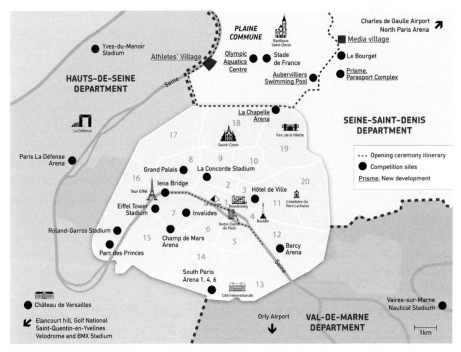

Figure 19.2. Schematic map of the Olympic and Paralympic competition sites and development in Greater Paris. (*Source*: Cécile Doustaly)

idea of using Parisian urban icons as shrines for sport competition is a simple but unprecedented one, matching both Parisian magic and luxurious brand identity.

The Olympic Games will be the most ambitious event organized in Paris (and France) but will also celebrate links with the two Olympic Games and the eight Great Exhibitions organized between 1844 and 1937. These, in their time, led to the building of new infrastructure which, like the Eiffel Tower (1889 Exhibition) and the Grand Palais (1900 exhibition), are now part of Paris's monumental legacy. It will also celebrate more ancient monuments like the Invalides and the Château de Versailles and more recent leisure infrastructures like the Bercy Arena or the new la Chappelle arena.

The opening ceremony will present: 'Paris, its River Seine, its Monuments, its banks, a unique event celebrating sport and the city'. Holding it outside a stadium for the first time will allow it to accommodate eight to ten times more spectators. The itinerary will run along 6 kilometres of the river Seine with 10,500 athletes parading from the Austerlitz Bridge to the Trocadéro and, *inter alia*, showcasing Notre Dame, the Grand Palais, and Les Invalides – all renovated for the occasion. Concerned about the planned figure of 600,000 spectators, the transport authorities have recently asked for to it to be limited to 400,000–500,000. Attendance will be mostly free but will include 100,000 who will occupy paid seating. According to some politicians, the Champs de Mars could have accommodated more people in more secure conditions.

For some actors, this reinforces a stereotype view of Paris and is a missed opportunity to promote the diversity of French heritage, from natural and rural spaces to industrial or intangible heritage, and multicultural communities. The Seine-Saint-Denis and Plaine Commune, which in 2020 lost the ceremonies initially planned at the Stade de France, will need to gain international attention through an alternative arts and heritage strategy.

As with many public sectors, culture and tourism tend to operate in silos, but the Cultural Olympiads have been identified as an opportunity for change (Doustaly, 2023), although the flexibility and creativity of large cultural festivals (Gold and Gold, 2020*a*) clash with the complexity of IOC rules and regulations. As a solution, some advocate creation of an alternative Off Festival as in the Festival of Avignon, given that the Olympiad is a protected brand.

The Games as a Lever for the Development of Greater Paris Metropolis

To spread development on the other side of central Paris's boundaries, the Games have been integrated in the development of the Greater Paris Metropolis. Smaller than the Region Île de France, this strategic inter-municipal authority was created in 2016 to administer an area of densely urbanized cities including central Paris with a population of twelve million. Relatedly, the Société du Grand Paris was set up in 2010 as a public institution designed to deliver the 'Grand Paris Express' circular metro,[6] a task it will need until 2030 to complete. The project has been affected by local political disputes, and the state may have seized the Olympics as a catalyst to resolve them (Lebeau, 2018).

The SOLIDEO is the commercial and industrial public organization created in 2017 to finance, supervise and deliver Olympic facilities, whether temporary or permanent, and to handle their repurposing after the Games as public amenities, new spaces, housing, and office units. It is also responsible for urban redevelopment works which have all been planned for legacy: improving transport, telecommunications, access to monuments (Grand Palais), connecting public spaces, regenerating canals, constructing new bridges and roads. Overall, it oversees building or renovation works on eleven competition, seventeen training, twenty infrastructural, and thirteen urban planning sites.

The SOLIDEO has benefitted from a positive context, reinforced by a better organizational stability and a more experienced and much smaller team (about 100) than the COJOP. It has also been able to rely on the experience from large developments associated with previous Olympic candidacies and recent innovations. Like the COJOP, it has drafted a mission statement and has identified four interrelated objectives to pursue: innovation and technology; local jobs and economic impact; a sustainable city; and universal accessibility.

Recent building innovation and digital tools have provided precious planning support and team motivation, advancing sustainable building methods. The new BIM (Building Information Modelling) digital platform has allowed the fusion of more than 700 digital models into the biggest three-dimensional model yet devised in Europe to cover the Olympic Village (an area of 65 hectares). It improves project management from conception through to execution. In the conception phase, it allows the teams responsible to share the plan and comment upon it, thus informing collaboration between actors to create reliable execution plans with associated budgets and deadlines. In the execution phase, BIM can identify lack of coherence between individual projects and other issues before construction starts. According to the teams, plans have never been so precise. The job shortages in the building industry, for lack of preparation, were one of the failures of London 2012. In Paris, an active strategy was devised to attract and train the 11,000 construction workers needed and allowed the filling of some gaps by complementing with subcontracting. Illegal works have been constrained as promised in the charter for work and place development. Other job opportunities, mostly in catering and security, lack attraction (Le Monde, 2023*a*; SOLIDEO, 2023; fieldwork, 2022–2023).

The legacy from new construction, mainly non-sport infrastructure for underserved areas, have benefitted from a new law creating 'two-phase (temporary and permanent) planning', building and developing permissions, with reversion limited to eighteen months after the Games. This signals the end of 2025 for final delivery, which aligns with the closure of SOLIDEO.[7] The project for a compact Olympics as laid out in the Candidacy documents was changed in 2022, with modifications in the allocation of competition sites being made in order to reduce costs and maximize reuse of existing premises. Although Paris will be the centre of media attention, it is too small to build new infrastructure and an Athletes' Village. Most other competitions will be held in Greater Paris, with the objective of leaving a lasting urban and sports legacy, mostly in Seine-Saint-Denis, which concentrates 80 per cent of SOLIDEO funding.

The Seine-Saint-Denis is the youngest and poorest *departement* in Metropolitan France. Densely populated (1.6 million inhabitants in 2019, as against 2.16 million for central Paris), it will benefit from new infrastructure and strategic urban regeneration projects. It has a significant lack of sport equipment, with only half of 11-year-olds knowing how to swim, for lack of adequate provision and transport. Both issues are being addressed by the Olympic and Paralympic Games, and the *departement* is trying to increase the figure to 75 per cent by 2024, as a clear legacy for its

Figure 19.3. The Olympic Aquatics Centre under construction, Saint-Denis. (*Source*: Photograph, CC Chabe01, August 2022)

inhabitants. However, the three planned swimming pools (see figure 19.2), will only partially cover the needs. The Athletes' and Media Villages and the Olympic Aquatics Centre (figure 19.3) are being built there, next to the Stade de France (constructed for the 2008 Olympic candidacy), in the inter-municipality of Plaine Commune, bordering the north of central Paris.

Planned for the Olympics, the new northern interconnected transport five-line hub Pleyel Saint-Denis and automated line 14 will provide strategic transport for 2024, but the other metro lines 15, 16, 17, 18 have been delayed until 2030 at least. More consensually, PRISME, a new inclusive training Centre, will be ready to support the Paralympic legacy. This thorough and fast urban change aims at modifying the attractivity model of northern Paris's poorer suburbs and improve the local quality of life. Extra SOLIDEO investments, like the Tour Pleyel 3–4 star hotel, criticized for being luxurious, will provide accommodation for the Olympics and be joined later by an adjacent Congress Centre (Pelloux *et al.*, 2017; Le Parisien, 2022).

The Athletes' Village: A New Model Neighbourhood?

For the Athletes' Village north of central Paris, the SOLIDEO coordinates planning and delivery on the public and privately owned plots, which will be subject to the democratic and administrative authority of three municipalities under the umbrella of Plaine Commune and the *departement*. Its perimeter overlaps three municipalities: Saint-Denis, Saint-Ouen and, an island across a branch of the Seine, the Île-Saint-Denis. Paris did not opt for an *ad hoc* extra-borough governance, unlike London where the London Legacy Development Corporation is still in place (Doustaly and Zembri-Mary, 2019). Contrary to London, the location of the Village was only partially a wasteland, since a mixed-development zone (*Zone d'Aménagement Concerté*, ZAC) had been created in 2009. The industrial site was redeveloped as the 'Cité du Cinéma', Luc Besson's 'Hollywood on Seine', with studios, offices, and cinema training, of which he rented large parts. Faced with economic issues, the Cité will house the athletes' canteen (for most of the daily 600,000 meals needed at the Village) and sports training halls, but its future activities are unknown. In contrast with Central Paris, the Village is an opportunity to showcase industrial French heritage and have space for urban experiments (SOLIDEO, fieldwork).

In 2018, the respected architect and urbanist Dominique Perrault produced the design for the Athletes' Village master plan in line with Paris 2024's candidacy, adapting to what he defined as a complex and overlooked site. The Village was to illustrate state of the art and 'exemplary' environmental standards, cater for athletes' needs during the Games, and be turned into a new neighbourhood immediately afterwards to benefit the local community. The vision was both to re-anchor the site to Paris and the Seine's history and geography and to produce an innovative and metropolitan plan. The two-phase planning permit was used to embed the finalization of this legacy stage within three years. Perrault had strong credentials, having often been associated with large-scale architectural and planning projects, notably in Paris along the Seine, and in Berlin as part of the 2000 failed Olympic candidacy.

SOLIDEO plans, finances, and supervises the Village. From 2019, fourteen operators and forty-one architects bidding as consortia were selected to develop the four plots of Village facilities. Construction works for the Village started in 2021, and should be delivered on time, mostly by early 2024 (figure 19.4). The Village is expected to accommodate around 14,000 athletes and 206 delegations during the Games, as well as 8,000 during the Paralympics. For the first time in the Games, a study was carried out by the Athletes' Commission of Paris 2024 to co-create the design of the Village. This involved in-depth interviews with fifty-three athletes and a consultation of 198 Olympians (twenty-three disciplines) and Paralympians (ten disciplines), from twenty-four countries North and South, who had previous experience of thirteen editions of the Games. The manifesto highlighting their main views and expectations influenced the Village design, 'building a Village by athletes, for athletes' (Paris 2024, 2020). Interestingly, their aspirations reflected twenty-first century urban planning best practice for

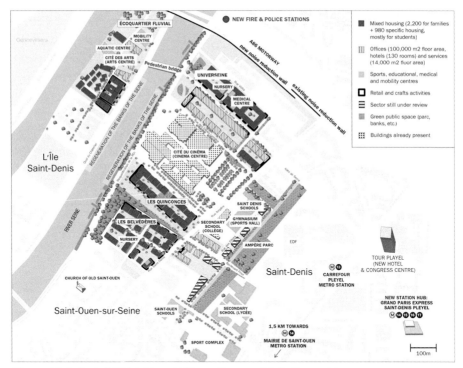

Figure 19.4. Paris 2024 Athletes' Village. (*Source*: Cécile Doustaly)

inclusive sustainable neighbourhoods, and SOLIDEO's view of the legacy. This stood for creating safe and green spaces that allowed for conviviality for diverse ages, gender, universal access, green spaces, respecting environmental objectives (47 per cent less carbon use compared to traditional building), and balancing work and leisure. An urban art programme with fifteen works reflecting this vision is scheduled to be ready for the Games ('Fertile currents', SOLIDEO).

After the Games and by the end of 2025, contractors have been tasked with repurposing most of the buildings in order to turn the Village into an 'eco-responsible, functional neighbourhood, which will blend into the city of the future'. The mixed-used neighbourhood of 52 hectares (330,000 square metres) is planned for 6,000 residents and 6,000 workers: 2,800 homes, a student residence, 72,000 square metres of tertiary activities, 20,000 square metres of neighbourhood shops and services, a 9,000 square metre hotel, a 15,000 square metre art centre, 9,000 square metres of public facilities (two nurseries, two schools, and a nautical centre), walking and cycling paths ('slow mobility'), parks, green spaces and regenerated Seine banks with a new footbridge to the Île-Saint-Denis (SOLIDEO, 2023).

The project also redefines environmental excellence as creating urban spaces adapted for the 2050 climate, a first in Olympic history:

◆   protecting and fostering biodiversity (e.g. insects, birds, and small animals);

◆   restricting carbon-emissions to achieve Paris Climate Plan's objectives and reach carbon neutrality by 2050 (e.g. use of wood and other organically sourced materials); limited cars and parking spaces; energy efficiency (solar and geothermal energy);

◆   adapt to climate change (e.g. use of plants, water, adapted surfaces). A 3-hectare landscaped park and, overall about 6 hectares of greenery have been planned, around 60 per cent more than previously existed, and 9,000 new trees and bushes.

SOLIDEO opted for a transparent communication tool by creating the House of the Project where diverse visitors, from the wider public including pupils, students, professionals, and sponsors can get an overview of the Olympic Village building project.[8]

The Paris 2024 Olympic Village will not become a park, but four neighbourhoods planned to be quickly occupied after the Games, leaving only a little to be developed later, as regeneration was already well under way in the area. This is in contrast with London and Sydney, for which legacy has spanned decades (see below). The Paris Village's size is indeed less than a quarter of London's Olympic Park (225 hectares compared with the LLDC area which spans 480 hectares) and a mere thirteenth of Sydney's footprint. Contrary to the initial compact Games described in the Paris bid, the more sustainable option chosen was to use existing sites in twelve departments of the country, with a trickle-down impact (table 19.2).

'The Games Finance the Games?'

The slogan used in relation to the hotly debated issue of the cost of the Paris Olympics was 'The Games finance the Games'. In the 2020 COJOP budget, 97 per cent of the budget was planned to come from the private sector, namely the IOC, partner companies, the Games ticket office, and licensing, with only 3 per cent from public funding, and ringfenced for the Paralympic Games. This budget covers only the cost of planning and organizing the event: adapting and operating facilities, renting premises, organizing competitions, setting up the Opening and Closing Ceremonies, housing athletes, welcoming and transporting athletes, delegations, and VIPs and ensuring security at competition venues (figure 19.5).

In December 2022, mainly due to inflation and increased energy costs, the COJOP reassessed its budget by 10 per cent to €4.4 billion. The contribution from public authorities (mainly the state for two-thirds, but also the City of Paris, Île de France region, and Greater Paris) doubled overall to reach €211 million, which included €170 million that was earmarked for the Paralympics as part of the policy of inclusion. The overall budget increased by

Table 19.2. Comparative analysis of Legacy Planning for the Sydney 2000, London 2012 and Paris 2024 Olympic Games Athlete's Village areas. (*Source:* Compiled by author)

	Stage 0 (Pre-Bid)	*Stage 1 (Bid)*	*Stage 2 (Accepted Bid)*	*Stage 3 (Post-Games)*	*Stage 4 Long term*
Sydney 2000[1] (bid won in 1993) 640 ha	Homebush Bay area attracted planning studies since the 1970s, polluted brownfield chosen already for 1988 Olympic failed bid.	Reactive engagement. Site selection (population, transport, environmental effect, cost); scoping site remediation.	Articulated Development. HBDC responsible for site remediation, environmental management, venue, facility, transport infrastructure development, creation of the parkland.	Consequential Legacy planning. SOPA ad-hoc agency takes on responsibility for the park. Finding a viable future through encouraging new development; testing market interest.	Metropolitan integration until 2050. Upscaling residential and commercial development; competitive development; role in the context of regional governance.
London 2012[2] (bid won in 2005) 225 ha (480 ha for the larger LLDC area)	Olympic Park was a complex, polluted brownfield cut through by railway tracks for which massive investment was needed.	Surprise win against Paris. Legacy focused on opportunities and social housing in a deprived area of East London in line with Mayor Ken Livingstone's regeneration politics.	Uncertainty about the legacy policy as Boris Johnson replaces Livingstone as London Mayor (2010) and supports a commodification approach to the site, serving London in general as well as East London (2013).	Ambitious Legacy strategy: 'live, work, visit' implemented by an *ad-hoc* body (LLDC, 2012–). Housing priority shifts from social to middle and high-end housing, new financial and cultural quarters.	Metropolitan integration until 2030: area partly cut off from its poorer surroundings; gradually becoming more attractive to Londoners; provides in demand housing; cultural quarter as social impact.
Paris 2024 Mayoral continuity ◆ new local transport and (bid won in 2017) 52 ha	After the 2012 failed bid (2005): a successful new ecological (50 ha) neighbourhood, Clichy-Batignole (started in 2001). Bid allowed consensus. The 2024 Olympic village site was only partially brownfield land, regeneration, and creation of the Cité du cinema started in 2009.	Most long-term planning devised and modified during stages 1 and 2. Low key strategy for a rather small mixed neighbourhood – mostly 'live and work: ◆ reactive engagement ◆ articulated development and consequential legacy planning ('opportunity investment') ◆ metropolitan integration planning (delays in metropolitan works).		Most planning will be over. Little land still to develop. End of SOLIDEO and retrofitting of constructions (2025). Area governance back to local authorities.	Planned for 2030: ◆ new local transport and activities plans finalized; ◆ increased quality of life; and opportunities ◆ socio-economic and cultural development aligned with Paris.

Notes:
1. Adapted from Freestone and Gunasekara (2017).
2. Doustaly and Zembri-Mary (2019).

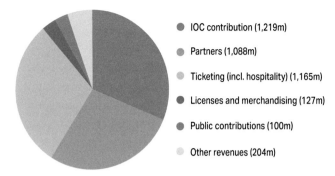

● IOC contribution (1,219m)

● Partners (1,088m)

○ Ticketing (incl. hospitality) (1,165m)

● Licenses and merchandising (127m)

● Public contributions (100m)

○ Other revenues (204m)

Figure 19.5. COJOP Organization Budget for Paris 2024, in million Euros (2020). (*Source*: Cécile Doustaly, using data from Paris 2024, 2022)

€400 million, also supported by growing commercial revenues (sponsorship €127 million; ticketing €143 million). Overall private investment is expected to reach about 95 per cent rather than the 97 per cent that was announced.

Experience suggests that total Olympic budgets generally double between the candidacy and the Games (see chapter 6), which inevitably alienates public opinion. In London, limited increases were decided before the Games, but the budget overspend still reached around 100 per cent (Poynter *et al.*, 2016; Doustaly and Zembri-Mary, 2019). While revisions seem unavoidable in such long-term mega projects, Paris has been bent on limiting increases and identifying cost saving solutions. Large use of existing equipment in Paris still means provisional adaptations are necessary. Many researchers consider that IOC funding is structurally insufficient. The way Olympic revenues are shared with the host city means tax-free re-transmission rights and sponsoring go to the IOC. Its €5 billion net gain from tax in Rio de Janeiro when the city itself was left to deal with inadequate structures and debt contributed to Paris's new approach. Furthermore, according to Boris Lebeau (2018, p. 4), the public–private partnerships devised to building projects 'often amounts to profit capture by a few investors and the socialization of the costs via the State and local authorities'. Olympic rhetoric tends to overlook this matter and local authorities present it more neutrally as a corollary of the market economy and unavoidable in large regeneration projects.

The original 2016 SOLIDEO budget, centralizing public fundings (state, region, local authorities), was evaluated at €1.4 billion. This was adjusted in July 2021 and aligned with inflation in December 2022, to reach €1.7 billion to allow for an additional cost of €140.1 million. With private investment (€2 billion) and complementary investments, the SOLIDEO budget reached €3.8 billion. Nicolas Ferrand, CEO, commented: 'Despite the obstacles … we will be able to deliver the works on time, within the set costs and the strong ambitions we have determined. The additional funding … is solely in response to the consequences of the war in Ukraine and the COVID crisis in China' (SOLIDEO, 2023).

It would be inaccurate to define the Olympic budget by simply adding the COJOP and SOLIDEO budgets. Some SOLIDEO works were started in advance of the Games. Others were added later, as some local authorities voted for the opportunity to invest, diverting existing budgets. For instance, Paris COVID-19 cycling routes have become permanent aligning Paris 2024 objectives with those of the City of Paris (€1.2 billion). Analysis of legacy also needs to consider the urban projects that were delayed or cancelled through diverting existing funds to the Olympics. For instance, regardless of delays following the coronavirus and due to high debt, Paris will not carry out building works in parallel with the Games. Redevelopments in central Paris of the Champs Elysées, the Trocadéro, and Notre-Dame de Paris forecourt into greener and more visitor friendly spaces will have to wait, with only minor improvements now planned, while the Tour Montparnasse will not be ready on time. Security costs, estimated at around €420 million, have not been included, with responsibility for those outside the immediate competition venues falling to local authorities. There are concerns as to the limited capacity of municipal police, leading to increased private security costs – concerns heightened by the safety incidents which disrupted the 2022 Champion's League final in Paris. Increased salaries which are expected to become necessary to attract hard-to-find workers have not been budgeted for either.

The costs do not include the public cost of tax relief for sponsors (Oméga could receive up to €4 billion). The multi-stakeholders' benefits from the new governance is constrained by the limitations placed on the use of the Olympic brand for the Organizing Committee's own sponsors or commercial operators. It leaves host territories without commercial sponsors, increasing reliance on public funds. The public–private partnership model of the Games and Paris 2024's decision that the event should largely pay for itself has therefore led to contradictory objectives: revenues depend on sponsors, while the public funders insist on an inclusive Games. There have been concerns that the COJOP and the IOC focus too much on accreditation (granted not only to people who have an essential or operational role in the Olympics, but also to accompanying guests and sponsors). To limit criticism, the IOC could reduce its number of accreditations and increase public outreach, from tourists to locals, as sponsors and ticketing bring similar funds. Commercial logic also contradicts Paris 2024's carbon limitation objectives (in this context, it is likely that statistics will be gathered on the number of guests travelling by air, staying in 5-star hotels, and so on).

In 2021 and again in 2023, the French national evaluating body imposed a responsibility on all Olympic partners to produce the detailed consolidated budget (functioning and investment) that it has been asking for without further delay. Its 2023 report, stating the impossibility of calculating the overall cost of the Games before the event, estimated that the total, including direct public spending, had gone from €6.9 billion in the candidacy to around €8.8 billion and that public investment could eventually reach €3 billion (CC, 2023).

A Limited Opposition to the Paris Games

By 2023, root and branch opposition to the Games has largely died out. However, if consensus to modify the project has been reached by actors in some domains, sensitive issues remain around transparency, the environment, surveillance, and a fair legacy. For instance, the Seine-Saint-Denis residents' collective *Saccage* (Rampage), created in 2020 to oppose the 'environmental, democratic and social ransacking' (author's translation) by Paris 2024, has not managed to create momentum. They defend the view that the Games do not uphold Olympic and sport values, but are a capitalist venture excluding the poor, whose promises are mere greenwashing and false social responsibility. As their concerns for the environment were central, they opposed several building projects restricting green and productive land, for instance the building on workers' gardens (4,000 square metres out of 25,000 square metres) of the large solarium outside the Aubervilliers training swimming pool. The delayed project was eventually defeated in the courts (7 July 2023), and the land use was retained, but only after the gardens had already been destroyed. The swimming pool, however, is expected to be finished on time. Local associations have documented the paradox between the contractors' environmental excellence in their specific zone (notably for the Village) and the concentration of road traffic and pollution around it for lack of coherent environmental planning (Gintrac, 2021). As with London, the Olympic Park margins were often overlooked in the project (Doustaly, 2023).

Saccage also organized a demonstration while awaiting the announcement of the 10 per cent Olympic budget increase on 14 December 2022, but this only attracted around fifty people. Experiencing a cost-of-living crisis, the participants wanted to continue to press for better accountability on the COJOP finances. Drawing a parallel with workers' life-threatening working conditions on Qatari building sites for the Football 2022 World Cup, a demonstrator accused the SOLIDEO of employing illegal migrants and disrespecting workers' rights (Saccage, 2020). The latter has put in place strict controls, including towards its sub-contractors, as illegal work is common in the French building industry. Despite this, only a few cases have been identified yet, with some regularized as a result.

The last main bone of contention underpinning opposition is that the government is accused by political and civic groups of instrumentalizing security threats in order to increase legal surveillance, notably through intelligent video protection with algorithms identifying crowd movement and suspect behaviour – although facial recognition has been ruled out.[9]

Conclusions

Academic literature has documented why the IOC has been faced with increased public hostility and why there has been a sharp decrease in the number of candidate cities (see chapters 1 and 2). Past Games have been associated with corruption and gentrification and have been exposed as commercial ventures lacking in proportionally sustainable impacts for local communities despite being largely financed with public funds. After the 2018 IOC 'New Norm', a global pandemic, and a war affecting the global economy, Paris 2024 appears at a turning point.

The Paris governance model and legislation (2023–2026) have reinforced the auditing and recommendation powers of the *Cour des Comptes* which reports regularly to Parliament on the organization, budget, and objectives of the Olympics, advising Olympic partners to improve reporting and evaluation towards its final report in October 2025 (CC, 2023). With the DIJOP, it confirms the role of the legislative, executive, and judiciary powers to oversee public, private, and voluntary budgets and commitments, balancing Macron's supposed centralizing and Colbertist tendencies. Nevertheless, some researchers question its true capacity to make assessments (Lebeau, 2018).

Various issues and controversies remain, and important risks have been identified particularly for the COJOP portfolio, but one can observe progress towards a more sustainable and inclusive Games, allowing for a larger base of stakeholders' legacies to be included. The Games can indeed initiate, accelerate or halt urban projects, making evaluation complex before and even after they are held. They attract close scrutiny and also can initiate positive or negative publicity. For Paris 2024, Île de France inhabitants, who would represent as many as 40 per cent of visitors, tend to be more critical than tourists (Gignon *et al.*, 2022) and will need convincing.

The Paris Games are associated with regained interest from politicians for ethics, transparency, the role of sport in identity politics, social cohesion, and individual emancipation, but also youth socialization or even acculturation (Hidalgo, 2020; Clastres *et al.*, 2022). Beyond economic development, soft power and tourism, the impact of the Games either to empower or deprive communities will affect the future of neighbourhoods, as material and immaterial legacies are linked in leading urban change (Delaplace and Schut, 2019).

The Paris 2024 Games in preparation offer an appealing vision for twenty-first century spectacular, innovative, and sustainable urban celebrations and legacies, promoting local jobs, socio-economic development, inclusion, culture, and quality of life. With these Olympics, France seeks to showcase French sport, heritage, and culture (Doustaly, 2023), but also to show its expertise in staging mega events and achieving sustainable planning and building (Cadot, 2020). World exposure will mostly focus on historical central Paris (with a cost for ceremonies reaching €168 million) while Seine-Saint-Denis will be the heart of the urban legacy. Beyond that, as noted, competitions will be organized in twelve *departements* and Olympic events will be widespread throughout France. The *Terre de Jeux* programme could be explored as a balancing act for the rest of French local authorities. The increased use of culture in the Games and France's ambition to achieve a dialogue between sport and culture still lack coherence and are not reflected by the limited direct budget for the Cultural Olympiads, with €13.4 million from the COJOP and €9 million from the Ministry of Culture (CC, 2023). However, it could mitigate some negative impacts from the Olympics and help reach sustainable goals through social cohesion, intercultural dialogue, participative governance, and local appropriation particularly in redeveloped areas (Doustaly, 2023).

Notes

1. See also: French State, Main Olympic and Paralympic Legislation (*Lois relatives aux jeux Olympiques et Paralympiques de 2024*): 2017–2023. Henceforth referred to simply as French State.
2. Paris 2024a; https://www.paris2024.org/fr/tony-estanguet-presentation.
3. *Société de Livraison des Ouvrages Olympiques*.
4. French State, 2017-1336.
5. See https://terredejeux.paris.2024.org.
6. Costed at €42 billion in 2020, reduced to €36 billion in 2021.
7. French State, 2018-512; Le Parisien, 2022.
8. https://projets.ouvrages-olympiques.fr/la-maison-du-projet/.
9. Saccage 2024 (2020); Interviews 2023; French State: 2023-96.

Acknowledgements

My thanks go to the professionals, civil society members, and academics who shared their expertise with me during informal conversations and formal interviews carried out between 2015 and 2022, in particular Plaine Commune (Céline Daviet, Head of Olympic Games); Paris Île de France Regional Tourism Office (Emmanuel Blum, Head of partnerships); the Maison du projet and Léa Marie (SOLIDEO), the Ministry of Culture, Mairie de Paris, firms, associations involved in Paris 2024 and academic colleagues. Research in Paris and London for this chapter was facilitated through two Cergy Paris Université projects I coordinate: HERITRISK (https://heritages.cyu.fr/version-francaise/programmes-scientifiques/projet-patrisque-heritrisk) with Geneviève Zembri-Mary, and OCC 'Olympic Cities and cultures' (https://heritages.cyu.fr/version-francaise/programmes-scientifiques/projet-olympic-cities-and-culture) (with Vanessa Castejon and Charlotte Gould).

Chapter 20

LOS ANGELES 2028

Sven Daniel Wolfe aviiind *Cerianne Robertson*

Los Angeles has a long Olympic history, paired with an equally long tradition of influencing how the Olympic Games are planned and deployed. Having hosted in 1932 and 1984, both times bestowing significant innovations on the institution of the Games, Los Angeles is one of the world's quintessential Olympic cities. Yet it is not the only one. It was therefore with some excitement that observers noted the competition for hosting the XXXIII Olympiad in 2024 came down to two cities with equally well-established Olympic credentials: Paris and Los Angeles. This contest emerged after the withdrawal of candidate cities Rome, Budapest, and Hamburg, due to a mixture of economic hardship, weak political support, popular protest, and adverse referenda (MacAloon, 2016; Maennig, 2019). Faced with a credibility and hosting crisis (Lauermann, 2022), the International Olympic Committee (IOC) shrewdly awarded hosting rights to both cities at the same time, granting 2024 to Paris and 2028 to Los Angeles (IOC, 2018*b*). This was an unprecedented move and required a special Executive Board proposal, an Extraordinary Session, a series of discussions and promises between the candidate cities and the IOC, a tripartite agreement between all parties, and finally ratification and voting at the 131st IOC Session in Lima, Peru, on 13 September 2017.

Even before this decision, however, there were already historic changes made to the processes of bidding and hosting due to the ongoing reforms under Olympic Agenda 2020 (IOC, 2014*a*, 2014*b*; see also chapter 1). One of the goals of Agenda 2020 was to align the Olympics better with the long-term plans of the host city, with a focus on increasing sustainability and lowering costs. Agenda 2020 was soon joined by a series of other Olympic reform packages, all of which affect the preparations for Los Angeles 2028. In the context of these widespread reforms, this chapter presents a forecast for the upcoming XXXIV Olympiad in Los Angeles. It includes an overview of the Games hosted by Los Angeles in 1932 and 1984, including the innovations they introduced and the controversies they engendered. The chapter then explores in more detail the awarding of the 2028 Games, as well as the implications of Olympic reform on hosting. Finally, the chapter details the preparations for 2028 and unpacks three emblematic sites of contestation tied to the Games.

A City Shaping and Shaped by the Olympics

It is impossible to discuss the 2028 Olympics in Los Angeles without first examining the context of nearly a century of Olympic history and influence in the city. Similarly, it is impossible to understand the modern Olympics without investigating the profound influence of the Los Angeles Games in 1932 and 1984. In both instances, Los Angeles was seen as 'saving' the Olympic movement from widespread political problems and fiscal catastrophe. On each occasion, Los Angeles was the only bidder (Dyreson and Llewellyn, 2008). Both events also left their mark on the city: a number of iconic stadiums, a major thoroughfare that sweeps across the city from east to west renamed as Olympic Boulevard, and to this day a variety of Olympic logos emblazoned in unexpected spots, from benches to buildings. Even the city's world-famous palm trees were said to be planted for the 1932 Games, though this could be an Olympic myth and instead may be the result of a massive unemployment relief programme (Masters, 2011). Regardless, the profound influence of the 1932 and 1984 Olympics can still be felt as the city gears up to host for a third time, and there are striking parallels between all events (Kassens-Noor, 2020).

The preparations for 1932 took place in the context of the global political strife that would lead to the Second World War, as well as the economic calamity of the Great Depression. People protested the folly of hosting a sporting celebration while so many suffered and starved, picketing the state capital under the slogan 'Groceries Not Games', and even throwing rocks through store windows that advertised the Olympics (Siegel, 2020). These challenges led many observers to doubt that the Games would occur at all, but the dismal mood began to dispel as the Olympics approached and the festival and fantasy atmosphere got underway (Henry and Yeomans, 1984).

Los Angeles 1932 also heralded a number of innovations and important changes for both event and city. Notably, these Games brought to fruition the longstanding plans for a *Cité Olympique* to house the athletes for the duration of the Games (Sainsbury, 2017). This first proper Olympic Village was sited in Baldwin Hills and founded on the ideals of bringing together athletes from disparate nations to find common ground in sportsmanship and shared humanity (TOC, 1933, pp. 233–235). The Village was built as a temporary infrastructure, with the individual bungalows disassembled and put up for sale after the Games. This clever marketing strategy capitalized on a red-hot market for anything associated with the elite athletes and the

Hollywood glamour of the 1932 Olympics. It also allowed the athletes to be housed in the Village at a modest and affordable cost, since organizers could balance the books after the event, and it contributed to the image of Los Angeles as a fiscally responsible host.

In many respects, the Olympic Village came to symbolize Los Angeles 1932 itself: a heady mixture of Hollywood stardom mixed with frictionless services for elite international athletes, all of whom were interacting freely without regard to race or creed. This is a powerful image which has not exhausted its fuel almost a century later. Nevertheless, in many respects it is also at least partly fiction. Despite fairytale reports in the press of the Village's harmonious mixing, there are important exclusions and oversights to note. For example, women athletes were forbidden entry to the Olympic Village and instead were relegated to a distant – though luxury – hotel. Further, while commentators claimed that the multicultural harmony of the Village eased the city's racial tensions, the reality was that only white spectators were allowed to attend the Games, while Black, Latino, and other minority residents could not even secure housing in many neighbourhoods due to the city's racist housing covenants (Dinces, 2005; Morgan, 2021). Despite the tension between the presentation of intercultural peace within the Olympic Village and the persistent inequalities outside it, Los Angeles 1932 commanded unprecedented soft power. It broadcast an extraordinarily attractive image of Californian and American style both around the world and to Los Angeles itself, and influenced global fashion, art, cinema, sport, and business. This image remains a powerfully seductive force, even as the tension between the imagination of Los Angeles and the reality for many residents remains salient to this day. These dynamics can be seen in the preparations for 2028.

After 1932, veterans from the Organizing Committee organized themselves into a booster group that agitated for the next four decades to host the Olympics again (Dyreson and Llewellyn, 2008). They finally succeeded in bringing the 1984 Games back to Los Angeles, though once again the city was the only bidder due to a spate of crises ranging from the terrorist attacks in Munich 1972 to the financial and planning catastrophes of Montreal 1976 (Large, 2012; Liao and Pitts, 2006). As in 1932, many observers predicted that the 1984 Olympics would spell the end of the Games, but once again Los Angeles imbued the ailing institution with new energy and direction, and inspired cities around the world to play host once more (Dyreson, 2015). Like its predecessor, this version of the Los Angeles Olympics was associated with significant innovations but also took place at the interface of Hollywood fantasy and a harsher reality for many residents.

Los Angeles 1984 is most famous for introducing the age of modern Olympic commercialism, producing a Games that was lean, efficient, and financially successful for the private organizing committee, boasting a $232.5 million surplus, excluding security costs (Llewellyn *et al.*, 2015). Peter Ueberroth, President of the Los Angeles Olympic Organizing Committee (LAOOC), is credited with managing a Games that emphasized existing infrastructure and strictly controlled expenditure, while maximizing revenues from broadcasting and sponsorship (Wenn, 2015). The surplus from the Games was ploughed into the LA84 Foundation, which provided significant funds for constructing and improving nearly 100 sports facilities in the subsequent decades (Wilson, 2015). At the same time, the event was marked by social and political controversies, some of which persist to this day in the city and indeed shape the production of Los Angeles 2028.

At the geopolitical scale, the Games were the site of a proxy Cold War, due to the famous boycott by the Soviet Union (D'Agati, 2013). Nationally, Los Angeles 1984 represented a triumph of neoliberal political-economic functioning, and further strengthened Ronald Reagan's hold on the American imagination (Gruneau and Neubauer, 2012). Domestically, too, the city was once again split between an image of Hollywood perfection and a reality for many residents that was much less romantic. At one end of this spectrum was a presentation of modernity, unity, celebration, and style that even included a man flying on a jetpack in the opening ceremonies (Sanders, 2013).[1] On the other, Olympic organizers reneged on contracts with minority business owners that promised them exclusive licensing rights; the businesspeople later filed a multimillion-dollar suit against the Los Angeles Olympic Organizing Committee (LAOOC) for excluding them from selling at the Games (Reich, 1985). Further, Los Angeles 1984 featured the nation's largest peacetime security operation, with thousands of militarized troops patrolling the city and monitoring the population with brand-new surveillance and security equipment, most of which remained with the Los Angeles Police Department and contributed to the continuing exclusionary policing processes that make up this paradigmatic carceral city (Davis, 2011). With sweeps to keep the homeless population out of sight of the world's television cameras, and the persistent spatial and economic exclusion of the city's non-white residents, Los Angeles 1984 exhibited the same mix of local inequalities hidden beneath a seductive and picture-perfect fantasy. This dynamic is fundamental to understanding the preparations for Los Angeles 2028, particularly within the context of the Olympic reforms that attempt to mitigate deleterious outcomes within the host city.

Olympic Reform

Overall, there are multiple common and well-documented problems related to hosting the Olympics and other mega-events (see Müller 2015*b*; Alm *et al.*, 2016; Flyvbjerg *et al.*, 2021). In the aftermath of a string of

Olympic-related scandals and controversies, numerous potential host cities withdrew their bids for both Summer and Winter Olympics (Lauermann and Vogelpohl, 2017; MacAloon, 2016; Maennig, 2019). This contributed to the wave of Olympic reforms that aim to restructure the ways in which the Games are bid for, planned, and deployed.

These are ambitious and wholesale organizational reforms launched by the IOC with Agenda 2020 (IOC, 2014*a*) and its partners, The New Norm (IOC, 2018*d*) and most recently, Agenda 2020+5 (IOC, 2021*e*). The scope of these reforms is covered elsewhere (see chapters 1 and 2), but insofar as they pertain to Los Angeles 2028, the most important aspect to note is the effort to change the relationships between the IOC and the host city, and the implications this has had on the preparations so far. One of the fundamental aspects of the reforms is an attempt to lower the costs and risks of bidding for and staging the Olympics by better aligning the needs of the Games with the city's development agenda. Although organizers in previous host cities such as Barcelona and Rio de Janeiro employed discourses of using the Olympics to serve their pre-existing development agendas, the recent reforms provide more concrete avenues for actually doing so. One result is the reformed event requirements, which foreground flexibility and optimization in favour of local Organizing Committees. Whereas previous Games imposed strict demands on the hosts, now – as a matter of policy – the Games endeavour to adapt to the city. This represents a power shift away from the IOC and towards local Organizing Committees, though there is debate about how effective this has been in producing better outcomes (Wolfe, 2023*a*, *b*). Nevertheless, one of the ways in which this shift is most visible is the requirement to maximize the use of existing infrastructure rather than building anew. Of all the Olympic reforms, this aspect has had the most profound implications on the preparations for Los Angeles 2028.

Bidding and Hosting: Legitimation and Opposition

Since Los Angeles already possesses the necessary infrastructure to host, the legitimation for bidding and hosting cannot be tied to local urban development agendas, as in many other pre-reform Olympics. Instead, the Los Angeles 2024 candidature files were framed very much in terms of what the city can do for the institution of the Games, rather than the other way around. Under the tagline 'Follow the Sun', the Los Angeles bidders presented a lean Olympics on the platform of existing sporting infrastructure that would simultaneously deliver the highest quality experience for athletes while also 'refreshing the Olympic brand around the world for a new generation' (LA24 Bid Committee, 2017*a*, p. 1). The bidders offered the next iteration of the LA Olympics as a low-risk choice, a dynamic and exciting host city but with no surprises (LA24 Bid Committee, 2017*c*, p. 2). Further, the bidders proudly presented California as a nexus for technology, entertainment, and youth culture, and touted their ability to promote the Olympics to new audiences via new technologies. Contextualizing their bid with the successes of 1932 and 1984, the bidders presented Los Angeles as the ideal choice to shepherd the reformed Olympics into a new era.

The candidature files also featured a narrative of strong local support for the Olympics, presented as a legacy from previous hosting successes. According to bidders, this history explains the 88 per cent support among the local public, as well as the full support of city, state, and federal governments (*ibid.*, p. 3). Yet in terms of what the Games might actually do for the city, bidders were rather vague. Locally, bidders promised that hosting would inspire healthy living and increase social cohesion, a promise that can be traced back to the discourses of unity in the 1932 Games. They also promised a number of environmental restoration projects within and adjacent to the four clusters of venues (*ibid.*, p. 66). Nationally, the Olympics were promised to enhance national unity while increasing youth participation in sport. These local and national selling points were more platitude than promise, and little more on them was said within the candidature files, much less after the bid was won. Instead, much of the space in the bid books dedicated to legitimation discussed how hosting would leverage Los Angeles' unique storytelling powers to launch the newly reformed Olympics into a sustainable and profitable future. Given recent Olympic scandals, it was indeed a compelling idea to organize a safe but exciting Games in Los Angeles, especially on the landscape of existing infrastructures. The bid committee presented themselves as just what the Olympic movement needed: an oasis of love for the Games, with a demonstrable record of leaving the institution on more stable ground than before.

There was no official campaign against the Olympics in Los Angeles while the bid books were being written and submitted which was in contrast to Boston where a dedicated opposition movement derailed that city's bid (Andranovich and Burbank, 2021). As plans for the Los Angeles Olympics percolated into the public sphere, thirty community and political organizations formed the NOlympics LA coalition in May 2017 (Boykoff, 2020). These groups worked on diverse issues such as housing and gentrification, homelessness, policing and racial justice, transit, and environmental justice. What bound them together was the notion that hosting would exacerbate the existing problems facing the city and distract from urban priorities, an argument they used to tie local issues into a multi-pronged critique of the Olympics both in Los Angeles and overall (NOlympics LA, 2017). These concerns and critiques were largely dismissed by the City Council, however, which voted to authorize the Host City Contract in August 2017, a month before the IOC officially selected Los Angeles to hold the 2028 Games.

Venues

As a global city, Los Angeles already possesses more than enough venues to host top-tier sporting and cultural events, while the city's grand Olympic history buttresses its claim that it can host again without undue disruption. This became particularly relevant after the public referendum that cancelled Boston's bid and thrust Los Angeles into the spotlight of the United States' Olympic ambitions (Andranovich and Burbank, 2021). In this context, it was not unrealistic when Los Angeles organizers promised that all venues were either already existing, under construction, or planned for temporary overlays, and thereby fulfilled the requirements of the Olympic reforms (LA24 Bid Committee, 2017*a*, p. 10). The IOC Evaluation Commission calculated that 97 per cent of venues were already in place and rated the bid very highly, particularly due to the inventory of facilities and the proven history of usage after 1932 and 1984 (IOC, 2017*b*, p. 20).

The venues themselves are grouped into four general clusters, the locations of which are determined by the presence of pre-existing infrastructure and span the length and breadth of the enormous Los Angeles County (figure 20.1). These clusters range from the Valley Sports Park in the north (oriented around the Sepulveda Basin Sports Complex), all the way to the Long Beach Sports Park in the south (sited on the famous Pacific Ocean beachfront and including the Belmont Veterans Memorial Pier). Inbetween these poles is the South Bay Sports Park (sited at the Dignity Health Sports Park) and the

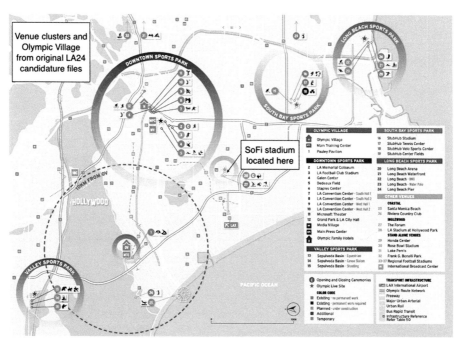

Figure 20.1. Venue map from original LA24 bid, showing the venues clustered into four Sports Parks. (*Source*: LA2024 Bid Committee)

Downtown Sports Park (an area spanning 4 km (2.5 miles) that features the legendary Memorial Coliseum and numerous facilities at the University of Southern California and in Downtown Los Angeles). In addition, the Games will feature an Olympic Village at University of California, Los Angeles, as well as a variety of ancillary venues scattered throughout the county, ranging from Santa Monica Beach on the west to the distant Lake Perris on the east.

The geographic footprint of the Los Angeles 2028 Olympics is gigantic. From the north cluster to the south cluster is a distance of 69 kilometres (42 miles), while from west to east is 140 kilometres (87 miles), or 71 kilometres (44 miles) if excluding faraway Lake Perris. Within this footprint, the impacts of hosting vary dramatically. A full nine cities in Los Angeles County will host Olympic venues, but many more will be traversed by athletes, officials, and spectators due to the dispersed geography of the Games and the emphasis on existing infrastructure.[2]

While laudable, the commitment to fulfilling the goals of Olympic reform and using existing venues brings up problems of attribution, already a challenge for mega-events research (Vanwynsberghe, 2015). Since the venues already exist or are planned and under construction, it is not a simple matter to determine whether a given intervention or impact is due to the Olympics or not. Indeed, there are a number of interventions that are linked with the 2028 Olympics, even though they do not appear in the Organizing Committee's budgets. Further, these interventions have had significant impacts on local populations, though there is debate over the extent to which the Olympics are implicated in these processes.

Inglewood

One such case is mentioned briefly in the IOC's bid evaluation report, which rated the LA bid highly for its attention to existing infrastructure. They noted that only one new venue would be constructed, but this was said to be planned irrespective of hosting. Listed as 'LA Stadium at Hollywood Park,' this single new venue is sited in Inglewood, not far from LAX Airport. Inglewood is one of the cities in LA County that stands to be most impacted by the 2028 Olympics.

Inglewood is a city of just over 100,000 residents, 50 per cent of whom are Hispanic and 41 per cent black (United States Census Bureau, 2021). Following the loosening of racial housing restrictions and white flight in the late 1960s and 1970s, Inglewood became a majority-black city that loomed large in the cultural imaginary of black Los Angeles. Like other black enclaves to its east, Inglewood experienced significant disinvestment in the late twentieth century. Nonetheless, it acquired the moniker 'City of Champions' as a result of hosting the Lakers (basketball) and Kings (ice hockey) teams in its Forum arena from 1967 to 1999. Since the early 2010s, it has undergone a period of intense reinvestment, focused on reinvigorating its status as a site for sports and entertainment. The Madison Square Garden Company poured $100 million into renovating the Forum and reopened it as a dedicated live music venue in January 2014 (Watt, 2014). In the same month, Stan Kroenke, the owner of the Rams (a top-level American football team), purchased 60 acres (~24 ha) in Hollywood Park, the site of a former racetrack, fuelling real estate speculation in the surrounding area. Two years later, the National Football League (NFL) approved the Rams' relocation from St. Louis, Missouri to Los Angeles, marking the first time in twenty-two years that Los Angeles would have its own NFL team. Construction then began on what would become the world's most expensive stadium: the $5 billion SoFi Stadium (Paris, 2020). This is the 3 per cent of Olympic venues named in the IOC's bid evaluation.

SoFi Stadium is the first of several developments planned for a 298-acre (120.6 ha) site (of which Kroenke owns a majority share): construction is also underway on a mall, close to 3,000 housing units (with no affordability requirements), and 75,000 square feet (6,970 m²) of office space (Stockbridge Capital Group, 2022). SoFi was not built primarily for the Olympics, but – as one of the world's most luxurious venues – it could not possibly be ignored for the Games (see figure 20.2). Indeed, the Los

Figure 20.2. View of SoFi stadium across the territory's water feature. Overhead an airplane prepares to land at nearby Los Angeles International Airport. (*Source*: Photograph, Sven Daniel Wolfe)

Angeles bidding materials touted it as a factor for why Los Angeles would make a good host, calling it 'the most modern sports stadium in the world … offering state-of-the-art technology and state-of-the-art facilities' (LA24 Bid Committee, 2017c, p. 4). Although it was constructed independently of the Olympics, it is inextricably linked to Los Angeles 2028 and will play a central role: SoFi is slated to host Olympic archery (in a temporary site next to the stadium) and to co-host the Opening and Closing Ceremonies in tandem with LA's historic Memorial Coliseum (LA28, p. 2022). It also sits at the heart of a slew of socio-spatial inequalities in Inglewood and beyond, of which the Olympics are undeniably a part, but not officially the cause. This suggests that the issues of attribution – already complicated but now rendered more complex due to the Olympic reforms – are not necessarily possible to unpack. Instead, it may be more productive to acknowledge that the Olympics play a role, though certainly not the only one, and then to explore the local impacts tied to these developments.

As plans for a new NFL stadium in Inglewood were made public, local tenants began reporting massive rent hikes: some landlords were doubling the rent overnight; others were adding $1,000 to the monthly price tag (Jennings, 2019). Between 2016 and 2022, median rents on one-bedroom apartments in Inglewood increased twice as fast as rents in the rest of Los Angeles (Fleming, 2022). The City of Inglewood saw the fastest rising property market in the Metro Los Angeles area (Theiss, 2019). In response to these spiralling costs, local housing and social justice organizations formed a coalition called Uplift Inglewood in 2015. The coalition's campaigns have included a successful push for city-wide rent control (passed in 2019), and an unsuccessful lawsuit against the development of a second new stadium in Inglewood.

This second stadium was sited directly across the street from SoFi Stadium. As SoFi developments commenced, the owner of the Clippers basketball team made moves to secure adjacent land – encompassing both publicly- and privately-held plots – to build a new basketball arena. The Uplift Inglewood coalition sued the Clippers team and the City of Inglewood on the basis that California's Surplus Land Act mandates that affordable housing development be prioritized on public land. Ultimately the coalition lost the lawsuit but managed to push back against the original plans, which would have led to the direct displacement of residents and churches. Instead, the new downsized plan featured a smaller area for purchase and eleven plots seized by eminent domain. The city justified this seizure by stating that the new privately-owned arena would bring 'substantial benefits to the local community', citing a $100 million community benefits package as one example (City of Inglewood, 2021a). Although the Clippers arena – now called the Intuit Dome – is not yet officially part of Los Angeles 2028's plans, it is frequently cited by local authorities as a likely Olympics venue.

It is difficult to assess the quantity of indirect displacement through rising rent prices and other exclusionary pressures tied to both new stadiums, but it is clear that these developments are having deleterious impacts on local communities. The Lennox Inglewood Tenants Union has documented continued displacement since the 2019 passage of rent control, including cases of landlords raising rents illegally or pressuring residents to move through harassment, intimidation, or neglect. Union members have argued Inglewood is witnessing the displacement of working-class black and brown residents, and the remaking of the city to serve tourists, wealthy event spectators, and the interests of capital. The expansion of Airbnbs and other short-term rentals aimed at stadium visitors risks intensifying displacement pressures in the area, in line with research on the links between tourism and gentrification (Cocola-Gant and Gago, 2021; Wachsmuth and Weisler, 2018). These impacts are concentrated in the areas around the new stadiums, which ties Los Angeles 2028 into these processes of development and displacement, even though the stadiums themselves are not directly the products of the Games.

Hotels and Housing

Aside from Inglewood, another area of concentrated Olympic sites is found at the University of Southern California (USC) and Exposition Park, home to the century-old Memorial Coliseum and the Banc of California Stadium. The latter opened in 2018 as the grounds of the Los Angeles Football Club, has since become home to Angel City FC as well, and is slated to host Olympics football preliminaries. The Coliseum is expected to co-host the Opening and Closing Ceremonies and stage track and field events. USC will

Figure 20.3. The interior of Memorial Coliseum during a football match in November 2019. (*Source*: Photograph, CC CanonStarGal)

host the Main Press Centre, the Media Village, badminton, and swimming and diving (in a temporary venue constructed on the university's baseball field, rather than in the 1984 Olympic pool). The neighbourhood is located in South Central Los Angeles just south of Downtown Los Angeles, which is in the midst of a southerly expansion. The majority-white, relatively affluent residents of new student housing complexes offer a visible contrast to the area's majority-racialized, working-class residents.

Since Los Angeles won hosting rights for 2028, at least two new hotel developments have been proposed for the streets adjacent to Exposition Park and the university. On the western perimeter of USC, a struggle is unfolding over the former site of the Bethune Library, a lot that has been vacant since 2009. For many years, community organizers have been calling for affordable housing to be built on the site, but at the time of writing, the project slated to be approved is a Marriott hotel, notably one with media facilities that could serve the Olympics press corps. As in Inglewood, a coalition of local organizations has arisen to oppose the development plans, aiming instead to advance projects that more clearly meet residents' needs (UNIDAD, 2020).

On the other side of the university, directly across from the Coliseum and LAFC stadium, city authorities approved a development project encompassing a hotel, apartment units, student housing, retail, and office space. The plan called for the displacement of residents from thirty-two rent-controlled apartment units. Los Angeles's City Council justified subsidizing this project by citing a need to accommodate growing tourism and the forthcoming Olympic and Paralympic Games (Alpert Reyes, 2019). Once they secured city approval, however, the project developers applied to adapt the project into a student housing facility for USC, excluding hotel rooms from the plan and distancing themselves from the Olympics. Nonetheless, the Olympics were a key discursive tool in initial project approval and served to justify the displacement of thirty-two families.

Homelessness

In 2018, Los Angeles' mayor, Eric Garcetti, said he was 'confident by the time the Olympics come, we can end homelessness on the streets of LA', (Internet Archive, 2018). At that time, the Los Angeles Homeless Services Authority (LAHSA) estimated that 31,285 people were unhoused in the City of Los Angeles, and 52,765 people across the county (LAHSA, 2018). As of 2022, the figures have increased substantially to 41,980 people across the city, and 69,144 people across the county (LAHSA, 2022). Although the county claims to be housing people more rapidly than ever before (LA County, 2022), rising rents are pushing people onto the streets at a faster rate. The visibility of some aspects of homelessness, particularly the sight of tents occupying some sidewalk and park spaces, has made it one of the most contentious issues in Los Angeles today. Angelenos are divided over appropriate policy responses and service priorities.

Los Angeles has long had a municipal law prohibiting sleeping, sitting, or lying in public space in ways that block pedestrian access, as well as a law prohibiting sleeping or camping in public parks. A 2018 US Court of Appeals decision stated that cities could not enforce anti-camping laws if they did not have sufficient shelter beds, as is the case in Los Angeles. In July 2021, Los Angeles's City Council amended Section 41.18 of the Los Angeles Municipal Code to allow enforcement of anti-camping provisions in areas within specified radiuses of 'libraries, parks, day-care centres, schools', and other locations including doorways and driveways (Zahniser and Oreskes, 2021). Critics have argued these criteria encompass such large swathes of the city that the ordinance effectively criminalizes homelessness, pushing unhoused Angelenos into different neighbourhoods (or into incarceration) rather than addressing systemic issues underlying homelessness (LACAN, 2021).

It is in this context of a dire homelessness crisis and intensive political debate that Los Angeles is preparing to host the 2028 Olympics. The mega-events literature documents a trend of intensified criminalization of homelessness before and during the Olympic Games, and Los Angeles 1984 was no exception to the trend. Police ramped up patrols to stop and search unhoused residents, pressuring them out of busy tourist areas and sometimes forcibly transporting them to jail, sparking legal claims against the city; one police captain said, 'we're trying to sanitize the area' (Roderick, 1984). Community organizers in groups like Skid Row's Los Angeles Community Action Network (LACAN) oppose the 2028 Games in part due to their community members' experiences of criminalization and aggressive policing during LA's previous five-ring festival, as well as concerns that the upcoming Games could serve as a justification for further criminalization.

While the city and Los Angeles 2028's plans regarding homelessness in the build-up to and during the Olympics remain unclear, the 2022 Super Bowl – hosted in the SoFi Stadium – heightened concerns. An encampment home to dozens of residents on the side of a road that connected LAX airport and SoFi Stadium was forcibly cleared three weeks before the event. The mayor of Inglewood denied any connection between the clearance and the Super Bowl (Venegas, 2022), yet residents who were forced to move reported that the workers conducting the clearance told them clearly that the action was due to the upcoming Super Bowl, directing them to move away from SoFi Stadium rather than towards it.

Clearly, the material crisis of homelessness in Los Angeles, as well as the contentious politics surrounding it, are grounded in conditions that would exist without the plans to host the Olympics in 2028. Nonetheless, hosting the Olympics may intensify the stakes, as Los Angeles faces intensified pressure to present a tourist-friendly version of 'cleanliness' to the global audience. This certainly has been the case in other Olympic host cities (Kennelly and Watt, 2011) and, given the scope of the homeless problem in Los Angeles, it is likely that the 2028 Games will follow the same pattern.

Transit

Successful transportation during Games-time is always a crucial element for hosting (Kassens-Noor, 2013*a*) but is particularly important in the preparations for Los Angeles 2028 due both to the event's large geographic footprint and also to the city's famously difficult traffic problems. Indeed, Los Angeles consistently rates as one of the worst cities for traffic in the United States, featuring eleven of the nation's twenty-five most congested freeway segments (Barragan, 2015; Pishue, 2021). Olympic travel will be impossible without using these freeways, so organizers face the challenge of ensuring timely and convenient transportation during the Games without disrupting travel for the rest of Los Angeles. In the candidature files, organizers established four overall objectives regarding transport: providing frictionless transit for the Olympic family, meaning athletes, officials, media figures, and other VIPs; transporting spectators and the Olympic workforce efficiently to their destinations; keeping the rest of Los Angeles in motion; and engaging the Games to accelerate Angelenos' adoption of expanded public transport systems (LA24 Bid Committee 2017*a*, p. 34).

In keeping with the use of existing venues, organizers stated that no transit investment was needed for the Olympics beyond projects already in progress. These included a $14 billion upgrade to Los Angeles's international airport and metro line extensions to link key Games sites including the airport, the Athletes' Village at UCLA, and Downtown. Despite the lack of projects linked directly to the Games, city officials clearly endeavoured to use hosting as a means to catalyse transportation developments – another longstanding strategy with mega-events worldwide (Kassens-Noor, 2013*b*). In Los Angeles, this attempt at event-led-catalysation was announced by Mayor Garcetti as the 'Twenty-Eight by '28 initiative', a plan to accelerate and complete a set of twenty-eight transport projects before the Games (Walker, 2018). Some of these had funding secured and were already scheduled for delivery prior to 2028, while others were planned for acceleration with an additional $26.2 billion beyond their initial budgets. Despite a sizeable media push at the time, this initiative appears to have been quietly abandoned in favour of more piecemeal investments. In 2021, the State of California allocated $1 billion to deliver 'critical projects in time for the Olympic Games', but did not define which projects were 'critical' (State of California, 2021, p. 183). In 2022, Los Angeles's Metro Authority identified over 200 projects that could help support the Games and thus merit priority funding (Uranga,

2022), but many of these were potentially problematic. For instance, the list includes a $1.4 billion automated 'people mover' connecting Inglewood's stadiums to Los Angeles's metro system, a key piece of potential Olympics infrastructure that was not included in the bid books. This project could wind up as another mega-event-related white elephant infrastructure: projections for peak ridership were 11,450 passengers per hour for a game at SoFi Stadium, compared to 414 passengers per hour on a normal weekend or weekday (City of Inglewood, 2021, p. 130).

Overall, the transit preparations for Los Angeles 2028 are marked by somewhat vague and undefined promises of beneficence for local populations, but there is little doubt that organizers will provide top-notch service for athletes, dignitaries, and spectators. Los Angeles authorities already have experience of limiting disruptions while managing traffic-related major events, ranging from the Super Bowl to the Oscars, and Los Angeles 2028 promises to build on this experience by advancing a fully integrated transport management system throughout Los Angeles County (LA24 Bid Committee, 2017c, p. 73). During Games-time, they plan to establish a comprehensive Olympic Route Network with dedicated lanes, automatic computer-controlled GPS venue access for VIPs, and Bus Rapid Transit lines for workers and fans (LA24 Bid Committee, 2017a, pp. 3, 4). However, whether hosting will truly catalyse a public transit boom for residents is another question.

Decorations and Festivities

Despite its stark racial and socioeconomic inequalities, in many areas Los Angeles is a hugely photogenic city. The Los Angeles 2028 hosting plan is intended to highlight these advantages for ticketed spectators and residents alike. Each of the four Sports Parks is sited to provide views of some of Los Angeles's most iconic landmarks and backdrops, such as the Hollywood Hills and Santa Monica Beach. Further, each of the Parks features more than clustered venues: within a securitized perimeter, visitors can partake in a festival atmosphere that includes food and drink, music, big screen Live Sites, and shopping (LA24 Bid Committee, 2017b, pp. 1–4). These Sports Parks will be linked by dedicated transport corridors, so that visitors technically should be able to travel between them without interfacing with the city proper.

Nevertheless, this idea of separating the Sports Parks from the rest of the city is challenged by the placement of certain stadiums within the urban fabric. For example, the size of the Downtown Sports Park makes it hard to imagine that the territory could be secured, and it is not clear how quotidian urban life will continue once the Games begin, should these festival plans take place. After all, it is a distance of over two miles between the Memorial

Coliseum at one end of the Park and the LA Live venue at the other, with a great deal of ordinary city between them. The bid books do not address this issue and organizers have so far remained silent.

In terms of communication, organizers promised to leverage the region's considerable storytelling soft power capacities in order to broadcast Los Angeles 2028 effectively to new audiences around the globe. The plan is to engage California's world-leading technology and social media companies to ensure global reach and engagement, thereby connecting the Olympics to new demographics via new technologies (LA24 Bid Committee 2017*a*, p. 27; 2017*c*, p. 6). Further, following the tradition of arts festivals tied to the 1932 and 1984 Games, the 2028 edition will feature a Cultural Olympiad that spans a range of leading institutions, including the Getty Museum and the California Institute of the Arts (LA24 Bid Committee, 2017*c*, p. 8). The arts campaign will reach from elite institutions down to the level of individual neighbourhoods, to include street art, food trucks, and music performances. Finally, when Games-time arrives, the built environment will be coordinated under a singular decorative vision to enhance the festival atmosphere throughout the city, but particularly along the Games routes (*ibid.*, p. 10). As a final touch, organizers plan to create a replicable model of the Live Site plan so that any of LA County's cities could organize an Olympic-related festival of their own.

Governance and Budget

One of the aspects that distinguishes the preparations for Los Angeles 2028 is the unique style of Olympic governance. Where other mega-events have established a specific delivery organization (such as SOLIDEO for Paris 2024, OlympStroy for Sochi 2014, or the Olympic Delivery Authority for London 2012), this edition features only the private LA28 organization. This is an echo of Ueberroth's lean organizational approach, which many continue to credit for the financial surplus of 1984. LA28 boasts a wealth of government and business connections and support, ranging from some of the globe's most recognized corporations to bipartisan political support at local, state, and national levels (LA24 Bid Committee, 2017*b*, p. 13).

Against this background, Los Angeles organizers promised an affordable Olympics with a balanced budget, slated for $5.32 billion at the time of the bid (LA24 Bid Committee, 2017*c*, p. 96). This has grown to an estimated $6.9 billion so far (CBS, 2021). This trend towards growth is consistent with the economic risks faced by other host cities, as every Olympics has suffered from busted budgets to greater or lesser degrees (Flyvbjerg *et al.*, 2021). Notably, taxpayers in both Los Angeles and the State of California will be held responsible for covering any financial shortfalls. Contractually, the city must first cover $270 million of any deficit, after which state guarantees will cover another $270 million. Anything over that must be paid again by Los Angeles taxpayers (Legislative Analyst's Office, 2017; Smith, 2021). Though city authorities made a wise financial decision in rejecting the initial proposal for a new $1 billion Olympic Village (Legislative Analyst's Office, 2016), Los Angeles 2028 still exposes residents of Los Angeles and California to financial risks.

Conclusion

For the third time in history, Los Angeles has been called to refresh and renew the Olympics. As in 1932 and 1984, the Games were awarded in a context of political and economic controversy, with Los Angeles as the sole bidder for its year (indeed, the IOC made history with its unprecedented and unanimous awarding of 2024 to Paris and 2028 to Los Angeles). This time, however, the Games will be held in the framework of the package of reforms that aim to realign the relationship between the Olympics and the host city. Among many other changes, these reforms emphasize the use of existing infrastructures rather than building anew. On its own, this represents significant progress in relation to previous mega-events and has the potential to reduce or even eliminate the risks of oversized and underused infrastructures geared to the event but not to the needs of the city. At the same time, this reform also brings up problems of attribution, as it is not clear to what extent the impacts of any given intervention can be tied to hosting.

Overall, the potential and the problems of 2028 should be seen in the context of previous editions. 1932 helped make the Olympics a mega-event both commercially and culturally, and 1984 helped revive the Games in the eyes of the world while introducing new strategies for profitable hosting. In this light, the salient question is related to a potentially new model of hosting, based on an array of existing infrastructure. Will the reformed Olympics only be granted to cities with a pre-existing portfolio of venues, and the proven capacity to fill them outside the Games? How will bidding authorities legitimize high costs to residents in the absence of promised improvements to the built environment? What will hosting look like in the aftermath of Los Angeles 2028, and what could a new Los Angeles Olympic model bring to the world?

There is little doubt that Los Angeles 2028 will be spectacular, producing a slick and beautiful event set against the background of the city's stunning and iconic monuments and landscapes. Sited in four Sports Parks that span a great swathe of the enormous Los Angeles County, organizers aspire once again to infuse the Games with the same Hollywood glamour and style as in 1932 and 1984. Yet, just as before, the Olympics are not arriving in a vacuum, and there is a chasm between the celebrated presentation of the city and the deep socio-spatial inequalities that persist in the lived city. The growing militarization of the Los Angeles Police Department, the relentless pressures of gentrification, and the overwhelming numbers of unhoused Angelenos mean that there is no lack of serious issues in the city. Many residents – particularly but not only those in affected areas – express real concern that hosting Los Angeles 2028 will exacerbate these problems rather than relieve them. Los Angeles will no doubt look stunning for the athletes, organizers, spectators, and the global audience. Yet outside the Olympic routes and the international broadcasting services, serious questions remain about whether hosting is in the best interests of the majority of residents.

Notes

1. It is worth watching the jetpack entry in the 1984 opening ceremonies and remembering how truly futuristic and fantastical this moment was for so many millions of people. This is available at: https://www.youtube.com/watch?v=yt0E-AkoM9U.

2. LA County is comprised of eighty-eight cities, but the Games will traverse three counties: Los Angeles, Orange, and Riverside counties. The 2028 Los Angeles Olympics will be held in venues in the cities of Los Angeles, Santa Monica, Carson, San Dimas, Anaheim (Orange County), Pasadena, Inglewood, Perris (Lake Perris, Riverside County), and the unincorporated area known as University City.

Chapter 21

BRISBANE 2032

Aysin Dedekorkut-Howes

Australia's third largest city and the capital of the state of Queensland, Brisbane, will be the country's third city to host the Summer Olympics. The selection of Brisbane makes Australia only the second country in the world, after the United States, to stage summer Olympic Games in three different cities. Nothing about the Brisbane Olympics has been typical so far. From its unusual bidding process to the regional spread of its venues it is a unique beast and a first in many ways. It has been awarded the Games eleven years prior to hosting, in an unrivalled bidding process with the outcome pretty much known months in advance. It is the first Olympics that is contractually obligated to be climate positive, meaning it must offset more carbon emissions than it produces. With 2.5 million residents, Brisbane will be the first mid-size city to host the Summer Games since Athens 2004, after a series of mega cities whose populations ranged from 8 million to 37 million residents at the time of the Games (McCormick, 2021).

Despite being called Brisbane 2032, the Games will be a regional Olympics spread around the South East Queensland (SEQ) region and beyond to the rest of the state rather than a traditional city-based event. Perhaps it is not surprising that the first ever regional Olympics will be held in the SEQ conurbation which Spearritt (2009) has called Australia's first '200 kilometre city' of continuous coastal urban and suburban development. For almost three decades Brisbane and SEQ have been among the most rapidly growing areas in Australia. The mining boom, sunbelt migration, the attraction of the warmer climate for retirees from the colder southern states of Victoria and New South Wales together with job opportunities offered by the booming economy for the younger population fuelled this growth. The region's current population of 3.5 million is projected to reach 5.9 million by 2050 (DILGP, 2017). Heynen and Vanaraja Ambeth (2023) likened Brisbane more to Winter Games hosts than the mega-city Summer Games hosts due to its smaller metropolitan region and the plan of a more decentralized Games. They suggested that successful delivery of the 2032

Games and achieving legacy benefits may again encourage other mid-size cities to aspire to host the Summer Games.

Brisbane had world city ambitions on its agenda for a long time and in 2009 the City Council rebranded it 'Australia's New World City' (Insch and Bowden, 2016). Critics of Brisbane 2032 argue that many of the expected benefits of Olympic events such as economic returns are not realizable, nor is the expected increase in sports participation likely in the long term, while the main aim of hosting the Olympics is to 'recast Brisbane as an international city able to hold its own alongside Australia's current Olympic cities, Melbourne and Sydney' (Rowe, 2021).

Brisbane has successfully hosted several major events, including the 1982 Commonwealth Games, 1988 World Expo, 2001 Goodwill Games, and 2014 G20 Leaders' Summit. Its first Olympic bid for the 1992 Games placed it third behind Barcelona and Paris in the 1986 decision (Rebgetz and Ford, 2015) due to lack of consideration of post-Olympics venue use and the location of the Athletes' Village in an environmentally sensitive wetland area (Hartigan, 2012). Brisbane's 2032 bid has a fifteen-year history (see table 21.1 for the Games timeline). In 2005, Queensland Premier Peter Beattie

Table 21.1. Timeline of key events. (*Source*: Compiled by Aysin Dedekorkut-Howes)

1 April 2005	Queensland premier announces Brisbane's intention to bid for 2024 Olympics
August 2008	AOC announces support for Brisbane Olympics bid
January 2009	AOC declares bidding for 2024 Olympics unrealistic
6 March 2015	2028 Olympics bid discussed in SEQ Council of Mayors meeting and pre-feasibility study commissioned
1 July 2016	*Pre-feasibility Analysis* of SEQ 2028 Olympics Bid released with positive findings
22 Feb 2019	*2032 SEQ Olympic and Paralympic Games Feasibility Study* released
26 June 2019	IOC changes Olympics bidding process
7–12 September 2019	Queensland Premier visits Switzerland for meetings
4 Mar 2020	IOC announces that Olympic Games will be climate positive from 2030
25 February 2021	IOC announces Brisbane as the preferred candidate city to host the 2032 Olympics
21 July 2021	IOC awards Brisbane the 2032 Games
21 March 2022	The SEQ City Deal announced
17 February 2023	State and federal governments sign funding agreement for Olympics sports infrastructure
23 July–8 August 2032	The Olympic Games
24 August–5 September 2032	The Paralympic Games

announced plans for Brisbane to bid to host the 2024 Olympic Games. On the eve of the opening of the Beijing Olympics in 2008, the Australian Olympic Committee (AOC) gave its support to Brisbane's Olympics bid and AOC president John Coates called for the Brisbane City Council and the Queensland Government to keep a future Olympic bid in mind in their infrastructure planning (Smith, 2008). However, he soon declared that 2024 was not a realistic target 'and it was unlikely a bid by an Australian city would be considered until the latter half of the 2020s, 2030s or beyond' (Draper and Dunlevy, 2009).

The seeds of Brisbane's second bid that led to its hosting of the 2032 Olympics were sown in 2015 on the heels of its successfully hosting the G20 summit and while neighbouring Gold Coast was preparing to host the 2018 Commonwealth Games. Brisbane Mayor Graham Quirk put the potential bid to host the 2028 Games on the agenda of the SEQ Council of Mayors meeting with the encouragement of the International Olympic Committee (IOC) president who suggested that Australia bid for a Games in the 2020s. The AOC president John Coates suggested Brisbane as the 'obvious choice' (Rebgetz and Ford, 2015). The 2018 Gold Coast Commonwealth Games provided the prospect of utilizing some of the infrastructure and accommodation in the proposed Brisbane 2028 Olympics, 'as well as monitoring the post-games use of the Gold Coast's facilities to understand how they are utilised in legacy mode' (Hartigan, 2012, p. 242).

The Council of Mayors commissioned a pre-feasibility study which indicated 'that the region has the capability and capacity to bid successfully for and host the 2028 Olympic and Paralympic Games' and 'that there are sufficient economic, social and cultural benefits to warrant further investigation' (COMSEQ, 2016). The follow-up feasibility study explored whether SEQ could or should stage the 2032 Games. The main motivation was using the Olympic Games bid 'as a catalyst to expedite infrastructure delivery' in one of Australia's fastest-growing regions with limited funding to meet the needs of the population, and to 'boost the economy and significantly raise the region's profile on the international stage' (COMSEQ, 2019). The 18-month study was released in 2019 and concluded that hosting the Games in SEQ was feasible and would generate significant opportunity for substantial economic and community benefits. It also suggested that underpinning incremental infrastructure projects by compelling production of legacy plans would optimize the impacts of the Games and complete alignment of the Games Master Plan with legacy needs the key to its success (Queensland Government, 2019). However, the study also revealed that the bid would require billions of dollars. Fortunately, significant changes in the bidding process announced months later by IOC made Brisbane's regional bid possible.

The New Bidding Process

In response to increasing event costs and the dwindling number of cities bidding to host ever larger and increasingly complex events, in the last decade the IOC has been exploring ways to decrease the costs and increase the attractiveness of hosting the Games. As noted elsewhere (see chapter 1), 'Olympic Agenda 2020' published in 2014 included measures to reduce bidding and staging costs, as well as expenditure sharing through joint bids (Gold and Gold, 2021).

The reform process culminated in a new approach to selection in 2019 with the goal of creating 'Olympic projects that are less expensive and that maximize operational efficiencies, while also unlocking greater value for future hosts, with a strong emphasis on legacy and sustainability' (IOC, 2021e). The reforms provide a streamlined approach to host elections and are underscored by increased flexibility and cooperation on a bilateral level. The key innovation of the process is the establishment of a permanent, non-committal and non-edition-specific ongoing dialogue. In this new approach, identification of preferred hosts for a specific event does not end dialogue with other bidders. Once the preferred hosts for a specific event are selected a Targeted Dialogue process explores proposals to host the specific event.

Two reforms in the new process enabled Brisbane Olympics to be different from previous events. First, it allows a more regional approach to hosting the Games with multiple venue hubs enabling maximum use of existing venues and distributing the event benefits to the host. The timeline of candidature is also more flexible. Rather than the traditional two-year candidature commencing nine years prior to the particular Games event that is awarded seven years in advance, the new flexible timeline allows cities to start the dialogue at any time with potential to award the Games earlier than before.

Tham (2022) reported that the IOC's announcement of Brisbane as the preferred bid in February 2021 caught competitor cities from Indonesia, India, Qatar, and a North/South Korea joint bid unaware and was criticized for not giving them adequate opportunity to present their cases before shortlisting candidates. The unprecedented July 2021 decision to award the 2032 Games to the sole candidate Brisbane allowed it to have the longest lead time of any host city to prepare for the Games and more than a decade to maximize the benefits of being a future host. Despite these purported advantages, this new bidding process has been criticized for being non-democratic and not transparent (Dubinsky, 2022). The IOC has cited Brisbane bid's sustainability, alignment with reforms and the Olympic agenda, support from all levels of government and the private sector, Brisbane's experience in handling major events, a high percentage of existing venues, and favourable weather among the reasons for its success.

Venue Master Plan

Brisbane 2032 proposed a polycentric venue master plan with three main zones containing seven venue clusters in the SEQ region (figure 21.1). The Brisbane zone at the centre is the main hub with twenty-one venues and includes Brisbane, Ipswich, Moreton Bay, Scenic Rim, and Redland local government areas (table 21.2). Gold Coast, 65 kilometres to the south of Brisbane, hosts seven venues and Sunshine Coast, 85 kilometres to the north, hosts four (Brisbane 2032 Consortium, 2021). The state's most populous cities outside the three major zones – Cairns, Townsville, and Toowoomba – will host football games to extend hosting benefits to key inland and coastal regional centres along with interstate venues in Sydney and Melbourne. Competition venues are distributed across eleven separate Queensland council areas, providing legacy benefits across the region and state, with additional regional opportunities for pre-Games training and festival or live sites (Queensland Government, 2019). Six of the thirty-seven competition venues will be new, and eight venues will receive major upgrades. No venues will be built just for the Games. All new and upgraded venue projects were pre-planned to meet the needs of the growth of the regions and brought forward for the Games (DSDILGP, 2023*a*).

Brisbane Cricket Ground, locally known as the Gabba, will receive the most significant upgrade that would increase its seating capacity from approximately 36–37,000 to 50,000 seats and create a pedestrian plaza

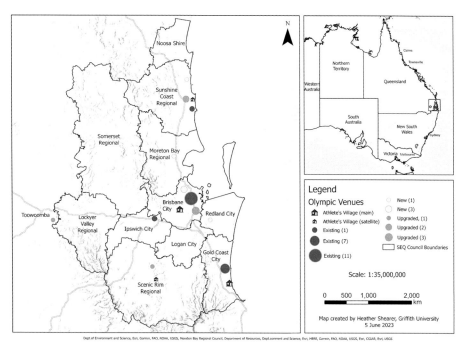

Figure 21.1. Brisbane 2032 Games venue locations. (*Source*: Compiled by Aysin Dedekorkut-Howes)

Table 21.2. Games venues. (*Source*: Compiled by Aysin Dedekorkut-Howes)

Venue	Council and Zone	Event	Status
Brisbane Arena	Brisbane	Aquatics	New
Brisbane Indoor Sports Centre	Brisbane	Basketball	New
Chandler Indoor Sports Centre	Brisbane	Gymnastics, Basketball	New
Moreton Bay Indoor Sports Centre	Moreton Bay, Brisbane	Boxing	New
Redland Whitewater Centre	Redland, Brisbane	Canoe (Slalom)	New
Sunshine Coast Indoor Sports Centre	Sunshine Coast	Basketball	New
Brisbane Aquatic Centre	Brisbane	Aquatics	Upgraded
Brisbane Cricket Ground (Woolloongabba), Brisbane	Brisbane	Opening and Closing Ceremonies, Athletics	Upgraded
Brisbane International Shooting Centre	Brisbane	Shooting	Upgraded
Wyaralong Rowing Centre	Scenic Rim, Brisbane	Canoe Sprint, Rowing	Upgraded
Sunshine Coast Mountain Bike Centre	Sunshine Coast	Mountain Biking	Upgraded
Sunshine Coast Stadium	Sunshine Coast	Football	Upgraded
Barlow Park, Cairns	Regional	Football	Upgraded
Toowoomba Sports Ground	Regional	Football	Upgraded
Anna Meares Velodrome	Brisbane	Cycling (BMX Racing)	Existing
Ballymore Stadium	Brisbane	Hockey	Existing
Brisbane Convention and Exhibition Centre	Brisbane	Badminton, Fencing, Table Tennis, Taekwondo	Existing
Brisbane Entertainment Centre	Brisbane	Handball	Existing
Brisbane Football Stadium	Brisbane	Football, Rugby	Existing
Brisbane Showgrounds	Brisbane	Equestrian	Existing
Ipswich Stadium	Ipswich, Brisbane	Modern Pentathlon	Existing
Manly Boat Harbour	Brisbane	Sailing	Existing
Queensland Tennis Centre	Brisbane	Tennis	Existing
South Bank Cultural Forecourt	Brisbane	Archery	Existing
South Bank Piazza	Brisbane	Basketball 3x3	Existing
Victoria Park	Brisbane	Cycling, Equestrian	Existing
Broadbeach Park Stadium	Gold Coast	Volleyball (Beach)	Existing
Broadwater Parklands*	Gold Coast	Aquatics, Triathlon	Existing
Coomera Indoor Sports Centre*	Gold Coast	Volleyball	Existing
Gold Coast Convention and Exhibition Centre*	Gold Coast	Volleyball, Weightlifting	Existing
Gold Coast Sports and Leisure Centre*	Gold Coast	Judo, Wrestling	Existing
Gold Coast Stadium*	Gold Coast	Football	Existing
Royal Pines Resort	Gold Coast	Golf	Existing
Alexandra Headland	Sunshine Coast	Athletics, Cycling, Sailing	Existing
North Queensland Stadium, Townsville	Regional	Football	Existing
Melbourne Rectangular Stadium	Interstate	Football	Existing
Sydney Football Stadium	Interstate	Football	Existing

Note:

* Venues used at the 2018 Gold Coast Commonwealth Games.

Figure 21.2. Architectural rendering of proposed new Gabba Stadium. (*Source*: Populous, 2021)

linking the stadium to the new Cross River Rail station, which is currently under construction (Riga, 2021; see figure 21.2). The A$2.7 billion redevelopment will be funded by Queensland Government with construction planned to start in 2026 and the venue be ready for use by 2030 (DSDILGP, 2023a).

The main Olympic Village that is planned to be developed in Northshore Hamilton in Brisbane will be the largest of the four Villages and accommodate 10,729 athletes and team officials (around two-thirds of the total) during the Olympics. It is located 6 kilometres from the city centre and within 12 kilometres and twenty minutes of fifteen venues housing twenty-four sports (figure 21.3). It will have a prime waterfront location and will comprise medium- and high-density apartments and townhouses, across a total of sixteen residential blocks rising to a maximum of fifteen storeys (figure 21.4). Residential blocks will include ground level retail space, podium, and underground parking (Brisbane 2032 Consortium, 2021).

The Gold Coast Olympic Village, with a capacity of 2,600 beds, is located adjacent to the major retail and entertainment precinct of Robina Town Centre (figure 21.5). Six of the Gold Coast venues hosting nine sports and disciplines are within 25 kilometres and twenty-five minutes of the Village site. This Village will be composed of medium-density apartments and townhouses, with a total of four residential blocks of maximum fourteen storeys and will offer a full Village experience. Both villages will be delivered through public–private partnerships. This approach saw the successful delivery of a very highly regarded Village of 1,252 units for the Gold Coast 2018 Commonwealth Games Village (*ibid.*).

Two primary satellite Villages will house the athletes outside the two main zones of Brisbane and the Gold Coast. Sunshine Coast Satellite Village leverages a housing development in the Maroochydore city centre within the heart of the Sunshine Coast, that is near competition and training venues

Figure 21.3. Location of Athletes' Village at Northshore Hamilton with respect to the city centre. (*Source*: Concept image, © Queensland Government)

Figure 21.4. Artist's impression of the main Athletes' Village at Northshore Hamilton. (*Source*: Concept image, © Queensland Government)

Figure 21.5. Proposed Olympic Village at Robina on the Gold Coast. (*Source*: Queensland Investment Corporation, 2021)

as well as beaches and entertainment districts. The residential buildings include ancillary space on the lower levels to be used for dining and other services. Kooralbyn Satellite Village will be located at the Kooralbyn Resort in the Scenic Rim and will accommodate rowing and canoe sprint athletes. The resort is within forty minutes of the venue in a scenic area and includes a range of amenities which will be available to the athletes. The existing accommodation will be supplemented by additional temporary accommodation for the Games. Both satellite villages will be connected to the venues and the Main Village in Brisbane with regular shuttles.

Olympics and Urban Development in SEQ

Reminiscent of Barcelona 1992's rationale of urban transformation (Cox and Searle, 2012), 'Brisbane is treating the Olympic Games as a platform for urban development that can transform how we travel, integrate multiple urban centres across South-East Queensland, and result in lasting changes to policies and behaviours' (Halog, 2022). One of the guiding principles informing the development of the Brisbane 2032 Olympic and Paralympic Games Master Plan is 'a legacy-led Master Plan' that will be evidenced by: alignment with federal, state and local government policies for infrastructure development supporting growth; delivering community legacy outcomes; and addressing environmental, accessibility and sustainability considerations (Brisbane 2032 Consortium, 2021, p. 12). Olympic Games are used as a catalyst for speeding up many projects included in the statutory SEQ Regional Plan (DILGP, 2017).

Brisbane's Cross River Rail line is being extended northwards through a new twin tunnel under Brisbane River with new underground stations. Gold Coast Light Rail (also known as the G:Link) extension south is currently under way and Brisbane Metro (despite the misleading name actually an electric bus rapid transit system described as a trackless tram) is under construction. The first two of the four new pedestrian 'green bridges' in the city bisected by the Brisbane River are expected to open in 2024 (Jackson, 2022). These major public mobility programmes are not only intended to shape how people move in the region but also change how they live. The green bridges, for example, are a part of the city's cycle network. Gold Coast's Light Rail line is intended to support the Regional Plan and the City Plan's aims of urban consolidation and densification along the rail route (Fainstein *et al.*, 2023).

The most significant urban transformation project facilitated by the Olympic Games is the redevelopment of the Northshore Hamilton district in Brisbane which is Queensland's largest waterfront urban renewal project. The Games Village site is in a state Priority Development Area (PDA). PDAs include parcels of land identified by the state for development to deliver significant benefits to the community. In PDAs Queensland Government's specialist land use planning and property development agency, Economic Development Queensland (EDQ), manages development rather than local governments. The main purpose of PDAs is to facilitate economic development. The former and transitioning industrial port area at Northshore Hamilton was declared a PDA on 27 March 2008 as a 304-hectare urban renewal area to be transformed into a vibrant, mixed-use precinct adjoining the Brisbane River. The Northshore Hamilton PDA Development Scheme that regulates development in the PDA was amended on 28 October 2022 to accommodate Brisbane 2032 and the Games Village (EDQ, 2022). The 40-hectare Village site is owned by EDQ.

The Planning Scheme views the Olympics and the location of the main Games Village in the PDA as a major opportunity that will provide multiple benefits to Northshore Hamilton, including showcasing Brisbane's waterfront to the world; accelerated delivery of development and infrastructure, such as roads, public spaces and new residential and mixed-use buildings; earlier delivery of the diverse housing already contemplated for the PDA, such as private, affordable, build to rent, retirement, aged care, hotel and short-term accommodation; opportunity for some existing buildings to be converted to new uses, such as commercial, community, and retail uses; economic opportunities for residents and business; and clarity and certainty for landowners and developers in the PDA to progress development proposals, noting their lands are not needed to deliver the Village (*ibid.*, p. 2). In summary, the Games in this case are used as a vehicle to implement the long-term plan for the area, seeking to rejuvenate the existing industrial land and fast-track what the scheme calls 'this significant city shaping project to deliver an indelible legacy for Brisbane' (*ibid.*). The Department of State Development website declares 'the Olympics will do for Northshore Hamilton what Expo 88 did for South Bank' and aims to make this area 'Brisbane's future premier riverfront lifestyle precinct' (DSDILGP, 2023*b*). Expo 1988 was used as a vehicle to transform the South Bank of the Brisbane River completely from a dilapidated old industrial area into parklands and Brisbane's major arts, culture, and entertainment precinct (Smith and Mair, 2018).

The Games Village will contain both permanent and temporary buildings, structures, public realm areas, and infrastructure. After the Games, the Village will be converted to provide 1,750 apartments as well as commercial and retail space. In legacy mode the Village will assist in meeting the housing needs of the increasing population by supplying various types of housing including social and affordable housing, aged care, retirement living, key worker and build-to-rent accommodation, hotel stock, and market housing. The expected legacy outcomes facilitated by the Games concept include: development of the proposed 'green street' connecting the waterfront and parkland to the future school precinct; delivery of a component of the future riverside parkland; construction of the new ferry (CityCat) terminal and the revitalization of existing warehouses along the waterfront (Brisbane 2032 Consortium, 2021, p. 28). Legacy community facilities will offer residents a recreational zone in the heart of the Village.

Robina Town Centre, where the Gold Coast Olympic Village will be located, is a special development zone established in 1992 for the creation of a central business district. It has its own Planning Agreement – Local Government (Robina Central Planning Agreement) Act 1992 – with the state government, within which development is regulated outside the local planning scheme. The existing town planning framework for the Robina Town Centre envisages intensive mixed-use development with an urban character relating to the adjacent waterway and core retail precinct and the Village development is fully aligned with this aspiration. The 8.1-hectare Village site is owned by the Queensland Government owned entity Queensland Investment Corporation (QIC). As in the case of the Brisbane Village, the Robina Village is designed as a legacy to deliver much needed housing supply to one of Australia's fastest growing regions (the average five-year population growth in the Gold Coast region is 2.5 per cent compared to 1.5 per cent for all of Australia) and contribute to the long-intended mixed-use centre (Brisbane 2032 Consortium, 2021).

Redevelopment of the Gabba stadium is also part of a major urban renewal project for the Woolloongabba precinct in Brisbane's inner south.

State Premier Annastacia Palaszczuk announced the state's intent to declare a PDA over the whole Gabba site leading into South Bank, declaring 'this is absolutely critical for urban renewal' (Jones, 2023). Prime Minister Anthony Albanese declared his support of the redevelopment, stating that this is 'more than just the stadium, it's about the way the city functions. It's all about urban redevelopment as well and making the city function and making it more liveable, the way that it works with the Cross River Rail project'. The redevelopment of the Gabba requires the controversial move of the heritage East Brisbane State School about two kilometres from its current location. The state government said the plans are for an active travel corridor to South Bank and the CBD through the area as well as more housing including social and affordable housing.

The proposed 18,000-seat new venue known as the Brisbane Arena is centrally located near the Roma Street Parklands and is intended to be Brisbane's new live entertainment arena. The arena will have a public pool that will be used for the swimming events at the Games. Queensland Government (2022a) states that it 'will catalyse renewal on the western edge of the city centre and aligns with long term plans for the area' (figure 21.6).

Figure 21.6. Artist's impression of Brisbane Arena. (*Source*: Concept image, © Queensland Government)

Transformation of the state-owned Victoria Park (Barrambin in Turrbal language) Golf Course into an iconic 64-hectare inner city public parkland is viewed as another significant project in building Brisbane up towards 2032 and beyond (BCC, 2023). The proposal was announced on 9 June 2019 by the Brisbane Mayor and, following two rounds of community engagement, Victoria Park Vision was released in December 2020. A draft master plan was released based on this vision in 2022. Implementation of early projects including an adventure playground, park furniture and shelters, and an urban pump track started in 2022. Consistent with the city's active transport initiatives the master plan proposes two new 'city-shaping' bridges to improve pedestrian and bicycle access between important inner urban precincts and

Figure 21.7. Artist's impression of inner-city pedestrian and cycle bridge at Victoria Park. (*Source*: Brisbane City Council, 2023)

key public transport nodes and overcome the barriers posed by the Inner-City Bypass and rail line (figure 21.7). The park has been named as the temporary venue for the equestrian cross country and BMX freestyle events.

Queensland is also accelerating the 'smart' and 'green' infrastructure projects such as 'sensor-triggered streetlights, automated air conditioning and watering of parks and green façades… robots for cleaning and construction, satmaps, swipe cards and QR codes', and use of data technology in thirty-two existing and planned Olympic venues, the future Athletes' Village, and the international media centres (Jackson, 2022).

The Legacy of Brisbane 2032: Sustainable and Climate Positive Games

Explicit evaluation of environmental concerns for Olympics Games dates back to the IOC's 1994 decision which was formalized through amending the Olympic Charter in 1996 and followed by the development of an Agenda 21 in 1999 (Gold and Gold, 2021; see chapter 1 above). Olympic Agenda 2020 led to sustainability and legacy strategies which advocated temporary structures, reuse of existing facilities and sustainable design in venues, sustainable infrastructure, travel, and transport and reducing greenhouse gas emissions. Legacy use of structures were embedded more firmly into the bidding process.

Desire to outdo previous events and failure to properly consider post-Olympics use of the new infrastructure has often left a legacy of overblown costs, large debts, and oversized and underused facilities (Gold and Gold, 2017*a*). However, since Sydney 2000 bid's far-reaching environmental benchmarks, cities started to aim to surpass each other using different targets as sustainability gained in importance. London 2012 Olympics took the guiding principles of legacy and sustainability further through the re-use of existing venues and installation of temporary seats where possible (Cox, 2012). Poynter and MacRury (2009) claimed that the plan to return to a more modest approach and stronger focus on urban regeneration and sporting legacy were key reasons for London's selection over Paris and Madrid for the 2012 Olympics.

Queensland Government in its *2032 Olympic and Paralympic Games Value Proposition Assessment* (2019, p. 13) suggested that:

> Harnessing the Olympic Games sustainability platform could drive Queensland's sustainability agenda. Stimulating new standards and innovation, the Games could provide a focal point for strategies that bring together expertise, industry and the community to address climate change and waste. These initiatives would provide a benchmark for Queensland and Australia, supporting long-term objectives.

The Assessment contained further proposals to use the Games to showcase sustainability initiatives, ecotourism opportunities and use of renewable and distributed energy resources to meet the Games' green energy requirements and to enhance market opportunities. The community vision that emerged from a recent survey of 897 respondents from the host region residents (Weaver *et al.*, 2022, p. 1) is of an 'efficient, affordable, and authentic Games that benefit and involve the host community and learn from the past'.

Tham (2022, p. 9) suggested that the Brisbane 2032 bid 'focuses on under-investigated aspects of socio-cultural sustainability and includes sustainability in all aspects of the Olympic Games from food and housing to cultural sustainability by advocating reconciliation to the First Nations roots and using Olympics as a catalyst for sporting participation in the elderly in the pursuit of active ageing as a state agenda'.

Economic Sustainability

The New Norm seemingly made Brisbane's bid much more affordable than previous Games. The projected cost of AU$4.45 billion (US$3.4 billion) at the time of the bid was less than a third of Tokyo's budget, or the US$15 billion cost of London 2012 or the US$13.2 billion cost of Rio 2016 (Holmes *et al.*, 2021). Furthermore, the Value Proposition Assessment (Queensland Government, 2019) claimed that the Games could be delivered at no cost to the State by recovering this estimated cost from IOC contributions and domestic revenues. However, due to post-pandemic construction cost inflation, there is already a substantial cost increase. In February 2023 the Queensland and federal governments reached a AU$7 billion funding agreement to overhaul Brisbane's sport and event venues ahead of the Olympics. Federal government will contribute around half, including all AU\$2.5 billion cost of the Brisbane arena as well as AU\$1 billion towards other new venues and upgrades. The Gabba redevelopment, initially proposed to cost about AU\$1 billion in 2021, is now estimated to cost about AU\$2.7 billion (Jones, 2023). The Committee for Brisbane's (2021) Phase One legacy planning document aims to achieve an interconnected, multimodal transport infrastructure and efficient, cost-effective public transport including a fast rail infrastructure and a 45-minute connected region (north to south and east to west). These infrastructure expenses are excluded from the cost projections. The Value Proposition Assessment for Brisbane (Queensland Government, 2019) provides estimates of around AU\$7.4 billion (US\$5.1 billion) economic benefits for the region and the creation of around 130,000 direct jobs and tens of thousands of indirect jobs, including 10,000 in the tourism industry. The Games are expected to generate more than AU\$20.2 billion (US\$13.9 billion) in international tourism growth between 2020 and 2036 and uplift in trade exports of up to AU\$8.63 billion (US\$5.96 billion) in the two decades before and after the Games (IOC, 2021*b*).

While at least thirty-one (84 per cent) of the venues planned to be used for Brisbane 2032 are existing or temporary (Brisbane 2032 Consortium, 2021), Foth *et al.* (2021) point out that this figure is lower than the upcoming two Olympics: 95 per cent for Paris 2024 and 100 per cent for Los Angeles 2028. However, it is important to note that both cities are holding the Olympics for the third time and are mega-cities with much larger populations – over four times the population of Brisbane and three times that of the SEQ region. Consistent with the guiding principle of the Games Master Plan of 'Embracing the IOC's New Norm reforms', Brisbane 2023 proposes new venues only when the venue is planned irrespective of the Games, is required for legacy, and explicitly supports the growth of the region (Brisbane 2032 Consortium, 2021, p. 12). Five of the seven Gold Coast venues were venues of the 2018 Commonwealth Games. Of these Coomera Indoor Sports Centre and Gold Coast Sports and Leisure Centre were built for the 2018 Games. Both facilities met an overwhelming demand upon opening and, according to Sheona Thomson (2018, p. 83): 'demonstrated through their popularity how needed they are in the context of their communities, where arguably infrastructure is playing catch-up to growth' (see figure 21.8). In her assessment immediately before the 2018 Commonwealth Games Thomson declared them already successes. Coomera Indoor Sports Centre functions today as an eight-court indoor community facility and has proven to be commercially sustainable and socially beneficial for the local government and the community (Brisbane 2032 Consortium, 2021). According to the City of Gold Coast Major Sporting Venues Executive Coordinator's assessment,

Figure 21.8. Legacy use of Coomera Indoor Sport Centre. (*Source*: MEGC, 2022)

Commonwealth Games legacy venues provided a real economic benefit for the region, and are used for local, national, and international events post Commonwealth Games. They are also emerging better and stronger from the coronavirus pandemic, having used the period of forced venue closures to improve the spaces, make some refurbishments, and set the venues up for the future creation of a sporting and leisure precinct (Luscombe, 2020). Brisbane Aquatic Centre slated for an upgrade for the 2032 Games was built for the 1982 Brisbane Commonwealth Games.

The vision of the Gold Coast 2018 Commonwealth Games of aligning the bid with existing infrastructural plans for the city to meet its growing population and increase sporting participation among its residents produced a positive legacy. There are no gigantic and unused 'white elephant' venues. The Athlete's Village was transformed into the Smith Collective, a mixed-use residential community of 1,170 apartments and eighty-two townhouses with shops and other communal facilities amidst 7 acres (2.8 ha) of landscaped open space (Farndon and Burton, 2019). Chandler Indoor Sports Centre, one of the new venues in Brisbane, is replacing a venue built for the 1982 Brisbane Commonwealth Games that will reach the end of its economic life in 2032.

One of the key characteristics of the Brisbane bid is how well the plans for the Games are linked to existing development plans for the city and region. Unlike past Olympics there are no new development projects solely for the Games. Instead, the Games are used as a catalyst for obtaining federal funding to bring forward existing infrastructure and urban development plans (Holmes *et al.*, 2021). Among these are many transport projects to ease traffic congestion in this rapidly growing region including Cross River Rail, Gold Coast Light Rail, Brisbane Metro, and a cycle network including the green bridges highlighted in the SEQ Regional Plan (DILGP, 2017).

Social Sustainability

Olympic Games may have various negative and positive impacts on the social dimensions of sustainability. KPMG's (2021) preliminary analysis identified community spirit, civic pride, increased physical activity and volunteering, and better mental health among the intangible benefits of the Games. Brisbane 2032 aims to achieve positive social impacts by building on the legacy of the Gold Coast 2018 Commonwealth Games, 'which set new standards for accessibility and equality for Para-sports and Para-athletes' and advancing the United Nation's Sustainable Development Goals, 'including promoting greater inclusion in sport for women with a disability' (Sygall, 2021, p. 32). One of the four outcomes sought in Committee for Brisbane's (2021, p. 2) legacy plan stated: 'First Nations and contemporary cultures are celebrated contributors to our community wellbeing and economic vitality'. The SMART goals (Specific, Measurable, Achievable, Relevant, Timely) developed for this outcome unfortunately are limited to increasing the awareness and knowledge of SEQ residents and visitors through promotion of the Indigenous place names. Despite this goal, none of the bid documents refer to Brisbane's Indigenous name Meeanjin (the place of the blue water lilies) in the language of Turrbal people, custodians of the Brisbane area for many thousands of years (Turrbal, 2022). A more ambitious goal under the outcome of equitable opportunities seeks to negotiate a treaty to record the history and preserve the culture of the region's Indigenous people, empower them to take responsibility for their communities and create commercial opportunities.

All new venues and venue upgrades are planned with their legacy in mind, to stimulate economic growth and support the recreational needs of a rapidly growing population. Four of the six proposed venues are planned to be 'Community Centres', collectively providing more than forty new multi-use court spaces within the SEQ region. These will build on the successful example of the Coomera Indoor Sport Centre built for the Gold Coast 2018 Commonwealth Games for the Gymnastics competition and will be reused in Brisbane 2032.

The Olympics and Paralympics Housing Trust is tasked with repurposing Games' infrastructure for social and affordable housing (Committee for Brisbane, 2021) and envisaged legacy impacts include catalysing development of social and affordable housing to meet the needs of Queensland's growing population (IOC, 2021b). The Games Feasibility Study (COMSEQ, 2019) includes use of Airbnb to supplement accommodation requirements. However, this may exacerbate the housing affordability crisis the region is already experiencing. While the flexibility introduced by the New Norm increases efficiency and reduces costs through reuse and sharing of facilities and smaller Games Villages due to athletes staying only during their competitions, Mair (2021) suggested that there will still be opportunity costs from delays to other needed facilities and inequal distribution of positive social impacts without benefit to disadvantaged communities in rural and regional Queensland.

Environmental Sustainability

Brisbane's most significant commitment regarding sustainability is to deliver the first contractually required climate positive Olympic Games. The legacy expected for the host region is the ambitious goal of making SEQ Australia's first zero carbon region (Committee for Brisbane, 2022). One of the five themes of the Brisbane Olympics vision is delivering a sustainable and resilient Games with a priority of achieving climate positive Games and as legacy create a transferable model for future hosts. This will help Queensland achieve its renewable energy and emissions reduction targets and support the UN Sustainable Development Goals (Brisbane 2032 Consortium, 2021). The Olympic commitment is consistent with Queensland's emissions reduction and renewable energy targets: zero net emissions by 2050, with an interim target to reduce emissions by 30 per cent below 2005 levels by 2030 (QDES, 2023). The former renewable energy target of 50 per cent by 2030 has recently been changed to 70 per cent by 2032 as part of the AU$62 billion set out in the 'Queensland Energy and Jobs Plan' (Queensland Government, 2022*b*).

The Queensland Government is planning to use a range of initiatives to minimize and mitigate against environmental impacts and deliver a Climate Positive Games. These include repurposing and upgrading existing infrastructure with enhanced green star credentials; encouraging behavioural change towards climate friendly policies and practices; reducing waste and pollution through reducing, reusing, and recycling initiatives before and during the event; and minimizing congestion and emissions through greater use of public transport and co-location of events (KPMG, 2021). Repurposing and upgrading existing infrastructure will use recycled materials and lower carbon options to support Queensland's 30 per cent emission reduction target 2030. Foth *et al.* (2021) found the wording of targeting all new infrastructure to obtain six-star Green Star for Buildings ratings noncommittal. They concluded that the IOC and the host cities have not undertaken a fundamental shift in their institutions to create climate-neutral or -positive Games but are relying on the existing rules, norms, and institutions. They argue that 'Brisbane 2032 … provides us with repackaged Games within its existing paradigm, not a new paradigm altogether' (*ibid.*, p. 242).

The climate positive Games commitment can be achieved through emission reduction measures and carbon offsets. From an environmental perspective carbon offsets should be the last solution. They are often criticized for allowing business-as-usual practices to continue, rather than cutting emissions at the source and their implementation involves various risks (Heynen and Vanaraja Ambeth, 2023). Development of a carbon budget for the Games is currently under way and will determine the extent of emission reduction and carbon offsets (QDES, 2022). Brisbane 2032 is committed to following best practice, aligning with recognized standards and reporting frameworks, and applying lessons from previous Games and other major sporting events. Its carbon management strategies to achieve climate positive Games will be guided by four key principles: first, minimizing the Games' footprint as much as possible before compensating more than 100 per cent of residual emissions; secondly, continuously improving emissions forecasting and measurement to support evidence-based decision making; thirdly, ensuring consistency and transparency across the event lifecycle to promote accountability and comparability; and finally, influencing matters to create change and deliver verifiable climate positive outcomes for Queensland and Australia, including by promoting shared responsibility. Halog (2022) identified exclusion of energy consumption and sourcing from the core principles of the Games Master Plan as a key shortcoming of Brisbane 2032 and argued that achieving a zero-emissions event by using renewable energy does not cover emissions of construction, particularly in a mostly coal-powered state. Early analyses of how to maximize social, economic, and ecological sustainability of Brisbane 2032 show that a higher reliance on carbon offsets results in poorer sustainability outcomes (Heynen and Vanaraja Ambeth, 2023). The most sustainable scenario with greater legacy requires large-scale renewable energy infrastructure investment for full decarbonization of the electricity sector and transport system and has significant costs.

Brisbane 2032 also aims to achieve zero waste and hopes to transform SEQ into Australia's first circular economy region (Committee for Brisbane, 2022). In addition to climate and waste related initiatives the value proposition mentioned provision of sustainable and locally produced food for Games clients (Queensland Government, 2019). Tham (2022, p. 9) suggested that the Brisbane 2032 bid 'focuses on under-investigated aspects of socio-cultural sustainability' and explains that sustainable food 'has a ripple effect on economic and environmental legacies, as they create jobs and support a more conscious form of agriculture'.

Engagement in Delivering Games Legacy

The Legacy Plan for the Games includes significant public consultation. Between December 2022 and March 2023 the Queensland Government conducted a survey asking Queenslanders and Australians their hopes, dreams, and aspirations for Brisbane 2032 and beyond. Receiving more than 12,000 submissions, responses included ideas ranging from high-level aspirations to tangible actions related to the environment, infrastructure, sport and physical activity, First Nations people and culture, transport, health and wellbeing, community connections, jobs and the economy, innovation and technology, diversity, equality, and inclusion. In March 2023, the Queensland Government also conducted a Brisbane 2032 Legacy Forum which brought together around 500 business leaders, sports stars, youth representatives, and Games representatives in a facilitated event. The synthesis of the ideas generated through these consultations will form the basis of the draft vision, themes, and priorities of the draft Legacy Plan and will be released for public consultation. In addition, the Brisbane 2032 Olympic and Paralympic Games Legacy Committee composed of twelve Queenslanders provides ongoing feedback to the government on what Queenslanders want in relation to Games legacy (Queensland Government, 2022*a*). Brisbane 2032 Coordination Office created in March 2023 will coordinate delivery of the Olympic and Paralympic Games in agreement with the Games partners. The Coordination Office will oversee many aspects of the games including legacy (DPC, 2023).

Fulfilling Olympic Commitments

Brisbane's bid is exemplary for not proposing any expensive and potentially white elephant stadia. The required infrastructure is already part of Queensland's plans for the next decade. In fact, the state Premier views it as 'transformational infrastructure' that will bring huge economic benefit and support economic recovery from the coronavirus pandemic (Eeles, 2021).

Following the award of the Games to Brisbane, SEQ City Deal, a twenty-year partnership between the Australian Government, Queensland Government, and 11 Councils which make up SEQ Council of Mayors, was announced in March 2022. This shared commitment to transform SEQ and deliver region-shaping infrastructure provides more than AU$1.8 billion investment with the aim of generating local jobs, boosting digital and transport connectivity, enhancing liveability, and supporting one of the fastest growing regions in the country. While this initiative was independent of the 2032 Games, this infrastructure investment aims to support the delivery of the Games and to use the Games as the catalyst for the region's transition to a more connected, integrated, liveable, sustainable, and innovative place, providing a lasting legacy for future generations (Australian Government *et al.*, 2022). Among other things, the deal will fund projects linked to the Brisbane Metro and green bridges.

While true legacy benefits in achieving carbon neutrality requires minimum reliance on carbon offsets and significant investment, the need to decarbonize to avoid the worst impacts of climate change may increase public support and demand for drastic action and may make this investment feasible. To enable Brisbane to benefit from the Olympic momentum, Heynen and Vanaraja Ambeth (2023) recommended improving Climate Positive Games governance through an independent committee in charge of developing detailed pathways and monitoring implementation, increasing public awareness of the climate positive Games commitment and legacy benefits, and increased engagement with the private sector. Halog (2022) argued that to be able to build on Sydney's success, Brisbane needs to go further than the Brisbane 2032 Master Plan that proposes integrating public transport services, strategically locating venues across Queensland, ensuring community needs across the state are met, investing in innovative solutions such as a sustainable hydrogen industry, and promoting policy and behavioural changes to help solve deep-rooted issues. Committing to lifecycle assessments of Olympic projects and follow up on promised outcomes over the years is necessary. Trying to achieve a 2032 climate-positive Games requires the city and the region to transform. Time will tell whether Brisbane can deliver on its promise of cost neutrality and commitment to be carbon positive.

Bibliography

The references listed in this bibliography include both the primary and secondary sources used in writing this book. Full publication details are not always given for the small number of sources listed here that were published before 1900, since some were privately published and bear only the names of their printers.

2010 Legacies Now (2008) *Collaborate, Participate, Celebrate: Annual Review 2007–08*. Vancouver: 2010 Legacies Now.

2010 Legacies Now (2009) *About Us*. Available at: http://www.2010legaciesnow.com/about_us/.

Acharya, S.K. (2005) Urban development in post-reform China: insights from Beijing. *Norsk Geografisk Tidsskrift*, **59**, pp. 229–236.

ACOG (Atlanta Committee for the Olympic Games) (1990) *Welcome to a Brave and Beautiful City*. Atlanta, GA: ACOG.

ACOG (1998) *Official Report of the XXVI Olympic Games*. Atlanta, GA: ACOG.

AEK (2016) Agia Sophia – Centre of sports, culture and memory. Available at: http://www.aekfc.gr/stp/agia-sofia-42938.htm?lang=en&path=-233246111.

AEKFC (2023) OPAP Arena. Available at: https://www.aekfc.gr/stp/opap-arena-2938.htm?lang=en&path=-233246111.

Agamben, G. (2005) *State of Exception*. Chicago, IL: University of Chicago Press.

Alaska Dispatch (2012) Anti-terrorism tool at forefront of 2012 London Olympic security. 4 May. Available at: http://www.alaskadispatch.com/article/anti-terrorism-tools-forefront-2012-london-olympics-security.

Alekseyeva, A. (2014) Sochi 2014 and the rhetoric of a new Russia: image construction through mega-events. *East European Politics*, **30**(2), pp. 158–174.

Alexandridis, T. (2007) *The Housing Impact of the 2004 Olympic Games in Athens*. Background paper. Geneva: Centre on Housing Rights and Evictions.

Allen, I. (2006) Should regeneration be based on a fleeting and extraordinary event? *Architects' Journal*, **224**, 30 November, p. 3.

Allen, N. (1965) *Olympic Diary: Tokyo 1964*. London: Nicholas Kaye.

Allen, J. and Cochrane, A. (2014) The urban unbound: London's politics and the 2012 Olympic Games. *International Journal of Urban and Regional Research*, **38**(5), pp. 1609–1624.

Alm, J., Solberg, H.A., Storm, R.K. and Jakobsen, T.G. (2016) Hosting major sports events: the challenge of taming white elephants. *Leisure Studies*, **35**(5), pp. 564–582.

Alpert Reyes, E. (2019) L.A. Planning Commission backs new hotel and housing development near USC. *Los Angeles Times*, 14 February. Available at: https://www.latimes.com/local/lanow/la-me-ln-fig-project-20190214-story.html.

Alpha Bank (2004) *The Impact of the Olympic Games on the Greek Economy*. Athens: Alpha Bank.

Amateur Photographer (2012) Fish photographer caught in Olympics terror alert. 23 May. Available at: http://www.amateurphotographer.co.uk/photo-news/538771/fish-photographer-caught-in-olympics-terror-alert.

Amnesty International (2021) *Brazil Country Report*. New York: Amnesty International, available from https://www.amnesty.org/en/location/americas/south-america/brazil/report-brazil/.

Andranovich, G. and Burbank, M.J. (2011) Contextualizing Olympic legacies. *Urban Geography*, **32**(6), pp. 823–844.

Andranovich, G. and Burbank, M.J. (2021) *Contesting the Olympics in American Cities: Chicago 2016, Boston 2024, Los Angeles 2028*. Singapore: Springer.

Andranovich, G., Burbank, M.J. and Heying, C.H. (2001) Olympic Cities: lessons learned from mega-event politics. *Journal of Urban Affairs*, **23**, pp. 113–131.

Anon (1904) *Universal Exposition, Saint Louis 1904: Preliminary Programme of Physical Culture, Olympic Games and World's Championship Contests*. St. Louis, MO: Organizing Committee.

Anon (1907) The Olympic Games. *The Times*, 30 March, p. 10.

Anon (1910) Dover, Robert. *Encyclopaedia Britannica*, 11th ed., vol. 8. Cambridge: Cambridge University Press, p. 453.

Anon (1987) The future of Athens: a city in transition. *Financial Times*, 6 May.

Anon (1994) Homebush: Games city to ghost town. *Sydney Morning Herald*, 22 November, p. 19.

Anon (2011) Greece's Olympic dream has turned into a nightmare for Village residents. *Daily Telegraph*, 23 June. Available at: https://www.telegraph.co.uk/finance/financialcrisis/8595360/Greeces-Olympic-dream-has-turned-into-a-nightmare-for-Village-residents.html.

Anon (2013) Boris Johnson: The Olympic Park will be the Albertopolis of the east. *Evening Standard*, 4 December. Available at: http://www.standard.co.uk/comment/comment/boris-johnson-the-olympic-park-will-be-the-albertopolis-of-the-east-8982871.html.

Anon (2015) 'Pre-legacy' of Rio 2016 Games begins as Olympic venue is opened to underprivileged communities. *Rio2016*, 23 December. Available at: http://www.rio2016.com/en/news/pre-legacy-of-rio-2016-games-begins-as-olympic-venue-is-opened-to-underprivileged-communities.

Anon (2021) Greece finally starts work on €28bn Athens 'Riviera'. *Financial Times*. Available at: https://www.ft.com/content/6bb37470-2441-4424-b5e3-8b322a73494c.

AOBC (Athens 2004 Olympic Bid Committee) (1997) *Athens Candidate City*. Athens: AOBC.

AOM (The Athens Olympic Museum) (2021) Athens welcomes its very own Olympic Museum at Golden Hall. Available at: https://athensolympicmuseum.org/en/newsroom/athens-welcomes-olympic-museum-at-golden-hall/.

Aoyama, Y. (2016) Urban planning challenge and the Olympic Games: Tokyo 1964 and 2020. *Research Series, Institute of Social Science, University of Tokyo*, **59**, pp. 115–128.

Aoyama, Y. (2017) Tokyo 2020, in Gold, J.R and Gold, M.M. (eds.) *Olympic Cities: Urban Planning, City Agendas and the World's Games, 1896 to the Present*. London: Routledge, pp. 424–437.

Aoyama, Y. (2022) The conflict between the country and the capital over the Olympics. *Review of Governance Studies, Meiji University Graduate School of Governance Studies*, 2022, pp. 73–85.

APO (Autoridade Pública Olímpica) (2017) Matriz de Responsabilidades 6ª atualização. Available at: http://rededoesporte.gov.br/pt-br/legado/matriz-de-responsabilidades.

Aragón-Pérez, A. (2017) Origins of the environmental dimension of the Olympic Movement. *Journal of Olympic History*, **15**(1), pp. 26–33.

Aragón-Pérez, A. (2019) The influence of the 1992 Earth Summit on the 1992 Olympic Games in Barcelona: awakening of the Olympic environmental dimension. *International Journal of the History of Sport*, **36**(2/3), pp. 244–266.

Arbaci, S. and Tapada-Berteli, T. (2012) Social inequality and urban regeneration in Barcelona city centre: reconsidering success. *European Urban and Regional Studies*, **19**(3), pp. 287–311.

Arbena, J.L. (1996) Mexico City 1968: the Games of the XIXth Olympiad, in Findling, J.E.

and Pelle, K.D. (eds.) *Historical Dictionary of the Modern Olympic Movement.* Westport, CN: Greenwood Press, pp. 139–147.

Armijo, L.E. (2007) The BRICS countries (Brazil, Russia, India and China) as an analytical category: mirage or insight? *Asian Perspective*, **31**(4), pp. 7–42.

Arnold, B. (1992) The past as propaganda. *Archaeology*, **45**(July/August), pp. 30–37.

Arnold, R. and Foxall, A. (2014) Lord of the (Five) Rings. *Problems of Post-Communism*, **61**(1), pp. 3–12.

Associated Press (2014) IOC struggling to find cities to host Olympics, 31 May. Available at: https://apnews.com/article/c95745845f07452db7ba143a1dc6287a.

Ataman, J. and Laborie, A. (2023) The world's biggest sporting event is coming to Paris. Not everyone's happy. *CNN Sport*, 11 June. Available at: https://edition.cnn.com/2023/06/11/europe/paris-france-olympics-mood-cmd-intl/index.html.

ATC (Australian Tourist Commission) (1998) *1996 Olympic Games Atlanta Report.* September. Sydney: ATC.

ATC (2000) *The Sydney Olympic Games.* ATC research update, April. Sydney: ATC.

ATC (2001) *Olympic Games Tourism Strategy: Overview.* Sydney: Australia Tourist Commission.

Athens Indymedia (2005) CCTV cameras all around us (but some destroyed). Available at: http://athens.indymedia.org/features.php3?id=394.

ATHOC (Athens Organizing Committee for the Olympic Games) (2004) Archery in the shadow of the Acropolis (advertisement), in Konstandaras, K. (ed.) *Greece: The Ideal Destination.* Athens: Hellenic Sun Editions.

ATHOC (2005) *Official Report of the XXVIII Olympiad*, 2 vols. Athens: Liberis Publications Group.

Audit Office (1999) *Performance Audit Report: The Sydney 2000 Olympic and Paralympic Games. Review of Estimates.* Sydney: Audit Office.

Australian Government, Queensland Government, and Council of Mayors South East Queensland (COMSEQ) (2022) *SEQ City Deal.* 21 March. Available at: https://seqmayors.qld.gov.au/documents/uX6PxQ4QY9Erz9eUjKRw.

Avarello, P. (2000) L'urbanizzazione, in De Rosa, L. (ed.) *Roma del Duemila.* Rome-Bari: Laterza, pp. 159–201.

Baade, R.A. and Matheson, V. (2002) Bidding for the Olympics: fool's gold, in Baros, C.P., Ibrahimo, M. and Szymanski, S. (eds.) *Transatlantic Sport: The Comparative Economics of North America and European Sports.* Cheltenham: Edward Elgar, pp. 127–151.

Baade, R.A., Baumann, R. and Matheson, V.A. (2008) Slippery Slope? Assessing the Economic Impact of the 2002 Winter Olympic Games in Salt Lake City, Utah. Department of Economics Faculty Research Series, Paper 08-15, College of the Holy Cross, Worcester, MA.

BAB (British Assessment Bureau) (2010) ISO 14001:2004 (ISO 14000) Certification. Available at: http://www.british-assessment.co.uk/ISO-14001-certification-services.htm.

Bachrach, S.D. (2001) *The Nazi Olympics Berlin 1936.* St. Louis, MO: Turtleback Books.

Baker, R.E. and Esherick, C. (2013) *Fundamentals of Sports Management.* Champaign, IL: Human Kinetics.

Bailey S. (2008) *Athlete First: A History of the Paralympic movement.* Oxford: Wiley-Blackwell.

BALASA (British Amputee and Les Autres Sports Association) (2007) *Les Autres Athletes.* Available at: http://www.patient.co.uk/showdoc/26739787/.

Barragan, B. (2015) The Worst Day and Time to Drive on Every Los Angeles Freeway. Curbed LA, 27 August. Available at: https://la.curbed.com/2015/8/27/9926230/worst-freeways-traffic-los-angeles.

Barnett, C.R. (1996) St. Louis 1904: the Games of the 3rd Olympiad, in Findling, J.E. and Pelle, K.D. (eds.) *Historical Dictionary of the Modern Olympic Movement.* Westport, CN: Greenwood Press, pp. 18–25.

Barringer, J.M. (2021) *Olympia: A Cultural History.* Princeton, NJ: Princeton University Press.

Bastéa, E. (2000) *The Creation of Modern Athens: Planning the Myth.* Cambridge: Cambridge University Press.

Batuhan, T. (2015) Olympic Strategy of Downtown Atlanta Business Elites: A Case Study of the 1996 Atlanta Summer Olympics. Unpublished PhD thesis, Department of Urban and Regional Planning, Florida State University-Tallahassee.

Bauman, Z. (2000) *Liquid Modernity*. Cambridge: Polity Press.

Bayle, E. (2016) Olympic social responsibility: a challenge for the future. *Sport in Society*, **19**(6), pp. 754–766.

Bazzanella, F., Bichler, B.F. and Schnitze, M. (2022) Collaboration and meta-organisation in event tourism – effects of the Olympic Agenda 2020 on planning the 2026 Winter Olympics. *Tourism Management Perspective*, **41**, January, 100939.

BBC (British Broadcasting Corporation) (2005) Games a £2bn UK tourism boost. 6 July. Available at: http://news.bbc.co.uk/1/hi/uk/4656771.stm.

BBC (2012) In pictures: Beijing's Olympic venue legacy. Available at: http://www.bbc.co.uk/news/in-pictures-18780003.

BBC News (2012a) London 2012: Major Olympic security test unveiled. 30 April. Available at: http://www.bbc.co.uk/news/uk-17891223.

BBC News (2012b) Typhoon jets arrive in London to test Olympic security. 2 May. Available at: http://www.bbc.co.uk/news/uk-17922490.

BBC News (2012c) Missiles may be placed at residential flats. 29 April. Available at: http://www.bbc.co.uk/news/uk-17884897.

BBC News (2013) Rio favela has 'more CCTV cameras than London. 11 January. Available at: http://www.bbc.co.uk/news/world-latin-america-20992062.

BBC News (2015) Beijing to host 2022 Winter Olympics and Paralympics, 31 July. Available at: http://www.bbc.co.uk/sport/0/winter-olympics/33730477.

BBC News London (2012) Sonic device deployed in London during Olympics, 12 May. Available at: http://www.bbc.co.uk/news/uk-england-london-18042528.

BBC Sport (2008) Olympic stadium 'hits £525m mark'. BBC News, 18 June. Available at: http:/news.bbc.co.uk/1/hi/England/London/7460188.

BCG (Boston Consulting Group) (2022) SNFCC Impact Study. Available at: https://www.snfcc.org/sites/default/files/sitefiles_2023-01/snfcc_impact_study_22_vf.pdf.

Bea, F.X. (1997) Shareholder value. *Wirtschaftswissenschaftliches Studium*, **29**(10), pp. 541–543.

Beard, M. (2004) The Greek heroes, a missed drugs test and a 'motorbike accident' that upset the Games. *The Independent*, 14 August.

Beriatos, E. and Gospodini, A. (2004) 'Glocalising' urban landscapes: Athens and the 2004 Olympics. *Cities*, **21**(3), pp. 187–202.

Berkeley, G. (2022a) NBCUniversal reports record viewing figures for Winter Paralympics after Olympics decline. *Inside the Games*, 20 March. Available at: https://www.insidethegames.biz/articles/1120785/nbcuniversal-figures-winter-paralympics.

Berkeley, G. (2022b) Olympic rights-holder Discovery takes channels off air in Russia after Ukraine invasion. Available at: https://www.insidethegames.biz/articles/1120452/discovery-take-channels-off-air-russia.

Bernal, M. (1987) *Black Athena: The Afroasiatic Roots of Classical Civilization*, vol. 1. New Brunswick, NJ: Rutgers University Press.

Bernstock, P. (2014) *Olympic Housing: A Critical Review of London 2012's Legacy*. Aldershot: Ashgate.

Bernstock, P. (2020) Evaluating the contribution of planning gain to an inclusive housing legacy: a case study of London 2012. *Planning Perspectives*, **35**(6), pp. 927–953.

Bernstock, P., Brownill, S., Davis, J., Melhuish, C., Minton, A. and Woodcraft, S. (eds.) (2022) *State of the Legacy: Reviewing a Decade of Writings on the Regeneration Promises of London 2012*. London: UCL Urban Laboratory.

Bianchini, F., Dawson, J. and Evans, R. (1992) Flagship projects in urban regeneration, in Healey, P., Davoudi, S., Tavsanoglu, S., O'Toole, M. and Usher, D. (eds.) *Rebuilding the City: Property-Led Urban Regeneration*. London: E and FN Spon, pp. 245–255.

Bingham Hall, P. (1999) *Olympic Architecture: Building Sydney 2000*. Sydney: Watermark Press.

Binyon, M. (1980) The way the Games were won. *The Times*, 4 August.

Blair, G. (2019) IOC 'very satisfied' with Tokyo 2020 preparations, say organisers. *The Guardian*, 24 July. Available at: https://www.theguardian.com/sport/2019/jul/24/ioc-tokyo-2020-olympic-games.

Blair, K. and Johnson, M. (2022) 'I am Invictus': parasport, the Invictus Games, and disability performance in Canada. *Theatre Research in Canada*, **43**(1), pp. 96–114.

Blake, A. (2005) *The Economic Impact of the London 2012 Olympics*. Nottingham: Christel DeHaan Tourism and Travel Research Institute.

Blowe, K. (2004) London's Olympics Myths. Radical Activist Network newsletter. Available at: *www.radicalactivist.net*.

BOC (British Olympic Council) (1907) *Olympic Games of London 1908: IVth International Olympiad*. London: British Olympic Council.

BOCOG (Beijing Organizing Committee for the Games of the XXXIX Olympiad) (2003) *Beijing Olympic Action Plan*. Beijing: BOCOG.

BOCOG (2010) *Official Report of the Games of the XXIX Olympiad in Beijing in 2008*. Beijing: BOCOG.

BOCOPG (Beijing Organizing Committee for the 2022 Olympic and Paralympic Winter Games) (2023) *Sustainability for the Future – Beijing 2022 Post-Games Sustainability Report*. Beijing: BOCOG.

BOGVWCG (Beijing Olympic Games Volunteer Work Coordination Group) 2008 *Manual for Being Olympic Volunteers*. Beijing: China Renmin University Press.

Bohotis, T.N. (2017) Archaeology and politics: The Greek–German Olympia excavations treaty, 1869–1875, in Voutsaki, S. and Cartledge, P. (eds.) *Ancient Monuments and Modern Identities*. London: Routledge, pp. 117–129.

Bokoyannis, D. (2006) Athens: The Making of a Contemporary and Friendlier City. Speech, 9 February, Athens Concert Hall. Available at: http://www.cityofathens.gr/files/pdf/highlights/apologismos_omilia_en.pdf.

Bondonio, P. and Campaniello, N. (2006) Torino 2006: what kind of Olympic Winter Games were they? A preliminary account from an organizational and economic perspective. *Olympika*, **15**, pp. 355–380.

Bondonio, P. and Guala, C. (2011) Gran Torino? The 2006 Olympic Winter Games and the tourism revival of an ancient city. *Journal of Sport and Tourism*, **16**(4), pp. 303–321.

Bonini, F. (2011) Le Olimpiadi nell'Italia che cambia. *Le Olimpiadi del 'miracolo' cinquant'anni dopo*. Milan: Franco Angeli, pp. 7–15.

Booth, D. (1999) Gifts of corruption? Ambiguities of obligation in the Olympic movement. *Olympika*, **8**, pp. 43–68.

Borja, F. (1992) *The Winter Olympic Games. Albertville 1992: A Case Study*. Paris: American University of Paris.

Borja, J. (ed.) (1995) *Barcelona: A Model of Urban Transformation 1980–1995*. Quito: Urban Management Series (PGU-LAC).

Bottero, M., Sacerdotti, S.L. and Mauro, S. (2012) Turin 2006 Olympic Winter Games: impacts and legacies from a tourism perspective. *Journal of Tourism and Cultural Change*, **10**(2), pp. 202–217.

Boukas, N., Ziakas, V. and Boustras, G. (2013) Olympic legacy and cultural tourism: exploring the facets of Athens' Olympic heritage. *International Journal of Heritage Studies*, **19**, pp. 203–228.

Bouras, S. (2007) Greek mall boom challenges tradition. Available at: http://www.nytimes.com/2007/06/11/business/worldbusiness/11iht-regreece.1.6096546.html.

Bourbillères, H. and Koebel, M. (2020) Les processus de contestation dans le cadre des candidatures des villes européennes aux Jeux olympiques et paralympiques 2024. *Movement and Sport Sciences*, **107**, pp. 17–29.

Bourbillères, H., Gasparini, W. and Koebel, M. (2023) Local protests against the 2024 Olympic Games in European cities: the cases of the Rome, Hamburg, Budapest and Paris 2024 bids. *Sport in Society*, **26**(1), pp. 1–26.

Boykoff, J. (2014) *Celebration, Capitalism and the Olympic Games*. New York: Routledge.

Boykoff, J. (2020) *Nolympians: Inside the Fight against Capitalist Mega-Sports in Los Angeles, Tokyo and Beyond*. Halifax, Nova Scotia: Fernwood Publishing.

Boykoff, J. and Fussey, P. (2013) London's shadow legacies: security and activism at the 2012 Olympics. *Contemporary Social Science*, **9**(2), pp. 253–270.

Boykoff, J. and Gaffney, C. (2020) The Tokyo 2020 Games and the end of Olympic history. *Capitalism Nature Socialism*, **31**(2), pp. 1–19.

Boyle, L. (2022) The Winter Olympics and the true cost of fake snow dominating the slopes. *The Guardian*, 2 February. Available at: https://www.independent.co.uk/climate-change/news/winter-olympics-fake-snow-2022-b2004826.html.

Boyle, P. and Haggerty, K.D. (2009) Spectacular security: mega-events and the security complex. *International Political Sociology*, **3**(3), pp. 257–274.

Boyle, P. and Haggerty, K.D. (2011) Civil cities and urban governance: regulating disorder for the Vancouver Winter Olympics. *Urban Studies*, **48**(15), pp. 3185–3201.

Boyle, P. and Haggerty. K. (2012) Planning for the worst: risk, uncertainty, and the Olympic Games. *British Journal of Sociology*, **63**(2), pp. 241–259.

BPA (British Paralympic Association) (2007) Sydney 2000. Available at: http://www.paralympics.org.uk/paralympic_games.asp?section=000100010003&games_code=00010003000300010003.

BPA (2015) National Paralympic Day 2015. Available at: http://paralympics.org.uk/npd2015.

Braconnier, S. (2018) Urbanisme, construction publique et Jeux olympiques Paris 2024. *Revue de Droit Immobilier*, No. 6.

Brent Ritchie, J.R. and Smith, B.H. (1991) The impact of a mega-event on host region awareness: a longitudinal study. *Journal of Travel Research*, **30**(1), pp. 3–10.

Brichford, M. (1996) Munich 1972: the Games of the 20th Olympiad, in Findling, J.E. and Pelle, K.D. (eds.) *Historical Dictionary of the Modern Olympic Movement*. Westport, CT: Greenwood Press, pp. 148–152.

Brisbane 2032 Consortium (2021) *IOC Future Host Commission Questionnaire Response: Final Submission*. Australian Olympic Committee. Available at: https://stillmed.olympics.com/media/Documents/International-Olympic-Committee/Commissions/Future-host-commission/The-Games-of-The-Olympiad/Brisbane-2032-FHC-Questionnaire-Response.pdf.

Brito, R. and Wade, S. (2017) AP Analysis: Rio de Janeiro Olympics cost $13.1 billion. *Associated Press*, 15 June. Available at: https://apnews.com/article/d1662ddb3bae4d2984ca4ab65012be78.

Brittain, I. (2008) The evolution of the Paralympic Games, in Cashman R. and Darcy S. (eds.) *Benchmark Games: The Sydney 2000 Paralympic Games*. Sydney: Walla Walla Press, pp. 19–34.

Brittain, I. (2010) *The Paralympic Games Explained*. London: Routledge.

Brittain, I. (2022) Tokyo 2020 Paralympic legacy, disability and Japan – Muzukashi desu ne? *Journal of Paralympic Research Group*, **17**, pp. 71–93.

Brittain, I. and Mataruna Dos Santos, L.J. (2018) The Rio 2016 Paralympic Games, in Brittain, I. and Beacom, A. (eds) *The Palgrave Handbook of Paralympic Studies*. London: Palgrave Macmillan, pp. 531–553.

Broudehoux, A.-M. (2004) *The Making and Selling of Post-Mao Beijing*. London: Routledge.

Brown, G. (2001) Sydney 2000: an invitation to the world. *Olympic Review*, **37**, pp. 15–20.

Brown, L.A. (2019) The Architectural Design and Planning Legacies of the European Summer Olympic Games 1948–2012. Unpublished PhD thesis. Newcastle: University of Northumbria.

Brown, L.A. (2020) Planning for legacy in the post-war era of the Olympic Winter Games. *International Journal of the History of Sport*, **37**(13), pp. 1348–1367.

Brownell, S. (2008*a*) *Beijing's Games: What the Olympics mean to China*. Lanham, MD: Rowman and Littlefield.

Brownell, S. (ed.) (2008*b*) *The 1904 Anthropology Days and Olympic Games: Sport, Race, and American Imperialism*. Lincoln, NE: University of Nebraska Press.

Brownell, S. (2013) 'Brand China' in the Olympic context. *Journal of the European Institute for Communication and Culture*, **20**(4), pp. 65–82.

Browning, M. (2000) Olympics under the gun. *The Guardian*, 8 March. Available at: http://www.cpa.org.au/gachive2/991games.html.

Brundtland, G.H. (1987) Chairman's foreword, in World Commission on Environment and Development, *Our Common Future*. Oxford: Oxford University Press, pp. ix–xv.

Brunet, F. (1993) *Economy of the 1992 Barcelona Olympic Games*. Lausanne: IOC.

Brunet, F. (1995) An economic analysis of the Barcelona '92 Olympic Games: resources, financing and impact, in Moragas, M. de and Botella, M. (eds.) *The Keys of Success: The Social, Sporting, Economic and Communications Impact of Barcelona '92*. Barcelona: Bellaterra, pp. 203–237.

Brunet, F. (2009) The economy of the Barcelona Olympic Games, in Poynter, G. and MacRury, I. (eds.) *Olympic Cities: 2012 and the Remaking of London*. Farnham: Ashgate, pp. 97–119.

Brunet, F. and Xinwen, Z. (2009) The economy of the Beijing Olympic Games: an analysis of prospects and first impacts, in Poynter, G. and MacRury, I. (eds.) *Olympic Cities: 2012 and the Remaking of London*. Farnham: Ashgate, pp. 163–180.

Buchanan, I. and Mallon, B. (2001) *Historical Dictionary of the Olympic Movement*. Lanham, MD: Scarecrow Press.

Buchanan, P. (1992) Barcelona: a city regenerated. *Architectural Review*, **191**(August), pp. 11–14.

Bukharov, E. (2018) Sochi 2014, in Brittain, I. and Beacom, A. (eds.) *The Palgrave Handbook of Paralympic Studies*. London: Palgrave Macmillan, pp. 507–530.

Bunning, W. (1973) *Report and Review of Moore Park and Alternative Sites in Sydney for a Major Sports Complex* [The Bunning Report]. Sydney.

Burbank, M.J., Andranovich, G.D. and Heying, C.H. (2001) *Olympic Dreams: The Impact of Mega-Events on Local Politics*. Boulder, CO: Lynne Rienner.

Burdett, M. (2017) Case study: Rio Olympics 2016. Available at: https://www.geography casestudy.com/case-study-rio-olympics-2016/.

Burnosky, R.L. (1994) The History of the Arts in the Olympic Games. Unpublished Master's Thesis, The American University, Washington, DC.

Burns, J. (2005) Written Statement to the US Senate Subcommittee on Trade, Tourism and Economic Development. *Field Hearing on The Economic Impact of the 2010 Vancouver, Canada, Winter Olympics on Oregon and the Pacific Northwest*. Washington, DC: US Government Printing Office.

Business File (2004) *Going for Gold? A Survey on the Economics of the 2004 Olympic Games*. Athens: Greek Special Survey Series.

Butler, T. (2007) Re-urbanizing London's Docklands: gentrification, suburbanization or new urbanism? *International Journal of Urban and Regional Research*, **31**(4), pp. 759–781.

Butterfield, H. (1931) *The Whig Interpretation of History*. London: George Bell and Sons.

Byun, J. and Leopkey, B. (2021) A resource-based view of post-Games legacy strategy: the case of the 2018 PyeongChang Olympic Games. *Sport in Society*, **24**(12), pp. 2139–2158.

Byun, J. and Leopkey, B. (2022) Exploring conflict among stakeholders in the governance of Olympic legacy. *Sport Management Review*, **25**, pp. 700–721.

Cadot, M. (2020) Préparer les jeux Olympiques et Paralympiques de 2024: une véritable course de fond. *Administration*, **268**, pp. 54–56.

Calavita, N. and Ferrer, A. (2000) Behind Barcelona's success story: citizens movements and planners' power. *Journal of Urban History*, **26**, pp. 793–807.

California Olympic Commission (1960) *VIII Olympic Winter Games Squaw Valley, California, Final Report*. Squaw Valley, CA: Organizing Committee.

Cannon, T. (2000) *China's Economic Growth: The Impact on Regions, Migration and the Environment*. London: Macmillan.

Cantelon, H. and Letters, M. (2000) The making of the IOC environmental policy as the third dimension of the Olympic Movement. *International Review for the Sociology of Sport*, **35**(3), pp. 294–308.

Capel, H. (2005) *El modelo Barcelona: un exámen crítico*. Barcelona: Edicions del Serbal.

Carisbroke, Lord, Porritt, A., Webb-Johnson, Lord, Heyworth, Lord, Templer, E.M., Londin, H., Summers, S., Bannister, R., Faure, J.C.A. and Guttmann, L. (1956) Games for the paralysed. *The Times*, 20 March, p. 11.

Carl Diem Institute (1966) *Pierre de Coubertin, The Olympic Idea: Discourses and Essays*. Lausanne: Editions Internationales Olympia.

Carson, R. (1962) *Silent Spring*. New York: Houghton Mifflin Harcourt.

Cartalis, C. (2015) Sport mega-events as catalysts for sustainable urban development: the case of Athens 2004, in Viegoff, V. and Poynter, G. (eds.) *Mega-Event Cities: Urban Legacies of Global Sports Events*. Farnham: Ashgate, pp. 205–218.

Cashman, R. (2006) *The Bitter-Sweet Awakening: The Legacy of the Sydney 2000 Olympic Games*. Sydney: Walla Walla Press.

Cashman, R. (2008) The Sydney Olympic Park model: its evolution and realisation, in Hay, A. and Cashman, R. (eds.) *Connecting Mega Events Cities: A Publication for the 9th World Congress of Metropolis*. Sydney: Sydney Olympic Park Authority, pp. 21–39.

Cashman, R. (2009) Regenerating Sydney's West: framing and adapting an Olympic vision, in Poynter, G. and MacRury, I. (eds.) *Olympic Cities: 2012 and the Remaking of London*, Farnham: Ashgate, pp. 133–143.

Cashman, R. (2011) *Sydney Olympic Park 2000 to 2010: History and Legacy*. Sydney: Walla Walla Press.

Cashman R. and Darcy S. (2008*a*) (eds.) *Benchmark Games. The Sydney 2000 Paralympic Games*, Sydney: Walla Walla Press, pp. 19–34.

Cashman, R. and Darcy, S. (2008*b*) Paralympic benchmarks before 2000, in Cashman, R. and Darcy, S. (eds.) *Benchmark Games: The Sydney 2000 Paralympic Games*. Sydney: Walla Walla Press, pp. 35–53.

Cashman, R. and Harris, R. (2012) *The Australian Olympic Caravan from 2000 to 2012*. Sydney: Walla Walla Press.

Cashman, R. and Hughes, A. (eds.) (1999) *Staging the Olympics: The Event and Its Impact*. Sydney: University of New South Wales Press.

Casciato, M. (2015) Sport and leisure in Rome from the Fascist years to the Olympic Games. *ICOMOS: Hefte des Deutschen Nationalkomitees*, **38**, pp. 29–36.

Cassar, S., and Creaco, S. (2012) Tourism aspects of the XVII Rome Olympiad. *Journal of Tourism and Cultural Change*, **10**(2), pp. 167–184.

CBS News (2009) IOC congratulates itself for the Beijing Olympics. 7 October. Available at: https://www.cbsnews.com/news/ioc-congratulates-itself-for-beijing-olympics/.

CBS News (2021) LA City Council approves Games agreement ahead of 2028 Olympics. 3 December. Available at: https://www.cbsnews.com/losangeles/news/la-city-council-approves-games-agreement-ahead-of-2028-olympics/.

CC (Cour des Comptes) (2023) *Organisation des JOP Paris 2024, Rapport au Parlement*, January. Paris: Cour des Comptes.

Cerqueira, S. and Pessoa, D. (2017) Ilha Pura se transforma em herança maldita da Olimpíada. *Veja*, 17 November. Available online: https://vejario.abril.com.br/cidade/ilha-pura-se-transforma-em-heranca-maldita-da-olimpiada/.

Chai, J.C.H. (1996) Divergent development and regional income gap in China. *Journal of Contemporary Asia*, **26**, pp. 46–58.

Chalip, L. (2004) Beyond impact: a general model for sport event leverage, in Ritchie, B.W. and Adair, D. (eds.) *Sport Tourism: interrelationships, impacts and issues*. Clevedon: Channel View Publications, pp. 226–252.

Chalip, L. and Leyns, A. (2002) Local business leveraging of a sport event: managing an event for economic benefit. *Journal of Sport Management*, **16**(2), pp. 132–158.

Chalkley, B. and Essex, S. (1998) Olympic Games: catalyst of urban change. *Leisure Studies*, **17**, pp. 187–206.

Chalkley, B. and Essex, S. (1999) Urban development through hosting international events: a history of the Olympic Games. *Planning Perspectives*, **14**(4), pp. 369–394.

Chandler, R. (1776) *Travels in Greece; or an Account of a Tour made at the Expense of the Society of Dilettanti*. Dublin.

Channel 4 (2012) The London 2014 Paralympic Games brought to you by Channel 4. Available at: http://www.channel4.com/media/documents/press/news/Paralympic%20Booklet.pdf.

Chappelet, J-L. (1997) From Chamonix to Salt Lake City: evolution of the Olympic Village concept at the Winter Games, in Moragas, M. de, Llines M. and Kidd, B. (eds.) *Olympic Villages: A Hundred Years of Urban Planning and Shared Experiences*. International Symposium on Olympic Villages. Lausanne: Documents of the IOC Museum, pp. 81–88.

Chappelet, J-L. (2002*a*) *A Short Overview of the Olympic Winter Games*. Barcelona: Centre d'Estudis Olimpics I de l'Esport, Universitat Autònoma de Barcelona.

Chappelet, J-L. (2002*b*) From Lake Placid to Salt Lake City: the challenging growth of the Olympic Winter Games since 1980. *European Journal of Sport Science*, **2**(3), pp. 1–21.

Chappelet, J-L. (2008) Olympic environmental concerns as a legacy of the Winter Games. *International Journal of the History of Sport*, **25**(14), pp. 1884–1902.

Chappelet, J-L. (2016) From Olympic administration to Olympic governance. *Sport in Society*, **19**(6), pp. 739–751.

Chappelet, J-L. (2021*a*) The governance of the Olympic system: from one to many stakeholders. *Journal of Global Sport Management*. https://doi.org/10.1080/24704067.2021.1899767.

Chappelet, J-L. (2021*b*) Winter Olympic referendums: reasons for opposition to the Games. *International Journal of the History of Sport*, **38**(13/14), pp. 1369–1384.

Charmetant, R. (1997) Albertville: Olympism and architecture, in Moragas, M. de, Llines M. and Kidd, B. (eds.) *Olympic Villages: A Hundred Years of Urban Planning and Shared Experiences*. International Symposium on Olympic Villages. Lausanne: Documents of the IOC Museum, pp. 109–115.

Charnock, G., March, H. and Ribera-Fumaz, R. (2021) From smart to rebel city? Worlding, provincialising and the Barcelona model. *Urban Studies*, **58**, pp. 581–600.

Chen, Y., Jin, G.Z., Kumar, N. and Shi, G. (2013) The promise of Beijing: evaluating the impact of the 2008 Olympic Games on air quality. *Journal of Environmental Economics and Management*, **66**(3), pp. 424–443.

Chestin, I. (2014) Sochi Olympics have left a trail of environmental destruction. *The Conversation*, 14 February. Available at: https://theconversation.com/sochi-olympics-have-left-a-trail-of-environmental-destruction-23112.

Chipperfield, M. (2000) Sydney in bad odour over toxic backyard for Olympic Games, *The Telegraph*, 27 August. Available at: https://www.telegraph.co.uk/news/worldnews/australiaandthepacific/1367883/Sydney-in-bad-odour-overtoxic-backyard-for-Olympic-Games.html.

Christensen, P. and Kyle, D.G. (2014) General introduction, in Christensen, P. and Kyle, D.G. (eds.) *A Companion to Sport and Spectacle in Greek and Roman Antiquity*. Chichester: Wiley Blackwell, pp. 1–15.

Church, B. (2005) Forgotten games. *Houston Chronicle*, 13 August.

CIIC (China Internet Information Centre) (2004) Beijing subways improve access for handicapped. *China Daily* (English language edition), 17 August. Available at: http://www.china.org.cn/english/2004/Aug/104219.htm.

City of Hellinikon-Argyroupoli (2013) Hellinikon: development for whom? Available at: http://www.elliniko-argyroupoli.gr/article.php?id=2569.

City of Inglewood (2021*a*) Resolution of Necessity – Hearing to Consider Adoption of Resolutions of Necessity to Acquire Property in the City of Inglewood for the Inglewood Basketball and Entertainment Center (IBEC) Project. 26 January. Available at: https://www.cityofinglewood.org/AgendaCenter/ViewFile/Item/10698?fileID=6795.

City of Inglewood (2021*b*) Inglewood Transit Connector Project. Draft Environmental Impact Report. November. Available at: https://www.cityofinglewood.org/DocumentCenter/ View/16869/Inglewood-Tranist-Connector-DEIR-Nov-2021.

Clastres, P., Vallotton, F. and Bancel, N. (eds.) (2022) Editorial: youth, young people, and sport in the twentieth century. *Frontiers in Sports and Active Living*, **4**, 25 April. Available at: https://www.frontiersin.org/articles/10.3389/fspor.2022.887919/full.

Close, P., Askew, D. and Xu, X. (2007) *The Beijing Olympiad: The Political Economy of a Sporting Mega-Event*. London: Routledge.

Club of Rome (2022) *Limits to Growth +50*. Available at: https://www.cluboframe.org/ ltg50/.

Coaffee, J. (2009) *Terrorism, Risk and the Global City: Towards Urban Resilience*. Farnham: Ashgate.

Coaffee, J. (2012) Resilience through lockdown: reflections on 'total security' preparations for London 2012. *British Society of Criminology Newsletter*, No. 70, pp. 7–10.

Coaffee, J. (2022) *The War on Terror and the Normalisation of Urban Security*. London: Routledge.

Coaffee J. and Fussey P. (2010) Olympic security, in Gold J.R. and Gold M.M. (eds.) *Olympic Cities: City Agendas, Planning, and the World's Games, 1896 to 2012*, 2nd ed. London: Routledge, pp. 167–179.

Coaffee, J. and Johnston, L. (2007) Accommodating the spectacle, in Gold, J.R and Gold, M.M. (eds. *Olympic Cities: Urban Planning, City Agendas and the World's Games, 1896 to the Present*. London: Routledge, pp. 138–149.

Coaffee J. and Murakami Wood, D. (2006) Security is coming home: rethinking scale and constructing resilience in the global urban response to terrorist risk. *International Relations*, **20**, 503–517.

Coaffee, J., Murakami Wood, D. and Rogers, P. (2008) *The Everyday Resilience of the City: How Cities Respond to Terrorism and Disaster*. Basingstoke: Palgrave Macmillan.

Coaffee, J., Fussey, P. and Moore, C. (2011) Laminating security for London 2012: enhancing security infrastructures to defend mega sporting events, *Urban Studies*, **48**(15), pp. 3311–3328.

Coaffee, J., Moore, C., Fletcher, D. and Bosher, L. (2008) Resilient design for community safety and terror-resistant cities, in *Proceedings of the Institution of Civil Engineers-Municipal Engineer*, **161**(2), pp. 103–110.

Coccossis, H., Deffner, A. and Economou, D. (2003) Urban/regional Co-operation in Greece: Athens, a Capital City under the Shadow of the State. Paper presented to 43rd European Congress of the Regional Science Association (ERSA), University of Jyväskylä, 27–30 August. Available at: http://www.jyu.fi/ersa2003/cdrom/papers/358.pdf.

Cocola-Gant, A. and Gago, A. (2021) Airbnb, buy-to-let investment and tourism-driven displacement: a case study in Lisbon. *Environment and Planning A*, **53**(7), pp. 1671–1688.

COF (Comité Olympique Français) (1924) *Rapport Officiel, Les Jeux de la VIII Olympiade Paris*. Paris: COF.

Cohen, P. (2013) *On the Wrong Side of the Track? East London and the Post Olympics*. London: Lawrence and Wishart.

Cohen, S. (1996) *The Games of '36: A Pictorial History of the 1936 Olympic Games in Germany*. Missoula, MT: Pictorial Histories Publishing Company.

COHRE (Centre on Housing Rights and Evictions) (2007*a*) *Fair Play for Housing Rights: Mega-Events, Olympic Games and Housing Rights*. Geneva: COHRE.

COHRE (2007*b*) *Hosting the 2012 Olympic Games: London's Olympic Preparations and Housing Rights Concerns*. Geneva: COHRE. Available at: http://www.cohre.org/store/ attachments/London_background_paper.pdf.

COHRE (2007*c*) One *World, Whose Dream? Housing Rights Violations and the Beijing Olympic Games*. Geneva: COHRE. Available at http://www.cohre.org/beijingreport.

COJO (Comité d'Organisation des Jeux Olympiques de 1924 à Paris) (1924) *Les Jeux de la Viiie Olympiade Paris 1924: Rapport Official*. Paris: Librarie de France.

COJO (Comité d'Organisation des Xemes Jeux Olympiques d'hiver) (1968) *Official Report Xth Winter Olympic Games.* Grenoble: Organizing Committee.

COJO (Comités d'Organisation des Jeux Olympiques) (1976) *Official Report of the XXI Olympiad, Montreal 1976.* Ottawa: COJO.

COJOP (Comité d'Organisation des Jeux Olympiques et Paralympiques de Paris 2024) (2023) Reinventing the Opening Ceremony in the Heart of the City. Available at: https://youtu.be/tqSEoFnHC88.

Collinet, C., Delalandre, M. and Beaudouin, S. (2020) L'opinion des Français sur les Jeux olympiques de Paris 2024. *Movement and Sport Sciences*, No. 107, pp. 31–40.

Collins, S. (2007) *The 1940 Tokyo Games: The Missing Olympics.* London: Routledge.

Colvin, S. (1878) Greek Athletics, Greek Religion and Greek Art at Olympia: An Account of Ancient Usages and Modern Discoveries. Paper given to the Liverpool Art Club, 4 February.

Commission of Inquiry (1977) *Report of the Commission of Inquiry into the cost of the 21st Olympiad*, 3 vols. Quebec: Éditeur Officiel du Québec.

Committee for Brisbane (2021) *Brisbane 2033: Our Olympics and Paralympics Legacies.* March. Available at: https://committeeforbrisbane.org.au/wp-content/uploads/2021/03/Brisbane-2033-Our-Olympics-and-Paralympics-Legacies_-Paper-01-2021.pdf.

COMSEQ (Council of Mayors South East Queensland) (2016) *Pre-Feasibility Analysis of a Potential South East Queensland Bid for the 2028 Olympic Games.* Available at: https://seqmayors.qld.gov.au/initiatives/olympic-games-pre-feasibility-study-20160726.

COMSEQ (2019) *2032 SEQ Olympic and Paralympic Games Feasibility Study.* Available at: https://seqmayors.qld.gov.au/initiatives/2032-seq-olympic-and-paralympic-games-feasibility-study-2032-olympics-20190221.

CONI (Comitato Olimpico Nazionale Italiano) (1956) *VII Giochi Olimpici Inversnali, Cortina D'Ampezzo, Rapporto ufficiale.* Rome: Comitato Olimpico Nazionale Italiano.

CONI (1963) *The Games of the XVII Olympiad, Rome 1960: the Official Report of the Organizing Committee.* Rome: CONI.

Connelly, B.L., Trevis Certo, S., Ireland, D. and Reutzel, C.R. (2011) Signaling theory: a review and assessment. *Journal of Management*, **37**(1), pp. 39–67.

Constandt, B. and Willem, A. (2021) Hosting the Olympics in times of a pandemic: historical insights from Antwerp 1920. *Leisure Sciences*, **43**, pp. 50–55.

COOB (Barcelona Olympic Organizing Committee) (1992) *Official Report of the Games of the XXV Olympiad*, 3 vols. Barcelona: COOB.

Cook, I.G. (2000) Pressures of development on China's cities and regions, in Cannon, T. (ed.) *China's Economic Growth: The Impact on Regions, Migration and the Environment.* London: Macmillan, pp. 33–55.

Cook, I.G. (2006) Beijing as an 'internationalized metropolis', in Wu, F. (ed.) *Globalisation and China's Cities.* London: Routledge, pp. 63–84.

Cook, I.G. (2007) Beijing 2008, in Gold, J.R. and Gold, M.M. (eds.) *Olympic Cities: City Agendas, Planning and the World Games, 1896–2016.* London: Routledge, pp. 287–314.

Cook, I.G. (2020) Twenty-first century issues and challenges in Chinese urbanisation: similarities and differences to the UK, in Goulder, R. (ed.) *Challenge and Change in the Urban Environment.* York: PLACE, pp. 21–40.

Cook, I.G. and Dummer, T.J.B. (2004) Changing health in China: re-evaluating the epidemiological transition model. *Health Policy*, **67**, pp. 329–343.

Cook, I.G. and Murray, G. (2001) *China's Third Revolution: Tensions in the Transition to Post-Communism.* London: Curzon.

Cook, T.A. (1909) *International Sport: A Short History of the Olympic Movement from 1896 to the Present Day, containing the Account of a Visit to Athens in 1906 and of the Olympic Games of 1908 in London together with the Code of Rules for 20 Different Forms of Sport and Numerous Illustrations.* London: Archibald and Constable.

Correa, F., Omena de Melo, E., Meza, H., Carvalho, N.R., Soldati, F. and Serodio, B., Lopes, A.B. (2022) Como e para quem se governa? Desafios para a governança urbana e metropolitana no Rio de Janeiro, in Ribeiro, L.C.Q. and Ribeiro, M. (eds.) *Reforma urbana e direito à cidade: Rio de Janeiro.* Rio de Janeiro: Letra Capital, pp. 119–143.

Correspondent (2010) Olympics sites to get new life. Available at: http://www.ekathimerini.com/4dcgi/_w_articles_politics_2_19/03/2010_115743.

COWGOC (Calgary Olympic Winter Games Organizing Committee/Calgary Olympic Development Association) (1988) *XV Olympic Winter Games: Official Report.* Calgary: Organizing Committee.

Cox, G. (2012) Sustaining a legacy: from Sydney 2000's environmental guidelines to the Commission for a Sustainable London 2012. *Australian Planner,* **49**(3), pp. 203–214.

Cox, G. and Searle, G. (2012) Planning for the Olympics – past, present, future. *Australian Planner,* **49**(3), pp. 190–192.

Cox, G., Darcy, M. and Bounds, M. (1994) The Olympics and Housing: A Study of Six International Events and Analysis of Potential Impacts of the Sydney 2000 Olympics. Paper prepared for the Shelter NSW and Housing and Urban Studies Research Group. University of Western Sydney-Macarthur, Sydney.

Coy, M. (2006) Gated communities and urban fragmentation in Latin America: the Brazilian experience. *GeoJournal,* **66**(1/2), pp. 121–132.

Crainz, G. (2001) *Storia del miracolo italiano. Culture, identità, trasformazioni fra anni '50 e '60.* Roma: Donzelli.

Craven, P. (2014) The Paralympic Movement takes off, LSE Public Lecture, 14 October 2014. Available at: http://www.lse.ac.uk/assets/richmedia/channels/publicLecturesAndEvents/slides/20131014_1830_paralympicMovement_sl.pdf.

Crowther, N.B. (2003) Elis and Olympia: city, sanctuary and politics, in Phillips, D.J. and Pritchard, D. (eds.) *Sport and Festival in the Ancient Greek World.* Swansea: Classical Press of Wales, pp. 75–100.

Cummins, S., Clark, C., Lewis, D., Smith, N., Thompson, C., Smuk, M., Stansfeld, S., Taylor, S., Fahy, A., Greenhalgh, T. and Eldridge S. (2018) The effects of the London 2012 Olympics and related urban regeneration on physical and mental health: the ORiEL mixed-methods evaluation of a natural experiment. *Public Health Research,* **6**(12), pp. 1–248.

CWS (Centre for Western Sydney) (2022) *Parramatta 2035: Vibrant/Sustainable/Global.* Sydney: Western Sydney University.

D'Agati, P. (2013) *The Cold War and the 1984 Olympic Games: A Soviet-American Surrogate War.* Basingstoke: Palgrave Macmillan.

Daily Mirror (2012) Armoured cars drafted in as security tightens ahead of the Olympic Games. 8 May. Available at: http://www.mirror.co.uk/sport/other-sports/london-2012-armoured-cars-drafted-824089.

Daily Telegraph (2012) London 2012 Olympics: Metropolitan Police double officers around torch as crowds bigger than predicted. 29 May. Available at: http://www.telegraph.co.uk/sport/olympics/torch-relay/9280127/London-2012-Olympics-Metropolitan-Police-double-officers-around-torch-as-crowds-bigger-than-predicted.html.

Dansero, E., Segre, A. and Mela, A. (2003) Spatial and environmental transformations towards Torino 2006: planning the legacy of the future, in Moragas, M. de, Kennett, C. and Puig, N. (eds.) *The Legacy of the Olympic Games 1984–2000.* Documents of the Museum. Lausanne: International Olympic Committee, pp. 83–93.

Darcovich, K. (2020) The road to recovery – delivering the ecological legacy of the Green Games, in Darcovich, K. (ed.) *20 years of Healing: Delivering the Ecological Legacy of the Green Games.* Sydney: Sydney Olympic Park Authority, pp. 5–17. Available at: file:///Users/Ann/Downloads/2021%20Biodiversity%20Ebook.pdf.

Darcy, S. (2001) The Games for Everyone? Planning for disability and access at the Sydney 2000 Paralympic and Olympic Games. *Disability Studies Quarterly,* **21**, pp. 70–84.

Darcy, S. (2003) The politics of disability and access: the Sydney 2000 Games experience. *Disability and Society,* **18**, pp. 737–757.

Darcy, S. (2017) Accessibility as a key management component of the Paralympics, in

Darcy, S., Frawley, S. and Adair, D. (eds.) *Managing the Paralympics*. London: Palgrave Macmillan, pp. 47–90.

Darcy, S. and Appleby, L. (2011) Sydney 2000: moving from post-hoc legacy to strategic vision and operational partnerships, in Legg, D. and Gilbert, K. (eds.) *Paralympic Legacies*. Champaign, IL: Common Ground Publishing, pp. 75–98.

Darcy, S., Dickson, T.J. and Benson, A.M. (2014) London 2012 Olympic and Paralympic Games: including volunteers with disabilities – a podium performance? *Event Management*, **18**, pp. 431–446.

Darcy, S., Frawley, S. and Adair, D. (2017) The Paralympic Games: managerial and strategic directions, in Darcy, S., Frawley, S. and Adair, D. (eds.) *Managing the Paralympics*. London: Palgrave Macmillan, pp. 1–19.

Daume, W. (1976) Organising the Games, in Lord Killanin and Rodda, J. (eds.) *The Olympic Games. 80 Years of People, Events and Records*, 1st ed. London: Barrie and Jenkins, pp. 153–156.

Davenport, J. (1996) Athens 1896: the Games of the 1st Olympiad, in Findling, J.E. and Pelle, K.D. (eds.) *Historical Dictionary of the Modern Olympic Movement*. Westport, CN: Greenwood Press, pp. 3–11.

Davidson, M. (2013) The sustainable and entrepreneurial park? Contradictions and persistent antagonisms at Sydney's Olympic Park. *Urban Geography*, **34**(5), pp. 657–676.

Davidson, M. and McNeill, D. (2012) The redevelopment of Olympic sites: examining the legacy of Sydney Olympic Park. *Urban Studies*, **49**(8), pp. 1625–1641.

Davies, F.A. (2014) Produzindo a 'região olímpica de Deodoro', in Rial, C. and Schwade, E. (eds.) *Anais da 29ª Reunião Brasileira de Antropologia*. Brasília: Kiron.

Davies, F.A. (2017) Deodoro: formas de governo para uma 'região olímpica'. Unpublished PhD thesis, Universidade do Estado do Rio de Janeiro.

Davies, M., Davies, J.P. and Rapp, D. (2017) *Dispersal: Picturing Urban Change in East London*. Swindon: Historic England.

Davis, E.L. (1996) Rome 1960: the Games of the XVII Olympiad, in Findling, J.E. and Pelle, K.D. (eds.) *Historical Dictionary of the Modern Olympic Movement*. Westport, CT: Greenwood, pp. 128–134.

Davis, J. (2014) A promised future and the open city: issues of anticipation in Olympic legacy designs. *Architectural Research Quarterly*, **18**, pp. 324–341.

Davis, J. (2020) Avoiding white elephants? The planning and design of London's 2012 Olympic and Paralympic venues, 2002–2018. *Planning Perspectives*, **35**(5), pp. 827–848.

Davis, M. (2011) Fortress Los Angeles: the militarization of urban space, in Ferrell, J. and Hayward, K. (eds,) *Cultural Criminology*. London: Routledge, pp. 287–314.

DCMS (Department for Culture, Media and Sport) (2004) *Tomorrow's Tourism Today*. London: DCMS.

DCMS (2006) *Welcome>Legacy*. London: DCMS.

DCMS (2007*a*) *Our Promise for 2012: How the UK will benefit from the Olympic Games and Paralympics Games*. Available at: http://www.culture.gov.uk/reference_library/pub lications/3660.aspx/.

DCMS (2007*b*) *Before, During and After: Making the Most of the London 2012 Games*. Available at: http://www.culture.gov.uk/images/publications/2012LegacyActionPlan.pdf.

DCMS (Department for Culture, Media and Sport) (2010) *London 2012: A Legacy for Disabled People*. London: Office for Disability Issues, DCMS.

DCMS (2012*a*) *Beyond 2012: The London 2012 Legacy Story*. London: DCMS.

DCMS (2012*b*) *London 2012 Olympic and Paralympic Games Quarterly Report December 2012*. London: DCMS.

De Coubertin, P. (1913) La question d'argent. *Revue Olympique*, **13**(12), pp. 183–185.

Degen, M. and García, M. (2012) The transformation of the 'Barcelona model': an analysis of culture, urban regeneration and governance. *International Journal of Urban and Regional Research*, **36**(5), pp. 1022–1038.

De Guzman, C. (2022) What artificial snow at the 2022 Olympics means for the future of

Winter Games. *Time Magazine*, 8 February. Available at: https://time.com/6146039/artificial-snow-2022-olympics-beijing/.

De Juliis, T. (2001) *Il CONI di Giulio Onesti: da Montecitorio al Foro Italico*. Roma: Società stampa sportiva.

De Moragas, M. and Botella, M. (1995) *The Keys to Success*. Barcelona: Centre d'Estudis Olímpics i de l'Esport.

De Moragas, M., Llinés, M. and Kidd, B. (eds.) (1997) *Olympic Villages: A Hundred Years of Urban Planning and Shared Experiences*. Lausanne: International Olympic Committee.

De Moragas, M., Kennett, C. and Puig, N. (eds.) (2003) *The Legacy of the Olympic Games 1984–2000*. Lausanne: International Olympic Committee.

Del Bianco, C. (2021) Porta Romana railyard and Olympic village: reflections and contributions from MIAW 2021, Del Bianco, C., Magni, C. and Setti, G. (eds.) *2026 Olympic Games and the City*. MIAW: Milan, pp. 171–179.

Delaplace M. and Schut, P.O. (eds.) (2019) *Hosting the Olympic Games: Uncertainty, Debate, Controversy*. London: Routledge.

Delgado, M. (2005) *Elogi del vianant: del 'model Barcelona' a la Barcelona real*. Barcelona: Edicions de 1984.

DeLisle, J. (2008) 'One world, different dreams': the contest to define the Beijing Olympics, in M.E. Price and D. Dayan (eds.) *Owning the Olympics: Narratives of the New China*. Ann Arbor, MI: University of Michigan Press, pp. 17–66.

Deloitte Australia (2015) *Restarting Sydney's Heart: Light Rail the Engine of Change*. Sydney: Deloitte Touche Tohmatsu.

Delsahut, F. (2014) Races on exhibit at the 1904 St. Louis Anthropology Days, in Bancel, N., David, T. and Thomas, D. (eds.) *The Invention of Race; Scientific and Popular Representations*. London: Routledge, pp. 247–258.

De Pauw, K.P. and Gavron, S.J. (2005) *Disability Sport*, 2nd ed. Champaign, IL: Human Kinetics.

Dichter, H.L. and Teetzel, S. (2020) The Winter Olympics: a century of games on ice and snow. *International Journal of the History of Sport*, **37**(13), pp. 1215–1235.

Dickson, G. and Schofield, G. (2005) Globalisation and globesity: the impact of the 2008 Beijing Olympics on China. *International Journal of Sport Management and Marketing*, **1**, pp. 169–179.

Dickson, T.J., Benson, A.M. and Blackman, D.A. (2011) Developing a framework for evaluating Olympic and Paralympic legacies. *Journal of Sport and Tourism*, **16**(4), pp. 285–302.

Diem, C. (1912) *Die Olympischen Spiele 1912*. Berlin: Ausgabe.

Diem, C. (1942) *Olympische Flamme: Das Buch vom Sport*. Berlin: Deutscher Archiv.

Dietschy, P. and Pivato, S. (2019) *Storia dello sport in Italia*. Bologna: il Mulino.

DILGP (Department of Infrastructure, Local Government and Planning) (2017) *ShapingSEQ: South East Queensland Regional Plan*. Brisbane: The State of Queensland.

Dinces, S. (2005) Padres on Mount Olympus: Los Angeles and the production of the 1932 Olympic mega-event. *Journal of Sport History*, **32**(2), pp. 137–165.

Dinces, S. (2018) The 1932 Olympics: spectacle and growth in interwar Los Angeles, in Wilson, W. and Wiggins, D.K. (eds.) *LA Sports: Play, Games, and Community in the City of Angels*. Fayetteville, AR: University of Arkansas Press, pp. 129–148.

Di Palma, D., Raiola, G. and Tafuri, D. (2016) Disability and sport management: a systematic review of the literature. *Journal of Physical Education and Sport*, **16**, pp. 783–793.

Dong, J. (2005) Women, nationalism and the Beijing Olympics: preparing for glory. *International Journal of the History of Sport*, **22**, pp. 530–544.

Dong, L. (1985) Beijing: the development of a socialist capital, in Sit, V.F.S. (ed.) *Chinese Cities*. Oxford: Oxford University Press, pp. 67–93.

Dost, S. (2003) *Das Olympische Dorf 1936 im Wandel der Zeit*. Berlin: Neddermeyer Verlag.

Doustaly, C. (2019) Comparative visions of heritage: holistic visions of heritage? in Doustaly,

C. (ed.) *Heritage, Cities and Sustainable Development, Interdisciplinary Approaches and International Case Studies*. Brussels: Peter Lang.

Doustaly, C. (2023) Has culture the transformative power to make the Olympic Games sustainable? *Local Economy* (in press).

Doustaly, C. and Zembri-Mary, G. (2019) The role of heritagization in managing uncertainties linked to major events and mega urban projects: comparing the Olympic Games in London (2012) and Athens (2004), in Delaplace, M. and Schut, P-O. (eds.) *Hosting the Olympic Games: Uncertainty, Debate, Controversy*. London: Routledge, pp. 93–126.

DPC (Department of the Premier and Cabinet) (2023) *Brisbane 2032 Coordination Office*. Available at: https://statements.qld.gov.au/statements/97364.

DPE (NSW Department of Planning and Environment) (2016) *Sydney Olympic Park: Review of Master Plan 2030 and State Significant Precinct*. Planning Report. Sydney: DPE.

DPIE (NSW Department of Planning, Industry and Environment) (2021) *Sydney Olympic Park Master Plan 2030* (Interim Metro Review). Explanation of Intended Effects. Sydney: DPIE.

Draper, M. and Dunlevy, G. (2009) AOC will not agree to bid for 2024 Olympics. *AAP General News Wire*, 18 January.

Drees, L. (1968) *Olympia: Gods, Artists, Athletes* (trans. G. Onn). London: Pall Mall Press.

DSDILGP (Department of State Development, Infrastructure, Local Government and Planning) (2023a) *The Gabba*. Available at: https://www.statedevelopment.qld.gov.au/industry/brisbane-2032/the-gabba.

DSDILGP (2023b) *Brisbane 2032 Athlete Village*. Available at: https://www.statedevelopment.qld.gov.au/industry/brisbane-2032/brisbane-2032-athletes-village.

Dubi, C. and Felli, G. (2006) Measuring global impact. *Olympic Review*, June. Available at: http://www.olympic.org/Documents/Reports/EN/en_report_1077.pdf.

Dubin, M.S., Ellingham, M., Fisher, J. and Jansz, N. (2002) *The Rough Guide to Greece*. London: Rough Guides.

Dubinsky, Y. (2019) Analyzing the roles of country image, nation branding, and public diplomacy through the evolution of the modern Olympic movement. *Physical Culture and Sport: Studies and Research*, **84**(1), pp. 27–40.

Dubinsky, Y. (2022) The Olympic Games, nation branding, and public diplomacy in a post-pandemic world: reflections on Tokyo 2020 and beyond. *Place Branding and Public Diplomacy*, **10**, pp. 1–12.

Duran, P. (2005) The impact of the Olympic Games on tourism. Barcelona: the legacy of the Games 1992–2002, in Urdangarin, I. and Torres, D. (eds.) *New Views on Sport Tourism*. Mallorca: Calliope Publishing, pp. 77–91.

Dyreson, M. (2015) Global television and the transformation of the Olympics: the 1984 Los Angeles Games. *International Journal of the History of Sport*, **32**(1), pp. 172–184.

Dyreson, M. and Llewellyn, M. (2008) Los Angeles Is the Olympic City: legacies of the 1932 and 1984 Olympic Games. *International Journal of the History of Sport*, **25**(14), pp. 1991–2018.

Ecologist, The (1972) *A Blueprint for Survival*. Harmondsworth: Penguin.

Edizel, O. (2014) Governance of Sustainable Event-led Regeneration: The Case of London 2012 Olympics, Unpublished PhD thesis, Brunel University, London.

Edizel, O., Evans, G. and Dong, H. (2013) Dressing up London, in Girginov, V. (ed.) *Handbook of the London2012 Olympic and Paralympic Games*, Vol.2. London: Routledge, pp. 19–35.

Edizel-Tasci, O. and Evans, G.L. (2021) Participatory mapping and engagement with urban water communities, in Ersoy, A. (ed.) *Co-Production and Social Justice*. Bristol: Policy Press, pp. 119–113.

EDQ (Economic Development Queensland) (2022) *Northshore Hamilton Priority Development Area Development Scheme Amendment 1*. Brisbane: Queensland Government. Available at: https://www.statedevelopment.qld.gov.au/__data/assets/pdf_file/0023/63707/northshore-hamilton-pda-proposed-development-scheme-amendment-1.pdf.

Edvinsson, T.N. (2014) Before the sunshine: organising and promoting the Olympic Games in Stockholm 1912. *International Journal of the History of Sport*, **31**, pp. 570–587.

Eeles, S. (2021) Queensland Premier flags possible new stadium, aquatic facility to be built for Brisbane Olympics 2032. *ABC News*, 25 February. Available at: https://www.abc.net.au/news/2021-02-25/olympic-games-brisbane-queensland-2032-mayor-premier/13190520.

Ehrlich, P.A. and Ehrlich, A.H. (1968) *Population Bomb*. New York: Ballentine Books.

Ekaterini.com (2016) Olympic venue to be turned into courtroom. 8 May. Available at: https://www.ekathimerini.com/news/208437/olympic-venue-to-be-turned-into-courtroom/.

Engel, S. (2012) Abandoned Olympic Cathedrals sit rotting in Beijing. Available at: http://www.bloomberg.com/news/videos/b/4b8bdf6c-52c0-4cf8-a334-46429da2413c.

ENIT (1962) Numero Speciale. *Statistica del turismo*, **13**(48).

Esparza, L.E. and Price, R. (2015) Convergence repertoires: anti-capitalist protest at the 2010 Vancouver Winter Olympics. *Contemporary Justice Review*, **18**(1), pp. 22–41.

Espy, R. (1979) *The Politics of the Olympic Games*. Berkeley, CA: University of California Press.

Essex, S. and Chalkley, B. (1998) Olympic Games: catalyst of urban change. *Leisure Studies*, **17**(3), pp. 187–206.

Essex, S. and Chalkley, B. (2002) Il ruolo dei Giochi Olimpici nella trasformazione urbana, in Bobbio, L. and Guala, C. (eds.) *Olimpiadi e Grandi Eventi*. Rome: Carocci, pp. 57–76.

Essex, S. and Chalkley, B. (2004) Mega-sporting events in urban and regional policy: a history of the winter Olympics. *Planning Perspectives*, **19**, pp. 201–232.

Esteban, J. (1999) *El Projecte Urbanístic: valorar la perifèria i recuperar el centre*. Barcelona: Aula Barcelona.

Evans, G.L. (1996a) Planning for the British Millennium Festival: establishing the visitor baseline and a framework for forecasting. *Journal of Festival Management and Event Tourism*, **3**, pp. 183–196.

Evans, G.L (1996b) The Millennium Festival and urban regeneration: planning, politics and the party, in Robinson, M. and Evans, N. (eds.) *Managing Cultural Resources*. Newcastle: Business Education Publishers, pp. 79–98.

Evans, G. (2007) London 2012, in Gold, J.R. and Gold, M.M. (eds.) *Olympic Cities: City Agendas, Planning and the World's Games 1896–2012*. London: Routledge, pp. 298–317.

Evans, G. (2010) London 2012, in Gold, J.R and Gold, M.M. (eds.) *Olympic Cities: City Agendas, Planning and the World's Games 1896–2016*, second edition. London: Routledge, pp. 359–389.

Evans, G.L. (2015) Designing legacy and the legacy of design: London 2012 and the regeneration games. *Architectural Review Quarterly*, **18**(4), pp. 353–366.

Evans, G.L. (1999) Last chance lottery and the Millennium City, in Whannel, G. and Foley, M. (eds.) *Leisure, Culture and Commerce: Consumption and Participation*, Publication 64. Eastbourne: Leisure Studies Association, pp. 3–22.

Evans, G.L. (2020) From Albertopolis to Olympicopolis: Back to the future? in Evans, G.L. (ed.) *Mega-Events: Placemaking, and Regeneration*. London: Routledge, pp. 35–52.

Evans, G.L. and Edizel, O. (2017) London 2012, in Gold, J.R. and Gold, M.M. (eds) *Olympic Cities. City Agendas, Planning and the World Games, 1896–2000*. London: Routledge, pp. 378–399.

Evans, G.L. and Shaw, S. (2001) Urban leisure and transport: regeneration effects. *Journal of Leisure Property*, **1**(4), pp. 350–372.

Evans, S.J. (2014) The new ruins of Athens: rusting and decaying 10 years on, how Greece's Olympics turned into a £7 billion white elephant. *Daily Mail*, 13 August. Available at: http://www.dailymail.co.uk/news/article-2723515/Athens-Olympics-leave-mixed-legacy-10-years-later.html.

Exército Brasileiro (2016) O legado dos Jogos Olímpicos e Paralímpicos Rio 2016. *Revista Verde-Oliva*, **235**, pp. 56–63.

Fahey, M.R. (2009) China, world affairs China. *Britannica Book of the Year: Events of 2008*. Chicago, IL: Encyclopaedia Britannica, pp. 383–386.

Fainstein, S.S., Forester, J., Lee, K.L., Na'puti, T., Agyeman, J., Stewart, N.J., Novy, J., Dedekorkut Howes, A., Burton, P., Norgaard, S., Smith, N.R., Zukin, S., Lubinsky, A. and Keith, M. (2023) Resistance and response in planning. *Planning Theory and Practice*, **24**(2), pp. 245–283.

Falk, N. (2003) Urban renaissance: lessons from Turin. *Town and Country Planning*, **72**(7), pp. 213–215.

Farndon, D. and Burton, P. (2019) Avoiding the white elephants: a new approach to infrastructure planning at the 2018 Gold Coast Commonwealth Games? *Queensland Review*, **26**(1), pp. 128–146.

Farrelly, E. (2012) Putting the home into Homebush. *Sydney Morning Herald*, 5 February, p. 5.

Faure, A. (2020) Les Jeux olympiques et paralympiques à l'heure des villes globales: analyse des candidatures ratées puis réussies de Paris et Tokyo. *Cybergeo Conversation*. Available at: https://cybergeo.hypotheses.org/610.

Faure, A. (2023) The preparation of the Tokyo 2020 Games: completing the waterfront sub-centre plan. *Journal of Convention and Event Tourism*, **24**, pp. 205–221.

FCO (Foreign and Commonwealth Office) (2011) Brazil: Rio 2016 Olympics – Sport Security. Rio de Janeiro: British Consulate General, March.

Felice, E. (2015) *Ascesa e declino. Storia economica d'Italia*. Bologna: il Mulino.

Fellmann, B. (1973) The history of excavations at Olympia. *Olympic Review*, **64/65**, pp. 109–118, 162.

Ferez, S., Ruffié, S., Joncheray, H., Marcellini, A., Pappous, S. and Richard, R. (2020) Inclusion through sport: a critical view on paralympic legacy from a historical perspective. *Social Inclusion*, **8**, pp. 224–236.

Fiadino, A. (2013) The 1960 Olympics and Rome's urban transformations. *Città e Storia*, **8**(1), pp. 173–214.

Filipo, L. (2015) Com 'invasores', prefeito passeia de barco e libera 'esquibunda' olímpico. *Globo Esporte*. Available at: https://ge.globo.com/olimpiadas/noticia/2015/09/prefeito-apresenta-slalom-olimpico-e-exalta-legado-do-local-antes-dos-jogos.html.

Finn, P. (2008) Putin directs organisers of 2014 Winter Olympics to protect wilderness. *The Washington Post*, 3 July. Available at: http://www.washingtonpost.com/wp-dyn/content/article/2008/07/03/AR2008070301912.html.

Fischer-Lichte, E. (2005) *Theatre, Sacrifice, Ritual: Exploring Forms of Political Theatre*. London: Routledge.

Fleming, J. (2022) A crisis for renters: football sent Inglewood home prices and rents sky-rocketing. *Los Angeles Times*, 9 February. Available at: https://www.latimes.com/business/story/2022-02-09/super-bowl-2022-inglewood-home-prices-rents-increase.

Fluid (2003) *London's Bid for the 2012 Olympic Games. Have Your Say*. London: Fluid/Lower Lea Valley Team.

Flyvbjerg, B. and Stewart, A. (2012) Olympic Proportions: Cost and Cost Overrun at the Olympics 1960–2012. Working Paper 3.3, Said Business School, University of Oxford.

Flyvbjerg, B., Bruzelius, N. and Rothengatter, W. (2003) *Megaprojects and Risk: An Anatomy of Ambition*. Cambridge: Cambridge University Press.

Flyvbjerg, B., Budzier, A. and Lunn, D. (2021) Regression to the tail: why the Olympics blow up. *Environment and Planning A*, **53**(2), pp. 233–260.

Forcellese, T. (2013) *L'Italia e i Giochi Olimpici. Un secolo di candidature: politica, istituzioni e diplomazia sportiva*. Milan: Franco Angeli.

Fortis, M. (2011) *Relazione di compatibilità economica per la valutazione della candidatura di Roma alle Olimpiadi e Paralimpiadi del 2020*. Rome.

Foth, M., Kamols, N., Turner, T.J., Kovachevich, A. and Hearn, G. (2021). Brisbane 2032: the promise of the first carbon-positive Olympics for regenerative cities, in Roggema, R. (ed.) *Regenerative Design for Cities and Landscapes*. Cham: Springer, pp. 227–248.

França, R. (2015) Transcarioca completa 1 ano com altos e baixos, transportando 230 mil passageiros por dia. *O Globo*, 24 May. Available at: http://oglobo.globo.com/rio/trans

carioca-completa-1-anocom-altos-baixos-transportando-230-mil-passageiros-por-dia-16247236.

Frasca, A. and Lòriga, V. (2010) *Roma Olimpica: la meravigliosa estate del 1960*. Rome: Comitato Olimpico Nazionale Italiano.

Freeman, J. (2012) Neoliberal accumulation strategies and the visible hand of police pacification in Rio de Janeiro. *Revista de Esutdos Universitários*, **38**(1), pp. 95–126.

Freeman, J. (2014) Raising the flag over Rio de Janeiro's favelas: citizenship and social control in the Olympic City. *Journal of Latin American Geography*, **13**(1), pp. 7–38.

Freeman, R.E. and McVea, J. (2001) A stakeholder approach to strategic management, in Hitt, M.A., Freeman, R.E. and Harrison, J.S. (eds.) *The Blackwell Handbook of Strategic Management*. Oxford: Blackwell, pp. 189–207.

Freestone, R. and Gunasekara, S. (2017) Sydney 2000, in Gold, J.R. and Gold, M.M. (eds.) *Olympic Cities: City agendas, planning and the World's games, 1896–2020*, 3rd ed. London: Routledge, pp. 317–332.

Freestone, R. and Pinnegar, S. (2021) Sydney: evolution towards a tri-city metropolitan region and beyond, in Neuman, M. and Zonneveld, W. (eds.) *Routledge Handbook for Regional Design*. London: Routledge, pp. 263–283.

French, S.P. and Disher, M.E. (1997) Atlanta and the Olympics, a one-year retrospective. *Journal of the American Planning Association*, **63**(3), pp. 379–392.

Friedman, J. (2005) *China's Urban Transition*. Minneapolis, MN: University of Minnesota Press.

Fussey, P., Coaffee, J., Armstrong, G. and Hobbs, R. (2011) *Sustaining and Securing the Olympic City: Reconfiguring London for 2012 and Beyond*. Farnham: Ashgate.

Gaffney, C. (2008) *Temples of the Earthbound Gods: Stadiums in the Cultural Landscapes of Rio de Janeiro and Buenos Aires*. Austin, TX: University of Texas Press.

Gaffney, C. (2010) Mega-events and socio-spatial dynamics in Rio de Janeiro, 1919–2016. *Journal of Latin American Geography*, **9**(1), pp. 7–29.

GamesBids.com (2007) Review of Olympic Bid news and information. Available at: http://www.gamesbids.com/english/index.shtml.

GamesBids.com (2009) Supreme Court rejects environmentalists appeal of Sochi 2014. 21 March. Available at: www.gamesbid.com/eng/other_news/1174503225.html.

García, B. (2001) Enhancing sports marketing through cultural and arts programmes: lessons from the Sydney 2000 Olympic Arts Festivals. *Sport Management Review*, **4**, pp. 193–220.

García, B. (2004) Urban regeneration, arts programming and major events: Glasgow 1990, Sydney 2000 and Barcelona 2004. *International Journal of Cultural Policy*, **10**, pp. 103–118.

García, B. (2007) Sydney 2000, in Gold, J.R. and Gold, M.M. (eds). *Olympic Cities: City Agendas, Planning and the World Games, 1896–2016*. London: Routledge, pp. 287–314.

García, B. (2012) *The Olympics Games and Cultural Policy*. London: Routledge.

García, B. (2013) *London 2012 Cultural Olympiad Evaluation*. Liverpool: The Institute of Cultural Capital: University of Liverpool and Liverpool John Moores University.

García, B. (2015) Placing culture at the heart of the Games: achievements and challenges within the London 2012 Cultural Olympiad, in Poynter, G. Viehoff, V. and Li, Y. (eds.), *The London Olympics and Urban Development: The Mega-Event City*. London: Routledge, pp. 255–270.

García, B. (2021) Summer of Seoul/Winter of Pyeongchang: contemporary art at the Korean Olympics. *Cultural Mega-Events Series*. Available at: https://medium.com/cultural-mega-events.

García, B. (2022) The Olympic Movement and cultural policy. *Journal of Olympic Studies*, **3**(2), pp. 44–66.

García, B. and Cox, T. (2013) *London 2012 Cultural Olympiad Evaluation*. London: Arts Council England.

García, B. and Miah, A. (2007) Ever decreasing circles? The profile of culture at the Olympics. *Locum Destination Review*, **18**, pp. 60–62.

Garcia, P. (1993) Barcelona and the Olympic Games, in Häussermann, H. and Birklhuber, D. (eds.) *Festivalisation of Urban Policies. Urban Development through Large-Scale Projects.* Opladen: Westdeutscher Verlag, pp. 251–277.

Gardner, J. (2022) *A Contemporary Archaeology of London's Mega Events: From the Great Exhibition to London 2012.* London: UCL Press.

Garst, W.D. (2015) Encourage super-rich to be more charitable. *China Daily*, 23 June. Available at: http://usachinadaily.com.cn/opinion/2015-06/23/content_21075607.

Gartner, W.C. and Shen, J. (1992) The impact of Tiananmen Square on China's tourism image. *Journal of Travel Research*, **30**(4), pp. 47–52.

Gaudette, M., Roult, R. and Lefebvre, S. (2017) Winter Olympic Games, cities, and tourism: a systematic literature review in this domain. *Journal of Sport and Tourism*, **21**(4), pp. 287–313.

Geeraert, G. and Gauthier, R. (2018) Out-of-control Olympics: why the IOC is unable to ensure an environmentally sustainable Olympic Games. *Journal of Environmental Policy and Planning*, **20**(1), pp. 16–30.

Geipel, R., Helbrecht, I. and Pohl, J. (1993) Die Münchener Olympischen Spiele von 1972 als Instrument der Stadtentwicklungspolitik (The Munich Olympic Games in 1972 as an instrument of urban policy), in: Häussermann, H. and. Siebel, W. (eds.) *Die Politik der Festivalisierung und die Festivalisierung der Politik: Große Ereignisse in der Stadtpolitik.* Wiesbaden: Verlag für Sozialwissenschaften, pp. 278–304.

Georgiadis, K. (2000) Die ideengeschichtliche Grundlage der Erneuerung der Olympischen Spiele im 19. Jahrhundert in Griechenland und ihre Umsetzung 1896 in Athen (The intellectual-historical foundations of the revival of the Olympic games in the nineteenth century in Greece and their 1896 transplantation into Athens). PhD Dissertation, Kassel: Agon-Sportverlag.

Georgiadis, K. and Theodonkako, P. (2016) The Olympic Games of Athens: 10 years later. *Sport in Society*, **18**(6), pp. 817–827.

Giannini, L. (2003) Profilo storico dell'impresa. *Società Generale Immobiliare Sogene: storia, archivio, testimonianze.* Rome: Palombi.

Gignon, A., Delaplace, M. and Pimenta De Souza, F. (2022) Jeux Olympiques et Paralympiques de Paris 2024 et images de Paris. *Via*, No. 22. Available at: https://journals.openedition.org/viatourism/8982?lang=en.

Gilbert, K. and Schantz, O.J. (2015) Paralympic legacy: what legacy? in Holt, R. and Ruta, D. (eds.) *The Routledge Handbook of Sport and Legacy: Meeting the Challenge of Major Sports Events.* London: Routledge, pp. 161–175.

Gintrac, C. (2021) La transition à Saint-Denis. Discours et réalités dans une banlieue du Grand Paris en mutation. *Bulletin de l'association de géographes français*, **97**(4), pp. 482–492.

Girginov, V. (2018) *Rethinking Olympic Legacy.* London: Routledge.

Giuntini, S. (2010) Il cappello del papa. *Lancillotto e Nausica*, **27**(1/2), pp. 36–47.

Giuntini, S. (2019) La storia del CONI: un libro con alcuni capitoli ancora da scrivere. *Clionet. Per un senso del tempo e dei luoghi*, **3**, pp. 33–50.

Giuntini, S. (2020) Recensione. Storia dello sport in Italia. *Storia dello sport. Rivista di studi contemporanei*, **2**(1), pp. 87–90.

GLA (Greater London Authority) (2012) *Olympic Legacy Supplementary Planning Guidance.* London: GLA.

Glasson, B. (2022) Environmental myth-work: the discursive greening of the Olympic Games. *Communication and Critical/Cultural Studies*, **19**(3), pp. 217–234.

Gleeson, B. (2001) Disability and the open city. *Urban Studies*, **38**, pp. 251–265.

Goggin, G. and Hutchins, B. (2017) Media and the Paralympics: progress, visibility, and paradox, in Darcy, S., Frawley, S. and Adair, D. (eds.) *Managing the Paralympics.* London: Palgrave Macmillan, pp. 217–239.

Gold, J.R. (2012) A SPUR to action: the Society for the Promotion of Urban Renewal, 'anti-scatter' and the crisis of reconstruction. *Planning Perspectives*, **27**(2), pp. 199–223.

Gold, J.R. and Gold, M.M. (2005) *Cities of Culture: Staging International Festivals and the Urban Agenda, 1851–2000*. Aldershot: Ashgate.

Gold, J.R. and Gold, M.M. (2007) Access for all: the rise of the Paralympics within the Olympic movement. *Journal of the Royal Society for the Promotion of Health*, **127**(3), pp. 133–141.

Gold, J.R. and Gold, M.M. (2008) Olympic cities: regeneration, city rebranding and changing urban agendas. *Geography Compass*, **2**, pp. 300–318.

Gold, J.R. and Gold, M.M. (2009) Future indefinite? London 2012, the spectre of retrenchment and the challenge of Olympic sports legacy. *London Journal*, **34**, pp.180–197.

Gold, J.R. and Gold, M.M. (2010) *Olympic Cities: City Agendas, Planning and the World's Games, 1896–2016*, 2nd ed. London: Routledge, pp. 1–13.

Gold, J.R. and Gold, M.M. (2011) The history of events: ideology and historiography, in Page, S. and Connell, J. (eds.) *Routledge Handbook of Event Studies*. London: Routledge, pp. 119–128.

Gold, J.R. and Gold, M.M. (eds.) (2012) *The Making of Olympic Cities*, 4 vols. London: Routledge.

Gold, J.R. and Gold, M.M. (2013) 'Bring it under the legacy umbrella': Olympic host cities and the changing fortunes of the sustainability agenda. *Sustainability*, **5**(8), pp. 3526–3542.

Gold, J.R. and Gold, M.M. (2014) Legacy, sustainability and Olympism: crafting urban outcomes at London 2012. *Revue Internationale des Sciences du Sport et de L'Éducation*, **37**(105), pp. 23–35.

Gold, J.R. and Gold, M.M. (2015) Framing the future: sustainability, legacy and the 2012 London Games, in Holt, R. and Ruta, D. (eds.) *The Routledge Handbook of Sport and Legacy: Meeting the Challenge of Major Sports Events*. London: Routledge, pp. 142–158.

Gold, J.R. and Gold, M.M. (2016) Urban segments and events spaces: World's Fairs and Olympic sites, in Hein, C. (ed.) *The Routledge Handbook of Planning History*. London: Routledge, pp. 350–365.

Gold, J.R. and Gold, M.M. (eds.) (2017*a*) *Olympic Cities: City Agendas, Planning, and the World's Game*s, *1896–2020*, 3rd ed. London: Routledge.

Gold, J.R. and Gold, M.M. (2017*b*) Olympic futures and urban imaginings: from Albertopolis to Olympicopolis, in Hannigan, J. and Richards, G. (eds.) *The Handbook of New Urban Studies*. London: Sage, pp. 514–534.

Gold, J.R and Gold, M.M (2019) Tales of the Olympic city: memory, narrative and the built environment. *ZARCH: Journal of Interdisciplinary Studies in Architecture and Urbanism*, **13**, pp. 12–33.

Gold J.R. and Gold M.M. (2020*a*) *Festival Cities. Culture, Planning and Urban Life*. London: Routledge.

Gold, J.R. and Gold, M.M. (2020*b*) Land remediation, event spaces and the pursuit of Olympic legacy. *Geography Compass*, **14**(8), e12495.

Gold, J.R. and Gold, M.M. (2021) Olympic legacies and the sustainability agenda. *Nature Sustainability*, **4**(4), pp. 290–291.

Gold, J.R. and Revill, G.E. (2006) Gathering the voices of the people? Cecil Sharp, cultural hybridity and the folk music of Appalachia. *GeoJournal*, **63**, pp. 55–66.

Gold, M. and Revill, G. (2007) The Cultural Olympiads: reviving the panegyris, in Gold, J.R. and Gold, M.M. (eds) *Olympic Cities. City Agendas, Planning and the World's Games, 1896–2012*. London: Routledge, pp. 59–83.

Goldstein, E.S. (1996) Amsterdam: the Games of the 9th Olympiad, in Findling, J.E and Pelle, K.D. (eds.) *Historical Dictionary of the Modern Olympic Movement*. Westport, CN: Greenwood Press, pp. 68–83.

González, M.J. and González, A.L. (2015) Strategic planning and change management. Examples of Barcelona, Seville and Saragossa (Spain). *Bulletin of Geography: Socio-economic Series*, **29**, pp. 47–64.

Good, D. (1998) The Olympic Games' Cultural Olympiad: Identity and Management. Un-published Master's Thesis, Faculty of the College of Arts and Sciences, American University, Washington DC.

Goodman, S. (1986) *Spirit of Stoke Mandeville: The Story of Sir Ludwig Guttmann*. London: Collins.

Gordon, B.F. (1983) *Olympic Architecture: Building for the Summer Games*. New York: John Wiley.

Gordon, H. (2003) *The Time of Our Lives: Inside the Sydney Olympics*. Brisbane: University of Queensland Press.

Goulartt, A. (2007) *XV Pan American Games Sailing Competition: Final Report*. Rio de Janeiro: Organizing Committee for the XV Pan American Games.

Grady, J. (2020) Legal aspects of the Olympics and ambush marketing, in Chatziefstathiou, D. García, B. and Séguin, B. (eds.) *Routledge Handbook of the Olympic and Paralympic Games*. London: Routledge, pp. 130–138.

Graham, S. (2010) *Cities Unger Siege: The New Military Urbanism*. London: Verso.

Graham, J., Gilbert, B., Minton, A., Perryman, M., Poynter, G. and Westall, C. (2013) Re-visiting the Olympic legacy. *Soundings*, **53**, pp. 82–92.

Grant Thornton, Ecorys, Loughborough University, Oxford Economics and Future Inclusion (2013) *Report 5: Post-Games Evaluation, Meta-Evaluation of the Impacts and Legacy of the London 2012 Olympic Games and Paralympic Games*. East London Evidence Base. London: DCMS.

Grey-Thompson, T. (2006) The Olympic Generation: How the 2012 Olympics and Paralympics can create the Difference. Inaugural Lecture, Staffordshire University, 26 October. http://www.staffs.ac.uk/news/article/dame_tanni.php.

Grix, J. and Brannagan, P.M. (2016) Of mechanisms and myths: conceptualising states' 'soft power' strategies through sports mega-events. *Diplomacy and Statecraft*, **27**(2), pp. 251–272.

Gruneau, R. and Horne, J. (eds.) (2016) *Mega-Events and Globalization: Capital and Spectacle in a Changing World Order*. London: Routledge.

Gruneau, R. and Neubauer, R. (2012) A gold medal for the market: the 1984 Los Angeles Olympics, the Reagan era, and the politics of neoliberalism, in Lenskyj, H.J. and Wagg, S. (eds.) *The Palgrave Handbook of Olympic Studies*. Basingstoke: Palgrave, pp. 134–162.

GSC (Greater Cities Commission) (2016*a*) *Greater Sydney Region Plan: A Metropolis of Three Cities*. Sydney: GCC.

GSC (2016*b*) *GPOP: Greater Parramatta and the Olympic Peninsula*. Sydney.

Gu, C. and Cook, I.G. (2011) Beijing: socialist capital and new world city, in Hamnett, S. and Forbes, D. (eds.) *Planning Asian Cities: Risks and Resilience*. London: Routledge, pp. 90–130.

Guimarães, R. (2015) Barra da Tijuca e o projeto olímpico: a cidade do capital. Unpublished Master's Dissertation, Federal University of Rio de Janeiro.

Guoqi, X. (2008) *Olympic Dreams: China and Sports, 1895–2008*. Cambridge, MA: Harvard University Press.

Guttmann, A. (2006) Berlin 1936: the most controversial Olympics, in Tomlinson, A. and Young, C. (eds.) *National Identity and Global Sports Events: Culture, Politics, and Spectacle in the Olympics and the Football World Cup*. Ithaca, NY: State University of New York Press, pp. 165–181.

Guttmann, L. (1976) *Textbook of Sport for the Disabled*. Aylesbury: H.M. & M. Publishers.

Hall, C.M. (1992) *Hallmark Tourist Events: Impacts, Management and Planning*. London: Belhaven.

Hall, P. (1980) *Great Planning Disasters*. London: Weidenfeld and Nicolson.

Halog, A. (2022) In a year of sporting mega-events, the Brisbane Olympics can learn a lot from the ones that fail their host cities. *The Conversation*, 16 August. Available at: https://

theconversation.com/in-a-year-of-sporting-mega-events-the-brisbane-olympics-can-learn-a-lot-from-the-ones-that-fail-their-host-cities-187838.

Hampton, J. (2008) *The Austerity Olympics*. London: Aurum Press.

Hanna, M. (1999) *Reconciliation in Olympism: The Sydney 2000 Olympic Games and Australia's Indigenous People*. Sydney: Walla Walla Press.

Hargreaves, J. (2000) *Freedom for Catalonia? Catalan Nationalism, Spanish Identity and the Barcelona Olympic Games*. Cambridge: Cambridge University Press.

Harjian, H. and Kashani, S.J. (2021) Evolution of the concept of sustainability: from Brundtland Report to sustainable development goals, in Hussain, C.M. and Velasco-Munoz, J. (eds) *Sustainable Resource Management: Modern Approaches in Context*. Oxford: Elsevier, pp. 1–24.

Harlan, H.V. (1931) *History of Olympic Games: Ancient and Modern*. Topanga, CA: Athletic Research Bureau.

Harloe, K. and Momigliano, N. (2018) Hellenomania: ancient and modern obsessions with the Greek past, in Harloe, K., Momigliano, N. and Farnoux, A. (eds.) *Hellenomania*. London: Routledge, pp. 1–19.

Hart Davis, D. (1986) *Hitler's Games: The 1936 Olympics*. London: Century.

Hartigan, M. (2012) Applying Olympic planning principles to assess Brisbane's potential as a 2028 Olympic host city. *Australian Planner*, **49**(3), pp. 239–248.

Hawken, S. (2014) Sydney Olympic Park 2030: the city in a park. *Landscape Architecture Australia*, **141,** pp. 21–22.

Hawthorne, F.H. and Price, R. (2001) *The Soulless Stadium: A Memoir of London's White City*. Upminster: 3-2 Books.

Haynes, J. (2001) *Socio-Economic Impact of the Sydney 2000 Olympic Games*. Lucerne: Olympic Studies Centre/Universitat Autònoma de Barcelona.

HCCPA (House of Commons Committee of Public Accounts) (2008) *The Budget for the London 2012 Olympic and Paralympic Games*. London: HMSO.

He, G. (ed.) (2008) *Olympic Architecture: Beijing 2008*. Basle: Birkhäuser.

Heath, J. (1996) 1996 Atlanta Paralympic Games. *Link*, **5**(4), pp. 16–23.

Heck, S. (2014) William Penny Brookes: the founding father of the modern pentathlon? *Sport in History*, **34**(1), pp. 75–89.

Hellenikon SA (2016) The company vision. Available at: http://www.hellinikon.com/en/the-company/vision.

Hemphill, L., McGreal, S. and Berry, J. (2004) An indicator-based approach to measuring sustainable urban regeneration performance: part 2, empirical evaluation and case-study analysis. *Urban Studies*, **41**(4), pp. 757–772.

Henry, B. and Yeomans, P.H. (1984) *An Approved History of the Olympic Games*, 4th ed. Sherman Oaks, CA: Alfred Publishing.

Hersh, P. (2008) Testament to progress atrophies after Games. Available at: https://www.de-chant.com/tim/files/clips/budburst.pdf.

Heynen, A.P. and Vanaraja Ambeth, P. (2023) Sustainable legacies of a climate positive Olympic games: an assessment of carbon offsets and renewable energy for Brisbane 2032. *Sustainability*, **15**(2), 1207. https://doi.org/10.3390/su15021207.

Hidalgo, A. (2020) Les nouveaux acteurs de la probité dans le sport. La probité des jeux olympiques: l'engagement de Paris. *Archives de politique criminelle*, **42**, pp. 111–112.

Hill, C.R. (1992, 1996) *Olympics Politics: Athens to Atlanta, 1896–1996*. Manchester: Manchester University Press.

Hill, D. (2022) *Olympic Park (When Britain Built Something Big)*. London: On London Books.

Hillenbrand, L. (2014) *Unbroken: A World War II Story of Survival, Resilience, and Redemption*. London: Random House.

Hiller, H.H. (1990) The urban transformation of a landmark event: the 1988 Calgary Winter Olympics. *Urban Affairs Quarterly*, **26**, pp. 118–137.

Hiller, H. and Moylan, D. (1999) Mega-events and community obsolescence: redevelopment versus rehabilitation in Victoria Park East. *Canadian Journal of Urban Research*, **8**, pp. 47–81.

Hilmes, O. (2018) *Berlin 1936: Fascism, Fear, and Triumph set against Hitler's Olympic Games*, trans. J. Chase. New York: Other Press.

HM Government (Her Majesty's Government/Mayor of London) (2011) *CONTEST: The United Kingdom Strategy for Countering Terrorism*. London: The Stationery Office. Available at: http://www.homeoffice.gov.uk/counter-terrorism.

HMG/ML (Her Majesty's Government/Mayor of London) (2013) *Inspired by 2012: The legacy from the Olympic and Paralympic Games*. London: Cabinet Office.

HMG/ML (2015) *Inspired by 2012: The Legacy from the Olympic and Paralympic Games. Third annual report – Summer 2015*. London: Cabinet Office.

HMG/ML (2016) *Inspired by 2012: The legacy from the Olympic and Paralympic Games, Fourth annual report*. London: Cabinet Office.

Hoberman, J. (1986) *The Olympic Crisis, Sport, Politics and the Moral Order*. New Rochelle, NY: Caratzas Publishing.

Hobhouse, H. (2002) *The Crystal Palace and the Great Exhibition, Art, Science and Productive Industry: A History of the Royal Commission for the Exhibition of 1851*. London: Athlone Press.

Hobsbawm, E. (1983) Mass-producing traditions: Europe, 1870–1914, in Hobsbawm, E. and Ranger, T. (eds.) *The Invention of Tradition*. Cambridge: Cambridge University Press, pp. 263–307.

Holden, M., MacKenzie, J. and VanWynsberghe, R. (2008) Vancouver's promise of the world's first sustainable Olympic Games. *Environment and Planning C: Government and Policy*, **26**(5), pp. 882–905.

Holmes, K., Mair, J. and Lockstone-Binney, L. (2021) Leaner, cost-effective, practical: how the 2032 Brisbane Games could save the Olympics. *The Conversation*, 21 June. Available at: https://theconversation.com/leaner-cost-effective-practical-how-the-2032-brisbane-gam es-could-save-the-olympics-162606.

Holt, R. and Mason, T. (2000) *Sport in Britain, 1945–2000*. Oxford: Blackwell.

Holthus, B., Gagné, I., Manzenreiter, W. and Waldenberger, F. (eds.) (2020) *Japan through the Lens of the Tokyo Olympics*. London: Routledge.

Home Office (2011) *London 2012: Olympic and Paralympic Safety and Security Strategy*. London: The Stationery Office. Available at: http://www.london2012.com/documents/ oda-industry-days/oda-security-industry-day-presentation.pdf.

Hooker, J. (2008) Before guests arrive, Beijing hides some messes. *New York Times*, 29 July. Available at: https://www.nytimes.com/2008/07/29/sports/olympics/29beijing.html.

HOOWI (Herausgegeben vom Organisationskomitee der IX Olympischen Winterspiele in Innsbruck) (1967) *Offizieller Bericht der IX Olympischen Winterspiele Innsbruck 1964*. Vienna: Österreichischer Bundesverlag für Unterricht, Wissenschaft und Kunst.

HOP (Hellenic Olympic Properties SA) (2006) Hellenic Olympic Properties: public real estate & sustainable commercial development. Available at: http://www.olympicproperties.gr/.

Hope, K. (1990) A chance to save Athens. *Financial Times*, 27 February.

Hopewell, J. (2018) PyeongChang is more than cold enough for the Winter Olympics. It's just not that snowy. *The Washington Post*, 9 February. Available at: https://www. washingtonpost.com/news/capital-weather-gang/wp/2018/02/06/pyeongchang-is-more-than-cold-enough-for-the-winter-olympics-its-just-not-that-snowy/.

Hornbuckle, A.R. (1996) Helsinki 1952: the Games of the 15th Olympiad, in Findling, J.E. and Pelle, K.D. (eds.) *Historical Dictionary of the Modern Olympic Movement*. Westport, CN: Greenwood Press, pp. 109–118.

Horne, J. and Silvestre, G. (2017) Brazil, politics, the Olympics and the FIFA World Cup, in Bairner, A., Kelly, J. and Lee, J.W. (eds.) *Routledge Handbook of Sport and Politics*. London: Routledge, pp. 483–496.

Host Boroughs (2011) *Convergence Framework and Action Plan 2011–2015*. London: Host Boroughs.

Howe, P.D. (2008) *The Cultural Politics of the Paralympic Movement through an Anthropological lens.* London: Routledge.

Howell, R.A. and Howell, M.L. (1996) Paris 1900: the Games of the 2nd Olympiad, in Findling, J.E. and Pelle, K.D. (eds.) *Historical Dictionary of the Modern Olympic Movement.* Westport, CN: Greenwood Press, pp. 12–17.

HRADF (Hellenic Republic Asset Development Fund) (2016) The Fund. Available at: http://www.hradf.com/en/the-fund/mission.

HRGSMC (Hellenic Republic General Secretariat for Media and Communications) (2015) Greece: dealing with the refugee crisis. Available at: http://www.mfa.gr/missionsabroad/images/stories/missions/geneva-pm/docs/factsheet.pdf.

Hughes, R. (1996) *Barcelona.* New York: Knopf.

Hulme, D.L. (1990) *The Political Olympics: Moscow, Afghanistan, and the 1980 US Boycott.* New York: Praeger.

IAAF (International Association of Athletics Federations) (2005) The International Museum of Athletics is born. Press Release, 23 June. Available at: http://www.iaaf.org/news/kind=101/newsid=29896.html.

Imrie, R. (1996) *Disability and the City: International Perspectives.* London: Sage.

Ilha Pura (2015) *Meu lugar.* Available at: http://ilhapura.com.br/meu-lugar/.

Innocenti, C. (2021) Greek Prime Minister unveils the new Athenian Riviera's plan with a 70 km cycle path. Available at: https://ecf.com/news-and-events/news/greek-prime-minister-unveils-new-athenian-rivieras-plan-70km-cycle-path.

Insch, A. and Bowden, B. (2016) Possibilities and limits of brand repositioning for a second-ranked city: the case of Brisbane, Australia's 'New World City', 1979–2013. *Cities*, **56**, pp. 47–54.

Inside the Games (2012) Rio 2016 Olympics will leave legacy of safety and security says city police chief. 15 March. Available at: http://www.insidethegames.biz/olympics/summer-olympics/2016/16233-rio-2016-olympics-will-leave-legacy-of-safety-and-security-says-city-police-chief.

Insolera, I. (2001) *Roma moderna. Un secolo di storia urbanistica 1870–1970.* Turin: Einaudi.

Insolera, I. (2011) Il 'piano regolatore' delle Olimpiadi, in IRSIFAR (ed.) *Le Olimpiadi del 'miracolo' cinquant'anni dopo.* Milan: Franco Angeli, pp. 17–22.

International Business Times (2012) London Olympics 2012: brand police on patrol to enforce sponsors' exclusive rights. 16 July. Available at: http://www.ibtimes.co.uk/london-2012-olympics-banned-words-advertising-gold-363429.

Internet Archive (2018) Late Night with Seth Meyers. March 7, 12:37am–1:38am EST. Available at: http://archive.org/details/WCAU_20180307_053700_Late_Night_With_Seth_Meyers.

Invictus Foundation (2016) *The Invictus Games Foundation.* Available at: https://invictusgamesfoundation.org/foundation.

Ioannou, T. (2014) Panathinaikos Stadium to be upgraded. *The Times of Change*, 29 April. Available at: http://www.thetoc.gr/eng/news/article/panathinaikos-stadium-upgraded.

IOC (International Olympic Committee) (1949) *44th IOC Session, Rome.* Lausanne: IOC.

IOC (1978) *Agreement between IOC and the city of Los Angeles.* Typescript, 27 October.

IOC (1991) *The Olympic Charter.* Lausanne: IOC.

IOC (1994) *Centenary Olympic Congress Report.* Tuesday 30th August 1994, Theme 1 the Olympic Movements' Contribution to Modern Society; sub-theme B: Sport and the Environment. Lausanne: IOC, pp. 97–145.

IOC (1996) *The Olympic Charter.* Lausanne: IOC.

IOC (1997a) *Manual on Sport and the Environment.* Available at: https://www.cipra.org/en/publications/3973.

IOC (1997b) *Memorias Olimpicas, por Pierre de Coubertin.* Lausanne: IOC.

IOC (1999a) Final Recommendations for IOC Reform Published. Press release, 24 November, Lausanne: IOC.

IOC (1999b) *IOC Crisis and Reform Chronology.* Lausanne: IOC.

IOC (1999*c*) *Olympic Movement's Agenda 2021 – Sport for Sustainable Development.* Lausanne: IOC.

IOC (2000) IOC and IPC Sign Cooperation Agreement. Press release, 20 October, Lausanne: IOC.

IOC (2001*a*) IOC and IPC Sign Agreement on the Organisation of the Paralympic Games. Press release, 10 June. Lausanne: IOC.

IOC (2001*b*) *Report of the IOC Evaluation Commission for the Games of the XXIX Olympiad in 2008.* Lausanne: IOC.

IOC (2003*a*) *The Legacy of the Olympic Games 1894–2000.* International symposium Lausanne, 2002. Lausanne: IOC. Available at: http://multimedia.olympic.org/pdf/en_report_635pdf.

IOC (2003*b*) *Olympic Games Study Commission: Report to the 115th IOC Session, Prague, July.* Lausanne: IOC.

IOC (2004*a*) *2012 Candidature Procedure and Questionnaire: Games of the XXX Olympiad in 2012.* Lausanne: IOC.

IOC (2004*b*) *The Olympic Charter.* Lausanne: International Olympic Committee.

IOC (2005) *Technical Manual on Olympic Village.* Available at: http://www.gamesmonitor.org.uk/files/Technical_Manual_on_Olympic_Village.pdf.

IOC (2006) *Olympic Movement's Agenda 21: Sport for Sustainable Development.* Lausanne: International Olympic Committee. Available at: http://www.olympic.org/Documents/Reports/EN/en_report_300.pdf.

IOC (2007) *IOC 2014 Evaluation Committee Report for XXII Olympic Winter Games in 2014.* Lausanne: IOC.

IOC (2008*a*) *2016 Candidature Procedure and Questionnaire: Games of the XXXI Olympiad.* Lausanne: IOC.

IOC (2008*b*) *Games of the XXXI Olympiad 2016 Working Group Report.* Lausanne: IOC.

IOC (2009) *The Olympic Movement in Society. IOC Final Report 2005–2008.* Lausanne: IOC.

IOC (2013*a*) *Olympic Legacy 2013.* Lausanne: IOC.

IOC (2013*b*) Sochi 2014's mountain venues set to provide lasting legacy. Available at: https://olympics.com/ioc/news/sochi-2014-s-mountain-venues-set-to-provide-lasting-legacy.

IOC (2014*a*) *Olympic Agenda 2020: Context and Background.* Lausanne: IOC.

IOC (2014*b*) *Olympic Agenda 2020: 20+20 Recommendations.* Lausanne: IOC.

IOC (2015*a*) Bidding for success: by invitation. *Olympic Review*, No 95 (April/June), pp. 31–33.

IOC (2015*b*) *Candidate Process Olympic Games 2024.* Lausanne: IOC

IOC (2015*c*) *Host City Contract operational requirements.* Lausanne: IOC.

IOC (2017*a*) *IOC Sustainability Strategy.* Lausanne: IOC.

IOC (2017*b*) *Legacy Strategic Approach: Moving Forward.* Lausanne: IOC.

IOC (2017*c*) *Report of the 2024 Evaluation Commission.* Lausanne: IOC.

IOC (2018*a*) *Carbon Footprint Methodology for the Olympic Games.* Lausanne: IOC.

IOC (2018*b*) Factsheet: Host City Election. 5 March.

IOC (2018*c*) *IOC Sustainability Report: Sharing Orogress on Our 2020 Objectives.* Lausanne: IOC.

IOC (2018*d*) *Olympic Agenda 2020: Olympic Games: The New Norm.* Lausanne: IOC.

IOC (2018*e*) PyeongChang Olympic Winter Games create legacy of environmental and social good. 24 February 2018. Available at: https://olympics.com/ioc/news/pyeongchang-olympic-winter-games-create-legacy-of-environmental-and-social-good.

IOC (2019*a*) *IOC Annual Report 2019: Credibility Sustainability Youth.* Lausanne: IOC.

IOC (2019*b*) *IOC Sustainability Progress Update. A Review or Our 2020 Objectives.* Lausanne: IOC.

IOC (2019*c*) *Olympic Games Guide on Sustainable Sourcing.* Lausanne: IOC.

IOC (2019*d*) *Future Host Commissions: Terms of Reference.* Lausanne: IOC.

IOC (2020/2021) Olympic Marketing Fact Files. Available at: http://www.olympic.org/Documents/IOC_Marketing/OLYMPIC–MARKETING–FACT–FILE–2012.pdf.

IOC (2021*a*) *Future Host Election*. Available at: https://olympics.com/ioc/future-host-election.

IOC (2021*b*) IOC Feasibility Assessment – Olympic Games Brisbane. February. Available at: https://olympics.com/ioc/brisbane-2032.

IOC (2021*c*) IOC reveals details of its 'Olympic Forest' project. Available at: https://olympics.com/ioc/news/ioc-reveals-details-of-its-olympic-forest-project.

IOC (2021*d*) *IOC Sustainability Report 2021*. Lausanne: IOC.

IOC (2021*e*) *Olympic Agenda 2020+ 5: 15 Recommendations*. Lausanne: IOC.

IOC (2021*f*) *Olympic Agenda 2020: Closing Report*. Lausanne: IOC.

IOC (2021*g*) *The Olympic Charter*. Lausanne: IOC.

IOC (2022*a*) *Annual Report 2021*. Available at: https://stillmed.olympics.com/media/Documents/International-Olympic-Committee/Annual-report/IOC-Annual-Report-2021.pdf.

IOC (2022*b*) *IOC Supplier Code*. Lausanne: IOC.

IOC (2022*c*) *Olympic Agora*. Available at: https://olympics.com/ioc/the-olympic-foundation-for-culture-and-heritage.

IOC (2022*d*) *Olympic Forest*. Available at: https://olympics.com/ioc/olympic-forest/.

IOC (2022*e*) *Olympic Marketing Fact File 2022 Edition*. Available at: https://stillmed.olympics.com/media/Documents/International-Olympic-Committee/IOC-Marketing-And-Broadcasting/IOC-Marketing-Fact-File.pdf.

IOC (2022*f*) *Over 125 years of Olympic Venues: Post-Games Use*. Executive Summary. Available at: https://stillmed.olympics.com/media/Documents/Olympic-Games/Olympic-legacy/Executive-summary-venues-post-games-use.pdf.

IOC (2022*g*) *Snow, Climate Change and the Olympic Winter Games*. Available at: https://olympics.com/ioc/news/snow-climate-change-and-the-olympic-winter-games.

IOC (2022*h*) *Studying Landscape of Winter Games 2030 and Beyond*. Available at: https://olympics.com/ioc/news/future-host-commission-studying-landscape-of-winter-sport-with-a-view-to-the-olympic-winter-games-2030-and-beyond.

IOC (2023*a*) *Commitment to Sustainability*. Available at: https://olympics.com/ioc/olympic-house/commitment-to-sustainability.

IOC (2023*b*) *Olympic Legacy*. Available at: https://olympics.com/ioc/olympic-legacy.

IOC (2023*c*) *Sustainability and Legacy Commission – Mission*. Available at https://olympics.com/ioc/sustainability-and-legacy-commission#:~:text=The%20IOC%20Sustainability%20and%20Legacy,and%20legacies%20in%20the%20social%2C.

IOC (2023*d*) *The Olympic Museum Network*. Available at: https://olympics.com/ioc/the-olympic-foundation-for-culture-and-heritage/communities/olympic-museums-network.

IOC (2023*e*) Tokyo 2020 goes beyond Carbon Neutrality and helps create a more 'Sustainable Society'. Available at: https://olympics.com/ioc/news/tokyo-2020-goes-beyond-carbon-neutrality-and-helps-create-a-more-sustainable-society.

IOC Committee Enquiry Commission (1993) *Report IOC Enquiry Commission for the Games of the XXVII Olympiad 2000*. Lausanne: IOC.

IOC OSC (IOC Olympic Studies Centre) (2022) *Candidature Files for the Winter Olympics*. Available at: https://library.olympics.com/default/candidatures.aspx?_lg=en-GB.

Iosa, I., Lallement, E. and Rozenholc-Escobar, C. (2022) *Le Pérenne et le temporaire dans la fabrique urbaine: la place des grands événements sportifs et culturels contemporains*. Paris: L'Harmattan.

IPC (International Paralympic Committee) (2005) *Annual Report 2004*. Bonn: IPC.

IPC (2006*a*) *About the IPC*. Bonn: IPC. Available at: http://www.paralympic.org/release/Main_Sections_Menu/IPC/About_the_IPC.

IPC (2006*b*) *Annual Report 2005*. Bonn: IPC.

IPC (2006*c*) *IPC Strategic Plan 2006–2009*. Bonn: IPC.

IPC (2008) New Russian law upholds Paralympic standards. Available at: http://www.paralympic.org/Media_Centre/News/General_News/2008_11_07_a.html).

IPC (2009) *Annual Report 2008*. Bonn: IPC. Available at: http://www.paralympic.org/

export/sites/default/IPC/Reference_Documents/2009_05_Annual_Report_2008_web. pdf.

IPC (2012) IOC and IPC Extend Co-operation Agreement Until 2020. Media Centre 9 May 2012. Available at: http://www.paralympic.org/news/ioc-and-ipc-extend-co-operation-agreement-until-2020.

IPC (2013*a*) *Accessibility Guide: An Inclusive Approach to the Olympic and Paralympic Games.* Bonn: IPC.

IPC (2013*b*) *Handbook: Paralympic Games.* Bonn: International Paralympic Committee.

IPC (2014*a*) Media Centre NBC TV deal monumental for Paralympic Movement. IPC Media Centre. Available at: http://www.paralympic.org/video/nbc-tv-deal-monumental-paralympic-movement-tatyana-mcfadden-alana-nichols-angela-ruggiero.

IPC (2014*b*) Sochi sets new barrier-free standards in Russia. Available at: https://www.paralympic.org/news/sochi-sets-new-barrier-free-standards-russia.

IPC (2015*a*) *International Paralympic Committee Annual Report 2014.* Bonn: IPC.

IPC (2015*b*) New law hailed as a landmark in Brazil, Media Centre. 8 July. Available at: http://www.paralympic.org/news/new-law-hailed-landmark-brazil.

IPC (2016) *About Us.* Available at: http://www.paralympic.org/the-ipc/about-us.

IPC (2022) *Tokyo 2020 Olympic and Paralympic Parks to be transformed into Games Legacy.* Available at: https://www.paralympic.org/news/making-the-olympic-and-paralympic-parks-a-legacy.

IPC (2023) *Paralympic and Para Sport Events.* Available at: https://www.paralympic.org/events.

IPP (Instituto Pereira Passos) (2011) *População residente e estimada – Brasil, Estado do Rio de Janeiro e Regiões Administrativas do Município do Rio de Janeiro – 2000/2010/2013–2016/2020* (Tabela N° 3261). Available at: https://www.data.rio/documents/ba877d53 302346eca990a47c99e15f74/about.

ISTAT (Istituto nazionale di statistica) (1962) *L'attrezzatura alberghiera in Italia.* Roma: Failli.

IVC (Inter Vistas Consulting) (2002) *The Economic Impact of the 2010 Winter Olympic and Paralympic Games: An Update.* Vancouver: State Government of British Columbia.

Jackson, D. (2022) Queensland's high-tech plan to make the 2032 Brisbane Olympic Games smarter and greener. *The Conversation*, 21 November. Available at: https://theconversation.com/queenslands-high-tech-plan-to-make-the-2032-brisbane-olympic-games-smarter-and-greencr-193949.

Jacomuzzi, S. (1976) *Storia delle Olimpiadi.* Turin: Einaudi.

Jefferys, K. (2014) *The British Olympic Association: A History.* Basingstoke: Palgrave Macmillan.

Jenkins, R. (2008) *The First London Olympics 1908.* London: Aurum Books.

Jennings, A. (2019) One of California's last black enclaves threatened by Inglewood's stadium deal. *Los Angeles Times.* 10 April. Available at: https://www.latimes.com/local/lanow/la-me-inglewood-gentrification-rent-crenshaw-rams-stadium-20190410-htmlstory.html.

Jennings, A. and Sambrook, C. (2000) *The Great Olympic Swindle: When the World wanted Its Games Back.* London: Simon and Schuster.

Johnson, C. (1999) Planning the Olympic site, in Bingham-Hall, P. (ed) *Olympic Architecture: Building Sydney 2000.* Sydney: Watermark Press, pp. 36–45.

Johnson, C. (2008) Introduction: New Event Horizon, in Hay, A. and Cashman, R. (eds.) *Connecting Cities: Mega Event Cities.* A publication for the 9th World Congress of Metropolis. Sydney: Sydney Olympic Park Authority for Metropolis Congress.

Jones, C. (2023) Gabba rebuild locked in as state and federal governments reach funding agreement for multiple 2032 Olympic projects. *ABC News*, 17 February. Available at: https://www.abc.net.au/news/2023-02-17/gabba-stadium-redevelopment-funding-2032-olympics-infrastructure/101988206.

Judge, L.W., Petersen, J. and Lydum, M. (2009) The best kept secret in sports: the 2010 Youth Olympic Games. *International Review for the Sociology of Sport*, **44**(2/3), pp. 173–191.

Kassens-Noor, E. (2012) *Planning Olympic Legacies: Transport Dreams and Urban Realities.* London: Routledge.

Kassens-Noor, E. (2013*a*) Managing transport during the Olympic Games, in Frawley, S. and Adair, D. (eds.) *Managing the Olympics*. Sydney: Palgrave Macmillan, pp. 127–146.

Kassens-Noor, E. (2013*b*) The transport legacy of the Olympic Games, 1992–2012. *Journal of Urban Affairs* **35**, pp. 393–416.

Kassens-Noor, E. (2020) *Los Angeles and the Summer Olympics: Planning Legacies*. Cham: Springer.

Kearins, K. and Pavlovich, K. (2002) The role of stakeholders in Sydney's Green Games. *Corporate Social Responsibility and Environmental Management*, **9**, pp. 157–169.

Keivani, R., Omena de Melo, E. and Brownill, S. (2020) Durable inequality and the scope for pro-poor development in a globalising world: Lessons from Rio de Janeiro. *City*, **24**(3-4), pp. 530–551.

Kennelly, J. (2016) *Olympic Exclusion: Youth, Poverty and Social Legacies*. London: Routledge.

Kennelly, J. and Watt, P. (2011) Sanitizing public space in Olympic host cities: the Spatial experiences of marginalized youth in 2010 Vancouver and 2012 London. *Sociology* **45**(5), pp. 765–781.

Keogh, L. (2009) *London 2012 Olympic Legacies: Conceptualising Legacy, the Role of Communities and Local Government and the Regeneration of East London*. London: Department of Communities and Local Government.

Kerr, S. and Howe, P.D. (2015) What do we mean by Paralympic legacy? in Poynter, G., Viehoff, V. and Li, Y. (eds.) *The London Olympics and Urban Development: The Mega-Event City*. London: Routledge, pp. 193–204.

Kettle, M. (1999) Corruption probe spares Samaranch, *The Guardian*, 2 March.

Keys, B.J. (2006) *Globalizing Sport: National Rivalry and International Community in the 1930s*. Cambridge, MA: Harvard University Press.

Kidd, B. (1996) Montreal 1976: the Games of the 21st Olympiad, in Findling, J.E. and Pelle, K.D. (eds.) *Historical Dictionary of the Modern Olympic Movement*. Westport, CN: Greenwood Press, pp. 153–160.

Kihara, L. (2020) Japan says not preparing for postponement of Olympic Games. *Reuters*, 20 March. Available at: https://www.reuters.com/article/us-health-coronavirus-olympics-aso-idUSKBN2150I4.

Killanin, Lord (1983) *My Olympic Years*. London: Secker and Warburg.

Kim, H-M. and Grix, J. (2021) Implementing a sustainability legacy strategy: a case study of PyeongChang 2018 Winter Olympic Games. *Sustainability*, **13**(9), 5141.

Kim, J. and Choe, S.-C. (1997) *Seoul: The Making of a Metropolis*. Chichester: John Wiley.

Kim, J.G., Rhee, S.W., Yu, J.C., Koo, K.M. and Hong, J.C. (1989) *Impact of the Seoul Olympic Games on National Development*. Seoul: Korea Development Institute.

Kimmorley, S. (2014) Sydney Olympic Park props up the NSW economy 14 years after the Olympics. *Business Insider Australia*, 31 May.

Kirakosyan, L. (2022) Legacy challenges and opportunities comparing the Rio 2016 and Tokyo 2020 Paralympics. *Journal of Paralympic Research Group*, **18**, pp. 19–46.

Kissoudi, P. (2008) The Athens Olympics: optimistic legacies: post-Olympic assets and the struggle for their realization. *International Journal of the History of Sport*, **25**(14), pp. 1972–1990.

Klassen, L. (2012) Participatory art at the Vancouver 2010 Cultural Olympiad. *Public*, **23**(45), pp. 212–223.

Korean Times (2021) Government decides to dismantle PyeongChang Olympics ski slope, restore forest. 11 June. Available at: https://www.koreatimes.co.kr/www/nation/2021/06/113_310370.html.

Kotogiannis, D. and Hope, K. (2014) Greece's tourism bounces back – now for a move upmarket. *Financial Times*, 5 July 2014. Available at: http://www.ft.com/cms/s/0/cda98386-fd41-11e3-bc93-00144feab7de.html#axzz3xVByLYL.

KPMG (2021) *Brisbane 2032 Olympic and Paralympic Games – Preliminary Economic, Social and Environment Analysis: Summary Report*. Brisbane: Department of Tourism, Innovation and Sport, Queensland Government. Available at: https://www.premiers.

qld.gov.au/publications/categories/reports/assets/2032-qld-games-economic-analysis-summary-report-final.pdf.

Kuhn, A. (2021) Toyota and other big Olympics sponsors are downplaying their ties to the Games. Available at: https:// www.npr.org/sections/tokyo-olympics-live-updates/2021/07/20/1018390493/toyota-and-other-big-olympics-sponsors-are-downplaying-their-ties-to-the-games.

Kyrieleis, H. (2003) The German excavations at Olympia: an introduction, in Phillips, D.J. and Pritchard, D. (eds.) *Sport and Festival in the Ancient Greek World*. Swansea: Classical Press of Wales, pp. 41–60.

Kyriakopoulos, V. (2009) *Athens Encounter*. London: Lonely Planet Publications.

L'Unità (1960) Insegnamenti di una competizione. *L'Unità*, 11 September.

LA County (2022) LA County Housed 80,000 People over 5 Years. Homeless Initiative. 5 May. Available at: https://homeless.lacounty.gov/uncategorized/la-county-housed-80000-people-over-5-years/.

LA24 Bid Committee (2017a) *Los Angeles Candidate City Olympic Games 2024*, Volume 1. Los Angeles, CA: Los Angeles Candidate City Olympic Games 2024.

LA24 Bid Committee (2017b) *Los Angeles Candidate City Olympic Games 2024*, Volume 2. Los Angeles, CA: Los Angeles Candidate City Olympic Games 2024.

LA24 Bid Committee (2017c) *Los Angeles Candidate City Olympic Games 2024*, Volume 3. Los Angeles, CA: Los Angeles Candidate City Olympic Games 2024.

LA28 (2022) Games Plan. Available at: https://la28.org/en/games-plan.html.

LACAN (Los Angeles Community Action Network) (2021) 41.18 Amendment: A Wolf in Wolfs Clothing. Available at: https://cangress.org/41-18-amendment-a-wolf-in-wolfs-clothing/.

Lamda Development (2016) Golden Hall – shopping centre expansion, Athens. Available at: http://www.lamdadev.com/en/investment-portfolio/future-developments/golden-hall-shopping-center-expansion,-athens.html.

Landry, F. and Yerles, M. (1996) *The International Olympic Committee One Hundred Years, the Idea, the Presidents, the Achievements*. Lausanne: IOC.

Lane, P. (2006) The Paralympics 2012. Unpublished lecture, symposium on 'Profiling London', London Metropolitan University, 26 April.

Langenbach, B. and Kruger, J. (2017) Emergence of the environmental policy of the International Olympic Committee: a historical analysis. *Journal of Qualitative Research in Sports Studies*, 11(1), pp. 15–32.

LAOOC (Los Angeles Olympic Organizing Committee) (1985) *Official Report of the Games of the XXIInd Olympiad Los Angeles, 1984*. Los Angeles, CA: Los Angeles Olympic Organizing Committee.

Lappo, G., Chikishev, A. and Bekker, A. (1976) *Moscow, Capital of the Soviet Union: A Short Geographical Survey*. Moscow: Progress Publishers.

Large, D.C. (2012) *Munich 1972: Tragedy, Terror, and Triumph at the Olympic Games*. Lanham, MD: Rowman and Littlefield.

Large, D.C. and Large, J.J.H. (2016) A most contentious contest: politics and protests at the 1936 Berlin Olympics, in Dart, J., Wagg, S. and Manganyi, N.C. (eds.) *Sport, Protest and Globalisation: Stopping Play*. Basingstoke: Palgrave Macmillan, pp. 51–75.

Larson, R. and Staley, T. (1998) Atlanta Olympics: the big story, in Thompson, P., Tolloczko, J.J.A. and Clarke, J.N. (eds.) *Stadia, Arenas and Grandstands: Design, Construction and Operation*. London: Spon, pp. 276–283.

LAHSA (Los Angeles Homeless Services Authority) (2018) 2018 Homeless Count Results. Available at: ttps://www.lahsa.org/news?article=410-2018-homeless-count-results.

LAHSA (2022) 2022 Greater Los Angeles Homeless Count Data. Available at: https://www.lahsa.org/news?article=893-2022-greater-los-angeles-homeless-count-data.

Latouche, D. (2007) Montreal 1976, in Gold, J.R. and Gold, M.M. (eds) *Olympic Cities: Urban Planning, City Agendas and the World's Games, 1896 to the Present*. London: Routledge, pp. 207–227.

Lauermann, J. (2016) Temporary projects, durable outcomes: urban development through failed Olympic bids? *Urban Studies,* **53**(9), pp. 1885–1901.

Lauermann, J. (2019) The urban politics of mega-events: grand promises meet local resistance. *Environment and Society,* **10**(1), pp. 48–62.

Lauermann, J. (2022) The declining Appeal of mega-events in entrepreneurial cities: from Los Angeles 1984 to Los Angeles 2028. *Environment and Planning C,* **40**(6), pp. 1203–1218.

Lauermann, J. and Vogelpohl, A. (2017) Fragile growth coalitions or powerful contestations? Cancelled Olympic bids in Boston and Hamburg. *Environment and Planning A,* **49**(8), pp. 1887–1904.

Leake, W.M. (1830) *Travels in the Morea,* 3 vols. London: John Murray.

Leary, M.E. and McCarthy, J. (2013) Introduction: urban regeneration, a global phenomenon, in Leary, M.E. and McCarthy, J. (eds.) *The Routledge Companion to Urban Regeneration.* London: Routledge, pp. 1–6.

Lebeau, B. (2018) Les Jeux olympiques de 2024: une chance pour le Grand Paris? *EchoGéo.* https://doi.org/10.4000/echogeo.15202.

Lee, C. (1988) From wartime rubble to Olympic host. *Far Eastern Economic Review,* **140**(36), pp. 60–65.

Lee, J.W. and Tan, T-C. (2021) Politics, policy and legacies of the Olympics in Asia Pacific: a panoramic view. *Sport in Society,* **24**(12), pp. 2067–2076.

Legislative Analyst's Office (2016) *Los Angeles' Bid for the 2024 Olympics and Paralympics.* Sacramento, CA: LAO. Available at: https://www.lao.ca.gov/reports/2016/3506/LA-Bid-2024-Olympics-Paralympics.pdf.

Legislative Analyst's Office (2017) *Los Angeles' Bid for the Olympics and Paralympics.* Sacramento, CA: LAO. Available at: https://lao.ca.gov/Publications/Report/3695.

Lehrer, U. and Laidley, J. (2008) Old mega-projects newly packaged? Waterfront redevelopment in Toronto. *International Journal of Urban and Regional Research,* **32**(4), pp. 786–803.

Lei, L. (2004) Beijing evolves into Olympic 'Green'. *China Daily,* 1 March. Available at: www.chinadaily.com.cn.

Le Monde (2022) A moins de deux ans des JO, les instances du sport français prennent l'eau. 30 September.

Le Monde (2023*a*) Paris 2024, la difficile bataille de la création d'emplois en Seine-Saint Denis. 25 January.

Le Monde (2023*b*) Tony Estanguet, l'autre mascotte des Jeux olympiques, 10 February.

Le Monde (2023*c*) JO 2024: avec 'Tous aux jeux', l'Etat lance son opération de billetterie 'populaire'. 5 April.

Lenskyj, H.J. (1996) When winners are losers, Toronto and Sydney bids for the Summer Olympics. *Journal of Sport,* **20**(4), pp. 392–410.

Lenskyj, H. (1998) Sport and corporate environmentalism: the case of the Sydney 2000 Olympics. *International Review for the Sociology of Sport,* **33**(4), pp. 341–354.

Lenskyj, H.J. (2000) *Inside the Olympic Industry: Power, Politics and Activism.* Albany, NY: State University of New York Press.

Lenskyj, H.J. (2002) *The Best Olympics Ever? The Social Impacts of Sydney 2000.* Albany, NY: State University of New York Press.

Lenskyj, H. (2004) Making the world safe for global capital: the Sydney 2000 Olympics and beyond, in Bale, J. and Christensen, M. (eds.) *Post-Olympism? Questioning Sport in the 21st Century.* Oxford: Berg, pp. 231–242.

Lenskyj, H.J. (2008) *Olympic Industry Resistance: Challenging Olympic Power and Propaganda.* Albany, NY: State University of New York Press.

Lenskyj, H. (2014) *Sexual Diversity and the Sochi 2014 Olympics.* Basingstoke: Palgrave.

Lenskyj, H.J. (2020) *The Olympic Games: A Critical Approach.* Bingley: Emerald Publishing.

Leontidou, L. (1990) *The Mediterranean City in Transition: Social Change and Urban Development.* Cambridge: Cambridge University Press.

Leopkey, B. and Parent, M.M. (2012) Olympic Games legacy: from general benefits to sustainable long-term legacy. *International Journal of the History of Sport*, **29**(6), pp. 924–943.

Le Parisien (2022) Paris2024. Series 07/07/2022-11/07/2022; 07/10/2022. Available at: https://www.leparisien.fr/jo-paris-2024/.

Lepre, A. (1999) *Storia della prima Repubblica. L'Italia dal 1943 al 1998*. Bologna: Il Mulino.

Lesjø, J.H. (2000) Lillehammer 1994: planning, figurations and the 'green' Winter Games. *International Review for the Sociology of Sport*, **35**(3), pp. 282–293.

Levett, R. (2004) Is green the new gold? A sustainable games for London, in Vigor, A., Mean, M. and Tims, C. (eds.) *After the Gold Rush: a sustainable Olympics for London*. London: IPPR/DEMOS, pp. 69–90.

Li, L.M., Dray-Novey, A.J. and Kong, H. (2008) *Beijing: From Imperial City to Olympic City*, Basingstoke: Palgrave Macmillan.

Li, X. (2017) From Beijing to Rio: rebranding China via the modern Olympic Games. *Journal of International Communication*, **23**(2), pp. 252–271.

Li, Y. (2006) Green Chaoyang part of Olympic preparations. *Beijing Today*, 24 March.

Li, Y. (2015) Measuring and assessing the impacts of London 2012, in Poynter, G., Viehoff, V. and Li, Y. (eds.) *The London Olympics and Urban Development: The Mega-Event City*. London: Routledge, pp. 35–47.

Lialios, G. (2021) Three revitalising redevelopments for Athens. 30 December. Available at: https://www.ekathimerini.com/society/1174638/three-revitalizing-redevelopments-for-athens/.

Liao, H. and Pitts, A. (2006) A brief historical review of Olympic urbanization. *International Journal of the History of Sport*, **23**(7), pp. 1232–1252.

Lin, X. (2004) Economic impact of Beijing Olympic Games 2008. *Proceedings of the 2004 Pre-Olympic Congress*, 6–11 August, Thessaloniki, Greece, Vol. 1, p. 100.

Little, C. (1997) From one brickpit to another: the ancient history of the Sydney Olympic bid. *Sporting Traditions*, **14**, pp.79–90.

Littlewood, A.R. (2000) Olympic Games, in Speake, G. (ed.) *Encyclopaedia of Greece and the Hellenic Tradition*, vol. 2. Chicago, IL: Fitzroy Dearborn, pp. 1176–1179.

LLDC (London Legacy Development Corporation) (2013) Mayor and Chancellor announce commitment to the development of major new education and arts centres, 4 December. Available at: http://queenelizabetholympicpark.co.uk/news/news-articles/2013/12/mayor-and-chancellor-announce-commitment-to-the-development-of-major-new-education-and-arts-centres.

LLDC (2014) *Ten Year Plan Draft V4* (9 June 2014). London: Greater London Authority.

LLDC (2016) *Ten Year Plan 2015/16–2024/25*. London: London Legacy Development Corporation.

LLDC (2021) *Queen Elizabeth Olympic Park Strategy to 2025*. London: London Legacy Development Corporation.

Llewellyn, M., Gleaves, J. and Wilson, W. (2015) The historical legacy of the 1984 Los Angeles Olympic Games. *International Journal of the History of Sport*, **32**(1), pp. 1–8.

Lloyds Banking Group (2012) *The Economic Impact of the London 2012 Olympic and Paralympic Games*. London: Lloyds Banking Group.

Lochhead, H. (2005) A new vision for Sydney Olympic Park. *Urban Design International*, **10**(3/4), pp. 215–222.

LOCOG (2011) *London 2012 Sustainability Report: A Blueprint for Change*. London: LOCOG.

LOCOG (2013a) *London 2012 Festival – 2012 Olympics*. Available at: http://www.london2012.com/join-in/festival.

LOCOG (2013b) *London 2012 Olympic Games Official Report*, 3 vols. London: LOCOG.

London2012 (2004) *London 2012: Candidate File*. London: LOCOG. Available at: http://www.london2012.com/en/news/publications/Candidatefile/Candidatefile.htm.

London Evening Standard (2012) Former Royal Marines to ferry around super-rich Games spectators. 28 May. Available at: http://www.thisislondon.co.uk/olympics/olympic-news/london-olympics-2012-former-royal-marines-to-ferry-around-superrich-games-spectators-7793520.html.

Long, X., Chen, B. and Park, B. (2018) Effect of 2008's Beijing Olympic Games on environmental efficiency of 268 China's cities. *Journal of Cleaner Production*, **172**, pp. 1423–1432.

Los Angeles Times (2007) Beijing Olympics visitors to come under widespread surveillance. *Los Angeles Times*, 7 August.

Loureiro, C., Coelho, H. and Rodrigues, M. (2021) Cinco anos depois, legado da Rio 2016 tem obras inacabadas, projeções fracassadas e projetos no papel. G1, 18 July. Available at: https://g1.globo.com/rj/rio-de-janeiro/noticia/2021/07/18/cinco-anos-depois-legado-da-rio-2016-especial.ghtml.

Lovett, C. (1997) *Olympic Marathon: A Centennial History of the Games Most Storied Race*. Westport, CN: Praeger.

LPOOC (Lake Placid Olympic Organizing Committee) (1932) *Official Report III Olympic Winter Games, Lake Placid*. New York: III Olympic Winter Games Committee.

LPOOC (1980) *Official Report XIII Olympic Winter Games, Lake Placid New York, Final Report*. Lake Placid: Lake Placid Olympic Organizing Committee.

Lucas, J.A. (1976) A history of the marathon race – 490 B.C. to 1975. *Journal of Sport History*, **3**, pp. 120–138.

Luscombe, G. (2020) Delivering for the Gold Coast. *Australasian Leisure Management*, **140**, pp. 20–24.

MacAloon, J.J. (1981) *This Great Symbol: Pierre de Coubertin and the Origins of the Modern Olympic Games*. Chicago, IL: University of Chicago Press.

MacAloon, J.J. (1989) Festival, ritual and TV (Los Angeles 1984), in Jackson, R. and McPhail, T. (eds.) *The Olympic Movement and the Mass Media*. Part 6. Calgary: Hunford Enterprises, pp. 21–40.

MacAloon, J.J. (2016) Agenda 2020 and the Olympic Movement. *Sport in Society*, **19**(6), pp. 767–85.

McCann, B. (2005) Complete the street! *Planning*, **71**(5), pp. 18–23.

McCormick, J. (2021) Brisbane to be smallest city to host Olympic Games in 80 Years. *SwimSwam*. 29 July. Available at: https://swimswam.com/brisbane-to-be-smallest-city-to-host-olympic-games-in-80-years/.

McGeoch, R. and Korporaal, G. (1994) *The Bid: How Australia won the 2000 Games*. Melbourne: Heinemann.

McIntosh, M.J. (2003) The Olympic bid process as a starting point of the legacy development, in De Moragas, M., Kennett, C. and Puig, N. (eds.) *The Legacy of the Olympic Games 1984–2000*. Lausanne: International Olympic Committee, pp. 450–456.

Macko, S. (1996) Security at the Summer Olympic Games is ready. *EmergencyNet NEWS Service*, **2**, p. 191.

McNamee, M.J. (2017) Paralympism, paralympic values and disability sport: a conceptual and ethical critique. *Disability and Rehabilitation*, **39**(2), pp. 201–209.

Maennig, W. (2019) Olympic Games: public referenda, public opinion and willingness to pay, in Downward, P., Frick, B., Humphreys, B. and Pawlowski, T. (eds.) *The SAGE Handbook of Sports Economics*. London: Sage, pp. 367–376.

Mahtani, K.R., Protheroe, J., Slight, S.P., Marcos, M., Demarzo, P., Blakeman, T., Barton, C.A., Brijnath, B. and Roberts, N. (2013) Can the London 2012 Olympics 'inspire a generation' to do more physical or sporting activities? An overview of systematic reviews. Available at: *BMJ Open* 013;**3**:e002058. doi:10.1136/bmjopen-2012-002058.

Mair, J. (2021) Reduce, re-use, recycle: how the new relaxed Olympic rules make Brisbane's 2032 bid affordable. *The Conversation*. March 9. Available at: https://theconversation.com/reduce-re-use-recycle-how-the-new-relaxed-olympic-rules-make-brisbanes-2032-bid-affordable-156100.

Mair, J. and Smith, A. (2021) Events and sustainability: why making events more sustainable is not enough. *Journal of Sustainable Tourism*, **29**(11/12), pp. 1739–1755.

Mallon, B. (1992) *The Unofficial Report of the 1920 Olympics*. Durham, NC: MOST Publications.

Mallon, B. (1998) *The 1900 Olympic Games: Results for All Competitors in All Events with Commentary. Results from the Early Olympics 2.* Jefferson, NC: McFarland and Company Inc.

Mallon, B. (1999*a*) *The 1904 Olympic Games: Results for All Competitors in All Events with Commentary. Results from the Early Olympics 3.* Jefferson, NC: McFarland and Company Inc.

Mallon, B. (1999*b*) *The 1906 Olympic Games: Results for All Competitors in All Events with Commentary. Results from the Early Olympics 4.* Jefferson, NC: McFarland and Company Inc.

Mallon, B. and Buchanan, I. (2000) *The 1908 Olympic Games: Results for All Competitors in All Events with Commentary. Results from the Early Olympics 5.* Jefferson, NC: McFarland and Company Inc.

Mallon, B. and Widland, T. (1998) *The 1896 Olympic Games: Results for All Competitors in All Events with Commentary. Results from the Early Olympics 1.* Jefferson, NC: McFarland and Company Inc.

Maloney, L. (1996) Barcelona 1992: the Games of the 25th Olympiad, in Findling, J.E. and Pelle, K.D. (eds.) *Historical Dictionary of the Modern Olympic Movement.* Westport, CN: Greenwood Press, pp. 185–193.

Mammarella, G. (1993) *L'Italia contemporanea*, vol. 5. Bologna: Il Mulino.

Mandell, R.D. (1976) *The First Modern Olympics.* London: Souvenir Press.

Mangan, J.A. (2008) Prologue: guarantees of global goodwill: post-Olympic legacies – too many limping white elephants, *International Journal of the History of Sport*, **25**(14), pp. 1869–1883.

Mapanti, A. (1999) *Olympia and the Olympic Games.* Athens: Michalis Toubis Editions.

Maraniss, D. (2008) *Rome 1960: The Olympics that Changed the World.* New York: Simon and Schuster.

Margaritis, G., Rozmiarek, M. and Malchrowicz-Mosko, E. (2017) Tangible and intangible legacy of the 19th century Zappas Olympics and their implications for contemporary sport tourism. *Physical Culture and Sport: Studies and Research*, **74**(1), pp. 54–60.

Markou, M. (2015) Renovation projects at Faliro Bay (Athens Social Atlas). Available at: https://www.athenssocialatlas.gr/en/article/faliro-bay/.

Marshall, T. (ed.) (2004) *Transforming Barcelona.* London: Routledge.

Martin, S. (2017) Rebranding the Republic: Rome and the 1960 Olympic Games. *European Review of History*, **24**(1), pp. 58–79.

Marvin, C. (2008) 'All under heaven': megaspace in Beijing, in Price, M.E. and Dayan, D. (eds.) *Owning the Olympics: Narratives of the New China.* Ann Arbor, MI: University of Michigan Press, pp. 229–259.

Masters, N. (2011) A Brief History of Palm Trees in Southern California. KCET. 7 December. Available at: https://www.kcet.org/shows/lost-la/a-brief-history-of-palm-trees-in-south ern-california.

Masterton, D.W. (1973) The contribution of the fine arts to the Olympic Games. *Proceedings of the International Olympic Academy.* Athens: IOA, pp. 200–213.

May, V. (1995) Environmental implications of the 1992 Winter Olympic Games. *Tourism Management*, **16**, pp. 269–275.

Mazzarini, F. (2010) Il miracolo di Onesti. Dalle fiamme di guerra alla fiaccola olimpica. *Lancillotto e Nausica*, **27**(1/2), pp. 26–35.

Meadows, D.H., Meadows, D.L., Randers, J. and Behrens, W.W. III (1972) *Limits to Growth: A Report for the Club of Rome's Project on the Predicament of Mankind.* New York: Universe Books. Available at: http://www.donellameadows.org/wp-content/userfiles/ Limits-to-Growth-digital-scan-version.pdf.

MEGC (Major Events Gold Coast) (2022) *Coomera Indoor Sports Centre*. Available at: https://majoreventsgc.com/venues/indoor/coomera-indoor-sports-centre/.

Menicucci, E. (2016) Raggi: Le Olimpiadi nel 2024? Pesa ancora il debito del 1960. *Corriere della Sera*, 29 August. Available at: https://www.corriere.it/politica/16_agosto_28/raggi-olimpiadi-2024-pesa-ancora-debito-60-0cb0df8e-6d5c-11e6-baa8-f780dada92e5.shtml.

Merkel, U. (2008) The politics of sport diplomacy and reunification in divided Korea. *International Review for the Sociology of Sport*, **43**(3), pp. 289–311.

Merkel, U. and Kim, M. (2011) Third time lucky!? PyeongChang's bid to host the 2018 Winter Olympics-politics, policy and practice. *International Journal of the History of Sport*, **28**(16), pp. 2365–2383.

Merlo, L. (1961) Risultati turistici delle Olimpiadi di Roma. *Revue de Tourisme*, **16**(4), pp. 151–156.

Metera, D., Pezold, T. and Piwowarski, W. (2005) *Implementation of Natura 2000 in New EU Member States of Central Europe: An Assessment Report*. Warsaw: The World Conservation Union.

METREX (The Network of European Metropolitan Regions and Areas) (2006) *The Legacies from Major Events: Findings and Conclusions*. Symposium on 'Planning for Major Events', Turin, 25–26 March. Glasgow: METREX. Available at: http://www.eurometrex.org/Docs/Expert_Groups/Major_Events/Torino_Report_2003.pdf.

Metropolitan Police Authority (2007) *Metropolitan Police Service Olympic Programme Update*. Available at: http://www.mpa.gov.uk/committees/x-cop/2007/070201/06/.

Meyer-Künzel, M. (2002) *Der planbare Nutzen: Stadtentwicklung durch Weltausstellungen und Olympische Spiele*. Hamburg: Dölling and Galitz.

MIC (Melbourne Invitation Committee) (1948) *The Melbourne Invitation Committee extends a most cordial Invitation to the Esteemed International Olympic Committee to celebrate the XVI Olympiad in Melbourne, Australia in 1956*. Melbourne: G.W. Grant and Sons.

Michaelidou, T. (2009) Main stream. *Athens 4U*, Spring, pp. 7–60.

Miller, D. (2003) *Athens to Athens: The Official History of the Olympic Games*. Edinburgh: Mainstream.

Miller, S.G. (2003) The organization and functioning of the Olympic Games, in Phillips, D.J. and Pritchard, D. (eds.) *Sport and Festival in the Ancient Greek World*. Swansea: Classical Press of Wales, pp. 1–40.

Millet, L. (1995) The Games of the city, in De Moragas, M. and Botella, M. (eds.) *The Keys to Success*. Barcelona: Centre d'Estudis Olímpics i de l'Esport, pp. 188–202.

Millington, V. (2009) London 2012: what legacy for artist's studios? *Axis webzine*, Autumn. Available at: http://www.axisweb.org/dlForum.aspx?ESSAYID=18066.

Milza, P. (2002) Un siècle de Jeux Olympiques. *Relations Internationales*, **111**(1), pp. 299–310.

Ministero del Turismo e dello Spettacolo (1960) *Lo stato Italiano e le Olimpiadi di Roma*. Roma: Editalia.

Minnaar, A. (2007) The implementation and impact of crime prevention/crime control open street closed-circuit television surveillance in South African Central Business Districts. *Surveillance and Society*, **4**(3), pp. 174–207.

Minnaert, L. (2012) An Olympic legacy for all? The non-infrastructural outcomes of the Olympic Games for socially excluded groups (Atlanta 1996–Beijing 2008). *Tourism Management*, **33**(2), pp. 361–370.

Misener, L., Darcy, S., Legg, D. and Gilbert, K. (2013) Beyond Olympic legacy: understanding Paralympic legacy through a thematic analysis. *Journal of Sport Management*, **27**, pp. 329–334.

Modrey, E. (2008) Architecture as a mode of self-representation at the Olympic Games in Rome (1960) and Munich (1972). *European Review of History*, **15**(6), pp. 691–706.

Monclús, F.J. (2000) Barcelona's planning strategies: from 'Paris of the South' to the 'Capital of West Mediterranean'. *GeoJournal*, **51**, pp. 57–63.

Monclús, F.J. (2003) The Barcelona Model: an original formula? From 'reconstruction' to strategic urban projects (1979–2004). *Planning Perspectives*, **18**, pp. 399–421.

Montalban, M.V. (1992) *Barcelonas*. London: Verso.

Monteiro, F. and Shropshire, K. (2010) How Rio won its Olympic bid. Available at: https://knowledge.wharton.upenn.edu/podcast/knowledge-at-wharton-podcast/brazils-gold-how-rio-won-its-olympic-bid/.

Moore M. (2008) Athens' deserted Games sites a warning to London Olympics. Available at: http://www.telegraph.co.uk/news/worldnews/europe/greece/2062541/Athens-des erted-Games-sites-a-warning-to-London-Olympics.html.

Moore, R. (2022) London's real Olympic masterstroke? *The Observer*, 24 July, pp. 30–31.

Morgan, E. (2021) L.A.'s 1932 Olympics Put the City on a World Stage. KCET. 14 July. Available at: https://www.kcet.org/shows/lost-la/a-boosters-dream-come-true-l-a-and-the-1932-olympics.

Morse, J. (2001) The Sydney 2000 Olympic Games: how the Australian Tourist Commission leveraged the games for tourism. *Journal of Vacation Marketing*, 7, pp. 101–107.

Moura, G. (1998) *O Rio corre para o Maracanã*. Rio de Janeiro: Fundação Getúlio Vargas.

MSNBC (Microsoft/National Broadcasting Corporation) (2004) No concrete plans for Greek athletics venues. 30 August. Available at: http://www.msnbc.msn.com.

Müller, M. (2011) State dirigisme in megaprojects: governing the 2014 Winter Olympics in Sochi. *Environment and Planning A*, **43**, pp. 2091–2108.

Müller, M. (2012) Popular perception of urban transformation through megaevents: understanding support for the 2014 Winter Olympics in Sochi. *Environment and Planning C*, **30**, pp. 693–711.

Müller, M. (2013) Greening Russia? Mobilising sustainability for the 2014 Olympic Games in Sochi, Working Paper, April. Available from www.martin-muller.net.

Müller, M. (2014) Introduction: Winter Olympics Sochi 2014: what is at stake? *East European Politics*, **30**(2), pp. 153–157.

Müller, M. (2015*a*) After Sochi 2014: costs and impacts of Russia's Olympic Games. *Eurasian Geography and Economics*, **55**(6), pp. 628–655.

Müller, M. (2015*b*) The mega-event syndrome: why so much goes wrong in mega-event planning and what to do about it. *Journal of the American Planning Association*, **81**(1), pp. 6–17.

Müller, M. (2017) Approaching paradox: loving and hating mega-events. *Tourism Management*, **63**, pp. 234–241.

Müller, M. (2018) How mega-events capture their hosts: event seizure and the World Cup 2018 in Russia. *Urban Geography*, **38**(8), pp. 1113–1132.

Müller, M., Wolfe, S.D., Gaffney, C., Gogishvili, D., Hug, M. and Leick, A (2021) An evaluation of the sustainability of the Olympic Games. *Nature Sustainability*, **4**, pp. 340–348.

Müller, M., Gogishvili, D., Wolfe, S.D., Gaffney, C., Hug, M. and Leick, A. (2023) Peak event: the rise, crisis and potential decline of the Olympic Games and the World Cup. *Tourism Management*, **95**, 104657.

Müller, N. (ed.) (2000) *Pierre de Coubertin, 1893–1937: Olympism, Selected Writings*. Lausanne: International Olympic Committee.

Mulley, C. and Moutou, C.J. (2015) Not too late to learn from the Sydney Olympics experience: opportunities offered by multimodality in current transport policy. *Cities*, **45**, pp. 117–122.

Muñoz, F. (1997) Historic evolution and urban planning typology of the Olympic Village, in Moragas, M. de, Llinés, M. and Kidd, B. (eds.) *Olympic Villages: A Hundred Years of Urban Planning and Shared Experiences*. Lausanne: International Olympic Committee, pp. 27–51.

Muñoz, F. (2006) Olympic urbanism and Olympic Villages: planning strategies in Olympic host cities, London 1908 to London 2012. *Sociological Review*, **54** (Supplement), pp. 175–187.

Murray, C. (2020) London's Olympic legacy: 'That feeling of normalness isn't quite here yet'. Interview with Selina Mason, Lendlease. London: *The Developer*, 7 January.

Mussi, E.T. (2017) The Emergence of Social Sustainability in the Development of Olympic Parks: The Case of Sydney Olympic Park. Unpublished PhD thesis, University of New South Wales.

Myer, A. (1996) *Millennium Park: Legacy of the Sydney Olympics*. Sydney: Green Games Watch 2000.

Myrdal, G. (1968) *Asian Drama: An Inquiry into the Poverty of Nations*. New York: Pantheon Books.

Nagata, K. (2014) Japan rises to challenge of becoming 'hydrogen society'. Available at: http://www.japantimes.co.jp/news/2014/10/12/national/japan-rises-challenge-becoming-hydrogen-society/#.VpQkdxV4aUk.

National Audit Office (2012) *The 2012 London Olympic and Paralympic Games: Post-Games Review*. London: National Audit Office. Available at: https://www.nao.org.uk/wp-content/uploads/2012/12/1213794fr.pdf.

National Bureau of Statistics (1999) *China Statistical Yearbook 1998*. Beijing: China Statistical Publishing House.

National Bureau of Statistics (2006) *China Statistical Yearbook 2005*. Beijing: China Statistical Publishing House.

Nel-lo, O. (1997) *The Olympic Games as a Tool for Urban Renewal: The Experience of Barcelona'92 Olympic Village*. Barcelona: Centre d'Estudis Olimpics, Universitat Autònoma de Barcelona. Available at: http://olympicstudies.uab.es/pdf/wp090_eng.pdf.

New York Times (2007) China finds American allies for security. 28 December. Available at: https://www.nytimes.com/2007/12/28/business/worldbusiness/28security.html.

New York Times (2012) Mission control, built for cities: I.B.M. takes 'Smarter Cities' concept to Rio de Janeiro. 3 March. Available at: http://www.nytimes.com/2012/03/04/business/ibm-takes-smarter-cities-concept-to-rio-de-janeiro.html?pagewanted=all&_r=0.

New York Times (2016) Security force of 85,000 fills Rio, unsettling rights activists. 7 August. Available at: https://www.nytimes.com/2016/08/08/world/americas/rio-olympics-crime.html.

Nichols, G. and Ralston, R. (2015) The legacy costs of delivering the 2012 Olympic and Paralympic Games through regulatory capitalism. *Leisure Studies*, **34**, pp. 389–404.

Nogueira, I. (2015) Acordo para Olimpíada tira 30 trens de moradores do RJ. *Folha de S. Paulo*, 14 May. Available at: http://www1.folha.uol.com.br/cotidiano/2015/05/1628801-acordo-para-a-olimpiadatira-30-trens-de-moradores-do-rj.shtml.

Noland, M. and Stahler, K. (2015) An Old Boys' Club no more: pluralism in participation and performance at the Olympic Games. *Journal of Sports Economics*, **18**(5), pp. 506–536.

NOlympics LA (2017) Platform. *NOlympics LA* (blog). 13 September. Available at: https://nolympicsla.com/platform/.

NPC (National People's Congress) (2011) *The Twelfth Five-Year Plan for the National Economic and Social Development of Beijing (2011–2015)*. Available at: http://www.bjpc.gov.cn/fzgh_1/guihua/12_5/Picture_12_F_Y_P/201208/P020120809377417514420.pdf.

NSW Government (1979) *Submission to the Australian Olympic Federation: 1988 Olympic Games, Sydney*. Sydney: NSW Government.

NSW Government (2001) *Budget Statement 2001–2002, Sydney 2000 Olympic and Paralympic Games*. Sydney: NSW Government.

Nuzman, C. (2002) 'O Rio nunca mais será o mesmo'. Interview with Pinto, M.B. and Grijó, F. *Jornal do Brasil*, 1 September, p.C5.

O'Bonsawin, C.M. (2010) 'No Olympics on stolen native land': contesting Olympic narratives and asserting indigenous rights within the discourse of the 2010 Vancouver Games. *Sport in Society*, **13**(1), pp. 143–156.

OCA (Olympic Co-ordination Authority) (1998) *State of Play '98 Update: A Report to the People of New South Wales*. Sydney: Olympic Co-ordination Authority.

O'Connor, A. (2008) Disabled groups outraged by Beijing snub. Available at: http://www. timesonline.co.uk/tol/sport/olympics/article4009610.ece.

O'Connor, A. (2009) Vancouver struggling to cover cost of Winter Olympics. *The Times*, 12 February 2009.

ODA (2015) *Report and Accounts presented to Parliament pursuant to articles 4(3) and 5(5) of the Olympic Delivery Authority (Dissolution) Order 2014/3184.* London: ODA.

ODPM (Office of the Deputy Prime Minister) (2004) *The English Indices of Deprivation 2004: Summary (revised).* London: ODPM.

Office for Disability (2009) New Legacy Promise puts Disabled People at the Heart of London 2012. Press release. Available at: http://www.officefordisability.gov.uk/docs/wor/new/0912-paralympics.pdf.

Ogura, K. (2018) Visions on the legacy of the Tokyo 2020 Paralympic Games, in Brittain, I. and Beacom, A. (eds.) *The Palgrave Handbook of Paralympic Studies.* London: Palgrave Macmillan, pp. 579–601.

Oliver, R. (2011) Toronto's Olympic aspirations: a bid for the waterfront. *Urban Geography*, **32**(6), pp. 767–787.

Olson, L.L.K. (1974) Power, Public Policy and the Environment: The Defeat of the 1976 Winter Olympics in Colorado. Unpublished PhD thesis, Department of Political Science, University of Colorado.

Omena de Melo, E. (2010) *Percepções urbanas em jogo: os impactos da Copa do Mundo de 1950 à luz da imprensa carioca.* Rio de Janeiro: Biblioteca Nacional. Available at: https://antigo.bn.gov.br/producao-intelectual/documentos/percepcoes-urbanas-jogo-impactos-copa-mundo-1950.

Omena de Melo, E. (2020) Just because of 20 cents? For a genealogy of the Brazilian 'Demonstrations Cup'. *International Journal of Urban Sustainable Development*, **12**(1), pp. 103–118.

OPLC (Olympic Park Legacy Company) (2010) *A Walk around Queen Elizabeth Olympic Park.* London: OPLC.

Øresundstid (2003) *History and Culture during the Past 1000 Years: The 19th Century.* Available at: http://www.oresundstid.dk/dansk/engelsk/oresundstid/1800/index.htm.

Organisasjonskomiteen (1952) *VI Olympiske Vinterleker Oslo 1952.* Oslo: Organisasjonskomiteen.

Organizing Committee (1928) *The Ninth Olympiad, Amsterdam 1928: Official Report.* Amsterdam: R.H. de Bussig.

Organizing Committee (1937) *The Eleventh Olympiad, Berlin 1936.* Berlin: Amtlicher Bericht.

Organizing Committee (1948) *The Official Report of the Organising Committee for the XIV Olympiad: London 1948.* London: British Olympic Association.

Organizing Committee (1958) *The Official Report of the Olympic Committee for the Games of the XVI Olympiad Melbourne 1956.* Melbourne: W.M. Houston, Government Printer.

Organizing Committee (1966) *The Official Reports of the Olympic Committee for the Games of the XVIII Olympiad.* Tokyo: Olympic Committee.

Organizing Committee (1969) *The Official Report*, 2 vols. Mexico City: Organizing Committee of the Games of the XIX Olympiad, Mexico.

Organizing Committee (1972) *The Official Report of the Olympic Committee for the Games of the XX Olympiad, Munich 1972*, 2 vols. Munich: Pro-Sport Munchen.

Organizing Committee (1976) *Official Report of the Games of the XXI Olympiad.* Ottawa: COJO-76.

Organizing Committee (1980) *Official Report of the Organizing Committee for the Games of the XXII Olympiad.* Moscow: Progress Publishers.

Organizing Committee (2018) *Olympic and Paralympic Games Rio 2016 Legacy.* Rio de Janeiro: OCOG Rio 2016.

Ortloff, G.C. and Ortloff, S.C. (1976) *Lake Placid: The Olympic Years, 1937–1980.* Lake Placid, NY: Macromedia.

Orttung, R.W. and Zhemukhov, S. (2014) The 2014 Sochi Olympic mega-project and Russia's political economy. *East European Politics*, **30**(2), pp. 175–191.

O'Sullivan, M. (2015) Parramatta light rail line via Sydney Olympic Park gets green light. *Sydney Morning Herald.* 8 December. Available at: http://www.smh.com.au/nsw/parra matta-light-rail-line-via-sydney-olympic-park-gets-green-light-20151207-glhxhg.html.

Owen, K.A. (2001) *The Local Impacts of the Sydney 2000 Olympic Games: Processes and Politics of Venue Preparation.* Sydney: Centre for Olympic Studies, University of New South Wales.

Owen, K.A. (2002) The Sydney 2000 Olympics and urban entrepreneurialism: local variations in urban governance. *Australian Geographical Studies,* **40**(3), pp. 323–336.

Owens, M. and Ward, R. (eds.) (2022) *Play the Game: How the Olympics came to East London.* London: Machine Books.

Oxford Economics (2007) *The Value of the London 2012 Olympic and Paralympic Games to UK Tourism.* London: VisitBritain/VisitLondon.

Papageorgiou-Ventas, A. (1994) *Athens: The Ancient Heritage and Historic Townscape in a Modern Metropolis.* Library Report 140. Athens: Archaeological Society at Athens.

Panagiotopoulou, R. (2014) The legacies of the Athens 2004 Olympic Games: a bitter-sweet burden. *Contemporary Social Science,* **9**(2), pp. 173–195.

Panagiotopoulou, R. (2016) The Cultural Olympiad of the Athens 2004 Olympic Games: a tribute to culture, tradition and heritage, in Müller, N., Messing, M. and Schormann, K. (eds.) *Cultural Views of the Olympics.* Kassel: Agon Sportverlag, pp. 133–158.

Papanikolaou, P. (2013) Athens 2004: ten years later the Olympic infrastructure, the Cultural Olympiad and the White elephant syndrome. *Journal of Power, Politics and Governance,* **1**, pp. 1–9.

Parent, M.M., Kristiansen, E., Skille, E.Å. and Hanstad, D.V. (2015) The sustainability of the Youth Olympic Games: Stakeholder networks and institutional perspectives. *International Journal of the History of Sport,* **50**(3), pp. 326–348.

Parienté, R. (1994) Centennial Olympic Congress of unity. *Olympic Review,* **322**, pp. 394–399.

Paris 2024 (2020) *Manifeste de l'expérience athlètes au village des Jeux Olympiques et Para-lympiques.* Paris: Comité d'organisation des Jeux Olympiques et Paralympiques de Paris.

Paris 2024 (2022) The Games finance the Games. Available at: https://www.paris2024.org/fr/financement-des-jeux/.

Paris 2024 (2023*a*) *A Social Charter for Responsible Games.* Available at: https://www.paris 2024.org/en/a-social-charter-for-responsible-games/.

Paris 2024 (2023*b*) Impact and Legacy. Available at: https://www.paris2024.org/en/impact-and-legacy/.

Paris 2024 (2023*c*) Halving the carbon footprint of the Games. Available at: https://www.paris2024.org/en/delivering-carbon-neutral-games/.

Paris, Y. (2020) Costly SoFi Stadium gets a Financial Handout from NFL. *Forbes,* 20 May 20. Available at: https://www.forbes.com/sites/jayparis/2020/05/20/costly-sofi-stadium-gets-a-financial-handout-from-nfl/.

Parismon, T. (2022) Five-minute city: Sydney Olympic Park Masterplan. *Urban Developer,* 1 August. www.theurbandeveloper.com.

Park, K. and Ok, G. (2018) 2018 PyeongChang Paralympic Games and the South Korean political intention, in Brittain, I. and Beacom, A. (eds.) *The Palgrave Handbook of Para-lympic Studies.* London: Palgrave Macmillan, pp. 555–577.

Park, S.-J. (1991) *The Seoul Olympics, the Inside Story.* London: Bellew Publishing.

Parry, J. (2012) The Youth Olympic Games: some ethical issues. *Sport, Ethics and Philosophy,* **6**(2), pp. 138–154.

Patel, A., Bosela, P.A. and Delatte, N.J. (2013) 1976 Montreal Olympics: case study of project management failure. *Journal of Performance of Constructed Facilities,* **27**, pp. 362–369.

Pavoni, A. (2015) Resistant legacies. *Annals of Leisure Research,* **18**(4), pp. 470–490.

Payne, M. (2006) *Olympic Turnaround: How the Olympic Games stepped back from the Brink of Extinction to become the World's Best Known Brand.* Westport, CT: Greenwood Press.

Payne, M. (2009) How Rio won the 2016 Olympic Games. *SportsPro,* November. Available at: http://www.michaelr payne.com/how_rio_won.html.

Payne, M. (2014) Ex-diretor diz que problema no Rio faz COI 'enfrentar pior crise em 30 anos'. Interview by P.R. Conde. *Folha de São Paulo*. Available at: http://olimpicos.blogfolha.uol.com.br/2014/05/09/ex-diretor-diz-que-problema-no-rio-faz-coi-enfrentar-pior-crise-em-30-anos/.

Peek, L. (2004) How I strolled into the heart of the Games. *The Times*, 14 May, p. 4.

Pelloux, P., Mariotte, C., Pépion, L., Vauléon, Y.-F. and Noury, A. (2017) *Étude: Les jeux olympiques et paralympiques de 2024, un levier pour la construction du Grand Paris*. Contributions de l'Atelier parisien d'urbanisme. Paris: Apur.

Peñalosa, E. (2013) Buses: not sexy but the only solution, in LSE Cities (ed.) *City Transformations*. Urban Age Conference, Rio de Janeiro. London: London School of Economics and Political Science, pp. 19–20. Available at: http://eprints.lse.ac.uk/60034/1/CityTransformationsConferenceNewspaper_2013.pdf.

Peng, J. and Yu, Y. (2008) Beijing Olympics Security Plan. Paper presented at Security and Surveillance at Mega Sport Events: from Beijing 2008 to London 2012 Conference, Durham University.

Pepper, D.M. (1996) *Modern Environmentalism: An Introduction*. London: Routledge.

Pereira, R.H. (2018) Transport legacy of mega-events and the redistribution of accessibility to urban destinations. *Cities*, **81**, pp. 45–60.

Perrottet, T. (2004) *The Naked Olympics: The True Story of the Olympic Games*. New York: Random House.

Perry, K-M.E. and Kang, H.H. (2012) When symbols clash: legitimacy, legality and the 2010 Winter Olympics. *Mass Communication and Society*, **15**(4), pp. 578–597.

Persson, C. (2000) The Olympic Host Selection Process. Unpublished PhD thesis, Luleå University of Technology.

Petrakos, G. and Economou, D. (1999) Internationalisation and structural changes in the European urban system, in Economou, D. and Petrakos, G. (eds.) *The Development of Greek Cities*. Athens: Gutenberg and University of Thessaly Publications.

Petrova, Y. (2014) Posle olimpiady chislo turistov v sochi vyrastet na 30%, no gostinitsy ne budut zapolneny [After the Olympics the number of tourists will grow by 30%, but the hotels won't be full]. *Vedomosti*, 24 February.

Pham, K. (2020) Beyond borders: steering metropolitan growth priorities through spatial imaginaries, *Australian Planner*, **56**(2), pp. 103–113.

Phillips, B. (2007) *The 1948 Olympics: how London rescued the Games*. Cheltenham: SportsBooks Limited.

Phillips, E. (2015) *The Olympic Century*. vol. 7. *VII Olympiad: Antwerp 1920, Chamonix 1924*. Leamington Spa: Warwick Press.

Pinson, G. (2002) Political government and governance: strategic planning and the reshaping of political capacity in Turin. *International Journal of Urban and Regional Research*, **26**(3), pp. 477–493.

Pinto, P.J. and Lopes dos Santos, G. (2022) Olympic waterfronts: an evaluation of wasted opportunities and lasting legacies. *Sustainability*, **14**(4), 1968.

Pishue, B. (2021) *2021 INRIX Global Traffic Scorecard*. Kirkland WA: INRIX. Available at: https://inrix.com/scorecard/.

Pitts, A. and Liao, H. (2009) *Sustainable Olympic Design and Urban Development*. London: Routledge.

Play the Game (2006) Greenpeace try to stop Olympic constructions at Sochi. Available at: https://www.playthegame.org/news/greenpeace-tries-to-stop-olympic-constructions-in-sochi/.

PMSU (Prime Minister's Strategy Unit) (2005) *Improving the Life Chances of Disabled People. Final Report*. Joint report with Department of work and Pensions; Department of Health; Department for Education and Skills; Office of the Deputy Prime Minister. London: PMSU.

Poast, P.D. (2007) Winning the bid: analyzing the International Olympic Committee's host city selections. *International Interactions*, **33**, pp. 75–95.

Pollalis, S., Kyriakopoulos, V., Papagianni, A., Papapetrou, N., Sagia, V. and Tritaki N. (2013) *The Urban Development of the Former Athens Airport.* Paper presented to AESOP-ACSP Joint Congress, 15–19 July, Dublin.

Polley, M. (2011) *The British Olympics: Britain's Olympic Heritage 1612–2012.* London: English Heritage.

POOC (PyeongChang Olympic Organizing Committee) (2019) *Official Report of the PyeongChang 2018, Olympic and Paralympic Winter Games*, Volume I. PyeongChang: POOC.

Porro, N. (2010) Il cemento e la ricotta. La capitale tra sviluppo e speculazione. *Lancillotto e Nausica*, **27**(1/2), pp. 16–23.

Porro, N., Martelli, S. and Russo, G. (2016) *Il mondiale delle meraviglie. Calcio, media e società.* Milan: Franco Angeli.

Poulios, P.C. (2006) The 2004 Athens Olympics: a cost-benefit analysis. *Entertainment and Sports Lawyer*, **24**(1), pp. 1, 18–31.

Pound, R.W. (2004) *Inside the Olympics: A Behind-the-Scenes look at the Politics, the Scandals, and the Glory of the Games.* Toronto: John Wiley.

Powell, H. and Marrero-Guillamon, I. (eds.) (2012) *The Art of Dissent.* London: Marshgate Press.

Poynter, G. and MacRury, I. (2009) London: preparing for 2012, in Poynter, G. and Macrury, I. (eds.) *Olympic Cities: 2012 and the Remaking of London.* Farnham: Ashgate.

Poynter, G. and Roberts, F. (2009) Atlanta 1996: the Centennial Games, in Poynter, G. and MacRury, I. (eds.) *Olympic Cities: 2012 and the Remaking of London.* Farnham: Ashgate, pp. 121–131.

Poynter, G., Viehoff, V., and Li, Y. (eds.) (2016) *The London Olympics and Urban Development: The Mega-Event City.* London: Routledge.

PPC (Public Properties Company SA) (2015) In a nutshell. Available at: http://www.etasa.gr/versions/eng/page.aspx.

Preuss, H. (2000) Electing to Olympic host city a multidimensional decision, in Wamsley, K.B., Martyn, S.G., Macdonald, G.H. and Barney, R.K. (eds.) *Bridging Three Centuries: Intellectual Crossroads and the Modern Olympic Movement.* Fifth International Symposium for Olympic Research, London, Ontario, International Centre for Olympic Studies, University of Western Ontario, pp. 89–104.

Preuss, H. (2004) *The Economics of Staging the Olympics: A Comparison of the Games, 1972–2008.* Cheltenham: Edward Elgar.

Preuss, H. (2005) The economic impact of visitors at major multi-sport events. *European Sport Management Quarterly*, **5**(3), pp. 283–305.

Preuss, H. (2007) The conceptualisation and measurement of mega sport event legacies. *Journal of Sport and Tourism*, **12**(3/4), pp. 207–-228.

Preuss, H. (2009) Opportunity costs and efficiency of investments in mega sports events. *Journal of Policy Research in Tourism, Leisure and Events*, **1**(2), pp. 131–140.

Preuss, H. (2011) *Kosten und Nutzen Olympischer Winterspiele in Deutschland, Eine Analyse von München 2018.* Wiesbaden: Gabler Verlag.

Preuss, H. (2015) A framework for identifying the legacies of a mega sport event. *Leisure Studies*, **34**(6), pp. 643–664.

Preuss, H. (2021) Financing the Olympic Movement and the Olympic Games, in Gangas, D. and Georgiadis, K. (eds.) *Looking Towards the Future with Hope.* Athens: International Olympic Academy, pp. 216–230.

Preuss, H. and Alfs, C. (2011) Signalling through the 2008 Beijing Olympics: using mega sport events to change the perception and image of the host. *European Sport Management Quarterly*, **11**(1), pp. 55–71.

Preuss, H. and Solberg, H.A. (2006) Attracting major sporting events: the role of local residents. *European Sport Management Quarterly*, **6**(4), pp. 391–411.

Preuss, H., Andreff, W., Weitzmann, M. (2019) *Cost and Revenue Overruns of the Olympic Games 2000–2018.* Wiesbaden: Gabler Springer.

Preuss, H., Scheu, A. and Weitzmann, M. (2020) Referendums at Olympic Games, in Chatziefstathiou, D., García, B. and Benoit, S. (eds.) *Routledge Handbook of the Olympic and Paralympic Games*. London: Routledge, pp. 183–200.

Preuss, H., Schallhorn, C., Schütte, N. (2022) *Olympic Sport Organisations in Times of Crisis and Change: Guide for Strategic Management and Good Governance*. Baden-Baden: Academia. Available at: https://www.nomos-elibrary.de/10.5771/9783985720644/olym pic-sport-organisations-in-times-of-crisis-and-change?l=en.

Price Waterhouse (1994) *Britain's Millennium Festival Project at Greenwich*. London: Price Waterhouse.

Promyslov, V. (1980) *Moscow: Past and Present*. Moscow: Progress Publishers.

Puls, S.L., Sonda, R., de la Rosa, M., Urbina, A.O. and Post, N.T. (2013) Analysis of the room supply in the hotel zone of Cancun, Mexico: EMU 9. *Journal of Tourism Research and Hospitality*, **2**, pp. 1–8.

Putin, V. (2007) Speech at the 119th International Olympic Committee Session, Guatemala 4 July. Available at: http://archive.kremlin.ru/eng/text/speeches/2007/07/04/2103_ type82912 type84779type127286_136956.shtml.

PyeongChang2018 (2016) *Actualising the Dream Project* (ADP). Available at: http://www. pyeongchang2018.com/horizon/eng/Paralympic_Games/ADP.asp.

Pyrgiotis, Y.N. (2001) The Games in the XXIst century, in IOC (ed.) *Olympic Games and Architecture. The Future for Host Cities*. Lausanne: IOC, pp. 25–29.

Pyrgiotis, Y.N. (2003) Athens 2004: planning and organising Olympic legacy, in De Moragas, M., Kennett, C. and Puig, N. (eds.) *The Legacy of the Olympic Games, 1984–2000*. Lausanne: IOC, pp. 414–418.

QDES (Queensland Department of Environment and Science) (2022) *Brisbane 2032 Climate Positive Games*. 26 July. Available at: https://www.des.qld.gov.au/climateaction/climate-positive-games.

QDES (2023) *Queensland's 2020 Greenhouse Gas Emissions and Targets*. Available at: https:// www.des.qld.gov.au/climateaction/emissions-targets.

Queensland Government (2019) *2032 Olympic and Paralympic Games Value Proposition Assessment: Executive Summary*. Brisbane: The Department of the Premier and Cabinet. Available at: https://www.premiers.qld.gov.au/publications/categories/reports/assets/ 2032-olympic-paralympic-games-vpa.pdf.

Queensland Government (2022*a*) *Brisbane 2032 Olympic and Paralympic Games*. Available at: https://www.qld.gov.au/about/Brisbane2032.

Queensland Government (2022*b*) *70% Renewables Target by 2032 announced in Landmark Energy Plan*. Available at: https://www.qld.gov.au/about/newsroom/queensland-energy-and-jobs-plan.

Raco, M. (2014) Delivering flagship projects in an era of regulatory capitalism: state led privatization and the London Olympics 2012. *International Journal of Urban and Regional Research*, **38**(1), pp. 176–197.

Raco, M. and Tunney, E. (2010) Visibilities and invisibilities in urban development: small business communities and the London Olympics 2012. *Urban Studies*, **47**(10), pp. 2069–2091.

Radio Free Asia (2008) China's empty protest zones. 18 August. Available at: https://www. refworld.org/docid/48b2a685c.html.

RBC (Rio 2016 Bid Committee) (2009*a*) *Candidature File for Rio de Janeiro to Host the 2016 Olympic and Paralympic Games*. 3 Vols. Rio de Janeiro: Rio 2016 Bid Committee.

RBC (2009*b*) OCOG and Non-OCOG Budget. *Documentos Candidatura Rio 2016*. https:// i3gov. Available at: planejamento.gov.br/balanco/2%2020CIDADANIA%20E%20INCLU SAO%20SOCIAL/7%20%20Esporte/1%20-%20Documentos/Candidatura%20Rio2016/ BGF%20-%20Candidatura%20Rio2016%20%20Dossi%ea %20de%20Candidatura/.

Rebgetz, L. and Ford, E. (2015) South-east Queensland mayors make move to bid for 2028 Olympics in Brisbane. *ABC News*, 6 March. Available at: https://www.abc.net.au/news/ 2015-03-06/mayors-move-to-bid-for-2028-olympics-in-brisbane/6287090.

Redmond, G. (1988) Toward modern revival of the Olympic Games: the various pseudo-

Olympics of the nineteenth century, in Seagrave, J.O. and Chu, D. (eds.) *The Olympic Games in Transition*. Champaign, IL: Human Kinetics, pp. 7–21.

Reef, P. (2021) NOlympics in Amsterdam! The struggle for urban space and the politics of Amsterdam's Olympic bid, 1984–1986. *Tijdschrift voor Geschiedenis*, **133**, pp. 659–686.

Reeve, S. (2001) *One Day in September: The Full Story of the 1972 Munich Olympic Massacre and Israeli Revenge Operation 'Wrath of God'*. New York: Arcade.

Regueira, C. (2021*a*) Legado Olímpico: arenas esportivas não deram lugar a escolas e têm aspecto de abandono. *G1*, 23 July. Available at: https://g1.globo.com/rj/rio-de-janeiro/noticia/2021/07/23/legado-olimpico-arenas-esportivas-nao-deram-lugar-a-escolas-e-tem-aspecto-de-abandono.ghtml.

Regueira, C. (2021*b*) Legado olímpico: moradores retirados da Vila Autódromo relatam problemas nas condições de condomínios. *G1*, 7 July. Available at: https://g1.globo.com/rj/rio-de-janeiro/noticia/2021/07/21/legado-olimpico-moradores-retirados-da-vila-autodromo-relatam-problemas-nas-condicoes-de-condominios.ghtml.

Reich, K. (1985) 12 Minority firms seeking $17 million: arbitration talks due in LAOOC suit. *Los Angeles Times*, 24 January. Available at: https://www.latimes.com/archives/la-xpm-1985-01-24-fi-11436-story.html.

Reich, K. (1986) *Making It Happen, Peter Ueberroth and the 1984 Olympics*. Santa Barbara, CA: Capra Press.

Reid, H. (2017) Athletes as heroes and role models: an ancient model. *Sport, Ethics and Philosophy*, **11**, pp. 40–51.

Renson, R. (1996) Antwerp 1920: the Games of the 7th Olympiad, in Findling, J.E. and Pelle, K.D. (eds.) *Historical Dictionary of the Modern Olympic Movement*. Westport, CN: Greenwood Press, pp. 54–60.

Renson, R. (2004) The cool games: the Winter Olympics 1924–2002, in Renson, R. and Gerlach, L.R. (eds.) *The Winter Olympics: from Chamonix to Salt Lake City*. Salt Lake City, UT: University of Utah Press, pp. 41–86.

Renson, R. and Den Hollander, M. (1997) Sport and business in the city: the Antwerp Olympic Games of 1920 and the urban elite. *Olympika*, **6**, pp. 73–84.

Repubblica (2012) Monti non firma garanzia: addio Olimpiadi Roma 2020. *Repubblica*, February. Available at: https://www.repubblica.it/sport/vari/2012/02/14/news/monti_olimpiadi_incontro-29856086/.

Reuters (2022) Beijing Games to bring in more spectators as COVID-19 under control. Available at: https://www.reuters.com/lifestyle/sports/beijing-2022-olympics-reports-6-new-covid-cases-among-games-personnel-2022-02-08/.

Rich, M., Futterman, M. and Panja, T. (2020) I.O.C. and Japan agree to postpone Tokyo Olympics. *New York Times*, 24 March. Available at: https://www.nytimes.com/2020/03/24/sports/olympics/coronavirus-summer-olympics-postponed.html.

Richard, R., Marcellini, A., Pappous, A., Joncheray, H. and Ferez, S. (2020) Construire et assurer l'héritage des Jeux olympiques et paralympiques. Pour une inclusion sportive durable des personnes vivant des situations de handicap. *Movement and Sport Sciences*, No. 107, pp. 41–52.

Richter, S., Singler, A. and Mladenova, D. (eds.) (2020) *NOlympics: Tokyo 2020/1 in der Kritik*. Leipziger Ostasien-Studien 20. Leipzig: Leipzig University Press.

Riga, R. (2021) Gabba earmarked to be 'home' of 2032 Olympic Games if Brisbane bid successful. *ABC News*. 20 April. Available at: https://www.abc.net.au/news/2021-04-20/gabba-stadium-brisbane-2032-olympics/100080058.

Riley, D. (2005) Written Statement to the US Senate Subcommittee on Trade, Tourism and Economic Development. *Field Hearing on The Economic Impact of the 2010 Vancouver, Canada, Winter Olympics on Oregon and the Pacific Northwest*. Washington, DC: US Government Printing Office.

Rio 2016 Bid Committee (2009) *Candidature File for Rio de Janeiro to Host the 2016 Olympics and Paralympics*, 3 Vols. Rio de Janeiro: Rio 2016 Bid Committee.

Ritchard, K. (2004) The hotel industry is pinning its hope on gold at Beijing in 2008: but is it a sure winner? *Hotel Asia Pacific*, December.

Roaf, V., van Deventer, K. and Houston, C. (1996) *The Olympics and Development: Lessons and Suggestions.* Observatory, South Africa: Development Action Group.

Roberts, P. (2000) The evolution, definition and purpose of urban regeneration, in Roberts, P. and Sykes, H. (eds.) *Urban Regeneration: A Handbook.* London: Sage, pp. 9–36.

Roche, M. (2000) *Mega-Events and Modernity: Olympics and Expos in the Growth of Global Culture.* London: Routledge.

ROCOG (Rio di Janeiro Organising Committee for the Olympic Games) (2009) *Candidature File for Rio de Janeiro to host the 2016 Olympic and Paralympic Games,* 3 vols. Rio di Janeiro: ROCOG.

Roderick, K. (1984) Horse patrols ride herd on transients. *Los Angeles Times*, 21 July. Available at: https://www.newspapers.com/clip/45695636/the-los-angeles-times/.

Rodrigues, J.M. (2015) Condições de mobilidade urbana e organização social do território. In Ribeiro, L.C.Q. (ed.) *Rio de Janeiro: Transformações na ordem urbana.* Rio de Janeiro: Letra Capital, pp. 287–319.

Rogan, M. and Rogan, M. (2010) *Britain and the Olympic Games: Past, Present, Legacy.* London: Matador.

Rognoni, G. (1996) The ideas and creativity of the Barcelona '92 Paralympic Ceremonies, in Moragas, M. de, MacAloon, J.J. and Llinos, M. (eds.) *Olympic Ceremonies: Historical Continuity and Cultural Exchange.* Lausanne: IOC, pp. 263–268.

Romanos, A., Vellissaraton, J. and Liveris, K. (2005) Re-shaping Urban Environment through Major Events: The Athens Olympic Games. Paper presented to the 41st ISOCARP Congress 2005. Available at: http://www.isocarp.net/Data/case_studies/665.pdf.

Rosso, E. (2004) Torino: Policies and Actions at a Metropolitan Level. Paper presented at the La Gouvernance Metropolitaine Conference, Montreal, 7–8 October.

Rothan, H.A. and Byrareddy, S.N. (2020) The epidemiology and pathogenesis of coronavirus disease (COVID-19) outbreak. *Journal of Autoimmunity*, **109**, 102433.

Rowe, D. (2021) The Brisbane Olympics are a leap into an unknowable future. *The Conversation*, 23 July. Available at: https://theconversation.com/the-brisbane-olympics-are-a-leap-into-an-unknowable-future-164933.

Rowe, P.G. (2006) *Building Barcelona: A Second Renaixenca.* Barcelona: Actar.

Rumsby, B. (2016) Paralympics in crisis after Rio runs out of money for Games. *The Telegraph*, 19 August. http://www.telegraph.co.uk/olympics/2016/08/19/paralympics-in-crisis-after-rio-runs-out-of-money-for-games/.

Rustin, M. (2009) Sport, spectacle and society: understanding the Olympics, in Poynter, G. and MacRury, I. (eds.) *Olympic Cities: 2012 and the Remaking of London.* Farnham: Ashgate, pp. 3–21.

Ryan, M. (2009) *For the Glory: Two Olympics, Two Wars, Two Heroes.* London: JR Books.

Ryzhkov, V. (2014) Controlling Russians through travel bans. *The Moscow Times*, 26 May.

Saccage 2024 (2020) No to Rampage 2024! Available at: https://saccage2024.noblogs.org.

Sainsbury, T. (2017) Olympic villages, in Gold, J.R. and Gold, M.M. (eds.) *Olympic Cities: City Agendas, Planning and the World Games, 1896–2020,* 3rd ed. London: Routledge, pp. 180–202.

Sales, E. (ed.) (2005) *Time Out: Athens,* 2nd ed. London: Ebury.

Samaranch, J.A. (1992) Message from the IOC President, in IOC (eds.) *Olympic Solidarity itinerant School: Marketing Manual.* Lausanne: IOC.

Samatas, M. (2004) *Surveillance in Greece: From Anticommunist to Consumer Surveillance.* New York: Pella Publishing.

Samatas, M. (2007) Security and surveillance in the Athens 2004 Olympics: some lessons from a troubled story. *International Criminal Justice Review*, **17**(3), pp. 220–238.

Sanahuja, R. (2002) Olympic City – The City Strategy 10 Years after the Olympic Games in 1992. Paper to the *International Conference on Sports Events and Economic Impact*, Copenhagen, Denmark, April.

Sanan, G. (1996) Olympic security operations 1972–94, in Thompson, A. (ed.) *Terrorism and the 2000 Olympics*. Sydney: Australian Defence Force Academy, pp. 33–42.

Sanchez, R.L.O. and Essex, S. (2018) The challenge of urban design in securing post-event legacies of Olympic Parks. *Journal of Urban Design*, **23**(2), pp. 278–297.

Sanchez, R.L.O., Koch, F. and Medrano, L. (2022) Olympic villages as heterotopias: contradictions between megaevents and quotidian urban life. *Housing, Theory and Society*, **39**(4), pp. 420–441.

Sanders, B.A. (2013) *The Los Angeles 1984 Olympic Games*. Charleston, SC: Arcadia Publishing.

Sandomir, R. (1999) Olympics: Inquiry cites Olympic 'culture' of impropriety. *The New York Times*, 2 March.

Saulwick, J. (2018) After three years, still no master plan for Sydney Olympic Park. *Sydney Morning Herald*, 21 May.

Savarese, M. (2019) Jailed former governor says he bought votes for Rio Olympics. *Associated Press*, 4 July. Available at: https://apnews.com/article/d22866041e754e638ed0863a6ff275c4.

Sbetti, N. (2012) *Giochi di potere: Olimpiadi e politica da Atene a Londra*. Florence: Le Monnier.

Schaap, J. (2008) *Triumph: The Untold story of Jesse Owens and Hitler's Olympics*. Bel Air, CA: Mariner Books.

Scharr, K., Steinicke, E. and Borsdorf, A. (2011) Sochi 2014: Olympic Winter Games between high mountains and seaside. *Revue de Géographie Alpine*, **100**, pp. 1–35.

Scharroo, P. (1928) The Olympic Stadium, in Feith, J.J., Hoven, J. and Linden, W.J.M. (eds.) *Officieel Feestnummer Olympische Spelen te Amsterdam 1928*. Amsterdam: Internationaal Federatie van Sportbonden, pp. 24–29.

Scherer, J. (2011) Olympic villages and large-scale urban development: crises of capitalism, deficits of democracy? *Sociology*, **45**, pp. 782–797.

Scheu, A., Preuss, H. and Könecke, T. (2021) The legacy of the Olympic Games: a review. *Journal of Global Sport Management*, **6**(3), pp. 212–233.

Schnitzer, M. and Haizinger, L. (2019) Does the Olympic Agenda 2020 have the power to create a new Olympic heritage? An analysis for the 2026 Winter Olympic Games bid. *Sustainability*, **11**, 442.

Scott, D., Steiger, R., Rutty, M. and Johnson, P. (2015) The future of the Olympic Winter Games in an era of climate change. *Current Issues in Tourism*, **18**(10), pp. 913–930.

Scott, D., Knowles, N.L.B., Ma, S., Rutty, M. and Steiger, R. (2023) Climate change and the future of the Olympic Winter Games: athlete and coach perspectives. *Current Issues in Tourism*, **26**(3), pp. 480–495.

Scott, M. (2010) *Delphi and Olympia: The Spatial Politics of Panhellenism in the Archaic and Classical Periods*. Cambridge: Cambridge University Press.

Scruton, J. (1998) *Stoke Mandeville: Road to the Paralympics: Fifty Years of History*. Aylesbury: Peterhouse.

Searle, G. (2002) Uncertain legacy: Sydney's Olympic stadiums. *European Planning Studies*, **10**, pp. 845–860.

Searle, G. (2012) The long-term urban impacts of the Sydney Olympic Games. *Australian Planner*, **49**(3), pp. 195–202.

SEC (Sport and Environment Commission) (1996) *Report of the Chairperson of the Sport and Environment Commission*. 105th session of the IOC, Atlanta 15–18 July, Annex 16, pp. 164–168.

Seefried, E. (2015) Rethinking progress. On the origins of the modern sustainability discourse 1970–2000. *Journal of Modern European History*, **13**(3), pp. 377–399.

Segrave, J.O. (2005) Pietro Metastasio's L'Olimpiade and the survival of the Olympic idea in eighteenth century Europe. *Olimpika*, **14**, pp. 1–28.

Séguillon, D. (2002) The origins and consequences of the first World Games for the Deaf: Paris, 1924. *International Journal of the History of Sport*, **19**, pp. 119–136.

Seine Saint Denis, Le Département (2021) Olympiade Culturelle. Available at: https://seinesaintdenis.fr/olympiade-culturelle.

Senn, A.E. (1999) *Power, Politics and the Olympic Games*. Champaign, IL: Human Kinetics.

Setzekorn, E. (2008) An Olympic evaluation. The China Beat (blog), 3 September. Available at: http://thechinabeat.blogspot.com/2008/09/olympic-evaluation.html.

Sheil, P. (1998) *Olympic Babylon*. Sydney: Pan Macmillan.

Shen, J. (2002) A study of the temporary population in Chinese cities. *Habitat International*, **26**, pp. 363–377.

Shibata, S. and Ito, Y. (2021) Tokyo official: no way we can assess economic impact of Games. *Asahi Shimbun*, 21 September. Available at: https://www.asahi.com/ajw/articles/1444480.

Shipway, R. (2007) Sustainable legacies for the 2012 Olympic Games. *Journal of the Royal Society for the Promotion of Health*, **127**, pp. 119–124.

Short, J.R. (2008) Globalization, cities and the Summer Olympics. *City*, **12**(3), pp. 321–340.

Short, J.R. (2018) *Hosting the Olympic Games: The Real Costs for Cities*. London: Routledge.

Siebel, W. (1994) *Was macht eine Stadt urban? Zur Stadtkultur und Stadtentwicklung*. Oldenburg: Universitätsreden 61, University of Olderburg.

Siegel, B. (2019, 2020) *Dreamers and Schemers: How an Improbable Bid for the 1932 Olympics Transformed Los Angeles from Dusty Outpost to Global Metropolis*. Berkeley, CA: University of California Press.

Silvestre, G. (2012) *An Olympic City in the Making: Rio de Janeiro Mega-Event Strategy 1993– 2016*. Lausanne: Olympic Studies Centre, International Olympic Committee.

Silvestre, G. (2017) O não legado e os Jogos que não foram. A primeira candidatura olímpica do Rio de Janeiro e o imaginário de legado urbano para a cidade. *Arquitextos*, 200.00.

Silvestre, G. (2020) Juegos Olímpicos y modelos urbanos: la influencia de Barcelona en la estrategia de megaeventos en Río de Janeiro (1995–2016). *Iberoamericana: América Latina-España-Portugal*, **20**(74), pp. 125–147.

Silvestre, G. (2022) Replicated or homegrown planning model? The mutual constitution of ideas, interests and institutions in the delivery of a megaproject in Rio de Janeiro. *International Planning Studies*, **27**(2), pp. 107–119.

Silvestre, G. and Oliveira, N.G. (2012) The revanchist logic of mega-events: community displacement in Rio de Janeiro's West End. *Visual Studies*, **27**(2), pp. 204–210.

Simson, V. and Jennings, A. (1992) *The Lord of the Rings: Power, Money and Drugs in the Modern Olympics*. Toronto: Stoddart.

SLOC (Salt Lake Organising Committee) (2002) *Official Report of the XIX Olympic Winter Games*, Salt Lake City: Salt Lake Organising Committee.

Smith, A. (2012) *Events and Urban Regeneration. The Strategic Use of Events to Revitalise Cities*. London: Routledge.

Smith, A. (2014) 'De-risking' East London: Olympic regeneration planning 2000–2012. *European Planning Studies*, **22**(9), pp. 1919–1939.

Smith, A. and Mair, J. (2018) *The Making of a City: How Expo 88 changed Brisbane Forever*. Bureau International des Expositions. Available at: https://www.bie-paris.org/site/en/blog/entry/the-making-of-a-city-how-expo-88-changed-brisbane-forever.

Smith, D. (2021) L.A. City Council approves agreement with 2028 Olympics organizers. *Los Angeles Times*, 4 December. Available at: https://www.latimes.com/california/story/2021-12-03/city-council-votes-to-back-olympic-games-agreement-with-la-2028.

Smith, H. (2003) Athens prays to Zorba to rescue its 'shambolic' Olympic Games. *The Observer*, 13 July.

Smith, H. (2004) Athens shows doubters it will hit games deadline. *The Guardian Online*. Available at: http://sport.guardian.co.uk/olympics/story/0,1278221,00.html.

Smith, W. (2008) London shows Brisbane a `smaller is better' way. *The Australian*, 6 August.

Smyth, H. (1994) *Marketing the City: The Role of Flagship Development in Urban Regeneration*. London: E and FN Spon.

Snaith, B. (2014) Olympic Park demonstrates ethnic preferences for landscape. *Landscape Institute*, 7 May. Available at: https://www.landscapeinstitute.org/blog/ethnic-preferences-in-olympic-park/.

SNF (Stavros Niarchos Foundation) (2023*a*) Identity since 1996. Available at: https://www.snf.org/en/about/identity/since-1996/.

SNF (2023*b*) SNF renews its support for the Stavros Niarchos Foundation Cultural Centre. 14 March. Available at: https://www.snf.org/en/news-stories/news/announcements/snf-renews-its-support-for-the-stavros-niarchos-foundation-cultural-center-snfcc-with-a-new-3-year-grant-of-up-to-30-million/.

Snyder, C.R., Lassegard, M.A. and Ford, C.E. (1986) Distancing after group success and failure basking in glory and cutting off shows no signs shows no signs failure. *Journal of Personality and Social Psychology*, **51**(2), pp. 382–388.

SOC (Stockholm Organizing Committee) (1913) *The Fifth Olympiad; The Official Report of the Olympic Games of Stockholm, 1912: Issued by the Swedish Olympic Committee* (ed. E. Bergvall and trans. E. Adams-Ray). Stockholm: Wahlstrom and Widstrand.

SOCOG (Sydney Organizing Committee for the Olympic Games) (2000) *Official Report of the XXVII Olympiad*. Available at: http://www.gamesinfo.com.au/postgames.

Solinger, D.J. (1995) The floating population in the cities: chances for assimilation? in Davis, D.S. Kraus, R. Naughton, B. and Perry, E.J. (eds.) *Urban Spaces in Contemporary China: The Potential for Autonomy and Community in Post-Mao China*. Cambridge: Cambridge University Press, pp. 113–139.

Söderlund, J., Sankaran, S. and Biesenthal, C. (2017) The past and present of megaprojects. *Project Management Journal*, **48**(6), pp. 5–16.

Sonne, W. (2003) *Representing the State: Capital City Planning in the Early Twentieth Century*. Munich: Prestel.

SOOC (Sochi Olympic Organising Committee) (2009) Games 2014 will double Sochi power supply. Available at: http://sochi2014.com/87868.

SOOC (2014) *Barrier-Free Environment at the Sochi 2014 Olympic and Paralympic Games*. Sochi: Sochi 2014 Organizing Committee.

SOPA (Sydney Olympic Park Authority) (2014) *Master Plan 2030*, revised version. Available at: http://www.sopa.nsw.gov.au/planning_and_development/master_plan_2030.

SOPA (2018) *Sydney Olympic Master Plan 2030* (2018 Review). Sydney: Sydney Olympic Park Authority.

SOPA (2022*a*) *Sydney Olympic Park 2050*. Draft Place Vision and Strategy, Wangal Country. Sydney: Sydney Olympic Park Authority.

SOPA (2022*b*) *Sydney Olympic Park 2050: Vision and Strategy*. Summary. Sydney: Sydney Olympic Park Authority.

Souza, B. (2014) Quando o Rio de Janeiro terá trens decentes? *Exame*. Available at: http://exame.abril. com.br/brasil/noticias/quando-o-rio-de-janeiro-tera-trens-decentes.

Spearritt, P. (2009) The 200 km city: Brisbane, the Gold Coast, and Sunshine Coast. *Australian Economic History Review*, **49**(1), pp. 87–106.

Special Correspondent (1948) Games for paralysed archery tournament at Ministry Hospital. *The Times*, 30 July, p. 7.

Special Correspondent (2004) Olympia shot put aims to revive stadium of ancient Games. *Financial Times*, 18 August.

Special Correspondent (2008) China hushes up Olympic deaths. *The Times*, 20 January. Available at: https://www.thetimes.co.uk/article/china-hushes-up-olympic-deaths-nz5wq ndvr0j.

Spencer, R. (2008) Beijing Olympic 2008 opening ceremony giant firework footprints 'faked'. Available at: http://www.telegraph.co.uk/sport/othersports/olympics/2534499/Beijing-Olympic-2008-opening-ceremony-giant-firework-footprints-faked.html.

Spilling, O. (1998) Beyond intermezzo? On the long-term industrial impacts of mega-events: the case of Lillehammer 1994. *Festival Management and Event Tourism*, **5**, pp. 101–122.

Sport England (2016) *The National Picture: Ethnicity and Disability*. Available at: http://www.sportengland.org/research/who-plays-sport/national-picture/.

Stanhope, J.S. (1824) *Olympia: Or Topography Illustrative of the Actual State of the Plain of Olympia, and of the Ruins of the City of Elis*. London.

Stanton, R. (2000) *The Forgotten Olympic Art Competitions: The Story of the Olympic Art Competitions of the Twentieth Century*. Victoria, BC: Trafford.

State of California (2021) *California Budget, May Revision 2021–2022*. Available at: https://www.ebudget.ca.gov/2021-22/pdf/Revised/BudgetSummary/FullBudgetSummary.pdf.

Sterken, E. (2007) Growth impact of major sporting events, in Preuss, H. (ed.) *The Impact and Evaluation of Major Sporting Events*. London: Routledge, pp. 63–78.

Stockbridge Capital Group (2022) Hollywood Park. Stockbridge Capital Group, LLC. Available at: https://stockbridge.com/property/hollywood-park/.

Stone, C.M. (1989) *Regime Politics: Governing Atlanta 1946–1988*. Lawrence, KS: University of Kansas Press.

Strangio, D. (2013) Mega events and their importance. Some frameworks for the city of Rome. *Città e Storia*, **8**(1), pp. 229–242.

Strickland, P. (2015) Anger in Greek refugee camp after Idomeni eviction. *Aljazeera*, 12 December. Available at: http://www.aljazeera.com/news/2015/12/anger-greek-refugee-camp-idomeni-eviction-151211143308010.html.

Stump, A.J. (1988) The Games that almost weren't, in Seagrove, J.O. and Chu, D. (eds.) *The Olympic Games in Transition*. Champaign, IL: Human Kinetics, pp. 191–199.

Sudjic, D. (2006) Where are the Olympic building plans heading? *The Observer*, 28 May.

Swart, K. and Bob, U. (2004) The seductive discourse of development: the Cape Town 2004 Olympic bid. *Third World Quarterly*, **25**, pp.1311–1324.

Swyngedouw, E., Moulaert, F. and Rodriguez, A. (2002) Neoliberal urbanization in Europe: large-scale urban development projects and the new urban policy. *Antipode*, **34**(3), pp. 542–577.

Sygall, D. (2021) Paralympics Australia aims for 2032 Brisbane games to deliver societal change. *Australasian Leisure Management*, **145**, pp. 32–33.

Sykianaki, C. (2003) Case Study: Athens and Olympic Games 2004. Paper given at symposium on 'The Legacies from Major Events', Turin, 25–26 March. Available at: http://www.eurometrex.org/Docs/Expert_Groups/Major_Events/Torino_Report_2003.pdf.

Sykianaki, C. and Psihogias, S. (2006) Athens Case Study. Paper given to symposium on 'Planning for Major Events', Turin, 24–25 March. Glasgow: METREX. http://www.eurometrex.org, accessed 2 March 2007.

Szymanski, S. (2002) The economic impact of the World Cup. *World Economics*, **3**(1), pp. 1–9.

Tabak, F. (2012) Em campanha, Paes tenta vincular sua imagem às transformações feitas por Pereira Passos. *O Globo*, 9 July. Available at: http://oglobo.globo.com/rio/em-campanha-paes-tenta-vincular-sua-imagem-as-transformacoes-feitas-por-pereira-passos-5433676.

Tagaris, K. (2014) Big dreams and angry protests swirl at abandoned Athens airport. *Reuters*, 26 June. Available at: http://uk.reuters.com/article/2014/06/26/us-greece-airport-idUKKBN0F10YI20140626.

Taillibert, R. with Harmel, F. (2000) *Notre cher Stade Olympique: lettres posthumes à mon ami Drapeau*. Montreal: Stanké.

Taylor, A. (2015) Greece's abandoned Olympic stadiums get a second life: housing refugees. *Washington Post*, 1 October. Available at: https://www.washingtonpost.com/news/worldviews/wp/2015/10/01/greeces-abandoned-olympic-stadiums-get-a-second-life-housing-refugees/.

Taylor, P. and Gratton, C. (1988) The Olympic Games an economic analysis. *Leisure Management*, **8**(3), pp. 32–34.

Te, B. (2009) Beijing Olympics: a new brand of China. *Asian Social Science*, **5**(3), 84–90.

Telesca, G. (2004) Le Olimpiadi di Roma e il miracolo economico. Unpublished MA dissertation. University of Florence.

Telesca, G. (2006) Tra Berruti e l'Immobiliare. Le Olimpiadi del 1960 e la trasformazione urbanistica di Roma. *Passato e Presente*, **67**(1), pp. 43–68.

Telesca, G. (2007) Sport, politica e affari. Le Olimpiadi di Roma del 1960. *Memoria e Ricerca*, **25**(2), pp. 153–169.

Telesca, G. (2014) Dealing with the past and planning the future: the urban renewal of Rome and Barcelona through the Olympic Games. *European Review of History*, **21**(1), pp. 19–36.

Terret, T. (ed.) (2008*a*) *Les Paris des Jeux Olympiques de 1924*, 4 vols. Biarritz: Atlantica.

Terret, T. (2008*b*) The Albertville Winter Olympics: unexpected legacies – failed expectations for regional economic development. *International Journal of the History of Sport*, **25**(14), pp. 1903–1921.

Thalis, P. and Cantrill, P.J. (1994) Reinventing the Australian suburb: the Olympic Village competition. *Polis*, **1**, pp. 44–45.

Tham, A. (2022) Getting a head start: the 2032 Olympic Movement through the preferred candidature bid involving Brisbane, Australia. *Sport in Society*, pp. 1–17.

The Guardian (2012*a*) Olympics welcome does not extend to all in London as police flex muscles, 4 May. Available at: http://www.guardian.co.uk/uk/2012/may/04/olympics-welcome-london-police.

The Guardian (2012*b*) Metropolitan police plastic bullets stockpile up to 10,000 after UK riots, 3 May. http://www.guardian.co.uk/uk/2012/may/03/metropolitan-police-plastic-bullets-stockpile-riots.

Theiss, E. (2019) Metro L.A. Residential Price Evolution 2014–2018: Beverly Hills Remains Most Expensive Market at $3M; Inglewood Leads Growth with 60% Median Gain. *PropertyShark Real Estate Blog* (blog), 8 October. Available at: https://www.propertyshark.com/Real-Estate-Reports/2019/10/08/metro-l-a-residential-price-evolution-2014-2018/.

Thompson, A. (1999) Security, in Cashman, R. and Hughes, A. (eds.) *Staging the Olympics: The Event and Its Impact*. Sydney: University of New South Wales Press, pp. 106–120.

Thompson, C., Lewis, D., Greenhalgh, T., Taylor, S. and Cummins, S. (2013) A health and social legacy for East London: narratives of 'problem' and 'solution' around London 2012. *Sociological Research Online*, **18**(2), pp. 144–149.

Thomson, S. (2018) Building for a future Gold Coast. *Architecture Australia*, **107**, pp. 82–89.

Thomson, G. and Newman, P. (2020) Cities and the Anthropocene: urban governance for the new era of regenerative cities. *Urban Studies*, **57**(7), pp. 1502–1519.

Thornley, A. (2012) The London 2012 Olympics: what legacy? *Journal of Policy Research in Tourism, Leisure and Events*, **4**(2), pp. 206–210.

Thorpe, G. (2017) Global TV figures for Rio 2016 Paralympic Games break records. *Inside the Games*, 16 March. Available at: https://www.insidethegames.biz/articles/1048178/global-tv-figures-for-rio-2016-paralympic-games-break-records.

Timms, A. (2021) NBC paid $7.75bn for its Olympic rights … and we got televisual vomit. *The Guardian*, 2 August.

Tjønndal, A. (2019) 'I don't think they realise how good we are': innovation, inclusion and exclusion in women's Olympic boxing. *International Review for the Sociology of Sport*, **54**, pp. 131–150.

TOC (Tenth Olympic Committee of the Games of Los Angeles) (1932) *Olympic Competition and Exhibition of Art 1932*. Los Angeles, CA: TOC.

TOC (1933) *Tenth Olympiad: Los Angeles 1932 Official Report*. Los Angeles: TOC.

TOCOPG (Tokyo Organizing Committee for the Olympic and Paralympic Games) (2016) *Tokyo 2020 Action and Legacy Plan 2016: Participating in the Tokyo 2020 Games, Connecting with Tomorrow*. Tokyo: TOCOPG.

Todd, J. (2016) The 40-year hangover: how the 1976 Olympics nearly broke Montreal. *The Guardian*, 6 July. Available at: https://www.theguardian.com/cities/2016/jul/06/40-year-hangover-1976-olympic-games-broke-montreal-canada.

Tomlinson, A. (1999) *The Game's Up: Essays in the Cultural Analysis of Sport, Leisure and Popular Culture*. Aldershot: Ashgate.

Tomlinson, A. (2014) Olympic legacies: recurrent rhetoric and harsh realities. *Contemporary Social Science*, **9**, pp. 137–158.

Tondelli, L. (2011) Andreotti, Roma, l'Olimpiade. *Le Olimpiadi del 'miracolo' cinquant'anni dopo*. Milan: Franco Angeli, pp. 37–46.

Toohey, K. (2008) The Sydney Olympics: striving for legacies – overcoming short-term disappointments and long-term deficiencies. *International Journal of the History of Sport*, **25**(14), pp. 1953–1971.

Toohey, K. and Veal, A.J. (2000, 2007) *The Olympic Games: A Social Science Perspective*. Wallingford: CAB International.

TOROC (2006) *Sustainability Report for XX Olympic Winter Games Torino 2006*. Turin: Organizing Committee of the XX Turin 2006 Olympic Winter Games.

Toshihiro, N. (2022) The Economic Impact of the Tokyo 2020 Games. Available at: https://www.tokyoupdates.metro.tokyo.lg.jp/en/post-603/#:~:text=In%20addition%2C%20the%20GDP%20boost,held%20in%20its%20full%20form.

Transparency International (2016) *Global Corruption Report: Sport*. London: Routledge.

Travel Utah (2002) *Beyond the Games: Assessing the Impact of the 2002 Olympic Winter Games and the Future of Utah Tourism*. Salt Lake City, UT: Utah Division of Travel Development.

Travlos, J. (1981) Athens after the liberation: planning the new city and exploring the old. *Hesperia*, **50**, pp. 391–407.

Trubina, E. (2014) Mega-events in the context of capitalist modernity: the case of 2014 Sochi Winter Olympics. *Eurasian Geography and Economics*, **55**(6), pp. 610–627.

Trust for London (2016) *Gentrification Index for Small Areas in London (2020–16)*. Available at: https://www.trustforlondon.org.uk/data/gentrification-across-london.

Tuppen, J. (2000) The restructuring of winter sports resorts in the French Alps: problems, processes and policies. *International Journal of Tourism Research*, **2**, pp. 327–344.

Turismo Torino (2004) *Olympic Games and Tourism: Turin's Tourist Strategy for the 2006 Winter Olympics*. Turin: Turismo Torino.

Turismo Torino (2006) *Torino 2006: One Year On*. Turin: Turismo Torino.

Turrbal (2022) *Our Story*. Available at: https://www.turrbal.com.au/our-story.

Tzonis, A. (2005) *Santiago Calatrava: The Athens Olympics*. New York: Rizzoli.

Ueberroth, P. with Levin, R. and Quinn, A. (1986) *Made in America: His Own Story*. New York: Morrow.

UEL (University of East London) (2015) *Olympic Games Impact Study – London 2012 Post-Games Report: December 2015*. London: University of East London.

UEL/TGIS (University of East London and the Thames Gateway Institute for Sustainability) (2010) *Olympic Games Impact Study – London 2012 Pre-Games Report: Final October 2010*. London: University of East London and the Thames Gateway Institute for Sustainability.

Ungood-Thomas, J. (2021) Mounting concern over environmental cost of fake snow for Olympics. *The Guardian*, 6 November. Available at: https://www.theguardian.com/world/2021/nov/06/mounting-concern-over-environmental-cost-of-fake-snow-for-olympics.

UNIDAD (2020) An Open Letter to City Leaders: Build Affordable Homes, Not A Hotel at the Former Site of the Bethune Library. Available at: https://www.unidad-la.org/wp-content/uploads/2020/08/UNIDAD-letter-re-Bethune-site-and-COVID-3.pdf.

United States Census Bureau (2021) U.S. Census Bureau QuickFacts: Inglewood City, California; Los Angeles City, California, 2021. Available at: https://www.census.gov/quickfacts/fact/table/inglewoodcitycalifornia,losangelescitycalifornia/POP010210.

Uranga, R. (2022) People mover, new bike paths and bus lanes: 2028 Olympics could fuel a transit boom in L.A. *Los Angeles Times*, 15 June. Available at: https://www.latimes.com/california/story/2022-06-15/how-l-a-is-building-transit-for-2028-olympics.

USA Today (2006) Host city hopes Games recast its image: Torino officials think new look will boost business, tourism. *USA Today*, 17 February.

Uzqueda, A., Garcia-Almirall, P., Cornadó, C. and Vima-Grau, S. (2021) Critical review of public policies for the rehabilitation of housing stock: the case of Barcelona. *Buildings*, **11**(3). Available at: https://www.mdpi.com/2075-5309/11/3/108.

V&A (Victoria and Albert Museum) (2015) The 2015 Henry Cole Lecture: Delivered by

Boris Johnson, 29 January. Available at: http://www.vam.ac.uk/content/articles/t/sackler-lectures/.

Van Harskamp, M. (2006) Lost in translation. *Rising East*, No. 3, January.

VANOC (2010) *Annual Report. Consolidated Financial Statements.* Vancouver: Vancouver Organizing Committee for the 2010 Olympic and Paralympic Winter Games.

Vanolo, A. (2015) The image of the creative city, eight years later: Turin, urban branding and the economic crisis taboo. *Cities*, **46**, pp. 1–7.

Van Rheenen, D. (2014) A skunk at the garden party: the Sochi Olympics, state-sponsored homophobia and prospects for human rights through mega sporting events. *Journal of Sport and Tourism*, **19**(2), pp. 127–144.

Vanwynsberghe, R. (2015) The Olympic Games Impact (OGI) Study for the 2010 Winter Olympic Games: strategies for evaluating sport mega-events' contribution to sustainability. *International Journal of Sport Policy and Politics*, **7**(1), pp. 1–18.

Vanwynsberghe, R., Surborg, B. and Wyly, E. (2013) When the Games come to town: neo-liberalism, mega-events and social inclusion in the Vancouver 2010 Winter Olympic Games. *International Journal of Urban and Regional Research*, **37**(6), pp. 2074–2093.

Varley, A. (1992) Barcelona's Olympic facelift. *Geographical Magazine*, **64**(7), pp. 20–24.

Varsori, A. (1998) *L'Italia nelle relazioni internazionali dal 1943 al 1992.* Rome-Bari: Laterza.

Veal, A.J. and Toohey, K. (2012) *The Olympic Games: A Bibliography.* Sydney: School of Leisure, Sport and Tourism, University of Technology. Available at: www.business.uts.edu.au/lst/research.index.

Vecchioli, D. (2021) Rio aprova projeto que protege floresta e enterra autódromo em Deodoro. *UOL.* Available at: https://www.uol.com.br/esporte/colunas/olhar-olimpico/2021/11/03/rio-aprova-projeto-que-protege-floresta-e-enterra-autodromo-em-deodoro.htm.

Venegas, G. (2022) Homeless encampment near SoFi Stadium cleared away ahead of Super Bowl. *NBC News*, 11 February. Available at: https://www.nbcnews.com/news/us-news/homeless-encampment-sofi-stadium-cleared-away-ahead-super-bowl-rcna14446.

Vidotto, V. (2006) *Roma contemporanea.* Rome-Bari: Laterza.

Vigor, A., Mean, M. and Tims, C. (eds.) (2004) *After the Gold Rush: A Sustainable Olympics for London.* London: IPPR/DEMOS.

Visit Britain (2010) *Britain Marketing and 2012 Games Global Strategy.* London: Visit Britain.

Voeltz, R.A. (1996) London 1948: the Games of the 14th Olympiad, in Findling. J.E. and Pelle, K.D. (eds.) *Historical Dictionary of the Modern Olympic Movement.* Westport, CN: Greenwood Press, pp. 103–108.

Vogel, R.K., Ryan, R. Lawrie, A., Grant, B., Meng, X., Walsh, P., Morris, A. and Riedy, C. (2020) Global city Sydney, *Progress in Planning*, **136**, 100426. https://doi.org/10.1016/j.progress.2018.09.002.

Vugts, J.F.T. (1992) *Olympiade: Geschiedenis van de Olympische Spelen vanaf het begin tot 1992.* Utrecht: SNS Bank.

Wachsmuth, D. and Weisler, A. (2018) Airbnb and the rent gap: gentrification through the sharing economy. *Environment and Planning A*, **50**(6), pp. 1147–1170.

Wainwright, O. (2022) A massive betrayal: the failed legacy of the London Olympics. *The Guardian*, 30 June, pp. 5–8.

Walker, A. (2018) The Olympics Fixed LAs Traffic Problem Once – Can the 2028 Games Do It Permanently? Curbed LA, 7 June. Available at: https://la.curbed.com/2018/6/7/17419270/olympics-2028-los-angeles-1984-traffic.

Wall Street Journal (2004) Securing the Olympic Games. *Wall Street Journal*, 22 August.

Wang, M. and Bao, H.X.H. (2018) Mega-event effects on the housing market: evidence from the Beijing 2008 Olympic Games. *Cities*, **72**, pp. 207–216.

Wang, T., Nie, W., Gao, J., Xue, L.K., Gao, X.M., Wang, X.F., Qiu, J., Poon, C.N., Meinardi, S., Blake, D., Wang, S.L., Ding, A.J., Chai, F.H., Zhang, Q.Z. and Wang, W.X. (2010) Air quality during the 2008 Beijing Olympics: secondary pollutants and regional impact. *Atmospheric Chemistry and Physics*, **10**, 7603–7615.

Warren, R. (2002) Situating the city and September 11th: military urban doctrine, 'pop-up' armies and spatial chess. *International Journal of Urban and Regional Research*, **26**(3), pp. 614–619.

Waterfield, R. (2004) *Athens: A History from Ancient Ideal to Modern City*. London: Macmillan.

Watt, B. (2014) The Forum in Inglewood Reopens with the Eagles. Southern California Public Radio. 15 January. Available at: https://archive.kpcc.org/blogs/economy/2014/01/15/15600/the-forum-reopens-in-inglewood/.

Watt, P. (2021) *Estate Regeneration and its Discontents: Public Housing, Place and Inequality in London*. Bristol: Policy Press.

Watts, J. (2005) Satellite data reveals Beijing as air pollution capital of world. *The Guardian*, 31 October.

Watts, J. (2006) Beijing Olympic official sacked over corruption. *The Guardian*, 13 June.

Watts, J. (2009) Beijing keeps Olympic restrictions on cars after air quality improves, *The Guardian*, 6 April.

WCED (World Commission on Environment and Development) (1987) *Our Common Future* (The Brundtland Report). Oxford: Oxford University Press.

WCOPCRJ (World Cup and Olympics Popular Committee of Rio de Janeiro) (2015) *Rio 2016 Olympics: The Exclusion Games*. Rio de Janeiro.

Weaver, C. (2014) Russia's Sochi loses tourism lustre to Crimea. *Financial Times*, 9 September.

Weaver, D., McLennan, C.L., Moyle, B. and Casali, G.L. (2022) Early community recommendations for sustainable mega-events: evidence from the 2032 Brisbane Olympic Games. *Journal of Sustainable Tourism*. https://doi.org/10.1080/09669582.2022.2149760.

Weed, M. (2008) *Olympic Tourism*. Oxford: Elsevier.

Weed, M. (2012) What's Worth Leveraging? A Meta-Analysis of the Volume and Value of Olympic Tourism Flows. Paper to the ESRC Seminar, Going for Gold: Leveraging the Olympic Tourism Legacy beyond 2012. Bournemouth, November.

Weed, M. (2014) Is tourism a legitimate legacy from the Olympic and Paralympic Games? An analysis of London 2012 legacy strategy using programme theory. *Journal of Sport and Tourism*, **19**(2), pp. 101–126.

Weed, M. (2017) Sport participation legacies of mega sporting events, in Brittain, I. Bocaro, J., Byers, T. and Swart, K. (eds.) *Legacies and Mega Events: Fact or Fairytale*. London: Routledge.

Weed, M. (2021) The geographies and psychologies of global transitions: implications for sport, tourism, climate, health, wellbeing and the economy. *Géocarrefour*, **95**(2).

Weed, M. and Bull, C. (2009) *Sports Tourism: Participants, Policy and Providers*, 2nd ed. Oxford: Elsevier.

Weed, M., Stephens, J. and Bull, C. (2011) An exogenous shock to the system? The London 2012 Olympic and Paralympic Games and British tourism policy. *Journal of Sport and Tourism*, **16**(4), pp. 345–377.

Wei, Y.H.D. and Yu, D.L. (2006) State policy and the globalisation of Beijing: emerging themes. *Habitat International*, **30**, pp. 377–395.

Weirick, J. (1999) Urban design, in Cashman, R. and Hughes, A. (eds.) *Staging the Olympics: The Event and Its Impact*. Sydney: University of New South Wales Press, pp. 70–82.

Welch, P.D. (1996) Paris 1924: the Games of the 8th Olympiad, in Findling, J.E. and Pelle, K.D. (eds.) *Historical Dictionary of the Modern Olympic Movement*. Westport, CN: Greenwood Press, pp. 61–67.

Wenn, S.R. (1993) Lights! Camera! Little action: television, Avery Brundage, and the Melbourne Olympics. *Sporting Traditions*, **1**, pp. 38–53.

Wenn, S.R. (1995) Growing pains: the Olympic movement and television, 1966–1972. *Olympika*, **4**, pp. 1–22.

Wenn, S.R. (2015) Peter Ueberroth's legacy: how the 1984 Los Angeles Olympics changed the trajectory of the Olympic Movement. *International Journal of the History of Sport*, **32**(1), pp. 157–171.

Whannel, G. (2012) The rings and the box: television spectacle and the Olympics, in Lenskyj,

H. and Wagg, S. (eds.) *The Palgrave Handbook of Olympic Studies.* New York: Palgrave MacMillan, pp. 261–273.

White, J.S. (2005) Constructing the Invisible Landscape: Organizing the 1932 Olympic Games in Los Angeles. Unpublished PhD thesis, School of Architecture, University of California at Berkeley.

Whitelegg, D. (2000) Going for gold: Atlanta's bid for fame. *International Journal of Urban and Regional Research*, **24**, pp. 801–817.

Williams, P. (1997) Out-foxing the people? Recent state involvement in the planning system. *Urban Policy and Research*, **15**(2), pp. 129–136.

Wilson, H. (1996) What is an Olympic City? Visions of Sydney 2000. *Media, Culture and Society*, **18**, pp. 603–618.

Wilson, S. (2014) Bach: 'I Am Still Assured' of security in Sochi. *Associated Press*, 3 February. Available at: http://bigstory.ap.org/article/bach-i-am-still-assured-security-sochi.

Wilson, W. (2015) Sports infrastructure, legacy and the paradox of the 1984 Olympic Games. *International Journal of the History of Sport*, **32**(1), pp. 144–156.

Wimmer, M. (1976) *Olympic Buildings.* Leipzig: Edition Leipzig.

Wingfield-Hayes, R. (2015) Japan scraps 2020 Olympic stadium design. BBC News, 17 July. Available at: https://www.bbc.co.uk/news/world-asia-33563243.

Winkler, A. (2007) *Torino: City Report.* London: Centre for Analysis of Social Exclusion, London School of Economics.

Wolfe, S.D. (2023*a*) Building a better host city? Reforming and contesting the Olympics in Paris 2024. *Environment and Planning* C, **41**(2), pp. 257–273.

Wolfe, S.D. (2023*b*) The juggernaut endures: protest, Potemkinism, and Olympic peform. *Leisure Studies*, https://doi.org/10.1080/02614367.2023.2195201.

WOS (Wenlock Olympian Society) (2006) *Wenlock Olympian Society.* Available at: http://www.wenlock-olympian-society.org.uk/.

Wu, F. (ed.) (2006) *Globalisation and China's Cities.* London: Routledge.

Wu, F. (ed.) (2007) *China's Emerging Cities.* London: Routledge.

WWF (World Wildlife Fund) (2004) *Environmental Assessment of the Athens 2004 Olympic Games.* Athens: WWF Greece.

Wynn, M. (ed.) (1984) *Planning and Urban Growth in Southern Europe.* London: Mansell.

Xin, Y. (2001) Olympic economy: a huge temptation. Available at: www.bjreview.com.cn/bjreview/EN/2001/200134/Nationalissues-200134(A).htm.

Xin, Y. and Kunzmann, K. R. (2020) Winter Olympics 2022 in Beijing: a must-be success story. *disP – The Planning Review*, **56**(2), pp. 78–90.

Yamawaki, Y. and Duarte, F. (2014) Olympic and urban legacy in Sydney: urban transformations and real estate a decade after the Games. *Journal of Urban Design*, **19**(4), pp. 511–540.

Yannopoulos, D. (2003) Entrepreneurs set eyes on Post-Olympic Windfall. *Athens News*, 26 August.

Yardley, J. (2005) Beijing's Quest for 2008: to become simply livable. *New York Times*, 28 August. Available at: https://www.nytimes.com/2005/08/28/world/asia/beijings-quest-for-2008-to-become-simply-livable.html.

Yardley, J. (2008) Beijing confirms deaths of 6 workers at Olympic construction sites. *New York Times*, 9 February. Available at: https://www.nytimes.com/2008/01/29/world/asia/29iht-29beijing.9568978.html.

Yew, W. (1996) *The Olympic Image: The First 100 years.* Edmonton, Alberta: Quon Editions.

Yoon, H. (2009) The legacy of the 1988 Seoul Olympic Games, in Poynter, G. and MacRury, I. (eds.) *Olympic Cities: 2012 and the Remaking of London.* Farnham: Ashgate, pp. 121–131.

Young, D.C. (1987) The origins of the modern Olympics: a new version. *International Journal of the History of Sport*, **4**, pp. 271–300.

Young, D.C. (1996) *The Modern Olympics: A Struggle for Revival.* Baltimore, MD: Johns Hopkins University Press.

Young, D.C. (1998) Further thoughts on some issues of early Olympic history. *Journal of Olympic History*, **6**(3), pp. 29–41.

Young, D.C. (2004) *A Brief History of the Olympic Games*. Oxford: Blackwell.

Zahniser, D. and Oreskes, B. (2021) L.A. finalizes its anti-camping law, setting the stage for vote-by-vote enforcement. *Los Angeles Times*, 8 July. Available at: https://www.latimes.com/california/story/2021-07-28/anti-camping-vote-la-homelessness.

Zhang, F. (2014) *China's Urbanization and the World Economy*. Cheltenham: Edward Elgar.

Zhang, J., and Wu, F. (2008) Mega-event marketing and urban growth coalitions: a case study of Nanjing Olympic New Town. *Town Planning Review*, **79**(2/3), pp. 209–226.

Zhang, J., Zhong, C. and Yi, M. (2016) Did Olympic Games improve air quality in Beijing? Based on the synthetic control method. *Environmental Economics and Policy Studies*, **18**, pp. 21–39.

Zhang, L. and Zhao, S.X. (2009) City branding and the Olympic effect: a case study of Beijing. *Cities*, **26**, pp. 245–254.

Zhang, Y., Ai, J., Bao, J.and Zhang, W. (2022) Lessons learned from the COVID-19 control strategy of the XXXII Tokyo Summer Olympics and the XXIV Beijing Winter Olympics. *Emerging Microbes and Infections*, **11**(1), pp. 1711–1716.

Zhou, S. (1992) *China: Provincial Geography*. Beijing: Foreign Languages Press.

Ziakas, V. and Boukas, N. (2012) A neglected legacy: examining the challenges and potential for sport and tourism development in post-Olympic Athens. *International Journal of Event and Festival Management*, **3**, pp. 292–316.

Zimbalist, A. (2021) Tokyo 2020 and its postponement: an economic prognosis. *Journal of Olympic Studies*, **2**(1), pp. 15–28.

Index

Spanning a period approaching two decades, the four editions of Olympic Cities *reveal the ideas and practices that have shaped and reshaped the relationship between the Olympics and their host cities.*

OLYMPIC CITIES
City Agendas, Planning, and the World's Games, 1896–2012
1st Edition
Edited by John R. Gold, Margaret M. Gold
Paperback
ISBN: 978–0–415–37407–1
First Published: 2007 by Routledge

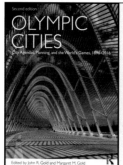

OLYMPIC CITIES
City Agendas, Planning, and the World's Games, 1896–2016
2nd Edition
Edited by John R. Gold, Margaret M. Gold
Paperback
ISBN: 978–0–415–48658–3
First Published: 2011 by Routledge

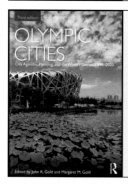

OLYMPIC CITIES
City Agendas, Planning, and the World's Games, 1896–2020
3rd Edition
Edited By John R. Gold, Margaret M. Gold
Paperback
ISBN: 978–1–138–83269–5
First Published: 2017 by Routledge

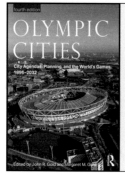

OLYMPIC CITIES
City Agendas, Planning, and the World's Games, 1896–2032
4th Edition
Edited By John R. Gold, Margaret M. Gold
Paperback
ISBN: 9781138832695
First Published: 2024 by Routledge